ONE WOMAN, ONE VOTE

VOTE FOR THE
WOMAN SUFFRAGE AMENDMENT
NOV. 2

ONE WOMAN, ONE VOTE

REDISCOVERING THE WOMAN SUFFRAGE MOVEMENT

EDITED BY
MARJORIE SPRUILL WHEELER

NEWSAGE PRESS

One Woman, One Vote

Rediscovering the Woman Suffrage Movement

Edited by Marjorie Spruill Wheeler

Copyright © 1995 by NewSage Press
and Educational Film Company
1995, 1996 Second Printing

Softcover ISBN 0-939165-26-0

Address inquiries to:
  NewSage Press
  P.O. Box 607
  Troutdale, OR 97060
  503-695-2211

Designed by Robert Cooney
Digital composition by Greg Endries
Printed in the United States

Cover Photo: Members of the Women's Political Union at
the State Fair suffrage tent, Syracuse, New York, c. 1915
Frank Corbeil Collection

Back Cover Photo: Suffrage parade, 1913
New York Public Library

Distributed by Publishers Group West
1-800-788-3123

Library of Congress Cataloging-in-Publication Data

One Woman, One Vote : rediscovering the
    woman suffrage movement / edited by Marjorie Spruill Wheeler.
        p.   cm.
    Includes biographical references and index.
    ISBN 0-939165-26-0
    1. Women—Suffrage—United States—History.   I. Wheeler, Marjorie
Spruill,
JK1896.054   1995
324.6 ' 23 ' 0973—dc20   95-34128
                                                                     CIP

Contents

Acknowledgments

It is my pleasure as editor to recognize and express my appreciation to all who were a part of this anthology's development.

One Woman, One Vote: Rediscovering the Woman Suffrage Movement is the companion volume to "One Woman, One Vote," the television special produced by the Educational Film Center (EFC) with major funding from the National Endowment for the Humanities, for the PBS "American Experience" series. The idea for the book came from Ruth Pollak, producer of the documentary, and Steve Rabin, President of EFC; I am grateful to them for recognizing the need for the anthology and giving me the opportunity to design and edit it; and to others at EFC who assisted with this project, including co-producer Felicia Widman, assistant producer Rachel Sweeney, and Tracy Rabin.

I am also grateful to the publisher, Maureen R. Michelson of NewSage Press, for taking on a task many believed could not be accomplished in such a short time—and making it happen. Like Steve, Ruth, and me, Maureen was determined that this book would bring the fascinating story of the woman suffrage movement to a general audience, as well as offer much to students and teachers of woman suffrage. In addition, I greatly appreciate the hard work and considerable talent of her associates at NewSage Press, including graphic designer Robert Cooney, who located and selected all the photographs and imagery; copy editor Tracy Smith; editorial assistant Susan McElroy; and Greg Endries for the digital composition of the book.

It has been an honor as well as a pleasure to work with the outstanding group of scholars who contributed essays to *One Woman, One Vote*. I am indebted to them for their willingness to write new essays for this volume or, in some cases, to revise existing works to make them accessible, as well as inviting to a general audience. Many of the contributors were also very helpful to me as informal consultants, particularly Sara Hunter Graham who "previewed" my introductions and offered useful suggestions.

The University of Southern Mississippi provided considerable support. A grant from the Aubrey Keith Lucas Faculty Excellence Endowment was invaluable, as was the support of the History Department chaired by Orazio Ciccarelli. Kim Jorns, departmental secretary, and university librarians Paul McCarver and Karolyn Thompson, were also especially helpful. I exhausted three talented graduate students during the preparation of this book: Audra Odom, who helped launch the project; Donna Sedevie, who aided in its development; and Karen Cox, who assisted me in proofreading and indexing at the end. And I am thankful for the help of two colleagues and friends, Mark Klinedinst and Michael Salda; by sharing their expertise, these computer wizards saved me countless hours.

Finally, I am indebted to my family. My mother, Edna Whitley Spruill, demonstrating by example how smart and strong women can be, has always inspired me and my sister Carol Spruill. I am grateful to my children Scott and Jesse for their love and for their pride and interest in my work. As Elizabeth Cady Stanton said of her son Theodore, to have sons interested in women's rights and women's history is "a source of intense satisfaction." My husband David wishes I wouldn't take on projects with such short and firm deadlines, but he has been wonderful nonetheless. As always, I appreciate his patience, support, and love.

—Marjorie Spruill Wheeler
Hattiesburg, Mississippi

Hundreds of women gave the
accumulated possibilities
of an entire lifetime,
thousands gave years of their lives,
hundreds of thousands
gave constant interest,
and such aid as they could.
It was a continuous, seemingly
endless, chain of activity.
Young suffragists who helped forge
the last links of that chain
were not born when it began.
Old suffragists who forged the
first links were dead when it ended.

—CARRIE CHAPMAN CATT AND
NETTIE ROGERS SHULER

**Woman Suffrage and Politics: The Inner
Story of the Suffrage Movement**

Introduction

A Short History of the Woman Suffrage Movement in America

Marjorie Spruill Wheeler

One Woman, One Vote: Rediscovering the Woman Suffrage Movement, and the documentary, "One Woman, One Vote," were inspired by the seventy-fifth anniversary of the Nineteenth Amendment that enfranchised American women. We honor those women who dedicated their lives to this great cause. Few Americans realize, however, that it required almost seventy-five years for suffragists to achieve this victory: between 1848, when a resolution calling for woman suffrage was adopted at the Seneca Falls Convention, to 1920, when the federal woman suffrage amendment was finally ratified, several generations of suffragists labored tirelessly for the cause. Many did not live to see its successful conclusion.

Origins: 1848–1869

The woman suffrage movement, which began in the northeastern United States, developed in the context of antebellum reform. Many women including Sarah and Angelina Grimké, Abby Kelley Foster, Lucretia Mott, Maria Stewart, Antoinette Brown Blackwell, Lucy Stone, Susan B. Anthony, and Elizabeth Cady Stanton, began speaking out for woman's rights when their efforts to participate fully in the great reform movements of the day—including antislavery and temperance—were rebuffed. These early feminists demanded a wide range of changes in woman's social, moral, legal, educational, and economic status; the right to vote was not their initial focus. Indeed, those present at the Seneca Falls Convention in upstate New York regarded the resolution demanding the vote as the most extreme of all their demands, and adopted it by a narrow margin at the insistence of Elizabeth Cady Stanton and Frederick Douglass.

After the Civil War, women's rights leaders saw enfranchisement as one of the most important, perhaps the most important of their goals. Enfranchisement, they believed, was essential both as a symbol of women's equality and individuality and a means of improving women's legal and social condition. They were extremely disappointed when the Fourteenth and Fifteenth Amendments did not provide universal suffrage for all Americans, but extended the

9

franchise only to black men. In fact, women's rights advocates divided acrimoniously in 1869 largely over the issue of whether or not to support ratification of the Fifteenth Amendment.

Suffrage Strategies During "The Schism": 1869–1890

Two woman suffrage organizations were founded in 1869, with different positions on the Fifteenth Amendment and different ideas about how best to promote woman suffrage. The National Woman Suffrage Association (NWSA) headed by Elizabeth Cady Stanton and Susan B. Anthony opposed the Fifteenth Amendment, but called for a Sixteenth Amendment that would enfranchise women. Led exclusively by women, the New York-based NWSA focused upon the enfranchisement of women through federal action, and adopted a more radical tone in promoting a wide variety of feminist reforms in its short-lived journal, *The Revolution*.

The other organization, the American Woman Suffrage Association (AWSA) with headquarters in Boston, was led by Lucy Stone with the aid of her husband Henry Blackwell, Mary Livermore, Julia Ward Howe, Henry Ward Beecher, Antoinette Brown Blackwell, Thomas Wentworth Higginson and others. It supported ratification of the Fifteenth Amendment while working for woman suffrage as well. While endorsing a federal amendment for female enfranchisement, this organization concentrated on developing grassroots support for woman suffrage. Employing agents who traveled all over the nation, establishing local and state suffrage organizations, speaking and circulating literature, and working through its newspaper, *The Woman's Journal*, the AWSA engaged in a massive educational campaign designed to make woman suffrage and other feminist reforms seem less radical and consistent with widely shared American values. AWSA members promoted state suffrage amendments and various forms of "partial suffrage" legislation, including bills giving women the right to vote on school or municipal issues or in presidential elections; they believed that these measures were desirable in themselves and a means to the eventual end—full suffrage for all American women.

Meanwhile, suffragists associated with the NWSA, disheartened by the response to the proposed federal amendment, and disdaining the state-by-state approach, tried to win their rights by other approaches, known collectively as the "New Departure." These suffragists challenged their exclusion from voting on the grounds that, as citizens, they could not be deprived of their rights as protected by the Constitution. Victoria Woodhull, a radical, iconoclastic, and beautiful figure who briefly gained the support of Stanton and Anthony in the 1870s (before her scandalous personal life and advocacy of free love were revealed at great cost to the movement), made this argument before Congress in 1871.

In 1872, Susan B. Anthony attempted to vote, hoping to be arrested and to have the opportunity to test this strategy in the courts; she was arrested and indicted for "knowingly, wrongfully and unlawfully vot[ing] for a representative to the Congress of the United States." Found guilty and fined, she insisted she would never pay a dollar of it. Virginia Minor, a suffrage leader in St. Louis, succeeded in getting the issue before the United States Supreme Court, but in 1875 the court ruled unanimously that citizenship did not automatically confer the right to vote and that the issue of female enfranchisement should be decided within the states.

The West Pioneers in Woman Suffrage

Even as the NWSA and the AWSA competed for support and tried several strategies for winning female enfranchisement to no avail, woman suffrage was making headway in the West. While most eastern politicians were dead set against woman suffrage, politicians and voters in several western states enfranchised women and, at times, battled Congress for the right to do so. In 1869 Wyoming led the nation in the adoption of woman suffrage while still a territory; in 1890, when it appeared that Congress would not approve its application for statehood as long as Wyoming allowed woman suffrage, the legislature declared "we will remain out of the Union a hundred years rather than come in without the women." Even the Mormon stronghold of Utah enacted woman suffrage as a territory in 1870 and came into the Union with woman suffrage in 1896. Colorado (1893) and Idaho (1896) were the other "pioneering" suffrage states.

Historians differ as to the reason why the West was so precocious in its adoption of woman suffrage. One theory was that frontier conditions undermined traditional gender roles and that women, having proven their ability to conquer difficult conditions and do "men's work," were rewarded with the vote. Another theory was that the politicians hoped that women voters would help to "civilize" the West. Most historians stress practical politics as opposed to advanced ideology as the explanation, arguing that western politicians found it expedient to enfranchise women for a variety of reasons. In Utah, for example, Mormons were confident that the votes of women would help preserve Mormon traditions—including polygamy—and that enfranchising women would help to dispel the idea widely accepted in the East that Mormon women were an oppressed lot.

For whatever reasons, these four western states were the *only* states to adopt woman suffrage in the nineteenth century. The next round of state victories did not come until 1910, and these were also in the West (Washington, 1910; California, 1911; Oregon, 1912; Kansas, 1912; and Arizona, 1912).

Woman Suffrage and Temperance

Meanwhile, the suffrage movement won a valuable ally when Frances Willard, as president of the Woman's Christian Temperance Union (WCTU), led thousands of otherwise quite traditional women to "convert" to the cause of woman suffrage as a way of protecting the home, women, and children. Following its official endorsement in 1880, the WCTU created a Department of Franchise under Zerelda Wallace and Dr. Anna Howard Shaw (later president of the NAWSA), which encouraged state WCTU chapters to endorse suffrage and distributed suffrage literature. Though Willard was a member of the AWSA and invited Susan B. Anthony to speak before the WCTU, the temperance organization's work for woman suffrage was particularly valuable in creating support for suffrage among women who might have considered the existing suffrage organizations and their leaders eccentric or radical.

The WCTU endorsement, however, gained for the suffrage movement a powerful opponent when the liquor industry concluded that woman suffrage was a threat to be stopped at all costs. Indeed, NAWSA President Carrie Chapman Catt later referred to the liquor industry as "the Invisible Enemy" and believed that its corrupt manipulation of American politics long delayed the coming of woman suffrage.

Unity Restored Through the NAWSA: 1890

One of the most important turning points in the history of the woman suffrage movement came in 1890 as the two national suffrage organizations reunited in one major organization. At the instigation of younger suffragists, the movement's aging pioneers put aside their differences sufficiently to merge their rival organizations into the National American Woman Suffrage Association (NAWSA). Elizabeth Cady Stanton was elected president; Lucy Stone, head of the executive committee; and Susan B. Anthony, vice president; but it was Anthony who actually took command of the new organization. (She became president officially in 1892 and remained in office until 1900.) While continuing to demand a federal amendment, NAWSA leaders concluded that they must first build support within the states, winning enough state suffrage amendments that Congress would approve a federal amendment and three-fourths of the states would be sure to ratify.

Though Stanton continued to address a wide range of feminist issues, many of them quite radical (including an indictment of Christianity in her 1895 *The Woman's Bible*), most NAWSA leaders including Anthony thought it imperative that the movement focus almost exclusively on winning the vote. In keeping with this new approach and influenced by the conservatism of new recruits, the suffragists went to great lengths to avoid association with radical causes.

Woman Suffrage and the Race Issue

This new approach included shedding the traditional association of women's rights with the rights of blacks. Although the NAWSA never stopped using natural rights arguments for woman suffrage, white suffragists—still indignant that black men were enfranchised ahead of them and angry at the ease with which immigrant men were enfranchised—drifted away from insistence upon universal suffrage and increasingly employed racist and nativist rhetoric and tactics.

The new NAWSA strategy included building support in the South. There the historic connection between the woman's movement and antislavery made suffrage anathema to the white conservatives who once again controlled the region and made advocacy of woman suffrage quite difficult for the influential white women the NAWSA wished to recruit. In the 1890s, however, with Laura Clay of Kentucky as intermediary, NAWSA leaders went to great lengths to, in Clay's words, "bring in the South."

Using a strategy first suggested by Henry Blackwell, northern and southern leaders began to argue that woman suffrage—far from endangering white supremacy in the South—could be a means of restoring it. In fact, they suggested that the adoption of woman suffrage with educational or property qualifications that would disqualify most black women, would allow the South to restore white supremacy in politics without "having to" disfranchise black men and risk Congressional repercussions.

The NAWSA spent considerable time and resources developing this "southern strategy," sending Catt and Anthony on speaking tours through the region, and holding the 1895 NAWSA convention in Atlanta. Eager to avoid offending their southern hosts they even asked their aging hero Frederick Douglass—who was an honored participant in women's rights conventions elsewhere in the nation—to stay away from the Atlanta meeting. By 1903, however, it was becoming clear that this southern strategy had failed; the region's politicians refused (in the words of one Mississippi politician) to "cower behind petticoats" and "use lovely women" to maintain white supremacy. Instead, they found other means to do so that did not involve the "destruction" of woman's traditional role.

White suffragists largely turned their backs on African American women in the late nineteenth and early twentieth centuries, and, in the South, excluded them totally from white suffrage organizations. Nevertheless, a growing number of African American women actively supported woman suffrage during this period. Following a path blazed by former slave Sojourner Truth and free blacks Harriet Forten Purvis and Margaretta Forten who spoke at antebellum women's rights conventions, and Massachusetts reformers Caroline Remond Putman and Josephine St. Pierre Ruffin who were active in the AWSA in the 1870s, black women persevered in their advocacy of woman suffrage even in these difficult times. Prominent African American suffragists included Ida B. Wells-Barnett of Chicago, famous as a leading crusader against lynching; Mary Church Terrell, educator and first president of the National Association of Colored Women (NACW); and Adella Hunt Logan, Tuskegee faculty member, who, in articles in *The Crisis,* insisted that if white women needed the vote to protect their rights, then black women—victims of racism as well as sexism—needed the ballot even more.

Still, white suffrage leaders, who either shared the nativism or racism endemic to turn-of-the century America or were convinced they must cater to it in order to succeed, continued in their attempts to shed the movement's radical image and enlarge their constituency.

Rebuilding: 1896—1910

From the late 1890s to around 1910, in a period historians once described as "the doldrums" of the woman suffrage movement, the NAWSA went through a major period of rebuilding—in regard to membership as well as image. Under the leadership of Carrie Chapman Catt, president from 1900 to 1904, the NAWSA began successful efforts (known as the "society plan") to recruit large numbers of socially prominent and politically influential women, such as Alva Smith (Vanderbilt) Belmont, who thereafter contributed lavishly to the suffrage movement. Rebuilding efforts also included convincing growing numbers of middle- and upper-class women involved in women's clubs that woman suffrage would be a boon to their civic improvement efforts. NAWSA leaders also reached out to the new generation of college-educated women, many of them professionals, reminding them that their opportunities were owed to the pioneers of the woman's rights movement, and challenging them to take up the torch.

The suffrage movement profited greatly from the new ideas and energy of younger leaders such as Maud Wood Park and Inez Haynes Irwin who formed the College Equal Suffrage League, and Mary Hutcheson Page of Massachusetts and Harriot Stanton Blatch (the daughter of Elizabeth Cady Stanton) of New York. These women reinvigorated the suffrage movements in their states by introducing new tactics borrowed from English suffragists or working-class political activists including open-air meetings and parades. Blatch also organized the Equality League of Self Supporting Women (1907), later called the Women's Political Union.

The NAWSA also expanded its educational efforts, distributing literature to schools and libraries, sponsoring debates, disseminating a new and less radical image of their movement's own history in which Anthony was virtually canonized. Together these rebuilding efforts greatly expanded the suffrage constituency, brought in able and talented workers, and made it much more difficult for anti-suffragists to label the movement as marginal or extreme. Yet, particularly after Catt resigned in 1904 (due to the illness of her husband) and Dr. Anna Howard Shaw inherited the presidency of the NAWSA, the de-centralized NAWSA provided little in the way of a national political strategy. Between 1896 and 1910, no new states were won for woman suffrage; only six state campaigns were attempted and all of them failed.

The Suffrage Movement and Progressivism

There was, however, considerable grounds for optimism in 1910. The Progressive Movement, which began around 1900 at the grassroots level and swept both national political parties, was proving to be a tremendous boon to the cause of woman suffrage. In all sections of the United States, women and men who supported Progressive reforms (including pure food and drug legislation, protection for workers, an end to child labor, and legislation to curb political corruption) believed that women's votes would help obtain such reforms. Countless women, many of them involved in civic improvement clubs, enlisted in the suffrage movement as they became frustrated at their inability to secure such reforms through "indirect influence" or lobbying.

Leading Progressive reformers including the revered Jane Addams, founder of the famous Chicago settlement house, Hull House, and Florence Kelley, Executive Secretary of the National Consumer's League, were strong supporters of woman suffrage. And labor leaders, including Rose Schneiderman, labor organizer and speaker with the Women's Trade Union League; and Leonora O'Reilly, who headed the industrial committee of the New York City Woman Suffrage Party, worked hard for suffrage as a means of achieving improved conditions for workers. Many working-class women joined the movement, welcomed by middle-class and elite leaders such as Harriot Stanton Blatch (who had objected to the NAWSA's "society plan") who worked to unite women of all classes into a revitalized suffrage movement. As opponents were quick to point out, many socialists supported woman suffrage, playing an important role in the suffrage movement particularly in New York, Wisconsin, and California—though some socialists including Emma Goldman thought it foolish to expect that much progress would come from female enfranchisement.

Anti-suffragists in the Progressive Era

As in the case of temperance and suffrage, however, the idea that women would support Progressive reforms provoked opposition. Industries that stood to lose from Progressive reform, such as the cotton textile industry of the South that employed large numbers of child laborers, joined the liquor industry as formidable opponents of woman suffrage, and worked together with the growing number of anti-suffrage organizations to oppose state suffrage referenda. They rarely attacked directly the idea of women exercising influence, however, instead arguing that *direct* involvement in politics rather than continued reliance upon *indirect* influence would be harmful to women, as politics was such a dirty game.

It is significant, however, that in the Progressive Era, female anti-suffragists (known as "Antis"), widely proclaimed that they *favored* woman's involvement in public affairs including nonpartisan political activity. Pointing to their own records of community service, they insisted that they opposed woman suffrage primarily out of the belief that involvement in partisan politics would dispel women's energies and dilute their influence. Indeed, as the suffrage movement entered what proved to be its last decade, a tradition of women's civic activism had developed—and been accepted—to the point that the argument over suffrage was more often framed in terms of how women could be most effective, rather than whether or not women should concern themselves with life outside a narrowly defined "woman's sphere."

Alice Paul and the National Woman's Party

Around 1912, the increased support for suffrage resulting from Progressivism, and the series of victories in the western states seemed to breathe new life into suffragists all over America. The return of Alice Paul from England, where she was inspired by the energy and boldness of the "militant" British suffragists, was also a major factor in the new suffrage activism.

Paul, her able associate Lucy Burns, and the circle of women who gathered around them, had no patience with the slow, state-by-state plodding that had consumed much of the NAWSA's energy since the 1890s. Working at first through the Congressional Union, the NAWSA-affiliated organization Paul organized to lobby for the federal amendment, these women insisted that the NAWSA focus its attention almost exclusively upon the federal route to enfranchisement. This infuriated some suffragists, particularly a small but vocal group of states' rights devotees led by Kate Gordon of New Orleans who favored woman suffrage by state action only. Still, the NAWSA did indeed renew its campaign for a federal amendment—but not before it parted company with Paul and her followers.

The central issue in this new rift in the suffrage forces was Alice Paul's advocacy of a strategy derived from the British suffragists, to oppose the "party-in-power" until it adopted woman suffrage, a strategy that violated the NAWSA's longstanding policy of non-partisanship. Forming a separate organization, soon known as the National Woman's Party (NWP), Paul and her associates continued to pursue a federal amendment using bold new tactics designed to force President Woodrow Wilson and the Democratic Party to support the federal amendment. These actions ranged from mobilizing women voters in western states against all Democrats in the 1916 election (especially Wilson who was running for re-election), to burning the president's war-time speeches in praise of democracy publicly in front of the White House.

Alice Paul proved to be brilliant at attracting and keeping the attention of the press—refusing to allow the press to continue to ignore the suffrage movement—and thereby forcing it to the forefront of public debate. The massive, dramatic suffrage parade that she organized during Wilson's inaugural celebration—featuring more than eight thousand suffragists spectacularly arrayed with costumes and banners and led by the striking Inez Milholland in flowing white robes on a white horse—captured the nation's attention. That the throngs assembled for the parade attacked the marchers after spitting on them and pelting them with lighted cigars, and that the police failed to protect them, led to a Congressional investigation—and attracted sympathy for the cause not unlike similar events during the Civil Rights Movement of the 1960s.

Indeed Paul and the NWP were among the first Americans to employ many of the tactics of civil disobedience: they were the first, for example, to picket the White House for a political cause. Again crowds attacked the demonstrators, but the pickets—not their attackers—were jailed. Imprisoned on charges of obstructing traffic, they were given prison terms of up to six months. When they protested this violation of their rights by going on hunger strikes, they were forcibly fed—a brutal and dangerous procedure—recorded in shocking detail in Doris Stevens's classic of 1920, *Jailed for Freedom*. All of this however, only increased their determination to expose the hypocrisy of a nation which, during World War I, proclaimed itself the leader of a crusade for democracy while jailing and abusing women for protesting the nation's denial of the vote to half of its adult citizens.

Carrie Chapman Catt and the "Winning Plan"

Carrie Chapman Catt was equally determined to bring the long struggle to a conclusion with the adoption of the federal suffrage amendment, but pursued this end with a strategy that contrasted sharply with that of Alice Paul. Catt's return to the NAWSA presidency in late 1915, and the adoption shortly thereafter of her then top secret "Winning Plan," harnessed the power of the massive but sluggish NAWSA and initiated a final, victorious suffrage drive. Catt insisted that further state work was vital, but made it clear that the federal amendment was still the ultimate goal. Her plan called for suffragists in states that had not adopted woman suffrage—and where a victory seemed possible—to launch campaigns at once. In states where defeat was likely, she insisted that suffragists avoid such an embarrassment to the cause and seek only partial suffrage—municipal, presidential, or primary suffrage—as they thought best. She urged suffragists in states where women already voted to pressure their national representatives to support the federal amendment.

Meanwhile Catt and her lieutenants, Maud Wood Park and Helen Gardener, worked hard to convince President Wilson to support woman suffrage by federal as well as state action, and conducted a massive lobbying effort to enlist congressional support. Dubbed by the press as the "Front Door Lobby" because of the contrast between their open and honest methods and those more common among Washington's lobbyists, the suffragists kept constant watch over members of Congress. Women from all parts of the nation came in "relays" to reinforce those stationed at NAWSA's Washington headquarters, who studied the congressmen with microscopic intensity, seeking the right words or arguments with which to persuade them to support the federal amendment. It had long since become clear to the suffragists that "justice" arguments alone would not be sufficient; politicians had to be convinced that it was expedient for them personally as well as for their party to support woman suffrage. Though some loved it and some loathed it, suffragists found it necessary to learn the art of "practical politics."

As Catt and Shuler later recalled in *Woman Suffrage and Politics,* this was an all-absorbing effort. "It is doubtful," they wrote, "if any man, even among suffrage men, ever realized what the suffrage struggle came to mean to women before the end was allowed in America. How much of time and patience, how much work, energy and aspiration, how much faith, how much hope, how much despair went into it. It leaves its mark on one, such a struggle." In these years Catt, like Anthony in final decades of her life, set aside other causes to focus exclusively upon winning the suffrage battle. When the United States entered World War I, Catt put her own pacifism on hold and urged suffragists to support the war effort—a policy that disappointed many peace advocates but enhanced the patriotic image of the movement with the public and powerful decision-makers, including Wilson.

A growing number of state victories and Woodrow Wilson's conversion (he began working for the federal amendment in 1918) finally led Congress to approve the Nineteenth Amendment and to submit it to the states in June 1919. Historians debate the relative contributions of Catt and the NAWSA versus Paul and the NWP to the victory in Congress. But clearly Catt's careful coordination of suffragists all over the nation and skillful political maneuvering, together with the pressure on Wilson and members of Congress that Paul and other militant suffragists applied by less orthodox methods of persuasion, were all major factors.

The Fight for Ratification

The final chapter in the suffrage story was still ahead: thirty-six states had to ratify the amendment before it could become law. As the struggle over ratification began, Illinois and Wisconsin competed for the honor of being the first to ratify, while Georgia and Alabama scrambled to be the first to pass a "rejection resolution." Most states took longer to act, and many battles were hard fought, with suffragists and anti-suffragists using all powers of persuasion at their command. By the summer of 1920, suffragists were dismayed to find that while only one more state was needed, no further legislative sessions were scheduled before the November 1920 election. Desperate, suffragists began pleading for special sessions. President Wilson was finally able to pressure the reluctant governor of Tennessee into calling such a session.

Thus the final battle over woman suffrage took place in Nashville, Tennessee in the long, hot summer of 1920. In that final, dramatic contest, anti-suffragists as well as suffragists from all over the nation descended upon the state in a bitter struggle over ideology and influence. That the suffrage movement's "Armageddon" took place in the South added to the suffragists' difficulties, as many white southerners regarded the federal amendment as "an extension" of the much-resented Fifteenth Amendment, and anti-suffragists presented the federal amendment as a threat to white supremacy and states' rights. The liquor industry and its corporate allies also appeared to be actively engaged in the struggle.

Despite the glare of national publicity, the suffragists watched with dismay as a comfortable margin in favor of ratification gradually disappeared, and they were quite uncertain of the result when the vote took place. When, on August 18, it appeared that Tennessee had ratified—the result of one twenty-four-year-old legislator from the mountains, Harry Burn, changing his vote at the insistence of his elderly mother, Febb King Ensminger Burn—the antis still managed to delay official ratification through parliamentary tricks. While anti-suffrage legislators fled the state to avoid a quorum, their associates held massive anti-ratification rallies and otherwise attempted to convince pro-suffrage legislators to oppose ratification. Finally, Tennessee reaffirmed its vote for ratification, and the Nineteenth Amendment was officially added to the United States Constitution on August 26, 1920.

One Woman, One Vote:
Rediscovering the Woman Suffrage Movement

This short history of the movement, as the reader will see, is drawn largely from the essays that follow. The nineteen essays, each focusing on a particular aspect of the suffrage story but presented in roughly chronological order, together tell the fascinating story of the woman suffrage movement from the failure of the Constitution to enfranchise women to the participation of women in politics after 1920. The authors of the essays, scholars in the fields of History, American Studies, Political Science, and Sociology, help us to "rediscover" the woman suffrage movement as they cover new ground, offer intriguing and sometimes conflicting interpretations, and challenge widely accepted theories about the movement's history.

Together the essays describe why a suffrage movement was necessary, how the movement began, and how it changed over time in response to changes in American society and politics. Through them we are introduced to several generations of suffrage leaders and learn of the supportive relationships as well as tensions that developed among them. We learn of the growing diversity of the suffrage constituency in terms of region, religion, race, class, ethnicity, and even attitude, and that the suffrage story included both a record of harmony and cooperation between diverse groups of suffragists, and a disturbing record of discrimination and betrayal. We come to a better understanding of the reasons that some American men and women opposed woman suffrage, and how—despite so many obstacles—suffragists finally prevailed. Finally, we discover that, though the diverse coalition known as the suffrage movement did not—and indeed, could not—turn into a united voting "bloc" after 1920, women continued to be politically active in a wide range of organizations and movements. Above all we learn that the franchise was not given to women when the Nineteenth Amendment was ratified seventy-five years ago: generations of suffragists labored long and hard to win this acknowledgment of woman's right to vote in the United States.

"Representative Women." 1870 lithograph. Clockwise from top: Lucretia Mott, Elizabeth Cady Stanton, Mary Livermore, Lydia Maria Child, Susan B. Anthony, and Grace Greenwood. Anna Dickinson is in the center. Library of Congress

One

"Ourselves and Our Daughters Forever":

Women and the Constitution, 1787–1876

Linda K. Kerber

Editor's Introduction: In this essay, Linda K. Kerber, one of the leading scholars of women in the American Revolution and the early national period, discusses why women were excluded from the vote as the new nation was launched and remained disfranchised during the nation's first one hundred years. Kerber makes it clear why a woman suffrage movement was necessary, and why suffragists came to focus on an amendment to the Constitution.

After describing the dramatic protest against women's political and legal inferiority, led by Susan B. Anthony and Elizabeth Cady Stanton at the 1876 celebration of the nation's centennial, Kerber examines the assumptions held by John Adams and the other Founding Fathers who implicitly excluded women from participation in the government of the new republic. These men, says Kerber, "Shared assumptions about women and politics so fully that they did not need to debate them," including the idea that women, like propertyless men, were dependent and "lacked a will of their own," and thus were appropriately excluded from suffrage. Significantly, the American Constitution did not *explicitly* exclude women from voting or other political rights. The states— assigned the task of establishing the requirements for voting—*could* have interpreted the Constitution to justify full enfranchisement of women, or the courts could have so ruled. "Women might have been absorbed fully into the American political community," writes Kerber, "without the necessity of constitutional amendment."

In the antebellum period, as the states dropped many of the restrictions on voting and extended the franchise to virtually all white men, however, no state moved to extend suffrage to women and the one state that had allowed women to vote rescinded this privilege. Thus, in the 1820s, 1830s, and 1840s, women began to protest publicly against their legal and political inferiority. In the Declaration of Sentiments adopted at the Seneca Falls Convention in 1848, participants demanded a wide range of constitutional, legal, and social reforms— including the right to vote.

After the Civil War, as the nation experienced a revolution in politics, and Congress amended the Constitution to address—for the first time—the issue of voter qualifications, women's rights advocates hoped that universal suffrage for *all* would be the result. As Kerber describes, however, the Fourteenth and Fifteenth Amendments, adopted to enfranchise the freedmen, actually added new obstacles to woman suffrage; not only did the amendment fail to include sex as a protected category along with race, but in the Fourteenth Amendment the word "male" was added to the Constitution for the first time. Ironically, the fact that women were now demanding the vote led the authors of the amendment to believe it was necessary to specify that the amendment would *not* enfranchise women.

Initially dismayed by these events, suffragists then tried the "New Departure," claiming suffrage and other rights based on a broad interpretation of the Fourteenth Amendment. As citizens, they claimed all the "privileges and immunities" of citizens, but were rebuffed by the courts. Thus, by the centennial celebration in 1876, it had become clear that woman suffrage was not going to emerge from reinterpretations of existing laws, either state or federal. If women were to be enfranchised, said Kerber, they would have to have "either an explicit constitutional amendment or a series of revisions in the laws of the states." Suffragists now knew what they would have to do to establish their right to the vote. The long and difficult fight for enfranchisement had only begun.

★   ★   ★   ★   ★

IN 1876, THE UNITED STATES celebrated one hundred years as an independent nation dedicated to the proposition that all men are created equal. The capstone of the celebration was a public reading of the Declaration of Independence in Independence Square Philadelphia, by a descendant of a signer, Richard Henry Lee.

Elizabeth Cady Stanton, who was then president of the National Woman Suffrage Association (NWSA), asked permission to present silently a women's protest and a written women's Declaration of Rights. Her request was denied. "Tomorrow we propose to celebrate what we have done the last hundred years," replied the president of the official ceremonies, "not what we have failed to do."

Led by Susan B. Anthony, five women appeared nevertheless at the official reading, distributing copies of their own Declaration. After this mildly disruptive gesture, they withdrew to the other side of the symmetrical Independence Hall, where they staged a counter-Centennial. "With sorrow we come to strike the one discordant note, on this one-hundredth anniversary of our country's birth," Susan B. Anthony declared.

Although the rhythms of her speech echoed the Declaration of Independence, as was fitting for the day—"The history of our country the past hundred years has been a series of assumptions and usurpations of power over woman..."—the substance of her speech was built on references to the Constitution. Anthony and the women for whom she spoke were troubled by the discrepancy between the universally applicable provisions of the Constitution and the specificity of the way in which these provisions were interpreted to exclude women. For example, since all juries excluded women, women were denied the right of trial by a jury of their peers. Although taxation without representation had been a rallying cry of the Revolution, single women and widows who owned property paid taxes although they could not vote for the legislators who set the taxes. A double standard of morals was maintained in law by which women were arrested for prostitution while men went free. The introduction of the word "male" into federal and state constitutions, Anthony asserted, functioned in effect as a bill of attainder, in that it treated women as a class, denying them the right of suffrage, and "thereby making sex a crime."

Anthony ended by calling for the impeachment of all officers of the federal government on the grounds that they had not fulfilled their obligations under the Constitution. Their "vacillating interpretations of constitutional law unsettle our faith in judicial authority, and undermine the liberties of the whole people," she declared.

> Special legislation for woman has placed us in a most anomalous position. Women invested with the rights of citizens in one section—voters, jurors, office holders—crossing an imaginary line, are subjects in the next. In some states a married woman may hold property and transact business in her own name; in others her earnings belong to her husband. In some states, a woman may testify against her husband, sue and be sued in the courts; in others she has no redress in case of damage to person, property, or character. In case of divorce on account of adultery in the husband, the innocent wife is held to possess no right to children or property, unless by special decrees of the court.... In some states women may enter the law school and practice in the courts; in others they are forbidden....
>
> These articles of impeachment against our rulers we now submit to the impartial judgment of the people... From the beginning of the century, when Abigail Adams, the wife of one president and mother of another, said, "We will not hold ourselves bound to obey laws in which we have no voice or representation," until now, woman's discontent has been steadily increasing, culminating nearly thirty years ago in a simultaneous movement among the women of the nation, demanding the right of suffrage.... It was the boast of the founders of the republic, that the rights for which they contended were the rights of human nature. If these rights are ignored in the case of one half the people, the nation is surely preparing for its downfall. Governments try themselves. The recognition of a governing and a governed class is incompatible with the first principles of freedom....[1]

The Founding Generation

Let us stand with Susan B. Anthony at her vantage point of 1876 and review the constitutional issues that touched women's lives in the first hundred years of the republic. During those hundred years, basic questions were defined and strategies for affecting legislation were developed. Not until after the Centennial would women direct their energies primarily to constitutional amendment. In the first century, the challenge was to understand whether and to what extent women's political status was different from that of men, and to develop a rationale for criticizing that difference.

It is intriguing to speculate how the Founders might have responded to Anthony's challenge. Throughout the long summer of 1787 in Philadelphia, the role of women in the new polity went formally unconsidered. Whether they came from small or large states, whether they favored the New Jersey or Virginia Plan, whether they hoped for a gradual end to slavery or a strengthening of the system, the men who came to Carpenters' Hall in 1787 shared assumptions about women and politics so fully that they did not need to debate them. Indeed, John Adams had missed the point in his now-famous exchange with Abigail Adams to which Anthony referred in her Centennial Address: Abigail Adams clearly had domestic violence as well as political representation in mind as she wrote; that is, she was thinking in both practical and theoretical terms.[2] Her husband refused to deal with the issue:

Abigail Adams to John Adams
March 31, 1776

...in the new Code of Laws which I suppose it will be necessary for you to make, I desire you would Remember the Ladies, and be more generous and favourable to them than your ancestors. Do not put such unlimited power into the hands of the Husbands. Remember all Men would be tyrants if they could. If perticular care and attention is not paid to the Laidies we are determined to foment a Rebelion, and will not hold ourselves bound by any Laws in which we have no voice, or Representation.

That your Sex are Naturally Tyrannical is a Truth so thoroughly established as to admit of no dispute.... Why then, not put it out of the power of the vicious and the Lawless to use us with cruelty and indignity with impunity....

John Adams to Abigail Adams
April 14, 1776

As to your extraordinary Code of Laws, I cannot but laugh. We have been told that our struggle has loosened the bonds of Government every where. That Children and Apprentices were disobedient—that schools and colleges were grown turbulent—that Indians slighted their guardians and Negroes grew insolent to their Masters. But your Letter was the first Intimation that another Tribe more numerous and powerfull than all the rest were grown discontented.... Depend upon it, We know better than to repeal our Masculine systems.... We have only the Name of Masters, and rather than give up this, which would compleatly subject Us to the Despotism of the Peticoat, I hope General Washington, and all our brave Heroes would fight....

Abigail Adams to John Adams
May 7, 1776

...Arbitrary power is like most other things which are very hard, very liable to be broken....[3]

The exclusion of married women from the vote was based on the same principle that excluded men without property from the vote. If the will of the people was in fact to be expressed by voting, it was important that each vote be independent and uncoerced. Men who had no property and were dependent on their landlords or employers for survival were understood to be vulnerable to pressure; they were, in John Adams's words, "too dependent upon other men to have a will of their own." Adams acknowledged, in fact, that excluding all women was somewhat arbitrary; but lines, as he explained in a thoughtful letter to the Massachusetts politician James Sullivan, had to be drawn somewhere.

John Adams to James Sullivan
May 26, 1776

It is certain, in theory, that the only moral foundation of government is, the consent of the people. But to what an extent shall we carry this principle? Shall we say that every individual of the community, old and young, male and female, as well as rich and poor, must consent, expressly, to every act of legislation? No, you will say, this is impossible. How then, does the right arise in the majority to govern the minority, against their will? Whence arises the right of the men to govern the women, without their consent? Whence the right of the old to bind the young, without theirs?...

But why exclude women?

You will say, because their delicacy renders them unfit for practice and experience in the great businesses of life, and the hardy enterprises of war.... Besides, their attention is so much engaged with the necessary nurture of their children, that nature has made them fittest for domestic cares. And children have not judgment or will of their own. True, but will not these reasons apply to others? Is it not equally true, that men in general, in every society, who are wholly destitute of property, are also too little acquainted with public affairs to form a right judgment, and too dependent upon other men to have a will of their own?... They talk and vote as they are directed by some man of property....

Your idea that those laws which affect the lives and personal liberty of all, or which inflict corporal punishment, affect those who are not qualified to vote, as well as those who are, is just. But so they do women, as well as men; children, as well as adults. What reason should there be for excluding a man of twenty years eleven months and twenty-seven days old, from a vote, when you admit one who is twenty-one? The reason is, you must fix upon some period in life, when the understanding and will of men in general, is fit to be trusted by the public. Will not the same reason justify the state in fixing upon some certain quantity of property, as a qualification?

The same reasoning which will induce you to admit all men who have not property, to vote, with those who have, for those laws which affect the person, will prove that you ought to admit women and children; for, generally speaking, women and children have as good judgments, and as independent minds, as those men who are wholly destitute of property; these last being to all intents and purposes as much dependent upon others, who will please to feed, clothe and employ them, as women are upon their husbands, or children on their parents.

Depend upon it, Sire, it is dangerous to open so fruitful a source of controversy and altercations as would be opened by attempting to alter the qualifications of voters; there will be no end of it. New claims will arise; women will demand a vote; kids from twelve to twenty-one will think their rights not enough attended to; and every man who has not a farthing, will demand an equal voice with any other; in all acts of state. It tends to confound and destroy all distinctions, and prostrate all ranks to one common level....[4]

John Adams spelled out with unusual frankness what most of his colleagues believed. If dependent men were to vote, the result would not be that the will of all individuals was counted; rather the result would be that landlords and employers would in effect exercise multiple votes. Married women were thought to be in much the same state as unpropertied men. Their property, according to the traditional British law of domestic relations, came under their husbands' power when they married, a practice known as coverture. The married woman, "covered" by her husband's civic identity, lost the power to manipulate her property independently. (She remained however, an independent moral being under the law, capable of committing crimes, even treason.) To give a vote to a person so dependent on another's will seemed to give a double vote to husbands, rather than to enfranchise wives. In a society in which it was assumed that the wife did the husband's bidding, it seemed absurd to give married men a political advantage over their unmarried brothers. Instead of revising the old law of domestic relations, and taking married women out from under the "cover" of their husbands' authority, virtually all the states denied the franchise to married women.

Roads Not Taken

The logic that excluded married women should not have, on the face of it, excluded unmarried women with property—including widows—who were not under the immediate influence of an adult man, who could buy and sell their property, and who paid taxes. Single adult women might have formed a substantial electorate, even in a system of coverture. But in practice custom rather than logic prevailed; single women were treated for the most part as were their married counterparts.

Only in New Jersey, where the state constitution of 1776 enfranchised "all free inhabitants" who could meet property and residence requirements did women vote; in 1790, possibly because of Quaker influence, an election law used the phrase "he or she" in referring to voters.

The New Jersey Constitution of 1776 provided that "All Inhabitants of this colony, of full age, who are worth fifty pounds proclamation money, clear estate in the same, and have resided within the county in which they claim a vote for twelve months immediately preceding the election, shall be entitled to vote for Representatives in Council and Assembly; and also for all other public officers, that shall be elected by the people of the county at large...."

In 1797, New Jersey law explicitly recognized that women voted: "No person shall be entitled to vote in any other township or precinct, than that in which he or she doth actually reside at the time of the election.... Every voter shall openly, and in full view deliver his or her ballot...."

The general tendency in suffrage law throughout the nineteenth century was to broaden the electorate by gradually eliminating property and racial qualifications; yet the New Jersey election statute did not become a model for other states. In 1797 the women's vote was thought to have been exercised as a bloc vote in favor of the Federalist candidate for Elizabethtown in the state legislature, and it was alleged to have made a real difference in the outcome of the election.

Faced with this gender gap, the defeated Democratic-Republicans launched a bitter campaign with two themes that were to appear and reappear as long as woman suffrage was debated in this country. First, they argued that women who appeared at the polls were unfeminine, forgetful of their proper place. Second, they asserted that women were easily manipulated, if not by husbands, then by fathers and brothers. It took ten years, but in 1807 New Jersey passed a new election law excluding all women from the polls, and no other state attempted New Jersey's 1776 experiment. In the absence of a collective political movement, no delegate came to Philadelphia in 1787 prepared to make an issue of woman suffrage or of any other distinctively female political concern; no one came prepared to engage in debate over the extent to which women were an active part of the political community.

With the benefit of hindsight, it is possible for historians to identify some substantive issues that politically empowered women might well have raised had the Constitution guaranteed their right to participate in a republican government. (Some of these issues would be addressed only a few years later, by Montagnards and Jacobins in France.) One obvious issue is divorce reform. In some states divorce was nearly impossible in 1787; in all it was extremely difficult. Since the majority of petitioners for divorce were women, the issue was one in which women had a distinctive interest. The language of republicanism, with its acknowledgment that the new order validated a search for happiness, was taken by a number of people to imply that divorce reform was a logical implication of republicanism. But the Constitution said nothing about it, and the states loosened restrictions only slowly. Two generations later women's rights activists would place divorce reform high on their political agenda; it is probable that it would also have been given priority on an agenda drafted in the 1780s.

A second concern might have been pensions for widows of soldiers. The Continental Congress authorized modest pensions for the widows of officers, but widows of soldiers would not be provided with pensions until 1832, by which time, of course, many of them were dead. It is easy to think of other issues: the

Women voting in New Jersey, c. 1800. Library of Congress

right of mothers to child custody in the event of divorce, restrictions on wife abuse, the security of dower rights. But expressions of opinion on these issues remained the work of individuals; no collective feminist movement gave them articulate expression as was the case in France. No organized female political pressure was brought to bear at the Constitutional Convention; there do not seem to have been American predecessors of the female Jacobin clubs of Paris.

The Constitution reflected the experience of the white middle- and upper-class men who wrote it and the experience of their constituents, the men of the upper- and lower-middle classes, the farmers and artisans, who had, as historian Edward Countryman has observed, "established their political identity in the Revolution." Although their political choices were characterized by what the historian Michael Grossberg has called their "deep aversion to unaccountable authority," they retained the authority of husbands over wives intact.[5] All free men, rich or poor, continued to gain control of their wives' bodies and property when they married. Women had not yet, as a group, firmly established their political identity.

Gender and the Language of the Constitution

The Constitution did not explicitly welcome women as voters or take particular account of them as a class. However, what the Constitution left unsaid was as important as what it did say. The text of the Constitution usually speaks of "persons"; only rarely does it use the generic "he." Women as well as men were defined as citizens. The Constitution establishes no voting requirements, leaving it up to the states to set the terms by which people shall qualify to vote.

> ***Article 1, Section 2:*** The House of Representatives shall be composed of Members chosen every Year by the People of the several States, and the Electors in each State shall have the qualifications requisite for Electors of the most numerous Branch of the State Legislature.

Thus women were not explicitly excluded from Congress, nor even from the presidency. The Constitution, in fact, left an astonishing number of substantive matters open to the choices of individual states; every part of it was open to change by amendment. This flexibility is an important reason for the survival of the American Constitution, as contrasted to the other republican constitutions of the era, like the French, which were far more detailed and explicit, but also less resilient. Women might have been absorbed fully into the American political community without the necessity of constitutional amendment.

Yet this absorption did not occur automatically. No state imitated New Jersey's experiment with suffrage before the Civil War; only a few—Utah, Wyoming, Colorado, Idaho—did so after the war. No state moved to place non-voters on juries, although there was obvious common sense in the argument that in order for a woman to be tried by her peers a jury should include women, whether or not women voted in that state. Although the old argument that the proper voter was a person of property eroded as liberals steadily decreased property requirements for voting by men, women were not enfranchised.

Attempts at Reform

Still, even without the vote, effective political coalitions of feminists and legal reformers developed at the end of the 1830s. They were interested in the codification and simplification of state laws. They pressed for the passage of Married Women's Property Acts that would enable married women to control property without necessitating cumbersome trusteeship arrangements. Beginning with a severely limited statute passed in Mississippi in 1839 and continuing throughout the century, state Married Women's Property Acts gradually extended the financial independence of married women, making it possible for a few feminists to entertain a vision of a full range of women's political activity, even under the older requirements of property holding. However, the new control that women achieved over their own property was not accompanied by the extension of the franchise.

The New York State Married Women's Property Act provides an example of this type of legislation:

> The real and personal property of any female [now married and] who may here-after marry, and which she shall own at the time of marriage, and the rents, issues and profits thereof shall not be subject to the disposal of her husband, nor be liable for his debts, and shall continue her sole and separate property, as if she were a single female.... It shall be lawful for any married female to receive by gift, grant, devise or bequest, from any person other than her husband and hold to her sole and separate use, as if she were a single female, real and personal property, and the rents, issues and profits thereof and the same shall not be subject to the disposal of her husband, nor be liable for his debts....
>
> A married woman may bargain, sell, assign, and transfer her separate personal property, and carry on any trade or business, and perform any labor or services on her sole and separate account, and the earnings of any married woman from her trade...shall be her sole and separate property, and may be used or invested by her in her own name....
>
> Any married woman may, while married, sue and be sued in all matters having relation to her...sole and separate property...in the same manner as if she were sole....
>
> Every married woman is hereby constituted and declared to be the joint guardian of her children, with her husband, with equal powers, rights, and duties in regard to them, with the husband....[6]

Elizabeth Cady Stanton, who had been a strong supporter of the New York Married Women's Property Acts, was also an energizing force behind the gathering of women in Seneca Falls in 1848. She and others who prepared and signed the Declaration of Sentiments at that meeting addressed forcefully the ways in which women had not been fully absorbed into the republican political order, although they were citizens. After a preface casting "Man" in a rhetorical role comparable to that played by King George III in the Declaration of Independence, the Declaration of Sentiments addressed constitutional and legal as well as social questions: trial by jury, the relationship between taxation and representation, the persistence of coverture.

> He has compelled her to submit to laws, in the formation of which she had no voice....

> He has made her, if married, in the eye of the law, civilly dead....

> He has taken from her all right in property, even to the wages she earns....

After depriving her of all rights as a married woman, if single, and the owner of property, he has taxed her to support a government which recognizes her only when her property can be made profitable to it....[7]

The legislative gains of the early part of the century and the emergence of a women's movement at mid-century were not, however, followed by a wave of enfranchisement. In fact, women found themselves excluded from the debate about the extension of the franchise that was engendered by the Civil War.

The Civil War Amendments, the New Departure and Its Defeat

The Civil War was not only a military crisis but also a revolution in politics, which would be validated by the Thirteenth, Fourteenth, and Fifteenth Amendments. By now there was most emphatically, a collective women's public presence—in the Sanitary Commission, the women's abolitionist societies, the Women's National Loyal League. But the "Woman Question" had not been central to the ideology of the Civil War, and once again, women found they could not claim the benefits. Abolitionist and Republican feminists had permitted themselves to anticipate that suffrage would be the appropriate reward for their sacrifices and support of the war effort. They also believed strongly that the authentic meaning of the expanded citizenship embedded in the Fourteenth Amendment was contradicted by its enforcement clauses. That is, if indeed "all persons, born or naturalized in the United States are citizens of the United States and the state in which they reside" then, they thought, women as well as men, black and white, should have the vote as one of the "privileges and immunities of citizenship." Their resentment was therefore all the greater when woman suffrage was not made part of the post-war amendments. The inclusion of the word "male" in the second section of the Fourteenth Amendment—a section never enforced—rubbed salt in a raw wound. The Fifteenth Amendment, guaranteeing the vote to all men despite race or previous condition of servitude, made explicit what the Fourteenth Amendment had left implicit.

Fourteenth Amendment, 1868
Section One

All persons born or naturalized in the United States, and subject to the jurisdiction thereof, are citizens of the United States and of the State wherein they reside. No State shall make or enforce any law which shall abridge the privileges or immunities of citizens of the United States; nor shall any State deprive any person of life, liberty or property, without due process of law; nor deny to any person within its jurisdiction the equal protection of the laws.

Section Two

Representatives shall be apportioned among the several States according to their respective numbers, counting the whole number of persons in each State, excluding Indians not taxed. But when the right to vote at any election for the choice of electors for President and Vice-President of the United States, Representatives in Congress, the executive and judicial officers of a State, or the members of the legislature thereof, is denied to any of the male inhabitants of such State, being twenty-one years of age and citizens of the United States, or in any way abridged, except for participation in rebellion, or other crime, the basis of representation therein shall be reduced in the proportion which the number of such male citizens shall bear to the whole number of male citizens twenty-one years of age in such State....

Holding their tempers, suffragists embarked on a national effort to test the universal possibilities of the first section of the Fourteenth Amendment, a strategy they called "the New Departure," only to discover that the Supreme Court rejected their arguments.[8] It was tested first in 1873 by Myra Bradwell, a Chicago woman who had studied law with her husband. She had been granted a special charter from the State of Illinois permitting her to edit and publish the *Chicago Legal News* as her own business, a business she carried on with distinction. (After the Chicago fire destroyed many law offices, it was the files of Bradwell's *Legal News* on which the city's attorneys relied for their records.) Bradwell claimed that one of the "privileges and immunities" of a citizen guaranteed by Section One was her right to practice law in the State of Illinois and to argue cases. The Illinois Supreme Court turned her down, on the ground that as a married woman, she was not a fully free agent.

In her appeal to the Supreme Court, Bradwell's attorney argued that among the "privileges and immunities" guaranteed to each citizen by the Fourteenth Amendment was the right to pursue any honorable profession. "Intelligence, integrity and honor are the only qualifications that can be prescribed.... The broad shield of the Constitution is over all, and protects each in that measure of success which his or her individual merits may secure." But the Supreme Court held that the right to practice law in any particular state was a right that might be granted by the individual state; it was not one of the privileges and immunities of citizenship. A concurring opinion added an ideological dimension:

> The natural and proper timidity and delicacy which belongs to the female sex evidently unfits it for many of the occupations of civil life. The constitution of the family organization, which is founded on the divine ordinance, as well as in the nature of things, indicates the domestic sphere as that which properly belongs to the domain and functions of womanhood. The harmony, not to say identity, of interests and views which belong or should belong to the family institution, is repugnant to the idea of a woman adopting a distinct and independent career from that of her husband. So firmly fixed was this sentiment in the founders of the common law that it became a maxim of that system of jurisprudence that a woman had no legal existence separate from her husband, who was regarded as her head and representative in the social state...many of the special rules of law flowing from and dependent upon this cardinal principal still exist in full force in most states. One of these is that a married woman is incapable, without her husband's consent, of making contracts which shall be binding on her or him. This very incapacity was one circumstance which the supreme court of Illinois deemed important in rendering a married woman incompetent fully to perform the duties and trusts that belong to the office of an attorney and counselor.[9]

Meanwhile, suffragists in a number of places attempted to test the other possibilities of the first section of the Fourteenth Amendment. In the presidential election of 1872, suffragist women in a number of districts appeared at the polls, arguing that if all citizens had the right to the privileges of citizenship, they could certainly exercise the right to vote. Susan B. Anthony presented herself at a barber shop in the eighth ward in Rochester, New York, which was serving as a polling place, and convinced two out of the three polling inspectors to register her, on the grounds that the New York State Constitution made no sex distinctions in the qualifications for voters. By the end of the day, fifteen more women had registered. On November 5, having first assured the inspectors that if they were prosecuted for admitting unauthorized persons to the polls, she would pay their legal fees, Anthony and the other women voted. It would be Anthony and the other women who were arrested for an illegal attempt to vote, not the inspectors. When she was judged guilty, she refused to pay her bail, hoping to force the case to the Supreme Court. A supporter, however, thinking he was doing Anthony a favor, paid it. The case was set for trial; in the interlude she voted in the Rochester city elections, and no one made a fuss. When the trial was moved to another county, Anthony and her colleagues made a whirlwind tour, speaking in approximately twenty towns each, ensuring that public opinion would not be uniformly against them even in a strange locale.

Anthony reasoned that sex was a characteristic markedly different from youth or being an alien. Although aliens could not vote, an individual alien man could choose to become a naturalized citizen. Minors could not vote, but minors, in the nature of things, grew to adulthood. "Qualifications," she argued, "can not be in their nature permanent or insurmountable. Sex can not be a qualification any more than size, race, color, or previous condition of servitude."

The judge, wanting to deny Anthony the legal system as a forum, directed the jury to bring in a verdict of guilty, and immediately discharged the jury. He fined Anthony $100. When she announced that she would "never pay a dollar of your unjust penalty," he declined to enforce the punishment. "Madam, the Court will not order you to stand committed until the fine is paid." Thus he had it both ways; a verdict of guilty, which would dissuade others from following Anthony's path, but a refusal to punish, thus avoiding making Anthony a martyr and making it impossible for her to bring the case to the U.S. Supreme Court.[10]

The president of the Woman Suffrage Association of Missouri was able to do what Anthony could not. Observing that the "power to regulate is one thing, the power to prevent is an entirely different thing," Virginia Minor attempted to vote in St. Louis. When the registrar refused to permit her to register, she and her husband Francis, an attorney who had developed the distinction between regulation and prohibition of suffrage, sued him for denying her one of the privileges and immunities of citizenship. When they lost the case they appealed to the Supreme Court.

In *Minor v. Happersett,* decided in 1875, the Court ruled that change must happen as a result of explicit legislation or constitutional amendment, rather than by interpretation of the implications of the Constitution. In a unanimous opinion the Court observed that it was "too late" to claim the right of suffrage by implication; the Founders had been men who weighed their words carefully. Nearly a hundred years of failure to claim inclusion by implication made a difference. What might have been gradual evolution in the founders' generation was avoidance of legal due process a hundred years later—"If suffrage was intended to be included...language better adapted to express that intent would most certainly have been employed." The Court was not prepared to interpret the Constitution freshly: "If the law is wrong it ought to be changed; but the power for that is not with us...." The decision meant that woman suffrage could not emerge from reinterpretation of the Constitution; it would require either an explicit constitutional amendment or a series of revisions in the laws of the states.

> ...For nearly ninety years the people have acted upon the idea that the Constitution, when it conferred citizenship, did not necessarily confer the right of suffrage. If uniform practice long continued can settle the construction of so important an instrument as the Constitution of the

United States confessedly is, most certainly it has been done here. Our province is to decide what the law is, not to declare what it should be.[11]

Reluctant Realignment of Suffrage Strategy

In the years between 1848 and 1876, American women had created a collective movement. It is true that it did not include the entire female population; many women were unaware and more were hostile. But the activists had brought into being an articulate and politically sophisticated pressure group which was prepared to offer an explicit and detailed criticism of the American political system and to make direct demands for inclusion in it.

When Susan B. Anthony rose to speak on July 4, 1876, the strategies of feminist politics were being realigned. She had the court decisions in *Bradwell* and *Minor* in mind as she spoke. She addressed not only the issue of suffrage but also the exclusion of women from multiple aspects of the political community that the Constitution had created. The right to serve on a jury had been so precious to American men that some states had refused to ratify the Constitution until they were convinced it would be added; yet "the women of this nation have never been allowed a jury of their peers," even in crimes like infanticide or adultery, where women's perspective might well be different from that of men. Anthony decried the division of the community into a class of men, which governed, and a class of women, which was governed.

Anthony's generation of feminists would begin their campaign for suffrage to restore what the second section of the Fourteenth Amendment—with its introduction of the word male—had killed by implication. But as historian Ellen DuBois has shrewdly discerned, this strategy abandoned the healthier, more inclusive strategy of the pre-1876 period, when claims for the vote as part of the privileges of *all* citizens meant that women understood themselves to be part of a community that included men and women, black and white. A suffrage amendment would be introduced in the Senate in 1878, and a new chapter in the political history of feminism would begin, one which emphasized the distinctive claims of women.

It is important to recognize that Stanton and Anthony began with a definition of equality under the Constitution that was considerably more inclusive than the vote alone. It included a vision of egalitarianism in the process of lawmaking as well as in the outcome. Ever since the 1848 Declaration of Sentiments, it had included a vision of equality within the family, between husbands and wives, as well as social equality, between male and female citizens, in the public realm. In her Centennial Address, Anthony expressed the full range of this vision, attacking double standards in moral codes, unequal pay scales, unequal treatment of adulterers. She would not be surprised today to see wife abuse, female health, or the feminization of poverty emerge as topics high on the contemporary feminist agenda. "It was the boast of the founders of the republic, that the rights for which they contended were the rights of human nature. If these rights are ignored in the case of one-half the people, the nation is surely preparing for its downfall," she declared.

Anthony ended her Declaration of Rights with a ringing conclusion. If there are any schoolchildren today who still—as children did in the nineteenth century—memorize great moments in the oratorical tradition of this country like Webster's reply to Hayne or Lincoln's Gettysburg Address, they should add this to their repertory:

And now, at the close of a hundred years, as the hour-hand of the great clock that marks the centuries points to 1876, we declare our faith in the principles of self government; our full equality with man in natural rights; that woman was made first for her own happiness, with the absolute right to herself—to all the opportunities and advantages life affords for her complete development; and we deny that dogma of the centuries, incorporated in the codes of all nations—that woman was made for man—her best interests...to be sacrificed to his will. We ask of our rulers, at this hour, no special privileges, no special legislation. We ask justice, we ask equality, we ask that all the civil and political rights that belong to citizens of the United States be guaranteed to us and our daughters forever.

Notes

This essay is a slightly expanded version of "'Ourselves and Our Daughters Forever': Women and the Constitution, 1787-1876," reprinted from *This Constitution: A Bicentennial Chronicle,* Spring 1985, 25-34, published by Project '87, of the American Historical Association and the American Political Science Association.

1. This account of the July 4, 1876 protest and the text of Anthony's speech is drawn from *History of Woman Suffrage,* eds., Elizabeth Cady Stanton, Susan B. Anthony, and Matilda Joslyn Gage, (Rochester, N.Y., 1886), 3: 31-34.

2. On this point, see the shrewd comments of Nancy F. Cott, "Passionlessness: An Interpretation of Victorian Sexual Ideology, 1790-1850," *Signs: A Journal of Women in Culture and Society* 4 (1978): 228-29.

3. L.H. Butterfield, ed., *Adams Family Correspondence* (Cambridge, Mass., 1963: New York, 1965) 1: 369-70, 382, 402.

4. John Adams to James Sullivan, 26 May 1776, in Robert J. Taylor, et al, *Papers of John Adams* (Cambridge, Mass., 1979) 4: 208-213.

5. Michael Grossberg, *Governing the Hearth: Law and the Family in Nineteenth-Century America* (Chapel Hill, 1985), 5-6.

6. *Laws of the State of New-York, Passed at the Seventy-First Session of the Legislature...* (Albany, 1848), 307-8; *Laws of the State of New York, Passed at the Eighty-Third Session of the Legislature...* (Albany, 1860), 157-59.

7. The complete text of the Declaration of Sentiments can be found in "The Seneca Falls Convention," *One Woman, One Vote,* below.

8. See two brilliant essays by Ellen DuBois, "Outgrowing the Compact of the Fathers: Equal Rights, Woman Suffrage, and the United States Constitution, 1820-1878," *Journal of American History* 74 (1987): 836-62, and "Taking the Law Into Our Own Hands: *Bradwell, Minor* and Suffrage Militance in the 1870s," in *One Woman, One Vote,* below.

9. *Myra Bradwell v. State of Illinois,* 83 U.S. 130 (1873).

10. See Ida Husted Harper, ed. *The Life and Work of Susan B. Anthony* (Indianapolis, 1899), 1: 423-53.

11. *Minor v. Happersett,* 88 U.S. 162 (1875).

Two

The Seneca Falls Convention

Editor's Introduction: In this passage from the six-volume suf-
frage classic, *History of Woman Suffrage,* (Volume 1, 1881), editors Elizabeth
Cady Stanton, Susan B. Anthony, and Matilda J. Gage tell the story of the 1848
convention in Seneca Falls, New York. Though there were individuals including
Abigail Adams, Frances Wright, Maria W. Stewart, Sarah and Angelina Grimké,
Maria Weston Chapman, Abby Kelley Foster, Ernestine Rose, Lydia Maria
Child, Margaret Fuller, and Lucy Stone, speaking out in favor of women's rights
before 1848, the Seneca Falls Convention is generally regarded as the origin of
the woman suffrage movement. The site of the Wesleyan Chapel where the convention took place and Stanton's Seneca Falls home are now National Historic
Sites.

The passage contains the famous "Declaration of Sentiments" adopted at the
convention, one of the most important documents in American history. The suffragists modeled their Declaration after the United States Declaration of Independence, enlisting for their cause the powerful, revolutionary rhetoric still much in
the public consciousness, and indirectly making the point that women had been
left out of the freedoms gained by white men as a result of the Revolution.

The women who organized the convention and drafted the Declaration—all
white, middle-class, married women—were, in the words of Stanton, Anthony,
and Gage, "fortunately organized and conditioned," and "had not in their own
experience endured the coarser forms of tyranny resulting from unjust laws or
association with unscrupulous men." As they compiled their list of grievances
to present to the world, these pioneering suffragists laughed at themselves for
having to go to the books to find a list sufficient to make a good case! They nevertheless felt "the wrongs of others" as well as the "insults incident to sex" contained in law, religion, literature, and custom that were an affront to "every
proud, thinking woman." Foreshadowing the elitism, nativism, and racism that
was later manifested in the suffrage movement, however, they expressed indignation that man "has withheld from her [woman] rights which are given to the
most ignorant and degraded men—both natives and foreigners."

The Declaration of Sentiments was a fitting document for the birth of the
women's movement as it addressed a wide range of issues: moral, political, religious, legal, educational, occupational, and even psychological, issues that the
women's movement *continues* to address. It comes as a surprise to most modern
readers that the ninth resolution calling for women to demand their "sacred

right to the elective franchise" was the most controversial. It was adopted by a slender margin owing to the strenuous efforts of Elizabeth Cady Stanton and Frederick Douglass who insisted the vote was the means by which their other demands could be realized.

That so many people (three hundred, including forty men) responded to their "call" surprised the convention's organizers but made it clear that the time was right for their venture. That women like Stanton and Mott were daunted at the prospect of chairing such a large gathering and drafted James Mott for the job, indicates the degree to which women—even *these* extraordinary women—were affected by the nearly universal disdain for women speaking in public. Several of the resolutions reflect their frustration at being denied the right to participate fully in the great antebellum reform movements of their day including temperance and antislavery. Given the prevailing view that women were morally superior to men, these women found it absurd that so many men engaged in moral reforms were attempting to deny them and other women the right to preach and teach versus the social evils of their day. In fact, Stanton and Mott first met in London at the 1840 World Anti-slavery Convention, where Mott and the other female delegates from America were rejected; rather than watch silently from the galleries, the two women took the opportunity to tour London "arm in arm" and talk of starting a women's rights movement in America.

As indicated by the concluding paragraph of the Declaration of Sentiments, the signers of the Declaration knew that they would be misrepresented and ridiculed, but they proclaimed that they would "use every instrumentality within our power to effect our object." All of this occurred as predicted. Outraged newspaper editors denounced the convention as shocking, unwomanly, monstrous, and unnatural, or ridiculed them as Amazons or love-starved spinsters. The ensuing storm of protest led some of the one hundred signers to retract their signatures. Frederick Douglass, one of their few champions in the press (and a supporter of women's rights until his death in 1895), defended the convention in *The North Star*. He was appalled that the women's rights advocates were abused and ridiculed even by those "who have at last made the discovery that negroes have some rights as well as other members of the human family." Indeed, said Douglass, "a discussion of the rights of animals would be regarded with far more complacency by many of what are called the *wise* and the good of our land."

However, the outraged editors inadvertently aided the movement; as word spread of the convention, women were inspired to call other conventions. In October 1850, the first National Woman's Rights Convention was held in Worcester, Massachusetts, and thereafter conventions took place every year (except 1857) until the Civil War led to a postponement of women's rights activities. Many of them were organized by the third member of the great suffrage triumvirate of the nineteenth century, Lucy Stone, who along with Susan B. Anthony, became fully engaged in this great movement soon after Seneca Falls.

★   ★   ★   ★   ★

Woman's Rights Convention—A Convention to discuss the social, civil, and religious condition and rights of woman, will be held in the Wesleyan Chapel, at Seneca Falls, N. Y., on Wednesday and Thursday, the 19th and 20th of July, current; commencing at 10 o'clock A.M. During the first day the meeting will be exclusively for women, who are earnestly invited to attend. The public generally are invited to be present on the second day, when Lucretia Mott, of Philadelphia, and other ladies and gentlemen, will address the convention.

This call, without signature, was issued by Lucretia Mott, Martha C. Wright, Elizabeth Cady Stanton, and Mary Ann McClintock....

The eventful day dawned at last, and crowds in carriages and on foot, wended their way to the Wesleyan church. When those having charge of the Declaration, the resolutions, and several volumes of the Statutes of New York arrived on the scene, lo! the door was locked. However, an embryo Professor of Yale College was lifted through an open window to unbar the door; that done, the church was quickly filled. It had been decided to have no men present, but as they were already on the spot, and as the women who must take the responsibility of organizing the meeting, and leading the discussions, shrank from doing either, it was decided, in a hasty council round the altar, that this was an occasion when men might make themselves pre-eminent]y useful. It was agreed they should remain, and take the laboring oar through the Convention.

James Mott, tall and dignified, in Quaker costume, was called to the chair; Mary McClintock appointed Secretary, Frederick Douglass, Samuel Tillman, Ansel Bascom, E.W. Capron, and Thomas McClintock took part throughout in the discussions. Lucretia Mott, accustomed to public speaking in the Society of Friends, stated the objects of the Convention, and in taking a survey of the degraded condition of woman the world over, showed the importance of inaugurating some movement for her education and elevation. Elizabeth and Mary McClintock, and Mrs. Stanton, each read a well-written speech; Martha Wright read some satirical articles she had published in the daily papers answering the diatribes on woman's sphere. Ansel Bascom, who had been a member of the Constitutional Convention recently held in Albany, spoke at length on the property bill for married women, just passed the Legislature, and the discussion on woman's rights in that Convention. Samuel Tillman, a young student of law, read a series of the most exasperating statutes for women, from English and American jurists, all reflecting the *tender mercies* of men toward their wives, in taking care of their property and protecting them in their civil rights.

The Declaration having been freely discussed by many present, was re-read by Mrs. Stanton, and with some slight amendments adopted.

DECLARATION OF SENTIMENTS

When, in the course of human events, it becomes necessary for one portion of the family of man to assume among the people of the earth a position different from that which they have hitherto occupied, but one to which the laws of nature and of nature's God entitle them, a decent respect to the opinions of mankind requires that they should declare the causes that impel them to such a course.

We hold these truths to be self-evident: that all men and women are created equal; that they are endowed by their Creator with certain inalienable rights; that among these are life, liberty, and the pursuit of happiness; that to secure these rights governments are instituted, deriving their just powers from the consent of the governed. Whenever any form of government becomes destructive of these ends, it is the right of those who suffer from it to refuse allegiance to it, and to insist upon the institution of a new government, laying its foundation on such principles, and organizing its powers in such form, as to them shall seem most likely to effect their safety and happiness. Prudence indeed, will dictate that governments long established should not be changed for light and transient causes; and accordingly all experience hath shown that mankind are more disposed to suffer, while evils are sufferable, than to right themselves by abolishing the forms to which they were accustomed. But when a long train of abuses and usurpations, pursuing invariably the same object evinces a design to reduce them under absolute despotism, it is their duty to throw off such government, and to provide new guards for their future security. Such has been the patient sufferance of the women under this government, and such is now the necessity which constrains them to demand the equal station to which they are entitled.

The history of mankind is a history of repeated injuries and usurpations on the part of man toward woman, having in direct object the establishment of an absolute tyranny over her. To prove this, let facts be submitted to a candid world.

He has never permitted her to exercise her inalienable right to the elective franchise.

He has compelled her to submit to laws, in the formation of which she had no voice.

He has withheld from her rights which are given to the most ignorant and degraded men—both natives and foreigners.

Having deprived her of this first right of a citizen, the elective franchise, thereby leaving her without representation in the halls of legislation, he has oppressed her on all sides.

He has made her, if married, in the eye of the law, civilly dead.

He has taken from her all right in property, even to the wages she earns.

He has made her, morally, an irresponsible being, as she can commit many crimes with impunity, provided they be done in the presence of her husband. In the covenant of marriage, she is compelled to promise obedience to her husband, he becoming, to all intents and purposes, her master—the law giving him power to deprive her of her liberty, and to administer chastisement.

He has so framed the laws of divorce, as to what shall be the proper causes, and in case of separation, to whom the guardianship of the children shall be given, as to be wholly regardless of the happiness of women—the law, in all cases, going upon a false supposition of the supremacy of man, and giving all power into his hands.

After depriving her of all rights as a married woman, if single, and the owner of property, he has taxed her to support a government which recognizes her only when her property can be made profitable to it.

He has monopolized nearly all the profitable employments, and from those she is permitted to follow, she receives but a scanty remuneration. He closes against her all the avenues to wealth and distinction which he considers most honorable to himself. As a teacher of theology, medicine, or law, she is not known.

He has denied her the facilities for obtaining a thorough education, all colleges being closed against her.

He allows her in Church, as well as State, but a subordinate position, claiming Apostolic authority for her exclusion from the ministry, and, with some exceptions, from any public participation in the affairs of the Church.

He has created a false public sentiment by giving to the world a different code of morals for men and women, by which moral delinquencies which exclude women from society, are not only tolerated, but deemed of little account in man.

He has usurped the prerogative of Jehovah himself, claiming it as his right to assign for her a sphere of action, when that belongs to her conscience and to her God.

He has endeavored, in every way that he could, to destroy her confidence in her own powers, to lessen her self-respect, and to make her willing to lead a dependent and abject life.

Now, in view of this entire disfranchisement of one-half the people of this country, their social and religious degradation—in view of the unjust laws above mentioned, and because women do feel themselves aggrieved, oppressed, and fraudulently deprived of their most sacred rights, we insist that they have immediate admission to all the rights and privileges which belong to them as citizens of the United States.

In entering upon the great work before us, we anticipate no small amount of misconception, misrepresentation, and ridicule; but we shall use every instrumentality within our power to effect our object. We shall employ agents, circulate tracts, petition the State and National legislatures, and endeavor to enlist the pulpit and the press in our behalf. We hope this Convention will be followed by a series of Conventions embracing every part of the country.

The following resolutions were discussed by Lucretia Mott, Thomas and Mary Ann McClintock, Amy Post, Catharine A. F. Stebbins, and others, and were adopted:

Whereas, The great precept of nature is conceded to be, that "man shall pursue his own true and substantial happiness." Blackstone in his Commentaries remarks, that this law of Nature being coeval with mankind, and dictated by God himself, is of course superior in obligation to any other. It is binding over all the globe, in all countries and at all times; no human laws are of any validity if contrary to this, and such of them as are valid, derive all their force, and all their validity, and all their authority, mediately and immediately, from this original; therefore,

Resolved, That such laws as conflict, in any way, with the true and substantial happiness of woman, are contrary to the great precept of nature and of no validity, for this is "superior in obligation to any other."

Resolved, That all laws which prevent woman from occupying such a station in society as her conscience shall dictate, or which place her in a position inferior to that of man, are contrary to the great precept of nature, and therefore of no force or authority.

Resolved, That woman is man's equal—was intended to be so by the Creator, and the highest good of the race demands that she should be recognized as such.

Resolved, That the women of this country ought to be enlightened in regard to the laws under which they live, that they may no longer publish their degradation by declaring themselves satisfied with their present position, nor their ignorance, by asserting that they have all the rights they want.

Resolved, That inasmuch as man, while claiming for himself intellectual superiority, does accord to woman moral superiority, it is preeminently his duty to encourage her to speak and teach, as she has an opportunity, in all religious assemblies.

Resolved, That the same amount of virtue, delicacy, and refinement of behavior that is required of woman in the social state, should also be required of man, and the same transgressions should be visited with equal severity on both man and woman.

Resolved, That the objection of indelicacy and impropriety, which is so often brought against woman when she addresses a public audience, comes with a very ill-grace from those who encourage, by their attendance, her appearance on the stage, in the concert, or in feats of the circus.

Resolved, That woman has too long rested satisfied in the circumscribed limits which corrupt customs and a perverted application of the Scriptures have marked out for her, and that it is time she should move in the enlarged sphere which her great Creator has assigned her.

Resolved, That it is the duty of the women of this country to secure to themselves their sacred right to the elective franchise.

Resolved, That the equality of human rights results necessarily from the fact of the identity of the race in capabilities and responsibilities.

Resolved, therefore, that, being invested by the Creator with the same capabilities, and the same consciousness of responsibility for their exercise, it is demonstrably the right and duty of woman, equally with man, to promote every righteous cause by every righteous means; and especially in regard to the great subjects of morals and religion, it is self-evidently her right to participate with her brother in teaching them, both in private and in public, by writing and by speaking, by any instrumentalities proper to be used, and in any assemblies proper to be held; and this being a self-evident truth growing out of the divinely implanted principles of human nature, any custom or authority adverse to it, whether modern or wearing the hoary sanction of antiquity, is to be regarded as a self-evident falsehood, and at war with mankind.

At the last session Lucretia Mott offered and spoke to the following resolution:

Resolved, That the speedy success of our cause depends upon the zealous and untiring efforts of both men and women, for the overthrow of the monopoly of the pulpit, and for the securing to woman an equal participation with men in the various trades, professions and commerce.

The only resolution that was not unanimously adopted was the ninth, urging the women of the country to secure to themselves the elective franchise. Those who took part in the debate feared a demand for the right to vote would defeat others they deemed more rational, and make the whole movement ridiculous.

But Mrs. Stanton and Frederick Douglass seeing that the power to choose rulers and make laws, was the right by which all others could be secured, persistently advocated the resolution, and at last carried it by a small majority.

WOMAN'S RIGHTS

CONVENTION!

COOPER UNION

New York City, Wednesday, March 20th '56,

at 8 P. M.

A Convention to discuss the social, civil, and religious
rights of women.

SUSAN B. ANTHONY

LUCRETIA MOTT

and other ladies and gentlemen will address the convention.

JAMES MOTT, Sec'y.   ELIZABETH CADY STANTON, Chairman.

ᴛ ᴜᴇ ᵖᵘᵇˡⁱᶜ e is requested to listen respectfully to the speeches but is invited to take part in the
discussion.

*Poster announcing an
1856 Woman's Rights
Convention in New York.
Frank Corbeil Collection*

Thus it will be seen that the Declaration and resolutions in the very first Convention, demanded all the most radical friends of the movement have since claimed—such as equal rights in the universities, in the trades and professions; the right to vote; to share in all political offices, honors, and emoluments; to complete equality in marriage, to personal freedom, property, wages, children; to make contracts; to sue, and be sued; and to testify in courts of justice. At this time the condition of married women under the Common Law, was nearly as degraded as that of the slave on the Southern plantation. The Convention continued through two entire days, and late into the evenings. The deepest interest was manifested to its close.

The proceedings were extensively published, unsparingly ridiculed by the press, and denounced by the pulpit, much to the surprise and chagrin of the leaders. Being deeply in earnest, and believing their demands pre-eminently wise and just, they were wholly unprepared to find themselves the target for the jibes and jeers of the nation. The Declaration was signed by one hundred men, and women, many of whom withdrew their names as soon as the storm of ridicule began to break. The comments of the press were carefully preserved [and are in the Appendix to Volume I. of *History of Woman Suffrage*], and it is curious to see that the same old arguments, and objections rife at the start, are reproduced by the press of today. But the brave protests sent out from this Convention touched a responsive chord in the hearts of women all over the Country....

Three

A Feminist Friendship:

Elizabeth Cady Stanton and Susan B. Anthony

Alice S. Rossi

Editor's Introduction: In this classic essay, a favorite of suffrage scholars and students for many years, Alice Rossi brings these two suffrage leaders to life. The essay originally appeared in *The Feminist Papers: From Adams to de Beauvoir*, a collection of documents by major feminist writers edited by Rossi. First published in 1973, this invaluable anthology is still in print today.

"A Feminist Friendship" describes Elizabeth Cady Stanton and Susan B. Anthony's extraordinary relationship, which lasted fifty-one years. Rossi explains how their contrasting but complementary skills and personalities empowered them both—making them such effective advocates for the cause of woman suffrage. In this essay, Rossi also offers an introduction to two of Stanton's writings: "Motherhood," and the Introduction to *The Woman's Bible.*

The two friends had quite different experiences and attitudes in regard to marriage and family. Married and the mother of seven children, Stanton took pleasure from her domestic life, but struggled to cope with the heavy burdens of housekeeping and children that left her little time to engage in the women's movement. Anthony, on the other hand, single and single-mindedly devoted to the cause of women's rights, resented the claims that marriage and childbearing exacted on other women's rights advocates. Yet she frequently came to Stanton's home and "stirred the pudding" and held the babies to free her hard-pressed friend for writing.

This feminist friendship afforded Stanton moral support as well. Her women's rights activities were opposed vigorously by her conservative father and resented by her politically ambitious husband who feared her controversial activities would cost him votes. Henry Stanton actually left town on the eve of the Seneca Falls Convention when he learned the proposed Declaration of Sentiments would include a demand for the vote!

Rossi's essay also demonstrates the wide range of Stanton's and Anthony's interests regarding women's rights beyond suffrage, and discusses how their contrasting family backgrounds led to contrasting political perspectives. Rossi's analysis of the way Stanton's views changed over time—along with her personal circumstances—is intensely interesting, as is the fact that Stanton recognized that Anthony was growing more conservative while she grew more radical.

★　★　★　★　★

THE TWO WOMEN most closely associated with the emergence of the woman's-rights movement in the nineteenth century are Elizabeth Cady Stanton and Susan B. Anthony. From the spring of 1851, when they first met, until Elizabeth's death in 1902 they were the most intimate of friends and the closest collaborators in the battle for women's rights in the United States. Together they were Lyceum lecturers in the 1850s, founders of equal rights and suffrage associations, organizers of annual conventions, hardy suffrage campaigners in the western states, and coeditors of the massive first three volumes of the *History of Woman Suffrage;* the contributions of these two pioneers are so intertwined that it is nearly impossible to speak of one without the other. They were in and out of each other's personal lives and households for more than fifty years. Their friendship and shared commitment to the cause of women's rights were the solid, central anchor in both their lives. As Elizabeth wrote to Susan in 1869, "no power in heaven, hell or earth can separate us, for our hearts are eternally wedded together."[1]

It is fitting, therefore, to introduce these two remarkable women in one essay and to focus on their friendship and the nature of their collaboration. The key to their effectiveness lies in the complementary nature of their skills. It can truly be said in this instance that the sum was greater than its parts, for either woman by herself would have had far less impact on the history of women's rights than they had in combination. Elizabeth had the intellect and ability to organize thought and evidence in a pungent, punchy prose. Susan was a master strategist, the "Napoleon" of the movement, as [Unitarian minister and friend] William Channing described her, superb at managing large-scale campaigns, quick and nimble in handling the give-and-take of convention meetings, and an effective public speaker. Elizabeth had only average stage presence and delivery as a speaker, and Susan's ability to conceptualize and develop her ideas was poor. Between them, Elizabeth's effective prose found its perfect outlet in Susan's public speaking. Elizabeth summed up their complementarity very well:

> In writing we did better work together than either could alone. While she is slow and analytical in composition, I am rapid and synthetic. I am the better writer, she the better critic. She supplied the facts and statistics, I the philosophy and rhetoric, and together we have made arguments that have stood unshaken by the storms of thirty long years.[2]

Down through the years Susan turned to Elizabeth for help in drafting speeches, testimony, and letters for presentation to conventions on education, temperance, and women's rights. A good example of this pressure on Elizabeth is in a letter appealing for her help in preparing a speech for a convention of school teachers which Susan was invited to give in 1856:

There is so much to say and I am so without constructive power to put in symmetrical order. So, for the love of me and for the saving of the reputation of womanhood, I beg you, with one baby on your knee and another at your feet, and four boys whistling, buzzing, hallooing "Ma, Ma," set yourself about the work.... Now will you load my gun, leaving me to pull the trigger and let fly the powder and ball? Don't delay one mail to tell me what you will do, for I must not and will not allow these school masters to say: "See, these women can't or won't do anything when we give them a chance." No, they sha'n't say that, even if I have to get a man to write it. But no man can write from my standpoint, nor no woman but you; for all, all would base their strongest argument on the unlikeness of the sexes.... And yet, in the schoolroom more than any other place, does the difference of sex, if there is any, need to be forgotten.... Do get all on fire and be as cross as you please.[3]

The letter captures several of Susan's qualities: blunt speech, a badgering of her associates to give her the help she needs (always in a hurry), a fighting spirit, and an ability to point to a central theme she wishes stressed. Elizabeth's response to this particular call for help came just five days later. She says in part:

Your servant is not dead but liveth. Imagine me, day in and day out, watching, bathing, dressing, nursing, and promenading the precious contents of a little crib in the corner of the room. I pace up and down these two chambers of mine, like a caged lioness longing to bring to a close nursing and housekeeping cares.... Is your speech to be exclusively on the point of educating the sexes together, or as to the best manner of educating women? I will do what I can to help you with your lecture.[4]

The "baby" referred to is five-month-old Harriot, Elizabeth's sixth child, and the speech, entitled "Co-education," was written by Elizabeth and delivered by Susan less than two months later.

This particular collaborative effort differed from most of their team work only in that it involved no face-to-face working out of the ideas to be developed in the speech. In most of their joint efforts they worked together more closely; Susan often visited the Stanton home in Seneca Falls for this purpose. Elizabeth described these occasions:

Whenever I saw that stately Quaker girl coming across my lawn, I knew that some happy convocation of the sons of Adam were to be set by the ears, by one of our appeals or resolutions. The little portmanteau stuffed with facts was opened.... Then we would get out our pens and write articles for papers, or a petition to the Legislature, letters to the faithful...call on *The Una, The Liberator,* and *The Standard,* to remember our wrongs as well as those of the slave. We never met without issuing a pronunciamento on some question.[5]

Thirty years later, when Elizabeth was no longer burdened with housekeeping and child-rearing responsibilities, she commented that in the 1850s, had it not been for Susan, who provided her with enough evidence of injustice to "turn any woman's thoughts from stockings and puddings," she might in time, "like too many women, have become wholly absorbed in a narrow family selfishness."

But a supportive friend who applied continual pressure to produce speeches and resolutions and articles for the press would hardly suffice to carry Elizabeth through the arduous years of child-rearing, from 1842 to the Civil War. During these years she not only bore seven children, but did a good deal of entertaining, produced reams of written material, served in temperance and abolition societies, lectured widely with the Lyceum circuit, and ran the household in Seneca Falls for long stretches of time without a man in the house. Elizabeth was clearly a woman of enormous physical energy coupled with a very strong will; these were needed to cope with such a regimen and to thrive on it. She was not a woman easily threatened by new experiences. Indeed, one of the best examples of her independence of mind and strength of body is the selection that follows, which describes her first experience of maternity. The reader will see how readily Elizabeth exercised her own judgment, even if it meant overriding medical advice. She seems to have given birth to all seven children with no aid beyond that of a friend and a nurse, commenting in a letter to Lucretia Mott after the fifth child's birth:

> Dear me, how much cruel bondage of mind and suffering of body poor woman will escape when she takes the liberty of being her own physician of both body and soul![6]

Among Elizabeth's prescriptions for a healthy womanhood was one she clearly followed herself, but which it would take many decades for medicine and psychiatry to learn: she insightfully put her finger on an important cause of hysteria and illness among the women of her day, in a 1859 letter to a Boston friend:

> I think if women would indulge more freely in vituperation, they would enjoy ten times the health they do. It seems to me they are suffering from repression.[7]

Elizabeth was not a woman to suffer from such repression herself. She showed none of the modern ambivalence about complaining when her responsibilities became onerous. One feels sure that in the intimacy of a friendly visit she let off steam in much the way she did in her letters during the 1850s, either by frankly admitting that she longed to be "free from housekeeping and children, so as to have some time to read and think and write" or by chafing at some affront to women and writing to Susan: "I am at a boiling point! If I do not find some day the use of my tongue on this question I shall die of an intellectual repression, a woman's rights convulsion."[8]

There was probably not another woman in the nineteenth century who put her tongue and pen to better use than Elizabeth Stanton. She and Susan clearly viewed themselves as rebels in a good fight for justice and equality for women. They wrote each other in martial terms full of "triggers," "powder and balls," "Thunderbolts." Locust Hill, Elizabeth's home in Seneca Falls, was dubbed "the center of the rebellion" and from here Elizabeth "forged the thunderbolts" and Susan "fired them."

But even a close friend was no solution to the heavy family responsibilities Elizabeth carried throughout the 1850s. In the early years of her residence in Seneca Falls she was full of complaints about the unreliability of household servants falling back on a dream of some "cooperative housekeeping in a future time that might promise a more harmonious domestic life" for women. But from 1851 on she had the help of a competent housekeeper, Amelia Willard, a capable woman who could readily substitute for Elizabeth herself. It was unquestionably this household arrangement which released Elizabeth for at least periodic participation in lecture tours and convention speeches during the years of heavy family responsibilities.

> It was while living in Seneca Falls and at one of the most despairing periods of my young life, that one of the best gifts of the gods came to me in the form of a good, faithful housekeeper. She was indeed a treasure, a friend and comforter, a second mother to my children, and understood all life's duties and gladly bore its burdens. She could fill any department in domestic life, and for thirty years was the joy of our household. But for this noble, self sacrificing woman, much of my public work would have been quite impossible. If by word or deed I have made the journey of life easier for any struggling soul I must in justice share the meed of praise accorded me with my little Quaker friend Amelia Willard.[9]

It is curious that it may be the help of a housekeeper and a friend that facilitates a woman's life's work, while the closest analogy to Elizabeth's tribute one would find from the pen of a man is typically a tribute to his wife.

It is an interesting aspect of the friendship between Elizabeth and Susan that, while Susan was extremely critical of the energy her woman's-rights friends gave to homemaking and "baby-making," as she put it, there is no written evidence that Elizabeth exerted any pressure on Susan to marry and have a family of her own, though Susan was only in her thirties during the first decade of their friendship. Elizabeth seems, in fact, to have been remarkably accepting of Susan exactly as she was; only a teasing quality in a few letters expressed any criticism of her. Susan, by contrast, showed little understanding of, and no hesitation in expressing herself strongly about, the diversion of her friends' energies away from reform causes. In the same 1856 letter in which she calls for Elizabeth's aid in writing a speech on coeducation Susan comments:

> Those of you who have the talent to do honor to poor womanhood, have all given yourself over to baby-making; and left poor brainless me

to do battle alone. It is a shame. Such a body as I might be spared to rock cradles. But it is a crime for you and Lucy Stone and Antoinette Brown to be doing it.[10]

In response, Elizabeth urged her friend to let "Lucy and Antoinette rest awhile in peace and quietness," since "we cannot bring about a moral revolution in a day or year."[11] This advice from Elizabeth had no effect on Susan, however. Two years later, in learning of the birth of Antoinette Brown's second child, she wrote the following revealing letter to Nettie (emphasis is by Susan):

> Dear Nettie: April 22, 1858
>
> A note from Lucy last night tells me that you have another *daughter*. Well, so be it. I rejoice that you are past the trial hour.
>
> Now Nettie, *not another baby* is my *peremptory command, two* will solve the problem whether a *woman can* be anything more than a *wife* and *mother* better than a half dozen or *ten even.*
>
> I am provoked at Lucy, just to think that she will attempt to speak in a course with such intellects as Brady, Curtis, and Chapin, and then as her special preparation, take upon herself in addition to baby cares, quite too absorbing for careful close and continued intellectual effort — the entire work of her house. A woman who is and must of necessity continue for the present at least, the representative woman, has no right to disqualify herself for such a representative occasion. I do feel it is so foolish for her to put herself in the position of *maid of all work and baby tender....*
>
> Nettie, I don't really want to be a downright scolder, but I can't help looking after the married sheep of the flock a wee bit.[12]

Three weeks later Susan sent another note to Nettie, this time adding a postscript to report:

> Mrs. Stanton sends love, and says "if you are going to have a large family go right on and finish up at once," as she has done. She has only devoted 18 years out of the very heart of existence here to the great work. But I say stop now, once and for all. Your life work will be arduous enough with two.[13]

Elizabeth Stanton softened this message with her own warm congratulations in an undated letter to Nettie that must have been written during this same spring:

> How many times I have thought of you since reading your pleasant letter to Susan. I was so happy to hear that you had another daughter. In spite of all Susan's admonitions, I do hope you and Lucy will have all the children you desire. I would not have one less than seven, in spite of all the abuse that has been heaped upon me for such extravagance.[14]

Quite another aspect of the place their friendship held in their personal lives is suggested by their terms of address and reference to each other. They were not terms of "sisterhood" but of "marriage." Their hearts "are eternally wedded together," as Elizabeth put it. In 1870, when the press circulated rumors that their partnership was "dissolving," Elizabeth wrote her friend, half in jest:

> Have you been getting a divorce out in Chicago without notifying me? I should like to know my present status. I shall not allow any such proceedings. I consider that our relations are to last for life; so make the best of it.[15]

Two such passionate and committed women were bound to have differences of opinion, but once again, Elizabeth drew the analogy to marriage in explaining their conviction that differences should be confined to their private exchanges while they presented a united front in public:

> So entirely one are we, that in all our associations, ever side by side on the same platform, not one feeling of jealousy or envy has ever shadowed our lives. We have indulged freely in criticism of each other when alone, and hotly contended whenever we have differed, but in our friendship of thirty years there has never been a break of one hour. To the world we always seem to agree and uniformly reflect each other. Like husband and wife, each has the feeling that we must have no differences in public.[16]

During these years the two women were firm in their belief that the differences between men and women were rooted purely in social custom; it may be that the cultural model of differences between husband and wife made the complementarity of marital roles a closer analogy to the nature of their own relationship than the presumed similarity of sisterhood. There is nevertheless some psychological validity in the symbolic use of the marriage bond to describe their friendship. Susan Anthony never married, and Elizabeth Stanton, though married for forty-six years, clearly received only shallow emotional support and no political support for her convictions from Henry Stanton. A warmth and effusiveness pervades Elizabeth's autobiography and her correspondence when she speaks of her children and of her close friends, but in hundreds of pages devoted to her personal life no comparable sentiment of warmth and mutuality appears in her rare references to her husband. It is not even clear whether Susan's frequent visits to the Stanton home coincided with Henry's stays at home. A politician, reformer, and journalist, he was clearly a traveling man. Seven children were born between 1842 and 1859, but there was a thinly disguised conflict between husband and wife on nonfamily matters. In 1855 Elizabeth wrote a few letters that permit a crack to show in the surface harmony. She had been developing plans that year to give a series of lectures on the Lyceum circuit and reports an exchange with her father concerning this plan in a letter to her cousin Elizabeth:

Susan B. Anthony (left) and Elizabeth Cady Stanton, c. 1870. Schlesinger Library, Radcliffe College

> We had a visit a little while ago from my venerable sire.... As we sat alone one night, he asked me: "Elizabeth, are you getting ready to lecture before lyceums?" "Yes sir," I answered. "I hope," he continued, "you will never do it during my lifetime, for if you do, be assured of one thing, your first lecture will be a very expensive one." "I intend," I replied, "that it shall be a very profitable one." [17]

Her father did in fact disinherit her at this time, though he relented before his death and altered his will once again. Elizabeth does not give vent to her acute distress over this altercation with her father in writing to her cousin, but during the same month she wrote in quite a different vein to Susan. Referring to a "terrible scourging" on her last meeting with her father, she wrote:

> I cannot tell you how deep the iron entered my soul. I never felt more keenly the degradation of my sex. To think that all in me of which my father would have felt a proper pride had I been a man, is deeply mortifying to him because I am a woman. That thought has stung me to a fierce decision—to speak as soon as I can do myself credit. But the pressure on me just now is too great. Henry sides with my friends, who oppose me in all that is dearest to my heart. They are not willing that I should write even on the woman question. But I will both write and speak. I wish you to consider this letter strictly confidential. Sometimes, Susan, I struggle in deep waters. [18]

This letter is a revealing one concerning both men in her life. Elizabeth had deeply ambivalent feelings toward her father. On the one hand she admired him for his mental abilities, was grateful for the understanding he gave her of the law, and was indebted to him for his continual financial support of her and her family over the years after her marriage. On the other hand she deeply

Susan B. Anthony (left) and Elizabeth Cady Stanton, c. 1888. Wyoming State Museum

resented the fact that none of her abilities or successes either as a schoolgirl or an adult could gain any praise at all from him. The same profile seems to hold for her marriage to Henry Stanton. Though they were both active in temperance and abolition agitation, they were completely at odds on her ideas and political activity on the woman's-rights issue. In the letter quoted above, the association of "father" and "husband" is immediate (Henry was ten years her senior), and Elizabeth feels herself a lone rebel in an unsympathetic social circle of family and neighbors, reaching out to the one sure friend who shares her commitments.

In this connection Henry Stanton's memoirs are interesting for what they leave unsaid. Though he wrote in the 1880s, when he was himself in his eighties, he seems unable even to mention the words "woman's rights." His wife is as absent from these pages as he is from her memoirs. The only reference in the entire book to Elizabeth's role in the woman's rights movement is the following passage, with its oblique reference to her leadership role—"in another department."

> The celebrity in this country and Europe of two women in another department has thrown somewhat into the shade the distinguished service they rendered to the slave in the four stormy years preceding the war and in the four years while the sanguinary conflict was waged in the field. I refer to Elizabeth Cady Stanton and Susan B. Anthony.[19]

The submerged conflict in the Stanton household was not confined to the husband and wife, for the seven children were drawn in as well. It is interesting to compare their separate memoirs on this point. Of the seven, the first four and the last-born were boys; yet it was the fourth child, a fourth son, who was to be the closest of the sons to Elizabeth. In the kind of leap across time that is perhaps characteristic of women's memories of their children she wrote:

I had a list of beautiful names for sons and daughters, from which to designate each newcomer; but, as yet, not one on my list had been used for my children. However, I put my foot down at number four, and named him Theodore, and, thus far, he has proved himself a veritable "gift of God," doing his uttermost, in every way possible, to fight the battle of freedom for woman.[20]

It was Theodore who studied the women's movement in Europe, where he lived for many years; he wrote a book entitled *The Woman Question in Europe*. In her autobiography Elizabeth noted:

To have a son interested in the question to which I have devoted my life, is a source of intense satisfaction. To say that I have realized in him all I could desire, is the highest praise a fond mother can give.[21]

Theodore's daughter was named Elizabeth Cady Stanton Jr. That Elizabeth took pride in her two daughters and lived in close contact with them, particularly Harriot, is clear throughout her memoirs. Both Harriot and her own daughter Nora were active in the suffrage movement, carrying Elizabeth's lead into the third generation.

In contrast, Henry Stanton makes no reference at all to the three children Elizabeth talked about so warmly, though he mentions the remaining four sons with pride. Speaking of his life as a lawyer, he added:

I have shown my regard for the profession by inducting four of my sons into its intricacies. Daniel Cady Stanton was for one year a supervisor of registration, and for two years a member of the legislature of Louisiana, in the turbulent era of reconstruction. Henry Stanton, a graduate of the law school of Columbia College, is now the official attorney of the Northern Pacific Railway Company. Gerrit Smith Stanton and Robert Livingston Stanton are also graduates of the Columbia School. The former cultivates the soil and dispenses the law in Iowa. The latter practices his profession in the city of New York.[22]

These are the only references Henry makes to any of his children. One senses a divisive line-up within the Stanton household that widened as the children grew up: Henry Sr. with sons Daniel, Henry, Gerrit, and Robert on the one side; Elizabeth with Theodore, Margaret, and Harriot on the other. The division, at least on the surface indications left to us, was rooted in Elizabeth's involvement in the "woman question."

It is little wonder that Elizabeth's friendship with Susan took on such intensity. While Elizabeth was torn between the love of her children and a sense of duty to home and spouse on the one hand, and the rebellious desire to be up and out fighting the battles dearest to her convictions on the other, Susan was a vital link that held these two worlds together in Elizabeth's heart and mind. Always the one to speak for both of them, and able to acknowledge tender sentiments to a far greater extent than the more purposive Susan, Elizabeth sums up the importance of their friendship:

> So closely interwoven have been our lives, our purposes, and experiences that, separated, we have a feeling of incompleteness—united, such strength of self-assertion that no ordinary obstacles, difficulties, or dangers ever appear to us insurmountable.[23]

The emotional quality of this assessment is one normally associated with the ideal, if not the reality, of a marital relationship; it is also a forerunner of the sisterly solidarity experienced in numerous feminist friendships in the 1970s.

It is much more difficult to gain a sense of Susan Anthony as a private person than it is of Elizabeth Stanton. Though she clearly reciprocated the deep friendship Elizabeth described, her personal style was quite different. The pressures on Susan were far more of a public than a private nature throughout her life, nor did she experience the deeply ambivalent relationship to a parent as Elizabeth did. Since she did not marry, Susan had no adult conflict of loyalties between family and a public career. Indeed, she showed great impatience with her women friends in the reform movements as they married and took on family responsibilities. That reticence in an autobiographic sense may be rooted in a past of greater serenity and lack of conflict is an insight for which we are indebted to Gordon Allport:

> Autobiographical writing seems to be preoccupied with conflict... happy, peaceful periods of time are usually passed over in silence. A few lines may tell of many serene years whereas pages are devoted to a single humiliating episode or to an experience of suffering. Writers seem driven to elaborate on the conditions that have wrecked their hopes and deprived them of satisfactions.[24]

This point may apply to correspondence as much as to autobiographies; and it is consistent that, from all one knows of Susan Anthony's family background, it was far more serene and conflict-free than Elizabeth's.

Susan Anthony's parents were happily married, and her father was a strong and beloved figure throughout her life. He was a strong supporter of temperance and antislavery, even at the risk of financial penalty to himself. He took an active role in the rearing and education of his children, with consistent encouragement of their independence and initiative, and drew no distinction in such matters between sons and daughters. He supported the girls in any desire to acquire skills, believing that every girl should be trained to be self-supporting— a view the Anthony neighbors clearly did not share. Susan's first biographer and friend, Ida Harper, suggests that Daniel Anthony saw in Susan an

> ability of a high order and that same courage, persistence and aggressiveness which entered into his own character. He encouraged her desire to go into the reforms which were demanding attention, gave her

financial backing when necessary, moral support upon all occasions and was ever her most interested friend and faithful ally.[25]

While many parents of the early woman's movement leaders shared commitments to temperance and abolition, few were full supporters of the woman's rights movement. Susan's family was exceptional in this regard; her parents and sister attended the earliest convention on woman's rights in Rochester and were among those signing petitions in support of the convention resolutions.

Drive, executive ability, and a single-mindedness of purpose became enduring characteristics of Susan Anthony. She was impatient with whatever did not contribute directly to the battles she waged in her various campaigns for reform. She began as a teacher at the age of seventeen, and for many years she was a critical observer and then vigorous participant at teachers' association conventions.

An early example of her courage and ability to press to the main point of an argument can be seen in her role at the 1853 state convention of schoolteachers. At this time women teachers could attend but could not speak at the convention meetings. Susan listened to a long discussion on why the profession of teaching was not as respected as those of law, medicine, and the ministry. When she could stand it no longer, she rose from her seat and called out, "Mr. President!" After much consternation about recognizing her, she was asked what she wished. When informed that she wished to speak to the question under discussion, a half-hour's debate and a close vote resulted in permission. Then she said:

> It seems to me, gentlemen, that none of you quite comprehend the cause of the disrespect of which you complain. Do you not see that so long as society says a woman is incompetent to be a lawyer, minister or doctor, but has ample ability to be a teacher, that every man of you who chooses this profession tacitly acknowledges that he has no more brains than a woman? And this, too, is the reason that teaching is a less lucrative profession, as here men must compete with the cheap labor of woman. Would you exalt your profession, exalt those who labor with you. Would you make it more lucrative, increase the salaries of the women engaged in the noble work of educating our future Presidents, Senators and Congressmen.[26]

Susan's point on the wage scale of occupations in which many women are employed is as pertinent today as it was in the 1850s. Equal pay for equal work continues to be seen as applying to equal pay for men and women in the same occupation, while the larger point of continuing relevance in our day is that some occupations have depressed wages because women are the chief employees. The former is a pattern of sex discrimination, the latter of institutionalized sexism.

Stanton and Anthony were of one mind on the issue of political rights for women, and this unanimity was at the core of their concerted organizational efforts during the long decades of the suffrage campaigns. Beyond this collaboration, however, they had complementary secondary interests. As a single woman and a Quaker, Susan was deeply concerned with opening the doors to women in the professions and with improving the pay scale of women workers. As a married woman and the more radical thinker of the two, Elizabeth was concerned with legislative reform of marriage, divorce, and property laws. There was much debate in the inner circle of woman's rights leaders in the 1850s on the expediency of pressing an issue such as divorce at woman's rights conventions, for it triggered far more violent responses from the public and was more divisive within their associations than even the political rights issue. It was also the case that the early leaders were not in agreement among themselves on the importance of marriage and divorce law reform or the solutions to sex inequity in the family sphere.

To trace these women leaders' views on marriage and divorce issues over the years would constitute a fascinating analysis that must remain for future scholars. I suspect, though only as a hypothesis, that the long-range trend of the woman's rights movement toward a narrower focus on the single issue of the vote was partially rooted in the aging of the leaders. Not only did these early pioneers live to a very old age, but they retained leadership positions in the movement well into their seventies. With increasing age, they may have felt far less personal involvement in such issues as marriage, child care, divorce, employment, and household management than they did in questions of political rights. Lucy Stone and Elizabeth Stanton were most concerned to press the issue of a woman's right to her own body in the 1850s, when they were young enough to be personally concerned. Thirty years later, the issue was no longer of high priority to them either personally or politically.

Some suggestion of the link between personal age and family status on the one hand and views on sex and maternity on the other can be seen in the following excerpts from writings of Elizabeth Stanton at various moments during her life. Elizabeth's age is recorded in parentheses along with the year in which she made each statement.

1853 (38) [Letter to Susan Anthony].

Man in his lust has regulated long enough this whole question of sexual intercourse. Now let the mother of mankind, whose prerogative it is to set bounds to his indulgence rouse up and give this whole matter a thorough, fearless examination.... I feel, as never before, that this whole question of woman's rights turns on the pivot of the marriage relation, and, mark my word, sooner or later, it will be the topic for discussion. I would not hurry it on, nor would I avoid it.[27]

1860 (45) [Letter to Susan Anthony].

Woman's degradation is in man's idea of his sexual rights. Our religion, laws, customs are all founded on the belief that woman was made for man. Come what will my whole soul rejoices in the truth that I have uttered. One word of thanks from a suffering woman outweighs with me the howls of all Christendom. How this marriage question grows on me. It lies at the very foundation of all progress. I never read a thing on this subject until I had arrived at my present opinion. My own life, observation, thought, feeling, reason, brought me to the conclusion. So fear not that I shall falter. I shall not grow conservative with age.[28]

1870 (55) [Letter to Susan Anthony].

Not only have I finished my lecture on marriage and divorce, but I have delivered it.... Women respond to this divorce speech as they never did to suffrage. In a word, I have had grand meetings. Oh, how the women flock to me with their sorrows. Such experiences as I listen to, plantation never equaled.[29]

1883 (68) [Excerpt from Diary].

I have been reading *Leaves of Grass*. Walt Whitman seems to understand everything in nature but woman. In "There is a Woman Waiting for Me," he speaks as if the female must be forced to the creative act, apparently ignorant of the great natural fact that a healthy woman has as much passion as a man, that she needs nothing stronger than the law of attraction to draw her to the male.[30]

1890 (75) [Excerpt from Diary].

Our trouble is not our womanhood, but the artificial trammels of custom under false conditions. We are, as a sex, infinitely superior to men, and if we were free and developed, healthy in body and mind, as we should be under natural conditions, our motherhood would be our glory. That function gives women such wisdom and power as no male ever can possess. When women can support themselves have their entry to all the trades and professions, with a house of their own over their heads and a bank account, they will own their bodies and be dictators in the social realm.[31]

There is an interesting progression in Elizabeth's ideas over the forty years covered by these excerpts, reflecting, one feels sure, not only the continuing evolution of her thought but also the subtle impact of her changing age and family status. Let us go back over these excerpts and try to see a connection between her ideas and the developmental stage she had reached in her own personal life.

The first two excerpts focus on sex and the power of men to impose their sexual demands on women: these are years during which Elizabeth was herself sexually active, with two pregnancies still ahead of her at the time of the 1853 writing, and a last birth just a year before she wrote the second excerpt in 1860.

The growing concern she felt for divorce reform was particularly apparent in the 1860s, culminating in the speech she delivered on marriage and divorce laws at numerous Lyceum lectures in 1870: with her own children now ranging in age from eleven to twenty-eight, she herself may have emerged from her peak dependent years. Indeed, since she was fifty-five years old in 1870, she was probably postmenopausal. Marital stability and termination now absorb her.

By 1883 there is a sharp shift in emphasis, with an image of woman as possessing a healthy sexual passion to match that of men: despite her age—sixty-eight—she had read and traveled widely and given much thought to the question of sexuality; but she no longer had any personal need to act upon them. She was now fully independent of her husband, seldom traveling with him, and perhaps learning a more modern view of sexuality from her own married children, Theodore and Harriot.

By 1890 the view of maternity had again shifted, and a strong positive view of women emerges: now she is no longer focusing on what women are deprived of by men or subjected to by men—a topic which had absorbed her as a younger woman; rather, she is taking pride in what women have that men do not have. Perhaps her own independence and the circumstance of married children who acknowledge her prominence and share her interests now permit her to see the power and privilege that flow from maternity at a more mature age. It may also be significant that by this date she is living in New York City, in an apartment overlooking the Hudson River, which she shared with her daughter Margaret and her youngest son, Robert. But it is also a tribute to the openness of her intellect at seventy-five that she could envisage the significance to women of an independent household and independent income, some thirty-five years before Virginia Woolf argued that "500 guineas" and a "room of one's own" were the symbols of what women needed to achieve real emancipation.[32]

Elizabeth and Susan began their lives in the same social and political climate of central New York State, absorbing the perspectives on benevolent reform that marked the region during the 1820s and 1830s. A critical difference between them was rooted in their families: Susan's family applied the lofty reformist values to their own personal lives, whereas Elizabeth's did not. Hence, when the two women turned to the cause of their own sex, it was a rebellious step for Elizabeth but an acting-out of parental values for Susan. This difference between the two women had consequences that showed throughout their lives. The more rebellious Elizabeth was in part motivated by the discord rankling within her as a result of the ambivalence in her relations with her parents and husband. She was driven to a search for a better vision of a better life, one grounded in cooperation and marked by domestic harmony. Her intellect was opened outward to the future, while her political action was held in check by the necessities of organization and the pressure of her far more conservative supporters. Since her past did not nourish her as Susan's did, the impulse to open inquiry and acceptance of change continued strong. For Susan the world looked rather different. She had no inner rebellious feelings rooted in her early family experiences, since she enjoyed the support and praise of the people important in her private life. She was therefore the executor of the reform ideas developed by her friend. But her mission was to make the system work, while Elizabeth was drawn to social innovation and more fundamental change in the system. From all the evidence available, Elizabeth seems to have been correct when she wrote, at the age of seventy-nine, that "I get more radical as I grow older, while she [Susan] seems to get more conservative."[33]

Notes

Reprinted from Alice S. Rossi, editor. *The Feminist Papers, From Adams to de Beauvoir,* Copyright 1973 by Alice S. Rossi. Reprinted with the permission of Northeastern University Press, Boston.

1. Theodore Stanton and Harriot Stanton Blatch, eds. *Elizabeth Cady Stanton as Revealed in Her Letters, Diary and Reminiscences,* 2 vols. (New York, 1922, 2: 125). This account of the friendship between Elizabeth Stanton and Susan Anthony is a partial one at best, and the interested reader can find more detail and a better chronology of their individual lives in several biographies (Ida H. Harper, *The Life and Work of Susan B. Anthony.* 3 vols. (Indianapolis, 1898); Katherine Anthony, *Susan B. Anthony: Her Personal History and Her Era.* (Garden City, N.Y., 1954); Alma Lutz, *Susan B. Anthony,* (Boston, 1959); see also, Alma Lutz, *Created Equal. A Biography of Elizabeth Cady Stanton,* (New York, 1940); and Stanton and Blatch, 1922) and memoirs by Elizabeth Stanton herself (E.C. Stanton, *Eighty Years and More: Reminiscences of Elizabeth Cady Stanton.* 2 vols. (New York, 1898). The best introduction to the political and organizational efforts of these two friends is in the volumes of the *History of Woman Suffrage* themselves.

2. Elizabeth Cady Stanton, Susan B. Anthony, and Matilda Joslyn Gage, eds., *History of Woman Suffrage,* (New York, 1881), 1: 459. Hereafter *HWS.*

3. Stanton and Blatch, *Elizabeth Cady Stanton as Revealed in Her Letters...,* 2: 64-66.

4. Ibid, 66-67.

5. *HWS* 1: 458-459. *The Una,* edited by Paulina Wright Davis, was one of the first women's rights newspapers. *The Liberator* was William Lloyd Garrison's antislavery newspaper in which he also supported women's rights.

6. Stanton and Blatch, *Elizabeth Cady Stanton as Revealed...,* 2: 45.

7. Ibid., 73-74.

8. Ibid., 41.

9. Ibid., 174.

10. Ibid., 65. Editor's note: Lucy Stone had one child and another that lived only briefly; her sister-in-law Antoinette Brown Blackwell, a Congregational and (later) Unitarian minister, author and lecturer, had seven children, though two died in infancy. Blackwell nevertheless managed to publish nine books over her long life including an attack on the antifeminist uses of Darwinism. She was the only one of the antebellum women's rights leaders who lived long enough to vote, at age ninety-five.

11. Stanton and Blatch, *Elizabeth Cady Stanton as Revealed...,* 2: 67.

12. Sarah Gilson, *Antoinette Brown Blackwell: Biographical Sketch,* 1909, 223-224. Unpublished manuscript in the Blackwell Family Papers, Schlesinger Library, Radcliffe College, Cambridge, Mass.

13. Ibid., 225.

14. Ibid., 233.

15. Stanton and Blatch, *Elizabeth Cady Stanton as Revealed...,* 2: 127.

16. *HWS* 1: 459.

17. Stanton and Blatch, *Elizabeth Cady Stanton as Revealed...,* 2: 61.

18. Ibid., 59, 60.

19. Henry B. Stanton, *Random Recollections.* (New York, 1887), 16.

20. Stanton and Blatch, *Elizabeth Cady Stanton as Revealed...,* 136.

21. E.C. Stanton, *Eighty Years and More,* 399-400.

22. Henry Stanton, *Random Recollections,* 1887, 147.

23. Stanton and Blatch, *Elizabeth Cady Stanton as Revealed...,* 1: 157.

24. Gordon W. Allport, *The Use of Personal Documents in Psychological Science,* Bulletin 49, (New York: Social Science Research Council), 78.

25. Harper, *The Life and Work of Susan B. Anthony,* 1: 57, 58.

26. *HWS* 1: 514.

27. Stanton and Blatch, *Elizabeth Cady Stanton as Revealed...,* 2: 49.

28. Ibid., 2: 82, 83.

29. Ibid., 2: 127. Editor's note: "plantation never equaled" presumably means that the problems of women needing divorces and unable to secure them exceeded even those of the slaves.

30. Ibid., 2: 210.

31. Ibid., 2: 270.

32. Virginia Woolf, *A Room of One's Own,* (London, 1931).

33. Stanton and Blatch, *Elizabeth Cady Stanton as Revealed...,* 2: 254.

Four

White Women's Rights, Black Men's Wrongs,

Free Love, Blackmail, and
the Formation of the American
Woman Suffrage Association

Andrea Moore Kerr

Editor's Introduction: In this article, Andrea Moore Kerr, author
of *Lucy Stone: Speaking Out for Equality* (1992), describes the dilemmas and difficulties the youthful suffrage movement encountered two decades after the
Seneca Falls Convention. After a "golden age" of woman suffrage activity in the
1850s under the leadership of Elizabeth Cady Stanton, Susan B. Anthony, and
Lucy Stone, the movement was temporarily suspended due to the Civil War.
During Reconstruction, the suffragists hoped that the expansion of the electorate that had begun before the war (the extension of the vote to all white
men) would continue, and that a reform-minded Congress dominated by the
Republican Party would enact universal suffrage for all. But when opponents of
black suffrage appeared to be using woman suffrage for their own ends, and
some who proposed an alliance with the woman suffrage movement were clearly hostile to black suffrage, the suffragists faced difficult decisions. And when
even former allies including Frederick Douglass asked the suffragists to accept
exclusion from the postwar suffrage amendments rather than endanger the
prospects of the newly freed black men, the suffragists did not all resolve their
dilemma in the same way.

In these troubled times, the movement was torn apart, and two rival suffrage
organizations were formed, creating a schism in the movement that lasted from
1869 to 1890. Anthony and Stanton, who believed that the enfranchisement of
black and immigrant men would actually make it even *more difficult* for women
to win the vote, formed the National Woman Suffrage Association (NWSA)—
opposing the Fifteenth Amendment and calling for a federal amendment for
woman suffrage. Lucy Stone, also distressed by the failure to seek universal suffrage but unwilling to oppose the enfranchisement of the freedmen, led those
who founded the American Woman Suffrage Association (AWSA)—supporting
the Fifteenth Amendment but working assiduously for woman suffrage. Unlike
some historians, Kerr insists that the issue of whether or not to support the Fif-

teenth Amendment was *the* issue leading to the great schism of 1869 and the creation of the rival suffrage associations and was recognized as such at the time.

Andrea Kerr describes these years—from the Civil War to the reunification of the AWSA and NWSA in 1890s—as very difficult ones for the movement, where support was limited and allies few. Yet accepting help from would-be allies sometimes proved to be very costly for the movement. Kerr argues that the NWSA's brief embrace of the infamous Victoria Woodhull tarnished the reputation of the entire movement despite the AWSA's attempts at "damage control."

Kerr also argues for the importance of Lucy Stone and the AWSA during these years, insisting that the AWSA was larger and better organized than the NWSA during the 1870s, and that their strategy was later vindicated. Though the NWSA deprecated the AWSA's state-by-state approach and willingness to work for partial suffrage, by the 1880s they recognized that these steps were necessary in order to build enough support for woman suffrage that a federal amendment could finally be won.

Of the great triumvirate of suffrage pioneers, Stanton, Anthony, and Stone, Stone is the least well known today. Many remember her primarily for her insistence on being known after her marriage to Henry Blackwell as "Lucy Stone only": shortly after her death in 1893 a Lucy Stone League, consisting of women who "kept their own names," was formed that continued into the 1970s. A charismatic and compelling orator, Stone had a talent for organization that greatly benefitted the nineteenth-century suffrage movement.

★ ★ ★ ★ ★

A S THE WOMAN SUFFRAGE MOVEMENT entered its second decade of activity in the early 1860s, its leaders could look back on a period of extraordinary accomplishment. From its modest beginnings—an 1846 public debate on woman suffrage at Oberlin College, the first public address on the subject of woman's rights in 1847, the Seneca Falls woman's rights convention of 1848—the movement for women's rights entered a period of growth unprecedented in the annals of reform. By the time of the first national convention held in 1850 in Worcester, Massachusetts, woman's rights, including the right of suffrage, had swept the land. The reform attracted so much attention that in 1854, P.T. Barnum sought to duplicate his success with the tour of Swedish singer Jenny Lind by hiring Lucy Stone to take her series of woman's rights lectures on a national tour.[1]

Antebellum Suffrage Activity: The "Golden Age"

The decade following the Worcester convention comprises a "golden age" of woman suffrage activity. Though the movement's proximate roots were intertwined with the antislavery organization, by the 1850s, woman suffrage had assumed a distinct reform identity. Loosely organized under the leadership of

Lucy Stone, Elizabeth Cady Stanton, and Susan B. Anthony, women raised funds and managed finances, organized conventions, developed strategies, delineated goals, and determined the direction of the movement. They planned and carried out petition drives and scheduled legislative hearings. With funds collected at meetings supplemented by earnings from lectures, women paid for the printing and distribution of books, tracts, and proceedings of the many local and national conventions. Groups of women formed education cadres and small political action committees in cities, towns, and rural hamlets.

The momentum gained by the fledgling movement in the 1850s came to a halt when Fort Sumter was fired upon in April of 1861. Woman suffrage activity ended while the American Civil War raged. In the war's aftermath, the fortunes of woman suffrage and the tangled politics of Reconstruction combined in a web of events and circumstances that threatened to reverse suffrage advances of the 1850s, making the enfranchisement of women an ever-more-distant goal. Out of this postwar chaos, two woman suffrage societies arose—the American and the National. For more than two decades, the two organizations labored separately toward the same goal. The story of one wing of suffragists—the National Woman Suffrage Association—has been told in the *History of Woman Suffrage*. A comprehensive history of the other wing—the American Woman Suffrage Association—has yet to be written.

Attempts to make clear distinctions between the two organizations falter before the changing tactics and strategies that marked both organizations for two decades after the war. Both labored more or less consistently for suffrage by Constitutional amendment; both eventually agreed on the need for state, municipal, and presidential suffrage. Lacking political experience, unschooled in consensus building, without the education formed in board room and back room, woman suffragists had to learn how to gain political ground the hard way—through trial and error. The ideologically driven but politically unwise actions of one wing of suffragists caused the woman suffrage movement to all but founder in the 1870s; the other association's attempt at damage control could not stem the flight of members nor turn the tide of public opinion that threatened to reverse the gains of two decades.

A look at events leading up to the division into two separate societies raises provocative questions about the politics of race and class. When the rights of two groups—in this instance, black males and white women—came into conflict, as they did in the post-Civil War period, present-day historians face a problem of interpretation that possesses many of the same features as the original dilemma. In the years immediately after the war, the rights of women— black and white, former slaves and free—came to be counterpoised against the rights of newly emancipated black males and free southern black males. The reaction to this conflict posed serious problems for woman suffragists then, and for women's historians now. In casting the Reconstruction dispute as hinging on universal suffrage versus black male suffrage, as some historians have done, we are at risk of replicating the mistakes of those whose political misalliances and poor judgment led to a brief-but-regrettable period of egregiously racist and elitist conduct. When a small splinter group of woman suffragists chose to lobby for educated suffrage and to campaign actively to prevent black freedmen from voting, the issues raised by their conduct transcend the theoretical. By casting this benighted campaign as a quest for universal rights, we risk perpetuating a means-and-ends argument that fails to take into account the political exigencies of a particular historical moment.[2]

The Competing Claims of Race and Sex

The first intimation of trouble arising from competing claims based upon race and sex came while the Civil War was still in progress. The war had occasioned a dramatic increase in both the size and scope of women's organized benevolent work. Seeking a wider political role for women, Elizabeth Cady Stanton and Susan B. Anthony issued a "call" in the spring of 1863 for a meeting of the "Loyal Women of the Nation." Its language both echoes Revolutionary-era notions of Republican Womanhood and rhetorically transforms them into ideas of women's full political equality. Drafted by Stanton, the call provoked women to think of themselves as equal political participants in the struggle: "Woman is equally interested and responsible with man in the final settlement of this problem of self-government; therefore let none stand idle spectators now.... [I]t is high time for the daughters of the revolution, in solemn council, to...lay hold of their birthright of freedom, and keep it a sacred trust for all coming generations."[3]

Lucy Stone presided over the gathering of leaders at the inaugural meeting of the Loyal Women. A series of resolutions committing women to an all-out effort to secure to all African Americans a full share of constitutional rights and privileges passed handily. The fifth resolution, calling for "no peace until the civil and political rights of all citizens of African descent and all women are practically established," provoked opposition from those who feared that adding woman's rights to antislavery would encumber the push for freedom and civil rights for slaves. Here was the first indication of future antagonism. Despite serious objections, the resolution passed.[4]

The women of the Loyal League, led principally by the efforts of Stanton and Anthony, eventually gathered four hundred thousand signatures on a petition urging Congress to pass a Thirteenth Amendment ending slavery. Their labors earned them praise and respect from reformers and politicians alike, but the small skirmish at the organizing convention was a bellwether of the larger conflict that would erupt over the inclusion of women in the push for civil rights at war's end. The history of events leading up to the 1869 split in the woman's rights movement furnishes a cautionary chapter on the perils of trying to compel the cart of ideology to pull the horse of politics.[5]

With the end of the war in sight in January, 1865, Stone and Anthony presented a resolution calling for combining woman's rights and antislavery organizations at a meeting of the New England Anti-Slavery Society. To their dismay, Wendell Phillips deferred action on their proposal until the May national meeting. In the months leading up to the May meeting, Stone and Anthony corresponded furiously with suffrage and antislavery leaders about the necessity for including woman suffrage in the press for black suffrage.[6]

At the May meeting, Wendell Phillips, a longtime friend of woman suffrage, insisted that this was the "Negro's Hour," and women must wait. Where the suffragists saw the hour as propitious, Phillips believed that adding woman suffrage would doom prospects for passage of a black suffrage amendment. The political situation of emancipated blacks was steadily deteriorating due to the passage of harsh and punitive Black Codes in the South. Northern Republicans were also aware that counting non-voting emancipated slaves as full persons, (rather than the three-fifths status apportioned by the Constitution), would gain fifteen potentially Democratic seats in Congress for the South. By enfranchising freedmen, Republicans hoped to gain substantial voters, a prospect appealing to non-reform as well as reform Republicans. Given the urgency of the moment, Wendell Phillips and other Republican leaders believed that passage of a black suffrage amendment was possible. They realized, however, that even if Congress were to pass the amendment, its ratification would be difficult, and they refused to endanger its passage by including women.[7]

Concerned that woman suffrage was to be abandoned in the push for black male suffrage, Stone, Stanton, and Anthony circulated woman suffrage petitions, lobbied for universal suffrage in the District of Columbia and organized a Woman's Rights convention at which they planned to go forward with plans for an Equal Rights Association with or without the cooperation of the existing antislavery organization. At the May 1866 convention, the two groups voted to merge, and the American Equal Rights Association (AERA) was born.[8]

In June of 1866, Congress passed the Fourteenth Amendment, introducing the word "male" into the Constitution as a qualification for voting. This dashed any lingering hopes suffragists might still have nurtured regarding universal suffrage. At an AERA convention in Albany, New York, that autumn, Stanton made a speech denouncing Republicans and praising Democrats, whose support she had hoped to gain—a hope that would later prove vain. Frederick Douglass objected, pointing out that the Democratic Party was on record as opposing any move to give suffrage or civil rights to blacks; their support for woman suffrage, warned Douglass, was but "a trick of the enemy" intended to split reformers on racial lines. Douglass begged suffragists to resist the ploy, but Stanton and Anthony ignored his warning.[9]

Following the Albany convention, Stone, Stanton, and Anthony embarked on a tour of New England and the Mid-Atlantic states. They set up AERA adjuncts, spearheaded petition drives and lobbied Republican legislators. Toward the end of January, the three suffragists were on board a train to New York when a blizzard stranded them for more than twenty-four hours. The snowbound train offered a captive audience of "doctors, lawyers, and legislators." Stanton, Stone, and Anthony "separated themselves far apart and each one gathered a crowd and talked and answered questions. They had a most merry time," an observer wrote, "and did a vast deal of good, I have no doubt." [10]

If suffragists gave the appearance of unity, differences were emerging. Though Stone protested "the poor half loaf of justice for the Negro, poisoned by its lack of justice for every woman in the land," she was growing more concerned about the deteriorating political condition of southern blacks. Matters came to a head in the Kansas campaign of 1867. The Kansas debacle began with a simple request to AERA headquarters from Sam Wood, a Kansas Republican. He asked if Lucy Stone and other woman suffrage workers would come to Kansas to campaign on behalf of a woman suffrage referendum. They agreed to his request. [11]

Kansas: Issues of Race and Sex Collide

Still bearing the scars of its recent bloody past, Kansas in 1867 was a hotbed of mistrust and malfeasance. The Republican-dominated legislature had ratified the Fourteenth Amendment; those who had labored since 1862 for black suffrage then called for a November referendum on a proposal to strike the word "white" from the state's list of voter qualifications. Sam Wood, a legislator who had voted against black suffrage every year since 1862, immediately proposed adding a referendum that would strike the word "male," thereby enfranchising women. Blacks accused Wood of deliberately trying to sabotage black suffrage by linking it to woman suffrage. [12]

Into this political quagmire came Lucy Stone and her husband Henry Blackwell, brimming with optimism and armed with two hundred and fifty pounds of suffrage leaflets they would distribute throughout the state. Blackwell, brother to the pioneer physicians Elizabeth and Emily Blackwell, was an ebullient optimist. "This is a glorious country, Mrs. S., and a glorious people," he wrote Stanton soon after their arrival. Stone and Blackwell stayed first at the home of former governor Charles Robinson, a relative of Stone's by marriage and a Republican Party leader who warned them that Sam Wood's proposal was an attempt to defeat black suffrage by splitting Republicans. Within weeks, it became clear that party unity was not going to withstand the test of woman suffrage. "I can not send you a telegraphic dispatch as you wish for just now there is a plot to get the Republican Party to...agree to canvass *only* for [striking] the word 'white,'" Stone wrote Anthony in early May. Soon afterward, Republicans voted by a very narrow majority to campaign for black suffrage only. [13]

Returning to New York, Stone took over the AERA office, while Stanton and Anthony went to Kansas to continue the campaign that was growing more and more bitterly divided along racial lines. Newspapers reported suffragist Olympia Brown as inveighing "against placing the dirty, immoral, degraded negro before a white woman." Sam Wood engaged in a nasty editorial exchange with black leaders. Long-time Republican friends of woman suffrage questioned

Lucy Stone, c. 1880.
Sophia Smith Collection

Poster from the 1867 Kansas campaign. Schlesinger Library, Radcliffe College

the political wisdom of continuing their support.[14] The situation worsened in late October when Stanton and Anthony joined forces with George Francis Train, a Copperhead (i.e. northerner who sympathized with the South in the Civil War) and a self-proclaimed candidate for president. He described his purpose: "By talking woman suffrage the Democrats 'beat the Republicans.' By stumping for woman suffrage Train 'beats the Republicans.' Copperheads know that the Republicans can carry Kansas unless they are divided."[15]

Back East, suffragists were dismayed to see an AERA-funded announcement of Train's entry into their campaign. Stone begged Anthony not to use AERA funds to campaign against black suffrage. Train was making woman suffrage "a laughingstock everywhere," she wrote, lamenting that Train's presence was "enough to condemn [woman suffrage] in the minds of all persons not already convinced." Anthony ignored her, and she and Train toured Kansas together, she speaking in favor of woman suffrage and denouncing the "rotten" Republican Party; he making derogatory and insulting remarks about blacks and uttering demagogic pronouncements about the dangers of black suffrage. "Carry negro suffrage," he warned, "and we shall see some white woman in a case of negro rape being tried by 12 negro jurymen." Train sent newspapers copies of his and Anthony's speeches and paid to publish and distribute booklets as well. Divisions within the Republican Party in Kansas and Train's association with the suffrage leaders drew national press attention. Train's anti-black campaign put Republicans who had remained staunchly pro-woman suffrage into an untenable position.[16]

Both woman suffrage and black suffrage proposals went down to defeat. Stanton and Anthony afterward publicly credited Train with delivering the 9,070 votes cast for woman suffrage, ignoring the evidence that showed that votes for woman suffrage came from heavily Republican counties. In the aftermath of the defeat, Republican Party leaders blamed the "side issue" of woman suffrage for the failure of black suffrage, sounding the alarm for any future attempts to combine both measures at the polls.[17]

Following the Kansas campaign, Stanton and Anthony announced that Train was financing a tour in which he would share the speakers' platform with them in cities and towns throughout the Midwest and East. Abolitionist and longtime friend of woman suffrage, William Lloyd Garrison, wrote that he was "mortified and astonished beyond measure in seeing Elizabeth Cady Stanton and Susan B. Anthony travelling about the country with that harlequin and semi-lunatic George Francis Train...denouncing Republicanism and lauding Copperheadism.... The colored people and their advocates have not a more abusive assailant than this same Train; especially when he...delights to ring the charges upon the "nigger," "nigger," "nigger," *ad nauseum.*"[18]

Stanton and Anthony turned a deaf ear to Train's anti-black invective, however. The connection did not end with the close of the speaking tour. Returning east, the two women accepted Train's offer to establish a newspaper that would jointly serve his political aims and the cause of woman suffrage. He named the paper *The Revolution.* "So long as Mr. Train speaks nobly for the woman," Anthony wrote, "why should we repudiate his services, even if he does ring the charges 'nigger, nigger, nigger'?" As Stanton explained, "All there is about [Train] is that he has made it possible for us to establish a paper. If the Devil himself had come up and said ladies I will help you establish a paper I should have said Amen!"[19]

Dissension Deepens, Conflict Erupts

At the May, 1868, meeting of the AERA, Olympia Brown, who had remained close to Stanton and Anthony, made a speech critical of the Republican Party. Frederick Douglass rose to object, characterizing Republicans as "largely in favor of enfranchising woman." He asked Brown: "Where is the Democrat who favors woman suffrage?" When a voice in the audience shouted "Train!" Douglass erupted: "Yes, he hates the negro, and that is what stimulates him to substitute the cry of emancipation for women." Following Douglass's speech, Anthony introduced a surprise resolution urging women to oppose the Fourteenth Amendment and to resolve to work for woman suffrage only. Her resolutions were defeated by the near-unanimous vote of all present. Immediately after the 1868 convention, Anthony set up a Woman Suffrage Society, with Stanton as president.[20]

In January 1869, Stone, Stanton, and Anthony were in Washington, where Congress was drafting the Fifteenth Amendment. The women unsuccessfully attempted to convince legislators, in particular Charles Sumner, to make it a universal suffrage amendment. Sumner apologized to the women, but he could see no political way to assure black enfranchisement if women were to be included. On February 27, Congress passed the proposed amendment, forbidding voter discrimination on the basis of "race, color, or previous condition of servitude." Immediately afterward, on March 15, 1869, George Julian proposed a Sixteenth Amendment forbidding voter discrimination based upon sex.[21]

Throughout the spring, Stanton continued to publish anti-Fifteenth Amendment editorials in *The Revolution*. In mid-April, Anthony called an emergency meeting of the executive committee of the AERA at which she tried and failed to get the committee to pass resolutions opposing ratification of the Fifteenth Amendment. If the AERA was willing to do all in its power to obtain suffrage for women, it refused to work to prevent black freedmen from voting. The stage was set for a major battle.[22]

"It is a pity that the cause of 'Equal Rights' should have been so disgraced by such a lawless scrabble for entrance tickets as occurred in the vestibule of the Hall last evening," said the Brooklyn *Daily Union*. "Men and women remorselessly crushing and tearing one another, and suffocating the solitary policeman who had the matter in charge." Indeed, throngs had besieged Steinway Hall, the site of the May 1869 AERA convention, hoping to witness the anticipated showdown.[23]

The opening salvo was fired by abolitionist Stephen Foster when he voiced objection to the nomination of Stanton to the vice presidency, because she had "publicly repudiated the principles of the society." Pressed by Stanton for particulars, Foster replied:

> These ladies stand at the head of a paper which has adopted as its motto "Educated Suffrage".... *The Revolution* lately had an article headed "That Infamous Fifteenth Amendment".... I am not willing to take George Francis Train on this platform with his ridicule of the negro and opposition to his enfranchisement.

Anthony responded with an impassioned defense of Train in which she protested that he had been "*almost* sent by God to furnish funds for *The Revolution*." This was too much for Foster, who replied angrily: "If you choose to put officers here that ridicule the negro and pronounce the Fifteenth Amendment infamous, why I must retire."[24]

Frederick Douglass then came forward and denounced Stanton's insistence on characterizing blacks as "Sambo" and "bootblacks" in *The Revolution*. He begged her to cease her anti-Fifteenth Amendment campaign. Anthony responded to his plea by laying a match to whatever oil remained on the troubled waters. If the "entire people" could not have suffrage, she said, then it must go "to the most intelligent first," for if "intelligence, justice, and morality, are to have precedence in the Government, let the question of woman be brought up first and that of the negro last." Anthony proceeded to introduce resolutions opposing ratification of the Fifteenth Amendment and in favor of educated suffrage. Lucy Stone rose and urged Anthony to withdraw the offending resolutions, arguing:

> We are lost if we turn away from the middle principle and argue for one class.... I thank God for the Fifteenth Amendment, and hope that it will be adopted in every State. I will be thankful in my soul if *any* body can get out of the terrible pit.[25]

Stanton's response to Stone's plea for withdrawal of the anti-black resolutions was to announce that she "did not believe in allowing ignorant negroes and foreigners to make laws for her to obey."[26]

Dissidents Form New Suffrage Organization

Put to the vote, both Anthony's anti-Fifteenth Amendment and the Educated Suffrage resolutions were defeated. Instead, the AERA body voted overwhelmingly to ratify resolutions favoring ratification of the Fifteenth Amendment and calling for adoption of a Sixteenth Amendment. They also passed a resolution calling for the establishment of a national woman suffrage organization comprising a network of state and local associations. Stanton and Anthony decided to pre-empt the AERA by forming a new "national" organization immediately, rather than after preliminary correspondence and meetings, as they had earlier agreed to do.[27]

The following week's *Revolution* noted that a national woman suffrage association had been formed in the parlor of the Woman's Bureau following the close of the AERA convention. The splinter group, calling itself the National Woman Suffrage Association, immediately passed a resolution opposing the proposed amendment. "All Wise Women Will Oppose the Fifteenth Amendment," editorialized Stanton. In the summer and fall of 1869, *The Revolution* stepped up its anti-black rhetoric, making references to the "barbarism," "brute force," and "tyranny" of black men.[28]

The majority of woman suffragists worried about the effect of Stanton and Anthony's campaign on the prospects for ratification of the Fifteenth Amendment. "Just arouse Mrs. Stanton's ire," wrote Stone, "and with her paper circulating largely in the doubtful Western States, she can defeat the 15th Amendment." An editorial in the *Woman's Advocate* of July 1869, called for "a National Organization," that would "be careful it deny no right, even to the most hapless or degraded of God's children." The organization must concentrate its efforts "on the proposed Sixteenth Amendment and such immediate legislation by Congress as may be obtained without any Amendment." At the next meeting of the New England Woman Suffrage Association, (NEWSA) members voted to work to form "an organization at once more comprehensive and more widely representative." [29]

Formation of the American Woman Suffrage Association

Writing to Elizabeth Buffum Chace, president of the Rhode Island Woman Suffrage Association, Stone explained the need for a new organization:

> I think it is a great pity to try and create or give currency to the idea that the Woman's Movement is opposed to the 15th Amendment.
> At every convention ... we have adopted resolutions heartily endorsing the 15th amendment.... It is not true that our movement is opposed to the negro. But it will be very easy to make it so, to the mutual harm of both causes....[30]

Modern-day historians who describe the differences between the two suffrage associations as lying in federal versus state suffrage work, or radical versus conservative ideologies, or who ascribe the division to "personal" factors ignore the clear and compelling reasons put forward at the time of the split.

Similarly, historians who conflate woman suffrage history in the decade after the Civil War with the National wing rather than with the larger American Woman Suffrage Association formed later that year at Cleveland, Ohio, ignore such critical factors as representation, size, membership, budget, tactics, and political impact. For more than a decade, the "National" organization consisted of small meetings held in New York City, its principal effort an annual January convention in Washington D.C. Mainstream suffragists—the great majority of those in attendance at the 1869 convention—had refused to be drawn into an either/or campaign to defeat black male suffrage, nor would they campaign for educated suffrage as a way of putting white women's interests ahead of those of freedmen.[31]

The American Woman Suffrage Association (AWSA) declared its purpose as securing the ballot to women, based upon the belief that "suffrage for woman is the great key that will unlock to her the doors of social and political equality." In pursuit of its goals, the AWSA proposed to organize for suffrage state by state, and to "prepare and circulate petitions to State Legislatures, to Congress, or to constitutional conventions in behalf of the legal and political equality of women," as well as to publish and distribute tracts and documents at below cost, and "employ lecturers and agents" to expand the organization.[32]

The volume of publications alone was staggering: in a single year AWSA sent out almost 216,000 leaflets from its Boston headquarters. At times, the organization had as many as four paid field agents who lectured and set up state and local societies in cities, towns, and villages throughout the country. AWSA's delegate basis ensured that state and local organizations would be represented at conventions held in different regions of the country so as to obtain the widest possible representation.[33]

In its early years, AWSA gained membership and auxiliaries at a rapid rate. In 1870, Lucy Stone began publication of a new woman's rights newspaper, *The Woman's Journal*. "Woman Suffrage has made astonishing progress," its editors reported. It had been "established in Wyoming, adopted in Utah, and submitted to the vote ... in Vermont," while "Minnesota has passed a bill to submit it to the concurrent votes of men and women." The article enumerated those states where woman suffrage was under consideration.[34]

In May of 1870, there were two woman suffrage conventions in New York City. At the AWSA meeting, a large crowd approved resolutions promising to continue state organizational work while supporting adoption of a federal woman suffrage amendment. Across town, at the NWSA convention, Stanton delineated what she called the "essential issue" dividing the two associations. The American society wished to "carry the measure step by step, year by year through the states" thereby forcing "educated refined women...to kneel at the feet of paupers, knaves, and drunkards." Stanton made clear her scorn for this approach, saying that "those who have the stomach for such work" could "canvass every state from Maine to California, and humbly ask Tom, Dick, and Harry, Patrick, Hans, Yung-Tung and Sambo, to recognize such women as Lucretia Mott, Ernestine Rose, Susan B. Anthony and Anna Dickinson as *their* political equals." [35]

The NWSA rejection of any state-by-state work held for almost a dozen years. The American wing, on the other hand, believed that intensive, state-by-state organization would lay the groundwork for eventual adoption and ratification of a federal amendment, should such an amendment prove constitutionally possible. The constitutionality of enfranchising women by federal amendment was brought into question by a number of court cases in the 1870s.[36]

Although partial forms of suffrage were problematic at best, they were nonetheless a factor in the final push for suffrage. When at last the Nineteenth Amendment was passed by Congress and sent to the state legislatures for ratification in June of 1919, its success was far from assured. Despite strong opposition, state legislators were aware that partial suffrage had made women's vote a force in national politics; women were able to vote for 339 of 531 presidential electors. The ratification margin was narrow, and in states where women could vote, the Nineteenth Amendment was ratified most easily.[37]

By the early 1880s, the National wing had come around to the American strategy. Anthony was quoted as saying, "I don't know the exact number of States we shall have to have...but I do know that there will come a day when that number will automatically and resistlessly act on the Congress of the United States to compel the submission of a federal suffrage amendment."[38]

The emphasis on state-by-state political organization, and the lobbying of legislators for various forms of partial suffrage was an arduous task. The slow but steady trickle of states and towns granting school suffrage, municipal suffrage, presidential suffrage, and occasionally, full voting rights to women kept suffragists' hopes alive, though the gains were painfully slow in coming, and losses often outnumbered gains.[39]

Suffrage campaigns and the weekly publication of a newspaper were costly. To raise funds, AWSA and *The Woman's Journal* editors staged a series of "bazaars" in Boston. These were enormous undertakings, usually occupying all three major public auditoriums, where merchants, entertainers, craftsmen, and restaurateurs donated time, goods, and services. There were daily theatrical and musical offerings, booths displaying crafts and various kinds of merchandise. Cakes, containing gold rings and little china dolls, were sold by the slice. At large concessions, women could buy "cooking-stoves, clothes-reels, bed-blankets, washing machines, wringers, pianos, sewing-machines of every variety, flowers, boxes of dried fish, soap, starch.... An art gallery displayed donated works, and one entire building had been "floored over and transformed into a large dining-room and restaurant." Hundreds of workers volunteered their time, and profits, usually eight to ten thousand dollars, went back into the suffrage effort.[40]

Woman Suffrage Linked to Free Love, Blackmail

Unfortunately, many of these organizational gains were undone by another misalliance. The NWSA leaders' actions in 1871 landed suffragists in an ever-widening net of scandal and intrigue that caused membership rolls to plummet and had hecklers shouting "Free Love!" at suffrage gatherings for decades to come. In January of 1871, Anthony welcomed Victoria Woodhull onto the NWSA platform in Washington following the latter's memorial before Congress claiming the right of suffrage for women based upon a Fourteenth Amendment argument. The possibility of a constitutional remedy for women's disfranchisement, accompanied by Woodhull's promise to donate ten thousand dollars to the NWSA won her acceptance among its leaders, a move they would bitterly regret.

Though only thirty-three at the time of her entrance into the woman suffrage movement, Victoria Woodhull had already led a full and remarkable life. She had worked variously as a prostitute, a mesmerist and spiritualist who claimed Demosthenes as her medium, a quack healer, blackmailer, extortionist, performance artist, stockbroker, journalist, and at the time of her entrance into the woman suffrage campaign, self-proclaimed candidate for president of the United States. Woodhull was simultaneously dubbed "Mrs. Satan" in a Nast cartoon, called "Queen of the Prostitutes" by the daily papers.[41]

Before she was eighteen, Woodhull had married, borne two children, and been charged along with other members of her family with numerous crimes. Following a "magnetic healing session" with millionaire financier Cornelius Vanderbilt, she and her sister, Tennie C. Claflin, suddenly came into enough money to purchase a stock brokerage on Wall Street and to begin publication of a newspaper, *Woodhull & Claflin's Weekly*. Both in her newspaper and in her public speeches, Woodhull championed "free love." News that Anthony had welcomed Woodhull onto the NWSA platform caused Stanton to write begging her not to "have another Train affair with Mrs. Woodhull." Stanton would come to embrace Woodhull too. The initial flurry of interest in Woodhull subsided, and for a brief period, calm reigned.[42]

The following May, Stone opened the AWSA meeting in New York City with an account of the year's progress: Woman suffrage proposals were under legislative consideration in nearly every eastern, northern, and western state, and despite repeated defeats, they drew larger average votes each year. Women were enfranchised in both Utah and Wyoming. Over fifty new county societies and five new state societies had been organized in Massachusetts alone. Stone and Livermore had been accredited party delegates to the Republican convention; the December bazaar netted close to $8,000; the Sixteenth Amendment was reintroduced in Congress, and the bill to grant woman suffrage in the District of Columbia had made a good legislative showing. With the circulation of *The Woman's Journal* nearing five thousand, she told the assembled gathering, there was much to celebrate.

Had Stone seen that day's New York *Tribune* with its bold headline—"Woman Suffrage and Free Love," she might have been less sanguine. The reference was to the rival NWSA convention and "[t]he people who 'work with and for' Mrs. Woodhull, new leader of the Woman Suffrage party, Woman Suffrage candidate for the Presidency and editor of *Woodhull & Claflin's Weekly*."[43]

Following the NWSA "Woodhull Convention," as it came to be known, membership in Anthony's society fell off so drastically that for the duration of 1871 and 1872, its leaders were able to hold "only parlor meetings." Former members set up separate suffrage organizations. Most of the New York women reorganized as the New York Central Woman Suffrage Association. The Connecticut Woman Suffrage Association led by Olympia Brown severed its tie to the NWSA and declared itself an independent society resolving to work "*only* for the elective franchise." In Iowa, Pennsylvania, Maryland, and Washington, resolutions were passed disavowing any tie to the Woodhull organization. By the end of 1871, fourteen of fifteen state suffrage societies had voted to become auxiliary to AWSA.[44]

In Boston in 1871, an Anti-Suffrage Committee was formed, and it was quick to offer Victoria Woodhull as "proof" of the serious threat to the sanctity of the family posed by those who claimed for women the right of suffrage. Propriety, no matter how numerous or decorous its adherents, was not news; Woodhull was. Waging a desperate counter-campaign, the Massachusetts AWSA paid three lecture agents/organizers to set up twenty to thirty meetings per week in cities and towns throughout New England, a prodigious political undertaking.[45]

Following a free-love speech by Victoria Woodhull, newspaper headlines proclaimed: "Died of Free Love, November 25th In Steinway Hall the Woman

Suffrage Movement." Woodhull's association with the NWSA lasted little more than a year; by May of 1872, its leaders had severed all ties to her. The New York suffragists' final disenchantment grew out of Woodhull's extortion campaign that spring, followed by her attempt to use the NWSA platform to campaign for the presidency of the United States. Woodhull's extortion methods consisted of presenting her victims with dummy copies of the front page of *Woodhull & Claflin's Weekly* that featured detailed, wholly spurious allegations of supposed sexual indiscretions. She then demanded $500 to keep the story out of print. Woodhull tried this with many suffragists, among them Elizabeth Phelps, Laura Curtis Bullard, Lillie Devereaux Blake, and even Susan B. Anthony herself.[46]

In May, Anthony learned that Woodhull intended to take over the 1872 NWSA convention and use it as a nominating meeting for her presidential candidacy. Cutting short a lecture trip, Anthony returned to New York and ordered the janitor to douse the gas lights as Woodhull mounted the stage, afterwards writing, "A sad day for me; all came near to being lost. Our ship was so nearly stranded by leaving the helm to others, that we rescued it only by a hair's breadth." The "ship" of suffrage was not yet stranded, but it was a vessel with a serious leak.[47]

Scandal Erupts

Woodhull's withdrawal in the summer of 1872 and a split in the ranks of Republicans resulted in a momentary political triumph for the suffragists. With Horace Greeley running as an independent candidate against them, Republicans were persuaded in the 1872 election to include in their platform a carefully worded and less-than-wholehearted woman suffrage plank—a promise of "respectful consideration" of the woman suffrage question.[48]

Buoyed by this political action and free of the Woodhull alliance, Anthony proposed having the two rival associations "cooperate and make a systematic campaign covering the whole ground." Stone, in the midst of an AWSA campaign to orchestrate demonstrations involving half a million Republican women throughout New England as a means of pressuring politicians to press their claim for suffrage after the election, ignored Anthony's peace overture.[49]

Days before the November election, *Woodhull & Claflin's Weekly* appeared on the newsstands. Its lead article accused Henry Ward Beecher, president of the AWSA and one of the most famous and respected clergymen in the nation, of having seduced a number of his female parishioners, among these women, suffragist Elizabeth Tilton. The entire first printing of the *Weekly* sold out within minutes. Copies commanded up to forty dollars apiece, and newsboys and carriages created gridlock on lower Broad Street as they awaited a second edition. Along with the allegations against Beecher, the paper accused Luther Challis, a wealthy Brooklyn stockbroker, of sexual misconduct in a story replete with lurid and sensational sexual details. Woodhull was arrested under the recently-

enacted Comstock Law and thrown into the Ludlow Street jail; Challis promptly sued for libel.[50]

Any hopes the suffragists had of escaping the scandal were quickly dashed.
The newspapers focused on the woman's rights connection. The accused adul-
terer, Beecher, was president of the AWSA; the presumably wronged husband,
Theodore Tilton, had headed the NWSA, and the imprisoned Victoria Woodhull was calling herself the woman suffrage candidate for president of the United States. If the connection to woman suffrage was inevitable, the tarring of all
suffragists with the brush of immorality seemed an unduly harsh consequence.
A midwestern editorialist described the irrationality of the public response to
the scandal, writing that he regretted the injustice to "hundreds of thousands of
honest men and pure women earnestly in favor of the [suffrage] reform to say
that they were following at the leadstring of the notorious female, Mrs. Woodhull...." Despite the "unreason" of linking the majority of suffragists to free
love, "five out of six people think so, and cannot be led to think anything
else."[51]

The Beecher-Tilton trial was the longest and most-publicized trial to have
occurred up to its time. For more than six months, the testimony of its various
witnesses occupied the front pages of newspapers across the country. Woman
suffragists struggled unsuccessfully to keep the political question of suffrage
separate from the public sensation. From Ohio, suffrage workers reported that
"'free love' (whatever it may mean) is the most efficient agent employed to
frighten people from our ranks." The Des Moines *Register* headlined its woman
suffrage report "Halt in Progress of Woman Suffrage." Indeed, throughout the
country, support at the state and local level evaporated rapidly. Formerly
friendly legislators advised woman suffragists that in the "current free-love
storm" it would be best to table woman suffrage legislation.[52]

Although a jury failed to convict Beecher, voting nine to three for his innocence, the damage had been done. The defection of formerly staunch supporters cut deeply into existing suffrage ranks and crippled the drive to recruit and
organize new members. Meetings were canceled; proprietors refused to rent
their halls to suffragists. Twenty years later, as suffragists tried to post notices of
their meetings, it was not unusual to hear some man shout across the street to
another, "Are you going to hear Woodhull tonight?" A Vermont suffragist
insisted that the Woodhull matter "set the cause back twenty years," and that
country people persisted in thinking as late as 1889 that women wanted suffrage "for free love."[53]

In the Wake of Disaster: Rebuilding Begins

Lucy Stone's anniversary address at the following spring's AWSA convention
was the most negative she had ever given. Though she tried to sound upbeat,
she had never felt less optimistic. Membership was falling off at such a rate that
the Massachusetts Woman Suffrage Association was forced to lower the number

required for a quorum at business meetings. Attendance at the May NEWSA anniversary had been down by more than a third.

As new women's organizations sprang up, leaders were careful to distance themselves from woman suffrage organizations. When the Association for the Advancement of Women was formed, newspapers characterized it as an attempt to "make a 'New Departure' from Woman Suffrage." When members tried to include woman suffrage as one of the aims of the new organization, their efforts went down to defeat.[54]

The Woodhull misalliance did incalculable harm. While present-day historians may sympathize with Woodhull's radical politics, it is nonetheless clear that Stanton and Anthony's embrace of an exotic, blackmailing, free-love advocate in the 1870s was a political disaster for woman suffrage. While the Woodhull connection directly tarnished the image of suffragists, it indirectly controlled the direction and tactics of the AWSA from the early 1870s on, as the "other" wing struggled to counter the image of impropriety with a purity crusade. "We *need* every clean soul to help us, now when such a flood of what is fatal to the peace, and purity of the family, is rolled in on our question," Lucy Stone wrote to a suffrage supporter in the midst of the Woodhull imbroglio.[55]

Eventually, memory of the scandals faded. The AWSA, which had been the larger and stronger organization, began to lose ground to the NWSA in the early 1880s as Anthony led the latter organization in a strong campaign to "capture" New England suffrage societies. Declining membership rolls and a shift by the NWSA to both state and federal work made Stone more amenable to merging the two societies. In 1887, Lucy Stone and her daughter, Alice Stone Blackwell, met with Susan B. Anthony and her protégée, Rachel Foster. Together, they agreed upon a committee to effect a reconciliation between the two societies. It was February 1890, before the two societies would formally merge as the National American Woman Suffrage Association, (NAWSA) but the groundwork for rapprochement had been laid.

Because Stanton and Anthony wrote the history of the movement, modern historians appear to accept the authors' *ex post facto* characterization of the 1869 split as devolving from tactical differences. All parties at the time of the split understood the issue to be the acceptance or rejection of Stanton and Anthony's campaign to defeat the Fifteenth Amendment. Mainstream suffragists in the American wing—the overwhelming majority—found the anti-Fifteenth Amendment campaign not only politically unwise, but morally repugnant.[56] Marginalized by their unpopular actions, the National wing—effectively a splinter group for more than a decade—found itself involved in a series of costly misalliances. In the decades that followed, Stanton and Anthony did extraordinary work for the cause of woman's rights; nevertheless, the political consequences of their earlier actions furnish a cautionary tale to those who continue to work for full equality for women today. Consensus building, the choice of rhetoric, decisions about which issues to include or exclude, and other strategic questions are as problematic to feminists today as those that confronted our foremothers. Ignoring what is painful in woman suffrage history diminishes the capacity to build on its strengths by learning from past mistakes. Even as today's historians acknowledge early suffragists' failings, we honor their legacy of courage, brilliance, fury, and power.

Notes

1. Carrie Chapman Catt and Nettie Rogers Shuler, *Woman Suffrage and Politics: The Inner Story of the Suffrage Movement* (New York, 1923), 31; P.T. Barnum to Dr. Trall, February 11, 1854; April 27, 1854; NAWSA Collection, Library of Congress (hereafter NAWSA LC).

2. Ellen Carol DuBois in "Outgrowing the Compact of the Fathers: Equal Rights, Woman Suffrage, and the United States Constitution, 1820-1878," in *Journal of American History* 74 (December, 1987), 841, casts the dispute in these terms. In her recent introduction to the revised edition of *The Elizabeth Cady Stanton-Susan B. Anthony Reader* (Boston, 1992), DuBois admits to a "profound sense of what was lost" in the break of Stanton and Anthony with abolitionists and Republicans. In identifying the 1869 break as the "moment the case for woman suffrage became simultaneously more gender-based and more elitist and racist," (xvi), DuBois conflates the woman suffrage movement with the actions of Stanton and Anthony, whose position on the issue was very much a minority position among suffragists.

3. See Lori Ginzberg, *Women and the Work of Benevolence: Morality, Politics, and Class in the Nineteenth-Century United States* (New Haven, 1990), chpt. 5; Elizabeth Cady Stanton, with Susan B. Anthony, Ida Husted Harper, *History of Woman Suffrage*, (Rochester, N.Y., 1889), 2: 53.

4. "The Loyal Women's National League" in *HWS*, Stanton, et. al., 2: 50-67.

5. Eleanor Flexner, *Century of Struggle: The Woman's Rights Movement in the United States* (Cambridge, Mass., 1959), 110-111.

6. 1865 letters in Blackwell Family Collection, Library of Congress, (hereafter B-LC).

7. *New York Times*, May 10, 1865; Ratification of the Fourteenth Amendment would take more than two years. Although northern sympathy for former slaves ran high, support for black suffrage did not. See William Gillette, *The Right to Vote: Politics and Passage of the Fifteenth Amendment* (Baltimore, 1965), 25-27.

8. *Proceedings of the 1866 Woman's Rights Convention,* (New York, 1866).

9. Ida Husted Harper, *Life and Work of Susan B. Anthony,* 3 vols. (New York, 1969), 1: 261-64.

10. Train incident in Ralph V. Harlow, *Gerrit Smith: Philanthropist and Reformer* (New York, 1972), 471. General suffrage activity in *HWS* 2: 172-82.

11. Lucy Stone to Abby Kelley Foster, January 24, 1867, B-LC.

12. See Eugene Berwanger, *The West and Reconstruction* (Urbana, Ill., 1981), 164-175.

13. Henry Blackwell to Elizabeth Cady Stanton, April 21, 1867, in B-LC; Andrea Moore Kerr, *Lucy Stone: Speaking Out for Equality* (New Brunswick, N.J., 1992), 124; Lucy Stone to Susan B. Anthony, May 9, 1867, B-LC; Daniel Wilder, *Annals of Kansas* (Topeka, 1875), 456.

14. Berwanger, *West*, 171.

15. George Francis Train, *The Great Epigram Campaign of Kansas* (Leavenworth, 1867), 47.

16. Elinor Rice Hays, *Morning Star: A Biography of Lucy Stone, 1818-1897* (New York, 1961), 197; Train, *Epigram*, 48, 58; Gillette, *Right,* 32-33.

17. Charles Robinson to Olympia Brown, December 22, 1867, Olympia Brown Collection, Schlesinger Library, Radcliffe; Emporia *News*, November 15, 1857; Gillette, *Right*, 31-40.

18. William Lloyd Garrison to Alfred Love, December 18, 1867, in Boston Public Library.

19. *The Revolution*, January 29, 1868; Elizabeth Cady Stanton to Olympia Brown, January, 1868, in Olympia Brown Collection.

20. Harper, *Susan B. Anthony*, 1: 304; *HWS*, 2: 341.

21. George W. Julian, *Political Recollections, 1840 to 1879* (Westport, Conn., 1884), 324.

22. Lucy Stone to Samuel May, April 9, 1869, in B-LC.

23. Brooklyn *Daily Union*, May 15, 1869.

24. *The Revolution*, May 20, 1869.

25. Brooklyn *Daily Union*, May 15, 1869; *The New York Times*, May 15, 1869; *HWS* 2: 383-84.

26. *The Revolution*, May 27, 1869.

27. *HWS* 2: 391-92, 320.

28. *The Revolution*, June 3, June 10, October 21, 1869.

29. Lucy Stone to Elizabeth Buffum Chace, July 11, 1869, in NAWSA-LC; *Woman's Advocate*, 2 (July, 1869).

30. Lucy Stone to Elizabeth Buffum Chace, July 11, 1869, in NAWSA-LC.

31. To date, no in-depth organizational history of either association has been done. Records indicate, however, that the AWSA dominated the 1870s, while the NWSA gained ascendance in the 1880s.

32. AWSA Convention in *HWS* 2: 763-64.

33. Lois Bannister Merk, "Massachusetts and the Woman Suffrage Movement," Ph.D. diss., Harvard University, 1961, 198.

34. *The Woman's Journal,* April 9, 1870.

35. Merk, "Massachusetts," 63; *The Revolution*, May 19, 1870.

36. See Catt and Shuler, *Woman Suffrage*, 96; and DuBois, "Outgrowing the Compact of the Fathers," 857-60.

37. See Catt and Shuler, *Woman Suffrage;* also see Appendix 5, "Partial Suffrage Gains," and chpt. 6, "Campaigning State by State" by Maud Wood Park in NAWSA, *Victory: How Women Won It* (New York, 1940), 69-80.

38. Anthony quote in Catt and Shuler, *Woman Suffrage*, 227.

39. See Catt and Shuler, *Woman Suffrage;* see also appendix and chart in NAWSA, *Victory.*

40. *The Woman's Journal,* December 31, 1870.

41. Emanie Sachs Arling, *The Terrible Siren* (New York, 1928), 1-15.

42. Elizabeth Cady Stanton to Susan B. Anthony, January 31, 1871, ECS Collection, LC.

43. *New York Tribune,* May 10, 1871.

44. *The Woman's Journal,* August 19, 1871; Katherine Deveraux Blake, *Champion of Woman: The Life of Lillie Deveraux Blake,* (New York, 1943), 91. Olympia Brown, *Acquaintances Old and New Among Reformers* (Milwaukee, 1911), 91; Louise Noun in *Strong-Minded Women: The*

Emergence of the Woman-Suffrage Movement in Iowa (Ames, Iowa, 1986), 177-197.

45. *The Woman's Journal*, March 11, 18, 25, 1871; Merk, "Massachusetts," chpt. 10.

46. Lancaster *Gazette*, November 25, 1871; Woodhull defended her use of blackmail in *Woodhull & Claflin's Weekly*, April 6, 1872; Accounts of the blackmail scheme (which in one case included a threat on the recipient's life if she did not pay up) in Arling, *Siren*, 164-65; NAWSA-LC; Blake, *Champion*, 90; Susan B. Anthony to Isabella Beecher Hooker, June 19, 24, 1872, in Stowe-Day Collection.

47. Harper, *Anthony*, 1: 413-15.

48. *The Woman's Journal*, June 15, 1872; *HWS* 2: 517-20.

49. *The Woman's Journal*, June 29, 1872; Susan B. Anthony to Lucy Stone, September 4, 1872, in NAWSA-LC.

50. Arling, *Siren*, 176; *Woodhull & Claflin's Weekly*, November 2, 1872; Challis case in New York *Herald*, November 3, 5, 6, 8, 10, 11, 19, 1872.

51. *The Woman's Journal*, November 30, 1872; Quote in Noun, *Strong-Minded*, 200.

52. *The Woman's Journal*, November 25, 1872; *Register* quote in Noun, 199. Blake, *Champion*, 91.

53. See Margaret Campbell to Lucy Stone, December 28, 1872; Alice Stone Blackwell to Mary Hunter, August 12, 1838; Alice Stone Blackwell to Lucy Stone, June 12, 1889. All in NAWSA-LC.

54. *The Woman's Journal*, October 25, 1873 and November 22, 1873.

55. Lucy Stone to John K. Wildman, November 7, 1871, in B-LC.

56. Although later accounts by Stanton and Anthony ascribed the split to different causes, (*HWS* 2: 400), there was no such confusion at the time of the formation of the new organization. Both *The Revolution* (May 20, 1869) and the *Woman's Advocate* (May 29, 1869) make it clear

THE DAILY GRAPHIC

AN ILLUSTRATED EVENING NEWSPAPER.

39 & 41 PARK PLACE.

VOL. VIII. | All the News. Four Editions Daily | NEW YORK, THURSDAY, OCTOBER 21, 1875.—TWELVE PAGES. | $12 Per Year in Advance. Single Copies, Five Cents. | NO. 816.

REAL vs. IMAGINARY WANTS.

Misses Anthony and Dickinson and Mrs. Stanton— We hold that this gives women the right to vote. Any way, you might let us."
Chief Justice Waite— In the opinion of the Court the XIV Amendment does not confer on women the right of suffrage."
Public Opinion— And you might add, Mr Chief Justice, that the great question of the day is, How to improve the suffrage—not how to extend it."

A satire of Anthony, Stanton, and Anna Dickinson claiming the right to vote under the Fourteenth Amendment, 1875. University of Illinois at Chicago

Five

Taking the Law Into Our Own Hands:

Bradwell, Minor, and
Suffrage Militance in the 1870s

Ellen Carol Dubois

Editor's Introduction: Ellen Carol Dubois, one of the most well-known and prolific scholars of the suffrage movement in the United States, describes the militant strategy pursued by the National Woman Suffrage Association (NWSA) between the schism of 1869 and the reunification of the two suffrage camps in 1890. In contrast with Andrea Kerr, Dubois presents the actions of the NWSA and its leaders as bold and principled. This includes their association with Victoria Woodhull, whom Dubois views as a courageous defender of women's right to control their own bodies as well as an articulate and intelligent advocate of woman suffrage.

Dubois sees Susan B. Anthony, Elizabeth Cady Stanton, and the NWSA as champions of political equality for all, demanding for women the protections afforded "citizens" in the Fourteenth and Fifteenth Amendments. Furious at their abandonment by former allies in the Republican Party, who insisted that the inclusion of woman suffrage would endanger the success of these two Reconstruction amendments, Stanton and Anthony initially protested the amendments even while they simultaneously called for a separate federal woman suffrage amendment. Yet, as Dubois explains in this essay, calling for a new amendment to the Constitution was not the only constitutional approach through which these suffragists tried to secure the vote in the 1870s.

After ratification of the Fourteenth and Fifteenth Amendments, NWSA leaders came up with a bold new strategy for winning the vote by claiming that the Fourteenth and Fifteenth Amendments actually *enfranchised* women. This approach, (also described in the previous essay by Linda Kerber), was known among the suffragists as the "New Departure." Initiated by Virginia and Francis Minor of St. Louis, who pursued it through the courts, it was the principal argument developed by Victoria Woodhull in her famous speech before Congress in 1871. It also inspired Myra Bradwell to claim the right to practice law as a *citizen's right.*

The New Departure emboldened many women including Susan B. Anthony to turn to "direct action," to go to the polls and claim their right to vote as citi-

zens of the United States. Anthony's subsequent trial for "knowingly, wrongfully, and unlawfully vot[ing]" was one of the most dramatic incidents in the history of the suffrage movement. The judge, in a statement prepared in advance
of the trial, directed the jury to find Anthony guilty, and ordered her to pay a
one hundred dollar fine that she, of course, refused to pay.

Rather than *plead* for the vote to be extended to them, the NWSA suffragists
demanded a right that they insisted was already theirs. In the 1870s, however,
the nation was in retreat from Reconstruction, and Congress and the courts
were increasingly unwilling to protect even the newly established black male
suffrage. The suffragists' militant strategy did not succeed, and direct action to
demand woman suffrage as a right rather than a privilege gave way to more conservative tactics—at least until militancy was revived during the last years of the
suffrage movement.

This essay makes it clear, however, that before suffragists reluctantly
embraced more conservative tactics—before they began arguing for enfranchisement on the basis of woman's ability to contribute to politics owing to
their differences from men—they first exhausted every possibility of gaining
the right to vote as citizens of the United States entitled to equal rights under
the United States Constitution. As DuBois so aptly phrases it: "They first
attempted to march into power directly through the main political entrance,
rather than indirectly, through the back door of the nursery or kitchen."

★　★　★　★　★

A
MONG THE MOST CONTESTED ELEMENTS of the Constitution have
been the Reconstruction amendments, and a crucial aspect of that contest has been the relation of the Fourteenth Amendment to women's
rights. This essay addresses the early history of women's rights claims to the
Fourteenth and Fifteenth Amendments. It explores the legal arguments with
which woman suffragists approached the Reconstruction amendments, the
popular support and militant activism they inspired, and the role that the
defeat of women's rights claims played in the larger history of Reconstruction
constitutionalism. This mid-nineteenth-century episode in women's rights history was extremely brief, but it reverberates richly with many important and
perplexing issues facing feminist thinkers and activists today. At various
moments during which I worked on this essay, I felt that this material provided
the historical key to current debates within feminism over "equality," over
"rights," and over "politics."

Here, in the post-Civil War years, we can see proponents of women's rights
as they move from universal to particularistic arguments, providing us with the
Gilded Age equivalent of the shift from "equality" to "difference" in the feminism of our own time. While many of my contemporaries emphasize the
abstract and "male" character of such universalistic categories as "person" or
"citizen," I have chosen to stress the many costs to the women's rights tradition

of moving away from such frameworks—however "hegemonic" they may seem to our postmodern consciousness—which have helped situate women's emancipation in the larger context of humanity's freedom.[1]

Here, too, we can trace the course of the demands of a disempowered group based on the venerable but problematic constitutional concept of "rights." Of late, "rights arguments" have been criticized, not only by conservatives but also by those on the left, for the assumption that entitlement inheres "naturally" in individuals, flourishing in a "private" realm that must be protected from interference, by others and by the state. Such a concept of "rights," it is argued, masks the workings of power and favors those already privileged by existing social and political structures—men, white people, and the propertied.[2] But this episode in women's rights, perhaps the entire tradition, treats rights quite differently: as something to be won and exercised collectively rather than individually; as the object of political struggle as much as of judicial resolution; as that which government affirmatively establishes rather than negatively shields; and above all as that which has greatest meaning not to the powerful, who already enjoy their entitlements, but to the powerless, who have yet to have their full place in society recognized.

Finally, this episode has implications for the character and place of the "political" in women's history. While women's historians have deepened our knowledge of the public activism of women, even—or especially—before their enfranchisement, much of this scholarship has followed what is called (in shorthand) "the separate spheres" model. Women, it is argued, have had—and may still have—their own political culture distinct from men's, and they have chosen to work for their own and society's betterment by embracing different institutions, following different rules, and adhering to different political values.[3] This essay suggests that to the degree that nineteenth-century women abandoned a political terrain also occupied by men—of partisan power and judicial contest—they were driven from it by defeat and forced to pursue politics by other, more indirect means. This essay considers women as they attempted to march into power directly, through the main political entrance, rather than indirectly, through the back door of the nursery or kitchen.

Introduction to the New Departure

Most histories of women's rights—my own included—have emphasized the initial rage of women's rights leaders at the Radical Republican authors of the Fourteenth and Fifteenth Amendments. In 1865 Elizabeth Cady Stanton was horrified to discover what she called "the word male" in proposals for a Fourteenth Amendment. The second section of the amendment defines the basis of congressional representation as "male persons over the age of twenty-one" and in doing so makes the first reference to sex anywhere in the Constitution. The passage of the Fifteenth Amendment in 1869, a much more powerful constitutional defense of political equality, only deepened the anger of women's rights advocates because it did not include sex among its prohibited disfranchise-ments.[4]

In 1869 the crisis split suffragists into two camps—the National Woman Suf-frage Association, which protested the omission of women from the Recon-struction amendments, and the American Woman Suffrage Association, which accepted the deferral of their claims. This part of the story is well known to stu-dents of woman suffrage, as is the National Association's concentration, through most of its twenty-one-year life (in 1890 it amalgamated with the American Association), on securing a separate amendment enfranchising women. Inasmuch as the form that federal woman suffrage ultimately took was precisely a separate constitutional amendment—the Nineteenth, ratified in 1920—this strategy is taken as the entirety of woman suffragists' constitutional claims. Yet, in the first few years after the passage of the Fourteenth and Fif-teenth Amendments, suffragists in the National Association camp energetically pursued another constitutional approach. They proposed a broad and inclusive construction of the Fourteenth and Fifteenth Amendments, under which, they claimed, women were already enfranchised. This constitutional strategy, known at the time as the New Departure, laid the basis for the subsequent focus on a separate woman suffrage amendment, even as it embodied a radical demo-cratic vision that the latter approach did not have.

The Fourteenth and Fifteenth Amendments

While the Fourteenth Amendment was in the process of being ratified, woman suffragists concentrated on its second clause, because of the offensive reference to "male persons." This phrase was included by the amendment's framers because in 1867 there was an active movement demanding the fran-chise for women, and it would no longer do to use such gender neutral terms as "person" to mean only men.[5] Yet such explicit exclusions of particular groups from the universal blessings of American democracy were not at all in the egali-tarian spirit of the age. Perhaps it was for this reason that in writing the first sec-tion of the Fourteenth Amendment, which defines federal citizenship, the framers could not bring themselves to speak of races or sexes but instead relied on the abstractions of "persons" and "citizens." In other words, the universali-ties of the first section of the Fourteenth Amendment, where federal citizenship is established, run headlong into the sex-based restrictions of the second sec-tion, where voting rights are limited. Those Reconstruction Era feminists angered at the restrictive clause quickly recognized these contradictions and became determined to get women's rights demands included in the broadest possible construction of the terms "persons" and "citizens" in the first section, to use, in other words, the first section to defeat the second.

After the Fifteenth Amendment was finally ratified, the suffragists of the National Association therefore shifted from the claim that the Reconstruction amendments excluded women and began to argue instead that they were broad enough to include women's rights along with those of the freedmen. This strategic turn, the New Departure,[6] was first outlined in October 1869 by a husband and wife team of Missouri suffragists, Francis and Virginia Minor. They offered an elaborate and elegant interpretation of the Constitution to demonstrate that women already had the right to vote. Their construction rested on a consistent perspective on the whole Constitution, but especially on a broad interpretation of the Fourteenth Amendment.[7]

The Minors' first premise was that popular sovereignty preceded and underlay constitutional authority. In exchange for creating government, the people expected protection of their preeminent and natural rights. This is a familiar element of revolutionary ideology. Their second premise was to equate the power of the *federal* government with the defense of individual rights, to regard federal power as positive.[8] Historically, the federal government had been regarded as the enemy of rights; the Bill of Rights protects individual rights by enjoining the federal government from infringing on them. In the wake of the devastating experience of secession, the Fourteenth Amendment reversed the order, relying on federal power to protect its citizens against the tyrannical action of the states. The Minors thus argued in good Radical Reconstruction fashion that national citizenship had finally been established as supreme by the first section of the Fourteenth Amendment: "the immunities and privileges of American citizenship, however defined, are national in character and paramount to all state authority."

A third element in the Minors' case was that the benefits of national citizenship were equally the rights of all. This too bore the mark of the Reconstruction Era. In the words of the amendment, "all persons born or naturalized in the United States" were equally entitled to the privileges and protections of national citizenship; there were no additional qualifications. In the battle for the rights of the black man, the rights of all had been secured. The war had expanded the rights of "proud white man" to all those who had historically been deprived of them, or so these radical reconstructionists believed.[9] In other words, the historic claim of asserting *individual* rights was becoming the modern one of realizing *equal* rights, especially for the lowly.

Finally, the Minors argued that the right to vote was one of the basic privileges and immunities of national citizenship. This was both the most controversial and the most important part of the New Departure constitutional construction. Popular sovereignty had always included an implicit theory of political power. The Minors' New Departure argument took this article of popular faith, reinterpreted it in light of Reconstruction Era egalitarianism, and gave it constitutional expression to produce a theory of universal rights to the suffrage. The New Departure case for universal suffrage brought together the Fourteenth Amendment, which nationalized citizenship and linked it to federal power, and the Fifteenth Amendment, which shifted the responsibility for the suffrage from the state to the national government.[10] This theory of the suffrage underlay much of the case for black suffrage as well, but because the drive for black suffrage was so intertwined with Republican partisan interest, it was woman suffrage, which had no such political thrust behind it, that generated the most formal constitutional expression of this Reconstruction Era faith in political equality.

Women Take the Vote

The New Departure was not simply a lawyer's exercise in constitutional exegesis. Reconstruction was an age of popular constitutionalism. Although presented in formal, constitutional terms, what the Minors had to say had much support among the rank and file of the women's rights movement. The underlying spirit of the Minors' constitutional arguments was militant and activist. The basic message was that the vote was already women's right; they merely had to take it. The New Departure took on meaning precisely because of this direct action element. Many women took the argument to heart and went to the polls, determined to vote. By 1871 hundreds of women were trying to register and vote in dozens of towns all over the country.[11] In 1871 in Philadelphia, to take one of many examples, Carrie Burnham, an unmarried tax-paying woman, got as far as having her name registered on the voting rolls. When her vote was refused, she formed the Citizens Suffrage Association of Philadelphia, dedicated not only to the defense of women's political rights but also to the greater truth that the right to vote was inherent, not bestowed. If the contrary were true, if the right to vote were a gift, this "implied a right lodged somewhere in society, which society had never acquired by any direct concession from the people." Such a theory of political power was patently tyrannical.[12]

That the first examples of women's direct action voting occurred in 1868 and 1869, before the Minors made their formal constitutional argument, suggests that the New Departure grew out of a genuinely popular political faith. In 1868 in the radical, spiritualist town of Vineland, New Jersey, almost two hundred women cast their votes into a separate ballot box and then tried to get them counted along with the men's. "The platform was crowded with earnest refined intellectual women, who feel it was good for them to be there," *The Revolution* reported. "One beautiful girl said 'I feel so much stronger for having voted.'"[13] The Vineland women repeated the effort for several years, and the ballot box eventually became an icon, which the local historical society still owns. From Vineland, the idea of women's voting spread to nearby towns, including Roseville, where, despite the American Association's official disinterest in the New Departure, Lucy Stone and her mother tried—but failed—to register their votes.

On the other side of the continent, Mary Olney Brown also decided she had the right to vote because the legislature of Washington Territory had passed an act giving "all white American citizens above the age of twenty-one years the right to vote." She wrote to other "prominent women urging them to go out and vote at the coming election ... [but] I was looked upon as a fanatic and the idea of woman voting was regarded as an absurdity." "Many [women] wished to vote…," she decided, "[but] had not the courage to go to the polls in defiance of custom." Finally, in 1869, she went to the polls with her husband, daughter, and son-in-law. Election officials threatened that she would not be "treated as a lady."

> Summoning all my strength, I walked up to the desk behind which sat the august officers of election, and presented my vote…. I was pompously met with the assertion, "You are not an American citizen; hence not entitled to vote." …I said… "I claim to be an American citizen, and a native-born citizen at that; and I wish to show you from the fourteenth amendment to the constitution of the United States, that women are not only citizens having the constitutional right to vote, but also that our territorial election law gives women the privilege of exercising that right."…I went on to show them that the…emancipation of the Southern slaves threw upon the country a class of people, who, like the women of the nation, owed allegiance to the government, but whose citizenship was not recognized. To settle this question, the fourteenth amendment was adopted.

Whereupon, the local election official, "with great dignity of manner and an immense display of ignorance," insisted "that the laws of congress don't extend over Washington territory" and refused her vote. When Brown was refused again, two years later, she concluded, "It amounts to this: the law gives women the right to vote in this territory, and you three men who have been appointed to receive our votes, sit here and arbitrarily refuse to take them, giving no reason why, only that you have decided not to take the women's votes. There is no law to sustain you in this usurpation of power."[14]

News of the efforts of women to register and vote spread through formal and informal means. Women's rights and mainstream journals reported on them, but information also might have been passed by word of mouth through networks of activists. Many sisters and friends, often in different states, turn up in the stories of New Departure voting women. In her account, Mary Olney Brown tells of her sister, who was inspired by her efforts to try to vote in a nearby town. Brown's sister took a different approach and was more successful. Eager to vote in a school election, she and her friends prepared a special dinner for election officials. "When the voting was resumed, the women, my sister being the first, handed in their ballots as if they had always been accustomed to voting. One lady, Mrs. Sargent, seventy-two years old, said she thanked the Lord that he had let her live until she could vote."[15]

The voting women of the 1870s often went to the polls in groups. They believed in the suffrage as an individual right but an individual right that would be achieved and experienced collectively. The most famous of these voting groups was the nearly fifty local activists, friends, and relatives who joined Susan B. Anthony in attempting to vote in Rochester, New York, in 1872. Virginia Minor herself was swept up in this collective activism. When she and some of her friends, all suffrage activists and Republican partisans, tried to register in St. Louis and were refused, she sued.

The congressional passage of the Enforcement Act in May 1870 to strengthen the Fifteenth Amendment greatly accelerated women's direct action voting. The Enforcement Act was meant to enforce the freedmen's political rights by providing recourse to the federal courts and penalties against local election officials who refused the lawful votes of citizens. Women who wanted to vote saw the act as a way to use the power of the federal government for their own benefit. Benjamin Quarles reports that freedwomen in South Carolina were encouraged by Freedmen's Bureau officials to attempt to vote by appealing to the Enforcement Act.[16] Some election officials responded to the Enforcement Act by accepting women's votes. When Nanette Gardner went to vote in Detroit in 1871, the ward official in her district was sympathetic to her protest and accepted her vote. The same man accepted Gardner's vote again in 1872, and she presented him with "a beautiful banner of white satin, trimmed with gold fringe on which was inscribed...'To Peter Hill, Alderman of the Ninth Ward, Detroit.... By recognizing civil liberty and equality for woman, he has placed the last and brightest jewel on the brow of Michigan.'"[17]

Most local officials, however, refused to accept women's votes. While Nanette Gardner voted successfully in Detroit, her friend Catherine Stebbins (the daughter of one of the Rochester voters) was turned away in the next ward. When Mary Brown's vote was refused in Olympia, she concluded that politicians more powerful than the local committeemen had decided to resist women's direct action efforts to vote and that "money was pledged in case of prosecution." In Santa Cruz, California, when Ellen Van Valkenberg was similarly turned back at the polls, she became the first woman to sue an election official under the Enforcement Act for refusing her vote.[18] By 1871 numerous New Departure woman suffrage cases were making their way through the federal courts.

Victoria Woodhull and the New Departure

Meanwhile, the New Departure gained an advocate who moved it from the local level into national politics: Victoria Woodhull. In January of 1871 Woodhull appeared before the House Judiciary Committee to make the constitutional case for women's right to vote. No woman had ever before been invited to address a committee of the United States Congress. Her appearance was sponsored by Massachusetts Republican Benjamin Butler, who may have helped her outline her constitutional case. The deeply felt conviction about women's rights underlying her argument was undoubtedly her own, however. Her memorial asked Congress to pass legislation clarifying the right of all women to vote under the new Reconstruction amendments.[19] The major difference between Woodhull and the Minors was tactical; she urged women to turn to Congress to resolve the question, while they relied on the courts.

Victoria Woodhull attempts to vote, 1871. Smithsonian Institution

Like all New Departure advocates, Woodhull embraced the premise that popular sovereignty was absolute: "the sovereign power of this country is perpetual in the politically-organized people of the United States, and can neither be relinquished nor abandoned by any portion of them." Her case for woman suffrage was simple and, from a radical Reconstruction perspective, virtually unassailable: inasmuch as the first section of the Fourteenth Amendment made no reference to sex, women along with men were citizens of the United States, and foremost among the "privileges and immunities" of national citizenship was the right to vote.[20] Like the Minors, Woodhull argued that the Fourteenth Amendment established the supremacy of national over state citizenship and the obligation of the federal government to protect the rights of all citizens equally.

Woodhull also argued from the Fifteenth Amendment, which she interpreted broadly, that voting is "a Right, not a privilege of citizens of the United States."[21] She directly confronted the most obvious objection to this interpretation, that the Fifteenth Amendment specifically prohibits only disfranchisements by race, color, and previous condition. First, she argued, the amendment's wording does not bestow the right to vote but assumes it to be preexisting. Although it explicitly prohibited certain disfranchisements, Woodhull argued that it could not be read to implicitly permit others. Second, the Fifteenth Amendment forbids disfranchisement "under three distinct conditions, in all of which," Woodhull argued, "woman is distinctly embraced." In other words, "a race comprises all the people, male and female." Woodhull here seems to grasp what many modern white feminists are still struggling to understand, that counterpoising the discriminations of race and sex obscures the experience of those who suffer both, that is, black women. Finally, Woodhull argued for her broad construction of the right of suffrage on the grounds of what she called "the blending of [the Constitution's] various parts," that is, the relation between the Fourteenth Amendment, which nationalizes citizenship and links it to the power of the federal government, and the Fifteenth Amendment, which shifts the responsibility for the suffrage from the state to the national government.[22]

The first official reaction to the New Departure came in response to Woodhull's memorial. The House Judiciary Committee issued two conflicting reports on the constitutional issues she raised.[23] Here we begin to see that debate over the feminists' particular constitutional arguments was inseparable from questions of the larger meaning of the Reconstruction amendments. The Majority Report rejected Woodhull's claims. Its author was John Bingham, one of the framers of the Fourteenth Amendment. Although Bingham conceded that women enjoyed the privileges of United States citizenship along with men, he disagreed that the Fourteenth Amendment added anything new to the content of national citizenship or altered the relationship between national and state citizenship. The Minority Report, signed by William Loughridge of Iowa and Benjamin Butler of Massachusetts, supported Woodhull's memorial and the generous and radical interpretation of the amendments on which it relied. The Minority Report interpreted the Fourteenth Amendment broadly, arguing that it was intended "to secure the natural rights of citizens as well as their equal capacities before the law." The Majority Report rejected Woodhull's argument that the Fifteenth Amendment shifted responsibility for the suffrage from the state to the national level, while the Minority Report agreed that the Fifteenth Amendment "clearly recognizes the right to vote, as one of the rights of a citizen of the United States."[24] "Thus it can be seen," Woodhull observed archly, "that equally able men differ upon a simple point of Constitutional Law."[25]

The mere fact of a congressional hearing was a victory for woman suffrage leaders, and the language of constitutional principle was an improvement over the semi-sexual innuendo with which their claims were often met.[26] The favorable Minority Report meant that some of the leaders of the Republican Party supported women's rights claims on the Constitution. In 1871 two committee rooms in the Capitol were put at the disposal of the suffragists to facilitate their lobbying efforts.[27] "Could you feel the atmosphere of...Congress, to-day, you would not doubt what the end must be, nor that it will be very soon," Isabella Beecher Hooker wrote.[28] The National Woman Suffrage Association urged women to put pressure on their congressmen to support the Butler Report, as well as to continue trying to vote and to work through the courts.[29]

Free Love and the Moral Divide

It was in this context, as Republicans struggled over the claims of the New Departure and suffragists grew hopeful, that the issue of "free love" was raised.

The sexual discourse that soon surrounded the New Departure played a role in shaping the political context and therefore the constitutional outcome. Woodhull is generally remembered in the history books not for her powerful constitutional arguments but for her shady sexual reputation. These sexual issues, however, were introduced not by Woodhull but by her opponents, who saw in them a way to divert attention from the constitutional arguments she made. Republican newspapers, notably the *New York Tribune,* accused Woodhull of multiple marriages, bigamy, and the advocacy of free love.[30] Suffrage leaders allied with Woodhull were either accused of sharing her "free love" sentiments or warned against the consequences of associating with disreputable women. As in other times, when politicians cannot face the genuine issues before them, the importance of "character" was asserted. "Men judge men's conventions not more by the formal platform they present than by...the character of those who are prominent in the proceedings," a New York periodical solemnly warned.[31]

Rather than react defensively to the attacks on her, Woodhull embraced the "free love" opprobrium with which she was charged. To her, the principles at the heart of sexual life were the same as those at the heart of political life, and the true basis of marriage was the same as the true basis of republican government: individual rights. Groping for a way to express her conviction that women, whether married or unmarried, must have unqualified control over their own reproductive and sexual lives, she used the language of Reconstruction constitutionalism to proclaim the doctrine of rights to and over one's own person. "Yes I am a Free lover," Woodhull responded to a heckler at one of her speeches. "I have an *inalienable, constitutional* and *natural* right to love whom I may,...to *change* that love *every day* if I please,...and it is your *duty* not only to *accord* [me my right], but, as a community, to see that I am protected in it."[32]

Such sex radicalism was not the predominant strain in nineteenth-century feminist circles. Most of the New Departure leaders (with the significant exception of Elizabeth Cady Stanton) were closer to the Victorian stereotype than Woodhull was, and they believed that the sex impulse must be tamed, not constitutionally secured. Nonetheless, even these "pious" women defended their alliance with Woodhull and rejected the conventional moral divide that separated "good" women from "bad." "God has raised up Woodhull to embody all questions of fellowship in political work [among] women irrespective of character," declared Isabella Beecher Hooker.[33] Instead of joining in a crusade against the immorality of women, New Departure suffragists began to attack the "hypocrisy" of men. Woodhull had been "raised up of God," suffragist and moral reformer Paulina Wright Davis claimed, to expose the perfidy of "a class that no one dares touch," men who said one thing and did another, men in power.[34] They shifted accusations of immorality not only from women to men but also from sexuality to politics. The true prostitutes, Woodhull asserted, were Republican leaders, who sold out principles for party power and wealth.[35]

The *Bradwell* Case

In late 1871, in the midst of this increasingly sexualized political context, the first New Departure cases began to reach the dockets of the federal courts. One was the case of Sara Spencer and seventy other women from the District of Columbia, who sued election officials under the Enforcement Act for refusing to permit them to vote. The District of Columbia was a deliberate choice for testing the New Departure argument. There, as advocates of black suffrage had first realized in 1867, the power of the federal government over the suffrage was not complicated by questions of dual sovereignty and states' rights.[36]

In October Judge Cartter of the Supreme Court of the District of Columbia ruled against Spencer. Cartter conceded that the Fourteenth Amendment included women along with men in the privileges and immunities of national citizenship; however, he rejected the democratic theory of suffrage on which the case rested. To concede that voting was a right was, in his opinion, to open the door to anarchy and would "involve the destruction of civil government." "The right of all men to vote is as fully recognized in the population of our large centres and cities as can well be done," wrote Cartter. "The result...is political profligacy and violence verging upon anarchy."[37] The larger context of the opinion, therefore, was anxiety about democratic politics, and Cartter's concern for the proper position of women in society was secondary. This was true of the entire New Departure debate (and perhaps of judicial disposition of women's rights claims more generally); it was conducted primarily in terms of "rights," not woman's sphere. What was claimed or denied for women was claimed or denied for all citizens, especially those previously excluded from rights due them. Whether this was because the question of women's place was subsumed in a more general struggle for political democracy or because sex-prejudice was still unspeakable in constitutional terms, the consequence was the same: denying women the rights they claimed under general provisions weakened those provisions in general.

The observation that general questions of constitutional rights had overtaken the specific discourse on woman's place is even clearer in the next major New Departure decision, the *Myra Bradwell* case. *Bradwell* was the first case touching on the New Departure to reach the Supreme Court. In 1869 Myra Bradwell, a Chicago feminist and pioneering woman lawyer, was refused admission to the Illinois bar. The grounds on which the state supreme court refused her application, along with the initial brief that Bradwell submitted in response, were concerned entirely with coverture, that is, with the question of the disabilities of married women before the law. By the time Bradwell brought her case before the United States Supreme Court in October 1871, she had changed the terms radically. Her case was no longer about coverture but had been reformulated in entirely New Departure terms. Her brief argued that her right to practice law was a citizen's right and that Illinois's action in refusing her was prohibited by the Fourteenth Amendment. As for coverture, she asserted that "the great innovation of the XIV Amendment...sweeps away the principles of the common law," so that even reforms of married women's property rights were no longer necessary. The *Bradwell* case is one of the few concerning women's rights commonly included in the history of constitutional law, but in my opinion it is not correctly situated, since it is usually cited to illustrate judicial assumptions about woman's place rather than the constitutional issues of citizenship on which it was actually argued and decided.[38]

Bradwell's case was closely watched by suffragists as an indication of how much support to expect from the Republican Party. Bradwell was represented before the Supreme Court by Senator Matthew Carpenter, one of the major second-generation leaders of the Republican Party. While Carpenter took up Bradwell's case and argued it in strong Fourteenth Amendment terms, he prefaced his case with an equally strong argument about why the right to vote was not covered by the Reconstruction amendments. He insisted, in other words, on a distinction between civil and political rights. While the federal government protected civil rights, women's as well as men's, Carpenter argued, the suffrage remained under the control of the states, beyond the lawful interference of federal power.[39]

Suffragists were understandably confused by the way Carpenter argued Bradwell's case. Was it an indication that Republican leaders were in favor of the New Departure or against it? Stanton allowed herself to be encouraged; if women were covered along with men under the Fourteenth Amendment, wasn't the fundamental point of equal rights won?[40] Victoria Woodhull, however, saw it differently; she argued that women might be admitted to the benefits of the postwar amendments only to find those amendments so narrowed that they bestowed virtually nothing at all, certainly not political rights. She charged that Republicans, "frightened by the grandeur and the extent" of the amendments they had enacted, had retreated to the enemies' doctrine of states' rights, where their own greatest achievements would ultimately be undone.[41]

The Supreme Court held back its decision on *Bradwell* until after the election. To trace the final judicial disposition of the suffragists' constitutional arguments, we have to understand what was at stake in this election and what a Republican victory would mean. The election of 1872 was a crisis for the Republicans.[42] In June 1872 an important group of reformers split off from regular Republicans to run an independent presidential campaign. These political rebels, the Liberal Republicans, based their revolt on the old opposition between central government and individual rights. From the perspective of feminists, who were also looking for a political alternative to the regular Republicans, the terms of the bolt were particularly disappointing. Feminists had learned from freedmen to see the federal government not as a threat to their rights but as the agency for winning them.

To add insult to injury, the Liberal Republicans picked as their candidate Horace Greeley, a man who had made his opposition to woman suffrage clear many years before. Infuriated by the nomination of Greeley, many New Departure suffragists campaigned actively for Ulysses Grant in 1872.[43] The regular Republicans cultivated their support, sending them about the country on official speaking tours and inserting a timid little reference to "additional rights" for women in their platform, a plank so insignificant that suffragists called it a "splinter." Holding off a decision on *Bradwell* was consistent with this temporary friendliness. Anthony expected that if Republicans won, they would reward women with the suffrage by recognizing the New Departure claims. She was so sure that when she came home from her last speaking tour on election day, she gathered together friends and relatives and went down to her local polling place to submit her vote for Grant. Although the local Republican official accepted the votes of fifteen of the demonstrators, including Anthony,[44] a few weeks later a United States marshall came to her house and arrested her for violation of federal law—the Enforcement Act.

Anthony's arrest was a signal that the Republicans were ready to dispose of the New Departure. Because she was the most famous woman suffragist in the nation, there is good reason to suspect her arrest had been authorized at the highest level of government. The conduct of her trial several months later reinforces this suspicion. The trial was moved from her home county, where she had lectured extensively to educate potential jurors, to another venue. The judge, Ward Hunt, was no small-town jurist but a recent appointee to the United States Supreme Court. He refused to submit the case to the jury, instead directing a guilty verdict from the bench, a practice that was later found unconstitutional. Years later, Anthony's lawyer observed, "There never was a trial in the country with one half the importance of Miss Anthony's.... If Anthony had won her case on the merit it would have revolutionized the suffrage of the country.... There was a prearranged determination to convict her. A jury trial was dangerous and so the Constitution was deliberately and openly violated." Anthony was not even permitted to appeal.[45]

In general, the outcome of the election cleared the way for the Republican Party to retreat from the radical implications of the postwar amendments. There is a link between the judicial dismissal of the feminists' New Departure and the larger repudiation of the postwar amendments. It is embodied in the fact that the Supreme Court's opinions on *Bradwell* and on the *Slaughterhouse* cases were delivered on the same day in 1873. *Slaughterhouse* is generally considered the fundamental Fourteenth Amendment Supreme Court decision. The case involved a group of Louisiana butchers who challenged a state law regulating their occupation on the grounds that it violated their rights as federal citizens (to practice their vocation—the same issue as *Bradwell*) and that the Fourteenth Amendment established the supremacy of national over state citizenship.[46]

Six months after the election, the Court delivered negative opinions in both cases, interpreting the Fourteenth Amendment very narrowly and finding it inapplicable in both cases. The case that the Court lingered over was *Slaughterhouse*.[47] By a bare majority, it ruled that the amendment's intent was only to ensure "the freedom of the slave race" and that it did not transfer the jurisdiction over fundamental civil rights from state to federal government. The opinion in *Bradwell* covered much less territory but did so by a larger majority. The Court merely rejected the claim that the right to practice law was one of the privileges and immunities of federal citizenship protected by the amendment. Beyond that, the Court simply commented that "the opinion just delivered in the *Slaughterhouse* Cases...renders elaborate argument in the present case unnecessary."[48] We should not be misled by this preemptory dismissal, however. The very interpretation under which the *Slaughterhouse* cases had been decided, that the Fourteenth Amendment was limited to matters of race and did not elevate national over state citizenship, had first been articulated in 1871 in the Majority Report of the House Judiciary Committee, rejecting Victoria Woodhull's claim that the Fourteenth Amendment guaranteed her right to vote.

The *Minor* Case

The Supreme Court ruled conclusively against the New Departure two years later, in 1875. The case in which it did so was *Minor v. Happersett,* brought, appropriately enough, by Virginia Minor, the woman who had first argued that as a citizen of the United States, she was constitutionally protected in her right to vote. Like Anthony, Minor had tried to vote in the 1872 election, but when her vote was refused, she brought suit under the Enforcement Act. The Missouri courts ruled against her, and she appealed to the United States Supreme Court on the grounds that constitutional protections of the citizen's right to vote invalidated any state regulations to the contrary. The Court ruled unanimously against her. Since the *Slaughterhouse* and *Bradwell* cases had disposed of the first element of the New Departure, that the Fourteenth Amendment established the supremacy of national citizenship, the decision in *Minor* concentrated on the second assertion, that suffrage was a right of citizenship. On this, the Court ruled starkly that "the Constitution of the United States does not confer the right of suffrage upon any one."[49]

Here, too, there was an intimate link between the fate of woman suffragists' constitutional claims and that of the Reconstruction amendments in general. The day after the Court delivered its opinion in *Minor,* it heard arguments in *United States v. Cruikshank.* In this case and in the *United States v. Reese,* black men for the first time brought suit under the Enforcement Act for protection of their political rights under the Fourteenth and Fifteenth Amendments, and the Court ruled against them. In the process of ruling against the plaintiffs, the Court found the Enforcement Act, under which both feminists and freedmen had sought protection, unconstitutional. Citing the recent decision in *Minor,* the Court ruled that inasmuch as the Constitution did not bestow the suffrage on anyone, the federal courts were outside their jurisdiction in protecting the freedmen's political rights.

The rejection of woman suffrage arguments on the grounds that the Fifteenth Amendment was only intended to forbid disfranchisement by race

WOMAN SUFFRAGE
CONVENTION.

The Connecticut Woman Suffrage Association will hold its Annual Convention

At NEW HAVEN,
ON

Thursday, December 11th, 1873,
AT

LOOMIS HALL.

The ladies of the New Haven Association will entertain all guests from abroad with lunch at noon and evening, at their Reading Room, in Hoadley's Building, opposite the Post Office. A business meeting will be held there for choice of officers, at ten o'clock, A. M.

Afternoon session at the hall at two o'clock,—free. Evening session at 7.30. Admission twenty-five cents.

Women having been denied the right of TRIAL BY JURY, (by a Judge of the Supreme Court of the United States,) in the person of SUSAN B. ANTHONY, and then fined for the *crime of voting*, her name having been duly registered by the proper officers, the statement of the whole case will be made by Miss ANTHONY in the evening. Rev. OLYMPIA BROWN will also speak then on " *Woman's place in Government.*"

In the afternoon, this question will be discussed:—"SHOULD WOMEN WHO ARE DENIED THE ELECTIVE FRANCHISE, BE COMPELLED TO PAY TAXES."

The members of the Society are earnestly invited to attend the business meeting in the morning, and all persons interested in establishing a truly republican form of Government, are cordially invited to attend the later sessions.

ISABELLA B. HOOKER, President.

F. ELLEN BURR, Secretary.

Announcement of an 1873 woman suffrage convention.
Woman Suffrage
Media Project

paved the way for a reading of the Fifteenth Amendment that was so narrow it did not even protect the freedmen themselves. In its decision in *United States v. Reese,* the Court argued that the plaintiff, although a black man, had not proved that his vote was denied on the grounds of race and so was not covered by constitutional protections. Eventually, of course, the freedmen were effectively disfranchised on grounds of income, residence, and education, all surrogates for race. Anthony had anticipated this connection. At her own trial, she predicted that the general narrowing of the Reconstruction amendments would follow on the heels of the repudiation of women's claims of equal rights under them. "If we once establish the false principle, that United States citizenship does not carry with it the right to vote in every state in this Union," she said, "there is no end to the petty freaks and cunning devices that will be resorted to exclude one and another class of citizens from the right of suffrage." [50]

Three years after the *Minor* defeat, suffragists began their pursuit of a separate constitutional amendment to prohibit disfranchisement on account of sex. At many levels, this was a less radical strategy. With the defeat of the New Departure, winning the vote for women was no longer tied to an overall democratic interpretation of the Constitution. To the degree that the struggle for women's votes was not strategically linked to the general defense of political democracy, that its goal was "woman suffrage" not "universal suffrage," elitist and racist tendencies faced fewer barriers, had freer reign, and imparted a more conservative character to suffragism over the next half-century.

Yet, despite this very important strategic shift, the New Departure period left a deep mark on the history of feminism. From time to time, some suffragist would see possibilities in the existing propositions of the Constitution and propose some clever legal mechanism for exploiting them.[51] Even direct action voting never completely died away. Twenty years after the *Minor* decision, Elizabeth Grannis of New York City made her eighth attempt to register to vote.[52] Certainly the larger spirit of militant direct action resurfaced in a spectacular way in the last decade of the American suffrage movement. The deepest mark of the New Departure, however, was to make women's rights and political equality indelibly constitutional issues. As Susan B. Anthony wrote, she "had learned... through the passage of the Fourteenth and Fifteenth amendments that it had been possible to amend [the Constitution] in such a way as to enfranchise an entire new class of voters."[53] The *Minor* case, the historian Norma Basch has observed, "drew the inferiority of women's status out of the grooves of common law assumptions and state provisions and thrust it into the maelstrom of constitutional conflict. The demand for woman suffrage...acquired a contentious national life."[54]

Notes

1. This essay is a reprint (with abbreviated notes) of an essay that first appeared in *Visible Women: New Essays on American Activism*, Nancy A. Hewitt and Suzanne Lebsock, eds., published in 1993 by the University of Illinois Press. It is reprinted here with permission of the press.
The literature generated by the contemporary feminist debate on equality versus difference is enormous. Two excellent analyses by historians are Linda Gordon, "On Difference," *Genders* 10 (Spring 1991): 91-111; and Joan Scott, "Reconstructing Equality-versus-Difference; or the Uses of Poststructuralist Theory for Feminism," *Feminist Studies* 14 (Spring 1988): 33-50.

2. For a sampling of critical legal studies scholarship on the limitations of rights thinking, see Mark Tushnet, "An Essay on Rights," *Texas Law Review* 62 (May 1984): 1386; and Peter Gabel, "The Phenomenology of Rights Consciousness and the Pact of Withdrawn Selves," ibid., 1563-99.

3. Paula Baker made this argument most forcefully for the pre-1920 period; see "The Domestication of Politics: Women and American Political Society, 1780-1920," *American Historical Review* 89 (June 1984): 620-47.

4. Ellen Carol DuBois, *Feminism and Suffrage: The Emergence of an Independent Women's Movement in America*,

1848-1869, (Ithaca, N.Y., 1978); Elizabeth Cady Stanton, *Eighty Years and More: Reminiscences, 1815–1897*, ed. Ellen Carol DuBois (1898; Boston, 1993), 242.

5. Stanton, *Eighty Years and More*, 242.

6. Elizabeth Cady Stanton, Susan B. Anthony, and Matilda J. Gage, eds., *History of Woman Suffrage*, Vol. 2 (Rochester, N.Y., 1881), 407-520; Ida Husted Harper, ed., *Life and Work of Susan B. Anthony*, (Indianapolis, 1899), 1: 409-48.

7. *HWS* 2: 407-10; on the Minors, see Louise R. Noun, *Strong Minded Women: The Emergence of the Woman Suffrage Movement in Iowa* (Ames, 1986), 168-69.

8. David Montgomery notes the importance of this Reconstruction Era shift in attitude to the positive state in *Beyond Equality: Labor and the Radical Republicans* (New York, 1967), 80-81.

9. On this aspect of Reconstruction Era constitutional thought, see Judith A. Baer, *Equality Under the Constitution: Reclaiming the Fourteenth Amendment* (Ithaca, N.Y., 1983).

10. While the Fifteenth Amendment was still pending, the Minors found an alternative constitutional basis for their claim that suffrage was a natural right in the fre-

quently cited 1820 case *Corfield v. Coryell,* which included the franchise as one of the privileges and immunities protected in Article 4.

11. In New Hampshire in 1870, Matilda Ricker tried to vote (*HWS* 2: 586-87). In New York in 1871, Matilda Joslyn Cage tried to vote in Fayetteville, and a group of women, led by Louise Mansfield, tried to vote in Nyack (Elizabeth Cady Stanton, Susan B. Anthony, and Matilda Joslyn Gage, eds., *History of Woman Suffrage,* [Rochester, N.Y., 1887], 3: 406; Isabelle K. Savelle, *Ladies' Lib: How Rockland Women Got the Vote* (New York, 1979), 13-16; in New York City, Victoria Woodhull and Tennessee Claflin tried to vote (Johanna Johnston, *Mrs. Satan* [New York, 1967], 110).

12. *HWS* 3: 461-62, and *HWS* 2: 600-601.

13. Eleanor Flexner, *Century of Struggle: The Women's Rights Movement in the United States* (Cambridge, Mass., 1959), 168, citing *The Revolution,* November 19, 1868, 307.

14. *HWS* 3: 780-86.

15. Ibid., 784.

16. Benjamin Quarles, "Frederick Douglass and the Woman's Rights Movement," *Journal of Negro History* 25 (June 1940): 35.

17. *HWS* 3: 523-24.

18. Ibid., 766.

19. Ibid., 2: 443-48.

20. Ibid., 445.

21. Victoria C. Woodhull, *Constitutional Equality: A Lecture Delivered at Lincoln Hall, Washington, D.C., February 16, 1871* (New York, 1871).

22. *HWS* 2: 445-46. The comment on "blending" was made in Woodhull's arguments in support of her congressional memorial. These are available in Victoria Woodhull, *The Argument for Woman's Electoral Rights under Amendment XIV and XV of the Constitution of the United States* (London, 1887), 44.

23. Both reports can be found in *HWS* 2: 461-82.

24. Ibid., 469, 478. In support of their interpretation, they cited the federal district court's decision in what was called the *Crescent City* case, later renamed the *Slaughterhouse* cases.

25. Woodhull, *Constitutional Equality,* 4.

26. Martha Wright complained to Elizabeth Stanton about a congressman who "said rudely to Mrs. Davis & Mrs. Griffing, 'You just call on us because you like to,'" to which Mrs. Griffing answered "'We call on you, because it is the only way known to us, to present our appeal to you,' & Mrs. Davis said 'You must remember that we are your constituents.'" Wright to Stanton, December 29, 1870, Garrison Family Collection, Smith College, Northampton, Mass.

27. *HWS* 2: 489.

28. Isabella Beecher Hooker to the Editor, *Independent,* February 11, 1871, reprinted in *Woodhull and Claflin's Weekly,* March 4, 1871, 10.

29. Ibid.; *An Appeal to the Women of the United States by the National Woman Suffrage and Educational Committee* (Hartford, Conn., April 19, 1871).

30. Woodhull's response to the charges can be found in the *New York World,* May 22, 1871, 3.

31. "The Voice of Apollo Hall," *Every Saturday,* June 17, 1871, 554.

32. Victoria C. Woodhull, *The Principles of Social Freedom, Delivered in New York City, November 20, 1871* (New York, 1871), 23-24.

33. Isabella Beecher Hooker to Anna E. Dickenson, April 22, (1871), box 9 Dickenson Papers, Library of Congress, Washington, D.C.

34. Paulina Wright Davis to Woodhull, May 29, 1871, Victoria Woodhull Martin Collection, Southern Illinois University, Carbondale.

35. Victoria C. Woodhull, "The Speech of Victoria C. Woodhull before the National Woman's Suffrage Convention at Apollo Hall, May 11, 1871," reprinted in Woodhull, *The Argument for Women's Electoral Rights,* 137.

36. *HWS* 2: 587-99.

37. Ibid., 598.

38. Ibid., 622. The opinion in Bradwell that is usually cited is not the terse dismissal of the Fourteenth Amendment argument that settled the case, but an individual concurring opinion by Justice Bradley that addressed the coverture issues that Bradwell had removed from her argument.

39. *HWS* 2: 618.

40. Elizabeth Cady Stanton, "Argument before the Senate Judiciary Committee," January 11, 1872, reprinted in *Woodhull and Claflin's Weekly,* January 27, 1872, 7; see also Stanton to Woodhull, December 29, [1872], Stanton Miscellaneous Papers, New York Public Library, New York.

41. Victoria Woodhull, *Carpenter and Cartter Reviewed: A Speech before the National Suffrage Association at Lincoln Hall, Washington, D.C, January 10, 1872* (New York, 1872), 20.

42. Montgomery, *Beyond Equality,* 379-86.

43. Anthony to Stanton, July 10, 1872, box 38, NAWSA Papers, Library of Congress.

44. Nancy A. Hewitt, *Women's Activism and Social Change: Rochester, New York, 1822-1872* (Ithaca, N.Y., 1984), 211. Anthony to Stanton, November 5, 1872, Harper Papers, Huntington Library, San Marino, California.

45. Harper, ed., *The Life and Work of Susan B. Anthony,* 1: 423-53; Charles Fairman, *History of the Supreme Court,* (New York, 1987), 7: 224.

46. Fairman, *History of the Supreme Court,* 285. Carpenter's argument in *Slaughterhouse* can be found in 21 Court Reporters Lawyers Edition, 399-401 (1872).

47. 16 Wall. 36 (1873).

48. 16 Wall. 130 (1873).

49. *HWS* 2: 734-42.

50. Ibid., 641.

51. The most important of these was Catherine McCullough's successful argument that the Constitution permitted states legislatively to enfranchise voters for presidential elections. In 1914 Illinois passed a "presidential suffrage" law, giving women votes in the 1916 presidential election. See Steven W. Buechler, *The Transformation of the Woman Suffrage Movement: The Case of Illinois, 1850-1920* (New Brunswick, N.J., 1986), 174-76.

52. Unidentified clipping, v. 12, 75, Susan B. Anthony Memorial Library Collection, Huntington Library, San Marino, Calif.

53. Susan B. Anthony and Ida Husted Harper, eds., *History of Woman Suffrage,* (Rochester, N.Y., 1902), 4: 10.

54. Norma Basch, "Reconstructing Female Citizenship" (Paper delivered at Women and the Constitution Conference, American University and the Smithsonian, October 1987).

Six

How the West Was Won for Woman Suffrage

Beverly Beeton

Editor's Introduction: In 1869 and 1870, as eastern suffrage forces were in disarray following the failure of the Reconstruction amendments to establish universal suffrage for all, the territories of Wyoming and Utah stunned the nation by announcing the enfranchisement of women. Later, as they entered the Union as states, Wyoming (1890) and Utah (1896) insisted on retaining woman suffrage despite considerable opposition from Congress. They were joined as suffrage states by Colorado (1893) and Idaho (1896), which enfranchised women through state constitutional amendments. These were the only four states to enfranchise women in the nineteenth century.

In this essay, historian Beverly Beeton answers the question students of the suffrage movement have always pondered: what was behind this pioneering embrace of woman suffrage? Why was it that the West was far ahead of the rest of the nation in enfranchising women? Beeton, the author of the book *Women Vote in the West: The Woman Suffrage Movement, 1869-1896* and numerous articles on woman suffrage in the West, explains that there were many factors contributing to the early victories in the West, and that each of the four territories/states has its unique story. She emphasizes, however, that practical politics rather than advanced ideology explain the West's precociousness in adopting woman suffrage. While most eastern and southern politicians saw woman suffrage as worthy of scorn or ridicule and unpopular with their constituents, western politicians embraced it as politically expedient for a fascinating variety of purposes. As Beeton explains, there *were* western men who wanted women enfranchised out of a sense of justice. But the votes necessary for passage of suffrage bills were there because woman suffrage served practical needs ranging from attracting women settlers (using woman suffrage as an advertising gimmick) to protecting polygamy.

Beeton also discusses the relationship between the eastern and western suffrage movements, a relationship of mutual influence. Some eastern proponents—including Congressmen—saw the territories as a good place to test this controversial new idea of woman suffrage. National suffrage leaders, including Lucy Stone, Elizabeth Cady Stanton, Susan B. Anthony, Anna Howard Shaw, and Carrie Chapman Catt, assisted with western suffrage campaigns, beginning with the unsuccessful Kansas campaign of 1867. But they benefited from the opportunity to test and develop strategies and tactics in the West that were later used elsewhere.

One fascinating aspect of the western story told by Beeton is the relationship between Mormon suffragists and eastern suffrage leaders who tried to welcome and support the Mormon women while avoiding the appearance of condoning polygamy. In the wake of the Victoria Woodhull affair, the public was prepared to believe the worst regarding suffragists and unconventional ideas about sex and marriage, and the National Woman Suffrage Association (NWSA) particularly was hurt by its defense of Mormon suffragists. Beeton also explains that in the West, as in the rest of the nation, racism and ethnic tensions played a role in the suffrage movement, and that in this region the controversy over voting rights involved Chinese and Native Americans as well as African Americans.

The early victories in the West were of tremendous importance in the history of the American woman suffrage movement. As Beeton notes, suffragists and anti-suffragists alike gathered data and published studies on the effects of woman suffrage on western society and politics, with each side insisting that the western experience proved *them* right. Of greater significance, however, was the inspiration these Rocky Mountain states provided to suffragists in other regions of the United States.

★　★　★　★　★

A HALF-CENTURY prior to the 1920 ratification of the Nineteenth Amendment women voted in the Rocky Mountain West. In December 1869, Wyoming women were granted the right to vote, and two months later in February of 1870, their sisters across the mountains in Utah gained access to polling places. In both cases, women were enfranchised through woman suffrage bills adopted by their territorial legislatures and signed by the territorial governors. As a result of an 1893 referendum women in Colorado were also enfranchised, and a state constitutional amendment in Idaho in 1896 provided woman suffrage there. Thus, Wyoming, Utah, Colorado, and Idaho were the *only* states where women were enfranchised in the nineteenth century.[1]

Why were women in the Rocky Mountain West the first to vote? There is no one simple answer. An examination of events in the four nineteenth-century suffrage states reveals a variety of motives that together caused a sufficient number of male legislators and voters to support woman suffrage. There *were* liberal-minded men who believed voting rights were an inherent right of citizenship; but pragmatic objectives, usually political ones, were necessary for enough men to vote for woman suffrage for it to become a reality. In short, women were enfranchised in the American West primarily as a matter of expediency, not ideology.

Move West and Vote

In the West, woman suffrage was often seen as a means to advertise a region in hopes of attracting settlers or investors. Sometimes it was proposed as a device to embarrass political opponents if they voted against it or vetoed it. Often, territorial residents saw it as a way to recruit eastern support for their bids for statehood. When black men, American-born Chinese men, and some Indian men voted, arguments for educated, property-owning, white women to have the same privilege appealed to many peoples' racial prejudices. Since the Rocky Mountain West was in the process of forming governments during the last quarter of the nineteenth century, the electorate had to be defined in the new laws and constitutions. Consequently, westerners were forced to think about and debate the issue of who would be allowed to vote.

The fact that there was no significant, organized opposition in the four states (as there was from liquor interests in the states of Washington and California) made passage of legislation and referenda easier. Another contributing factor was the completion of the transcontinental railroad in 1869 that facilitated the quick transportation of people and ideas. Eastern lecture-bureau circuit riders, many of whom addressed women's issues, immediately toured the West, and westerners traveled to the East more frequently and received news in a more timely fashion—including reports on eastern debates regarding political rights for former slaves and women.

The existence of a post-Civil War woman suffrage movement also contributed to the early enfranchisement of western women because eastern suffragists kept the discussion of women's rights alive. It was in response to lobbyists' pressure for passage of a woman suffrage constitutional amendment that some eastern newspapers and politicians proposed testing woman suffrage in the territories. Also, when campaigns were waged in the West, eastern suffrage associations provided money and organizational expertise. Conversely, the suffrage movement as a whole benefited when strategies and campaign techniques were developed and tested in the western states.

In 1867, when the Fourteenth Amendment defining national citizenship to include black men was being ratified, a number of campaigns to amend state and territorial constitutions to provide for woman suffrage took place in the American West. The most vigorous effort was staged in Kansas where two amendments were proposed: one enfranchising black men and one enfranchising women. Initially, the prospects appeared to be good because the 1861 Kansas constitution included school suffrage for women.[2]

Representing the American Equal Rights Association, the postwar organization advocating universal suffrage, Lucy Stone and her husband, Henry Blackwell, campaigned for a month in Kansas, and returned to Boston with optimistic reports that the Republicans had launched an irreversible movement for equal rights. However, this optimism proved premature. As the debate intensified, editors of national and local Republican and reform newspapers supported political privileges for black men but failed to endorse equal rights for women. In the words of Horace Greeley, chair of the American Equal Rights Association, the extension of the franchise to women would be too revolutionary for public acceptance.

As the sunflowers blossomed in the late summer of 1867, Susan B. Anthony and Elizabeth Cady Stanton toured Kansas and found sentiment against woman suffrage growing. A month before the vote on the amendments, they were joined by George Francis Train, an avid Democrat and railroad financier, who brought money to the campaign. But association with Train caused abolitionists and Republicans to criticize severely Anthony and Stanton because Train used white supremacy arguments overtly to advance the women's cause. Responding to Republican critics, Anthony exclaimed: "Your test of faithfulness is the Negro, ours is the woman."[3]

Belatedly, many national newspaper editors tried to convince Kansas voters that the question was one of universal suffrage. Even Horace Greeley grudgingly acknowledged in his *New York Tribune* that while he regarded woman suffrage with distrust, he was willing to see it pioneered in Kansas.[4] Nevertheless, when the votes were tallied, both propositions failed. Neither women nor black men were enfranchised as a result of the Kansas campaign in 1867.

Following the Kansas campaign, however, the woman suffrage movement adopted sunflower yellow as its campaign color, and the movement began to assume the form that it would take for the next quarter century. Feeling betrayed by the male equal rights reformers they had worked with for years before and after the Civil War, Stanton and Anthony launched a new organization in 1869 dedicated to woman suffrage, the National Woman Suffrage Association (NWSA), with headquarters in New York. They also founded a woman suffrage newspaper, *The Revolution,* which they used to oppose the Fourteenth and Fifteenth Amendments, advocating instead for suffrage for the educated, irrespective of sex or color. Immediate enfranchisement of all women through a federal constitutional amendment was their major focus. That same year, led by Lucy Stone, Henry Blackwell, and Julia Ward Howe, more moderate suffragists rallied to the banner of the American Woman Suffrage Association (AWSA) based in Boston. This group, which supported the Fourteenth and Fifteenth Amendments, endorsed the constitutional amendment for woman suffrage, but emphasized building support for woman suffrage in the states. This schism on goals and methods persisted until 1890 when the two factions merged into the National American Woman Suffrage Association (NAWSA).

Meanwhile, Congressmen continued to consider the idea of enfranchising women in the territories as an experiment. During the Kansas campaign, Hamilton Willcox, a representative of the New York Universal Franchise Association, proposed that women in *all* the territories be enfranchised, and *The New York Times* publicized this scheme for testing woman suffrage. Given legislative form by George Washington Julian, Republican Congressman from Indiana, the idea of women voting in the territories was appealing because it appeared to be safe from a political point of view.[5] Neither the political stability of the established states nor the national political scene would be seriously altered (since territorial residents were not allowed to vote for their own governors or the president), and the definition of the electorate could be reexamined by Congress when the territories applied for admission to the Union as states. Moreover, since Congress controlled the territories, the experiment could be halted if it went awry. And the possible defeminizing impact that politics might have on women and the impact women would have on politics could be tested safely.

In addition, Willcox and others predicted that woman suffrage would be advantageous in relieving the problem of "surplus women" in the East (more women than men available for marriage as a result of the Civil War casualties, a problem exacerbated by male migration to the West). The adoption of woman suffrage in the West, they believed, would encourage eastern women to move to the frontier.[6] These men also predicted that woman suffrage would lead to the elimination of polygamy—the Utah Mormon practice of men marrying multiple wives.

Of course, population redistribution and Mormon plural marriage were not the primary concerns of women's rights advocates who insisted that women had inherent natural rights and demanded a constitutional amendment protecting women's political rights as the proposed Fifteenth Amendment protected the rights of freedmen. Yet, as the Fifteenth Amendment was approved, the proposed woman suffrage amendment and the proposal to test woman suffrage in the territories languished. Representative Julian's bill on woman suffrage in the territories was now limited to Utah Territory where the bill's sponsors hoped woman suffrage could eradicate polygamy—a "relic of barbarism."

While eastern suffragists divided over the best means of attaining the vote and eastern politicians contemplated the theoretical consequences of woman suffrage, however, women in the Rocky Mountain West were voting.

Women's Rights in Wyoming

In December of 1869, the Wyoming territorial legislature surprised the nation by passing a bill enfranchising women. While there was no organized suffrage campaign in this new territory with fewer than nine thousand residents of which only slightly more than one thousand were women of voting age, the arguments for woman suffrage were well known. Traveling on the newly completed transcontinental railroad, the lyceum bureau's stellar speaker, Anna Dickenson, visited Wyoming on her western tour. And Redelia Bates, a woman suffrage lecturer from St. Louis, spoke to the Wyoming territorial legislature. In addition, eastern debates over women's rights were covered by local newspapers. Yet, though there were individuals in Wyoming such as the suffrage bill's introducer, William H. Bright, who believed in women's right to vote as a matter of citizenship, the bill passed because lawmakers believed woman suffrage was a way to advertize the territory to potential investors and settlers. Some Democrats thought it would embarrass the Republican governor, John A. Campbell, who would (they presumed) veto it, but he surprised them by quickly signing the law that even went beyond suffrage to allow women to serve on juries and hold public office.

A jubilant Susan B. Anthony reported the news of the enfranchisement of women in Wyoming to the suffragists assembled for the first NWSA convention. She urged women "to emigrate to Wyoming and make a model State of it by sending a woman Senator to the National Capital,"[7] though she planned to stay home and work for a federal constitutional amendment enfranchising all women. While eastern women did not heed the call to go west, they did use the Wyoming example to urge their own state legislatures to extend equal rights to them and to encourage Congress to amend the Constitution.

In the summer of 1871, Stanton and Anthony went west to "the land of freedom," as they called Wyoming, where they were warmly greeted by government officials and leading citizens. Returning east in December, Anthony learned that some Wyoming Democrats, unhappy about the election of several Republicans, were trying to repeal the woman suffrage law. However, Governor Campbell vetoed the repeal act, saying, "No legislature has the right to disfranchise it own constituents."[8] When an attempt was made to overturn his veto, the members of the Council and the House divided along party lines defeating the measure by one vote.

As the first and only place where women voted and sat on juries, Wyoming was an object of curiosity. Easterners were eager to question travelers and Wyoming residents to determine what impact woman suffrage had on women and on society. Two years after passage of the law, Edward M. Lee (who reportedly had been removed as Secretary of Wyoming Territory for public drunkenness and enjoying the company of a prostitute known as "the Circassian Girl") told *The Galaxy* magazine that the powers of the ballot had not caused women to abandon any of their womanly or wifely qualities. As he saw it, the time-honored ordinance of marriage seemed to be as everlasting as the mountains; moreover, there were no signs of that "pestiferous freelove doctrine" that seemed to be gaining converts in the East.[9] At the 1874 NWSA convention, Aaron Sargent, a Congressman from California, praised woman suffrage in Wyoming "where women hold office, where they vote, where they have the most orderly society of any of the Territories."[10]

While Sargent was applauding the results of Wyoming women's new-found freedoms, however, a number of newspaper editors were questioning the experiment. When the *New York Independent* charged that only twenty-five women had voted in the last election, the AWSA investigated and its newspaper *The Woman's Journal* countered with assurances from citizens of Wyoming that women's participation in elections had "become a matter of course." Having observed women voting for four years, Governor Campbell testified he was convinced of the justice and wisdom of the measure. In 1888, the NWSA expressed its confidence in its convention banner proclaiming: "The vote of women transformed Wyoming from barbarism to civilization."

A year later, over one hundred Wyoming women demanded that woman suffrage be affirmed in the statehood constitution. Few convention delegates openly opposed woman suffrage, but nearly a third subscribed to the idea of separate submission (of woman suffrage and statehood) arguing that the citizens of Wyoming had not had an opportunity to vote on the proposition because voting rights had been granted to women by the territorial legislature. However, when the debates ended, woman suffrage was included, and two-thirds of the voters registered their support for the constitution. When Congress was about to reject Wyoming's admission into the Union because of the clause enfranchising women, Wyoming legislators telegraphed Congress saying they would remain out of the Union a hundred years rather than join without woman suffrage. Finally, the constitution was approved by a narrow margin with the controversial clause intact, and Wyoming became the first state to allow its female citizens to vote.

Utah Suffrage a Vote for Mormons

Two months after the 1869 passage of the initial woman suffrage bill in Wyoming, the Utah territorial legislature enfranchised Utah women. This move received considerable national attention because it admitted nearly forty times as many women to the polling places as had the Wyoming action; moreover, most of these women were members of the Mormon church that practiced plural marriage. Arguing that polygamy only existed where women were degraded, reformers predicted the ballot would be used to eradicate the practice. Even the NWSA proclaimed its confidence that the enfranchisement of women in Utah was the one safe, sure, and swift means to abolish polygamy. Reformers refrained, however, from claiming the vote would cause women to migrate to the territory because the Mormons promoted their marital system as a means to deal with "surplus women."

Generally, the national concern about Utah women amused the Mormons. Assuring readers that Utah women could vote "without running wild or becoming unsexed," George Q. Cannon, editor of the Mormon-controlled newspaper, the *Deseret News,* expressed pleasure in the opportunity to be an example to the world.[11]

The Mormons, of course, expected that woman suffrage would reinforce rather than undermine Mormon traditions. In fact, enfranchisement of women in Utah was primarily an effort by the Mormons to counter the image painted by lecture-bureau circuit riders of Mormon women as downtrodden slaves and to stop national efforts to eliminate polygamy. Furthermore, in 1870, just before the territorial legislature acted, reports arrived in Salt Lake City that Congress was considering a variety of threatening legislation ranging from schemes to partition Utah and give segments to the surrounding territories and states, to proposals to disfranchise the Mormons, disqualify them from holding public office and sitting on juries, and deprive them of the right to homestead or preempt public lands, or disinherit their children. Mormons were also concerned about new threats to polygamy; when enforcement of the anti-polygamy law of 1862 seemed imminent, five thousand women gathered in the Mormon Tabernacle on Temple Square for a "great indignation meeting" to decry the "mean, foul" legislation.

It was against this background that the Utah legislature passed the bill extending the ballot to women, and on February 12, 1870, the non-Mormon, Territorial Secretary S.A. Mann, serving as acting governor, signed the bill into law. Responding to a resolution of appreciation from a delegation of Utah women, Mann penned a letter philosophizing about the intelligent use of the ballot. Mormon faithful, William Clayton, was less philosophical when he noted, "The poor, enslaved downtrodden!!! women of Utah can now act for themselves and take revenge on the men of Israel." Then he gleefully exclaimed that those who expected Mormon women to use the vote against polygamy would "gnash their teeth with rage" and "foam worse than ever," for "there are not many women here but will sustain all the measures of the authorities [of the church] better than some of the men do." [12]

There were individuals in Utah in 1870 who advocated woman suffrage for liberal, human rights reasons, and there was some concern about non-Mormons coming into the territory now that the transcontinental railroad was completed. But the compelling reasons for passage of the legislation were related to polygamy and statehood. "Bah!" was the Salt Lake Herald's response to the accusation that the Mormon-dominated legislature gave the vote to women to strengthen Mormon political power against non-Mormons. With a total population of 87,000 of which only about 4,500 were non-Mormons, doubling the Mormon voting power was not necessary. [13]

Ironically, now that Mormon women had proven to be supporters of polygamy, Congress began to try to strip them of the franchise. During the 1870s and 1880s, Utah repeatedly petitioned for statehood as Congress continually proposed legislation designed to take voting privileges from Utah women as part of the anti-polygamy effort. And Mormons repeatedly reminded Congress that the idea of enfranchising women in Utah was being considered in the East when the Utah territorial legislature acted.

Using the church's women's auxiliary, the Relief Society, as the communications network, Mormon women became skilled at holding "mass meetings" and producing "mammoth petitions" in opposition to hostile legislation or in support of statehood. Utah women and the territory's delegate to Congress were in regular communication with national suffrage leaders and were able to solicit suffragists to lobby Congress on Utah's behalf.

In 1883, when Congress was considering a number of measures to "elevate" the women of Utah and "relieve" them from their "bondage" by repealing the territorial act conferring the vote, the Washington, D.C., attorney, suffragist, and soon-to-be presidential candidate, Belva Lockwood, launched an aggressive campaign against the legislation saying: "It is not only a fight for `Mormon' female votes—it is a contest for woman's equal rights in principle." Persuading the NWSA to adopt a resolution against the legislation, Lockwood declared: "Only a fool or a knave would deny" the bill is a direct blow at woman suffrage. [14]

When suffragists were accused by anti-polygamists of being in "an attitude not unfriendly to polygamy" and anti-polygamy societies reported that Mormon women voted as instructed by the church hierarchy, national suffrage leaders realized their image was being tarnished by identification with Utah women. Thus, Anthony went to great lengths to clarify that the NWSA's only interest in Utah was woman suffrage. As the concern with polygamy intensified in Congress, suffrage leaders continued their support of Utah women's voting rights while trying to distance themselves from polygamy.

Reverend Anna Howard Shaw, Henry Blackwell, and Mary A. Hunt presented the arguments of the AWSA to the House Committee on Territories, objecting to the proposed disfranchisement of Utah women. Instead, they petitioned for a law to give women equal suffrage in all the territories. In 1887, the NWSA urged President Grover Cleveland to veto the Edmunds-Tucker Bill that proposed to take the vote from Utah women. He responded by allowing the bill to become law without his signature.[15] And the national suffrage cause was set back further when Congress once again refused to pass the Anthony Amendment.

The suffrage movement and the NWSA in particular were greatly weakened by identification with the Mormons and their marital system. Belva Lockwood's defense of the Mormons brought the wrath of society down on the NWSA and the cause. In the 1870s, society had a similar negative reaction to feminist Victoria Woodhull who was opposed to legal and clerical marriage and instead advocated "free love" with the assumption that each woman had the right to decide whether, when, and with whom to become sexually active.[16] Women's rights advocates could no longer be critical of the institution of marriage without being accused of favoring polygamy. It was now necessary for feminists to shun all criticisms of marital and family relations and pledge their belief in the sanctity of monogamous marriage.

Elizabeth Cady Stanton and Susan B. Anthony's methods and philosophy lost credibility after 1887, and American feminism took a conservative turn. The state-by-state approach to gaining enfranchisement dominated the movement until 1914, and feminist critiques of marriage and women's roles in society were set aside as priority was given to securing the ballot. Susan B. Anthony continued to be revered, but a new and more conservative generation of suffragists emerged, and temperance was accepted as part of the movement in spite of warnings that it would rally liquor interests to work against woman suffrage. When the NWSA and the AWSA merged in 1890, only the women of Wyoming were enfranchised, because Utah women had lost the vote by Congressional action, and Washington women had, for the second time, seen their suffrage law declared invalid by that territory's supreme court.

While the relationship between women's rights leaders and the Mormons was strained, suffragists continued to visit Utah. In the spring of 1895, Anthony and Anna Howard Shaw led a three-day Rocky Mountain Suffrage Conference in Salt Lake City attended by women from Wyoming, Utah, and Colorado. National suffragists also assisted Utah women with the development of a territorial suffrage association—a step that seemed necessary because many Utah men were willing to abandon woman suffrage now that it could no longer be used to protect polygamy or advance the statehood cause. This became evident when Utah made a new bid for admission into the Union (still unsuccessful) with a constitution prohibiting polygamy and limiting suffrage to adult men.

The Utah feminist, Charlotte Ives Cobb Godbe Kirby, who was known for her radical rhetoric calling for women of the world to unite, wrote numerous articles and letters on behalf of the Utah Territory Woman Suffrage Association and sometimes vied with Emmeline B. Wells for the leadership role in the Utah woman suffrage movement.[17] Active on the local and national scenes, Kirby and Wells were both involved in the discussion about woman suffrage in 1895 when the territory prepared to make a new bid for statehood and debated the provisions of the proposed state constitution.[18] However, two Mormon men, both of whom were historians and members of the Democratic party, led the convention debate over inclusion of women in the electorate. Brigham H. Roberts argued that women could not act independently because of relationships in the family; besides, he said, women are sufficiently represented in poli-

Rocky Mountain Suffrage Conference, May 1895. In the front row are Margaret N. Caine (far right) and Susan B. Anthony (third from right). In the second row are Zina D. H. Young (second from right), Emmeline B. Wells (third from right), Sarah M. Kimball (fourth from right), and Anna Howard Shaw (fifth from right). In the third row are Mary C.C. Bradford (far right) and Estelle Kesl (third from right). Theresa A. Jenkins is in the fourth row, (third from right). In the back row are Mattie Hughes Cannon (far left), Emily S. Richards (fourth from left), and Ellis Meredith Stansbury (fifth from left). Schlesinger Library, Radcliffe College tics by husbands, fathers, sons, or brothers.[19] Orson F. Whitney, who compared Roberts to a bull standing in front of a train attempting to prevent it from passing ("I admire your courage but d__n your judgement"), insisted, "it is woman's destiny to have a voice in the affairs of government. She was designed for it. She has a right to it."[20]

Finally, Utah approved a constitution containing woman suffrage in 1895. Since the Mormon Church had officially abandoned polygamy in 1890, Congress approved the constitution with little protest about the enfranchisement of women, and President Cleveland did not raise the issue when he issued the proclamation admitting the territory of Utah as a state on January 4, 1896.

Colorado Suffrage, a Matter of Race

While polygamy was the major issue tied to woman suffrage in Utah, across the Rockies in Colorado racial concerns were predominant. The territorial legislature and newspapers had been discussing woman suffrage since the late 1860s, and Governor Edward M. McCook had called for Colorado to join its sister territory, Wyoming, as a leader in the cause of universal suffrage. Advocates argued it was taxation without representation when women were prohibited from voting. Opponents warned: women do not want to vote; involvement in politics might destroy "the symmetry of women's character"; only the class that goes to war should be allowed to vote; and the enfranchisement of women at this time is premature. But race was the major issue.[21]

Representative M.S. Taylor warned Colorado territorial legislators in 1870 that black women, as well Chinese women, will vote if the woman suffrage bill passes.[22] After studying the legislation, a house committee chaired by Representative A.H. DeFrance urged passage and argued it was unfair for uneducated, non-property-holding black men to vote on matters concerning the property of white women who were not allowed to vote. He went on to suggest that women's presence in politics would have a "purifying influence" on society and politics. It was in response to DeFrance that Taylor warned of the folly of allowing "Negro wenches" and Chinese women to vote.

Unmoved by petitions from women requesting suffrage, lawmakers refused to approve the legislation. Thus, DeFrance sought a compromise by proposing that the suffrage bill be submitted to the qualified electorate of the territory, including women, for ratification or rejection.[23] After considerable parliamentary maneuvering by the friends and foes of woman suffrage, Taylor moved for postponement, and the house effectively killed the bill by voting fifteen to ten to delay action.

Even though the legislative measure was dead, the debate was kept alive in the newspapers and was periodically enlivened by the visit of a suffrage speaker. In July of 1870, the eastern actress and lecturer Olive Logan spoke in Denver, and one year later, Stanton and Anthony lectured to a responsive crowd in the Denver Theater. As Colorado drafted a constitution in preparation for admis-

sion as the Centennial State, woman suffrage was a major issue. Fearing rejection by the Colorado electorate or the national Congress, constitutional convention delegates limited women's involvement in the political process to
school district elections, but provided for a vote on woman suffrage in the first
general election after statehood.

Consequently, in 1877 a major campaign began to persuade the Colorado
male electorate to fully enfranchise women. The Colorado Suffrage Association
coordinated speaking tours throughout the state that included local advocates
such as William H. Bright, who had initiated the suffrage bill in Wyoming and
was now living in Denver, and many eastern headliners. Susan B. Anthony
stumped mining towns and outlying communities speaking in saloons, in hotel
dining rooms, at railroad stations, and on a soapbox in front of a courthouse.

While newspapers in Denver generally supported the referendum, Pueblo's
Colorado Chieftain editorialized against suffragists. Denver's Catholic Bishop
Machebeuf continued his pulpit campaign against woman suffrage and was
soon joined by the Presbyterian Reverend Bliss, who referred to suffragists as
"bawling, ranting women, bristling for their rights." If women vote, he told
parishioners, married women will live in endless bickering with their husbands
and single women will never marry. On election day when Reverend Bliss
encountered women handing out fliers urging men to vote in the affirmative,
he identified himself and reiterated his objections to women voting. The
AWSA's Lucy Stone countered, and a loud exchange ensued. Yet, when the day
ended, Reverend Bliss's point of view was victorious; woman suffrage was
defeated by a vote of two to one.[24]

Sixteen years passed before Colorado suffragists were once again able to get a
referendum on the ballot in 1893—thanks to the support of Populist legislators
and the Populist governor, David H. Waite. Colorado suffragists concentrated
on converting male voters through newspapers and political parties. While
they organized local suffrage leagues throughout the state, they limited the
number of eastern speakers invited to the state. When suffragists pledged their
support of silver as a currency basis along with gold, miners and unionized
workers seemed willing to support the referendum, and victory came within
grasp when the Republican, Prohibitionist, and Populist parties endorsed equal
suffrage. With strong support and little opposition the referendum passed.

National suffragists quickly seized Colorado as an attractive example because
it had a large population and an urban center where the impact of women voting could be closely observed. Unlike Wyoming, Colorado did not have a reputation as a wild frontier with a high crime rate, and it was not tainted by
polygamy as was Utah. Moreover, Colorado was unique as the first state to grant
woman suffrage by referendum. The aggressive campaign methods used by Colorado suffragists with organizational and financial support from eastern suffrage associations became the model for other states. The strategies of converting the male electorate through speeches, political parties, and public demonstrations, which were developed in Colorado under the guidance of NAWSA

leader Carrie Chapman Catt, would be employed in other states, notably California and Idaho.

Idaho, Suffrage in Snake River Country

One year after women were enfranchised in Wyoming and Utah, Dr. Joseph William Morgan, a Democratic representative from Oneida County, announced that women in Idaho should enjoy the same rights and introduced a woman suffrage bill in the territorial legislature. However, Republican W.H. Van Slyke appealed to Blackstone's theory of the legal and political merger of the woman with the man upon marriage and warned, "that to give her the ballot would work an entire social revolution, disrupting the family tie, and bringing a conflict of sexes in the land."[25] When lawmakers put the issue to a vote, it resulted in a tie. Thus, Idaho's first woman suffrage bill died.

Occasionally, an Idaho suffragist would lecture or Abigail Scott Duniway,[26] the Oregon suffrage leader and editor of *The New Northwest* suffrage newsletter, would tour the territory speaking and soliciting subscribers, but for a decade and a half there was only limited discussion of woman suffrage in Idaho. Immigration, Mormons, prohibition, and woman suffrage were intertwined in a complex way in Idaho. One-fourth of the residents were Mormons, most of whom lived in Dr. Morgan's southeastern part of the state along the Utah-Idaho border, and there were fears woman suffrage would give Mormons disproportionate political power because there were large numbers of women in Mormon settlements. Fearing voting rights for women might encourage more Mormons to move to Idaho some people reported: "The impression was getting abroad that Idaho was controlled by the leading Mormons in Salt Lake, and that this impression would tend to discourage [non-Mormon] immigration."[27] The underlying cause of most of this anxiety was political; at the time, most Mormons voted Democratic.

Concerns about prohibition posed a bigger problem for woman suffrage advocates in Idaho; Duniway and some other suffragists blamed the Woman's Christian Temperence Union (WCTU's) efforts to stop liquor traffic for a woman suffrage law being declared unconstitutional in Washington territory. Consequently, in 1889—when the constitutional convention was being lobbied to include woman suffrage and a clause prohibiting the sale of liquor— Duniway rushed to Boise. Arguing temperance and woman suffrage were not inexorably tied, she assured statehood constitution writers that women would not vote away beer and whiskey. However, delegates were more concerned that the document would not be accepted if Idaho was associated with the Mormons and woman suffrage than they were that women would use the ballot to bring about prohibition. Thus, both women and Mormon men were denied political rights and the opportunity to vote on the constitution that was submitted to the Idaho electorate and the United States Congress in 1890.

Abigail Scott Duniway, who now spent part of her time in Custer County, Idaho, where her sons had a homestead claim, thought woman suffrage would be submitted to the Idaho electorate in the first election after statehood as had been the case in Colorado. This did not happen, however. While Duniway, temperance advocates, and Mormon women worked in their own ways to advance the cause, six years passed before a woman suffrage amendment received the required two-thirds vote in the Idaho legislature. Anticipating that a major campaign was needed to persuade the electorate to support the amendment, Anthony told Duniway to leave suffrage in Idaho to the eastern managers and to confine her activities to Oregon.[28] Thus, Emma Smith DeVoe of Illinois went to Idaho to manage the campaign, and Mell Woods, an active suffrage worker from Wallace, Idaho, (the daughter of the Utah's Mormon suffragist Emmeline B. Wells), was assigned to assist DeVoe.

Organizing local suffrage clubs as she traveled, DeVoe toured Idaho giving suffrage lectures. In November of 1895, delegates from these suffrage clubs converged in Boise to found the Idaho Equal Suffrage Association. Having just returned to her home in Buffalo, New York from California where she had worked on that state's unsuccessful suffrage campaign, Anthony sent a telegram to Idaho suffrage conventioneers saying, "Women speakers can not reach them [male voters]."[29] Instead she advised Idaho suffragists to educate voters through political party newspapers and public meetings. Heeding Anthony's advice, Idaho suffragists organized for the upcoming campaign. In the spring of 1896, Laura M. Johns, a campaign organizer from Kansas, was coordinating activities in the southwest part of the state. Helen Young, a lawyer from Wallace, Idaho, was in charge of the northern part of the state, and Blanche Whitman of Montpelier was responsible for rallying the predominantly Mormon communities in the southeast region, where Mormon men were now allowed to vote.

This approach minimized regional tensions and allowed suffragists to focus on gaining support for political rights for women. In their resolutions urging support for the amendment, Idaho suffragists pointed to the examples of women voting in the neighboring states, and called forth the principle of no taxation without representation. Appealing to racial biases, suffragists argued that white, native-born American women should be at least equal in political rights with Chinese men, who if born in the United States were allowed to vote, and Indian men, who under the 1887 Dawes Severalty Act [mandating an end to Indian reservations] were allowed citizenship and voting rights. In her Fourth of July speech, suffragist Laura M. Johns referred to the enfranchisement of Nez Pierce Indian men and said she believed, "Women were as much entitled to privileges of citizenship as those savages."[30] NAWSA organizer Carrie Chapman Catt, who had refined campaign strategies in Colorado, came to Idaho during the summer to assist the Idaho association's advisory board with the preparation of instructions to the local suffrage clubs. As the election approached, most of the state's newspapers declared their support, and all four political parties—Populists, Democrats, Republicans, and Silver Republicans—endorsed the amendment.

On election day men cast 12,126 votes in support and 6,282 against. However, before celebrations proclaiming Idaho the fourth woman suffrage state

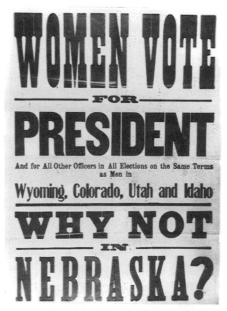

Flag with four stars representing states where women could vote, c. 1900. Smithsonian Institution

Poster from the 1911 Nebraska campaign. Nebraska State Historical Society

could be staged, the board of canvassers ruled the measure was defeated because it had not received a majority of all votes cast in the election, just a majority cast on the amendment. Determined, the Idaho suffrage association commissioned lawyers, William E. Borah and James H. Hawley, who would eventually become Idaho's senator and governor, to carry the issue to the Idaho Supreme Court where the ruling was favorable. Idaho now joined the ranks of suffrage states.

Woman suffrage was realized in Idaho in 1896 because the political parties (especially the Populists) as well as the Mormons and the WCTU supported it, and there was no significant organized opposition from liquor interests as there was in the Pacific Coast states. Idaho suffragists perfected campaign techniques developed in Colorado that proved to be the major strategies of the women's movement for the next quarter century. In 1897, Catt instructed the NAWSA conventioneers to study the Idaho methods and improve them, for: "Until we do this kind of house-to-house work we can never expect to carry any of the states in which there are large cities."[31]

Four Experiments Examined

Idaho was the last and the least famous of the nineteenth-century woman suffrage states. The Wyoming experience was the best known and the longest tested. While the Utah example was considered anomalous by some as a result of the association of polygamy, Colorado—with its large population and urban center—was considered the most reliable test of suffrage strategies and suffrage itself.

Suffragists gathered data on the four states in an attempt to demonstrate the positive impact of woman suffrage. They concluded from their findings that women's involvement in politics had resulted in calmer and more orderly polling places, in the selection of candidates of higher moral character, in better schools, in more moral and sanitary legislation, and in making "intemperance and other bad habits unpopular."[32] More colorful, but less positive conclusions appeared in popular publications. The well-known western novelist William Macleod Raine reported access to polling booths had not "unsexed" women, and they had not "regenerated the world" with their ballots.[33] Examining the experiences in the Rocky Mountain states, the editor of the Utah *Deseret News* found the promised purification of politics had "not panned out to any very extraordinary extent"; moreover, partisanship had "taken hold of the lady voter with equal if not greater force than" it had the men.[34] As one Colorado woman phrased it: "They vote with men, and for men, and just about like men."[35] A writer for *Pearson's Magazine* concluded women had used the ballot to do "nothing revolutionary, startling, uplifting, or sensational."[36]

Woman suffrage is usually viewed by historians as a middle-class reform movement; this view holds in the early experiences in the West. Most leaders and supporters of the movement in the four Rocky Mountain states were white, Protestant, protectors of the community. There was some identification of woman suffrage with temperance and Populism, but generally woman suffrage in the American West was not led by people who sought to overthrow or even radically reform the established social, economic systems. Even in the cases where the Populist Party was a prime force in bringing about their enfranchisement, after a year or two, women tended to vote for the more conventional political parties. Most western suffragists held conservative political views and defended tradition, especially the role of wife and mother.

Arguments for and against political rights for women were often based on racist assumptions in the last quarter of the nineteenth century, in the West as elsewhere in the nation. Since white women were generally better educated and often owned property, it was argued, they should not be the political inferiors of black, Chinese, or Indian men. The emotional appeals of equal rights workers and politicians that "my wife" or "my mother" is surely as good as a black man were provocative, and the cry of white women's superiority to Indians and Chinese had a special appeal in the American West. On the other hand, an often-heard condemnation of woman suffrage was that black women, Chinese women, and Indian women could not be kept out of the voting booths if women were enfranchised. These arguments were frequently used by westerners and by eastern politicians and suffragists who kept woman suffrage alive on the national scene.

The fact that a national suffrage movement existed in the East and that governments were in a formative stage in the West also contributed to the establishment of women's rights during the last three decades of the nineteenth century. The West was a dynamic, evolving region. Railroads ended the isolation, the frontier was closing, and territorial status was being traded for statehood. In those days of boosterism, westerners were promoters; so it was natural for them to seize on a non-threatening scheme such as woman suffrage as a means to publicize their regions and hopefully attract settlers, investors, and support for their admission to the Union as states.

The fact that Wyoming and Utah were territories in 1869 and 1870 allowed for quick enactment of woman suffrage. Once a territorial legislature approved a bill, only the governor's signature was needed for it to become law. Moreover, when westerners were writing statehood constitutions and preparing themselves for self-government, they had to think through and vote consciously on a form of government including a definition of the electorate.

Certainly, there were liberal, egalitarian-minded individuals in the West who supported woman suffrage for human rights reasons, but enfranchisement became a reality as a result of expediency. The motives of the legislators and governors responsible for enfranchising women were usually conservative and political rather than progressive, ideological, and egalitarian. These men were not afraid that western women would use the ballot to reform society or seize political power; after all, with the exception of Utah, there were not many women.[37] Moreover, in these four regions, women had not formed significant social reform movements. Even the WCTU was not considered a serious threat.

Fourteen Years to Light the Other Forty-Four States

After the 1896 amendment of the Idaho constitution, however, it was fourteen years before Wyoming, Utah, Colorado, and Idaho, were joined by another suffrage state and a new star was added to the woman suffrage flag displayed annually at the national suffrage meeting. Yet, when at last the woman suffrage movement emerged from its string of defeats and began to win battles in the states, the first victories *again* were in the American West. In 1910, Washington added its star to the suffrage flag, followed by California in 1911, Oregon, Arizona, and Kansas in 1912, the Territory of Alaska in 1913, and Montana and Nevada in 1914. Thus, at the beginning of World War I, woman suffrage existed in eleven western states and the territory of Alaska. It would be seven more years before the Nineteenth Amendment would be ratified in 1920.

Notes

1. This essay is based on Beverly Beeton's book *Women Vote in the West: The Woman Suffrage Movement, 1869-1896*, published in the American Legal and Constitutional History series, edited by Harold Hyman and Stuart Bruchey, Garland Publishing, New York, 1986.

2. Ellen Carol DuBois, *Feminism and Suffrage: The Emergence of an Independent Woman's Movement in America, 1848-1869* (Ithaca, 1978).

3. Elizabeth Cady Stanton, Susan B. Anthony, Matilda J. Gage and Ida H. Harper, eds. *History of Woman Suffrage*, 6 vols. 1881-1922. (Reprint edition, New York: Arno, 1969), 2: 264.

4. *New York Tribune*, October 1, 1867.

5. *HWS* 2: 324-325.

6. In the post-Civil War years there was a great deal of concern about what the newspapers called the "surplus women" problem. Yet census data for 1890 reveals that there were 32,067,880 men in the nation and only 30,554,370 women. It seems to have been a problem more of perception than reality; to the extent that a marriage gap existed, it was a matter of age and geographical distribution, not of actual numbers.

7. As quoted in Katharine Anthony, *Susan B. Anthony: Her Personal History and Her Era* (New York, 1954), 248.

8. Hamilton Willcox, pamphlet, "Wyoming: The True Cause and Splendid Fruits of Woman Suffrage There from Official Records and Personal Knowledge correcting the errors of Horace Plunkett and Professor Bryce and supplying omissions in the *History of Woman Suffrage* by Mrs. Stanton, Mrs. Gage, and Miss Anthony, and in the *History of Wyoming* by Hubert Howe Bancroft with other information about the state." (New York: November 1890), 17, Bancroft Library, Berkeley, Calif.

9. Extract from *The Galaxy* article, 13 (June 1872): n.p., located in the Susa Young Gates papers, Widtsoe Collection at the Utah State Historical Society, Salt Lake City, Utah.

10. *HWS* 2: 545.

11. *Deseret News*, February 15, 1870.

12. William Clayton to Brother Jesse, and Clayton to Brother East, February 13, 1870. Clayton Letterbooks, Bancroft Library.

13. In *The Puritan Ethic and Woman Suffrage* (New York, 1967), Alan P. Grimes, employing status anxiety techniques similar to those developed by Richard Hofstadter, argues that "the constituency granting woman suffrage was composed of those who also supported prohibition and immigration restriction and felt woman suffrage would further their enactment." Grimes errs in his analysis when he reads backwards into history. The issues of prohibition and immigration restriction were not significant factors in Wyoming, Utah, Colorado, and Idaho when woman suffrage was enacted there.

14. Belva A. Lockwood's speech before the NWSA, January 24, 1883, as printed in the *Ogden Daily Herald*, June 9, 1883.

15. *Salt Lake Herald*, January 29, 1887; and *Deseret News*, March 4, 1887.

16. In *Everyone Was Brave: The Rise and Fall of Feminism* (Chicago, 1969), William L. O'Neil argues that suffragists' identification with Victoria Woodhull and her views on monogamy made it impossible for women's rights advocates to be critical of the institution of marriage without being accused of favoring free love. The same thesis is valid when applied to Lockwood and the identification with polygamy.

17. Beverly Beeton, "'I Am an American Woman': Charlotte Ives Cobb Godbe Kirby," *Journal of the American West*, 27 (April 1988): 13-19.

18. See Jean Bickmore White article, *Utah Historical Quarterly*, 42 (Fall 1974): 344-69.

19. Brigham Henry Roberts autobiography, copy of manuscript at Utah State Historical Society, Salt Lake City, Utah, 117-78.

20. O.F. Whitney speech, March 30, 1895, *Men and Woman* (May 14, 1895): 10-12.

21. William B. Faherty, "Regional Minorities and the Woman Suffrage Struggle," *Colorado Magazine* (July 1956), 1.

22. "Speech of M.S. Taylor on Suffrage," *Colorado Transcript*, January 26, 1870.

23. Billie Barnes Jensen, "Woman Suffrage in Colorado," M.A. thesis, University of Colorado, 1959, 20-21.

24. *HWS* 3: 723.

25. *Idaho Statesman*, January 10, 1871; also see the January 5, 1871 issue.

26. Abigail Scott Duniway's *Path Breaking: An Autobiographical History of the Equal Suffrage Movement in Pacific Coast States* (Portland, Oregon, 1914) is a detailed record of events in Idaho; however, Duniway had her prejudices and made herself and her point of view most important in her narration of events. *HWS* 4: 589-97 has a chapter on the suffrage campaign in Idaho written by two participants—Eunice Pond Athey and William Balderston, editor of the *Idaho Statesman*.

27. An article from the *Avalanche* as cited in the *Idaho Democrat*, a Mormon newspaper published in southern Idaho, March 24, 1883.

28. T.A. Larson, "Woman's Rights in Idaho," *Idaho Yesterdays* 16 (Spring 1972): 2-15, 9. Larson published numerous articles on woman suffrage in the West. The most detailed version is "Emancipating the West's Dolls, Vassals and Hopeless Drudges: The Origins of Woman Suffrage in the West," in Roger Daniels, editor, *Essays in Western History in Honor of T.A. Larson*, v. 37 (Laramie: University of Wyoming Publications, 1971).

29. As quoted in *Idaho Statesman*, November 21, 1895; also see, Anthony Diary, November 18, 1895, in the Library of Congress, Manuscript Division, Washington, D.C.

30. *Caldwell Tribune*, July 4, 1896; also see, "Equal Suffragists' Desires," in the Equal Suffrage Association of Idaho file, Idaho State Historical Society, Boise, Idaho.

31. *HWS* 4: 293.

32. For detailed information on the impact of woman suffrage in the four states see Beeton, *Women Vote in the West*, 136-156.

33. As quoted in *Deseret News*, February 13, 1902.

34. *Deseret News* editorial, October 12, 1906.

35. Priscilla Leonard, "Woman Suffrage in Colorado," *Outlook*, 55 (March 2, 1897): 791.

36. Ike Russell, "What Women Have Done with Votes," *Pearson's Magazine*, n.d., 538, clipping in The Church Archives, Historical Department of the Church of Jesus Christ of Latter-day Saints, Salt Lake City, Utah.

37. The census data for 1870 indicates that when woman suffrage was being considered in the four territories the population was approximately 9,000 in Wyoming, 87,000 in Utah, 40,000 in Colorado, and 15,000 in Idaho. Utah was the only place where women represented nearly half of the total; in the other territories women composed one-fourth, or less, of the population.

Seven

Frances Willard
and the Woman's Christian Temperance Union's Conversion to Woman Suffrage

Carolyn De Swarte Gifford

Editor's Introduction: In the early 1880s, the woman suffrage movement received one of the most important endorsements in its history when the new president of the Woman's Christian Temperance Union (WCTU), Frances Willard, "converted" the WCTU to the suffrage cause. Willard thus brought into the movement large numbers of moderate women who were activists and would labor mightily for the "Home Protection Ballot"—women who otherwise might have avoided association with woman suffrage in an era when its national leaders were considered by many to be radical if not disreputable.

Carolyn De Swarte Gifford, editor of the forthcoming book *"Writing Out My Heart": Selections from the Journal of Frances E. Willard, 1855-1896* and author of several articles on Willard and the WCTU, explains here that converting the WCTU to woman suffrage meant redefining the influential image of the "True Christian Woman." It meant convincing women that their God-given duty was to use their moral influence for good in the larger society—not just in the home as tradition required.

This was no easy task in late nineteenth-century America. Several generations of women had been influenced by a flood of prescriptive literature defining the "True Woman" as (in the words of historian Barbara Welter), "pure," "pious," "submissive," and "domestic." Most American women and men assumed that women were innately more religious than men and morally obligated to exercise influence for good in the world—but only through woman's "indirect influence" over husbands and children in the home. It was widely believed that participation in public affairs, particularly in the disreputable world of politics, would rob women of that very innocence and ignorance of evil that so inspired men to rule wisely for their sakes.

As early as the 1870s and 1880s, however, the women of the WCTU experienced the disillusionment with "indirect influence" that later converted many women reformers to the suffrage cause during the Progressive Era, which began around 1900. The WCTU women were convinced that their crusade would not succeed until women were enfranchised; and they insisted that if

117

women were (as most people believed) morally superior to men, it was their *solemn duty* to enter the political arena and clean it up—if only to protect the home.

Thus many evangelical Christian women were "converted" to woman suffrage, and convinced—like Frances Willard—that God had called them to serve the cause of woman suffrage as well as temperance. Through the WCTU, the influential concept of the True Woman was revised and expanded to include, as Gifford writes, the "public space" beyond the home. The WCTU, which in the late nineteenth century was the largest woman's organization yet in existence, had branches in twenty-one countries, and opened new doors for countless women. This was true even in the South, a stronghold of evangelical Christianity and conservatism, where resistance to expansion of woman's role was strong. Not every woman in the WCTU became a suffragist; but hundreds of thousands responded to Willard's message that it was not only *acceptable* to work for woman suffrage—it was their Christian duty.

The endorsement of woman suffrage by the WCTU was a mixed blessing for the cause, however, as it attracted a formidable opponent, the liquor industry. The so-called "whisky interest," composed of brewers, distillers, distributors, and saloon keepers, often combined forces with other industries that felt threatened by woman suffrage and spent heavily to defeat it. Carrie Chapman Catt and Nettie Rogers Shuler, in their 1923 retrospective *Woman Suffrage and Politics: The Inner Story of the Suffrage Movement,* devoted an entire chapter to the "corrupt manipulations" of American politics by the liquor industry. The industry, claimed Catt and Shuler, "dictat[ed] terms to parties and politicians," "kept Legislatures from submitting suffrage amendments," "organized droves of ignorant men to vote against suffrage amendments at the polls," and "restrained both dominant parties from endorsing woman suffrage,"—an "invisible and invincible power that for forty years kept suffragists waiting for the woman's hour." The "forty years" to which Catt and Shuler referred were the years between 1880, when the WCTU endorsed woman suffrage, to 1920 when suffragists were at last victorious.

THE SIXTH ANNUAL CONVENTION of the Woman's Christian Temperance Union in November 1879 promised fresh direction for the organization. Its newly elected leader, Frances E. Willard, a young, vigorous educator from the West, advocated woman suffrage as the means necessary to insure prohibition. The choice of Willard as president indicated that many WCTU leaders supported her suffrage position, a stance well known to them (and to her opposition within the organization) since she had been speaking about it publicly for several years. The WCTU could expect to enter the new decade of the 1880s faced with a difficult task: convincing its rapidly growing membership of mainly evangelical Christian women that woman suffrage was not a radical idea espoused by women whose behavior was at least question-able, if not outrageous. The vote for women must be made acceptable, respectable, and in fact a part of woman's duty as a Christian. For this to occur the image of the True Christian Woman had to be redefined and broadened to include enfranchisement. This redefinition began for many WCTU members through a religious experience that they described as a conversion to woman suffrage. They claimed that God called them to work for the vote for women. Increasingly during the 1880s, evangelical women entered the struggle for woman suffrage, convinced that it was God's will that they do so.

Redefining True Womanhood

In 1880 the WCTU suffrage goal must have appeared as a vision far off in the future. Nevertheless, WCTU leaders began a campaign for woman suffrage throughout the country. Willard and other WCTU organizers traveled thou-sands of miles by rail and horse-drawn wagons stumping for the twin aims of prohibition and the vote for women. As they tirelessly crisscrossed the United States with their message, *Our Union* (after 1882 *The Union Signal*), the official organ of the WCTU, began to print a barrage of articles, editorials, columns, and letters, pushing woman suffrage from every angle that might appeal to its readership. Through the decade of the 1880s the organization labored to per-suade its members that woman's sphere should be widened to include numer-ous activities believed by most Americans to be the prerogative of men.

Frances Willard announced the widening of woman's sphere in what became a favorite motto of the WCTU: "Woman will bless and brighten every place she enters, and she will enter every place."[1] The first half of the motto was not particularly alarming since "brightening every place she enters" had been woman's traditional duty and, moreover, her greatest pleasure, if one could believe the volumes of prescriptive literature written for and by women throughout the nineteenth century. The second half of the motto might prove disconcerting, however, if one grasped its full import. It boldly stated that women intended to move from the private, domestic sphere into the public world. Although the motto was constructed in the declarative rather than the imperative mode, as befitted a ladylike statement, Willard meant what she said. She was to spend her many years as WCTU president working out with determi-nation her conviction that women belonged in every place, whether it be in the pulpit and in delegations to national church conferences or in the voting booth and in the conventions of national political parties. She envisioned a limitless space for women's abilities and talents.

Willard faced a dilemma in the 1880s: how was she to encourage and enable others to share in her vision for women? How would she inspire WCTU women to examine and reinterpret prescriptive images of woman that had shaped their lives? What motivation would compel evangelical women to work slowly and at times painfully toward a redefinition of the Christian woman?

There is power for change as well as for proscription inherent in symbols and images since they are, by their very nature, capable of revealing new depths of meaning and lending themselves to nuances of interpretation. Particular persons and specific historical contexts may shape and alter traditional symbols and images, reinvesting them with further content and renewed vigor. Such a process of change occurred in the image of the True Christian Woman during the decades of the 1870s and 1880s. Certainly it had begun earlier in the century, but the women and men who initiated the task were often isolated from one another or involved in reform goals other than that of re-visioning woman's image. Other more radical women's rights reformers such as Elizabeth Cady Stanton and Susan B. Anthony, failed to evoke images of woman that appealed to the majority of mainstream evangelical Protestant women who were more timid and loath to challenge the status quo, than Stanton and Anthony.

In order to understand how vast numbers of WCTU women accepted a redefinition of the True Woman image that included enfranchisement, it is necessary to follow several lines of investigation. First, one must examine the image of woman current in the evangelical milieu from which most of the WCTU women came. Second, one must determine how closely the image or ideal of Christian womanhood conformed to the realities of women's lives. Third, one must assess the ways in which influential leaders such as Frances Willard were able to infuse ideals and images with new possibilities of content and meaning. Finally, one must seek to discover what other forces were at work in the last third of the nineteenth century, in both the church and the larger world, which might call forth or allow for enlarged roles for women. In short, one must try to recreate the historical moment in which the image of woman was opened up to dimensions previously unthinkable and thus unattainable for the majority of American evangelical Protestant women during the nineteenth century.

The Traditional Meaning of True Womanhood

These evangelical Protestant women who filled the ranks of the "white ribbon army" of the WCTU proudly displayed the tiny emblem of their membership on respectable, drab-colored, high-collared dresses. The simple grosgrain ribbons, in white to symbolize the purity of the True Woman, identified those who wore them as sisters battling for prohibition, but also for the elevation of women in all areas of their lives. Quite often the white ribbon was entwined with a yellow ribbon signifying woman suffrage.[2] Both colors were worn proudly and in many cases with more than a hint of defiance. And no wonder, since these women were daring to stand up to the mighty weight of centuries of Christian tradition which taught that women were subordinate to men and to be governed by them, and therefore women had no justification for demanding the enfranchisement of their sex.

The authority of scripture was unquestionable for evangelical woman. They had grown up hearing, reading, and believing that the Bible, the word of God, decreed the dominant/subordinate male/female relationship. God had created it so, and Eve's rebellious refusal to obey God's word served to emphasize woman's fundamental irresponsibility with the corresponding necessity for male governance. The Pauline Epistles elaborated on woman's subordinate status, enjoining wives to submit to their husbands and ordering all women to keep silent in church. Along with the biblical injunctions came enormous numbers of sermons, homilies, home Bible study groups, and advice books based on biblical texts, which commented further on the attitudes and activities proper to the True Christian Woman. Often these commentaries included warnings to women who overstepped the bounds of woman's sphere, putting themselves in danger of becoming "unwomanly."

The editorial page of the February 1880 issue of *Our Union* featured an article containing such a warning, which was reprinted from an Indianapolis newspaper. The first paragraph of the article quoted from a Sunday evening sermon given November 2, 1879, by the Reverend J. Saunders Reed, priest of St. Paul's Episcopal Cathedral in Indianapolis. Reed had delivered his message just as the National WCTU, meeting in the same city, decided to embrace the goal of woman suffrage. He was obviously disturbed by the public behavior of women.

> It worries, it angers, it disheartens me to see women thrusting themselves into men's places and clamoring to be heard in our halls and churches. A woman-man I have always nauseated and loathed; but, oh, from a man-woman I would make haste to get me away as from a monstrosity of nature, a subverter of society, the cave of despair, the head of Medusa, a bird of ill-omen, a hideous specter, a travesty of all that is sacred and divine.[3]

Here was an example of a vicious verbal assault on women who ventured beyond their proper place. Why would the editors of *Our Union* choose to print such a diatribe, one invoking symbols and images that had served for centuries to proscribe women's activities and confine them to a restricted sphere?

Reed attacked women who entered the public arena, that "male territory" of church pulpit and lecture hall, and probably the city council and state legislature as well, since WCTU members had already appeared before these bodies seeking the passage of prohibition legislation. He accused women who acted in this manner of breaking down sanctified gender expectations, assuming male prerogatives, and thereby becoming masculinized. Such an accusation could not be shrugged off lightly by a generation of women who had been socialized to understand that women and men were created by God for different though complementary tasks and spheres. Usurping a role of the opposite sex was deviant behavior as Reed so clearly charged. The woman who stepped out of her space was unnatural, even monstrous. She risked destroying the social order; worse, in committing "a travesty of all that is sacred and divine" she sinned willfully against God's plan for creation.

Reed's rhetoric played upon the powerful prescriptive symbol of the woman as Other—shameful, sinful, and, finally, less than fully human. In an age that was familiar with classical Greek mythology, he called up the horrible image of Medusa with her grotesque face surrounded by ringlets of writhing serpents, a monster turning those who looked upon her to stone. He might as effectively have chosen a biblical symbol of woman as Other—Eve, Mary Magdalene, Jezebel—whose mere mention would have served the same purpose as the name of Medusa, suggesting to his listeners woman's potential for unnaturalness and wickedness. Moreover, the priest was not alone in his opinion of woman's proper sphere and the qualities of those who overstepped its bounds. Undoubtedly the majority of Americans agreed with him. Even as late as 1879 few women had the courage to challenge the men (and women as well) who employed such evocative symbols of deviance and evil to keep women in their place.[4] Wouldn't the editors of *Our Union* have been wiser to leave this attack on "the public woman" out of the WCTU paper? Why not downplay such virulent criticism by ignoring it? But the editors of *Our Union* were neither stupid nor naive; rather, they were quite shrewd. They had an excellent reason for printing Reed's thoughts on the "man-woman."

The sermon excerpt had originally appeared as the lead paragraph in an article by a reporter covering the WCTU national convention for the *Indianapolis Journal*. The entire piece was printed in *Our Union*. In it, the *Journal* reporter took Reed to task for his statements and ridiculed him for being "angered, disheartened and worried" by such women as J. Ellen Foster, Mary Livermore, Mary T. Lathrap, Annie Wittenmyer, and Frances E. Willard, the convention's leaders. These women and others, according to the reporter, were the equals of any minister in an Indianapolis pulpit: "They were logical, forcible and concise, and held the attention of an audience from their first utterance to the close. They were conservative and sensible—much more so than a like number of men have usually been when convened on a similar occasion."[5] The writer thus captured in a paragraph the tone and demeanor that the WCTU as an organization would assume throughout the 1880s. He went on to accuse Reed and those who held similar opinions about woman's sphere, of being "many generations behind the age." The article closed with a veiled challenge: "The men have not all the brains, nor all the morals, nor all the religion, and should not be afraid to compete with the women in any place they can fill with equal ability and propriety."[6]

The interplay of Reed's attack and its vigorous rebuttal by a newspaper completely independent of the WCTU served an important strategic function. The points made in the article, though thoroughly endorsed by the union, did not appear to be special pleading by a self-interested group. The newspaper labeled as old-fashioned those who conformed to the prevalent attitude toward women and pronounced a rallying cry for WCTU women in the 1880s. Although this particular challenge came from the *Indianapolis Journal*, it was in fact similar to many such challenges and exhortations from the WCTU leaders to the membership that were regularly printed in *Our Union* and *The Union Signal*. Through its national newspaper as well as through its leaders' speeches, the WCTU directly confronted the issue with which nineteenth-century American women struggled: the binding force of the American religious-cultural tradition whose institutions interlocked to uphold the image of the ideal woman as pious, pure, domestic, and submissive, shut up in the private sphere of the home and its extension, the church.[7]

Many of the women who joined the WCTU spent all their time in their homes and their churches. These two areas were literally their lives. Even as late as the 1870s only a few exceptional women had rebelled against this pleasant prison, woman's sphere. Indeed, many enjoyed and took pride in their woman-ly tasks. Nothing could be more satisfying they felt, than providing a haven of peace and rest from the cares of the world for the True Man, counterpart of the True Woman. If the True Woman was to be dependent, passive, yielding, the True Man, her complement, was to be independent, aggressive, and a good provider for his family.

The earliest issues of *Our Union* abounded with descriptions of the gentle wife as the "soul force" of the home, welcoming her weary husband back to his domestic retreat and comforting him after his day of battle with the bustling economic enterprises of the nation. In this shelter she was also to nurture her children in a pure, protected environment. The frequency of these cloying portrayals moved Mary A. Livermore, Massachusetts WCTU leader and woman suffrage worker, to dismiss the contents of the paper as "pious blarney."[8] Yet alongside these glorifications of the home as haven, *Our Union* printed grue-some cautionary tales depicting the disintegration of families and homes through the drunkenness of husbands and fathers. It ran true stories, con-tributed by readers, about young boys eight or nine years old "led down the road to ruin" by saloon keepers who tempted them with liquor-filled candies and free lunches. Always the tales included descriptions of helpless wives and mothers wringing their hands and weeping but unable to do anything to stop their men and boys from the onslaught of "Demon Rum." The apparently naive and unintended juxtaposition of the ideal of True Man and True Woman with the stark reality of women's actual experience pointed out the failure of many families to live up to the expectations generated by powerful ideal images.

Clearly a terrible tension had developed between the ideal and the real. Such tension had always existed, but events during the 1870s brought many women to the point of admitting the strain they felt themselves or observed in other women's lives. Male alcoholism was a key factor in creating this tension. Men who were drunkards often did not support their families and thus did not live up to the responsibilities of the True Man. Indeed, they were apt to abandon their families for long periods of time while they went on "binges," a pattern that one contemporary historian has described as a uniquely American phe-nomenon.[9] Women were unprepared to support their families economically and were thus in dire circumstances if the family wage earner disappeared or became disabled through chronic alcoholism. Excessive alcohol consumption had long been an American characteristic. Alcohol consumption had fallen in the decades just before the Civil War, partly through the efforts of the temperance movement. But it rose again rapidly during and after the war, and the number of saloons per capita grew as well. Faced with an intolerable situation, women acted in protest. In the winter of 1873-74 occurred the Ohio Women's Crusade, a spontaneous series of praying demonstrations by women aimed at forcing saloon keepers to shut down their establishments. In a welcoming address to the Fifth Annual Convention of the California WCTU in 1884, a member reminded the delegates of the crucial significance of the crusade as the start of a consciousness-raising process for women. As the news of the praying bands of women spread rapidly by telegraph throughout the nation:

> Men read and laughed and sneered; women, busy women stopped their work, read the strange lines, thought and lifted up their hearts to God in prayer. Had the time come for women to take the forefront in the battle against intemperance? Was it right? Had she not learned, and learned at her mother's knee that home is woman's sphere? Home her only safe abiding place?
>
> But on the other hand, had she not through long years been the sufferer? It was her frame that blighted and withered under the curse of this vile traffic. No wonder she was ready for acting. No wonder she sprang to the front.[10]

What had been implicit earlier in the pages of Our Union—the discontinuity between the ideal of the True Woman in her home and the awful reality of many women's lives—became explicit. Woman was not "safe" in her home. The lessons about womanhood that generations of mothers had taught their daughters were being seriously questioned. Woman was not necessarily the "queen" of the domestic realm; she was, in far too many cases, its victim. The corrupt world that she had attempted to shut out of the home invaded her supposedly pure, inviolate space, often through the saloon and its influence. Saloons were not a part of most women's experience. For many they epitomized male and thus public territory. The decision to move from the private to the public sphere, to assail the enemy on his own ground, was a tremendous and frightening one for women. Yet clearly, as the quote suggests, they were fed up with their situation. And just as clearly, they believed they were being called by God out of their homes into active temperance agitation.[11]

The Traditional Meaning Loses Its Power

The women of Ohio were temporarily successful in achieving their goals. Some saloon keepers actually closed their businesses and took up other lines of work or moved west, at times assisted by crusade women who provided them with small sums of money to make a new start. During the crusade, however, women discovered to their dismay how powerless they really were. They had been taught that the moral and spiritual influence they exerted over men was enormous though indirect, and thus consistent with their subordinate status. While women provided pure home life and noble Christian example, men would somehow carry that atmosphere with them into the halls of government and law and guide public life accordingly. Believing this, the Ohio Crusade women, going to court on behalf of wives who were beaten and abandoned by drunken husbands, expected to find a sympathetic hearing. When they attempted to prosecute liquor dealers under statutes that made dealers responsible for selling liquor to known drunkards, they found that the male-run judicial system figuratively (and often literally) laughed in their faces. Occasionally, at the local level where a woman did wield some influence through her husband's position, a guilty verdict was brought against a liquor dealer. But it was swiftly appealed and thrown out in appellate court.[12] When women appeared before city councils and state legislatures all over the country lobbying for various prohibition measures, they encountered male reactions ranging from polite boredom to sarcastic ridicule to open hostility. In fact Reed's sermon, quoted earlier, was typical of the hostile reactions women provoked.

At first the women were merely puzzled. They had been told that they were the guardians of morality. Sometimes it was even suggested that women were spiritually and ethically superior to men, and yet they were ignored, ridiculed, or verbally attacked by men when they attempted to raise ethical issues in saloons, courtrooms, and legislatures. Some WCTU women discovered that men found it convenient to let women attend to morality while they attended to business, law, and politics. There was, in effect, a double standard of morality in regard to the public and private spheres.

Women became painfully aware that they and their spiritual, moral influence were not welcome in men's public life. Many husbands instructed their wives, politely and no doubt gently, to stay where they belonged—at home. There women could be as pious and pure as they pleased. And men could get on with the work of the public world, where the values of home and woman seemed not to operate. Many women sensed that a deep ethical split had occurred between the public and private spheres. Different moral systems prevailed in the two separated sectors.

Drusilla Wilson, president of the Kansas WCTU, addressed herself to the conflict that had developed between women's private and men's public values, as she spoke about her leadership of Lawrence, Kansas women who knelt on the floors of saloons, fervently praying that saloon keepers would stop selling liquor.

> Indelibly stamped upon some of our minds during the Crusade was the need of Prohibition, for then some of us learned that the [liquor] traffic was a child of the law. Woman saw it was inconsistent for our fathers

and brothers and husbands to make laws protecting [liquor traffic] and the women follow in the wake pleading with men thus licensed [to sell liquor] to quit the business. A change must be brought about.[13]

Obviously, what many women viewed as moral—temperance, in this instance—did not accord with what the men in their own households believed to be in the interests of good business.

Wilson also emphasized what would become increasingly evident to the WCTU organization during its first decade (1874-84): "following in the wake pleading" was not an effective long-term strategy for reform. Women questioned both the dignity and the efficacy of such tactics. Drusilla Wilson, in her reserved Quaker manner, had described the methods as "inconsistent." Other women were humiliated and extremely angered by the failure of praying and pleading, typical women's tactics, to move men to support temperance reform measures. Their humiliation reflected their recognition of women's total powerlessness in the public sphere. It also reflected women's consternation in the face of the breakdown of the ideal complementary relationship of True Man and True Woman in the ethical realm.

Additionally, women began to perceive that although they were placed on a pedestal in much male rhetoric and there honored, adored, and cared for, men showed little actual sympathy for women who were victims of their dependent status, left without ways to support themselves and their children when men abandoned them. Nor did men really seem to take seriously women's ethical concerns, women's thoughts, women's activities, or women in general. It was a cruel hoax to be placed on a pedestal and dismissed with laughter, and women did not like it. Again and again in their accounts of temperance work, references appear to the indignation women felt when men found their public appearances, both praying and pleading, occasions of humorous diversion. Apparently the True Woman image functioned for many men only as a way to keep women from meddling in the male world. It was no longer an ideal they believed in but a convenient mechanism to put women in their place and out of men's way.

If this were the case, women would not be able to accomplish their temperance goals. They had to depend on male cooperation with their reform efforts, since these efforts increasingly involved legislative measures for prohibition. With few exceptions, in the 1870s and 1880s women could not vote and were not members of legislative bodies. If they were not able to persuade men to vote for prohibition they could pray and plead, but to no effect. Definitely, as Drusilla Wilson maintained, a change must be brought about.

Woman suffrage was the change for which Wilson and other WCTU leaders called.... Furthermore, as evangelical Christians they had to be able to justify their political and suffrage activity religiously. It was absolutely essential for them to believe that their behavior sprang from an experience that convinced them that God wanted them, indeed called them, to vote.

God Calls WCTU Women to Vote

During the nineteenth century, the individual conversion—a personal experience of God's saving power and will for one's life—was a weighty source of authority for religious behavior. Revivals centering on such conversions were a fundamental characteristic of American evangelical Protestant life. Within such a religious climate, if one claimed to receive a changed, reinterpreted image of woman as the content of the conversion experience, the claim would be difficult for another to challenge, particularly if the challenger shared a belief in the possibility of individual conversion. Many WCTU women came from a background of revivalism. The Ohio Women's Crusade, which came to be looked upon as the formative event for the WCTU, had strong revivalistic features, including the participants' testimony that they received a pouring out of the Holy Spirit upon them, a fresh baptism of power renewing and deepening the baptism they had previously received upon entry into the Christian faith.

Frances Willard herself claimed to have experienced God's call to advocate woman suffrage. As she traveled through Ohio in the winter of 1876 organizing for the WCTU, she took time out from her hectic schedule for Bible study and prayer on Sunday morning:

> Upon my knees alone, in the room of my hostess who was a veteran Crusader, there was borne in upon my mind, as I believe from loftier regions, the declaration, "You are to speak for woman's ballot as a weapon of protection to her home and tempted loved ones from the tyranny of drink." [14]

Not only did Willard hear God's will that she work for what she labeled "The Ballot for Home Protection," she also received "a complete line of argument and illustration" [15] for her first speech on Home Protection which she delivered later in the year at the Woman's Congress in Philadelphia and at the National WCTU Annual Meeting in Newark.

An intense wave of revivalism led by Dwight L. Moody was sweeping through America's large eastern and mid-western cities during the 1870s. Willard worked with Moody in Boston for a short time during the winter of 1877 but left his revival circuit to devote her energy to her own methods of temperance reform. In a letter to Moody's wife explaining why she was leaving, Willard set forth her differences with Moody's approach to the temperance aspect of his revivals. He expected and sought individual regeneration with an accompanying pledge by the saved person to drink no more. Willard noted sharply in her letter that Moody emphasized the regeneration of men and that she as a woman found his approach inadequate. She advocated the WCTU goals of prevention through education and legislation especially, she wrote, "putting the ballot in woman's hand for the protection of her little ones and her home." [16] Willard saw no distinction as Moody did between the religious activity of revival and the political activity of securing temperance legislation. A

Christian, she felt, should work through any and every means available and consonant with her faith to reform the world and its institutions as well as individual believers. She understood no separation between the public and private spheres; both were arenas for reform and they overlapped. Women must strive for the reform of society in all its aspects and one of the most powerful means toward this aim was woman suffrage. In order to be effective reformers, women must have the ballot. After all, had not God himself validated this means of reform in Willard's personal religious experience "on her knees in prayer"?

For the next two years Willard "evangelized" for her belief in woman suffrage, managing to persuade a significant number of WCTU leaders and a portion of the membership of the rightness of her position. She became president in November 1879, an event that signaled the beginning of the National WCTU campaign for endorsement of a suffrage position among its member state organizations.

On January 1, 1880, *Our Union* featured the story of "One Woman's Experience." It was nothing less than a paradigmatic example of a conversion, that form of religious experience so prevalent in American Protestant life. However, its content was quite unusual. The anonymous writer claimed a conversion to woman suffrage:

> It would sound very strange and far-fetched to many ears, even absurd, that a woman should be morally and religiously converted to Home Protection. I feel I was actually converted by the Lord's Spirit, and led to a deeper feeling, if not a deeper knowledge of the truth.[17]

She described her attendance at a WCTU Annual Meeting, where, for the first time, she had the opportunity to see and hear the "consecrated women" who led the organization. She was convinced of the sincerity of their efforts in temperance reform and of their selfless dedication to the cause.

She contrasted their demeanor with her impressions of others who advocated woman suffrage. She had come to the convention believing that suffragists were "party aspirants and women who were always howling over the wrongs of woman, and the Lord had been so good to me I did not think women had such a hard time after all; nor in fact, do I now."[18] Her attitude toward suffragists was typical of that of many WCTU women. They saw them as self-serving power seekers whose activities went beyond the bounds of propriety and who thus did not conform to the image of True Womanhood.

WCTU women were not iconoclastic. They had not abandoned or destroyed the ideal of True Woman but were in the process of dealing with some of its negative, prescriptive aspects and seeking to broaden and re-vision its possibilities. Thus they were frightened of radical suffragists who seemed to go too far, to act too boldly, and to take anticlerical, antireligious positions. Historians Nancy F. Cott and Ellen Carol DuBois have created a phrase to describe the change in religious attitude more radical suffragists underwent: "de-conversion," meaning "ideological disengagement from the convincing power of evangelical

Protestantism (or inability to accept the whole of it)."[19] In contrast, one might call the experience of many WCTU women "re-conversion," an intense conviction that God demanded yet more from women, further consecration that would lead them toward places and forms of activity formerly thought off limits. "One Woman's Experience" continues with a vivid description of just such a "re-conversion."

> I had thought I had consecrated myself to the Lord, to work for Him both in the Church and in Temperance work; I thought I was willing to use any weapon for truth, justice and virtue He should place in my hand. But when I came into convention, the conviction kept forcing itself upon me that I was not wholly consecrated to His service: I was not willing to do anything and everything for Him. There was that fearful ballot woman "unsexing herself," etc., etc., according to Dr. Bushnell, whose arguments you know, and of which every letter I have hitherto endorsed.[20]

"De-conversion" implies a sharp breaking away, a definite denial of one's former tradition; "re-conversion" indicates not a rupture, but rather a deepening or re-dedication of one's life to God's service in new ways.

The Dr. Bushnell to whom the anonymous writer referred was the Reverend Horace Bushnell, a leading nineteenth-century evangelical theologian, dead for three years by the time this article was written, but whose thought obviously still wielded tremendous influence over American churchgoers. He had written a book, *Woman Suffrage: The Reform against Nature,*[21] which developed the argument that man was to govern, woman to be governed, and thus that woman could not vote since voting was governing. His views on woman's unsexing herself by the act of voting (woman as unnatural, as other) were so well known that the writer assumed she did not have to elaborate on them for her readers. And yet she was able to defy such a powerful theological figure on the strength of her personal experience of God's call to vote.

Her conversion did not come easily. She mentioned nights of "waking and weeping," during which God allowed her to "gather up her prejudices [against woman suffrage] as a bundle and lay them aside." She felt her conversion as an easing of heart and conscience, accompanying her decision to work for woman's vote as an expression of God's will for her. Historian Donald M. Scott, in his article, "Abolition as a Sacred Vocation," describes the conversion to a reform, using as his example the position of Immediatism held by radical abolitionists. "Immediatism," Scott writes, "was less a program of what to do about slavery than, in evangelical terms, a 'disposition,' a state of being in which the heart and will were irrevocably set against slavery.... Immediatism became a sign of whether or not one was a saved Christian in abolition circles."[22] Although the reform is different, the "disposition" of the convert is very similar to that described in "One Woman's Experience." Belief in woman suffrage for Home Protection signified for a large number of WCTU members the deepest commitment to temperance and to woman. The belief in temperance was assumed, but support for woman suffrage became the mark of a truly consecrated worker.

Testimonies of conversion to woman suffrage multiplied on the pages of *Our Union* as WCTU women throughout the country felt a clear call from God to support the ballot for women as a means of Home Protection. A "Home Protection" column, running throughout the 1880s in *Our Union* and *The Union Signal,* carried reports of state and local efforts for woman's vote in school, municipal, state, and territorial elections and referenda. Each new gain was celebrated on the pages of the WCTU paper and announced in meetings where it was greeted with a restrained but enthusiastic waving of handkerchiefs and the singing of the "Temperance Doxology." A Boston prayer meeting in January 1880 with several hundred women and men present was described as exceeding the great revivals of Moody in the felt presence of the Holy Spirit.[23] At the end of a long day of prayer women left the church with petitions in their hands, determined to canvass Boston for woman's limited right to vote on the single issue of prohibition.

Mary A. Livermore wrote one of the more dramatic accounts of a conversion to woman suffrage in a memorial eulogy for a Massachusetts WCTU leader. Livermore quoted a letter written in the woman's last illness and addressed to the membership of the Massachusetts Union.

> Standing on the threshold of the better land, I see more clearly. I would like to urge the dear workers in our great cause to acquaint themselves more fully with the evil that destroys the beauty and glory of our nation. The desire comes strongly to me to entreat them to put aside all narrowness and prejudice in their methods of work. Dear sisters, hold yourselves open to conviction! If the ballot were in the hands of women as a temperance measure, it would be powerful for the overthrow of the liquor traffic. *Then do not fight against the movement to give the ballot to woman "lest haply you be found fighting against God."*[24]

The women of the Massachusetts WCTU were not noted at that time for their enthusiastic support of woman suffrage. But surely the deathbed pleading of one of their own would make them reexamine their "prejudices," particularly when their dying sister strongly hinted that they might be defying God by not supporting the ballot for Home Protection.

The True Woman as Voter

WCTU women were beginning to reverse the arguments used against them by those who warned that woman's voting would be an act of rebellion against God. With the strength and validation they gained from personal experience of God's will for them, the women were able to stand up to persons who cited the authority of scripture against woman's moving outside her sphere. Writings and speeches began to include many references to women of the Old and New Testaments who served God through entering the public sphere and engaging in the

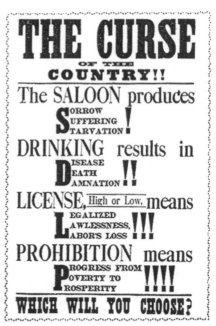

Frances Willard.
Frances Willard Memorial Library

Prohibition poster.
Woman Suffrage Media Collection

religious and political processes of their times. Deborah, judge of the people of Israel and leader of its armies, was a great favorite. Zerelda Wallace from Indiana, head of the WCTU franchise [suffrage] department during the 1880s and an outspoken supporter of woman suffrage, was fondly referred to as "the Deborah of the franchise movement."[25] Biblical women served as models of courage and power for WCTU women who were attempting to initiate new modes of behavior. They did not intend to question the authority of scripture but to enlist the weight of scripture in support of what they had experienced as the will of God for them. In doing so, they launched upon an extensive hermeneutical task as they pored over scriptural passages for fresh insight into their meaning.

WCTU speakers and writers began to place Galatians 3:28 ("There is neither Jew nor Greek, there is neither bond nor free, there is neither male nor female: for ye are all one in Christ Jesus" [KJV]) alongside Paul's more restrictive passages in recognition that the Bible lent itself to differing interpretations and emphases. Jesus was hailed as the friend of woman and, more boldly, as her Emancipator.[26] The WCTU had a number of excellent preachers in its membership, and these women filled pulpits across the nation speaking on temperance and other issues of concern to women. Wherever the National WCTU Annual Meeting was held, arrangements were made so that WCTU women spoke in as many churches as would receive them. Often over fifty women preached both Sunday morning and evening to packed sanctuaries. In their sermons they delivered powerful alternative understandings of scripture that inspired their listeners to re-vision woman's possibilities.

Thus the image of the True Woman went through a process of extensive reinterpretation in the 1880s. As more and more WCTU women experienced a "reconversion" to woman suffrage, they could imagine the True Woman as a voter and her sphere as extending out from her home to include the public space beyond. The WCTU encouraged its members to try out their newly claimed power and define new roles for themselves. The WCTU functioned, historian Estelle Freedman notes, as "a strong public female sphere...mobiliz[ing] women [to gain] political leverage in the larger society."[27] As such it became far more than a temperance organization....

Frances Willard and other leaders repeatedly emphasized that the WCTU was a sisterhood that brought together women from all areas of the nation, as well as an educational endeavor that prepared them for intelligent and responsible participation in public life. As Willard declared in 1885:

> Our WCTU is a school, not founded in that thought or for that purpose, but sure to fit us for the sacred duties of patriots in the realm that lies just beyond the horizon of the coming century. Here [at the close of the nineteenth century] we try our wings that yonder [in the twentieth century] our flight may be strong and steady. Here we prove our capacity for great deeds. There we shall perform them.[28]

In this "school" WCTU members would be "educated up to the level of the equal suffrage movement" where there would be "no sex in citizenship."[29]

...The WCTU had struggled for nearly two decades reinterpreting the traditional image of woman.... The WCTU women were not discouraged from their suffrage goals by suggestions of unnaturalness or accusations of unwomanly behavior, as they had been earlier. Their deep conviction that God called them to work for the vote for women enabled thousands of WCTU members to accept wholeheartedly Frances Willard's challenging statement to them: "Woman will bless and brighten every place she enters, and she will enter every place." For the WCTU in 1890, this was a vision in the process of becoming a reality.

Notes

This is a shortened version of Gifford's original article entitled "Home Protection: The WTCU's Conversion to Woman Suffrage," that appeared in *Gender, Ideology, and Action: Historical Perspectives on Women's Public Lives*, Janet Sharistanian, ed., (Greenwood Press, 1986), 95-120, and is reprinted with permission of Greenwood Publishing Group, Inc., Westport, CT.

1. Frances E. Willard, "Work of the W.C.T.U.," in Annie Nathan Meyer, *Woman's Work in America* (New York, 1891), 410. Also see Frances E. Willard, annual address at St. Louis NWCTU Convention, in *The Union Signal*, October 30, 1884, 2.

2. In "Politics and Culture in Women's History: A Symposium," *Feminist Studies* 6, no. 1 (Spring 1980): 26-64, Ellen DuBois and Mari Jo Buhle refer to the WCTU as a

key organization for understanding the nineteenth-century woman's movement. Buhle identifies the twenty-year period from 1870 to 1890 as an important gap which historians need to fill in from a feminist historical approach. Contemporary work has begun on the WCTU: See Ruth Bordin, *Woman and Temperance: The Quest for Power and Liberty, 1873-1900* (Philadelphia, 1982); Barbara Leslie Epstein, *The Politics of Domesticity: Women, Evangelism and Temperance in Nineteenth Century America* (Middletown, Conn., 1981); and, Jack S. Blocker Jr., "*Give to the Winds Thy Fears*": *The Women's Temperance Crusade, 1873-1874* (Westport, Conn., 1985).

3. "They Say: From Four Standpoints," *Our Union*, February 1, 1880, 1.

4. Ellen Carol Dubois, in *Feminism and Suffrage: The Emergence of an Independent Women's Movement in America, 1848-1869* (Ithaca, 1978), mentions Elizabeth Cady Stanton's 1869 meeting with Bloomington, Ill., women who had been reminded by a clergyman of their inferiority to men. Stanton reports (in *History of Woman Suffrage*, 2: 372) that she had to moderate her usually radical stance in the face of the women's resulting demoralization. Over a decade later, the situation had not much changed.

5. "They Say: From Four Standpoints," *Our Union*, February 1, 1880, 1.

6. Ibid.

7. Barbara Welter, *Dimity Convictions: The American Woman in the Nineteenth Century* (Athens, Ohio, 1976); Nancy F. Cott, *The Bonds of Womanhood: "Woman's Sphere" in New England, 1750-1835* (New Haven, 1977); and Kathryn Kish Sklar, *Catharine Beecher: A Study in American Domesticity* (New York, 1976) on the antebellum cult of True Womanhood and women like Catharine Beecher who sought to make of woman's sphere a shaping force for American society. See Carolyn De Swarte Gifford, "For God and Home and Native Land: The WCTU's Image of Woman in the Late Nineteenth Century," in Hilah F. Thomas and Rosemary Skinner Keller, eds., *Women in New Worlds: Historical Perspectives on the Wesleyan Tradition* (Nashville, 1981): 310-27.

8. Mary A. Livermore to Frances E. Willard, November 21, 1876. WCTU National Headquarters Historical Files (joint Ohio Historical Society-Michigan Historical Collections), WCTU microfilm edition, roll 11.

9. William J. Rorabaugh, *The Alcoholic Republic: An American Tradition* (New York, 1979), 163-68. See also Jacquie Jessup, "The Liquor Issue in American History: A Bibliography," in Jack S. Blocker, Jr., ed., *Alcohol, Reform and Society: The Liquor Question in Social Context* (Westport, Conn., 1979): 259-79; and Bordin, *Women and Temperance*, intro., chpts. 1 and 2.

10. "News from the Field," *The Union Signal*, October 2, 1884, 11.

11. Carolyn De Swarte Gifford, "For God and Home and Native Land," 8, 9, 15.

12. See Eliza Daniel Stewart, *Memories of the Crusade: A Thrilling Account of the Great Uprising of the Women of Ohio in 1873, against the Liquor Crime*, (Columbus, Ohio, 1889).

13. *Minutes of the Fourth Annual Meeting held at Burlingame, Kansas, September 27, 28, 29, 1882, State Woman's Christian Temperance Union of Kansas*, (Burlingame, Kans., 1882), 11.

14. Frances E. Willard, *Glimpses of Fifty Years: The Autobiography of an American Woman* (Chicago, 1892), 351.

15. Ibid.

16. Ibid., 360.

17. "One Woman's Experience," *Our Union*, January 1, 1880, 3.

18. Ibid.

19. Nancy F. Cott, *Bonds of Womanhood*, 204, n. 10.

20. "One Woman's Experience," 3.

21. Horace Bushnell, *Woman Suffrage: The Reform against Nature*, (New York, 1869).

22. Donald M. Scott, "Abolition as a Sacred Vocation," in Lewis Perry and Michael Feldman, eds., *Antislavery Reconsidered: New Perspectives on the Abolitionists* (Baton Rouge, 1979), 53, 54, 72.

23. "Home Protection," *Our Union*, February 1, 1880, 3.

24. "In Memoriam" by Mary A. Livermore. For Mrs. Lucinda B. Barrett of the Massachusetts WCTU in *The Union Signal*, July 3, 1884, 2. Emphasis added. The phrase "Lest haply you be found fighting against God" paraphrases Acts 5: 39 (KJV).

25. "Annual Convention," *Our Messenger*, December 1887, 4.

26. In *Our Messenger*, September 1887, the Wichita, Kans. WCTU announced that it was sending Rev. Hana's leaflet "Jesus Christ, the Emancipator of Women" to every minister in town.

27. Estelle Freedman, "Separatism as Strategy: Female Institution Building and American Feminism, 1870-1930," in *Feminist Studies* 5, 3 (Fall 1979): 513.

28. Frances E. Willard, Address to the Woman's Congress at Des Moines, Iowa, 1885, as quoted in Annie Nathan Meyer, *Woman's Work in America*, 408.

29. Ibid., 404. "No sectarian in religion, no sectionalism in politics, no sex in citizenship" was a popular slogan of the WCTU.

Mary Church Terrell (center), and her two sisters, Annette (left) and Sarah Church.
Moorland-Spingarn Research Center, Howard University

Eight

African American Women and the Woman Suffrage Movement

Rosalyn Terborg-Penn

Editor's Introduction: In this essay, historian Rosalyn Terborg-Penn, widely recognized as the foremost authority on African American women in the suffrage movement, provides an overview of their involvement in the movement's long and complex history. African American suffragists played an active role in the fight for female enfranchisement despite many obstacles. These included obstacles placed in their path by other suffragists—white women—who were willing, in many cases, to win their own enfranchisement at the expense of leaving their African American sisters behind.

The women's rights movement and the movement for justice for African Americans had a close, albeit erratic, relationship throughout American history. Women—black and white—played an active role in the fight to abolish slavery. Yet discrimination against women who took on a highly visible role in the fight led antislavery feminists to begin an independent movement for women's rights. Just after the Civil War, supporters of the rights of blacks and women again worked together—for *universal* suffrage—in the American Equal Rights Association founded in 1866. However, they divided rancorously in 1869 over the exclusion of women from enfranchisement through the Fourteenth and Fifteenth Amendments. As Terborg-Penn reminds us, supporters of woman suffrage broke into two woman suffrage organizations over this issue, with some suffragists refusing to accept the idea that this was "the Negro's Hour" and that women must await their turn.

The situation was drastically different in the last three decades of the woman suffrage movement when the historic connection between women's rights and the rights of African Americans became a distinct liability for advocates of *woman* suffrage. The 1890s and early 1900s was an era in which the vast majority of southern black men were disfranchised through legislation and constitutional amendments—unchallenged by the federal government. In addition, Jim Crow laws were adopted establishing segregation in nearly every aspect of life, resulting in one of the worst periods in the history of American race relations. At this time, many national suffrage leaders working with white southern suffragists, tried unsuccessfully to promote woman suffrage by saying that the enfranchisement of women—with educational requirements that would effectively limit the vote to white women—would actually help restore white supremacy in southern politics. In the last decade of the suffrage movement, after disfranchisement had been completed, white suffragists insisted that woman suffrage and black suffrage were *unrelated* issues. They countered antisuffragists' claims that state or federal suffrage amendments threatened white supremacy by insisting that the same discriminatory provisions that kept black men from voting would apply to black women.

Victims of both racism and sexism and eager to fight against both, African American women were in a difficult position as relations between these two great social movements fluctuated. Not enfranchised along with the men of their race in the Reconstruction amendments, African American women faced a cruel dilemma when asked to wait patiently for their own enfranchisement. Their predicament worsened in the late nineteenth and early twentieth centuries. Black women who were eager to participate in the woman suffrage movement often found it difficult to do so, as white suffragists not only embraced racist tactics but excluded black women from membership in suffrage organizations. When at last the long-awaited "woman's hour" seemed to be at hand, white suffragists deliberately avoided any action that might alarm white racists and endanger the suffrage cause—and *again* African American women were expected to understand.

As Terborg-Penn explains, African American women nevertheless played an active role in every stage of the suffrage movement from the antebellum period through the suffrage victory in 1920, working sometimes with white suffragists and sometimes in separate African American women's clubs. Among American suffragists, black women were, perhaps, the most unwavering advocates of universal suffrage for all. Yet, as Terborg-Penn argues, they also understood and proclaimed publicly that the vote was essential for their own protection, the protection of their children, and the progress of their race.

African American suffragists did *not* understand or accept their exclusion from white suffrage organizations or the racist tactics employed by white suffragists. Neither did they accept the efforts of southern state governments to exclude them from voting after the victory of the Nineteenth Amendment or the failure of white women's organizations to assist them in claiming that right. Though some African American women were able to register and vote even in the South, the vast majority remained disfranchised. Not until 1965 would black women—and black men—be fully enfranchised, after a new suffrage movement in which African American women *again* played a leading role. Only then was America, at last, a nation in which there was universal suffrage.

★　★　★　★　★

A FRICAN AMERICAN WOMEN participated in the woman suffrage movement from the antebellum period through to the passage of the Nineteenth Amendment. Legal status, class, region of residence, gender, and racial identification determined the degree to which black women could participate in the movement. Multiple forms of oppression, primarily slavery and then poverty, restricted many black women from working to gain women's right to vote in the nineteenth century. Nevertheless, African American women resisted the many barriers put against their political participation. Similar categories bound all American women, and most African American men, all of whom were also disfranchised. However, during the seventy-two years of the movement, limitations on these groups were never as restricting as those set by the society for black women.

Throughout the history of the movement, but particularly in the nineteenth century, black women had little opportunity to participate in organized woman suffrage activities. During the antebellum period, only the relatively small number of legally free African American women were privileged enough to lobby for the right to vote. After emancipation during the post-Civil War years, impoverished southern black women seeking work, fleeing physical threats to their lives, and struggling with survival strategies for their families, could little afford to make the organized woman suffrage movement a priority. At this time, the large majority of black women fell into this category. Nonetheless, there were always African American woman suffragists and as the century turned, more and more black women, inside and outside of the South, began to flex their political muscles and demand the right to vote.

Although blacks and whites developed similar suffrage strategies and formed coalitions, differing experiences among the races and conflicts between the two groups resulted. The disfranchised all agreed that rational individuals could not argue against the ideas of freedom and justice for all adult citizens, though some educated white suffragists attempted to exclude immigrant women who did not speak English from qualifying to vote. Nonetheless, by the late nineteenth century an anti-black woman suffrage strategy, more insidious than the anti-immigrant woman agenda, reinforced differences among African American and white woman suffragists, some of whom hoped to exclude black women from gaining the right to vote. This anti-woman suffrage agenda further divided black and white woman suffragists.

Class was another factor that influenced women's participation in the organized woman suffrage movement. Just as the majority of white women who actively participated in the organized movement were of the middle class, the majority of black women suffragists appeared to have enjoyed higher status than the masses of women of their race. Because many of the activities of African American women participants were not recorded in the official histories of the movement, it is difficult to be sure that more middle-class black women were suffragists than those of the working class. The changing status of

African American women during the duration of the movement—from slave to free, from rural to urban, from illiterate to literate—can be seen as factors which encouraged black strategies to achieve women's enfranchisement. One thing is certain: for various reasons more and more black women, like white women, joined the ranks of suffragists as the movement progressed in the twentieth century. This survey of African American women in the woman suffrage movement focuses on their reasons for supporting the "Votes for Women" campaign, but also on the obstacles they met along the way to enfranchisement.

Nineteenth-Century Black Woman Suffragists

There were two fundamental reasons why African Americans supported the woman suffrage movement during the nineteenth century. At mid-century their argument was based upon the belief, which was also held by white woman suffragists, that women were second-class citizens who needed the vote to improve their status in society. However, by the late nineteenth and early twentieth centuries, the rationale had grown to include the argument that black women needed the vote in order to help uplift the race and to obtain their own rights. A discussion of the activities and views of black female suffragists from the antebellum period to the turn of the century reveals that woman suffrage, to them, was a just and a practical cause.[1]

Although black women participated throughout the nineteenth-century woman suffrage campaign, their views were seldom recorded during the antebellum period. During these years, most of the African Americans commonly associated with the leadership of the struggle were men. Nonetheless, several African American women were among the ranks of antebellum woman's rights advocates. The most renowned among them was Sojourner Truth, who attended several woman's rights meetings beginning with the Worcester, Massachusetts Convention of 1850. Ironically, she was quite unlike the other African American suffragists of her time. She was an emancipated slave who was illiterate and labored in various menial capacities for her keep. Her African American sisters in the movement were literate, privileged women who had been born free. Truth is known to the movement because the white leadership recorded her outspoken sentiments, often citing them as anomalous to those of the other women in the movement. In 1851, for example, at Akron, Ohio, Truth gave a remarkable address that made her famous in the annals of the movement, despite the attempts of some white feminists to thwart her efforts to be heard. From that time on, Truth's views on women's rights and woman suffrage, spoken in folk dialect, were highly publicized. At the New York City convention held in 1853, for example, Truth commented publicly about white prejudice against her, when she said: "I know that it feels a kind O'hissin' like to see a colored woman get up and tell you about things, and Woman's Rights."[2]

Unlike those of Sojourner Truth, the words of suffragists Harriet Forten Purvis and her sister, Margaretta Forten, were not recorded. Both women were founding members of the Philadelphia Female Anti-Slavery Society and daughters of the wealthy reformer James Forten, Sr. The sisters helped to lay the groundwork for the first National Woman's Rights Convention ever held, in October 1854. Another early black female suffragist was abolitionist lecturer Sarah Remond from Salem, Massachusetts. She was honored in 1858, when she spoke at the Ninth National Woman's Rights Convention held at New York City, but her remarks were not recorded. According to the recollections of Susan B. Anthony, journalist and militant abolitionist Mary Ann Shadd Cary began her support of woman's rights during the late 1850s. However, it appears that none of her statements on woman suffrage during the antebellum period have survived.[3]

After the Civil War, these black female abolitionists and feminists were joined by Hattie Purvis, who was Harriet Purvis's daughter, and by abolitionist and poet Frances Ellen Watkins Harper. Both women participated in the American Equal Rights Association (AERA). In an effort to campaign for universal suffrage, this organization of men and women was founded in 1866 during a woman's rights convention. Frances Harper spoke at the convention and also served on the financial committee, but there appears to be no record of her remarks. Aside from her participation as a committee member, during this period, little is known about her reasons for supporting woman suffrage. Nevertheless, during the years in which the AERA functioned, from 1866 through 1869, black women served on committees and contributed financial as well as moral support.[4]

If Sojourner Truth is best remembered for her folk words of wisdom, Harriet and Hattie Purvis can be remembered for their consistent service in a variety of roles in the AERA. In 1866 Harriet and black abolitionist William Still were elected to the Executive Committee. In 1867 she and black abolitionist Charles Lenox Remond appeared as the blacks elected to the Finance Committee. In 1868, Hattie Purvis was elected recording secretary, along with Henry Blackwell. Both were reelected the following year.[5]

By 1869, differences in ideology among suffragists in the AERA over the proposed Fifteenth Amendment split the membership. Although the association members all supported the goal of universal suffrage, they disagreed on the means by which this goal was to be achieved. Some felt that a just amendment should include all disfranchised Americans, despite widespread public opposition to woman suffrage. Others believed that universal suffrage would have to be achieved in stages and that the most politically advantageous means was to enfranchise black men first, the campaign for which was called "Negro suffrage." As a result of this controversy, the AERA ceased to function. Elizabeth Cady Stanton, Susan B. Anthony, and their supporters abandoned the AERA and formed the National Woman Suffrage Association (NWSA) in May 1869 and divorced themselves from the "Negro suffrage" issue. Although men were allowed to participate in the NWSA, they were excluded from official positions. By November 1869, Lucy Stone and Henry Ward Beecher had led their followers into the American Woman Suffrage Association (AWSA), which supported the Fifteenth Amendment and allowed males to hold office in the AWSA.[6]

Black suffragists, both males and females, became involved in this ideological dispute. Mary Ann Cary, for example, disagreed with the final form of the Fifteenth Amendment because it included the word "male." On the other hand, Frances Harper, although committed to woman suffrage, felt that it was politically expedient to fight first to enfranchise black men despite the setback to the woman suffrage cause.[7] Divisions among female suffragists affected black affiliation in the resulting suffrage associations. Hattie Purvis attended NWSA meetings, as did Cary. Harper affiliated with the AWSA. Sojourner Truth attended meetings of both groups.[8]

During the 1870s, the AWSA attracted several additional black women. Among them was Caroline Remond Putman of the crusading Remond family of Salem, Massachusetts, whose members actively lectured against slavery. In 1870 she helped to found the Massachusetts Woman Suffrage Association under the auspices of the AWSA.[9] Josephine St. Pierre Ruffin was another Massachusetts black woman suffragist. She has been described as having played a leading role in every movement to emancipate black women. Ruffin began her suffrage activities during 1875 as a member of the Massachusetts Woman Suffrage Association. A Bostonian, she affiliated with the group as a result of the welcome she received from Lucy Stone, Julia Ward Howe, and other pioneers in the Massachusetts movement.[10] Perhaps Ruffin's positive assessment of these prominent AWSA leaders gives clues as to why more African American women appear to have affiliated with the AWSA rather than the NWSA.

The first South Carolina delegate to a woman suffrage convention was a black woman, Charlotte Rollin (known as Lottie) of Charleston. Along with her sisters, Frances, Louisa, and Kate, the Rollin sisters were influential in Reconstruction politics during the late 1860s and 1870s. Frances Rollin worked for and later married William J. Whipper who, as a delegate to the South Carolina Constitutional Convention of 1868, pleaded for the enfranchisement of women as well as black men. Lottie Rollin worked for black congressman Robert Brown Elliott. Rollin spoke on the floor of the South Carolina House of Representatives in 1869 to urge support of universal suffrage. By 1870, she chaired the founding meeting of the South Carolina Woman's Rights Association and was elected secretary. In 1871 her sister Louisa led a meeting at the state capital to promote woman suffrage. The following year Kate Rollin was elected treasurer of the association, and Lottie Rollin represented South Carolina as an ex-officio member of the Executive Committee of the AWSA, which met in New York City that year.[11]

Not until the 1870s do we find black female arguments on behalf of woman suffrage preserved in written form—other than those attributed to Sojourner Truth. At this time, Lottie Rollin addressed the chairman of the South Carolina Woman's Rights Convention in 1870 and said: "We ask suffrage not as a favor, not as a privilege, but as a right based on the ground that we are human beings, and as such entitled to all human rights."[12] The Rollin rationale on behalf of woman suffrage reflected the contemporary rhetoric that women were second-class citizens who needed the vote to improve their status in society.

One strategy used by blacks as well as whites to obtain the ballot for women was an appeal for female enfranchisement based on the Fifteenth Amendment. In 1872, white suffragist Mary Olney Brown of Washington State wrote a letter to Frederick Douglass, editor of the black newspaper, *The New National Era* (Washington). Offering an emotional plea for black male support of the vote for black women, Brown argued that the Fifteenth Amendment, which had enfranchised black men in 1870, should be applied to the enfranchisement of women because it did not exclude them in the definition of citizenship. Douglass printed the letter, wherein Brown encouraged voting black men to support her strategy. This appears to be the first in many efforts made by white suffragists to reestablish the political coalition they had severed with African American men.[13]

Brown's strategy to demand suffrage as woman's legal right, a strategy frequently employed in the 1870s, could very well have come from journalist Mary Ann Cary, who had argued on behalf of the ballot for black women in the 1860s and became one of the few women during this period who successfully registered to vote. She did this in 1871 in the District of Columbia, although like Susan B. Anthony and others, Cary was prohibited from voting. Cary is an example of the women historian Ellen DuBois calls radical feminists, who emerged in the 1870s as independent suffragists.[14] Cary attended the NWSA Convention that met in Washington in January of 1871 while she was a student in the Howard University Law School, and supported the memorial that Victoria Woodhull presented before the House Judiciary Committee the previous December. Woodhull had argued, like Mary Olney Brown, that the proposed Sixteenth Amendment to enfranchise women was not necessary, for as citizens, women had the right to vote under the Fourteenth and Fifteenth Amendments. She appealed to Congress merely to pass a declaratory resolution to that effect since the Constitution made no distinction between citizens based on gender.[15]

In support of this strategy, Cary prepared a testimony for the Judiciary Committee of the House of Representatives about the need for black women to vote in the District of Columbia. She noted that she was a taxpayer with the same obligations as the black male taxpayers of the city. Cary felt, therefore, that suffrage should be her right just as it was theirs. She noted that many women of her race in the nation's capital supported the other women of the nation who demanded not only the vote, but the striking of the word "male" from the Constitution.[16]

Supporting her claim about black female support for woman suffrage, Cary wrote the NWSA in 1876 on behalf of ninety-four black women from the District of Columbia. Her letter requested that their names be enrolled in the July 4, 1876 centennial autograph book, as signers of the NWSA's Woman's Declaration of Rights. This declaration called for the immediate enfranchisement of American women.[17]

Cary and Mary Olney Brown were not alone in identifying woman suffrage as a potential source of strength to black women during the Reconstruction years. Frances Harper argued similarly. In 1873, she attended the AWSA Convention at the Cooper Institute in New York City. In making the closing speech, Harper declared that "as much as white women need the ballot, colored women need it more." She indicted what she called the "ignorant and often degraded men" who subjected black women in the South to arbitrary legal authority. Acknowledging the progress already made by women of her race, Harper pleaded for equal rights and equal education for the African American women of the nation.[18]

The post-Civil War years were not only an era of change for white woman suffragists, they marked a time for expanding the rationale for woman suffrage among African American women. Even though black women continued to express the original argument in support of woman suffrage—women are second-class citizens who need the vote—by the late nineteenth and early twentieth centuries, the rationale began to reflect more specifically needs of African American women. For example, in 1880 Cary organized the Colored Women's Progressive Franchise Association in the District of Columbia. Among the purposes of the group was what Cary called "an aggressive stand against the assumption that men only may begin and conduct industrial and other things." This idea was in keeping with the radical feminist belief that women, like men, should take leadership roles in developing industrial sectors in the economy. Cary even made plans to start a newspaper to support the rights and interests of women and to establish a joint stock company in which women were to have the controlling official power. There is no evidence, however, that she was ever able to accomplish these goals.[19]

Cary was not the only black female journalist to favor woman suffrage in the 1880s. Gertrude Bustill Mossell of Philadelphia, like Cary, was from a prominent antebellum free-Negro family of reformers. Mossell initiated a woman's column in T. Thomas Fortune's first newspaper, *The New York Freeman,* a nationally oriented black newspaper. In her first article, entitled "Woman Suffrage" published in 1885, she encouraged blacks to read the *History of Woman Suffrage,* the *New Era,* the essays of John Stuart Mill, and other works about woman's rights to familiarize them with the woman suffrage movement and perhaps change the minds of those who opposed it. Mossell argued also that despite the anti-suffragists' charges to the contrary, most housewives supported woman suffrage.[20]

Other veteran suffragists continued their activities in the movement during the 1880s. Hattie Purvis was actively involved in the Pennsylvania Woman Suffrage Association. Frances Harper was a director of the Women's Congress, and by 1887 she was the Superintendent of Work Among Colored People for the Woman's Christian Temperance Union (WCTU), a national body quite supportive of woman suffrage. Josephine St. Pierre Ruffin was a member of the first board of the Massachusetts School Suffrage Association, which was founded in 1880.[21]

In the last decade of the nineteenth century, more and more African American women began to organize, raising their voices in support of woman suffrage. One of the reasons for this was the rising number of educated blacks who emerged during the first generation out of slavery. With this new freedom, black women, like white women, actively developed the women's club movement as a vehicle for change.

The first fifty-two delegates who met to organize the National Federation of Afro-American Women at Boston in August of 1895, were eager supporters of woman suffrage. The women cheered suffragist William Lloyd Garrison, Jr., who spoke of the need for political equality for women. Among the members of the Federation were veteran suffragists Frances Harper and Josephine Ruffin, who had made the initial call for an organization representative of African American women throughout the nation. Among the younger members destined to become prime movers among the black woman suffragists of the twentieth century was Washington, D.C. educator Mary Church Terrell, a native of Memphis and an Oberlin graduate.[22]

In 1896 the National Federation of Afro-American Women merged with the National League of Colored Women to form the National Association of Colored Women (NACW). Mary Church Terrell was elected the first president. She and several other newly emerging black female leaders included woman suffrage in their campaign to lead the nation's black women toward self-help and racial uplift. Among this group was journalist Ida B. Wells-Barnett, who had been driven out of Memphis in 1892 because of her antilynching crusade. She later married, had a family, and settled in Chicago. Margaret Murray Washington, principal of the secondary school at Tuskegee Institute in Alabama and Booker T. Washington's wife, was also among this group. By 1900, Susan B. Anthony listed these three women among the prominent advocates of woman suffrage.[23]

A lesser-known southern black woman of the 1890s was Mary McCurdy, a temperance leader and advocate of woman suffrage whose views echoed the changing rationale for woman suffrage exemplified by racial and gender identification. She personified the growing number of southern women, educated during Reconstruction, who sought political means to solve the social ills of black communities. While living in Rome, Georgia, McCurdy was president of the local black woman's temperance union and an official in the state temperance organization. She also edited the *National Presbyterian,* a temperance paper published in 1890. A firm believer in woman suffrage, McCurdy saw the franchise as the means to prohibit the liquor traffic, a major vehicle for political corruption. Not only did she blame white men for keeping the ballot from the women of the nation, she also blamed them for the political corruption in the South. McCurdy felt that the majority of African American men who had voted in the South after the Fifteenth Amendment enfranchised them had either been robbed of that right, or had allowed their ballot to be purchased. African American women, she predicted, would never allow their votes to be bought.[24]

"Woman to the Rescue," a pro-suffrage cartoon from The Crisis, *May 1916.*
Woman Suffrage Media Collection

While touring the South during the Reconstruction years, Frances Harper observed the results of political corruption. She echoed McCurdy's opinion when she expressed her sentiments against corruption, published in a poem of 1896. Harper spoke in dialect through "Aunt Chloe," who said:

> And this buying up each other
>   Is something worse than mean.
> Though I think a heap of voting,
>   I go for voting clean.[25]

Although white women complained about political corruption in the South and in immigrant communities in the Northeast, they were usually on the offensive with their criticism of others. African American women were always on the defensive, defending their race as well as criticizing the ills that kept many former slaves powerless. Mary Church Terrell responded to white women's criticism of the purchase of the "Negro vote" at the National American Woman Suffrage Association (NAWSA) meeting that she attended in Washington in 1904. By then a national figure, she felt that black men were being unduly condemned for selling their votes and she said: "They never sold their vote til they found that it made no difference how they cast them." Terrell noted also that there were many cases of black men who were tempted, yet never sold their right to the ballot. Furthermore, she suggested that the white suffragists should aid rather than merely condemn black voters: "My sisters of the dominant race, stand up not only for the oppressed sex, but also for the oppressed race!"[26]

At the turn of the century, Terrell, like other black suffragists before her, admonished America for violating the principle "government of the people, for the people and by the people," by denying women the right to the ballot. As a result of male-dominated politics, she asserted, women were held in subjugation by men, many of whom she called "illiterate, debauched, and vicious."[27] The Terrell rationale for support of woman suffrage included both themes—suffrage as the right of women as citizens and woman suffrage as a means to uplifting African Americans.

Twentieth-Century Black Woman Suffragists

By the first decade of the twentieth century, more black women began to speak out about how important their right to vote could be to black people as a whole and to black women in particular. Yet, as growing numbers of African American women supported and joined the organized woman suffrage movement, their potential political influence stimulated the creation of greater obstacles blocking their attempts to achieve the right to vote.[28]

With the creation of the "colored" women's club movement, more and more resourceful women had a means of spreading the word about strategies for uplifting themselves and their race. Adella Hunt Logan was one of them. She was the only Alabama woman, black or white, listed in 1900 by the NAWSA as a life member. A native of Georgia who joined the Tuskegee Institute faculty in 1883 as principal of the training school, Logan wrote one of the most comprehensive arguments in support of woman suffrage. In 1905, she argued similarly to Terrell: "Government of the people, for the people and by the people is but partially realized so long as woman has no vote."[29] She could not understand why women were treated as citizens in other aspects of American life, but not when it came to the exercise of the franchise. Her words were similar to those of Cary, who had indicted America for imposing taxation without representation upon the majority of women of the nation. Noting the suffrage victories for women in various western states, Logan argued that as a result of woman suffrage in those states, civic affairs had improved.[30]

Logan rejected the argument of anti-suffragists who alleged that women did not need the ballot because they were not interested in politics. She opposed the view that woman suffrage would bring women into politics and, as a result, cause them to neglect the home. Logan went further and also dismissed the theory that exercising the franchise was a complicated process that women could not understand. She concluded, as did Terrell, that the right of suffrage was withheld from women for political reasons by those she called "ignorant and vicious men." Finally, like Cary, Truth, Harper and other black women of the nineteenth century, Logan argued that if white women needed the vote in order to acquire advantages as well as protection of their rights, then black women needed the ballot even more, because they carried the double burden of racism and sexism.[31] Numerous African American women followed in this tradition, formulating arguments that emphasized why black women, specifically, needed the vote.

When given the opportunity, African American women exercised the right to vote. For instance, black women voted in Colorado at the turn of the century. Their political activities were noted by Helen Woodbury, who in 1909 published a study of the equal suffrage movement in Colorado. She commented that black women were interested in politics because in 1901 there was a "colored woman's" Republican club in Denver. In addition, she found that 1,373 blacks voted in Denver during the 1906 election, of whom 45.2 percent were women. From Woodbury's overall statistics, she concluded that a larger percentage of black women than white women voted in that Denver election.[32] Needless to say, reports like Woodbury's sent up red flags in front of those who feared the potential power of black women voters, especially the power of black club women.

Woodbury's findings are not surprising because, during the last quarter of the nineteenth century, the woman's club movement had expanded dramatically, usually with clubs developing membership and reform strategies along racially separate lines. Perhaps one reason for this separate development lay in the unique needs of black women during the period. Native-born white women had no need to defend their dignity against widespread assumptions that they were wanton, immoral, and socially inferior. White women did not have the severe problems of racial discrimination that compounded black women's plight in employment and education. Moreover, race consciousness was evident among African Americans in general as growing numbers of race-specific civil rights organizations, business groups, and self-help societies emerged at the century's end.[33]

Racism in the Suffrage Movement

Another reason for the development of racially separate women's groups was the exclusion of black women from most white female clubs. Despite the differences between the two groups, there were some common causes and attempts at unity on local levels. Journalist Paula Giddings refers to the women who made these attempts as "radical interracialists"—black women who were determined to enter the mainstream.[34] Nevertheless, doing so was not easy, for this was the era of "Jim Crow" nationwide. African American women were involved in temperance work, suffrage groups, and club work. The experiences of many of their leaders indicated the pervasiveness of white female prejudice and discrimination against black females in women's groups, even those who were part of the woman suffrage coalition.[35]

Throughout the 1890s, Josephine St. Pierre Ruffin had challenged white women to unite with blacks for the benefit of humanity, but her words went virtually unheeded outside of Massachusetts. She was discriminated against personally when attending the General Federation of Women's Clubs, which met in Wisconsin in 1900. Disillusioned by the incident, the black woman's club she represented, The Woman's Era Club, made an official statement which included the view "that colored women should confine themselves to their clubs and the large field of work open to them there."[36]

At the same convention of the General Federation of Women's Clubs, Mary Church Terrell, representing the NACW, was refused permission to bring the group greetings on behalf of her association because the southern clubs objected, threatening resignation. Despite this rebuff, Terrell was invited to speak before other white groups during the early years of the twentieth century. At the Minneapolis Convention of Women in 1900 she addressed the group not only about the needs of black women, but also about the prejudice and lack of sympathy on the part of white women. Terrell indicted them for not extending a helping hand to African Americans whose aims were similar to their own. The same year, she made a similar speech at the NAWSA meeting in the District of Columbia.[37]

Ida B. Wells-Barnett reported how Fannie Barrier Williams, an African American club woman in Chicago, attempted to join the Chicago Woman's Club in 1894. The all-white group split over the controversy created by those who wanted a black member and those who did not. After fourteen months of controversy, Williams was admitted. At the turn of the century, Wells-Barnett noted that the issue was still significant in Illinois when the State Federation of Women's Clubs membership made it impossible for African American clubs to become members. Nonetheless, black women's clubs were so numerous that by the second decade of the twentieth century a large federation of "colored" women's clubs was active in black communities throughout Illinois. By 1914, Wells-Barnett helped to organize the Alpha Suffrage Club of African American women, who were influential later in electing a black man to Congress, Oscar DePriest.[38]

The experiences of Ruffin, Terrell, Williams, and Wells-Barnett were not unique. During the same period, the woman suffrage campaign gained momentum, but the national leadership emulated the racial attitudes of white women's clubs around the nation. As historian Aileen Kraditor has observed, white supremacy was an influential factor in the strategy of the suffragists as the need developed for southern support for a woman suffrage amendment. As early as the 1890s, Susan B. Anthony realized the potential to the woman suffrage cause in wooing southern white women. She chose expedience over loyalty and justice when she asked veteran feminist Frederick Douglass not to attend the 1895 NAWSA Convention scheduled in Atlanta. Anthony explained to Wells-Barnett that Douglass's presence on the stage with the honored guests, his usual place at these conventions, would have offended the southern hosts. Wells-Barnett, however, admonished Anthony for giving in to racial prejudice.[39]

By the 1903 NAWSA Convention in New Orleans, the board of officers prepared a statement endorsing the organization's position to allow states the right to develop their own woman suffrage positions, which was tantamount to an endorsement of white supremacy in most states, particularly in the South. The statement was signed by Susan B. Anthony, Carrie C. Catt, Anna Howard Shaw, Kate N. Gordon, Alice Stone Blackwell, Harriet Taylor Upton, Laura Clay, and Mary Coggeshall. During the convention week, Susan B. Anthony visited the black Phillis Wheatley Club in New Orleans. In presenting flowers to Anthony on the occasion, Sylvamie Williams, president of the club, indicated that black women were painfully aware of their "down trotten" [sic] position among white suffragists.[40]

Fear of offending southern white suffragists in Atlanta and in New Orleans is one thing, but how can the prejudice against African American club women in Wisconsin, and in Chicago be explained? There was a nationwide, not just a southern prejudice against African American women. It appears that white women outside of the South used southern white women's overt prejudice as an excuse for the NAWSA's discriminatory policies, while hiding their own similar feelings about black women, although they shared many of the black women's goals for reform and women's political equity. African American woman suffragists were quite aware of their position, and they were determined to move beyond the attempts to keep them disfranchised.

Black suffragists knew that although those national suffrage leaders who courted black support endorsed equal suffrage among the races while in African American circles, their public actions and statements to the mainstream society often contradicted their professed egalitarianism. For example, Alice Paul, organizer of the National Woman's Party (NWP) and the suffrage parade in front of the White House in 1913, had expressed her sympathy for black woman's enfranchisement. Yet before the parade the leaders asked Wells-Barnett, who was representing the Alpha Suffrage Club, not to march with the white Chicago delegates. Again the rationale was fear of offending white southern women. Terrell marched in the parade with African American women from Howard University, assembled in the section reserved for black women—at the end of the line. By 1919, she confided her feelings about Paul to Walter White of the National Association for the Advancement of Colored People (NAACP). Both questioned Paul's loyalty to black women, concluding that if she and other white suffragist leaders could get the amendment through without enfranchising African American women they would.[41]

Why this suspicion among African American leaders on the eve of the passage of the Nineteenth Amendment? By this time, nearly all the major white suffrage leaders had compromised their support of black woman suffrage. For example, despite endorsing black suffrage, Anna Howard Shaw had been accused of refusing to allow an African American delegate at the Louisville NAWSA convention of 1911 to propose an anti-discrimination resolution. As president of the NAWSA from 1910 to 1915, Shaw avoided offending white, southern suffragists, and supported the states' rights position of the association.[42]

The strength of the states' rights strategy among southern, white suffragists can be observed as early as the 1890s, when, they sought suffrage for white women through new state constitutions, which had been drafted to disenfranchise black men. Historian Marjorie Spruill Wheeler confirms that white suffragists believed votes for white women could be used as a way of countering the "Negro vote" in the South. The dynamics of this southern woman suffrage strategy can be seen in looking at the similar positions of two leaders of the southern movement. Laura Clay came from Kentucky, a state with a small black population—which could hardly have affected the balance of political power in the state—whereas Kate Gordon came from Louisiana, a state where the black population was very large, and had held considerable political influence in the state during the Reconstruction Era. By 1906, however, Clay had come to agree with Gordon that southern suffragists should campaign for state suffrage amendments containing "whites-only" clauses.[43]

African American leaders directed their displeasure upon southern suffragists like Clay. For example, NAACP officials noted that at the Jubilee Convention of the NAWSA in 1919, Clay proposed "that certain sections [of the proposed amendment] be amended with particular reference to those parts that would permit the enfranchisement of Negro women in the South."[44] It appears that as the success of a non-restrictive woman suffrage amendment became apparent, some southern leaders feared the potential threat to the status quo that an active and fast-growing black woman suffrage movement would have in states such as Tennessee and Kentucky.

By 1919 a united front began to develop among African American suffragists nationwide, as black women feared the growing alliance between national woman suffrage leaders and those who hoped to eliminate blacks from the so-called Anthony Amendment being debated in Congress. As the amendment was debated in the Senate, several southern senators attempted to alter it in ways that would either restrict the vote to white women, or restrict implementation to the states. For example, in 1918 Mississippi Senator John Sharp Williams proposed to amend the resolution to make it read, "The right of white citizens to vote shall not be denied."[45] However, the vote was laid on the table. Again in 1919, Mississippi Senator Pat Harrison attempted unsuccessfully to have the word "white" placed in the original amendment, while Louisiana Senator Edward J. Gay called for an amendment providing the states instead of the Congress the power to enforce it.[46]

Throughout the Congressional debates, the NAACP, representing black and white supporters of enfranchising African American women, lobbied for the defeat of such efforts. In addition, the NACW took action by encouraging African American women in states where black men still retained the franchise to pressure the NAWSA and the NWP to oppose any changes to the Anthony Amendment. In the meantime, NACW leaders knew that white woman suffragists, despite their reluctance to enfranchise black women, needed the votes of black men outside of the South. These African American women developed a strategy designed to expose the hypocrisy of the white suffrage leadership. In 1918, the leaders of the Northeastern Federation of Women's Clubs, which represented six thousand black women from nine states, applied for NAWSA membership.[47] Carrie Chapman Catt, who was president of the NAWSA at the time, asked Ida Husted Harper, editor of the *History of Woman Suffrage* and a long-time friend of the late Susan B. Anthony, to discourage the Northeastern Federation from applying for membership. Both women felt NAWSA membership for the black group would offend the white southern organizations and hamper passage of the Anthony Amendment. Both Catt and Harper had argued in favor of black woman suffrage in the past and apparently thought the Federation would understand their position and not be offended by their request.[48]

However, African American club women understood what white club women did not. Blacks were seeking more than NAWSA membership; they were seeking NAWSA support for the enfranchisement of African American women. Elizabeth C. Carter, president of the Federation, admonished Harper for her arrogance and patronizing testimony, which presumed that African American women were not politically sophisticated enough to use NAWSA membership as a strategy to gain the vote.[49] Fortunately amendments seeking to enfranchise white women only failed with the close of the Sixty-Fifth Congress and the Anthony Amendment was passed by Congress in June 1919. However, African Americans understood how vulnerable their women were as the amendment made the rounds in the states toward ratification.

By the summer of 1920, only one state was needed for ratification and President Wilson successfully appealed to the governor of Tennessee for a special legislative session to consider the amendment. Tennessee appeared to be the only hope, but even in this state the legislature could not resolve the stalemate. Once again, the white suffrage leaders realized that African Americans may be needed to break the deadlock. Alice Paul turned to the NAACP for help. At this point, NAACP leaders lent their support by urging black voting men in Tennessee to lobby their state legislators to support the amendment, but not before taking the opportunity to remind Paul how white women had either worked against black political leaders who were males, or ignored the plight of black suffragists who were females. Nonetheless, these women had no compunction about asking black people for their help.[50]

Fortunately for woman suffragists, the Tennessee deadlock ended positively for the Nineteenth Amendment, which was ratified in August 1920. Despite the white suffragists' record of discrimination, most African American leaders, both men and women, welcomed woman suffrage. Naively, they hoped that black women could help uplift the standards of their race through exercising the franchise. Like many white woman suffragists, blacks believed the vote to be the panacea to their social problems.

The Disfranchising of Black Women in the South

African American hopes for political equity were quickly dashed as the majority of black women who still lived in the South were quickly disfranchised. In addition, the black Republican women and men outside the South began to lose their political influence within a decade after the passage of the Nineteenth Amendment.

Disfranchisement had been predicted by several white southern suffragists. Kentucky's Madeline McDowell Breckinridge, for one, considered herself a liberal on racial issues, but did not believe African American women should be voters until they could be properly educated. Breckinridge advocated educational requirements at the state level that would eliminate most potential black voters. Nonetheless, she opposed the blatantly racist statements made by southern suffragists like Louisiana's Kate Gordon and Mississippi's Belle Kearney. Of the two, Gordon opposed a federal amendment, saying it invited northern intervention in the affairs of the states that would endanger white supremacy. However, by the eve of the Nineteenth Amendment's ratification, Kearney attempted to change Gordon's mind about opposing the amendment, arguing that the South need not fear northern intervention on behalf of disfranchised black women. Kearney had been convinced that northerners were sympathetic with the South's "negro problem."[51] Indeed, she was correct.

African Americans, nonetheless, rallied nationwide to the woman suffrage victory. The enthusiastic responses of black women may have seemed astonishing when one realizes that woman suffrage was a predominantly middle-class movement among native-born white women and that the black middle class remained very small during the early twentieth century. Furthermore, the heyday of the woman suffrage movement embraced an era that historian Rayford Logan called "the nadir" in African American history, characterized by racial segregation, defamation of the character of black women, and lynching of black Americans, both men and women. It is a wonder that African American women dared to dream a white woman's dream—the right to enfranchisement.[52]

Apprehensions from discontented black leaders about the inclusion of black women as voters, especially in the South, had been evident throughout the second decade of the twentieth century. African American fears went beyond misgivings about white women in states like New York and Texas, where women gained the franchise before the ratification of the Nineteenth Amendment. In 1917, while the New York State woman suffrage referendum was pending in the legislature, black suffragists in the state had complained of discrimination against their organizations by white suffragists during the state-wide convention at Saratoga. White suffrage leaders assured black women that they were welcome in the movement. Although the majority of the African American delegates were conciliated, a vocal minority remained disillusioned. In 1918 the black editors of the *Houston Observer* responded to black disillusionment when they called upon the men and women of their race to register to vote in spite of the poll tax, which was designed especially to exclude Texas's African American voters.[53] Black women, nevertheless, were discriminated against. Six of them were refused the right to vote at Fort Worth on the grounds that the primaries were open to white Democrats only. Efforts to disfranchise black women in Houston failed, however, when the women took legal action against the registrar who attempted to apply the Texas woman suffrage law to white women only. A similar attempt to disqualify African American women in Waxahachie, Texas failed also.[54]

After the ratification of the federal amendment, black women registered in large numbers throughout the South, especially in Georgia and Louisiana, despite major obstacles placed against them by the white supremacists. In defense, African American women often turned to the NAACP for assistance. Field Secretary William Pickens was sent to investigate the numerous charges and recorded several incidents that he either witnessed personally or about which he received reports. In Columbia, South Carolina, for example, a requirement that a voter pay taxes on property valued at three hundred dollars or more was made mandatory for black women. If they passed that test, the women were required to read from and to interpret the state or the federal constitutions. No such tests were required of white women. Although the *Columbia State,* a local newspaper, reported disinterest in registering among African American women, Pickens testified to the contrary. By the end of the registration period, twenty Columbia black women had signed an affidavit against the registrars who had disqualified them. In the surrounding Richland County, African American women were disqualified when they attempted to register to vote. As a result, several of them made plans to appeal the ruling.[55]

Many cases like these were handled by the NAACP, and after the registration periods ended in the South, its board of directors presented the evidence to Congress. The NAACP officials and others testified at a 1920 congressional hearing in support of the proposed Tinkham Bill that would have reduced representation in Congress from states where there was restriction of woman suffrage and thus protected African American women from disfranchisement. Belle Kearney's prediction was right, however. The North did not intervene in the southern "negro problem." White supremacy prevailed, as southern congressmen successfully claimed that blacks were not disfranchised, just disinterested in voting. Despite the massive evidence produced by the NAACP, the Tinkham Bill failed to pass.[56]

White southern apprehensions of a viable black female electorate were not illusionary. "Colored women voter's leagues" were growing throughout the South, where the task of the leagues was to give black women seeking to qualify to vote instructions for countering white opposition. Leagues could be found in Alabama, Georgia, Tennessee, and Texas. These groups were feared also by white supremacists because the women sought to qualify black men as voters as well.[57]

During the November 1920 elections, southern whites also expected black women to vote in larger numbers than white women. If this happened, they feared, the ballot would soon be returned to African American men. Black suffrage, it was believed, would also result in the return of the two-party system in the South, because African Americans would consistently vote Republican. These apprehensions were realized in Florida after the election. Black women in Jacksonville had registered and voted in greater numbers than white women. In reaction, the Woman Suffrage League of Jacksonville was reorganized into the Duval County League of Democratic Women Voters. The members were dedicated to maintain white supremacy and pledged to register white women voters.[58]

The inability of Congress and the NAACP to protect the rights of black women voters led the women to seek help from national woman suffrage leaders. Not surprisingly, these attempts failed also. In 1919, anticipating victory, the NAWSA had changed its name to the League of Women Voters (LWV), a

African American women organize for suffrage, c. 1919.
Schomburg Center, New York Public Library

non-partisan organization designed to maintain women's political participation on national and local levels. At the 1921 national LWV convention held at Cleveland, African American women brought their complaints about disfranchisement before the LWV. The white southern delegates at the convention threatened to walk out if the "negro problem" was debated. In typical League fashion, a compromise resulted, wherein African American women were allowed to speak before the body, but no action was taken by the organization.[59]

When the African American women suffragists sought assistance from the National Woman's Party, they were rebuffed totally. The NWP leadership position was that since black women were discriminated against in the same ways as black men, their problems were not woman's rights issues, but race issues. Therefore, the NWP felt no obligation to defend the right of African American women as voters.[60]

Abandonment by white women suffragists in 1920 really came as no surprise to most black women leaders. The preceding decade of woman suffrage politics had reminded them of the assertions of black woman suffrage supporters of the past. Frederick Douglass had declared in 1868 that black women were victimized mainly because they were blacks, not because they were women. Frances Ellen Watkins Harper answered in 1869 that for white women the priority in the struggle for human rights was sex, not race. By 1920 the situation had changed very little, and many African American suffragists had been thoroughly disillusioned by the racism of the white feminists they had encountered.[61]

A significant number of black women and black women's organizations had not only supported woman suffrage on the eve of the passage of the Nineteenth Amendment, but attempted to exercise their rights to vote in the elections immediately following the amendment's ratification in 1920. Unfortunately for them, African American women confronted racial discrimination in their efforts to support the amendment and to win the vote. Consequently, discontented black feminists anticipated the disillusionment that their white counterparts encountered within a decade following amendment ratification, as women's votes did not become the panacea to social problems of the larger society.

Notes

1. Rosalyn Terborg-Penn, "Nineteenth Century Black Women and Woman Suffrage," *The Potomac Review* 7 (Spring/Summer 1977): 13-24, 13.

2. Elizabeth Cady Stanton, Susan B. Anthony, and Matilda J. Gage, eds., *History of Woman Suffrage*, 6 vols., (New York, 1969), 1: 115, 546, 567.

3. Ibid., 386, 668; *HWS* 3: 72.

4. *HWS* 2: 168, 222.

5. Ibid., 191, 221, 378-79; *HWS* 3: 457.

6. *HWS* 2: 400, 406.

7. Speech to the Judiciary Committee, Mary Ann Shadd Cary Papers, Folder No. 2, Moorland-Spingarn Research Center, Howard University, Washington, D.C.; *HWS* 2: 215, 391-92; *HWS* 3: 346-47, 358.

8. See the proceedings for the NWSA and the AWSA for 1869 to 1876 in *HWS* 2.

9. *HWS* 3: 268-69.

10. *The Crisis*, 10 (August 1915), 188; Booker T. Washington, ed., *A New Negro for a New Century* (Chicago, 1900), 392.

11. *HWS* 3: 821, 827-28; Carole Ione, *Pride of Family: Four Generations of American Women of Color* (New York, 1991), 74-75; Joel Williamson, *After Slavery: The Negro in South Carolina During Reconstruction*, *1861-1877* (New York, 1975), 338; Nearly three decades later, in *HWS* 4 (1900), Virginia D. Young, president of the South Carolina suffragists, dated the beginning of the suffrage movement in her state as 1890, the year her association was founded, completely ignoring the activities of the inter-

racial woman's rights association founded twenty years before. Terborg-Penn, "Nineteenth Century Black Women and Woman Suffrage," 16.

12. *HWS* 3: 828.

13. Terborg-Penn, "Nineteenth Century Black Women and Woman Suffrage," 17.

14. Ellen Carol DuBois, *Feminism and Suffrage: The Emergence of an Independent Women's Movement in America, 1848-1869* (Ithaca, 1978), 201-02.

15. Speech of A.G. Riddle to the NWSA Anniversary Meeting, January 11, 1871, Washington, D.C., Cary Papers, Folder No. 7A.

16. Speech to the Judiciary Committee, Cary Papers, Folder No. 2.

17. *HWS* 3: 31, 72, 955.

18. *HWS* 3: 828, 833-834; Terborg-Penn, "Nineteenth Century Black Women and Woman Suffrage," 18.

19. Statement of Purpose, Colored Women's Progressive Franchise Association, Cary Papers, Folder No. 5.

20. Gertrude Mossell, "Woman Suffrage," *The New York Freeman,* December 26, 1885.

21. *HWS* 4, (reprint, New York, 1969), 898, 1104; F.E.W. Harper, "A Factor in Human Progress," *AME Church Review* 2 (1885), 14; *HWS,* 3: 273.

22. T. Thomas Fortune, "The New Afro-American Woman," *The New York Sun,* August 7, 1895; *The Woman's Era* (Boston), July 1896; Terborg-Penn, "Nineteenth Century Black Women and Woman Suffrage," 19.

23. Terborg-Penn, "Nineteenth Century Black Women and Woman Suffrage," 19.

24. M.A. McCurdy, "Duty of the State to the Negro," *Afro-American Encyclopedia,* ed. James T. Haley (Nashville, 1895), 141-45.

25. Frances E. Harper, *Sketches of Southern Life* (Philadelphia, 1896), 16.

26. Ida H. Harper, *History of Woman Suffrage,* vols. 5 and 6, (New York, 1900-1920), 105-06.

27. *HWS* 4: 358-59.

28. Rosalyn Terborg-Penn, "Discrimination Against Afro-American Women in the Woman's Movement, 1830-1920," 17-27, in *The Afro-American Woman: Struggles and Images,* Sharon Harley and Rosalyn Terborg-Penn, eds. (Port Washington, N.Y., 1978), 24-27.

29. Adella Logan, "Woman Suffrage," *The Colored American Magazine,* 9 (September 1905), 487.

30. Ibid., 488.

31. Ibid., 489.

32. Helen Laura Sumner Woodbury, *Equal Suffrage: The Results of an Investigation in Colorado Made for the Collegiate Equal Suffrage League of New York State* (New York, 1909), 70, 114-17.

33. Terborg-Penn, "Discrimination Against Afro-American Women," 21.

34. Paula Giddings, *When and Where I Enter: The Impact of Black Women on Race and Sex in America* (New York, 1984), 154.

35. Terborg-Penn, "Discrimination Against Afro-American Women," 21.

36. J.W. Gibson and W.H. Crogman, *Progress of a Race, Or the Remarkable Advancement of the Colored American* (Naperville, Ill., 1902, 1912), 216-20.

37. *Minneapolis Journal,* November 1900, Mary Church Terrell Papers, Manuscript Division, Library of Congress, Washington, D.C.; *HWS* 4: 358-59.

38. Ida B. Wells-Barnett, *Crusade for Justice: The Autobiography of Ida B. Wells-Barnett,* Alfreda Duster, ed. (Chicago, 1970), 345-47.

39. Aileen Kraditor, *The Ideas of the Woman Suffrage Movement, 1890-1920* (Garden City, N.Y., 1971), 213-14: Wells-Barnett, *Crusade for Justice,* 229-30.

40. *HWS* 5: 55, 59, 60 n. 1.

41. Walter White to Mary Church Terrell, March 14, 1919, Terrell Papers.

42. Terborg-Penn, "Discrimination Against Afro-American Women," 25.

43. Kraditor, 144-154; Marjorie Spruill Wheeler, *New Women of the New South: The Leaders of the Woman Suffrage Movement in the Southern States,* (New York, 1993), 101-102, 104, 110, 113-125.

44. *The Crisis* 17 (June 1919), 103.

45. *HWS* 5: 640.

46. *HWS* 5: 645-46.

47. Terborg-Penn, "Discrimination Against Afro-American Women," 25-26; *New York World,* March 1, 1919, Suffrage File, NAACP Papers, Manuscript Division, Library of Congress, Washington, D.C.

48. Terborg-Penn, "Discrimination Against Afro-American Women," 26.

49. Elizabeth C. Carter to Ida Husted Harper, April 10, 1919, Suffrage File, NAACP Papers.

50. *HWS* 6: 617; Giddings, 164.

51. Wheeler, 100-105, 143.

52. See Rayford W. Logan, *The Negro in the United States* (Princeton, 1957).

53. Rosalyn Terborg-Penn, "Afro-Americans in the Struggle for Woman Suffrage," Ph.D. diss., Howard University, 1977, 295-96.

54. Ibid, 301-02.

55. William Pickens, "The Woman Voter Hits the Color Line," *Nation* 3 (October 6, 1920): 372-73.

56. *Eleventh Annual Report of the NAACP for the Year 1920* (New York, 1921), 15, 25-30; Terborg-Penn, "Discontented Black Feminists," 267.

57. *The Crisis* 19 (November 1920), 23-25; *Negro Year Book,* 1921, 40.

58. Kenneth R. Johnson, "White Racial Attitudes as a Factor in the Arguments Against the Nineteenth Amendment," *Phylon* 31 (Spring 1970): 31-32, 35-37.

59. Giddings, 166.

60. Rosalyn Terborg-Penn, "Discontented Black Feminists: Prelude and Postscript to the Passage of the Nineteenth Amendment," 261-78, in *Decades of Discontent: The Women's Movement, 1920-1940,* edited by Lois Scharf and Joan M. Jenson (Westport, Conn., 1983), 267.

61. Ibid., 261, 267.

Page from The San Francisco Call, *July 4, 1909.* Sophia Smith Collection

Nine

The Suffrage Renaissance:

A New Image for a New Century, 1896–1910

Sara Hunter Graham

Editor's Introduction: One of the clearest and most fascinating examples in this volume of "rediscovering the woman suffrage movement" is this essay by historian Sara Hunter Graham who challenges long-accepted ideas about the woman suffrage movement at the turn of the century.

As the end of the nineteenth century approached, American suffragists were at last united in a single organization. The National Woman Suffrage Association and the American Woman Suffrage Association had come together to form the National American Woman Suffrage Association (NAWSA) in 1890. Susan B. Anthony quickly emerged as the organization's principal leader, serving as president from 1892 to 1900. Lucy Stone died in 1893, and Elizabeth Cady Stanton became somewhat estranged from the suffrage movement after the publication in 1895 of *The Woman's Bible* in which Stanton indicted Christianity for contributing to the subordination of women. Anthony, setting aside the militant tactics of the 1870s, now urged suffragists to avoid controversy and focus exclusively on gaining the vote. The NAWSA dedicated itself to building support throughout the nation and securing enough state victories that a federal amendment could be won.

The NAWSA leaders assisted suffragists throughout the nation in their efforts to obtain state suffrage amendments. The four thrilling victories in the Rocky Mountain states, however, stood out in contrast to countless defeats. The NAWSA's vigorous campaign in the South, an attempt to gain woman suffrage through the new state constitutions adopted during the 1890s, was unsuccessful. In fact, after the victories in Utah and Idaho in 1896, not a single state fell into the suffrage column until 1910.

The suffrage movement entered a stage that historian Eleanor Flexner in 1959—and suffrage historians ever since—describe as "the doldrums." As Flexner noted in her influential study, *Century of Struggle: The Woman's Rights Movement in the United States,* between 1896 and 1910 only six state referenda were held, and three of these were in Oregon. All of these failed, and the federal suffrage amendment "appeared moribund." Anthony retired from leadership, and her promising successor, Carrie Chapman Catt, rose to the presidency in 1900

157

only to be forced into retirement four years later due to the illness of her husband. Dr. Anna Howard Shaw, who served as NAWSA president from 1900 to 1915, is generally regarded by historians as an extraordinary orator but an inept administrator who presided over a highly de-centralized and ineffective NAWSA.

In this essay, however, Sara Hunter Graham offers a revisionist view of "the doldrums." Rather than a period of indecision and inactivity, Graham sees the period from 1896 to 1910 as one of careful and successful rebuilding, in which the leaders of the NAWSA deliberately reshaped the image of their movement. They also expanded their ranks in ways that greatly enhanced the prestige and effectiveness of the suffrage movement, recruiting wealthy and socially prominent women as well as a new generation of energetic and talented college-educated women.

The leadership for this "suffrage renaissance" came largely from Carrie Chapman Catt who, before having to resign as president, strengthened the NAWSA in many ways. This included the introduction at the national level of the "society plan," tested earlier in Colorado, that brought women of wealth, prestige, and influence into the suffrage movement—and made it quite difficult for anti-suffragists to stigmatize suffragists as fanatics.

Graham also informs us that determination to create a new and more saleable image led NAWSA leaders to rewrite the history of the woman suffrage movement, de-emphasizing controversial aspects of its past and virtually canonizing early leaders, particularly Anthony. They emphasized the progress women had made in terms of educational, professional, and legal reforms and pictured suffrage as the next logical step. Through new rituals, symbols and rhetoric, they promoted solidarity throughout an enlarged and diverse constituency united only by the desire to gain the vote for women. They also, Graham concludes, brought women into the movement by creating a new political culture based on membership in a single-interest pressure group that was far more attractive to women than the male political culture of saloons and smoke-filled rooms.

Thus, writes Graham, "the visionary cause of the pioneers" was transformed into "an eminently safe program" acceptable to middle-class club women and the social elite—a development NAWSA leaders regarded as "a necessary precondition that would eventually win the vote." As we will see in subsequent essays, other women who were not of the nation's elite would also be an important part of the massive and diverse coalition amassing in support of woman suffrage in the first two decades of the twentieth century; but as Graham makes clear, the NAWSA's successful efforts to make the movement attractive to women with leisure, funds, and influence to contribute to the cause played a crucial role in the success of the woman suffrage movement.

★　★　★　★　★

S UFFRAGISM IN THE EARLY 1900S was burdened with an image arising from its history that was in many respects a hindrance to further progress. Suffragists' advocacy of divorce reform, experimental dress, and feminist interpretations of the Bible had given the nineteenth-century movement a reputation of radicalism that was exploited by the enemies of suffrage to dissuade more conventional women from participating in the movement. Consequently, during the years 1896 to 1910 suffragists made little tangible progress in state referenda or federal amendment campaigns. No new states were won for suffrage and the federal amendment lay dormant in committee, prompting one historian to label the period "the doldrums."[1]

Despite the poor record generated by state suffrage campaigns, however, the "doldrums" were in reality an important period of growth and renewal for the movement. So significant were these years of regeneration that the period might more appropriately be called "the suffrage renaissance." Aware of the movement's negative image but unwilling to disavow the contributions of the pioneers, the suffragists of the National American Woman Suffrage Association (NAWSA) sought to create a tradition that could reconcile their heroic and somewhat controversial past with the association's pragmatic plans for the future. Developing a reinterpreted, sanitized version of the past, coupled with a sincere celebration of the heroism of pioneer suffragists, NAWSA leaders forged a link between the heroic age of confrontational politics and the new organizational approach to reform that appealed to mainstream American women.

The Referendum of 1895: An Anti-suffrage Victory

A turning point for the woman suffrage movement came on election day, 1895, when the Massachusetts State Legislature held a mock, or nonbinding, suffrage referendum. The State Legislature had been besieged for years by both suffragists and their opponents to act on the issue. In an effort to determine public opinion on the question, the legislature ruled that both women and men would vote in the mock referendum. In a singularly odd twist, both suffragists and anti-suffragists opposed the contest. The former objected to the nonbinding status of the vote, while the latter expressed disgust at being forced to cast a vote in order to demonstrate their aversion to voting. Anti-suffragists resolved their dilemma, however, by clever strategy, good organization, and effective propaganda.[2]

The Massachusetts Association Opposed to Further Extension of the Suffrage to Women (MAOFESW), founded in 1882 by Mrs. Henry O. Houghton and revitalized several months before the November 1895 referendum, attempted to persuade women to abstain from voting on the issue. Arguing that a low female voter turnout would indicate the wishes of Massachusetts women far more convincingly than a large "no" vote, anti-suffragists solicited contributions from well-wishers and embarked on a house-to-house canvass of Boston in order to bring their message to the people. Aiding the MAOFESW workers was a group of prominent Boston men who formed the Man Suffrage Association (MSA). Boasting a membership that included two ex-governors of the state, the president of Harvard University, noted religious leaders, professors, business men and attorneys, the MSA raised over $3,600 in less than two months at a time when the combined expenditures of all suffrage advocates was a mere $1,300.[3]

In contrast to the wealthy and prestigious individuals that opposed woman suffrage, suffragists relied on reformers such as Henry Blackwell, his daughter Alice Stone Blackwell, Julia Ward Howe, and Thomas Wentworth Higginson for leadership and support. Blackwell and Higginson had served together in the abolition movement, and along with Julia Ward Howe, were among the pioneers of the nineteenth-century woman's rights crusade. In addition to the aging but able reformers, Senator George F. Hoar agreed to preside over the Suffrage Referendum State Committee, formed in July 1895, to coordinate the suffrage forces. Unfortunately, most suffragists continued their long-time practice of suspending suffrage work during the summer months. By the time the committee reassembled in October, its members faced a well-organized and active opposition. The anti-suffragists had used the summer to their advantage, circularizing each ward, publicizing their position in the press, and plastering walls and fences with huge placards bearing the message, "Men and Women, Vote No!"[4]

More effective than these publicity measures, however, was the anti-suffrage strategy that encouraged women to abstain from voting. On November 5, antis gleefully pointed to the low female turnout as proof that the vast majority of Massachusetts women did not want the vote. Of approximately 612,000 women eligible to register only 42,676 did so, and of those, only 23,065 actually cast a vote. Although women voters supported the measure 22,204 to 861, not a single female vote was cast in forty-four towns. Of the 273,946 male votes cast, a resounding 186,976 men voted against the measure.[5] By shifting attention away from the actual female vote in the mock referendum and emphasizing instead the percentage of the female population that stayed away from the polls, the anti-suffragists managed to interpret the referendum as an overwhelming victory for their position.

The 1895 referendum cast a long shadow: never again would suffragists call for a test of strength if that test was to include the disfranchised members of their own sex, and never again would anti-suffragists believe that the majority of women favored woman suffrage. Although suffrage leaders continued to maintain that a large latent sentiment for their reform existed, the strategic course that they pursued as the new century unfolded revealed a pragmatic acceptance of the weakness of their position. There was little doubt among suffragists that the majority of Americans accepted the idea of a separate domestic sphere for women. Moreover, in taking the position of defending the status quo and opposing any change in the status of women, the anti-suffragists had occupied the high ground in the coming battle for the vote.

During the Massachusetts referendum campaign, MAOFESW had demonstrated its ability to mobilize an influential constituency, utilize modern advertising methods, and raise large sums of money to finance their work. The suffragists, although dedicated to their cause, were unable to compete with the superior funding and efficiency of their opponents. Moreover, the anti-suffragists had effectively turned the referendum into a demonstration of indifference on the part of Massachusetts women, and had placed the suffrage forces in the defensive position of supporting a democratic reform that the majority of women did not desire. In the aftermath of the contest, many Massachusetts suffrage clubs lost members or disbanded completely, while MAOFESW and other anti-suffrage organizations grew in size and strength. The referendum of 1895, repeatedly cited in national periodicals and in anti-suffrage tracts as proof of female indifference to woman suffrage, shaped the opposition to suffrage for years to come.

More immediately, however, the 1895 Massachusetts referendum forced suffragists to reassess the strengths and weaknesses of their organization. The lesson of 1895 seemed to point toward a continuation of the NAWSA policy of educating the public to the benefits of woman suffrage, but with a new emphasis on effective organization and strong financial support. In addition, suffragists slowly began to recognize the need for a new public image. In response to anti-suffrage propaganda that characterized them as fanatics, and in an effort to attract a larger, more stable membership, suffragists in the first decade of the twentieth century attempted to win respect for their cause and legitimize their organization through a variety of tactics. Their efforts demonstrated a new awareness of the importance of public opinion and marked a turning point in the movement itself. Suffragism of old, shaped by the dedication of a few faithful friends, was to become the movement of the masses, and as such, had to be packaged in a form more attractive to a wider audience.

The Society Plan

Most suffragists believed that the greatest obstacle to woman suffrage was not anti-suffrage opposition or male recalcitrance but rather the indifference of American women. Doubtless many agreed with one anti-suffragist's diagnosis of the problem her opponents faced. "What [the suffrage movement] has to overcome," she explained, "is not an argument but a feeling."[6] Even when this "feeling" manifested itself in overt hostility to the movement, suffrage leaders remained convinced that their foremost task was to exorcise the demon of indifference by converting the apathetic masses to the idea of distaff democracy. And in an age that saw the proliferation of female associations and voluntary societies, it is not surprising that suffrage advocates turned to women's clubs for their organizational model and to society women for the talisman of respectability.

The active recruitment of prominent women by NAWSA officials was not an innovation at the turn of the century; pioneer suffragists had made repeated efforts along those lines throughout the Gilded Age. One of the first successful attempts, however, came in 1893, when Lucy Stone and Carrie Catt attempted to organize the prominent women of Denver, Colorado, according to the "society plan." Although the Colorado Equal Suffrage Association claimed a small but dedicated number of "respectable middle class women," Stone believed that an untapped reservoir of suffrage support existed among wealthy Denver clubwomen. Stone wrote to Denver civic leader Mrs. John R. Hanna, imploring her to make Catt's acquaintance and help her protégée organize the city's leading citizens for suffrage. Hanna duly asked the young suffragist to dinner, and after a long discussion, the two embarked upon an ambitious plan to recruit the city's society women for woman suffrage. Within weeks of their initial meeting, the Denver Equal Suffrage League was formed, composed almost entirely of wealthy clubwomen and socialites. One of the League's first functions, a large public meeting ostensibly in honor of Catt, featured a long list of distinguished speakers from Denver's political and financial circles and was attended by what local suffragists considered the city's "best people." "A most marked result," wrote one Denver suffragist, "was that not one paper in Denver said a word of ridicule or even mild amusement concerning suffragists," and went on to attribute the press's favorable coverage to the presence for the first time of prominent citizens among the suffrage ranks.[7] Moreover, Catt's society plan was hailed as the crucial factor in the suffrage referendum in 1893, when Colorado joined Wyoming as the second woman suffrage state.

With her election to the NAWSA presidency in 1900, Catt laid plans to recruit prestigious women of wealth to the suffrage fold at the national level. Initially, most of the NAWSA leadership agreed with Catt's society plan. Susan B. Anthony, for example, endorsed the idea, and urged NAWSA Corresponding Secretary Rachel Foster Avery to include in the annual convention program a list of all delegates and alternates in order to display prominently the names and addresses of prestigious converts to the cause.[8] Moreover, Catt asked Business Committee members to compile lists of influential clubwomen, ministers and politicians from which to solicit new members, and included well-heeled men as well as society women in her recruitment scheme. Suffragists also sought to win over influential labor and agricultural leaders, and drew up lists of union officials and Grangers for postal propaganda.[9]

In 1904, the Association acknowledged the society plan at the annual convention, when the official plan of work for the year recommended that suffragists become active in civic, charitable, or educational work in their communities.[10] Through local clubs and organizations, suffrage advocates could recruit wealthy women with both time and money to devote to the cause. Experience gained in club work could be turned to account in suffrage societies, enabling suffrage leaders to draw on a ready-made constituency already trained in parliamentary procedure, public speaking and fund-raising. Notably missing in the list of organizations to recruit, however, was the burgeoning black women's club movement. The unspoken assumption of NAWSA leaders was that the society plan was for whites only.

In addition to recruiting from white civic or charitable organizations, suffragists sought new members through parlor meetings, the traditional form of middle-class female assembly. Held in the privacy of the home, parlor meetings were deemed respectable by even the most modest Victorian women, and served to attract a conservative set that would have blanched at attending a public lecture or rally. One suffrage advocate described her role as a parlor meeting speaker in St. Paul:

> You had these little afternoon gatherings of women, maybe six or eight women. You had a cup of tea. A little social gathering. While we were drinking tea, I gave them a little talk and they asked questions about what was going on.... It was alot [sic] better, I thought at the time, than to have a lecture. Because a lot of them wouldn't go to a lecture. And it was what I could do.[11]

Occasionally, professional suffrage speakers would address parlor gatherings in the afternoon before a major nighttime suffrage rally. In this way advocates could reach both the timid and the bold; suffragists believed that through gradual education, encouragement, and attention to individual sensibilities, even the most timid souls could be transformed into "new women."

Although the days of ridicule experienced by nineteenth-century female reformers had passed, speaking in a public forum remained unthinkable for many women. Through the parlor meeting, elite women could gather in a nonthreatening environment to discuss a wide range of topics. Woman suffrage, birth control, municipal reform, and labor conditions found their way into parlor conversations, along with the more traditional subjects of literature, history, and religion. Some women, like those who attended the Monday Club of Richburg, New York, combined the new with the old: on alternating weeks, club members turned their attention from New York history and bird-watching to the history of women and pro-suffrage arguments.[12] The growing interest in nontraditional subjects was reflected in other conservative women's groups like the General Federation of Women's Clubs (GFWC), an organization that refused to endorse woman suffrage until the second decade of the twentieth century. Evidence of this trend was demonstrated by the newly elected president of the GFWC when she informed the biennial convention that:

> Dante is dead. He has been dead for several centuries, and I think it is time that we dropped the study of his *Inferno* and turned our attention to our own.[13]

By concentrating their efforts on prosperous though conservative women, NAWSA suffragists sought to take advantage of the awakened interest in public affairs manifested by the GFWC and other women's organizations.

Initially, the "society plan" drew applause from many suffragists who had labored unsuccessfully to recruit new members in the past. Active recruitment in the woman suffrage state of Colorado, for example, drew influential women

Carrie Chapman Catt, c. 1890.
University of Rochester

NAWSA headquarters in Warren, Ohio,
c. 1900. Frank Corbeil Collection

into the crusade and provided workers in non-suffrage states with ammunition with which to refute the negative stereotypes that had plagued the movement. One suffragist told congressmen at the 1904 Judiciary Hearing on Woman Suffrage that a leading anti-suffragist, when introduced to several prominent Colorado women, expressed admiration of their ability and dedication. "As social leaders, as philanthropists, as club women and church women, she had swallowed them whole and found them delicious"; the suffragist testified, they only disagreed with her after she knew them also to be suffragists."[14]

While many society women limited their involvement in the suffrage crusade to timely financial support, others played a more important part in the movement. Wealthy New York socialite Mrs. Clarence McKay, for example, organized her own suffrage league, contributed large sums to the cause, and recruited many of that state's most influential women into the suffrage camp.[15] Virginia's Equal Suffrage League included prominent Virginia writers Ellen Glasgow and Mary Johnston, as well as the great-granddaughters of Thomas Jefferson and George Mason.[16] Name recognition, handsome contributions, and social prestige were welcome boons to an organization that had borne the stigma of fanaticism for decades.

Though few NAWSA members questioned the strategy that brought such bounty, the "society plan" led a minority to protest. To some suffragists the "society plan" smacked of impropriety and elitism. "I could not help wondering what Lucy Stone would have thought to have seen the Special representative of the cause she gave her life to, promenading in low neck and arms bare to the shoulders at the Governor's reception," one elderly suffragist wrote in despair. "Mrs. [Evelyn H.] Belden worked bravely...according to her ideas of the right way—*the Society Way*—but there are some old workers who do not think that some of the methods tended to elevate the cause." [17] Others, like Harriet Stanton Blatch, chafed under the yoke of gradualism. Blatch characterized the suffrage movement at the turn of the century as "a rut worn deep and ever deeper," and in 1907 founded the League of Self-Supporting Women in an effort to escape the tedium and elitism embodied in the NAWSA's "society plan." [18] New York Socialists like Ida Crouch Hazlett viewed with apprehension the new emphasis on upper-class status, and spoke out against mainstream suffragists' "snobbish truckling to the women of influence and social position." [19] So pronounced was the effort to woo socialites that one popular periodical labeled the suffrage crusade a "gilt-chair movement" in reference to suffragists' swank gatherings.[20]

Creating a Suffrage Tradition

Though the "gilt-chair movement" offended some, most suffragists believed that their newly won sense of respectability more than compensated for what little criticism the society plan generated. And in keeping with the new emphasis on image at the expense of ideological unity, NAWSA leaders took steps to legitimize their organization through the creation of a formal suffrage historical tradition. On a simple level, tradition may be used to legitimize events, groups, or causes by associating them with the rhetoric, rituals, or personalities of an historic past. A political party, for example, may employ tradition to establish a link between its heroic past and its present platform, as in the recurrent allusions to "The Great Emancipator" made by Republicans trolling for black votes. Used in this way, tradition may represent a series of unspoken assumptions and loyalties, and serve as a symbol of organizational unity.

At a deeper level, however, tradition may mask the varied ideological perspectives of a diverse constituency with what one historian has called its "undefined universality." [21] The trappings of tradition allow leaders to de-emphasize conflicting opinions and ideals by focusing attention on non-controversial rituals and rhetoric. Moreover, the creation or reinterpretation of traditions may help to steer a group or movement away from an unsavory past or a discarded ideology without the discussion or disagreement engendered by the democratic process. A salient characteristic of tradition is that, for all its presumed foundation in the past, it can be manipulated with singular ease to suit the purposes of the present.

The chief components of the "new" suffrage tradition were a mixture of established, or genuine, rituals, and reinterpreted symbols, rhetoric, and practices that had been customized over time to suit the changing nature of the movement. One of the oldest and most important elements of suffrage tradition was an authorized history of women, with suffrage activism as its focal point. Suffragists had long insisted on the place of women in history. In this regard, nineteenth-century suffrage associations may be considered to have been the first American organizations to promote actively women's history as a discipline. The monumental *History of Woman Suffrage,* begun by Elizabeth Cady Stanton, Susan B. Anthony, and Matilda Joslyn Gage in 1881, was more than propaganda for the cause; to suffrage advocates it filled the void in history textbooks left by the omission of American women.[22] The multi-volume history was continued until the passage of the Nineteenth Amendment in 1920, and remains a testimony to the suffragists' conviction that the women's rights movement deserved a permanent place in history. One of Susan B. Anthony's last acts was to arrange for shipment of the unsold volumes, totaling over ten tons in weight, to NAWSA headquarters, from which the books were distributed to every major library in the country.[23]

The NAWSA showed a commitment to women's history by its efforts to disseminate works on or by women. Beginning in 1902, provisions were made to establish circulating suffrage libraries. These libraries gave women access to the major works on feminist theory and literature, as well as to biographies of famous women and histories of the women's rights movement. The 1903 NAWSA Plan of Work included the compilation of a catalog of woman suffrage literature, to be donated to libraries to encourage the use of such materials. Carrie Chapman Catt showed great enthusiasm for both the catalog and suffrage libraries, and urged each NAWSA suffrage league to appoint a committee on libraries to keep women's history before the public. "Perhaps someday we shall have in the Congressional Library in Washington a story of the work of women...," Catt mused to her friend Alice Stone Blackwell. "We must keep a careful record of our progress for the story is an important one."[24]

Many suffragists shared Catt's vision of the long-term significance of their cause, and despaired over the omission of women from traditional American histories of the period. "There never was another nation with as many parents as we have had," one suffragist wrote in disgust, "but they have all been fathers—Pilgrim Fathers, Plymouth Fathers, Forefathers, Revolutionary Fathers, City Fathers, Church Fathers—fathers of every description but no mothers!"[25] In response to such discontent, Pauline Steinem, chairman of NAWSA's Committee of Education, conducted a rudimentary investigation in 1909 of history and civics textbooks used in the public schools. Steinem wrote to four hundred school superintendents and twenty-six textbook publishing companies in an attempt to survey educators and publishers on the extent of female representation in history books. Although some responses pointed to a handful of famous women like Martha Washington and Betsy Ross who had found their way into the schoolbooks, most of those surveyed replied that they had never considered the problem at all. Steinem attributed lack of recognition to the "masculine point of view which has dominated civilization," and vehemently protested against the impression conveyed by textbooks "that this world has been made by men and for men."[26]

Steinem's findings, coupled with a growing frustration with "the masculine point of view" as it related to suffragism, led NAWSA officials to take their message directly into the schools in 1910. One plan of attack was the idea of suffrage debates to be held in classrooms across America. The NAWSA initially furnished a packet of debate material at a modest price, including citations for both pro- and anti-suffrage works, but by 1912 debaters could turn to the latest volume in the Debaters Handbook Series, *Selected Articles on Woman Suffrage*.[27] School debates offered an opportunity to educate the young on the role of women in history, as well as attracting free publicity for the movement. As one suffragist pointed out, "get the young people involved and you [also] catch mothers!"[28] The injection of women's history or woman suffrage into the schools, while applauded by suffrage advocates, outraged anti-suffragists. "The woman suffrage question has no place in the schools," one anti-suffrage press release maintained, and went on to insist that as long as parents were divided on the issue, school boards should refrain from tampering with textbooks.[29]

Evolution of American Women

Suffragists' efforts to place women's history, and particularly suffrage history, in classrooms and public libraries reflects the NAWSA's belief in the importance of suffrage recruitment. On the one hand, suffragists' enthusiasm for women's history could be interpreted as the natural desire for self-gratification and glory that a heroic history can bestow upon its participants. Legendary feats and heroine-worship can help to sustain an organization in the face of adversity, and so it was with the suffrage movement. But beyond its capacity to distract and sustain a troubled membership, suffragists used the idea of women's history to provide justification for their cause while simultaneously shaping that history to fit the needs of their movement. In a sense, the suffragists created a "great woman" history that ran parallel to the contemporary historical works that excluded them. And throughout that history runs the recurrent theme of the steady evolution of women toward a egalitarian, if distant, utopia.

Advocates of suffrage did not question the belief that women were subject to the forces of evolution and were making progress throughout the ages. This sense of progress marked the rhetoric of suffrage orators like Anna Howard Shaw, who made repeated references in her speeches to the gains that women had won through decades of sacrifice. Shaw told one audience:

> The real reformer does not judge of the reform from the day or of an hour, but traces its progress from the beginning, and no human being with the eye of faith can fail to see traversing the whole progress of our movement a divinity shaping our ends…and that divinity is the gospel of democracy.[30]

Others, like writer Ida Husted Harper, drew on the theory of female evolution in widely circulated articles and pamphlets. In a *North American Review* article, for example, Harper first traced the history of the franchise in America, and pointed out that religious, property, educational, and racial qualifications had all been abandoned for male Americans. She then cited the changing status of women from colonial times to the twentieth century that resulted from hard-won legal reforms and educational advancements. In the area of education Harper found the most conclusive evidence of progress: in 1902, for example, there were more girls than boys enrolled in high, normal, and manual-training schools, and over a third of all college students were female. Moreover, of the total number of college degrees conferred in 1902, almost half went to female graduates. Coupled with statistics on the dramatic rise in the number of women entering the professions, Harper's findings documented the evolution of American women to an audience eager to believe in progress.[31]

From an unenlightened past into a clean, well-lighted future, the women of an unwritten history were made to march, and their suffragist creators made the most of their progress. "Women [of the past] lived in a twilight life, a half-life apart, and looked out and saw men as shadows walking," wrote M. Cary Thomas, president of Bryn Mawr and ardent suffragist:

> Now women have won the right to higher education and to economic independence. The right to become citizens of the State is the next and inevitable consequence of education and work outside the home. We have gone so far; we must go farther. We cannot go back.[32]

If evolution of women and the inevitability of their progress provided the philosophical foundation of early women's history, accounts of educational, legal, and professional advances served as testimonials to the doctrine of female progress. Women's history as seen by suffragists was comprised of a factual body shaped by an ideologically informed philosophy, or in other words, a content and meaning that were intricately entwined and mutually supportive.

History of this sort was important to the suffrage movement in several ways. First, NAWSA leaders drew from women's, and particularly suffrage, history a tradition of leadership handed down from pioneer suffragists and women's rights activists, canonized in the *History of Woman Suffrage* and hagiographic accounts of the movement's early workers, and imbued with the legacy of a century of heroic struggle. As the lineal successors of Anthony, Stanton, and Stone, twentieth-century leaders found legitimation for their position through the celebration of, and association with, what might be called the "founding mothers" of their organization.

The Creation of Consensus

For the NAWSA rank and file the reinterpreted suffrage tradition bridged the gap between the content and meaning of their history. NAWSA membership rolls contained the names of radical feminists, timid society women, socialists, moderates, and states' rights southerners; the old adage that "politics makes strange bedfellows" was especially true of the suffrage movement at the turn of the century. Suffragist leaders used both genuine and reinterpreted traditions to bind this diverse constituency together and to create what may be called a movement psychology. Through ritual and pageantry, selected events and individuals were molded into a form of popular history that encapsulated both the pasteurized version of the past and a diluted dose of suffrage ideology.

Perhaps the most revered of all NAWSA traditions centered on the veneration of selected suffrage pioneers. Since the formation of the NAWSA in 1890, a generous part of every convention was dedicated to the movement's early adherents. This celebration of the pioneers took several forms, including memorials for deceased workers, greetings from those too old or too infirm to attend, and tributes from younger members who recognized the contributions of their predecessors. During her years as president, Susan B. Anthony often spoke of the pioneers' achievements, using the time between speakers to recognize informally members of the audience who had served the cause for years. Moreover, her stories of what one suffragist called "the cabbage and rotten-egg days" served to immerse converts in a kind of "living suffrage history," providing both role models and a heroic legacy to inspire the new recruits.[33] Formal recognition for the movement's early advocates was also included in convention programs in the form of "Evenings with the Pioneers," and in 1910, a "Decoration Day for our Heroines" became a permanent suffrage tradition.[34]

NAWSA leaders' interpretation of the suffrage pioneers, however, was strangely reticent about some of their predecessors' more controversial actions. Retaining the philosophy of female progress and the legend of heroism and self-sacrifice, NAWSA leaders presented to their constituents a sanitized version of the past that robbed the pioneers of much of their color, complexity, and principles. Issues such as divorce reform, racial equality, and feminist religious reinterpretations were quietly dropped from the suffrage liturgy in an effort to pasteurize the pioneer experience. Most notable in this reinterpreted history of the movement was the disappearance from the suffrage canon of none other than Elizabeth Cady Stanton, one of the founders of the Seneca Falls Convention and, with Anthony, a dynamic force in the nineteenth-century suffrage crusade. Although both women worked together for decades and shared many of the same ideas and goals for the movement, Anthony's vision of the cause was more pragmatic and in some ways more limited than that of Stanton. For Anthony, the primary goal of the suffrage crusade was unity with other women's groups to form a broad-based constituency for the vote for women. As time passed, Anthony became convinced that rather than addressing working women's issues in order to bring them into the suffrage fold, it was easier to recruit elite women to the cause. Moreover, their advocacy of suffrage would provoke less hostility among the public and the press.

Stanton shared Anthony's vision of unity, but envisioned the movement as an open platform for any issue that concerned women. Rather than narrowing the focus of the NAWSA to elites, Stanton urged suffragists to "stir up a whole group of new victims from time to time, by turning our guns on new strongholds."[35] True to her word, she had over the years endorsed a variety of reforms considered

Maud Wood Park (left) and Florence Luscomb, 1913.
Schlesinger Library, Radcliffe College

radical for the time. Divorce reform, feminist revision of the Bible, dress reform, separation of church and state—all were subjects for her pen. Stanton's writings and speeches constantly put forward the notion that once women had the vote, they would use their ballots to enact an explicit political agenda including these and other reforms. Her radicalism can best be seen in her belief that all movements for freedom were linked inextricably, and that suffrage was part and parcel of that radical tradition. Stanton's radicalism, however, was on a collision course with the NAWSA's growing conservatism. By the time of her death in 1902, she was largely eclipsed in suffrage hagiography by the less-threatening image of her old friend Anthony. More importantly, the NAWSA's disavowal of Stanton signaled the narrowing of the movement's goals and constituency that was to be a crucial component of the twentieth-century campaign for the vote.[36]

Building a Suffrage Constituency

A second and equally important suffrage tradition, although similar in some respects to that of the pioneers, was in fact the creation of twentieth-century suffragists. Beginning in 1906, NAWSA conventions regularly featured "College Evenings," events designed to appeal to the young, well-educated recruits who increasingly flocked to suffrage functions. Active recruitment of college women was the brainchild of Boston suffragists Maud Wood Park and Inez Haynes Gillmore. While students at Radcliffe, Park and Gillmore had been initiated into the suffrage ranks by Massachusetts Woman Suffrage Association (MWSA) president Alice Stone Blackwell. With Blackwell's encouragement, Park and Gill-more founded the Massachusetts College Equal Suffrage League in 1900.[37] Their efforts were so successful that at the NAWSA annual convention in 1906, dele-gates overwhelmingly voted to establish a national College Equal Suffrage League.

The delegates' enthusiasm for the new organization was in part a result of the first of many NAWSA "College Evenings," held at the Lyric Theater in Baltimore on February 8, 1906. Susan B. Anthony, M. Carey Thomas, and Mary E. Garrett had conceived the idea of such an evening in the fall of 1905, when Anthony, worried that the suffrage convention would not be well received in conserva-tive Baltimore, urged her two co-workers to do what they could "to make [the convention] respectable."[38] The three women planned the event both to involve new workers in the convention program and to "illustrate distinctly the new type of womanhood—the College Woman" as an integral part of their movement. Together they incorporated the disparate yet vital elements of hero-ism, respectability, and progress into a suffrage tradition that symbolized the new membership, methods, and image of twentieth-century suffragism.

The president of The Johns Hopkins University presided over the 1906 "Col-lege Evening," and area college women clad in cap and gown served as ushers for the event. With pioneer suffragists Clara Barton and Julia Ward Howe seated on the podium, an array of college presidents, professors, and deans spoke on the topic, "What has been accomplished for the higher education of women by Susan B. Anthony and other woman suffragists." One by one, the distinguished guests reminded the audience of the pioneers' achievements, and lauded their efforts to open the doors of higher education for women. "We are indebted to [the pioneer women]," Vassar historian Lucy M. Salmon told the audience, "for making it possible for us to spend our lives in fruitful work rather than in idle tears."[39] Others singled out Susan B. Anthony for special praise. "The women of today," one speaker maintained, "may well feel that it is Miss Anthony who has made life possible for them."[40] By linking the advancement of women's educa-tion to the pioneers, and in particular, to pioneer suffragists, College Evening dignitaries firmly bound a new generation of women to the historical continu-um of the movement. Moreover, by presenting carefully selected early suffrag-ists in a light that was clearly attractive to a college audience, College Evening speakers attributed to them an inflated influence on a development that was both respectable and popular.

In the years that followed the first College Evening, NAWSA leaders increas-ingly exploited this pioneer/college connection, and in doing so further steered clear of the radicalism of the movement's origins. According to Maud Wood Park, the purpose of the College Equal Suffrage League was to help college women "realize their debt to the women who worked so hard for them, and to make them understand that one way to pay that debt is to fight the battle in the quarter of the field in which it is still to be won, to make them realize the oblig-ation of opportunity."[41] The "debt to the pioneers" became a kind of suffrage slogan, and was even adopted as the title of a 1907 Boston program to honor long-time suffrage workers. At that event, Park listed in her concluding remarks the names of women's rights activists including Frances Wright, Margaret Fuller, Ernestine Rose, and the Grimké sisters and the dates that they began their agitation, pointing out that many women's colleges were founded at the same time. "It seems to me," Park concluded, "that the so-called higher education, along with many other improvements in the standing of women, owes a heavy debt to the movement which advocated equal rights." [42] The debt to the pioneers would also resurface yearly at NAWSA conventions, as College Evening took its place beside such regular traditions as pioneer memorials and the president's address.

The Suffrage Saint

A third and final suffrage tradition grew out of both College Evening and pioneer memorials, and served as the touchstone of twentieth-century suffrage ideology, rhetoric, and ritual. The creation of this potent symbol occurred over a number of years, but reached fruition in March 1906, with the death of Susan B. Anthony. As past president of the NAWSA and as a representative of pioneer activism, Anthony had attained celebrity status within the movement long before her death. NAWSA conventions were carefully scheduled to coincide with the aging reformer's birthday, and convention-goers could count on lavish celebrations, emotional speeches, and a personal word or two from the celebrity herself. In addition to her appearances at the annual conventions, Anthony had travelled extensively for years and was well-known to suffragists throughout America, who increasingly viewed her as the living embodiment of their cause. Local fund-raisers often took the form of "Susan B. Anthony Day," and state suffrage convention badges and programs routinely bore her picture. [43] Such was her stature in the movement that during her later years she often witnessed her own apotheosis. In 1903, for example, while dining on bluefish and "diplomate pudding" with a Brooklyn, New York, suffrage league, she heard a series of speeches presented on the topic "Susan B. Anthony: Lessons and Inspirations from Her Life." [44]

Ida Husted Harper was in part responsible for Anthony's transformation from reviled fanatic to adored leader. Her two-volume biography of the reformer was published in 1898, and provided readers with the day-to-day occurrences of her subject's life in almost Boswellian detail. A third volume, added after Anthony's death, extended the work to more than sixteen hundred pages and included excerpts from over a hundred highly favorable editorials on Anthony that appeared after her death. [45] In addition to her work as a hagiographer, Harper proved to be unsurpassed as a nascent press agent. In keeping with the NAWSA's new emphasis on respectability, she composed an article in 1903 for *Pearson's Magazine* entitled "Miss Anthony at Home" that portrayed the aging suffragist as "domestic in every fiber of her body." [46] With an eye to her prospective female audience, Harper cloaked her subject in the rhetoric of domesticity with such "feminine" attributes as neatness, hospitality, self-sacrifice, patience, and loyalty. According to the article, "Aunt Susan" sat down at the breakfast table looking "like a lovely grandmother," to a meal "strictly of the feminine order." Later she embarked upon a day of womanly pursuits that included cooking, cleaning, and sewing. "Miss Anthony," concluded the article, "never has suggested ways for repairing the damages of society with one-half the skill she employed in teaching her nieces her wonderful method of darning rents in garments and household linens."[47] Through her literary efforts, Harper helped to replace the stereotypical image of masculinized fanatic with a non-threatening feminine heroine imbued with domestic virtues.

The sanctification of Susan B. Anthony, however, was not completed until her death in 1906. At the NAWSA convention of that year, the aging reformer appeared before her devoted disciples for the last time. Her health gone, she exhorted the delegates in a faltering voice to continue in the great work begun at Seneca Falls, and closed her remarks with the words, "Failure is impossible!" After the convention closed, she traveled to Washington to attend the annual Congressional Hearings but was too ill to leave her bed. Returning for the last time to her home in Rochester, New York, Anthony was attended by her niece and sister, and in her final hours, by Anna Howard Shaw. Profoundly shaken by the loss of her closest friend, Shaw would help to create the most enduring and vital of suffrage traditions: the suffrage saint.[48]

Like Harper, Anna Howard Shaw was uniquely fitted to the role of hagiographer. She met Anthony at a suffrage meeting in 1888, and a lifelong friendship had ensued. Shaw clearly worshipped the older woman. One of her favorite stories featured the seventy-year-old Anthony, wrapped in a dressing gown and talking until dawn, "foreseeing everything, forgetting nothing, and sweeping me with her in her flight toward our common goal until I...experienced an almost dizzy sense of exhilaration."[49] Such was Shaw's devotion that, in her 1915 autobiography, Anthony figures almost as prominently as does the author herself. As both president of the NAWSA and an Anthony disciple, Shaw hurried to Rochester when word came that the end was near. What followed would provide an important source of inspiration for the cult of personality that adopted Anthony as its patron saint.

Deathbed scenes were a popular literary device for turn-of-the-century novelists, and it is therefore not surprising that Shaw chose to record the scene she witnessed in both the periodical press and in her autobiography. Indeed, her vivid description of Anthony's pale visage and prophetic words lend credence to the expression, "life imitates art." Two passages in particular express the motif Shaw sought to capture. On the last afternoon of her life, Anthony suddenly began to recite the names of the women as this "final roll-call...seemed to file past her dying eyes that day in an endless, shadowy review," Shaw wrote, and she quoted Anthony as saying "I know the sacrifices they have made, but it has all been worth while!" With this benediction, Anthony lapsed into silence for a time, but rallied once more in order to assure Shaw that, after death, she would continue to be an active force in the woman suffrage movement. "Who knows?" Anthony speculated, "Perhaps I may be able to do more for the Cause after I am gone than while I am here." [50]

In a sense she was right. Anthony's vision (or Shaw's invention?) of "the shadowy review," coupled with her prophecy of a kind of mystic activism beyond the grave, suggests a type of secular sanctification well-known to readers of sentimental fiction of the period. The theme of suffrage saint was also conspicuous in a selection of poems written about Anthony and published after her death in Volume Three of Harper's biography. "She is not dead but more alive/ than in her fairest earthly days," one poet proclaimed, while another pictured her "with eyes that looked beyond the gates of death" and crowned by a "halo of her venerable age." [51] Perhaps the most explicit example of sanctification was by John Russell Hayes, who poetically recorded Anthony's entry into a supernatural suffrage procession:

> And then my vision faded,
> And a lordly melody rolled
> As down celestial vistas
> The saintly company strolled.
> But the face of that latest comer
> I longest kept in sight—
> So ardent with consecration,
> So lit with angelic light...
> Crowned is she and sainted
> In heavenly halls above
> Who freely gave for her sisters
> A life of boundless love. [52]

On March 15, 1906, the suffrage saint was buried in Rochester, New York. The mayor of Rochester, the president of Rochester University, and other local dignitaries were present, in addition to suffrage and temperance leaders, aging abolitionists, college women, friends, and family members. Despite a heavy snowfall, an estimated crowd of ten thousand assembled outside the church, pressing against the doors and windows in order to hear Anna Howard Shaw's eulogy. Touching briefly upon Anthony's "womanly attributes," she then described her subject's heroism and devotion to the cause. "There is no death for such as she," Shaw concluded, and predicted that "the ages will come to revere her name." [53] When the church doors were opened at the close of the service, crowds of mourners streamed past the body. One mourner in particular caught the attention of some reporters: an elderly black woman, covered with snow and leaning heavily on a crutch, paused by the coffin and sobbed aloud into a frost-covered handkerchief. Other journalists chose to feature an aged black man, also limping, who took as a *memento mori* a single leaf from the funeral wreath. The heroic eulogies, patriotic rhetoric and weeping black spectators reminded some witnesses of another fallen emancipator. Describing the long line of mourners who filed past the body, one observer called them "the plain people, the people Susan B. Anthony and Abraham Lincoln loved." After the long procession had passed, a female honor guard from the university escorted the coffin past houses draped in black to the grave site where Shaw delivered the final words.[54]

In the days that followed, friends worked to ensure a lasting memory for their patron saint. Rochester educators named an elementary school after Susan B. Anthony, a local church commissioned a stained-glass window bearing her likeness, and women's clubs, temperance groups, and civic organizations honored her with memorials. Ida Husted Harper collected over a thousand editorials that eulogized Anthony, including one from the anti-suffrage *New York Times* lauding "the tender, womanly loveliness of the great reformer."[55]

Suffragists across the nation held memorial services similar to the one conducted by the Kentucky Equal Rights Association a week after Anthony's death. Mary Clay, a long-time suffragist and descendant of Henry Clay, "The Great Compromiser," presided over the service that took place in the Clay family home. In the center of the parlor draped in yellow satin and black crepe stood a large picture of Susan B. Anthony, flanked by a small candle in a pink candlestick, a souvenir from the suffrage leader's eightieth birthday celebration. On a nearby table was a smaller portrait of the reformer, surrounded by photographs of Lucy Stone, Elizabeth Cady Stanton, and Isabella Beecher Hooker. After a roll call of pioneer suffragists and a sketch of the reformer's work for women's rights, the assembly heard a series of elegies and a dramatic reading based on Anthony's final days. Following a rosary and benediction, the women sang "Nearer, My God, To Thee" and adjourned for refreshments.[56]

The nature of the Kentucky memorial service closely followed the form routinely employed by literary, church, or civic gatherings of women, but with a suffrage theme. Within this structure, songs, poems, and dramatic readings provided a thread of continuity between old forms and new meanings. The intimate atmosphere of the parlor meeting encouraged participation by women who would have shied away from speaking to a larger audience. Overtones of religious ritual endowed the service with both familiarity and stately respectability in accord with the tastes of the times. The parlor decor approached ecclesiastical parody with its makeshift altar and display of icons. In addition, the service followed a quasi-liturgical pattern, employing both poetic and prose readings and ending with the litany of the rosary and the benediction.

Kentucky suffragists also shaped the memorial service to suit the private agenda of their movement. Tradition played an important role: the veneration of the pioneers, the idea of a parallel women's history, and the philosophy of female progress were all incorporated into the ceremony. In her posthumous role, Susan B. Anthony became what no living woman could be: a universally shared symbol of the cause whose very name could conjure a constellation of images and sentiment. Across the nation clubwomen and suffragists met for similar services.[57] Within a decade Anthony had become, like Lincoln and Altgeld before her, part of the common mental property of Progressive Americans. Her picture was hung beside those of the Founding Fathers' in schoolrooms across America, her memory achieving a measure of the vague immortality accorded to the heroes of American democracy. In 1917, for example, Eugene V. Debs characterized her as "synonymous with the cause of human freedom and equal rights,...a moral heroine, an apostle of progress, a herald of the coming day."[58]

The Formation of a Female Political Culture

Mary Clay's memorial service, with its quaint sentimentality and solemn naiveté, summons up a lost world of women, conceived within the pages of popular fiction of the period, adorned with the trappings of Victorian respectability, and bound by parlor walls. Although trivial when compared to the larger course of world affairs, it reminds us that political participation for women at the turn of the century was not accomplished merely by the conversion of Congress or the ratification of an amendment. Instead, women entered the political arena through a lengthy process that included such seemingly apolitical institutions as historical biography, sentimental fiction and parlor meetings, as well as more familiar processes of state referenda campaigns, lobbyist activity, and direct political coercion. It would be unjust to downplay the early efforts of women's political organization. Given the high degree of female participation in Progressive Era movements like temperance, child-labor reform, and civic betterment crusades, the timid parlor meetings of the 1900 to 1910 period should be seen as the training ground for many Progressive activists.

Thus by 1910 the visionary cause of the pioneers had been transformed into an eminently safe program for middle-class club meetings. This stage of development, which first brought a wealthy, "respectable" class of women into comfortable participation in suffrage, was seen by NAWSA leaders as a necessary precondition of the movement that would eventually win the vote. For better or worse, these middle-class leaders could not conceive of conducting a successful campaign without the approval and the financial support of the social elite.

As tangible proof of the wisdom of their strategy, leaders of the NAWSA could point to a dramatic increase in support for their reform. Membership rolls soared from about 12,000 in 1906, the year of Anthony's death, to over 117,000 in 1910. After 1910, a widescale organizational scheme was put into effect, and a corps of dedicated organizers largely drawn from the ranks of college-educated women was active throughout the country. Moreover, by 1914 a professional lobby was at work to push the federal amendment through Congress. This expanded effort was fueled by an ample treasury; in 1916, for example, the NAWSA's operational budget stood at $100,000 annually. The suffrage political strategy, based on the precondition of a respectable image, had paid high dividends and was the foundation of their victory in 1920.

In a few years' time, NAWSA leaders had built a solid political base for suffrage by attracting into the movement large numbers of women who previously were uninvolved in politics. They had accomplished this by giving a political meaning to traditional forms of female assembly, organization, and entertainment. For the women involved, the familiar surroundings and rituals legitimized and demystified the alien world of political action. Anti-suffrage propaganda and the unflattering stereotype of nineteenth-century suffragists had hammered home the proposition that femininity and politics could never mix. In the first decade of the new century, however, a generation of women drew a different message from what they soon would call the "suffrage ideal." Women who had always been excluded from political participation were drawn, not to party affiliations, bosses, and smoke-filled rooms, but rather to a new kind of political activity: active membership in a reform or single-interest pressure group. Scholars who lament the decline of popular political participation in the Progressive Era fail to take into account this shift from party affiliation to interest group loyalty. In fact, movements like suffrage, temperance, child-labor reform, and other Progressive causes involved and included vast numbers of people who had had no part in the political process during the hey day of the parties, yet were involved in a popular politics of their own making.

In the first decade of the twentieth century, suffrage leaders set out to create a new image for their movement. Their basic goal was to forge a notion of women's history and female progress that could be accepted as consonant with the wider aspirations of mainstream society. In a sense they banished the radical past, turned their back on nonconformity, and in the process captured the support of quietly influential groups of women. Gone was the taint of extremism that suffragists believed had haunted the movement for decades; the parlor meeting had adopted "Aunt Susan" as its patron saint, and suffragism had come of age.

Notes

This article is drawn from the author's book, *Woman Suffrage and the New Democracy*, forthcoming from Yale University Press.

1. Eleanor Flexner, *Century of Struggle: The Woman's Rights Movement in the United States*, (1959; Cambridge, Mass., 1975), 256.

2. Ibid., 230.

3. James J. Kenneally, "Woman Suffrage and the Massachusetts Referendum of 1895," *The Historian* 30 (August, 1968): 620-623.

4. Susan B. Anthony and Ida Husted Harper, eds., *History of Woman Suffrage*, vol. 4 (1883-1900; reprint, New York, 1969), 735-737; and Kenneally, "Woman Suffrage and the Massachusetts Referendum of 1895," 625.

5. Ibid., 630. In *HWS*, Alice Stone Blackwell's account of the 1895 referendum emphasizes the positive aspects of the contest.

6. Priscilla Leonard, "The Ladies Battle," *Current Literature* 36 (April, 1904): 386-389.

7. Minnie Reynolds to Alice Stone Blackwell, December 12, 1930, National American Woman Suffrage Association Papers (hereafter cited as NAWSA), Reel 17, Library of Congress (hereafter cited as LC).

8. Susan B. Anthony to Rachel Foster Avery, January 22, 1900, Papers of Susan B. Anthony, Reel 1, LC.

9. Carrie Chapman Catt to Catherine Waugh McCullough, August 8, 1900, Dillon Collection, Box 9, Schlesinger Library, Radcliffe College, (hereafter cited as SL).

10. *Proceedings of the Thirty-Sixth Annual Convention of the National American Woman Suffrage Association*, 1904, 14-15; *Current Literature* 36 (April, 1904): 386-389.

11. Sherna Gluck, ed. *From Parlor To Prison: Five American Suffragists Talk About Their Lives* (New York, 1976); Calendar for 1912, NAWSA, Reel 48, LC.

12. Monday Club of Richburg, New York, Calendar for 1912, NAWSA, Reel 48, LC.

13. Quoted in Gluck, *From Parlor To Prison,* 12-13.

14. House Committee on the Judiciary Hearing on Woman Suffrage, February 16, 1904, Statement of Mary C.C. Bradford, Women's Rights Collection, Folder 42, SL.

15. Carrie Chapman Catt to Mrs. Millicent Garrett Fawcett, October 19, 1909, Carrie Chapman Catt Papers, Reel 3, LC.

16. See Dorothy Scura, "Ellen Glasgow and Women's Suffrage," *Research in Action* 6 (Spring 1982): 12-15. For Mary Johnston, see Elizabeth D. Coleman, "Penwoman of Virginia's Feminists," *Virginia Cavalcade* 6 (Winter 1956): 8-11; and Marjorie Spruill Wheeler, "Mary Johnston, Suffragist," *Virginia Magazine of History and Biography* 100 (January 1992): 99-118.

17. Margaret Campbell to Henry B. Blackwell, May 14, 1900, NAWSA Reel 5, LC.

18. Harriet Stanton Blatch and Alma Lutz, *Challenging Years: The Memoirs of Harriet Stanton Blatch,* (New York, 1940), 91-92.

19. *New York Call,* March 11, 1917. Quoted in Mari Jo Buhle, *Women and American Socialism, 1870-1920* (Urbana, Ill., 1983), 225.

20. *Literary Digest* 36 (February 29, 1908): 290-292.

21. For a detailed discussion of tradition and its uses, see Eric Hobsbawm and Terence Ranger, eds., *The Invention of Tradition* (Cambridge, 1983), 1-12.

22. Ida Husted Harper, *History of Woman Suffrage* vol. 5 (Reprint, New York, 1969): 228.

23. *HWS* 5: 204-206. Anthony's interest in placing the work is documented in Ida Husted Harper, *The Life and Work of Susan B. Anthony,* 3 vols., (Indianapolis, 1898 and 1908), 1278-1279.

24. Carrie Chapman Catt to Alice Stone Blackwell, November 6, 1908, Carrie Chapman Catt Papers, Reel 2, LC.

25. Speech by Anna Howard Shaw, "The Fate of the Republic," (1892) Dillon Collection, Folder 499, SL. "That is where the weakness of every Republic lies," Shaw continued, "they have been fathered to death."

26. *HWS* 5: 263.

27. Edith M. Phelps, ed., *Selected Articles on Woman Suffrage,* Debaters Handbook Series, (Minneapolis, 1912).

28. Mary Gray Peck, Report of the Headquarters Secretary, quoted in *HWS* 5: 266-268.

29. Press Release, "Anti Suffrage News and Comment" (n.d.), issued by New York State Association Opposed Women's Suffrage, Folder 2, SL.

30. Speech by Anna Howard Shaw to the NAWSA Convention, April 14, 1910, Women's Rights Collection, Folder 514, SL.

31. Ida Husted Harper, "Why Women Cannot Vote in the United States," *North American Review* 179 (July, 1904): 30-35.

32. Pamphlet by M. Cary Thomas, "A New Fashioned Argument for Woman Suffrage," (October 17, 1908) Women's Rights Collection, Folder 730, SL.

33. Volume 5 of *HWS* devotes ample coverage to the pioneers in its chapters on the annual conventions. For the quotation, see *HWS* 5: 123.

34. Anna Howard Shaw, Letter to "Progress," (March, 1910) Dillon Collection, Box 22, SL. For examples of pioneer celebrations, see *HWS* 5: 30-31 and 219-220.

35. Ellen Carol DuBois, *Elizabeth Cady Stanton/Susan B. Anthony: Correspondence, Writings, Speeches* (New York, 1981), 226.

36. Not only were Stanton's more radical activities omitted from the suffrage pioneer tradition, but her role in founding the American women's rights movement was also forgotten. According to historian Ellen DuBois, Stanton's papers were not collected and she found no biographer until 1940. See DuBois, *Elizabeth Cady Stanton/Susan B. Anthony...,* 191-192.

37. Maud Wood Park, "The College Equal Suffrage League: Introductory notes," (1942), Women's Rights Collection, Folder 696, SL; *HWS* 5: 660-662.

38. *HWS* 5: 167; and Anna Howard Shaw, *The Story of a Pioneer* (New York, 1915), 221-223.

39. *HWS* 5: 170.

40. Ibid., 171.

41. Maud Wood Park, "Address to the 28th Annual Convention of NAWSA, College Night," February 8, 1906, Women's Rights Collection, Folder 855, SL.

42. Typescript of *Woman's Journal* article, "Debt to the Pioneers," March 30, 1907, Women's Rights Collection, Folder 855, SL. For examples of this theme, see *HWS* 5: 173 and 226.

43. *HWS* 5: 1373; *Life and Work of Susan B. Anthony,* 1355.

44. Program, Kings County Political Equality League, Brooklyn, New York, February 14, 1903, NAWSA, Reel 26, LC.

45. Harper, *The Life and Work of Susan B. Anthony.*

46. *Pearson's Magazine* March, 1903. Excerpts from this article also appear in Harper, *Life and Work of Susan B. Anthony,* 1298-1304.

47. Ibid., 1295-1304.

48. Ellen DuBois used the term "suffrage saint" in reference to Anthony in a conversation with the author in 1986.

49. Anna Howard Shaw, *The Story of a Pioneer,* 189-190.

50. Ibid., 232-234.

51. Harper, *Life and Work of Susan B. Anthony,* 1604 and 1606-1607.

52. Ibid., 1607-1610.

53. Anna Howard Shaw, "Address at Memorial Service for Susan B. Anthony," March 15, 1906, Dillon Collection, Box 22, SL.

54. Accounts of the Anthony funeral are drawn from Shaw, *Story of a Pioneer,* 235-238; and Harper, *Life and Work of Susan B. Anthony,* 1429-1444.

55. *New York Times,* March 18, 1906. Clipping in the Breckinridge Family Papers, Box 700, LC.

56. Notes from KERA Memorial Service for Susan B. Anthony by Mary Clay, March 22, 1906, NAWSA, Reel 5, LC.

57. For example, see Program, ERA Club Memorial Service for Susan B. Anthony, May 8, 1906, NAWSA, Reel 26, LC.; and Program, "A Meeting of Appreciation of the Life and Work of Susan B. Anthony," Interurban Political Equality Council of Greater New York, April 1, 1906, NAWSA, Reel 26, LC.

58. Eugene V. Debs, "Susan B. Anthony: Pioneer of Freedom," *Pearson's Magazine* (July, 1917). Copy in NAWSA, Reel 26, LC.

Ten

Jane Addams, Progressivism, and Woman Suffrage:

An Introduction to "Why Women Should Vote"
Victoria Bissell Brown

and

"Why Women Should Vote"
Jane Addams

Editor's Introduction: In the passage that follows, historian Victoria Bissell Brown illuminates for us one of the most popular and influential pro-suffrage documents written during the long campaign for woman suffrage, Jane Addams's "Why Women Should Vote." Brown, who is writing a two-volume biography of the revered Progressive reformer and suffragist, discusses the popularity of Addams's essay and analyzes it in the context of Progressive reform philosophy and pro-suffrage rhetoric.

An understanding of the Progressive movement and its relationship to woman suffrage as explained by one of the movement's luminaries is crucial to our understanding of the success of the woman suffrage movement. For of all the factors leading to the victory in 1920, the emergence around 1900 of this new era of reform—the "Progressive Era"—is one of the most important.

Progressivism, which energized American politics until World War I, began at the grassroots level and strongly affected American politics at all levels—including both major political parties. Indeed, in 1912, Progressives in the Republican Party bolted and formed the "Progressive Party" with Theodore Roosevelt as their candidate, after the Republicans chose to back President William Howard Taft for re-election. Roosevelt and Taft then lost to Woodrow Wilson, the Progressive politician nominated by the Democrats.

This reform zeal arose in response to the many ills that plagued American society in the last half of the nineteenth century as a result of massive industrialization, urbanization, and immigration. Progressives insisted that the hands-off, non-interventionist style of government demanded by conservatives, while appropriate, perhaps, for a rural, agrarian society, was no longer adequate in a new era in which an individual's pursuit of happiness brought him or her constantly into conflict with others, when large corporations ran roughshod over smaller businesses and exploited workers without restraint, and large numbers of people lived in close proximity in cities without adequate provision for sanitation, disease control, or recreation. Progressives demanded that government—from municipal to federal—*take action* on a variety of fronts, including (to name a few): regulating corporations to protect workers and consumers; safeguarding public health; banning child labor; establishing compulsory education, juvenile courts and public playgrounds; and reforming government to make it more responsible, accountable, and free of corruption!

The Progressive coalition included a diverse group of people determined to remedy the social evils produced by unrestrained capitalism but not always in agreement about solutions. In fact, Progressivism was riddled with contradictions. For example, Progressives generally supported democratic reforms including the secret ballot, the nomination of candidates by primaries rather than meetings in "smoke-filled rooms," and the direct election of United States Senators by the voters rather than the state legislatures. But some Progressives, believing that corrupt urban political machines were manipulating the "ignorant immigrant vote," favored undemocratic reforms such as literacy tests to eliminate the uneducated from the electorate. Most Progressives were middle class, and many patronizingly believed that the working class needed to be protected more than empowered: they believed that citizens like themselves should shape social policy out of a sense of noblesse oblige.

Progressivism aided the woman suffrage movement in several ways. New ideas about the functions of government were more in line with old ideas about woman's nature and abilities: a government that was expected to nurture and protect and arbitrate conflicts rather than focus exclusively on national defense and economic development might benefit from woman's presumably innate characteristics and domestic experience. In addition, public support for woman suffrage grew as a result of the widespread belief that women—if enfranchised—would support Progressive reforms because they were more moral, compassionate, and nurturing than men. People also assumed that woman suffrage would be a boon to Progressivism because hundreds of thousands of women were clearly demonstrating their support for Progressive reform as lobbyists and political activists. Indeed, many of these reform-minded women were converted to the suffrage movement out of frustration when politicians failed to take their lobbying seriously and/or opposed the reforms they supported. Like the women of the WCTU before them, women Progressives—and their male supporters—believed that they would be much more effective if women were able to vote rather than rely exclusively upon "indirect influence."

Suffragists recognized the advantages offered by this political climate. As the previous essay by Sara Hunter Graham demonstrates, early twentieth-century suffragists were eager to avoid the taint of radicalism, to counter the anti-suf-fragists' claim that suffrage was unwomanly, and to link their movement with popular ideas. Indeed, though suffragists never ceased to argue for woman suf-frage on the grounds that it was *right* and *just* and due to them as citizens of the United States, they were at all times searching for ways to persuade politicians that enfranchising women was politically *expedient.*

In the Progressive Era, rather than arguing against the idea of separate spheres, suffragists typically proclaimed that woman suffrage was completely compatible with woman's traditional duties. They often argued that, as a result of industrialization and urbanization, women were no longer able to protect their homes and children without the vote! Some suffragists, either believing in women's innate differences from men or pandering to this popular supposi-tion, insisted that women would *naturally* support the new nurturing role many believed government should adopt. As one widely used suffrage poster stated: "Women are by nature and training housekeepers. Let them help in the city housekeeping. They will introduce an occasional spring cleaning."

As Victoria Brown explains, Jane Addams's "Why Women Should Vote" is in some ways consistent with and in other ways different from the prevailing usage of Progressive ideology in pro-suffrage rhetoric. Addams's essay is extremely important as one of the strongest statements of the argument that changed conditions *require* women to vote in order to continue to fulfill their traditional functions. Publishing this powerful endorsement of woman suffrage as inextricably linked to Progressivism was of inestimable value to the suffrage cause—the seal of approval from America's best-loved Progressive.

Brown insists, however, that Addams—though a leading suffragist—was not necessarily typical of suffragists and did not focus her political energies primar-ily on this cause. In fact, she presented woman suffrage as of crucial importance primarily as an *implement* through which women could more effectively reach their political goals, a way for women to assert their political values while still fulfilling their traditional functions.

Brown defends Addams against charges that have been leveled against her by some historians, accusations that she pandered to popular ideas and prejudices. For example, Brown rejects the idea that Addams "grounded her suffrage rea-soning in biological essentialism." Rather, Brown insists, Addams believed that whatever differences existed in the political values of men and women were attributable to women's *experience,* not innate habits or instincts. Furthermore, Addams did not employ the nativist, elitist, or racist arguments embraced by some suffragists. Brown insists that Addams was a woman of principle, and that this essay is a sincere statement of her Progressive reform philosophy—not mere suffrage propaganda.

Still, Brown concedes that Jane Addams was a brilliant strategist and a habit-ual diplomat, owing to her desire to avoid conflict and promote harmony. In this and other works, writes Brown, Addams astutely presented woman suffrage as inevitable given the new focus of government in the Progressive Era. Many a suffragist would follow her lead, presenting suffrage as something women were *compelled* to embrace given changed historical circumstances rather than the result of woman's desire for equality and power. "If there was any guile in Addams's pro-suffrage position," writes Brown, "this was surely it."

Yet Brown's emphasis here is on the sincerity of Addams's essay. The power of the essay, she argues, was in the neat fit between Addams's focus on the connection between suffrage and reform and the appeal of Progressivism. That the essay was so popular was a testimony to Addams's "unusual ability" to weave her Progressive concerns "into a pro-suffrage argument that appealed to mainstream sensibilities without bowing to mainstream prejudices."

★　　★　　★　　★　　★

IN THE YEARS between 1900 and 1915, close to two hundred articles appeared in popular American magazines concerning American woman suffrage. In the year 1910 alone, the interested American reader could sample some twenty-five articles on the subject. Perched at the top of this stack of articles for and against and about woman suffrage sits Jane Addams's editorial, "Why Women Should Vote," published in the January 1910 edition of *The Ladies' Home Journal.* Of all the popular articles on suffrage that appeared in these years, Addams's has probably been reprinted the most often, quoted the most regularly, cited the most frequently. The modern reader must ask, has this pro-suffrage essay received such attention over the years simply because it was written by the most famous woman of her day or because it best reflects the era's pro-suffrage ideology? Are the arguments Addams put forth in *The Ladies' Home Journal* unique to her or representative of the dozens of pro-suffrage articles Americans were reading in these years?

The answers to all of those questions are "yes." The article has, of course, received special attention because of Jane Addams's fame. But Addams's fame was due in no small part to her ability to craft popular articles that resonated with strong currents in public opinion while still marking out a unique philosophical position. Scholars have not always appreciated this particular talent in Jane Addams, nor have they always looked favorably on Addams's position in "Why Women Should Vote" that women "need this implement in order to preserve the home."

Back in the 1970s, when scholars of women were measuring every text by the single ideological yardstick of "liberal" feminism, Jane Addams's pro-suffrage argument appeared to fall short because she did not put the classical liberal emphasis on women's individual right to the vote. At that time, it was thought that her embrace of women's traditional domestic role in this *Ladies' Home Journal* essay, along with her focus on the social good women could perform with the vote, constituted an accommodation to, even a pandering to, popular gender politics.[1] Current scholarship, however, allows for a new reading of "Why Women Should Vote." This scholarship reminds us that women's progress depends as much on "republican" commitments to the common good as on "liberal" rights and individual autonomy. Read in the light of contemporary research on female culture and moral values, Addams's assumption that women speak "in a different voice" appears to be more a positive assertion of the need for that particular ideological voice in politics than a capitulation to existing notions of women's innate moral nature.[2] Read, too, in light of the work of current historical research on women reformers in the Progressive Era, Jane Addams's focus on women's collective duty to reform (rather than their individual right to autonomy) in "Why Women Should Vote" appears to be more a reflection of the political climate unique to the Progressive Era, and more a function of the very particular emphasis Addams placed on economic democracy, than an accommodation to conservative nostalgia for selfless womanhood.[3]

Understanding "Why Women Should Vote" requires understanding that Jane Addams's central political goal was the legislative enactment of a Progressive social agenda, including protective labor legislation, health and welfare programs, educational reform, and legal equity for blacks and immigrants. When she said that woman suffrage was an "implement" women needed to "preserve the home," she was saying that she regarded the achievement of the Progressive agenda as essential to the preservation of the homes of millions of poor and working-class Americans. Further, she was saying that woman suffrage was crucial to enacting that agenda because women occupied the homes that needed preserving and, therefore, were most likely to support Progressive reform. It was this set of assumptions that motivated her active support for woman suffrage and that shaped the arguments she crafted for woman suffrage.

Placed alongside the other pro-suffrage articles published at the time, "Why Women Should Vote" thus appears to be quite representative of the pro-reform, "Progressive" mood dominant in American political life in 1910. And in being representative of Progressives, Addams appears unique among suffrage leaders. Her devotion to improving the lives of the working class by creating an interdependent polity as responsive to domestic as to commercial needs meant that questions of women's particular situation were subordinated, in her writing, to questions of women's duty to demand expansion of the nation's entire political agenda. Whatever readers today may think of this approach, its popularity at the time may be detected in the fact that a year after this essay appeared in *The Ladies' Home Journal,* Addams was elected to a vice presidency in the National American Woman Suffrage Association (NAWSA).

Close inspection of "Why Women Should Vote" suggests that Jane Addams's popularity derived not only from her Progressive concern for economic and political democracy, but from her unusual ability to weave that concern with her own mediating temperament, diplomatic style, and genuine respect for domesticity into a pro-suffrage argument that appealed to mainstream sensibilities without bowing to mainstream prejudices. "Why Women Should Vote," is, first and foremost then, a statement of Jane Addams's Progressive reform philosophy. As such, the essay serves to inform our understanding of the ways in

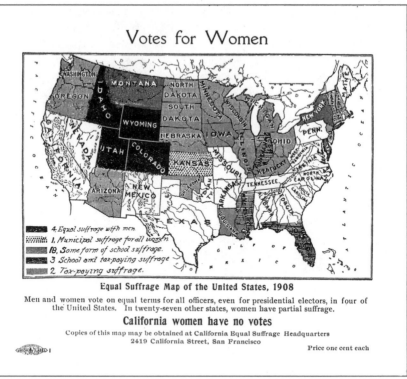

Votes for Women

4. *Equal suffrage with men.*
1. *Municipal suffrage for all women.*
18. *Some form of school suffrage.*
3. *School and tax-paying suffrage.*
2. *Tax-paying suffrage.*

Equal Suffrage Map of the United States, 1908

Men and women vote on equal terms for all officers, even for presidential electors, in four of the United States. In twenty-seven other states, women have partial suffrage.

California women have no votes

Copies of this map may be obtained at California Equal Suffrage Headquarters
2419 California Street, San Francisco

Price one cent each

By 1908 only four states allowed women the vote. Sophia Smith Collection

which woman suffrage and Progressivism were mutually reinforcing movements in the early twentieth century and the role Addams played in linking the success of one movement to the success of the other.

Jane Addams and Progressive Era Reform

When Jane Addams wrote "Why Women Should Vote" in 1910, she was fifty years old and enjoying a decade, 1905-1915, that would mark the peak of her power and influence in America. Four years before her pro-suffrage essay appeared in *The Ladies' Home Journal,* an article on Addams in *Current Literature* was published with the title, "The Only Saint America Has Produced." And in the year following her *Ladies' Home Journal* essay, when *The Independent* asked its readers to name "the most useful Americans," Addams was ranked second, behind Thomas Edison but ahead of Andrew Carnegie. Indeed, when *The Ladies' Home Journal* invited Addams to write "Why Women Should Vote," the magazine itself was on record in opposition to woman suffrage. Still, it gave Addams space to make a case for suffrage that was bound to be very appealing to *Journal* readers, and, three years later, hired her to write a monthly column on civic matters. The

Journal introduced that column with the claim that "no woman in America today is so closely in touch with those great social and economic movements that are outside the home and yet vitally touch the home as Jane Addams."[4]

Addams had launched her reform career by opening, in 1889, the second, and by far the most famous, social settlement house in the United States, Hull-House on Halstead Street in Chicago. The settlement began as one building, but by 1910 it comprised thirteen buildings encircling an entire square block of a working-class, immigrant neighborhood on Chicago's west side. Addams's settlement served as a meeting place for political activists, workers, students, immigrants, women's groups, unionists, artists and reformers, children and teenagers. It served as well as a catalyst for social legislation, political reform, social science theory, and labor organizing at the city, state, and national levels. Until her death in 1935, Jane Addams presided as the calm center of the storm that was Hull-House, attracting extraordinarily gifted, innovative people around her and adroitly leading them in the development of all the sorts of social service programs and legislative agendas that have come to typify the "Progressive Era" of the 1890s and early 1900s.

Because of her close ties to the University of Chicago during that institution's glory years around the turn of the century, Addams is often called the founder of the academic discipline of social work. She was by nature more a sociologist than a social worker, however, and with the eye of a sociologist—and the voice of a kind and tactful but brutally honest aunt—she delivered thousands of speeches both in the United States and around the world, wrote over a dozen books, and published over five hundred articles for magazines and journals ranging from *The Ladies' Home Journal* to the *Annals of the American Academy of Political and Social Sciences*. She was active with labor unions in strike mediation and labor legislation, was a founding member of the NAACP, served on the Chicago School Board, was the paid garbage inspector for her ward (the only paid position she ever held), staged unsuccessful political campaigns against corrupt ward bosses, worked on state programs for the criminal and the insane, was president of the National Conference of Charities and Corrections, and, as noted, served as a vice president of the National American Woman Suffrage Association from 1911 until 1914. Addams was a leading figure in Teddy Roosevelt's Progressive Party, becoming in 1912 the first American woman to give a nominating speech at a presidential political convention. In the course of her career, she traveled to every continent as a distinguished visitor, sat on countless boards and advisory committees, and counseled presidents, governors, mayors, senators, and congressmen as well as leaders of anarchist, socialist, feminist, immigrant, African American, and labor organizations.

Finally, Jane Addams was a peace activist who held out against supporting America's participation in World War I and formed, in protest, the Women's International League for Peace and Freedom. This unpopular political stance, the only political stance she ever adopted that was completely out of sync with her times, transformed Addams from a beloved American icon into public enemy number one. Almost fifteen years after the war was over, however, in 1931, Addams's on-going peace activism was vindicated when she became the first American woman to win the Nobel Peace Prize. But during the interim years, when she was vilified as a dangerous subversive, her critics published elaborate "spider web" charts on which they demonstrated that Jane Addams was the secret link connecting every reform and radical group in the country. Whatever we may now think of her critics' politics, we have to concede to the accuracy of their claim: Jane Addams was the secret link connecting every reform and radical group in the country in the years between 1890 and her death in 1935.[5]

The Appeal of Jane Addams

There were myriad reasons for Addams's enduring stature, not the least among them her ability to write about contentious public issues like woman suffrage in a persuasive but non-argumentative voice. Her argument for woman suffrage in *The Ladies' Home Journal* of 1910 is an excellent example of her unique stylistic ability to disarm opponents by gliding past fundamental disagreements, presuming shared goals, focusing almost entirely on the great good to be gained, and ignoring the position that was to be defeated. Though she herself would detest a military analogy, the contemporary reader cannot help but picture Addams striding untouched through battlefields where her comrades were engaged in bloody combat, always pointing to the hill that was to be captured and paying little heed to the enemy all around. Indeed, she was a master at occupying the enemy's ground. Her argument in "Why Women Should Vote" that the suffrage would help, not hurt, the home was not unusual; plenty of other suffragists made the same case. But other suffragists made this, and other arguments, in a contentious way, directly attacking the antis' claim that woman suffrage would destroy the home. Addams, by contrast, never once mentioned that opponents of woman suffrage claimed to be preserving the home. She simply refused to contend that point and thus rose above the fray. This was vintage Addams.

A non-confrontational style is not the only feature distinguishing Jane Addams's approach in "Why Women Should Vote." There is, as well, her targeted deployment of woman suffrage as part of the Progressive assault on Gilded Age greed in politics and the economy, and there is her careful derivation of female values from history and experience, not biology and intuition. But in order to appreciate fully Addams's idiosyncratic handling of these issues and their relationship to woman suffrage, it is perhaps useful to examine first some of the popular magazine articles on suffrage appearing contemporaneously with "Why Women Should Vote."

Popular Suffrage Arguments of the Day

A chronological survey of articles published between 1900 and 1915 makes several points quite clear: first, that pro-suffrage arguments were one half of an active, national debate with anti-suffrage arguments, and both sides in that debate were shaped by the other. Second, suffragists and anti-suffragists alike had, by 1900, moved away from the broad philosophical debates over women's "rights" and "female nature" that typified the latter half of the nineteenth century. The debate after 1900 centered on more prosaic discussions of whether the majority of women actually wanted the vote and whether women's votes would actually bring about the benefits to Progressive reform that suffragists claimed. It is here that another point comes clear, and that is the extent to which woman suffrage had become linked in the public mind with the Progressive movement for political and economic reform, but also the degree to which it was easier for conservatives to attack woman suffrage than to attack Progressive reform. Anti-suffragists never openly opposed woman suffrage on the grounds that women voters would enact reform; rather, they tried to argue that woman suffrage was irrelevant to reform. This development in the debate was partially rooted in the peculiarities of United States suffrage history, which was distinguished by women's state-by-state, city-by-city acquisition of voting rights. The discussion of suffrage in popular magazines was, thus, not occurring in a political vacuum; it was all being conducted while women were actually going to the polls and voting in an increasing number of states and in dozens of municipalities. As the aged reformer Julia Ward Howe pointed out in 1909, concrete events meant that the whole question of woman suffrage had become entirely practical.[6]

Given the gradual accretion of women's voting rights in the United States, it is hardly surprising to find that over a third of the fifty articles surveyed for this essay were devoted to descriptions of woman suffrage campaigns, debates over whether woman suffrage in Colorado or Wyoming or Idaho or Utah had achieved the Progressive benefits suffragists predicted, and arguments over whether women were actually going to the polls. By the first decade of the twentieth century, the time for philosophical debates about female nature and women's rights had pretty much passed.

This is not to say that the suffragists never mounted a principled argument for their position in popular magazines. On the contrary, the magazine evidence strongly supports the recent claim by historian Paula Baker that "the suffragists made every conceivable argument, from equal rights to home protection to the need for an intelligent electorate."[7] But what is interesting here is not that one pro-suffrage article would argue for equal rights while another would argue for home protection. The most striking characteristic of the popular pro-suffrage literature of the day is that within a single article could be found the whole array of justifications possible for woman suffrage.

So we find suffragists like Frank Parsons arguing on one page of *The Arena* in 1908 that "sex has nothing to do with the reasons on which the suffrage rests," and arguing two pages later that "women have a higher regard for principle than men…their gentleness, sympathy, refinement and incorruptibility are sadly needed in our politics." Or Rosamond Sutherland, another pro-suffrage writer, arguing in a 1910 issue of *North American Review* that "the emancipation of women is a natural evolution which can no more be stopped than the tides of the sea," while at the same time arguing that "woman is instinctively a home-maker," and the vote would not wash away that apparently non-evolving fact. Or the editors of *The Independent* asserting in 1915 that "partial suffrage—the suffrage of men alone—is a denial of democracy. Democracy will never be full and complete until every individual in the community has an equal right to determine how the affairs of the community shall be managed," and, in the same article, also asserting that "women, by the very nature of their being,...are experts on certain vital subjects.... Women have different qualities of mind from men. Men are...reasoning beings. Women are creatures of intuition."[8]

None of the authors of these articles worried about the inconsistencies now detectable in their positions; they slipped and slid easily from democratic principle to practical politics to biological determinism. As Julia Ward Howe said in 1909, "the fundamental argument for woman suffrage, of course, is its justice; and this would be enough were there no other. But a powerful argument can also be made for it from the standpoint of expediency."[9]

This "flexibility" in the pro-suffrage position allowed considerable room for volleying with the anti-suffragists. When the antis argued that women should rely on men for protection, not the ballot, the wealthy widow and suffrage militant Alva Belmont retorted that experience proved women could most definitely not rely on men for protection. When the antis argued that politics was a dirty, bloody battlefield that would soil and injure women, the suffrage movement's most prodigious publicist Ida Husted Harper said that politics should be a cooperative effort, not a bloody battle. And in mock sympathy for the adversarial mess she said men had made of civic life, the attorney and suffragist Florida Pier offered women's help with the cleanup. (This was the sort of help, said Pier, that any human being would offer to another who was in a "pickle.") When the antis said that women's domesticity had made them too narrow-minded to vote, the suffragists responded that the vote would expand women's horizons. When the antis said that the majority of women did not wish to vote, Sutherland responded that in matters of principle, numbers were irrelevant. When the antis said that ignorant, immoral, and immigrant women would vote, some suffragists retorted that citizens in a democracy should have more faith in the common folk and others argued that women would double the "respectable" vote and out-poll the already-enfranchised unfit men. Finally, and most importantly, when the antis—skirting the knotty question of biology—argued that woman's social function as a mother was far too demanding and far too important to afford them the time and energy for civic activities, the suffragists turned that argument right on its head, insisting that it was precisely because their maternal duties were so vital to national life that they needed a voice in government. "Woman has a right to this most effective means of transforming the social environment into greater fitness for herself and all her loved ones," wrote Frank Parsons in 1908.[10] This, as it turned out, was the suffragists' most unassailable argument. And it was this argument that Jane Addams made most eloquently in her pro-suffrage writings.

Jane Addams's Progressive Suffrage Argument

The Ladies' Home Journal essay was one of dozens of speeches and articles Addams penned on woman suffrage in the years between 1897 and 1920. Comparing the *Journal* piece to her other writings makes clear that "Why Women Should Vote" was typical of her approach to woman suffrage and illuminates how her approach was both similar to and different from that of the other popular arguments being made at the time. Addams's writings on woman suffrage are distinctive because they do not "make every conceivable argument"; she did not blend a biological argument with a human rights argument with an elitist argument with a utilitarian argument. Like the proverbial hedgehog, Addams knew one thing, she knew it well, and she repeated it often: "Only when all the people become the governing class can the collective resources and organizations [of the society] be consistently utilized for the common weal."[11] As has already been noted, in applying this overarching Progressive philosophy to the question of woman suffrage, Addams was unique among suffrage advocates. Unlike other suffrage leaders, Addams subordinated women's particular gender-based situation to the broader, class-based concerns of the Progressive program. In addition, she was uniquely consistent, single-minded, even redundant, in not mixing her fierce commitment to democracy and practical results with abstract liberalism. In "Pragmatism and Politics," written for *The Survey* in 1912, Addams declared:

> The American voter is not content with the 18th century formulae of liberty and equality, high-flown as they are, for they do not apply to the situation. Liberty has come to be a guarantee of equal opportunity to play our parts well in primary relations, and the elemental processes of birth, growth, nutrition, death are the great levellers that remind us of the essential equality of human life. No talk of liberty or equality "goes" that does not reckon with these.[12]

The pro-suffrage arguments Addams made must be viewed within the very particular political and historical context of the Progressive Era's assertion of collective over individual interests. Considered in terms of her outrage at Gilded-Age selfishness gone wild, Addams's focus on women's vote as a potential tool in the service of community interests makes all the sense in the world.

"Why Women Should Vote" requires no apology for its lack of attention to individual rights. In Jane Addams's world, individual rights had created the urban, industrial problems she and her neighbors battled every day. Her emphasis on the community good that housewives could enact with the vote does not make her a sellout to comfortable, bourgeois domesticity. Rather, it marks her as a fully engaged, Progressive Era reformer whose daily life was consumed with solving serious urban problems evident in every household in her neighborhood. From where Addams sat in Chicago's crowded, dirty Nineteenth Ward, living with other college-educated women who had joined her Hull-House settlement in order to use their privileges on behalf of the working poor, it was not gender per se that distinguished the disadvantaged in American society, it was class. And the remedy for that disadvantage was not, in Addams's experience, more individualism. Whatever "personal ambition" might have accomplished in the past, said Addams in 1912, "it is certainly too archaic to accomplish anything now. Our thoughts, at least for this generation, cannot be too much directed from mutual relationships and responsibilities."[13]

Contrary to what her critics have suggested, Addams did not focus on the collective utility of woman suffrage in order to take the sting out of female independence. Her focus derived honestly out of her political priorities; she was intent on eradicating the evils of economic inequality in American society and believed collective action was the only means to that end. She did not emphasize women's domestic role because she wished to placate the patriarchs or because she did not understand the power of patriarchy to manipulate women's traditional work to its own ends. She assigned great significance to female domesticity because her daily experience taught her that domesticity was no bourgeois ideal but a utilitarian reality for her working-class neighbors, and one that could be powerful if deployed in the political arena against America's individualistic patriarchs.

Addams never openly argued with the antis' claims that the mass of women were too weak or passive or uninterested to vote. Instead, she silently smothered those claims with her argument that the vote would make women stronger, more responsible, and more civic-minded. Note that the editorial for *The Ladies' Home Journal* is not titled "Why Women Should HAVE the Vote," but, rather, "Why Women Should Vote." She was not arguing constitutional principles here; she was talking about the pragmatic effect—on women and on men—of the act of voting.

Jane Addams, Biology, and Elitism

If all Jane Addams had cared about was the attractiveness of her pro-suffrage arguments to middle-class audiences, she would have done what so many of her peers in the movement did; she would have "made every conceivable argument." The fact that she did not, the fact that editorials like "Why Women Should Vote" made such a consistent and relatively narrow set of democratic and utilitarian arguments, deserves notice. Examination of her pro-suffrage language makes clear, for example, that Addams did not ground her suffrage reasoning in biological essentialism. Despite what some critics have charged, she did not claim that women were innately, "essentially," more moral than men.[14] Nor did she say that women were biologically destined for domesticity. In the opening paragraph of "Why Women Should Vote" Addams states that she regards women's domesticity as a product of history that could only be ended by "social change." She speaks of "tradition" in this and other pro-suffrage writings, and she speaks of women's "different experience." But this most careful of writers did not speak of biology determining women's nature or women's role. Yes, she does refer in *The Ladies' Home Journal* to "those affairs which naturally and historically belong to women," but readers familiar with Addams's phrasing as well as her psychology will agree that she used the word "naturally" in all sorts of arguments. It was, for her, a synonym for "logically," and served her need to sweep past opponents, leaving them with the burden of proving that she was not merely stating the obvious.

Back in the early 1970s, the historian Jill Conway claimed that Addams "accepted [the] idea of biologically determined masculine and feminine temperaments," and argued that Addams was incapable of "seeing men and women as moral equals."[15] But these claims are not supported by the language in Addams's own texts. Her argument in *The Ladies' Home Journal* against women influencing men's votes rests on the assumption that a man's "point of view" was "quite as honest and valuable" as a woman's. Indeed, in her first public address on woman suffrage in 1897, speaking before the Chicago Political Equality League, Addams stated:

> I am not one of those who believe—broadly speaking—that women are better than men. We have not wrecked railroads, nor corrupted Legislatures, nor done many unholy things that men have done; but then we must remember that we have not had the chance. But my understanding of the matter is that woman should have the ballot because without this responsibility she cannot best develop her moral courage. As Mazzini once said...we have no right to call our country a country until every man has a vote, and surely no logical mind can stop at sex in granting suffrage.[16]

Seventeen years later, writing for the *Annals of the American Academy of Political and Social Science,* Addams would still claim, "good government is not a matter of sex when it means...defending little children."[17] She did believe, and recent historical research has borne Addams out on this, that women's daily experience made them more likely than men to place human welfare and aesthetics above concerns with profit—but she rooted that difference in nurture, not nature.[18]

The one possible exception to this general rule can be found in *The Ladies' Home Journal* for June of 1913 when Addams wrote an atypically ironic essay titled, "If Men Were Seeking the Franchise." There, in tones suggesting the influence of radical feminist philosopher Charlotte Perkins Gilman, Addams showed what women's objections to men voting would be if women controlled the government. Some of her arguments there—that men might not be good voters because they are "always so eager to make money," are "so reckless," think "so little of dust," and "are so fond of fighting...you always have been since you were little boys"—could be read as a biological, essentialist view of masculine and feminine nature. But it seems just as likely that Addams was trying to show the absurdity of essentialist claims. Certainly her concluding remarks for that article indicate that "such talk" was not serious, that "as far as the guardianship of the State is concerned there is no distinction between the powers of men and women save those which custom has made."[19] It would not be until the masculine carnage of World War I had seared her soul that Addams's language would begin to imply that female nature had any corner on morality. This was not her approach during the woman suffrage campaign.[20]

Just as she did not join other suffragists in making biological claims for women's right to the vote, so, too, Addams did not join the chorus of elitists, racists, and nativists who tried to argue that woman suffrage would double the "respectable," white, native-born vote more than it would expand the votes of the rabble. "Why Women Should Vote" is an excellent example of her view that working women and immigrant women and poor women not only needed the vote in order to protect their own interests and those of their families, but also wanted the vote in order to be responsible, active agents in their communities. By telling her largely white, largely middle-class readership that Scandinavian women were accustomed to the vote, that Jewish women had "covered markets" in Russia and Poland, and that Italian women saw no distinction between voting in school board elections to protect the education of older children and voting in state or federal elections to protect the milk drunk by younger children, Addams was slyly shaming those who had been surprised by the suffrage enthusiasm among these groups of women. True, she did romanticize her neighbors by implying that ethnic women's naivete gave them an organic grasp of political common sense, but in the context of the era's ethnocentric elitism, Addams's romanticism looks more like protection than pandering.

Had Addams been purely a strategist, she would have brushed past her working-class women's suffrage enthusiasm in the way she brushed past other potentially controversial points. But Addams calculated where to earn and where to spend her political capital. She ignored questions of women's individual rights precisely because she did not want to ignore the political aspirations of the women in her neighborhood. It was her concern for their collective need to improve their lives, rather than her concern for her own individual right to vote, that fueled Addams's suffrage energies in the first place. To say that she fashioned a palatable domestic argument for woman suffrage in order to make female voters less threatening completely overlooks the very real political risk she took by predicting that working-class, immigrant women would, as voters, actively demand services and legislative protections from federal, state, and municipal governments. This was hardly a neutral stance to take during the Progressive Era, and it speaks volumes about the class-oriented nature of Addams's political activism.

Twelve Reasons Why Women Should Vote

1. BECAUSE those who obey the laws should help to choose those who make the laws.
2. BECAUSE laws affect women as much as men.
3. BECAUSE laws which affect WOMEN are now passed without consulting them.
4. BECAUSE laws affecting CHILDREN should include the woman's point of view as well as the man's.
5. BECAUSE laws affecting the HOME are voted on in every session of the Legislature.
6. BECAUSE women have experience which would be helpful to legislation.
7. BECAUSE to deprive women of the vote is to lower their position in common estimation.
8. BECAUSE having the vote would increase the sense of responsibility among women toward questions of public importance.
9. BECAUSE public spirited mothers make public spirited sons.
10. BECAUSE about 8,000,000 women in the United States are wage workers, and the conditions under which they work are controlled by law.
11. BECAUSE the objections against their having the vote are based on prejudice, not on reason.
12. BECAUSE to sum up all reasons in one—IT IS FOR THE COMMON GOOD OF ALL.

VOTES FOR WOMEN

NATIONAL WOMAN SUFFRAGE PUBLISHING CO., INC.
171 Madison Avenue,   New York City

Jane Addams, 1898.
Swarthmore College Peace Collection

Woman suffrage leaflet, c. 1915.
Smithsonian Institution

The Strategic Power of Addams's Argument

The modern feminist may well cringe at the link Addams made between women's traditional domestic duties and the vote. But that reaction should not blind us to the sincerity of her argument—or to the strategic value of her argument.

While it took political risks, Addams's "spin" on suffrage was also strategically brilliant. In her hands, suffrage advocates became steadfast defenders of women's right to care for home and family, not the destroyers of domesticity depicted in anti-suffrage lore. In her hands, the feminine powers of "persuasion" which anti-suffragists preferred in place of voting became dishonest tools of manipulation, just as unworthy of women as they were unfair to men. Finally, and most interestingly, in Addams's hands, it was historical inevitability that required women to move their caregiving into the public sector, not some feminist scheme to alter the course of history. With a curious but very characteristic mix of assertiveness and self-effacement, Addams trumpeted women's ability to rise to history's challenge while sliding right past the role women reformers like herself had played in changing history by placing women's traditional concerns on the political agenda.

In "Votes for Women and Other Votes," which appeared in *The Survey* in 1912, Addams expanded on the argument for historical inevitability implicit in "Why Women Should Vote" and downplayed the role of historical agents like herself. Addams claimed in this article that history is "merely a record of new human interests" becoming "the subjects of governmental action and the incorporation into government itself of those classes who represented new interests." As government became involved in commerce, merchants became voters; as government became involved in industrial affairs, workers became voters. The campaign for woman suffrage, reasoned Addams, was the inevitable, sensible result of contemporary government's involvement with "the basic human interests with which women have been traditionally concerned." Thus skirting the female activism that had placed these "basic human interests" on the Progressive Era's political agenda, Addams argued that these new public duties had fallen to women simply through the natural unfolding of history. Pushing this argument even further, Addams claimed that women were only demanding a new household tool—the vote—"because they insist that they will not cease to perform their traditional duties, simply because these duties have been taken over by existing governments."[21]

If there was any guile in Addams's pro-suffrage position, this was surely it. According to her construction, the link between Progressive Era reforms and woman suffrage had arisen organically. Women's political activism was a result, not a cause, of the Progressive Era, and women's need for the vote was a result, not a cause, of historical change. Addams knew different, of course, but this approach satisfied her political and temperamental need to soothe the nerves of those dizzied by the explosion of Progressivism's government activism and women's connection to that activism. Rather than pandering to Americans' elitism or their nativism or their affection for biological essentialism, Addams instead insisted on democracy—economic, social, and legal—and then played to Americans' comfort with historical inevitability and with women's role as dutiful servants to posterity.

Conclusion

As one of America's most revered public figures, Jane Addams played an important role in the campaign for woman suffrage. Since her fame and stature did not reside in the woman suffrage movement, and since Americans perceived her as sincerely committed to the common good, her arguments for woman suffrage as a tool of reform carried special weight. It is doubtful that the majority of the readers of "Why Women Should Vote" in 1910 shared Addams's deep convictions about economic democracy, the dignity of immigrants and workers, or the historical (rather than biological) roots of female domesticity. But it is likely that they were sympathetic to her view that enfranchised women would strengthen contemporary efforts to clean up the factories and the cities, reduce poverty, and improve education and public health. And while Addams fashioned an emphasis on domesticity out of her desire to show the interdependence of the public and the private in modern life, it is also likely that readers found in Addams's domestic emphasis a comforting reassurance that woman suffrage would not destroy the traditional family. In this way, then, Addams maintained her own principles while still achieving popular appeal. The argument here is that Jane Addams's particular approach to woman suffrage, specifically her lack of attention to women's individual rights, arose less from political timidity about gender than from overriding, firm convictions about social and economic reform. As it happened, this focus on the link between suffrage and reform intersected sufficiently with the Progressive attitudes of many Americans to be attractive—despite the fact that Addams was more democratic in her goals than the majority of her readers.

Women's rights were always an avenue to matters of class for Addams; they were never the final destination on her political journey. "Why Women Should Vote" is just one piece of evidence that Addams's support for woman suffrage was rooted in her primary commitment to economic democracy, but it is a very strong piece of evidence. In addition, her writing in this essay, as in so many others, makes clear that, just as Addams always felt more comfortable privileging class issues over gender issues, so, too, she always felt more comfortable arguing for her causes in non-argumentative language. Over the course of her life, consciously and unconsciously, Addams trained the stream of her thinking to flow in elegantly diplomatic channels. Her personal recoil from conflict, coupled with her conviction that all conflict should be mediated, meant that she always presented her case in terms of ultimate harmony, not ultimate victory; this was no more or less true of her suffrage writings than of her writings about labor or militarism.

"Why Women Should Vote," like all of Jane Addams's contributions to the suffrage cause, is thus an exquisitely clever, carefully phrased, determinedly practical, democratic argument. One need not agree with it in order to appreciate its brilliance and its sincerity.

Why Women Should Vote
by Jane Addams, of Hull-House, Chicago

For many generations it has been believed that woman's place is within the walls of her home, and it is indeed impossible to imagine the time when her duty there shall be ended or to forecast any social change which shall release her from that paramount obligation.

This paper is an attempt to show that many women today are failing to discharge their duties to their own households properly simply because they do not perceive that as society grows more complicated it is necessary that woman shall extend her sense of responsibility to many things outside of her own home if she would continue to preserve the home in its entirety. One could illustrate in many ways. A woman's simplest duty, one would say, is to keep her house clean and wholesome and to feed her children properly. Yet if she lives in a tenement house, as so many of my neighbors do, she cannot fulfill these simple obligations by her own efforts because she is utterly dependent upon the city administration for the conditions which render decent living possible. Her basement will not be dry, her stairways will not be fireproof, her house will not be provided with sufficient windows to give light and air, nor will it be equipped with sanitary plumbing, unless the Public Works Department sends inspectors who constantly insist that these elementary decencies be provided. Women who live in the country sweep their own dooryards and may either feed the refuse of the table to a flock of chickens or allow it innocently to decay in the open air and sunshine. In a crowded city quarter, however, if the street is not cleaned by the city authorities no amount of private sweeping will keep the tenement free from grime; if the garbage is not properly collected and destroyed a tenement-house mother may see her children sicken and die of diseases from which she alone is powerless to shield them, although her tenderness and devotion are unbounded. She cannot even secure untainted meat for her household, she cannot provide fresh fruit, unless the meat has been inspected by city officials, and the decayed fruit, which is so often placed upon sale in the tenement districts, has been destroyed in the interests of public health. In short, if woman would keep on with her old business of caring for her house and rearing her children she will have to have some conscience in regard to public affairs lying quite outside of her immediate household. The individual conscience and devotion are no longer effective.

Chicago one spring had a spreading contagion of scarlet fever just at the time the school nurses had been discontinued because business men had pronounced them too expensive. If the women who sent their children to the schools had been sufficiently public-spirited and had been provided with an implement through which to express that public spirit they would have insisted that the schools be supplied with nurses in order that their own children might be protected from contagion. In other words, if women would effectively continue their old avocations they must take part in the slow upbuilding of that code of legislation which is alone sufficient to protect the home from the dangers incident to modern life. One might instance the many deaths of children from contagious diseases the germs of which had been carried in tailored clothing. Country doctors testify as to the outbreak of scarlet fever in remote neighborhoods each autumn, after the children have begun to wear the winter overcoats and cloaks which have been sent from infected city sweatshops. That their mothers mend their stockings and guard them from "taking cold" is not a sufficient protection when the tailoring of the family is done in a distant city under conditions which the mother cannot possibly control. The sanitary regulation of sweatshops by city officials is all that can be depended upon to prevent such needless destruction. Who shall say that women are not concerned in the enactment and enforcement of such legislation if they would preserve their homes?

Even women who take no part in public affairs in order that they may give themselves entirely to their own families, sometimes going so far as to despise those other women who are endeavoring to secure protective legislation, may illustrate this point. The Hull-House neighborhood was at one time suffering from a typhoid epidemic. A careful investigation was made by which we were able to establish a very close connection between the typhoid and a mode of plumbing which made it most probable that the infection had been carried by flies. Among the people who been exposed to the infection was a widow who had lived in the ward for a number of years, in a comfortable little house which she owned. Although the Italian immigrants were closing in all around her she was not willing to sell her property and to move away until she had finished the education of her children. In the mean time she held herself quite aloof from her Italian neighbors and could never be drawn into any of the public efforts to protect them by securing a better code of tenement-house sanitation. Her two daughters were sent to an Eastern college; one June, when one of them had graduated and the other still had two years before she took her degree, they came to the spotless little house and to their self-sacrificing mother for the summer's holiday. They both fell ill, not because their own home was not clean, not because their mother was not devoted, but because next door to them and also in the rear were wretched tenements, and because the mother's utmost efforts could not keep the infection out of her own house. One daughter died and one recovered but was an invalid for two years following. This is, perhaps, a fair illustration of the futility of the individual conscience when woman insists upon isolating her family from the rest of the community and its interests. The result is sure to be a pitiful failure.

One of the interesting experiences in the Chicago campaign for inducing the members of the Charter Convention to recommend municipal franchise for women in the provisions of the new charter was the unexpected enthusiasm and help which came from large groups of foreign-born women. The Scandinavian women represented in many Lutheran Church societies said quite simply that in the old country they had had the municipal franchise upon the same basis as men since the seventeenth century; all the women formerly living under the British Government, in England, Australia or Canada, pointed out that Chicago women were asking now for what the British women had long had. But the most unexpected response came from the foreign colonies in which women had never heard such problems discussed and took the prospect of the municipal ballot as a simple device—which it is—to aid them in their daily struggle with adverse city conditions. The Italian women said that the men engaged in railroad construction were away all summer and did not know anything about their household difficulties. Some of them came to Hull-House one day to talk over the possibility of a public wash-house. They do not like to wash in their own tenements, they have never seen a washing-tub until they came to America, and find it very difficult to use it in the restricted space of their little kitchens and to hang the clothes within the house to dry. They say that in the Italian villages the women all go to the streams together; in the town they go to the public wash-house; and washing, instead of being lonely and disagreeable, is made pleasant by cheerful conversation. It is asking a great deal of these women to change suddenly all their habits of living, and their contention that the tenement-house kitchen is too small for laundry-work is well taken. If women in Chicago knew the needs of the Italian colony they would realize that any change bringing cleanliness and fresh clothing into the Italian household would be a very sensible and hygienic measure. It is, perhaps, asking a great deal that the members of the City Council should understand this, but surely a comprehension of the needs of these women and efforts toward ameliorating their lot might be regarded as matters of municipal obligation on the part of voting women.

The same thing is true of the Jewish women in their desire for covered markets which have always been a municipal provision in Russia and Poland. The vegetables piled high upon the wagons standing in the open markets of Chicago become covered with dust and soot. It seems to these women a violation of the most rudimentary decencies and they sometimes say quite simply: "If women had anything to say about it they would change all that."

...The duty of a woman toward the schools which her children attend is so obvious that it is not necessary to dwell upon it. But even this simple obligation cannot be effectively carried out without some form of social organization as the mothers' school clubs and mothers' congresses testify, and to which the most conservative women belong because they feel the need of wider reading and discussion concerning the many problems of childhood. It is, therefore, perhaps natural that the public should have been more willing to accord a vote to women in school matters than in any other, and yet women have never been members of a Board of Education in sufficient numbers to influence largely actual school curriculi. If they had been kindergartens, domestic science courses and school playgrounds would be far more numerous than they are. More than one woman has been convinced of the need of the ballot by the futility of her efforts in persuading a business man that young children need nurture in something besides the three r's. Perhaps, too, only women realize the influence which the school might exert upon the home if a proper adaptation to actual needs were considered. An Italian girl who has had lessons in cooking at the public school will help her mother to connect the entire family with American food and household habits. That the mother has never baked bread in Italy—only mixed it in her own house and then taken it out to the village oven—makes it all the more necessary that her daughter should understand the complication of a cooking-stove. The same thing is true of the girl who learns to sew in the public school, and more than anything else, perhaps, of the girl who receives the first simple instruction in the care of little children, that skillful care which every tenement-house baby requires if he is to be pulled through his second summer. The only time, to my knowledge, that lessons in the care of children were given in the public schools of Chicago was one summer when the vacation schools were being managed by a volunteer body of women. The instruction was eagerly received by the Italian girls, who had been "little mothers" to younger children ever since they could remember.

As a result of this teaching I recall a young girl who carefully explained to her Italian mother that the reason the babies in Italy were so healthy and the babies in Chicago were so sickly was not, as her mother had always firmly insisted, because her babies in Italy had goat's milk and her babies in America had cow's milk, but because the milk in Italy was clean and the milk in Chicago was dirty.... She also informed her mother that the "City Hall wanted to fix up the milk so that it couldn't make the baby sick, but that they hadn't quite enough votes for it yet." The Italian mother believed what her child had been taught in the big school; it seemed to her quite as natural that the city should be concerned in providing pure milk for her younger children as it should provide big schools and teachers for her older children. She reached this naïve conclusion because she had never heard those arguments which make it seem reasonable that a woman should be given the school franchise but no other.

But women are also beginning to realize that children need attention outside of school hours; that much of the petty vice in cities is merely the love of pleasure gone wrong, the overrestrained boy or girl seeking improper recreation and excitement. It is obvious that a little study of the needs of children, a sympathetic understanding of the conditions under which they go astray, might save hundreds of them. Women traditionally have had an opportunity to observe the plays of children and the needs of youth, and yet in Chicago, at least, they had done singularly little in this vexed problem of juvenile delinquency until they helped to inaugurate the Juvenile Court movement a dozen years ago. The Juvenile Court Committee, made up largely of women, paid the salaries of the probation officers connected with the court for the first six years of its existence, and after the salaries were cared for by the county the same organization turned itself into a Juvenile Protective League, and through a score of paid officers are doing valiant service in minimizing some of the dangers of city life which boys and girls encounter....

The more extensively the modern city endeavors on the one hand to control and on the other hand to provide recreational facilities for its young people the more necessary it is that women should assist in their direction and extension. After all, a care for wholesome and innocent amusement is what women have for many years assumed. When the reaction comes on the part of taxpayers women's votes may be necessary to keep the city to its beneficent obligations toward its own young people.

...Ever since steam power has been applied to the processes of weaving and spinning woman's traditional work has been carried on largely outside of the home. The clothing and household linen are not only spun and woven, but also usually sewed, by machinery; the preparation of many foods has also passed into the factory and necessarily a certain number of women have been obliged to follow their work there, although it is doubtful, in spite of the large numbers of factory girls, whether women now are doing as large a proportion of the world's work as they used to do. Because many thousands of those working in factories and shops are girls between the ages of fourteen and twenty-two there is a necessity that older women should be interested in the conditions of industry. The very fact that these girls are not going to remain in industry permanently makes it more important that some one should see to it that they shall not be incapacitated for their future family life because they work for exhausting hours and under insanitary [sic] conditions.

If woman's sense of obligation had enlarged as the industrial conditions changed she might naturally and almost imperceptibly have inaugurated the movements for social amelioration in the line of factory legislation and shop sanitation. That she has not done so is doubtless due to the fact that her conscience is slow to recognize any obligation outside of her own family circle, and because she was so absorbed in her own household that she failed to see what the conditions outside actually were. It would be interesting to know how far the consciousness that she had no vote and could not change matters operated in this direction. After all, we see only those things to which our attention has been drawn, we feel responsibility for those things which are brought to us as matters of responsibility. If conscientious women were convinced that it was a civic duty to be informed in regard to these grave industrial affairs, and then to express the conclusions which they had reached by depositing a piece of paper in a ballot box, one cannot imagine that they would shirk simply because the action ran counter to old traditions.

To those of my readers who would admit that although woman has no right to shirk her old obligations, that all of these measures could be secured more easily through her influence upon the men of her family than through the direct use of the ballot; I should like to tell a little story. I have a friend in Chicago who is the mother of four sons and the grandmother of twelve grandsons who are voters. She is a woman of wealth, of secured social position, of sterling character and clear intelligence, and may, therefore, quite fairly be cited as a "woman of influence".... I happened to call at her house on the day that Mr. McKinley was elected President against Mr. Bryan for the first time. I found my friend much disturbed. She said somewhat bitterly that she had at last discovered what the much-vaunted influence of woman was worth; that she had implored each one of her sons and grandsons, had entered into endless arguments and moral appeals to induce one of them to represent her convictions by voting for Bryan! That, although sincerely devoted to her, each one had assured her that his convictions forced him to vote the Republican ticket.... I contended that a woman had no right to persuade a man to vote against his own convictions; that I respected the men of her family for following their own judgement regardless of the appeal which the honored head of the house had made to their chivalric devotion. To this she replied that she would agree with that point of view when a woman had the same opportunity as a man to register her convictions by vote. I believed then as I do now, that nothing is gained when independence of judgement is assailed by "influence," sentimental or otherwise, and that we test advancing civilization somewhat by our power to respect differences and by our tolerance of another's honest conviction.

This is, perhaps, the attitude of many busy women who would be glad to use the ballot to further public measures in which they are interested and for which they have been working for years. It offends the taste of such a woman to be obliged to use "indirect influence" when she is accustomed to well-bred, open action in other affairs, and she very much resents the time spent in persuading a voter to take her point of view, and possibly to give up his own, quite as honest and valuable as hers, although different because resulting from a totally different experience. Public-spirited women who wish to use the ballot, as I know them, do not wish to do the work of men nor to take over men's affairs. They simply want an opportunity to do their own work and to take care of those affairs which naturally and historically belong to women, but which are constantly being overlooked and slighted in our political institutions....

To turn the administration of our civic affairs wholly over to men may mean that the American city will continue to push forward in its commercial and industrial development, and continue to lag behind in those things which make a city healthful and beautiful. After all, woman's traditional function has been to make her dwelling-place both clean and fair. Is that dreariness in city life, that lack of domesticity which the humblest farm dwelling presents, due to a withdrawal of one of the naturally cooperating forces? If women have in any sense been responsible for the gentler side of life which softens and blurs some of its harsher conditions, may they not have a duty to perform in our American cities?

In closing, may I recapitulate that if woman would fulfill her traditional responsibility to her own children; if she would educate and protect from danger factory children who must find their recreation on the street; if she would bring the cultural forces to bear upon our materialistic civilization; and if she would do it all with the dignity and directness fitting one who carries on her immemorial duties, then she must bring herself to the use of the ballot—that latest implement for self government. May we not fairly say that American women need this implement in order to preserve the home?

Notes

The article, "Why Women Should Vote," was first published in The Ladies Home Journal, 27, (January 1910): 21-22.

1. For examples of this critical view of Addams, see: Jill Conway, "Women Reformers and American Culture, 1870-1930," Journal of Social History 5 (Winter, 1971-72): 164-177; Jill Conway, "Stereotypes of Femininity in a Theory of Sexual Evolution," Victorian Studies 14 (September, 1970): 47-62; Judith Lacerte, "If Only Jane Addams Had Been a Feminist," Social Casework 57 (December, 1976): 656-660; William O'Neill, Everyone was Brave: A History of Feminism in America (Chicago, 1971), 120; Aileen Kraditor, The Ideas of the Woman Suffrage Movement (New York, 1965).

2. Carol Gilligan, In a Different Voice: Psychological Theory and Women's Development (Cambridge, Mass., 1982); Joan Tronto, "Beyond Gender Difference Toward a Theory of Care," Signs 12 (Summer, 1987): 644-663; Jean Bethke Elshtain, "Antigone's Daughters," Democracy 2 (April, 1982): 46-59; Mary Dietz, "Context is All: Feminism and Theories of Citizenship," Daedalus (1987): 1-24; Kathleen B. Jones, "Citizenship in a Woman-Friendly Polity," Signs 15 (Summer, 1990).

3. Paula Baker, "The Domestication of Politics: Women and American Political Society, 1780-1920," American Historical Review 89 (June, 1984): 620-647. Kathryn Kish Sklar, "Hull House in the 1890's: A Community of Women Reformers," Signs 10 (Summer, 1985): 658-677; and "The Historical Foundations of Women's Power in the Creation of the American Welfare State, 1830-1930," 43-93 and Eileen Boris, "The Power of Motherhood: Black and White Activist Women Redefine the 'Political,'" both in Mothers of the New World: Maternalist Politics and the Origins of Welfare States, Seth Koven and Sonya Michel, eds. (New York, 1993), 213-245.

4. "The Only Saint America Has Produced," Current Literature 40 (April, 1906); "The Most Useful Americans," The

Independent 74 (May 1, 1913): 956-957; Editor's introduction to Addams's 1913 column, *The Ladies' Home Journal*, 30 (January, 1913): 25.

5. The best published biography of Jane Addams is *American Heroine: The Life and Legend of Jane Addams* by Allen F. Davis, (New York, 1973). Davis includes a copy of a "spider web" chart on p. 265.

6. Julia Ward Howe, "The Case for Woman Suffrage," *The Outlook* 91 (April 3, 1909): 780.

7. Baker, "The Domestication of Politics," 642.

8. Frank Parsons, "Shall Our Mothers, Wives and Sisters Be Our Equals or Our Subjects?" *The Arena* 40 (July, 1908): 92-94; Rosamond Sutherland, "The Appeal of Politics to Woman," *The North American Review* 191 (January, 1910): 82, 85; "The Justice and Desirability of Woman Suffrage," *The Independent* 82 (April 5, 1915): 3-4.

9. Howe, "The Case for Woman Suffrage," 781.

10. Alva P. Belmont, "Woman's Right to Govern Herself," *The North American Review* 190 (November, 1909): 664-674; Florida Pier, "The Delightfully Quaint Antis," *Harper's Weekly* 53 (December 11, 1909): 34; Harper, "Would Woman Suffrage Benefit the State, and Woman Herself?" 374; Sutherland, "The Appeal of Politics to Woman," 82; "Margaret vs. Bridget," *The Independent* 67 (1909): 1394; Parsons, "Shall Our Mothers, Wives and Sisters Be Our Equals or Our Subjects?" 93; Molly Warren, "The Housekeeper's Need of the Ballot," *The World Today* 12 (January-June, 1907): 418-421. For examples of anti-suffrage arguments in popular magazines in these years, see: "Concerning Woman's Suffrage," *The Outlook* 64 (March 10, 1900); Lyman Abbott, "Why Women Do Not Wish the Suffrage," *The Atlantic Monthly* 92 (September, 1903); Elizabeth McCracken, "The Women of America: Woman's Suffrage in Colorado," *The Outlook* 75 (November 28, 1903): 737-744; Annie Nathan Meyer, "Woman's Assumption of Sex Superiority," *North American Review* 178 (January, 1904): 103-109; Lyman Abbott, "The Assault on Womanhood," *The Outlook* 91 (April 3, 1909): 784-788; "Do Women Wish to Vote?" *The Outlook* 94 (February 19, 1910): 375-377; Molly Elliot Seawell, "The Ladies' Battle," *The Atlantic Monthly* 106 (September, 1910): 289-303; Jessie Atkinson McGriff, "Before the American Woman Votes," *The Ladies' Home Journal* 27 (April, 1910): 56.

11. Jane Addams, "Votes for Women and Other Votes," *The Survey* 29 (June 1, 1912): 368.

12. Jane Addams, "Pragmatism in Politics," *The Survey* 29 (October 5, 1912): 12.

13. Jane Addams, "A Modern Lear," *The Survey* 29 (November 2, 1912): 137.

14. Conway, "Women Reformers," and "Stereotypes of Femininity"; Davis, *American Heroine*, 187, 316.

15. Conway, "Women Reformers," 174, and "Stereotypes of Femininity," 58.

16. Jane Addams, "The Working Woman's Need of the Ballot," *The Woman's Journal* (November 20, 1897).

17. Jane Addams, "The Larger Aspects of the Woman's Movement," *Annals of the American Academy of Political and Social Science* 56 (November, 1914): 6.

18. See, for example, Maureen Flanagan, "Gender and Urban Political Reform: The City Club and the Woman's Club of Chicago in the Progressive Era," *American Historical Review* 95 (October, 1990): 1032-1050.

19. Jane Addams, "If Men Were Seeking the Franchise," *The Ladies' Home Journal* 30 (June, 1913): 21.

20. Jane Addams, "Women, War, and Suffrage," *The Survey* 35 (November 6, 1915): 148-149. This article indicates that Addams did not, in the years before 1920, rest her claims for women's role in international relations on biological essentialism.

21. Addams, "Votes for Women and Other Votes," 367-368.

Eleven

"Better Citizens Without the Ballot":

American Anti-suffrage Women
and Their Rationale
During the Progressive Era

Manuela Thurner

Editor's Introduction: In this fascinating essay, Manuela Thurner discusses the women who organized to *oppose* woman suffrage, the anti-suffrage women popularly known as the "Antis." Thurner insists that these women are often misunderstood—when they are discussed at all—by historians who have accepted without sufficient examination the suffragists' characterization of their despised female adversaries as: "puppets of more powerful male forces"; selfish, pampered socialites, motivated by a desire to maintain their own highly privileged status; and reactionaries with an extremely narrow view of woman's proper role. Misunderstanding of the anti-suffrage women also stems from the fact that historians have at times generalized about anti-suffragists after studying only the writings of anti-suffrage men—who, in many cases, *were* reactionaries disturbed by the increasing public activity of women, or claimed that woman suffrage would "ruin women" and "destroy the home" out of fear that it would threaten their economic interests.

Thurner's own study, focusing particularly on Antis in the Northeast between 1900 and 1920 and based on the writings of anti-suffrage women and major Anti periodicals, avoids both of these pitfalls—and offers very different conclusions about anti-suffrage women. Thurner rejects the idea that the Antis were controlled by male anti-suffragists, and downplays the socio-economic differences between anti-suffragists and suffragists.

Most significantly, Thurner challenges prevailing assumptions about the *ideology* of the female anti-suffragists, who "portrayed themselves as very much in line with and in favor of turn-of-the-century Progressive reform and female activism." According to Thurner, the Antis *urged* women to play an active role in public affairs, but believed that this could best be done "without the ballot" by disinterested, nonpartisan women. They opposed woman's entry into politics believing that political activity—like participation in the woman suffrage movement itself—would diffuse women's energies and lessen their effectiveness by diverting them away from all-female clubs and organizations through which women had already proven to be very influential. And they argued (like some feminists and scholars today) that female separatism might be more effective in achieving reforms women desire than the dilution of women's efforts in gender-integrated political organizations.

Indeed, Thurner insists that this set of ideas regarding women's participation in public affairs was one of the reasons the Antis were initially successful and able to forestall the suffrage victory as long as they did. She implies that had Progressive-Era Antis insisted on women remaining completely in the domestic sphere—like some suffrage opponents who denounced public activism on the part of women as unwomanly and ungodly—they might have been less convincing. This in itself is strong testimony concerning the degree of change that had taken place in the late nineteenth century in ideas about woman's sphere.

★   ★   ★   ★   ★

"WILL HISTORY REMEMBER the heroines of feminism...? It will not." Thus anti-suffragist Florence R. Hall expressed her optimism about her opponents' fate in the September 1915 issue of *The Woman's Protest,* the official publication of the National Association Opposed to Woman Suffrage (NAOWS).[1] Seventy-five years after the passage of the Nineteenth Amendment, and after three decades of feminist scholarship, which has produced a huge body of literature on exactly those "heroines of feminism," Hall's assertion sounds peculiar, if not outright absurd. Yet, in the fall of 1915, this assessment on the part of an anti-suffrage woman was by no means far-fetched or unrealistic. The "Antis"—as the female anti-suffragists came to be known—accurately predicted victories for their cause in the November state suffrage referenda of New York, New Jersey, Massachusetts, and Pennsylvania. Coming, as they did, after a host of preceding suffrage defeats throughout the country, the Antis' triumphs in those four eastern states constituted their latest and most promising success. That very same year, they could also point to the fact that suffrage amendments had been lost in twenty state legislatures. It was not until New York State finally passed woman suffrage in November of 1917 and the House of Representatives voted in favor of a federal amendment, in the year following, that signs of disillusion and resignation began to show within the ranks of the organized anti-suffragists. Ultimately defeated in 1920 when Tennessee cast the necessary thirty-sixth vote to ratify the Nineteenth Amendment, anti-suffragists disappeared from the public stage—and from the subsequent historical record. Now, it was the suffragists' turn to invoke the dictum that "[v]ictorious movements record their history, vanquished ones rarely do."[2]

Historians and the Anti-suffrage Movement

Feminist scholarship has indeed recounted women's collective endeavors and triumphs more extensively than the manifold conflicts and tensions among women of different ethnic, racial, religious, political, and class backgrounds. Women's historians all too often uncritically adopt feminist perspectives and judgments when they set out to write women into history. In the historiography of the woman suffrage movement, this point of view has led to various misconceptions about the women who opposed their own enfranchisement. Reiterating the assessments of prominent suffragists, later historians of the suffrage movement have dismissed the female antis as insignificant and have elaborated instead on the male liquor, business, political, and southern states' rights interests as the more important and potent anti-suffrage forces.[3] The small body of secondary literature focusing on the anti-suffragists does little to modify these interpretations or to dispel the myths. While minutely exploring the organizational history and makeup of the more important anti-suffrage associations, it does not, surprisingly, take much care to investigate more fully those women's motivations for opposing their enfranchisement.[4]

The majority of scholars have accepted the "woman's place is in the home" argument as the fundamental and most frequently invoked rationale of the Antis. For the most part, historians have depicted the opponents of woman suffrage as late Victorians who, married with children, were not ready or willing to accommodate themselves to the individualistic tendencies and altered social and gender relations of the modern era, and whose adherence to an ideology of domesticity was doomed to failure in an era of widespread Progressive reform and public activism. However, an analysis of the female anti-suffragists' major periodicals and writings of the first two decades of the twentieth century, the most active and successful phase of the organized Antis' short history, reveals the relative insignificance of this argument. Instead, the Antis not only actually but also ideologically ventured considerably beyond the domestic sphere in their effort to forestall women's enfranchisement. They, in fact, portrayed themselves as very much in line with and in favor of turn-of-the-century Progressive reform and female activism. This may not only help to explain the fact that the Antis were able to prolong the suffrage fight considerably; it also promises an analysis of their arguments in terms that are of relevance to current debates about women's relationship to the public and political realms.

Women as Anti-suffrage Theorists and Activists

The organized anti-suffrage movement started in 1882 with the founding of the Massachusetts Association Opposed to the Further Extension of Suffrage to Women (MAOFESW). By 1900, there were female anti-suffrage associations in New York, Illinois, California, South Dakota, Washington, and Oregon. In 1911, the National Association Opposed to Woman Suffrage (NAOWS) opened its headquarters in New York City, from which it moved to Washington, D.C. in 1917. Due to the NAOWS's vigorous recruitment efforts, twenty-five state associations with combined membership estimated at 200,000 subscribed to the anti-suffrage cause by 1915.[5] Yet it is of minor significance to recollect the exact founding dates, membership figures, and organizational structures of the twenty-odd anti-suffrage associations (the data offered on those counts by both contemporary observers and historians are incomplete and often contradictory) or to remember the names of the participating states (which varied from year to year). The crucial point is to realize that the movement was commonly understood to be founded, staffed, and led by women. Although men's anti-suffrage organizations existed, they did not issue their own periodicals or engage in the kind of sustained publicity work that became the hallmark of the older and more seasoned female organizations. In keeping with their avowed philosophy to steer clear of politics and to concentrate instead on educating the public about their beliefs, female antis occasionally voiced their resolve to "leav[e] the political end entirely to men."[6] Yet, in practice, it was usually representatives of female anti-suffrage organizations who appeared before congressional committees or other political forums to speak out against women's enfranchisement.

Women also came to be the most prolific theorists of the anti-suffrage movement. Not only did the bulk of articles and essays in the anti-suffrage periodical press stem from the pen of female contributors; women also authored the more elaborate treatises and tracts delineating a rationale for opposing women's enfranchisement. When Helen Kendrick Johnson's *Woman and the Republic* was first published in 1897, reviews across the nation were full of praise. *The St. Paul Pioneer-Press* termed it the "most temperate, concise, and well-conducted argument against woman suffrage which has yet appeared in book form."[7] One newspaper declared: "If the woman suffrage movement is ever to be finally defeated, it will be by women themselves, and by arguments and considerations like those so ably stated in this remarkable book."[8] Heartened by the press's generally favorable attitude towards their cause, other female anti-suffragists followed in Johnson's footsteps. Virginian Molly Elliot Seawell's *The Ladies' Battle* (1911); journalist Ida Tarbell's *The Business of Being a Woman* (1912); Grace Duffield Goodwin's *Anti-Suffrage: Ten Good Reasons* (1915), a booklet written by the president of the Washington, D.C. anti-suffrage association; and Annie Riley Hale's *The Eden Sphinx* (1916) were other well-received books that more or less forcefully advanced a coherent rationale for opposing women's enfranchisement.[9] Though none of these works achieved the popularity or critical acclaim of Johnson's treatise, their mere existence and wide circulation nevertheless testified to the fact that women not only worked but wrote to thwart their own enfranchisement.

Who were these women? In addressing this question, one encounters a host of stereotypes and clichés that have been transmitted through the suffragist record. "A little band of rich, ultra society women," "the candied fruit of a generation characterized by 'frenzied finance,'" "butterflies of fashion" who "move in a limited though most unimpeachable circle" were only a few of many unflattering epithets the suffragists held in store for their opponents.[10] Some sociologists and historians have in fact argued that the female anti-suffragists were mostly upper-class women whose primary motivation for their vehement opposition to the ballot was their fear of a decline in status. According to this interpretation, the Antis were most of all wary of the democraticizing tendencies of suffragist politics and thus eager to safeguard their class privileges.[11]

However, the class-related differences between the proponents and the opponents of women's enfranchisement should not be overemphasized. To be sure, many of the female Antis came from old and well-established families whose names were often known well beyond their native states' boundaries for the social, political, and economic clout they had carried for decades or

"The New Woman—Wash Day." A satirical photograph inspired by woman suffrage. Library of Congress

even centuries. It is also true that the organized leadership's particular make-up did not facilitate or encourage the participation of women of non-white, non-Protestant backgrounds. African American, immigrant, and working-class women may very well have harbored anti-suffrage sentiments, but they were not represented in the movement's front ranks or on the editorial boards of the anti-suffrage periodicals. Yet the suffrage movement, too, especially in its later phase, counted a fair number of socially prominent women among its activists and, moreover, had its own share of elitist, nativist, and racist rhetoric.

Most importantly, a college education, professional employment, and a life without a husband and children were not infallible indicators of a woman's pro-suffrage stance. Indeed, most anti-suffragists would have had no difficulty in embracing the label of the "New Woman" as appropriate designation for themselves. Alike in many biographical particulars, pro- and anti-suffrage women shared above all one crucial conviction: both groups declared themselves to be deeply committed to women's public activism and social reform.

The Anti-suffragist as "New Woman"

In March 1909, *The Anti-Suffragist,* a publication of the New York State Association Opposed to Woman Suffrage (NYSAOWS), reprinted a comment by well-known suffragist Florence Kelley, general secretary of the National Consumer's League, in which she branded the Antis as "shirks," "lazy, comfortable, sheltered creatures, caring nothing for the miseries of the poor."[12] Few other accusations could have struck more to the heart of the anti-suffrage women's self-definition and could have provoked a more indignant reaction. Addressing the Judiciary Committee of the House of Representatives in 1914, Massachusetts Anti Mrs. Henry Preston (Sarah C.) White took pains to refute such claims. Listing a long catalog of the MAOFESW members' and leaders' manifold philanthropic, charitable, educational, and civic activities, White asserted that the anti-suffragists, all widely publicized stereotypes to the contrary, were "disinterested, public-spirited citizens who give their time and service to questions of public service without the hope of political reward or preference."[13]

Similar assertions resounded throughout the anti-suffrage literature of the first two decades of the twentieth century. In a prefatory chapter to a collection of anti-suffrage essays by Massachusetts women, published on the occasion of the defeat of the state's 1915 suffrage referendum, Mrs. John (Katharine Torbert) Balch, then president of the MAOFESW, emphasized that its members represented a fair cross section of the population, comprising women of every "class or type." Even more importantly, she asserted that she "could fill pages with the record" of the Antis' "public welfare activities."[14] As if to underscore that claim, every one of the seventeen anti-suffrage essays following Balch's introduction was prefaced by a roster of the various public activities of their respective authors—activities that included work in educational associations, municipal, health, consumer, and trade union leagues, women's clubs, settlement houses, state boards of charity, prison, playground, and child reform organizations.[15]

The public activities or the professional experiences of an anti-suffrage woman were often cited as if they conferred upon her the very legitimacy and authority to speak out in opposition to women's enfranchisement and to make her opinion one of particular interest and value to the female population of America. When addressing themselves to the public, whether in the form of legislative committees or a more general audience, Antis emphatically underscored their public commitment and thus took pains to dissociate themselves from the image of sheltered, domestic creatures foisted upon them by their opponents. Yet references to civic activities did more than boost the Antis' stature in public. The anti-suffragists' involvement in all kinds of reform and associational endeavors was reflected by and shaped the rationale of the women opposed to their enfranchisement. I want to argue that the arguments turn-of-the-century Antis most frequently invoked against women's enfranchisement had less to do with woman's place in the home than with her appropriate role in the public realm.

A Woman's Place Is in Public

Just as the Antis rejected their image as idle, elitist, "bridge-playing" socialites,[16] they steadfastly sought to refute the suffragists' assertions that the domestic sphere was the only one they allegedly considered appropriate for women. They continually pointed out that they did *not* "make a fetish of the home as a place, nor of woman in the home, merely because she happens to be there."[17] On the contrary. Turn-of-the-century anti-suffrage leaders constantly urged women to leave the household to engage in a multitude of extra-domestic activities. In what came to be the unofficial creed of NAOWS, reiterated time and again in *The Woman's Protest,* president Mrs. Arthur M. (Josephine) Dodge stated at the organization's fourth annual meeting in January 1916:

> We believe that women according to their leisure, opportunities, and experience should take part increasingly in civic and municipal affairs as they always have done in charitable, philanthropic and educational activities and we believe that this can best be done without the ballot by women, as a non-partisan body of disinterested workers.[18]

Another Anti put it even more forcefully: "Do not mistake me. No woman should spend all her time at home. Public needs and social duties must be attended to."[19] In an attempt to clarify the Antis' position on this issue, Mrs. J.B. Gilfillan, president of the Minnesota Association Opposed to Woman Suffrage, announced that:

> Anti-Suffragists are opposed to women in political life, opposed to women in politics. This is often interpreted to mean opposition to women

in public life, which is a profound mistake. We believe in women in all the usual phases of public life, except political life. Wherever woman's influence, counsel or work is needed by the community, there you will find her, so far with little thought of political beliefs.... The pedestals they are said to stand upon move them into all the demands of the community.[20]

In keeping with their own public activism and visibility, anti-suffrage leaders, speakers, and authors thus saw women's legitimate sphere of action not reduced to or circumscribed by domestic concerns. Rather, they stimulated women to venture beyond the home dutifully to shoulder their responsibilities in the public realm of reform and civic activities.

Given their obvious advocacy of women's presence in public life, both in theory and in practice, the question becomes *why* the anti-suffragists shied away so vehemently from the political realm. What explains the resolute stance of New York journalist Jeanette L. Gilder who wrote: "Give woman everything she wants, but not the ballot. Open every field of learning, every avenue of industry to her, but keep her out of politics"?[21] What made the vote so unpalatable to those women who otherwise embraced a host of public duties and responsibilities?

Anti-suffragists of the Progressive Era provided two answers. Some, by far the minority among them, argued that women were already overburdened, "with the demands of society, the calls of charity, the church, and philanthropy constantly increasing."[22] They thus could not possibly take on other, i.e. political duties, which would include not only casting the ballot, but also serving on juries or running for office. A further diffusion of women's energies would not increase their positive effect on society, as the suffragists argued, but entail a lessening of female influence as women would be forced to sacrifice quality for quantity in their attempt to add another weighty task to their already packed agenda.

More often, however, the Antis' rejection of the vote reflected not so much their dread of overwork and exhaustion, as it was based on a more sophisticated and recommendable rationale. "For me, the vital argument against suffrage for women is that it would hamper them in their more effective work in social and political lines," social worker Mary Ella Swift wrote in the lead article of a 1913 issue of *The Woman's Protest*.[23] Most Antis would certainly have agreed with this observation. Swift and other anti-suffragists insisted that political beliefs and the ballot would not only be of little value to the female reformer, but would in fact constitute a serious handicap in her work for the social good. Since casting the ballot would necessitate a woman's alignment with a political party, to become a voter would rob her of her political neutrality and non-partisanship. This in turn would diminish her influence with legislative or other governmental authorities that had so far been responsive to women's requests on the very grounds of their political disinterestedness.[24] Standing "apart from and beyond party politics," unenfranchised women, the Antis argued, were especially effective in addressing social problems and bringing about much-needed reform legislation.[25] "Outside the political machinery," *The Anti-Suffragist* announced in its December 1908 issue, "there is a world...where all reform begins."[26] "The more reform movements are separated from politics the better for them," the journal declared again in April 1912.[27]

It was largely for this reason that the powerful umbrella organization of the nation's myriad female literary and educational groups, the General Federation of Women's Clubs, did not officially endorse woman suffrage until 1914. When it did, this came as a serious blow to the Antis. For years, they had tried to prevent this development by insisting that the collective work of the women's clubs was "more potent" than women's individual exercise of political privileges, which would only splinter female solidarity along party lines.[28] Likewise, the Antis considered trade unions, not political organizations, the better representatives of working women's interests and the more effective agents in providing good working conditions and propagating fair labor legislation.[29] To alleviate and remedy all kinds of social ills, concerning all classes and segments of society, anti-suffragists preferred non-partisan to partisan bodies, and politically neutral women to male voters whose reform intentions they found to be inevitably compromised by their affiliations to a political party.

Far from supposedly urging women to stay in or retreat into a narrowly circumscribed domestic realm and to "shirk" their public responsibilities, the female anti-suffragists advanced arguments that derived from and reflected their sincere efforts to discharge those responsibilities with the best possible results. In their opinion, it was the advocates of woman suffrage who egotistically dodged all civic obligations, attending suffrage meetings instead of "giv[ing] hours, days, thought and energy to quiet, persistent, unheralded work toward the amelioration of the condition of women, children, and the unfortunate."[30] When the suffragists announced that they would stop contributing to civic and philanthropic causes until they were given the vote, the Antis uttered a collective cry of indignation. Taking this as further example of the suffragists' selfishness and unscrupulousness, they grasped the opportunity to portray themselves as the truly reform-oriented and caring social force of the two.

Nonpartisan Women, Society, and the State

The fight for woman suffrage, at least during the Progressive Era, was not a conflict between women who were active in public and those who advocated that a woman's place was in the home. Rather, it was two different notions of women's relationship to the public and the political realm that were at odds in the debates concerning women's enfranchisement. In an essay entitled "Woman's Civic Work Better Done Without Suffrage," Anti Elizabeth McCracken summarized the controversy's underlying issue as follows:

[O]ur position, as Anti-Suffragists, is not negative, but positive. We are not so much opposing the policy of the Suffragists as we are presenting a policy of our own. The Suffragists have one conception of the relation of women to good government—and we Anti-Suffragists have another—which seems to us better. Just as fervently as the Suffragists, do the Anti-Suffragists desire to be citizens, and intend to be citizens.... We Anti-Suffragists feel that we not only can be and are citizens without the ballot, but that we shall remain better citizens without it than with it.[31]

Mrs. Andrew J. (Alice N.) George, a principal secretary of both the Massachusetts and the National Association Opposed to Woman Suffrage, also asserted that "[w]oman's citizenship is as real as man's. The question we must answer is one of social efficiency."[32] Thus, the issue at stake was not, as many historians have argued implicitly or explicitly, one of anti-suffragists pitting their private female sphere of domestic concerns against a male public sphere of political affairs in a vestigial Victorian scenario. Rather, in the social and political context of the Progressive Era, Antis tried to hold on to what they considered to be a distinctive female public realm, different from the male realm of politics in its functions, but equal or even superior in its societal ramifications.

In order to bring women's positive influence to bear even more successfully upon public life, anti-suffragists believed that the boundaries between men's and women's public activities should not be erased, but rendered even more distinct. Such was the gist of a lecture Mrs. Barclay Hazard held before the New York State Federation of Women's Clubs in 1907:

[W]e must accept partisanship, political trickery and office-seeking as necessary evils inseparable from modern conditions, and the question arises what can be done to palliate the situation. To our minds, the solution has been found by the entrance of women into public life. Standing in an absolutely independent position, freed from all party affiliations, untrammeled by any political obligations, the intelligent, self-sacrificing women of to-day are serving the State (though many of them hardly realize it) as a third party whose disinterestedness none can doubt.[33]

The successful continuation of women's disinterested work, "untainted by political ambition" and motives, would only be ensured, according to the anti-suffragists, by keeping men and women in their separate public spheres and by recognizing their respective promises as well as limitations.[34]

In the eyes of the anti-suffragists, the vote threatened to divest women of their public power. By forcibly redirecting women's attention and energies to politics, the proponents of women's enfranchisement were about to undermine the non-partisan foundation of the all-female clubs, societies, and associations, i.e., women's citadels of public power. Seeing the suffragists' demand for the vote as an indication of their willingness to sacrifice women's social activism in the arena of male electoral politics, the Antis were upset by this apparent denial of the efficiency and validity of women's public influence as manifested through channels other than electoral politics. Women's strength in the public sphere, the Antis argued, could be more fully developed if they remembered their difference, not their sameness with male political actors. What was at stake for the Antis in the debates about woman suffrage was not women's domesticity, but women's effectiveness as non-voting, yet public-spirited citizens and agents of social change.

In order to show that their claims about the reform successes and social efficiency of unenfranchised women were not just sheer hypotheses or wishful thinking on their part, the Antis cited a variety of evidence in their favor. Their preferred strategy was to enlist the testimony of a host of female social workers, reformers, and activists who maintained that they would have never accomplished what they did if they had been entitled to cast the ballot and thereby been asked to abdicate their political neutrality. Furthermore, the anti-suffragists buttressed their assertions with "empirical evidence" from the states that had already granted the franchise to their female populations. Charts unfavorably comparing the reform legislation as well as the laws pertaining to women in Colorado, the Antis' exemplary suffrage state, to those of the eastern non-suffrage states filled the pages of the anti-suffrage periodicals.[35] Such legal documentation also constituted the basis for Minnie Bronson's influential anti-suffrage tract, "The Wage-Earning Woman and the State," reprinted annually in the early 1910s, which tried to disprove contentions about working women's need for the ballot.[36] Finally, the Antis cited statistical as well as impressionistic evidence to announce the numerical decline of women's civic and reform associations in the suffrage states.

The years during World War I seemed to be an especially propitious time for the Antis to advance their argument of the efficiency of politically neutral women carrying out disinterested relief service in the name of peace and patriotism. While the suffragists proclaimed that they ranked their efforts to win the vote above the country's commitment to win the war, the Antis instead never tired of highlighting their self-sacrificing and loyal stance towards the nation. In fact, they channeled much of their associational, human, and financial resources into war relief work, which was extensively documented in the war-year issues of *The Woman's Protest*. Asserting that the "importance of nonpolitical women to the state [was] greater than ever before," the anti-suffragists saw the global conflict as an opportunity to put an end to allegations about their idleness and to demonstrate the validity and relevance, not to mention the patriotic implications, of their rationale against women's enfranchisement.[37] Ironically, what had looked like a perfect opportunity to underscore the logic of the Anti position turned out to be one of the major determining factors in their ultimate defeat. In recognition of the invaluable aid and service women had rendered to their country during this time of crisis, many formerly undecided

WHY WE DO NOT APPROVE
OF
WOMAN SUFFRAGE

BECAUSE: We feel that the ballot makes absolutely no difference in the economic status of woman. Whether she votes or not, her charities, great and small, will continue, professions will extend diplomas to her intelligence, and trade will grant recompense to her ability. As for the protection of the ballot to working women, it will protect them no farther than it protects men who, in spite of their voting power, find themselves unable to cope with labor conditions by legislation and form themselves into unions outside of law and law making.

BECAUSE: Our hospital Boards, our social and civic service work, our child welfare committees and countless other clubs and industries for the general welfare and uplift need women who can give non-partisan and unselfish service, the worth of which service would be greatly lessened by political affiliations.

BECAUSE: Behind law there must always be force to make it effective. If legislation was shaped by a majority of women over men we should soon have, not government, but chaos.

BECAUSE: It is an attested fact that politics degrade women more than women purify politics.

BECAUSE: We believe that American men would speedily remedy all conditions needing reform if urged with half the force now brought to bear in favor of suffrage.

BECAUSE: We believe that the interests of all women are as safe in the hands of men as in those of other women.

BECAUSE: Thorough investigation of the laws of suffrage states shows that non-suffrage states have by far the better and more humane laws, and that all laws are more strictly enforced than in suffrage states.

BECAUSE: We believe that if franchise for women would better general conditions, there would be some evidence of that betterment in states where it has been exercised for twenty and up to forty-four years.

BECAUSE: Women make little use of suffrage when it is given them. School suffrage has been a lamentable failure, the women vote averaging scarcely two per cent in any state.

BECAUSE: The energies of women are engrossed by their present duties and interests, from which men cannot relieve them, and there is great need of better performance of their present work rather than diversion to new fields of activity.

BECAUSE: The suffrage movement develops sex hatred which is a menace to society.

BECAUSE: Of the alliance of suffrage with socialism which advocates free love and institutional life for children.

BECAUSE: The greatest menace to the morals of today lies in the efforts of suffragists to convince the world that vice is predominant. In the mad rush for the ballot and the consequent advertisement of immorality, reverence has been dethroned and reticence annihilated. It is high time for the right thinking, purity-loving women to arise and undo the terrific impress made on the public mind by the preachments of these pursuers of vice.

BECAUSE: The great majority of intelligent, refined and educated women do not want enfranchisement. They realize no sense of injustice such as expressed by the small minority of suffragists. They have all the rights and freedom they desire, and consider their present trusts most sacred and important. They feel that the duties which naturally must ever revert to their sex are such that none but themselves can perform and that political responsibilities could not be borne by them without the sacrifice of the highest interests of their families and of society.

Nebraska Association Opposed to Woman Suffrage.

Anti-suffrage leaflet, c. 1914. Denison Library, Scripps College legislators finally acceded to the Nineteenth Amendment, granting women the vote in 1920.

Anti-suffragism, Female Activism, and Progressive Reform

The emergence, in the 1890s and the first two decades of the 1900s, of an anti-suffrage rationale that centered on the public activities rather than the domestic "nature" and destiny of American women reflected and drew upon certain historical developments and circumstances that made the argument both timely and persuasive. This is not to say that *all* female or, for that matter, male, opponents of women's suffrage espoused the reasoning outlined in this essay. Nor do I want to argue that this has been the dominant anti-suffrage rationale ever since women first demanded their enfranchisement. Rather, it was an argument particularly suited to the Progressive Era. In that particular period of American history, which was characterized by a near-universal preoccupation with reform and enthusiasm for progress, women gained new visibility and clout. Women founded and participated in a variety of associations, organizations, clubs, and societies; they entered many educational institutions that had formerly been the exclusive preserve of men; and they were newly visible in the public as clerical workers, department store employees, professionals, and social reformers.[38] Contrary to common historical wisdom, the female Antis were not opposed to but actively involved in such and similar developments. Their associational and sometimes (semi-)professional experiences did not only provide them with the expertise and the know-how to establish an organized anti-suffrage movement; they also became an integral part of their anti-suffrage rationale. Far from divorcing themselves from the activist and reformist traditions and tendencies of the past and the present, the anti-suffrage women eagerly stressed their indebtedness to nineteenth-century female reformers and emphasized their firm commitment to the reform agenda of the Progressive Era.

As a matter of fact, early twentieth-century Antis cited the female notables of the preceding century as fitting exemplars of women whose fame and reputation rested upon a host of extraordinary achievements, all of which had been possible without the ballot. The Antis were not at a loss to find distinguished nineteenth-century women who had combined public activism with a resolute anti-suffrage stance. English relief worker Octavia Hill was occasionally introduced as the prototypical woman whose distinctive and invaluable contribution was not that of a "politician," but of "a disinterested factor working to render public service uncolored by political motives."[39] Closer to home, educators Catharine Beecher, Emma Willard, and Civil War nurse Dorothea Dix, "the Florence Nightingale of this country," led the throng of influential women whom the American Antis took to be their sisters in spirit and action as well as the truly progressive forces in society.[40]

Claiming to be the rightful descendants of this distinctively female tradition of public activism, the anti-suffragists aligned themselves with the "true woman" ideology that they saw as the driving force behind all major reform achievements of the nineteenth and early twentieth centuries.[41] Anti Lilian Bayard Taylor Kiliani cited the entrance of women into institutions of higher education, industry, and the professions as well as the profusion of female reform associations and movements as irrefutable proof of how much women were able to achieve, "without going to the polls or becoming involved in party politics."[42] Helen Kendrick Johnson, in particular, made it her avowed objective to wrest praise for women's progress and manifold accomplishments from the suffragists. She asserted that "'Movement' and 'Progress' [were] not synonymous terms," but with regard to woman suffrage virtually irreconcilable opposites. In her *Woman and the Republic,* she argued that wherever advocates of woman suffrage had meddled in matters of major national concern—be it abolitionism, temperance, or woman's rights—they had only caused delays, dissensions, and serious disturbances, which had frustrated a more prompt and efficient approach to these affairs.[43]

Aware that "next to being unpopular, to be unprogressive, is the worst thing that can be said of an American, male or female,"[44] Antis were especially sensitive to criticism of that kind and went to great lengths to refute allegations about their aversion to change. New York Anti Annie Nathan Meyer, one of the driving forces behind the foundation of Barnard College and an associate editor of the anti-suffrage, anti-feminist, anti-socialist *The Woman's Patriot,* was especially insistent in refuting the widespread assumption that the "movement to obtain the ballot for women is identical with and not to be separated from all other movements for women's progress." In the spring of 1910, she indignantly wrote:

> The suffragists have battled for suffrage the past forty years in America—on the whole with rather conspicuous unsuccess. Some of them—fewer by far than is claimed—also incidentally battled for other reform, but never without the help and enthusiasm of convinced anti-suffragists.... The women who really blazed the paths of education and reform in this country were either outspoken antisuffragists or at best lukewarm suffragists who were too busy doing their work to bother about imaginary wrongs. This confusion of the suffrage movement with every movement that made for advance goes merrily on, and few take the trouble to stop it.[45]

Turning the tables on the suffragists, the Antis characterized the votes-for-women movement as "fifty years behind the time," calling it a "movement backward towards men and mastodons, the miocene hipparion and eocene anchitherium."[46] In comparison, the average female anti-suffragist was seen as standing "in the very front rank of progress for she [was] a preventive philanthropist," she was "the newest new woman,... at work at home and in public."[47]

Because it allowed them to combine their rejection of women's enfranchisement with an unequivocal affirmation of the ideas of social progress and women's advancement, such reasoning understandably attracted many women to the anti-suffrage cause. The appeal of this particular argumentation could largely be explained by the fact that it built on and embraced several assumptions that were shared by most women—and men—during the Progressive Era, regardless of their stance on the question of suffrage.

In fact, agreement on women's public influence and the need for social reform often brought opponents and proponents of woman suffrage alike together in their common concern for the public good. In 1891, Annie Nathan Meyer edited a book called *Woman's Work in America,* a collection of essays on women's manifold contributions to education, literature, journalism, medicine, ministry, law, industry, philanthropy, and the state.[48] Ironically, and significantly, most of the contributors to this volume, which was compiled by an ardent anti-suffragist, professed to be in favor of women's enfranchisement; the preface, for example, was written by well-known Bostonian suffragist Julia Ward Howe.

Suffragists were in fact willing to acknowledge the successes and positive changes in social work that women had wrought without the vote. In an essay entitled "The Legislative Influence of Unenfranchised Women," historian and activist Mary Ritter Beard conceded that "other influences than those of the ballot box operate on" legislators and state representatives.[49] Elaborating on this point, Beard in 1915 published her *Woman's Work in Municipalities,* an impressive compendium of the various types of women's activities on the local and communal levels—paying no heed to those women's opinion on the suffrage issue.[50]

While anti-suffragists most probably wholeheartedly welcomed Beard's observations, they could not assent to her suggestion that women's influence would reach even further if they were given the vote. For the Antis, it was the very fact of their disfranchisement and concomitant disinterestedness that had made women such efficient reformers. Looking back on women's multitudinous accomplishments over the past decades, they saw no reason to believe that the continuing success and expansion of women's charitable, philanthropic, and civic reform activities depended on the ballot. It was at this crucial juncture where anti- and pro-suffrage women's opinions took different turns. While the demand for the vote, in some instances, served as a unifying cause for many women of different backgrounds and interests, it became the divisive issue for many female activists who otherwise found themselves in general accord on matters concerning women's prominent role in turn-of-the-century social reform.[51] Agreeing on social reform as the desirable objective of women's public involvement, Antis and suffragists differed on which way was the better and more efficient to that end.

Conclusion

Such findings not only correct or modify traditional accounts concerning the female anti-suffragists' makeup and motives, but also carry with them implications that are relevant to larger debates in the field of women's history.

It would not be an exaggeration to claim that women's involvement in reform associations, institutions, and movements is probably the most widely studied area of American women's history. Much of the secondary literature has focused on the question of whether or to what extent women's manifold organizational activities foreshadowed and/or constituted the necessary prerequisites of suffragism and feminism. For the most part, historians have tried to establish a continuum between early- and mid-nineteenth-century women's participation in a variety of reform movements and turn-of-the-century women's espousal of suffrage and feminist principles. Earlier abolitionist, moral reform, temperance, and other largely single-sex reform societies have been seen as consciousness-raising training-grounds for later avid suffragists. Similarly, historians have argued that nineteenth-century women's activism gave them an incentive to expand their sphere of influence and provided them with a rationale to demand the vote to that end.[52]

The example of the female anti-suffragists, however, calls for a more complex interpretation. As their case demonstrates, women's public activities have not always been put to feminist ends nor have they necessarily bred ideas critical of the patriarchal organization of the state as women, so the story goes, came to realize their powerlessness and ineffectiveness in the political arena.[53] The Antis, as discussed in this essay, opposed women's enfranchisement not in spite of, but *because of* their involvement and experiences in a huge number of extra-domestic organizations, which they came to look upon as their bulwarks of public power and influence. The majority of organized Antis were women who occupied many public positions and offices and who brought their experiences and expertise in the public realm to bear on their anti-suffrage labor. While they saw suffragism and feminism as dangerous to the progress of society, they, at the same time, had no difficulty proclaiming their affinities with various pioneering women activists of the nineteenth century, or welcoming every possible development that they perceived as furthering women's progress. Both the Antis' own activism and their interpretations of women's historical and social mission combined to generate strong anti-feminist, defined as anti-suffrage beliefs and convictions.

Yet, strangely and ironically, anti-suffrage women have something to tell the late twentieth-century feminist historian and theorist. Although the turn-of-the-century Antis' own definition of politics as a male, partisan enterprise was a very narrow one, which did not encompass their reform activities, this fact should not and cannot prevent us from regarding women's public activism in the realm of social reform legislation as highly political. Recent feminist scholarship has expanded traditional definition of politics so as to incorporate many areas, activities, and actors that have generally been excluded by political theory. Some scholars have even gone so far as to suggest that there were times, the Progressive Era prominent among them, when women's distinctive contributions to society had more far-reaching social and political implications than men's exercise of their voting privileges.[54] Emphasizing the integrity and importance of a distinctively female tradition of public activism and asserting that women's citizenship did not, for its valuation, depend on the vote, the turn-of-the-century anti-suffrage women styled themselves as champions and defenders of an area and of ideas that are of increasing interest to feminist political theorists who are trying to introduce an "alternative concept of public life" deriving its force from non-electoral, non-partisan forms of political participation.[55] Once historians and political theorists start to examine more closely the workings and the concerns of the female public culture of the past to gain insights for the present and the future, they cannot afford to ignore the voices of the women who opposed woman suffrage.

Notes

This essay is a revised version of an article originally published in the *Journal of Women's History* 5, no. 1 (Spring 1993), 33-60, and appears here with the permission of the journal.

1. Florence R. Hall, "Disinterested, Appealing to All Humanity," *The Woman's Protest* 7, no. 5 (September 1915), 6.

2. Carrie Chapman Catt and Nettie Rogers Shuler, *Woman Suffrage and Politics: The Inner Story of the Suffrage Movement* (1923; reprint, Seattle, 1969), 132.

3. See Eleanor Flexner, *Century of Struggle: The Woman's Rights Movement in the United States* (Cambridge, 1968), 294-305; Alan P. Grimes, *The Puritan Ethic and Woman Suffrage* (New York, 1967), 78-98; Aileen S. Kraditor, *The Ideas of the Woman Suffrage Movement, 1890-1920* (New York, 1965), 14-42; William L. O'Neill, *Feminism in America: A History* (New Brunswick, 1989), 55-64; and Carl N. Degler, *At Odds: Women and the Family in America from the Revolution to the Present* (New York, 1980), 349-355.

4. See, Jane Jerome Camhi, "Women Against Women: American Anti-Suffragism, 1880-1920," Ph.D. diss., Tufts University, 1973; Thomas J. Jablonsky, "Duty, Nature, and Stability: The Female Anti-Suffragists in the U.S., 1894-1920," Ph.D. diss., University of Southern California, 1978; See also Mara Mayor, "Fears and Fantasies of the Anti-Suffragists," *Connecticut Review* 7, no. 2 (April 1974): 64-74; Catherine Cole Mambretti, "The Battle Against the Ballot: Illinois Woman Antisuffragists," *Chicago History* 9, no. 3 (Fall 1980): 168-177; and Louise L. Stevenson, "Women Antisuffragists in the 1915 Massachusetts Campaign," *New England Quarterly* 52, no. 1 (March 1979): 80-93.

5. For more information see, Camhi, "Women Against Women," and Jablonsky, "Duty, Nature, and Stability."

6. *The Woman's Protest* 7, no. 1 (May 1915): 16.

7. *The St. Paul Pioneer-Press*, cited in Helen Kendrick Johnson, *Woman and the Republic: A Survey of the Woman-Suffrage Movement in the United States and a Discussion of the Claims and Arguments of Its Foremost Advocates* (1897; New York, 1913), 364, 367, 368.

8. *The Brooklyn Standard-Union*, quoted in Rossiter Johnson, *Helen Kendrick Johnson: The Story of Her Varied Activities* (New York, 1917), 51.

9. Molly Elliot Seawell, *The Ladies' Battle* (New York, 1911); Ida Tarbell, *The Business of Being a Woman* (New York, 1912); Grace Duffield Goodwin, *Anti-Suffrage: Ten Good Reasons* (New York, 1915); and Annie Riley Hale, *The Eden Sphinx* (New York, 1916).

10. Quotes are taken from *The Woman's Standard* (May 1906): 3, ibid. (February 1905): 1, cited in Jablonsky, "Duty, Nature, and Stability," 10; *The Woman's Protest* 8, no. 5 (March 1916): 13; and Susan B. Anthony and Ida Husted Harper, *History of Woman Suffrage* 4 (New York, 1969), 716.

11. Susan E. Marshall, "In Defense of Separate Spheres: Class and Status Politics in the Antisuffrage Movement," *Social Forces* 65, no. 2 (December 1986): 327-351; and Susan E. Marshall and Anthony M. Orum, "Opposition Then and Now: Countering Feminism in the Twentieth Century," in *Research in Politics and Society: A Research Annual; Vol. 2: Women and Politics: Activism, Attitudes and Office-Holding*, eds. Gwen Moore and Glenna Spitze (Greenwich, Conn., 1986), 23.

12. Florence Kelley, quoted in *The Anti-Suffragist* 1, no. 3 (March 1909): 2.

13. Mrs. Henry White, "Who Are the Anti-Suffragists—And Why," *The Woman's Protest* 4, no. 6 (April 1914): 5, 6.

14. See Mrs. John Balch, "Who the Massachusetts Anti-Suffragists Are," in *Anti-Suffrage Essays by Massachusetts Women*, ed. Ernest Bernbaum (Boston: Forum Publications, 1916), 21-23.

15. That this self-representation on the part of the Antis did indeed correspond with their actual experiences and employments is corroborated by a look at the 1914-1915 edition of the *Woman's Who's Who of America*. In this biographical dictionary of American and Canadian women who "are leading in or contributing to women's larger participation in the good causes and higher endeavors of our time," one finds a great number of women who, while actively engaged in a host of leagues, clubs, societies, and voluntary organizations, declared themselves opposed to or undecided with regard to woman suffrage; see John William Leonard, ed., *Women's Who's Who of America: A Biographical Dictionary of Contemporary Women of the United States and Canada, 1914-1915* (New York, 1914), 22.

16. Laura Fay-Smith, quoted in Marshall, "In Defense of Separate Spheres," 341.

17. *The Woman's Protest* 5, no. 6 (October 1914): 14.

18. Mrs. Arthur M. Dodge, "The Report of the President," *The Woman's Protest* 8, no. 3 (January 1916): 6.

19. Mrs. Charles Burton Gulick, "The Imperative Demand Upon Women in the Home," in *Anti-Suffrage Essays by Massachusetts Women*, 133.

20. Mrs. J.B. Gilfillan, "Work and the Home," *The Woman's Protest* 7, no. 1 (May 1915): 17.

21. Jeanette L. Gilder, "Why I am Opposed to Woman Suffrage," pamphlet, 1894, MAOFESW, Mudd Library, Yale University (hereafter cited as Mudd).

22. Quoted in Kraditor, *The Ideas of the Woman Suffrage Movement*, 27-28; also *The Anti-Suffragist* 1, no. 1 (July 1908): 4; and Emily Bissell, "A Talk to Women on the Suffrage Question," pamphlet, 1909, 2, NYSAOWS, Mudd.

23. Mary Ella Swift, "Suffrage for Women a Handicap in Civic Work," *The Woman's Protest* 3, no. 4 (August 1913): 3.

24. See *The Anti-Suffragist* 1, no. 2 (December 1908): 11, 13; 2, no. 1 (September 1909): 5; 3, no. 3 (March 1911): 3; 3, no. 4 (June 1911): 8; 4 no. 2 (April 1912): 2; *The Woman's Protest* 1, no. 4 (August 1912): 12; 6, no. 3 (January 1915): 9; and 7, no. 5 (September 1915): 19. See also the contributions of Mrs. A.J. George, Monica Foley, Dorothy Godfrey Wayman, and Margaret C. Robinson in *Anti-Suffrage Essays by Massachusetts Women*.

25. *The Anti-Suffragist* 1, no. 2 (December 1908): 11.

26. *The Anti-Suffragist* 1, no. 2 (December 1908): 13.

27. *The Anti-Suffragist* 4, no. 2 (April 1912): 2.

28. Anon., "Women's Clubs More Potent Than the Ballot," *The Woman's Protest* 5, no. 3 (July 1914): 5.

29. See Anon., "Working Women and Suffrage," *The Anti-Suffragist* 2, no. 2 (December 1909): 1; and Adeline Knapp, "Do Working Women Need the Ballot?—An Address to the Senate and Assembly Judiciary Committee of the New York Legislature," NAOWS, Mudd.

30. Anon., "Missing the Opportunities," *The Woman's Protest* 1, no. 5 (September 1912): 4.

31. Elizabeth McCracken, "Woman's Civic Work Better Done Without Suffrage," *The Woman's Protest* 4, no. 3 (Jan 1914): 16.

32. Mrs. A.J. George, "Efficiency the Real Test of Woman Suffrage," *The Woman's Protest* 8, no. 6 (April 1916): 5.

33. Mrs. Barclay Hazard, "How Women Can Best Serve the State" (Chicago: Illinois Association Opposed to the Extension of Suffrage to Women; reprinted by courtesy of the NYSAOWS, n.d.), 2, Mudd.

34. *The Woman's Protest* 2, no. 2 (December 1912): 6; see also Annah Robinson Watson, "The Attitude of Southern Women on the Suffrage Question," *The Arena* 11 (February 1895): 366.

35. See Eliza D. Armstrong, "Non-Partisan Woman Wins Where Voters Fail," *The Woman's Protest* 4, no. 3 (December 1913): 21; Mrs. Rowland G. Hazard, "Some Reasons Why We Oppose Suffrage; Its Effect on the State," pamphlet, 1911, Rhode Island Association Opposed to Woman's Suffrage, Mudd; Ellen Mudge Burrill, "Some Practical Aspects of the Question"; and Catherine Robinson, "Massachusetts Compared With Suffrage States," in *Anti-Suffrage Essays by Massachusetts Women*, 43-52, 62-66.

36. Minnie Bronson, "The Wage-Earning Woman and the State," 1912, 1913, 1914, NAOWS, Mudd.

37. *The Woman's Protest* 7, no. 4 (August 1915): 7-8.

38. For an excellent overview of this period, see Sara M. Evans, *Born for Liberty: A History of Women in America* (New York, 1989), 145-173.

39. Mrs. Arthur M. Dodge, "Woman Suffrage Opposed to Woman's Rights," in *Women in Public Life*, ed. James P. Lichtenberger, *The Annals of the American Academy of Political and Social Science* 56 (November 1914), 104.

40. *The Woman's Protest* 8, no. 5 (March 1916): 19.

41. Mrs. Herbert Lyman, "The Anti-Suffrage Ideal," in *Anti-Suffrage Essays by Massachusetts Women*, 121; *The Woman's Protest* 5, no. 2 (June 1914): 10.

42. Lilian Bayard Taylor Kiliani, "Women Without Ballot Do Greater Work," *The Woman's Protest* 3, no. 2 (June 1913): 8.

43. See especially the introduction and the chapter on "Woman Suffrage and Philanthropy" in Johnson, *Woman and the Republic*, 5-9, 104-155; quotation on 104.

44. Mrs. Robert McVickar, "What is an Anti-Suffragist?," undated pamphlet, NAOWS, Mudd.

45. Annie Nathan Meyer, "Miss Johnston and Woman Suffrage," *The Bookman* 31 (May 1910): 314.

46. Alice Hill Chittenden, "The Inexpediency of Granting the Suffrage to American Women—An Address at the Tenth Biennial of the General Federation of Women's Clubs, Cincinnati, May 14, 1910," pamphlet, NAOWS, Mudd; Anon., "A Movement Toward Mastodons," *The Woman's Protest* 4, no. 1 (November 1913): 14.

47. Margaret H. Freeman, "The Voice of the Majority," *The Anti-Suffragist* 2, no. 1 (September 1909): 3; and Margaret Doane Gardiner, "A Mining Experiment," *The Anti-Suffragist* 3, no. 1 (September 1910): 3.

48. Annie Nathan Meyer, ed., *Woman's Work in America* (New York, 1972).

49. Mary Ritter Beard, "The Legislative Influence of Unenfranchised Women," in *Women in Public Life*, 54, 60.

50. Mary Ritter Beard, *Woman's Work in Municipalities* (1915; New York, 1972).

51. See Lucy Jeanne Price, "Lessons Learned From the Campaign," *The Woman's Protest* 8, no. 1 (November 1915): 5-6.

52. See especially Keith Melder, "Ladies Bountiful: Organized Women's Benevolence in Early Nineteenth-Century America," *New York History* 48, no. 3 (July 1967): 231-255; Alice Rossi, "Social Roots of the Woman's Movement in America," in *The Feminist Papers*, ed. Alice Rossi (New York, 1973), 241-281; Barbara Berg, *The Remembered Gate: Origins of American Feminism. The Woman and the City*, 1800-1860 (New York, 1978); and Lori Ginzberg, "'Moral Suasion is Moral Balderdash': Women, Politics, and Social Activism in the 1850s," *Journal of American History* 73, no. 3 (December 1986): 601-622.

53. Studies that have acknowledged the anti-feminist potential of women's associations include: Mary Ryan, "The Power of Women's Networks: A Case Study of Female Moral Reform in Antebellum America," *Feminist Studies* 5, no. 1 (Spring 1979): 66-85; Nancy Cott, *The Bonds of Womanhood: "Woman's Sphere" in New England, 1780-1835* (New Haven, 1977); and Nancy A. Hewitt, *Women's Activism and Social Change: Rochester, N.Y., 1822-1872* (Ithaca, 1984).

54. See Estelle Freedman, "Separatism As Strategy: Female Institution Building and American Feminism, 1870-1930," *Feminist Studies* 5, no. 3 (Fall 1979): 512-529; Paula Baker, "The Domestication of Politics: Women and American Political Society, 1780-1920," *American Historical Review* 89, no.2 (June 1984): 620-647; idem., *The Moral Frameworks of Public Life: Gender, Politics, and the State in Rural New York, 1870-1930* (New York, 1991); and Maureen A. Flanagan, "Gender and Urban Political Reform: The City Club and the Woman's City Club of Chicago in the Progressive Era," *American Historical Review* 95 (October 1990): 1032-1050.

55. Sara M. Evans, "Women's History and Political Theory: Towards a Feminist Approach to Public Life," in *Visible Women: New Essays on American Activism*, Nancy A. Hewitt and Suzanne Lebsock, eds. (Urbana, 1993), 121.

Twelve

Working Women, Class Relations, and Suffrage Militance:

Harriot Stanton Blatch and the New York Woman Suffrage Movement, 1894–1909

Ellen Carol DuBois

Editor's Introduction: Rediscovering the woman suffrage movement means revising a number of widely held but inaccurate ideas about the movement and its history. One of these misconceptions is that the woman suffrage movement in America was a "middle-class movement." Though it is true that many suffragists and suffrage leaders were middle-class, characterizing the movement as such, as Ellen Carol DuBois explains, "homogenizes" the movement. It distorts the picture by ignoring the presence in, and the contributions to, the suffrage movement of women from both ends of the economic scale.

As DuBois makes clear in this essay, elite women and working-class women were increasingly involved in the suffrage movement around the turn of the century. And in New York, a coalition of these women headed by Harriot Stanton Blatch, Elizabeth Cady Stanton's daughter, created a new tradition of class relations among women—one on which, writes DuBois, a "thriving, modern woman suffrage movement could be built." DuBois, who has just completed a biography of Harriot Stanton Blatch, describes Blatch as a born politician with the "combination of suffrage convictions and class awareness to lead New York suffragists through that transition." After a fascinating discussion of the attitudes of the wealthy suffragists who became prominent in the movement in the 1890s, DuBois explains how Blatch rejected the pattern of class relations favored by many elite suffragists and pointed the way to a new and far more productive working relationship between women from both ends of the socioeconomic spectrum that would transform and invigorate the entire suffrage campaign.

Though from an elite background, Blatch rejected the maternalistic attitudes toward working-class women held by many elite suffragists who presumed that working-class women should defer to their leadership in return for their protection. And she emphatically denounced the idea endorsed by some suffrage leaders in the 1890s (including Elizabeth Cady Stanton) that suffragists should call for woman suffrage with an educational qualification that would curtail the number of working-class women who would be enfranchised. A college-educated woman with B.A. and M.A. degrees from Vassar, Blatch's view of work as the key to women's independence, dignity, and freedom was similar to that of her contemporary, the feminist intellectual, Charlotte Perkins Gilman. Indeed, Blatch saw working-class women more as exemplars for women like herself rather than "victims to be succored."

Blatch, like Jane Addams, was convinced that working-class women not only understood their own interests but needed the vote in order to represent those interests and support reform. Impressed by the successful efforts of some British suffragists to organize across class lines (Blatch had married an Englishman and lived in Great Britain from 1882 to 1902), and by the partnership created between working-class and wealthy women in the Women's Trade Union League, she was also convinced that working-class women were able co-workers in the fight for woman suffrage.

Blatch urged established suffrage societies "to recognize the importance of the vote to wage-earning women and the importance of wage-earning women to winning the vote." However, writes DuBois, when existing groups failed to respond, Blatch formed her own society, the "Equality League of Self-Supporting Women." This organization, which harnessed the talents of educated professionals and the power and political sagacity of trade-union women, provided the medium for introducing a new and aggressive—indeed militant—style of activism into the suffrage movement.

Indeed, DuBois helps us "rediscover" the suffrage movement in yet another very important way as she demonstrates that the militant tactics embraced by American suffragists in the twentieth century were not entirely imported, but partly home grown—a contribution of working-class suffragists. Their involvement in the movement "broaden[ed] the class basis and the outlook of American suffragism" and thus prepared the way for American women "to respond to the heroism of the British militants."

Following a 1907 visit to New York by a leader of the British militants, Blatch and other "new" suffrage leaders introduced their tactics into the American movement. Some New York suffragists even adopted the name "suffragette"—a term embraced by the British militants, but generally shunned by moderate or conservative American suffragists precisely because it associated them with the British militants and was used by American anti-suffragists to diminish or denigrate suffrage advocates. But the embrace of the term by some New York suffragists—as well as their participation in public demonstrations—suggested just how willing these suffragists had become to part with genteel tradition.

Militant tactics, including parades and open-air (as opposed to parlor) meetings, and other such attention-getting tactics, would soon be embraced by the mainstream suffrage movement all over the nation (though the NAWSA continued to shun picketing and civil disobedience). These tactics proved to be extremely important to the cause, as they made it impossible for the press to continue to ignore the movement as they seemed determined to do. And, as Blatch shrewdly comprehended, participation in these public acts by women who had been taught to shun publicity was in itself good for the cause, in that it forced a re-examination of assumptions about definitions of femininity and cemented the participants' commitment to the cause.

★ ★ ★ ★ ★

THE POLITICS of Harriot Stanton Blatch illuminates the origin and nature of the woman suffrage movement in the Progressive Era. Blatch was the daughter of Elizabeth Cady Stanton, the founding mother of political feminism. Beginning in the early twentieth century, she was a leader in her own right, initially in New York, later nationally. As early as 1903, when politics was still considered something that disreputable men did, like spitting tobacco, Blatch proclaimed: "There are born politicians just as there are born artists, writers, painters. I confess that I should be a politician, that I am not interested in machine politics, but that the devotion to the public cause…rather than the individual, appeals to me."[1]

Just as her zest for politics marked Blatch as a new kind of suffragist, so did her efforts to fuse women of different classes into a revitalized suffrage movement. Blatch's emphasis on class was by no means unique; she shared it with other women reformers of her generation. Many historians have treated the theme of class by labeling the organized women's reform movement in the early twentieth century "middle-class." By contrast, I have tried to keep open the question of the class character of women's reform in the Progressive Era by rigorously avoiding the term. Characterizing the early twentieth-century suffrage movement as "middle-class" obscures its most striking element, the new interest in the vote among women at both ends of the class structure. Furthermore, it tends to homogenize the movement. The very term "middle-class" is contradictory, alternatively characterized as people who are not poor, and people who work for a living. By contrast, I have emphasized distinctions between classes and organized my analysis around the relations between them.

Class Complexities and Progressive Era Suffragism

No doubt there is some distortion in this framework, particularly for suffragists who worked in occupations like teaching. But there is far greater distortion in using the term "middle class" to describe women like Blatch or Carrie Chapman Catt or Jane Addams. For example, it makes more sense to characterize an unmarried woman with an independent income who was not under financial compulsion to work for her living as "elite," rather than "middle class." The question is not just one of social stratification, but of the place of women in a whole system of class relations. For these new style suffragettes, as for contemporary feminists who write about them, the complex relationship between paid labor, marital status, and women's place in the class structure was a fundamental puzzle. The concept of "middle class" emerged among early twentieth-century reformers, but may ultimately prove more useful in describing a set of relations between classes that was coming into being in those years, than in designating a segment of the social structure.

Blatch, examined as a political strategist and a critic of class relations, is important less as a unique figure than as a representative leader, through whose career the historical forces transforming twentieth-century suffragism can be traced. The scope of her leadership offers clues to the larger movement: She was one of the first to open up suffrage campaigns to working-class women, even as she worked closely with wealthy and influential upper-class women; she pioneered militant street tactics and backroom political lobbying at the same time. Blatch's political evolution reveals close ties between other stirrings among American women in the Progressive Era and the rejuvenated suffrage movement. Many of her ideas paralleled Charlotte Perkins Gilman's influential reformulation of women's emancipation in economic terms. Many of Blatch's innovations as a suffragist drew on her prior experience in the Women's Trade Union League. Overall, Blatch's activities suggest that early twentieth-century changes in the American suffrage movement, often traced to the example of militant British suffragettes, had deep, indigenous roots. Among them were the growth of trade unionism among working-class women and professionalism among the elite, changing relations between these classes, and the growing involvement of women of all sorts in political reform.

Wealthy Women and Suffragism in the 1890s

The suffrage revival began in New York in 1893-1894, as part of a general political reform movement. In the 1890s New York's political reformers were largely upper-class men concerned about political "corruption" which they blamed partly on city Democratic machines and the bosses who ran them, partly on the masses of voting men, ignorant, immigrant, and ripe for political manipulation. Their concern about political corruption and about the consequences of uncontrolled political democracy became the focus of New York's 1894 constitutional convention, which addressed itself largely to "governmental procedures: the rules for filling offices, locating authority and organizing the different branches."[2]

The New York woman suffrage movement, led by Susan B. Anthony, recognized a great opportunity in the constitutional convention of 1894. Focusing on political corruption, Anthony and her allies argued that women were the political reformers' best allies. For while men were already voters and vulnerable to the ethic of partisan loyalty—indeed a man without a party affiliation in the 1890s was damned close to unsexed—everyone knew that women were naturally nonpartisan. Enfranchising women was therefore the solution to the power of party bosses. Suffragists began by trying to get women elected to the constitutional convention itself. Failing this, they worked to convince the convention delegates to include woman suffrage among the proposed amendments.[3]

Anthony planned a house-to-house canvass to collect signatures on a mammoth woman suffrage petition. For the $50,000 she wanted to fund this effort, she approached wealthy women in New York City, including physician Mary Putnam Jacobi, society leader Catherine Palmer (Mrs. Robert) Abbe, social reformer Josephine Shaw Lowell, and philanthropist Olivia (Mrs. Russell) Sage. Several of them were already associated with efforts for the amelioration of working-class women, notably in the recently formed Consumers' League, and Anthony had reason to think they might be ready to advocate woman suffrage.[4]

The elite women were interested in woman suffrage, but they had their own ideas about how to work for it. Instead of funding Anthony's campaign, they formed their own organization. At parlor meetings in the homes of wealthy women, they tried to strike a genteel note, emphasizing that enfranchisement would *not* take women out of their proper sphere and would *not* increase the political power of the lower classes. Eighty-year-old Elizabeth Stanton, observing the campaign from her armchair, thought that "men and women of the conservative stamp of the Sages can aid us greatly at this stage of our movement."[5]

Why did wealthy women first take an active and prominent part in the suffrage movement in the 1890s? In part they shared the perspective of men of their class that the influence of the wealthy in government had to be strengthened; they believed that with the vote they could increase the political power of their class. In a representative argument before the constitutional convention, Jacobi proposed woman suffrage as a response to "the shifting of political power from privileged classes to the masses of men." The disfranchisement of women contributed to this shift because it made all women, "no matter how well born, how well educated, how intelligent, how rich, how serviceable to the State," the political inferiors of all men, "no matter how base-born, how poverty stricken, how ignorant, how vicious, how brutal." Olivia Sage presented woman suffrage as an antidote to the growing and dangerous "idleness" of elite women, who had forgotten their responsibility to set the moral tone for society.[6]

Yet, the new elite converts also supported woman suffrage on the grounds of changes taking place in women's status, especially within their own class. Jacobi argued that the educational advancement of elite women "and the new activities into which they have been led by it—in the work of charities, in the professions, and in the direction of public education—naturally and logically tend toward the same result, their political equality." She argued that elite women, who had aided the community through organized charity and benevolent activities, should have the same "opportunity to serve the State nobly." Sage was willing to advocate woman suffrage because of women's recent "strides...in the acquirement of business methods, in the management of their affairs, in the effective interest they have evinced in civic affairs."[7]

Suffragists like Jacobi and Sage characteristically conflated their class perspective with the role they saw for themselves as women, contending for political leadership not so much on the grounds of their wealth, as of their woman-liness. Women, they argued, had the characteristics needed in politics—benevo-lence, morality, selflessness, and industry; conveniently, they believed that elite women most fully embodied these virtues. Indeed, they liked to believe that women like themselves were elite *because* they were virtuous, not because they were wealthy. The confusion of class and gender coincided with a more general elite ideology that identified the fundamental division in American society not between rich and poor, but between industrious and idle, virtuous and vicious, community-minded and selfish. On these grounds Sage found the purposeless leisure of wealthy women dangerous to the body politic. She believed firmly that the elite, women included, should provide moral—and ultimately politi-cal—leadership, but it was important to her that they earn the right to lead.[8]

The problem for elite suffragists was that woman suffrage meant the enfran-chisement of working-class, as well as elite, women. Jacobi described a promi-nent woman who "had interested herself nobly and effectively in public affairs,…but preferred not to claim the right [of suffrage] for herself, lest its con-cession entail the enfranchisement of ignorant and irresponsible women." An elite anti-suffrage organization committed to such views was active in the 1894 campaign as well, led by women of the same class, with many of the same beliefs, as the pro-suffrage movement. As Stanton wrote, "The fashionable women are about equally divided between two camps." The antis included prominent society figures Abby Hamlin (Mrs. Lyman) Abbott and Josephine Jewell (Mrs. Arthur) Dodge, as well as Annie Nathan Meyer, founder of Barnard College and member of the Consumers' League. Like the elite suffragists, upper-class antis wanted to insure greater elite influence in politics; but they argued that woman suffrage would decrease elite influence, rather than enhance it.[9]

Elite suffragists' willingness to support woman suffrage rested on their confi-dence that their class would provide political leadership for all women once they had the vote. Because they expected working-class women to defer to them, they believed that class relations among women would be more coopera-tive and less antagonistic than among men. Elite women, Jacobi argued before the 1894 convention, would "so guide ignorant women voters that they could be made to counterbalance, when necessary, the votes of ignorant and interest-ed men." Such suffragists assumed that working-class women were too weak, timid, and disorganized to make their own demands. Since early in the nine-teenth century, elite women had claimed social and religious authority on the grounds of their responsibility for the women and children of the poor. They had begun to adapt this tradition to the new conditions of an industrial age, notably in the Consumers' League, formed in response to the pleas of women wage earners for improvement in their working conditions. In fact, elite antis also asserted that they spoke for working-class women, but they contended that working-class women neither needed nor wanted the vote.[10]

From an exclusively elite perspective, the anti-suffrage argument was more consistent than the pro-suffrage one; woman suffrage undoubtedly meant greater political democracy, which the political reform movement of the 1890s most fundamentally feared. Elite suffragists found themselves organizing their own arguments around weak refutations of the antis' objections.[11] The ideological weakness had political implications. Woman suffrage got no serious hearing in the constitutional convention, and the 1894 constitutional revisions designed to "clean up government" ignored women's plea for political equality.

The episode revealed dilemmas, especially with respect to class relations among women, that a successful suffrage movement would have to address. Elite women had begun to aspire to political roles that led them to support woman suffrage, and the resources they commanded would be crucial to the future success of suffrage efforts. But their attraction to woman suffrage rested on a portrait of working-class women and a system of class relations that had become problematic to a modern industrial society. Could elite women sponsor the entrance of working-class women into politics without risking their influence over them, and perhaps their position of leadership? Might not working-class women assume a newly active, politically autonomous role? The tradition of class relations among women had to be transformed before a thriving and modern woman suffrage movement could be built. Harriot Stanton Blatch had the combination of suffrage convictions and class awareness to lead New York suffragists through that transition.

Bringing Working Women Into Suffragism

The 1894 campaign, which confronted suffragists with the issue of class, also drew Blatch actively into the American woman suffrage movement. She had come back from England, where she had lived for many years, to receive a master's degree from Vassar College for her study of the English rural poor. A powerful orator, she was "immediately pressed into service...speaking every day" at parlor suffrage meetings, often to replace her aged mother.[12] Like her mother, Blatch was comfortable in upper-class circles; she had married into a wealthy British family. She generally shared the elite perspective of the campaign, assuming that "educated women" would lead their sex. But she disliked the implication that politics could ever become too democratic and, virtually alone among the suffragists, criticized all "those little anti-republican things I hear so often here in America, this talk of the quality of votes." And while other elite suffragists discussed working-class women as domestic servants and shop clerks, Blatch understood the centrality of industrial workers, although her knowledge of them was still primarily academic.[13]

Blatch's disagreements with the elite suffrage framework were highlighted a few months after the constitutional convention in an extraordinary public debate with her mother. In *The Woman's Journal*, Stanton urged that the suffrage movement incorporate an educational restriction into its demand, to respond to "the greatest block in the way of woman's enfranchisement...the fear of the 'ignorant vote' being doubled." Her justification for this position, so at odds with the principles of a lifetime, was that the enfranchisement of "educated women" best supplied "the imperative need at the time...woman's influence in public life." From England, Blatch wrote a powerful dissent. Challenging the authority of her venerated mother was a dramatic act that—perhaps deliberately—marked the end of her political daughterhood. She defended both the need and the capacity of the working class to engage in democratic politics. On important questions, "for example...the housing of the poor," their opinion was more informed than that of the elite. She also argued that since "the conditions of the poor are so much harder...every working man needs the suffrage more than I do." And finally, she insisted on the claims of a group her mother had ignored, working women.[14]

The debate between mother and daughter elegantly symbolizes the degree to which class threatened the continued vitality of the republican tradition of suffragism. Blatch was able to adapt the republican faith to modern class relations, while Stanton was not, partly because of Blatch's participation in the British social democratic movement known as Fabianism. As a Fabian, Blatch had gained an appreciation for the political intelligence and power of the working class very rare among elite reformers in the United States. When she insisted that the spirit of democracy was more alive in England than in the United States, she was undoubtedly thinking of the development of a working-class political movement there.[15]

Over the next few years, Blatch explored basic assumptions of the woman suffrage faith she had inherited in the context of modern class relations. In the process, like other women reformers of her era, such as Charlotte Perkins Gilman, Florence Kelley, Jane Addams, and numerous settlement house residents and supporters of organized labor, she focused on the relation of women and work. She emphasized the productive labor that women performed, both as it contributed to the larger social good and as it created the conditions of freedom and equality for women themselves. Women had always worked, she insisted. The new factor was the shift of women's work from the home to the factory and the office, and from the status of unpaid to paid labor. Sometimes she stressed that women's unpaid domestic labor made an important contribution to society; at other times she stressed that such unpaid work was not valued, but always she emphasized the historical development that was taking women's labor out of the home and into the commercial economy. The question for modern society was not whether women should work, but under what conditions, and with what consequences for their own lives.[16]

Although Blatch was troubled by the wages and working conditions of the laboring poor, her emphasis on work as a means to emancipation led her to regard wage-earning women less as victims to be succored, than as exemplars to their sex. She vigorously denied that women ideally hovered somewhere above the world of work. She had no respect for the "handful of rich women who have no employment other than organizing servants, social functions and charities." Upper-class women, she believed, should also "work," should make an individualized contribution to the public good, and where possible should have the value of their labor recognized by being paid for it.[17] As a member of the first generation of college-educated women she believed that education and professional achievement, rather than wealth and refinement, fitted a woman for social leadership.

Turning away from nineteenth-century definitions of the unity of women that emphasized their place in the home, their motherhood, and their exclusion from the economy, and emphasizing instead the unity that productive work provided for all women, Blatch rewrote feminism in its essentially modern form, around work. She tended to see women's work, including homemaking and child rearing, as a mammoth portion of the world's productive labor, which women collectively accomplished. Thus she retained the concept of "women's work" for the sex as a whole, while vigorously discarding it on the individual level, explicitly challenging the notion that all women had the same tastes and talents.[18]

Her approach to "women's work" led Blatch to believe that the interconnection of women's labor fundamentally shaped relations among them. Here were the most critical aspects of her thought. Much as she admired professional women, she insisted that they recognize the degree to which their success rested on the labor of other women, who cared for their homes and their children. "Whatever merit [their homes] possess," Blatch wrote, "is largely due to the fact that the actress when on the stage, the doctor when by her patient's side, the writer when at her desk, has a Bridget to do the homebuilding for her." The problem was that the professional woman's labor brought her so much more

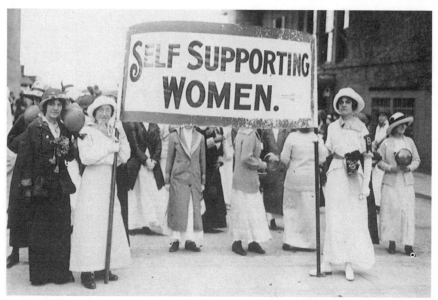

A New York City suffrage parade, c. 1912. Schlesinger Library, Radcliffe College

freedom than the housemaid's labor brought her. "Side by side with the marked improvement in the condition of the well-to-do or educated woman," Blatch observed, "our century shows little or no progress in the condition of the woman of the people." Like her friend Gilman, Blatch urged that professional standards of work—good pay, an emphasis on expertise, the assumption of a lifelong career—be extended to the nurserymaid and the dressmaker, as well as to the lawyer and the journalist. Until such time, the "movement for the emancipation of women [would] remain…a well-dressed movement." [19]

But professional training and better wages alone would not give labor an emancipatory power in the lives of working-class women. Blatch recognized the core of the problem of women's work, especially for working-class women: "How can the duties of mother and wage earner be reconciled?" She believed that wage-earning women had the same desire as professional women to continue to enjoy careers and independence after marriage. "It may be perverse in lowly wage earners to show individuality as if they were rich," Blatch wrote, "but apparently we shall have to accept the fact that all women do not prefer domestic work to all other kinds." But the problem of balancing a career and a homelife was "insoluble—under present conditions—for the women of the people." "The pivotal question for women," she wrote, "is how to organize their work as home-builders and race-builders, how to get that work paid for not in so called protection, but in the currency of the state." [20]

As the female labor force grew in the late nineteenth century, so did the number of married women workers and demands that they be driven from the labor force. The suffrage movement had traditionally avoided the conflict between work and motherhood by pinning the demand for economic equality on the existence of unmarried women, who had no men to support them. Blatch confronted the problem of work and motherhood more directly. In a 1905 article, she drew from the utopian ideas of William Morris to recommend that married women work in small, worker-owned manufacturing shops where they could have more control over their hours and could bring their children with them. Elsewhere, she argued that the workplace should be reorganized around women's needs, rather than assume the male worker's standards, but she did not specify what that would mean. She never solved the riddle of work and children for women—nor have we—but she knew that the solution could not be to force women to choose between the two nor to banish mothers from the labor force. [21]

Blatch's vision of women in industrial society was democratic—all must work and all must be recognized and rewarded for their work—but it was not an egalitarian approach nor one that recognized most working women's material concerns. According to Blatch, women worked for psychological and ethical reasons, as much as for monetary ones. "As human beings we must have work," she wrote; "we rust out if we have not an opportunity to function on something." She emphasized the common promises and problems work raised in women's lives, not the differences in how they worked, how much individual choice they had, and especially in how much they were paid. She was relatively unconcerned with the way work enabled women to earn their livings. No doubt, her own experience partially explains this. As a young woman fresh out of college in the 1870s, she had dared to imagine that her desire for meaningful work and a role in the world need not deprive her of marriage and motherhood, and it did not. Despite her marriage, the birth of two children, and the death of one, she never interrupted her political and intellectual labors. But she also never earned her own living, depending instead on the income from her husband's family's business. In later years, she joked about the fact that she was the only "parasite" in the organization of self-supporting women she headed.[22]

But the contradictions in her analysis of the problem of work and women reflected more than her personal situation. There were two problems of work and women: the long-standing exploitation of laboring women of the working classes and the newly expanding place of paid labor in the lives of all women in bourgeois society. While the two processes were not the same, they were related, and women thinkers and activists of the Progressive period struggled to understand how. As more women worked for pay and outside of the home, how would the meaning of "womanhood" change? What would be the difference between "woman" and "man" when as many women as men were paid workers? And what would be the class differences between women if all of them worked? Indeed, would there be any difference between the classes at all, once the woman of leisure no longer existed? Virtually all the efforts to link the gender and class problems of work for woman were incomplete.

Blatch rethought the principles of political equality in the light of her emphasis on women's work. At an 1898 congressional hearing, Blatch hailed "the most convincing argument upon which our future claims must rest—the growing recognition of the economic value of the work of women."[23] Whereas her mother had based her suffragism on the nineteenth-century argument for natural rights and on the individual, Blatch based hers on women's economic contribution and their significance as a group.

The contradictions in Blatch's approach to women and work also emerged in her attempts to link work and the vote. On the one hand, she approached women's political rights as she did their economic emancipation, democratically: Just as all sorts of women must work, all needed the vote. Wealthy women needed the vote because they were taxpayers and had the right to see that their money was not squandered; women industrial workers needed it because their jobs and factories were subject to laws, which they had the right to shape. On the other hand, she recognized the strategic centrality of the enormous class of industrial workers, whose economic role was so important and whose political power was potentially so great. "It is the women of the industrial class," she explained, "the wage-earners, reckoned by the hundreds of thousands,...the women whose work has been submitted to a money test, who have been the means of bringing about the altered attitude of public opinion toward woman's work in every sphere of life."[24]

New York City and Political Reform

Blatch returned to New York for several extended visits after 1894, and she moved back for good in 1902. She had two purposes. Elizabeth Stanton was dying, and Blatch had come to be with her. Blatch also intended to take a leading role in the New York City suffrage movement. On her deathbed in 1902, Stanton asked Anthony to aid Blatch. However, hampered by Anthony's determination to keep control of the movement, Blatch was not able to make her bid for suffrage leadership until Anthony died, four years later.[25]

Meanwhile, Blatch was excited by other reform efforts, which were beginning to provide the resources for a new kind of suffrage movement. During the first years of the twentieth century two movements contributed to Blatch's political education—a broadened, less socially exclusive campaign against political corruption and a democratized movement for the welfare of working women. By 1907, her combined experience in these two movements enabled her to put her ideas about women and work into practice within the suffrage movement itself.

Women had become more active in the campaign against political corruption after 1894. In New York City Josephine Shaw Lowell and Mary Putnam Jacobi formed the Woman's Municipal League, which concentrated on educating the public about corruption, in particular the links between the police and organized prostitution. Women were conspicuous in the reform campaigns of Seth Low, who was elected mayor in 1901.[26]

By the early 1900s, moreover, the spirit of political reform in New York City had spread beyond the elite. A left wing of the political reform movement had developed that charged that "Wall Street" was more responsible for political corruption than "the Bowery." Women were active in this wing, and there were women's political organizations with links to the Democratic party and the labor movement, a Women's Henry George Society, and a female wing of William Randolph Hearst's Independence League. The non-elite women in these groups were as politically enthusiastic as the members of the Woman's Municipal League, and considerably less ambivalent about enlarging the electorate. Many of them strongly supported woman suffrage. Beginning in 1905, a group of them organized an Equal Rights League to sponsor mock polling places for women to register their political opinions on election day.[27]

Through the 1900s Blatch dutifully attended suffrage meetings, and without much excitement advocated the municipal suffrage for propertied women favored by the New York movement's leaders after their 1894 defeat. Like many other politically minded women, however, she found her enthusiasm caught by the movement for municipal political reform. She supported Low for mayor in 1901 and believed that his victory demonstrated "how strong woman's power really was when it was aroused." By 1903 she suggested to the National American Woman Suffrage Association (NAWSA) that it set aside agitation for the vote, so that "the women of the organization should use it for one year, nationally and locally, to pursue and punish corruption in politics." She supported the increasing attention given to "the laboring man" in reform political coalitions, but she pointedly observed that "the working woman was never considered."[28]

However, working-class women were emerging as active factors in other women's reform organizations. The crucial arena for this development was the Women's Trade Union League (WTUL), formed in 1902 by a coalition of working-class and elite women to draw wage-earning women into trade unions. The New York chapter was formed in 1905, and Blatch was one of the first elite women to join. The WTUL represented a significant move away from the tradition of elite, ameliorative sisterhood at work in the 1894 campaign for woman suffrage. Like the Consumers' League, it had been formed in response to the request of women wage earners for aid from elite women, but it was an organization of both classes working together. Blatch had never been attracted to the strictly ameliorative tradition of women's reform, and the shift toward a partnership of upper-class and working-class women paralleled her own thinking about the relation between the classes and the role of work in women's lives. She and other elite women in the WTUL found themselves laboring not for working-class women, but with them, and toward a goal of forming unions that did not merely "uplift" working-class women, but empowered them. Instead of being working-class women's protectors, they were their "allies." Instead of speaking on behalf of poor women, they began to hear them speak for themselves. Within the organization wage earners were frequently in conflict with allies. Nonetheless, the league provided them an arena to articulate a working-class feminism related to, but distinct from, that of elite women.[29]

Although prominent as a suffragist, Blatch participated in the WTUL on its own terms, rather than as a colonizer for suffrage. She and two other members assigned to the millinery trade conducted investigations into conditions and organized mass meetings to interest women workers in unions. She sat on the Executive Council from 1906 through 1909 and was often called on to stand in for President Mary Dreier. Her academic knowledge of "the industrial woman" was replaced by direct knowledge of wage-earning women and their working conditions. She was impressed with what she saw of trade unionism, especially its unrelenting "militance." Perhaps most important, she developed working relations with politically sophisticated working-class women, notably Leonora O'Reilly and Rose Schneiderman. Increasingly she believed that the organized power of labor and the enfranchisement of women were closely allied.[30]

Working-class feminists in the league were drawn to ideas like Blatch's—to conceptions of dignity and equality for women in the workplace and to the ethic of self-support and lifelong independence; they wanted to upgrade the condition of wage-earning women so that they, too, could enjoy personal independence on the basis of their labor. On the one hand, they understood why most working-class women would want to leave their hateful jobs upon marriage; on the other, they knew that women as a group, if not the individual worker, were a permanent factor in the modern labor force. Mary Kenney O'Sullivan of Boston, one of the league's founders, believed that "self support" was a goal for working-class women, but that only trade unions would give the masses of working women the "courage, independence, and self respect" they needed to improve their conditions. She expected "women of opportunity" to help in organizing women workers, because they "owed much to workers who give them a large part of what they have and enjoy," and because "the time has passed when women of opportunity can be self respecting and work *for* others." [31]

Initially, the demand for the vote was less important to such working-class feminists than to the allies. Still, as they began to participate in the organized women's movement on a more equal basis, wage-earning women began to receive serious attention within the woman suffrage movement as well. Beginning about 1905, advocates of trade unionism and the vote for women linked the demands. At the 1906 suffrage convention WTUL member Gertrude Barnum pointed out that "our hope as suffragists lies with these strong working women." Kelley and Addams wrote about the working woman's need for the vote to improve her own conditions. In New York, Blatch called on the established suffrage societies to recognize the importance of the vote to wage-earning women and the importance of wage-earning women to winning the vote. When she realized that existing groups could not adapt to the new challenges, she moved to form her own society. [32]

The Equality League of Self-Supporting Women

In January 1907 Blatch declared the formation of a new suffrage organization, the Equality League of Self-Supporting Women. The *New York Times* reported that the two hundred women present at the first meeting included "doctors, lawyers, milliners and shirtmakers." [33] Blatch's decision to establish a suffrage organization that emphasized female "Self-support"—lifelong economic independence—grew out of her ideas about work as the basis of women's claim on the state, the leadership role that she envisioned for educated professionals, and her discovery of the power and political capacity of trade-union women. The Equality League provided the medium for introducing a new and aggressive style of activism into the suffrage movement—a version of the "militance" Blatch admired among trade unionists.

Initially, Blatch envisioned the Equality League of Self-Supporting Women as the political wing of the Women's Trade Union League. All the industrial workers she recruited were WTUL activists, including O'Reilly, the Equality League's first vice president, and Schneiderman, its most popular speaker. To welcome working-class women, the Equality League virtually abolished membership fees; the policy had the added advantage of allowing Blatch to claim every woman who ever attended a league meeting in her estimate of its membership. She also claimed the members of the several trade unions affiliated with the Equality League, such as the bookbinders, overall makers, and cap makers, so that when she went before the New York legislature to demand the vote, she could say that the Equality League represented thousands of wage-earning women.[34]

Blatch wanted the Equality League to connect industrial workers, not with "club women" (her phrase), but with educated, professional workers, who should, she thought, replace benevolent ladies as the leaders of their sex. Such professionals—college educated and often women pioneers in their professions—formed the bulk of the Equality League's active membership. Many were lawyers, for instance, Ida Rauh, Helen Hoy, Madeleine Doty, Jessie Ashley, Adelma Burd, and Bertha Rembaugh. Others were social welfare workers, for instance the Equality League's treasurer, Kate Claghorn, a tenement housing inspector and the highest paid female employee of the New York City government. Blatch's own daughter, Nora, the first woman graduate civil engineer in the United States, worked in the New York City Department of Public Works. Many of these women had inherited incomes and did not work out of economic need, but out of a desire to give serious, public substance to their lives and to make an impact on society. Many of them expressed the determination to maintain economic independence after they married.[35]

Although Blatch brought together trade-union women and college-educated professionals in the Equality League, there were tensions between the classes. The first correspondence between O'Reilly and Barnard graduate Caroline Lexow was full of class suspicion and mutual recrimination. More generally, there were real differences in how and why the two classes of working women demanded the vote. Trade-union feminists wanted the vote so that women industrial workers would have power over the labor laws that directly affected their working lives. Many of the college-educated self-supporters were the designers and administrators of this labor legislation. Several of them were, or aspired to be, government employees, and political power affected their jobs through party patronage. The occupation that might have bridged the differences was teaching. As in other cities, women teachers in New York organized for greater power and equal pay. The Equality League frequently offered aid, but the New York teachers' leaders were relatively conservative and kept their distance from the suffrage movement.[36]

Blatch's special contribution was her understanding of the bonds and common interests uniting industrial and professional women workers. The industrial women admired the professional ethic, if not the striving careerism, of the educated working women, and the professionals admired the matter-of-fact way wage-earning women went out to work. The fate of the professional woman was closely tied to that of the industrial worker; the cultural regard in which all working women were held affected both. Blatch dramatized that tie when she was refused service at a restaurant because she was unescorted by a man (that is, because she was eating with a woman). The management claimed that its policy aimed to protect "respectable" women, like Blatch, from "objectionable" women, like the common woman worker who went about on her own, whose morals were therefore questionable. Blatch rejected the division between respectable women and working women, pointing out that "there are five million women earning their livelihood in this country, and it seems strange that feudal customs should still exist here."[37]

The dilemma of economically dependent married women was crucial to the future of both classes of working women. Blatch believed that if work was to free women, they could not leave it for dependence on men in marriage. The professional and working-class members of the Equality League shared this belief, one of the distinguishing convictions of their new approach to suffragism. In 1908, Blatch and Mary Dreier chaired a debate about the housewife, sponsored by the WTUL and attended by many Equality League members. Charlotte Perkins Gilman took the Equality League position, that the unemployed wife was a "parasite" on her husband, and that all women, married as well as unmarried, should work, "like every other self-respecting being." Anna Howard Shaw argued that women's domestic labor was valuable, even if unpaid, and that the husband was dependent on his wife. A large audience attended, and although they "warmly applauded" Gilman, they preferred Shaw's sentimental construction of the economics of marriage.[38]

A month after the Equality League was formed, Blatch arranged for trade-union women to testify before the New York legislature on behalf of woman suffrage, the first working-class women ever to do so. The New York Woman Suffrage Association was still concentrating on the limited, property-based form of municipal suffrage; in lethargic testimony its leaders admitted that they had "no new arguments to present." Everyone at the hearing agreed that the antis had the better of the argument. The Equality League testimony the next day was in sharp contrast. Clara Silver and Mary Duffy, WTUL activists and organizers in the garment industry, supported full suffrage for all New York women. The very presence of these women before the legislature, and their dignity and intelligence, countered the antis' dire predictions about enfranchising the unfit. Both linked suffrage to their trade-union efforts: While they struggled for equality in unions and in industry, "the state" undermined them, by teaching the lesson of female inferiority to male unionists and bosses. "To be left out by the State just sets up a prejudice against us," Silver explained. "Bosses think and women come to think themselves that they don't count for so much as men."[39]

The formation of the Equality League and its appearance before the New York legislature awakened enthusiasm. Lillie Devereux Blake, whose own suffrage group had tried "one whole Winter...to [interest] the working women" but found that they were "so overworked and so poor that they can do little for us," congratulated Blatch on her apparent success. Helen Marot, organizing secretary for the New York WTUL, praised the Equality League for "realizing the increasing necessity of including working women in the suffrage movement." Blatch, O'Reilly, and Schneiderman were the star speakers at the 1907 New York suffrage convention. "We realize that probably it will not be the educated workers, the college women, the men's association for equal suffrage, but the people who are fighting for industrial freedom who will be our vital force at the finish," proclaimed the newsletter of the NAWSA.[40]

Militance for American Suffragists

The unique class character of the Equality League encouraged the development of a new style of agitation, more radical than anything practiced in the suffrage movement since...since Elizabeth Stanton's prime. The immediate source of the change was the Women's Social and Political Union of England (WSPU), led by Blatch's comrade from her Fabian days, Emmeline Pankhurst. Members of the WSPU were just beginning to be arrested for their suffrage protests. At the end of the Equality League's first year, Blatch invited one of the first WSPU prisoners, Anne Cobden-Sanderson, daughter of Richard Cobden, to the United States to tell about her experiences, scoring a coup for the Equality League. By emphasizing Cobden-Sanderson's connection with the British Labour party and distributing free platform tickets to trade-union leaders, Blatch was able to get an overflow crowd at Cooper Union, Manhattan's labor temple, two-thirds of them men, many of them trade unionists.[41]

The Equality League's meeting for Cobden-Sanderson offered American audiences their first account of the new radicalism of English suffragists, or as they were beginning to be called, suffragettes. Cobden-Sanderson emphasized the suffragettes' working-class origins. She attributed the revival of the British suffrage movement to Lancashire factory workers; the heroic figure in her account was the working-class suffragette, Annie Kenney, while Christabel Pankhurst, later canonized as the Joan of Arc of British militancy went unnamed. After women factory workers were arrested for trying to see the prime minister, Cobden-Sanderson and other privileged women, who felt they "had not so much to lose as [the workers] had," decided to join them and get arrested. She spent almost two months in jail, living the life of a common prisoner and coming to a new awareness of the poor and suffering women she saw there. Her simple but moving account conveyed the transcendent impact of the experience.[42]

Cobden-Sanderson's visit to New York catalyzed a great outburst of suffrage energy; in its wake, Blatch and a handful of other new leaders introduced the WSPU tactics into the American movement, and the word suffragette became as common in New York as in London. The "militants" became an increasingly distinct wing of the movement in New York and other American cities. But it would be too simple to say that the British example caused the new, more militant phase in the American movement. The developments that were broadening the class basis and the outlook of American suffragism had prepared American women to respond to the heroism of the British militants.[43]

The development of militance in the American suffrage movement was marked by new aggressive tactics practiced by the WSPU, especially open-air

A crowd outside of New York's City Hall to hear suffragists speak, October 1908.
Library of Congress

meetings and outdoor parades. At this stage in the development of British militance American suffragists generally admired the heroism of the WSPU martyrs.
Therefore, although the press emphasized dissent within the suffrage movement—it always organized its coverage of suffrage around female rivalries of
some sort—the new militant activities were well received throughout the movement. And, conversely, even the most daring American suffragettes believed in
an American exceptionalism that made it unnecessary to contemplate going to
prison, to suffer as did the British militants.[44]

Despite Blatch's later claims, she did not actually introduce the new tactics
in New York City. The first open-air meetings were organized immediately after
the Cobden-Sanderson visit by a group called the American Suffragettes. Initiated by Bettina Borrman Wells, a visiting member of the WSPU, most of the
American Suffragettes' membership came from the Equal Rights League, the
left-wing municipal reform group that had organized mock polling places in
New York since 1905. Feminist egalitarians with radical cultural leanings, its
members were actresses, artists, writers, teachers, and social welfare workers—
less wealthy versions of the professional self-supporters in the Equality League.
Their local leader was a librarian, Maud Malone, whose role in encouraging new
suffrage tactics was almost as important as, although less recognized than,
Blatch's own.[45]

The American Suffragettes held their first open-air meeting in Madison Square on New Year's Eve, 1907. After that they met in the open at least once a week. Six weeks later, they announced they would hold New York's first all-woman parade. Denied a police permit, they determined to march anyway. The twenty-three women in the "parade" were many times outnumbered by the onlookers, mostly working-class men. In a public school to which they adjourned to make speeches, the American Suffragettes told a sympathetic audience that "the woman who works is the underdog of the world"; thus she needed the vote to defend herself. Socialists and working women rose from the floor to support them. Two years later the Equality League organized a much more successful suffrage parade in New York. Several hundred suffragettes, organized by occupation, marched from Fifty-ninth Street to Union Square. O'Reilly, the featured speaker, made "a tearful plea on behalf of the working girl that drew the first big demonstration of applause from the street crowd."[46]

Perhaps because the American Suffragettes were so active in New York City, Blatch held the Equality League's first open-air meetings in May 1908 upstate. Accompanied by Maud Malone, she organized an inventive "trolley car campaign" between Syracuse and Albany, using the interurban trolleys to go from town to town. The audiences expressed the complex class character of the suffrage movement at that moment. In Syracuse Blatch had her wealthy friend Dora Hazard arrange a meeting among the workers at her husband's factory. She also held a successful outdoor meeting in Troy, home of the Laundry Workers' Union, one of the oldest and most militant independent women's trade unions in the country. Albany was an anti-suffrage stronghold, and its mayor tried to prevent the meeting; but Blatch outwitted him. The highlight of the tour was in Poughkeepsie, where Blatch and Inez Milholland, then a student at Vassar College, organized a legendary meeting. Since Vassar's male president forbade any woman suffrage activities on college grounds, Blatch and Milholland defiantly announced they would meet students in a cemetery. Charlotte Perkins Gilman, who was extremely popular among college women, spoke, but it was the passionate trade-union feminist, Rose Schneiderman, who was the star.[47]

Blatch believed that the first function of militant tactics was to gain much-needed publicity for the movement. The mainstream press had long ignored suffrage activities. If an occasional meeting was reported, it was usually buried in a small back-page article, focusing on the absurdity and incompetence of women's efforts to organize a political campaign. Gilded Age suffragists themselves accepted the Victorian convention that respectable women did not court public attention. The Equality League's emphasis on the importance of paid labor for women of all classes struck at the heart of that convention. Blatch understood "the value of publicity or rather the harm of the lack of it." She encouraged open-air meetings and trolley car campaigns because they generated much publicity, which no longer held the conventional horror for her followers.[48]

Militant tactics broke through the "press boycott" by violating standards of respectable femininity, making the cause newsworthy, and embracing the subsequent ridicule and attention. "We...believe in standing on street corners and fighting our way to recognition, forcing the men to think about us," an *American Suffragette* manifesto proclaimed. "We glory...that we are theatrical." The militant pursuit of publicity was an instant success: Newspaper coverage increased immediately; by 1908 even the sneering *New York Times* reported regularly on suffrage. The more outrageous or controversial the event, the more prominent the coverage. Blatch was often pictured and quoted.[49]

The new methods had a second function; they intensified women's commitment to the movement. Militants expected that overstepping the boundary of respectability would etch suffrage beliefs on women's souls, beyond retraction or modification. Blatch caught the psychology of this process. "Society has taught women self sacrifice and now this force is to be drawn upon in the arduous campaign for their own emancipation," she wrote. "The new methods of agitation, in that they are difficult and disagreeable, lay hold of the imagination and devotion of women, wherein lies the strength of the new appeal, the certainty of victory." Borrman Wells spoke of the "divine spirit of self-sacrifice" which underlay the suffragette's transgressions against respectability and was the source of the "true inwardness of the movement."[50]

If suffrage militants had a general goal beyond getting the vote, it was to challenge existing standards of femininity. "We must eliminate that abominable word ladylike from our vocabularies," Borrman Wells proclaimed. "We must get out and fight." The new definition of femininity the militants were evolving drew, on the one hand, on traditionally male behaviors, like aggression, fighting, provocation, and rebelliousness. Blatch was particularly drawn to the "virile" world of politics, which she characterized as a male "sport" she was sure she could master. On the other hand, they undertook a spirited defense of female sexuality, denying that it need be forfeited by women who participated vigorously in public life. "Women are no longer to be considered little tootsey wootseys who have nothing to do but look pretty," suffragette Lydia Commander declared. "They are determined to take an active part in the community and look pretty too." A member of a slightly older generation, Blatch never adopted the modern sexual ethic of the new woman, but she constantly emphasized the fact that women had distinct concerns that had to be accommodated in politics and industry. These two notes—the difference of the sexes and the repressed ability of women for manly activities—existed side by side in the thought of all the suffrage insurgents.[51]

The militant methods, taking suffrage out of the parlors and into the streets, indicated the new significance of working-class women in several ways. Blatch pointed out that the new methods—open-air meetings, newspaper publicity—suited a movement whose members had little money and therefore could not afford to rent halls or publish a newspaper. As a style of protest, "militance" was an import from the labor movement; WTUL organizers had been speaking from street corners for several years. And disrespect for the standards of ladylike respectability showed at least an impatience with rigid standards of class distinction, at most the influence of class-conscious wage-earning women.[52]

Working-class feminists were eager to speak from the militants' platform, as were many Socialists. A Socialist cadre, Dr. Anna Mercy, organized a branch of the American Suffragettes on the Lower East Side, which issued the first suffrage leaflets ever published in Yiddish. Militants also prepared propaganda in German and Italian and, in general, pursued working-class audiences. "Our relation to the State will be determined by the vote of the average man," Blatch asserted. "None but the converted...will come to us. We must seek on the highways the unconverted."[53]

Shoulder to Shoulder for Woman Suffrage

However, it would be a mistake to confuse the suffragettes' radicalism with the radicalism of a working-class movement. The ultimate goal of the suffragettes was not a single-class movement, but a universal one, "the union of women of all shades of political thought and of all ranks of society on the single issue of their political enfranchisement." While the Equality League's 1907 hearing before the state legislature highlighted trade-union suffragists, at the 1908 hearing the league also featured elite speakers, in effect de-emphasizing the working-class perspective.[54] Militants could neither repudiate the Socialist support they were attracting, and alienate working-class women, nor associate too closely with Socialists and lose access to the wealthy. Blatch—who actually became a Socialist after the suffrage was won—would not arrange for the Socialist party leader Morris Hillquit to join other pro-suffrage speakers at the 1908 legislative hearing. Similarly, the American Suffragettes allowed individual Socialists on their platform but barred Socialist propaganda. Speaking for Socialist women who found the "idea of a 'radical' suffrage movement...very alluring," Josephine Conger Kaneko admitted that the suffragettes left her confused.[55]

Moreover, the militant challenge to femininity and the emphasis on publicity introduced a distinctly elite bias; a society matron on an open-air platform made page one while a working girl did not, because society women were obliged by conventions and could outrage by flouting them. In their very desire to redefine femininity, the militants were anxious to stake their claim to it, and it was upper-class women who determined femininity. In Elizabeth Robin's drama about the rise of militance in the British suffrage movement, *The Convert*, the heroine of the title was a beautiful aristocratic woman who became radical when she realized the emptiness of her ladylike existence and the contempt for women obscured by gentlemen's chivalrous gestures. The Equality League brought *The Convert* to New York in 1908 as its first large fund-raising effort; working-class women, as well as elite women, made up the audience. Malone was one of the few militants to recognize and to protest against excessive solicitousness for the elite convert. She resigned from the American Suffragettes when she concluded that they had become interested in attracting "a well-dressed crowd, not the rabble." [56]

Blatch's perspective and associations had always been fundamentally elite. The most well connected of the new militant leaders, she played a major role in bringing the new suffrage propaganda to the attention of upper-class women. She presided over street meetings in fashionable neighborhoods, where reporters commented on the "smart" crowds and described the speakers' outfits in society-page detail. Blatch's first important ally from New York's social leaders (the "Four Hundred") was Katherine Duer Mackay, wife of the founder of the International Telephone and Telegraph Company and a famous society beauty. Mackay's suffragism was very ladylike, but other members of her set who followed her into the movement were more drawn to militancy. Alva Belmont, a veritable mistress of flamboyance, began her suffrage career as Mackay's protégée. The elitist subtext of militance was a minor theme in 1908 and 1909. But by 1910 becoming a suffragette was proving "fashionable," and upper-class women began to identify with the new suffrage style in significant numbers. By the time suffragette militance became a national movement, its working-class origins and trade-union associations had been submerged, and it was in the hands of women of wealth. [57]

From the beginning, though, class was the contradiction at the suffrage movement's heart. In the campaign of 1894, elite women began to pursue more power for themselves by advocating the suffrage in the name of all women. When Cobden-Sanderson spoke for the Equality League at Cooper Union in 1907, she criticized "idle women of wealth" as the enemies of woman suffrage, and she was wildly applauded. But what did her charge mean? Were all rich women under indictment, or only those who stayed aloof from social responsibility and political activism? Were the militants calling for working-class leadership of the suffrage movement or for cultural changes in bourgeois definitions of womanhood? This ambiguity paralleled the mixed meanings in Blatch's emphasis on working women; it coincided with an implicit tension between the older, elite women's reform traditions and the newer trade-union politics they had helped to usher in; and it was related to a lurking confusion about whether feminism's object was the superfluity of wealthy women or the exploitation of the poor. It would continue to plague suffragism in its final decade, and feminism afterwards, into our own time.

Notes

This essay is an abridged version of the essay by the same title that appeared in the *Journal of American History*, 74 (1987), 34-58, and is printed here with the permission of the journal. The author wishes to thank the Papers of Elizabeth Cady Stanton and Susan B. Anthony, University of Massachusetts, Amherst, for providing generous research assistance.

1. "Mrs. Blatch's Address," clipping, 1903, Women's Club of Orange, N.J., Scrapbooks, v. 4 (New Jersey Historical Society, Trenton). Thanks to Gail Malmgreen for this citation.

2. Richard L. McCormick, *From Realignment to Reform: Political Change in New York State, 1893-1910*, (Ithaca, 1979), 53.

3. Susan B. Anthony and Ida Husted Harper, eds., *History of Woman Suffrage* (Rochester, 1902), 4: 847-52; New York State Woman Suffrage Party, *Record of the New York Campaign of 1894* (New York, 1895); Ida Husted Harper, *The Life and Work of Susan B. Anthony* 3 vols. (Indianapolis, 1898-1908), 2: 758-76, esp. 759.

4. Mary Putnam Jacobi, "Report of the Volunteer Committee in New York City," in *Record of the New York Campaign*, 217-20; Maud Nathan, *The Story of an Epoch-Making Movement* (Garden City, 1926); William Rhinelander Stewart, ed., *The Philanthropic Work of Josephine Shaw Lowell* (New York, 1911), 334-56.

5. *New York Times*, April 14, 1894, 2; ibid., April 15, 1894, 5 Suffrage scrapbooks, Mrs. Robert Abbe Collection (Manuscript Division, New York Public Library). Theodore Stanton and Harriot Stanton Blatch, eds., *Elizabeth Cady Stanton As Revealed in Her Letters, Diary and Reminiscences*, 2 vols. (New York, 1922), 2: 299.

6. Mary Putnam Jacobi, "Address Delivered at the New York City Hearing," in *Record of the New York Campaign*, 17-26; Olivia Slocum Sage, "Opportunities and Responsibilities of Leisured Women," *North American Review*, 181 (Nov. 1905): 712-21.

7. Ibid.

8. Ibid.

9. Jacobi, "Report of the Volunteer Committee," 217; Stanton and Blatch, eds., *Elizabeth Cady Stanton*, 2: 305; *New York Times*, May 3, 1894, 9.

10. Jacobi, "Address Delivered at the New York City Hearing," 22; *New York Times*, April 12, 1894, 5.

11. *Woman's Journal*, May 12, 1894, 147.

12. Ibid., May 19, 1894. The study, patterned after Charles Booth and Mary Booth's investigation of the London poor, on which Blatch worked, was published as Harriot Stanton Blatch, "Another View of Village Life," *Westminster Review*, 140 (Sept. 1893): 318-24.

13. Stanton and Blatch, *Elizabeth Cady Stanton*, 11, 304: unidentified clipping, April 25, 1894, Scrapbook 20, Susan B. Anthony Collection (Manuscript Division, Library of Congress); *New York Times*, April 25, 1894, 5; ibid., May 3, 1894, 9; *New York Sun*, April 15, 1894, n.p.

14. *Woman's Journal*, Nov. 3, 1894, 348-49; ibid., Dec. 22, 1894, 402; ibid., Jan. 5, 1895, 1. Blatch wrote that her mother's position "pained" her but there is no evidence of any personal conflict between them at this time. Ibid., Dec. 22, 1894, 402.

15. Harriot Stanton Blatch and Alma Lutz, *Challenging Years: The Memoirs of Harriot Stanton Blatch* (New York, 1940), 77. *Woman's Journal*, Jan. 18, 1896, 18.

16. *Woman's Journal*, May 12, 1900, 146-47. Along with Blatch and Charlotte Perkins Gilman, Florence Kelley and Jane Addams were the most important figures to focus on women and class. See Charlotte Perkins Gilman, *Women and Economics: A Study of the Economic Relation*

between Men and Women as a Factor in Social Evolution (Boston, 1898).

17. Harriot Stanton Blatch, "Specialization of Function in Women: *Gunton's Magazine* 10 (May 1896): 349-56, esp. 350.

18. Ibid.

19. Ibid, 354-55.

20. Blatch, "Specialization of Function in Women," 350, 353.

21. Harriot Stanton Blatch, "Weaving in a Westchester Farmhouse," *International Studio*, 26 (Oct. 1905): 102-5: *Woman's Journal*, Jan. 21, 1905; ibid., Dec. 31, 1904, 423.

22. Blatch, "Weaving in a Westchester Farmhouse," 104; Blatch and Lutz, *Challenging Years*, 70-86; Rhoda Barney Jenkins interview by Ellen Carol DuBois, June 10, 1982 (in DuBois's possession); Ellen DuBois, "Spanning Two Centuries: The Autobiography of Nora Stanton Barney," *History Workshop*, no. 22 (Fall 1986), 131-52, esp. 149.

23. *HWS* 4: 311.

24. "Mrs. Blatch's Address," Women's Club of Orange, N.J., Scrapbooks; *HWS* 4: 311.

25. Harriot Stanton Blatch to Susan B. Anthony, Sept. 26, 1902, in *Epistolary Autobiography*, Theodore Stanton Collection (Douglass College Library, Rutgers University, New Brunswick, N.J.).

26. Oswald Garrison Villard, "Women in New York Municipal Campaign," *Woman's Journal*, March 8, 1902.

27. *New York Times*, Jan. 14, 1901, 7.

28. *HWS* 4: 861; Ida Husted Harper, ed., *History of Woman Suffrage*, (New York, 1922), 6: 454; *New York Times*, March 2, 1902, 8; *Woman's Tribune*, April 25, 1903, 49.

29. Minutes, March 29, 1906, reel 1, New York WTUL Papers (New York State Labor Library, New York).

30. Nancy Schrom Dye, *As Equals and As Sisters: Feminism, the Labor Movement, and the Women's Trade Union of New York* (Columbia, 1980), 63; Minutes, April 26, Aug. 23, 1906, New York WTUL Papers; *New York Times*, April 11, 1907, 8.

31. Mary Kenney O'Sullivan, "The Need of Organization among Working Women (1905)," Margaret Dreier Robins Papers (University of Florida Library, Gainesville).

32. *Woman's Journal*, March 17, 1906, 43; Kelley, *Woman Suffrage*; Jane Addams, *Utilization of Women in Government*, in *Jane Addams: A Centennial Reader* (New York, 1960), 117-18; *Woman's Journal*, Dec. 31, 1904, 423; "Mrs. Blatch's Address," Women's Club of Orange, N.J., Scrapbooks.

33. *New York Times*, Jan. 3, 1907, 6; *Woman's Journal*, Jan. 12, 1907, 8.

34. *Progress*, June 1907. Carrie Chapman Catt to Millicent Garrett Fawcett, Oct. 19, 1909, container 5, Papers of Carrie Chapman Catt (Manuscript Division, Library of Congress).

35. *Woman's Journal*, Aug. 17, 1907, 129. On Nora Blatch (who later called herself Nora Stanton Barney), see DuBois, "'Spanning Two Centuries," 131-52. Those self-supporters who, I believe, had independent incomes include Nora Blatch, Caroline Lexow, Lavinia Dock, Ida Rauh, Gertrude Barnum, Elizabeth Finnegan, and Alice Clark.

36. Caroline Lexow to Leonora O'Reilly, Jan. 3, 1908, reel 4, Leonora O'Reilly Papers (Schlesinger Library, Radcliffe College, Cambridge, Mass.); O'Reilly to Lexow, Jan. 5, 1908, ibid; Robert Doherty, "Tempest on the Hudson: The Struggle for Equal Pay for Equal Work in the New

York City Public Schools, 1907-1911," *Harvard Educational Quarterly* 19 (Winter 1979): 413-39. The role of teachers in the twentieth-century suffrage movement is a promising area for research. For information on teachers' organizations in the Buffalo New York, suffrage movement, I am indebted to Eve S. Faber, Swarthmore College, "Suffrage in Buffalo, 1898-1913" (unpublished paper in DuBois's possession).

37. *New York Times,* June 6, 1907, 1.

38. On self-support for women after marriage, see *New York World,* July 26, 1908, 3; and Lydia Kingsmill Commander, "The Self Supporting Woman and the Family," *American Journal of Sociology,* 14 (March 1909), 752-57. On the debate, see *New York Times* Jan. 7, 1909, 9.

39. *New York Times,* Feb. 6. 1907, 6.; Harriot Stanton Blatch, ed., *Two Speeches by Industrial Women* (New York, 1907), esp. 8.

40. *Woman's Tribune,* Feb. 9, 1907, 12; Minutes, April 27, 1909, New York WTUL Papers; *Progress,* Nov. 1907.

41. Blatch and Lutz, *Challenging Years,* 100-101; *Progress,* Jan. 1908.

42. *Woman's Journal,* Dec. 28, 1907, 205, 206-7.

43. By 1908, there was a racehorse named "Suffragette," *New York Evening Telegram,* Sept. 16, 1908. Blatch noted that once she left England in the late 1890s, she and Emmeline Pankhurst did not communicate until 1907, after they had both taken their respective countries' suffrage movements in newly militant directions. Blatch to Christabel Pankhurst, in Christabel Pankhurst, *Unshackled: How We Won the Vote* (London, 1959), 30.

44. The first American arrests were not until 1917. For American suffragists' early response to the WSPU, see *Woman's Journal,* May 30, 1908, 87. Even Carrie Chapman Catt praised the British militants at first. *Woman's Journal,* Dec. 12, 1908, 199. For an example of divisive coverage by the mainstream press, see "Suffragist or Suffragettes," *New York Times,* Feb. 29, 1908, 6.

45. On Bettina Borrman Wells, see A.J.R., ed., *Suffrage Annual and Women's Who's Who* (London, 1913), 390. Thanks to David Doughan of the Fawcett Library for this reference. The American Suffragettes found a predecessor and benefactor in seventy-five-year-old Lady Cook, formerly Tennessee Claflin, in 1909 the wife of a titled Englishman. "Our Cook Day," *American Suffragette* I (Nov. 1909): 1.

46. On the first open air meeting, see *New York Times,* Jan. 1, 1908, 16. On the parade, see ibid., Feb. 17, 1908, 7; there is also an account in Dorr, *What Eight Million Women Want,* 298-99; *New York Evening Journal,* May 21, 1910.

47. Equality League of Self-Supporting Women, *Report for Year 1908-1909* (New York, 1909), 2; Blatch and Lutz, *Challenging Years,* 107-9. On Vassar, see also *New York American,* June 10, 1908.

48. Harriot Stanton Blatch, "Radical Move in Two Years," clipping, Nov. 8, 1908, suffrage scrapbooks, Abbe Collection. Blatch "starred" in a pro-suffrage movie, *What Eight Million Women Want,* produced in 1912. Kay Sloan, "Sexual Warfare in the Silent Cinema: Comedies and Melodramas of Woman Suffragism," *American Quarterly* 33 (Fall 1981): 412-36. She was also very interested in the propaganda possibilities of commercial radio, according to Lee de Forest, a pioneer of the industry who was briefly married to her daughter. Lee de Forest, *Father of Radio: The Autobiography of Lee de Forest* (Chicago, 1950), 248-49.

49. Mary Tyng, "Self Denial Week," *American Suffragette,* 1 (Aug. 1909); *New York Herald,* Dec. 19, 1908.

50. Blatch, "Radical Move in Two Years"; Mrs. B. Borrman Wells, "The Militant Movement for Woman Suffrage," *Independent,* April 23, 1908, 901-3.

51. "Suffragettes Bar Word Ladylike," clipping, Jan. 13, 1909, Suffrage scrapbooks, Abbe Collection; Blatch and Lutz, *Challenging Years,* 91-242; *New York Herald,* March 8, 1908.

52. Blatch and Lutz, *Challenging Years,* 107; Dye, *As Equals and As Sisters,* 47.

53. *Woman's Journal,* May 30, 1908, 87; Blatch, "Radical Move in Two Years."

54. Borrman Wells, "Militant Movement for Woman Suffrage," 901, *Woman's Journal,* Feb. 29, 1908, 34.

55. *New York Times,* Feb. 11, 1908, 6; [Josephine C. Kaneko], "To Join, or Not to Join," *Socialist Woman,* 1 (May 1908): 6.

56. On *The Convert,* see Equality League, *Report for 1908-1909,* 4; Jane Marcus, "Introduction," in *The Convert* (London, 1980), v-xvi; *New York Call,* Dec. 9, 1908, 6; and Minutes, Dec. 22, 1908, New York WTUL Papers.

57. *New York Times,* May 14, 1909, 5. On Mackay and her Equal Franchise Society, see *New York Times,* Feb. 21, 1909, part 5, 2. On Blatch's relation to Mackay, see Blatch and Lutz, *Challenging Years,* 118.

Thirteen

A Politics of Coalition:

Socialist Women and the California Suffrage Movement, 1900–1911

Sherry J. Katz

Editor's Introduction: In this study of the California suffrage movement, Sherry J. Katz illustrates the increasing diversity of the early twentieth-century suffrage movement as she highlights the contributions of socialist women to the successful California suffrage campaign of 1911. Socialist women, Katz explains, had an unusual degree of prominence and influence among California's suffragists. Though socialist women were active in state suffrage movements elsewhere, "mainstream suffragists" in the Northeast, Midwest, and South tended to marginalize or shun socialist women—even before World War I when socialists were persecuted for alleged disloyalty and subversiveness.

Socialist women had been active in the first attempt to gain a state suffrage amendment in California, the failed referendum of 1896. As the state's suffrage movement revived in the early 1900s, socialist women contributed to the revival. Particularly after 1907, writes Katz, California socialist women made a deliberate effort to broaden the perspective and the constituency of what they perceived to be a "bourgeois movement." From middle-class or stable working-class families, often well-educated and employed in professional or clerical positions, these socialist suffragists proved to be crucial intermediaries between the middle-class and elite suffragists and the working class. They were highly effective in recruiting working-class women into the movement and winning support from the labor movement and working-class men. After the success of California's state suffrage campaign in 1911—the second in a new round of twentieth-century victories that helped breathe new life into the national suffrage movement—mainstream suffragists in the state freely acknowledged the crucial role of the socialist suffragists.

Like the working-class suffragists in New York described by Ellen Carol DuBois, these suffragists introduced new arguments and modern tactics that contributed to the success of the suffrage movement. Though many of the arguments used by the socialists were similar to those of other suffragists, including the idea that women's "social housekeeping" talents would be useful in politics, the socialist suffragists emphasized that women were entitled to political rights because of their economic contributions. "The heart of their argument," writes Katz, was "the idea that women's labor, inside and outside the home, had always contributed to 'social wealth' and that women, as social producers, deserved the ballot." California's socialist women employed some of the modern tactics used to attract publicity by working-class suffragists and their allies in New York, but they also invented new tactics—from door-to-door canvassing to the use of electric signs—that would become common during the movement's last decade. Significantly, the socialist suffragists' innovative tactics included printing campaign literature and conducting suffrage rallies in foreign languages, indicating a desire to attract the support of new immigrants. Yet even these women were affected by the racism that was so common among white suffragists in the early twentieth century.

The 1911 campaign seemed to socialist women to be a fulfillment of their dream of a cross-class sisterhood, writes Katz. After the victory, however, the level of unity and cooperation that marked the state suffrage campaign declined to a degree. Still, socialist and "mainstream" women's groups continued to work together and to achieve much. Indeed, Katz concludes, "socialist women's influence on the legislative proposals advocated by mainstream women's groups helps explain why California was at the forefront of social welfare legislation for women during the Progressive Era."

★　★　★　★　★

DURING THE EARLY TWENTIETH CENTURY the woman suffrage movement experienced a revitalization and expansion, becoming for the first time a mass coalition utilizing militant tactics and modern methods. The California suffrage campaign provides an illuminating case study of the political and social diversity of this mass movement, and sheds light on the process and success of coalition-building. Although socialist women in many regions of the country joined suffrage organizations or campaigned for suffrage through the Socialist Party, California socialist women achieved an apparently unprecedented level of integration, leadership, and influence. Their prominence depended, in part, on California's congenial political and social context, and on an effective strategy that socialist women devised to forge an influential left-wing constituency within the larger movement.

This case study demonstrates the critical role that socialists played in expanding the boundaries of the suffrage coalition, contributions less visible in states where they participated as individuals or achieved less prominence as an organized subgroup. By spearheading efforts to recruit wage-earning women, win the support of organized labor, and court the working-class vote, socialist women broadened the suffrage movement's base. In providing leadership and strategies for class-bridging, they emphasized new arguments for women's enfranchisement and introduced modern methods of suffrage agitation, including militant and flamboyant street tactics. Socialist women's vigorous grassroots campaigns in urban, working-class communities, especially in Los Angeles, proved critical to the success of California's 1911 suffrage referendum.

Socialist women made California, along with New York, a center of working-class coalition building and experimentation in militant strategies that influenced the trajectory of both state and national campaigns after 1911.

Socialism and Woman Suffrage: Linkages and Chasms

From 1890 to 1920, powerful international socialist and feminist movements helped to reinvigorate the woman suffrage demand and to create mass, militant, and modern suffrage movements. In the United States, the activism of both independent feminists sympathetic to socialism and female members of the Socialist Party of America helped to transform the suffrage movement into a broad and diverse coalition in the early twentieth century. Although the Second Socialist International instructed socialist women in 1907 to reject collaboration with mainstream suffragists and to conduct separate campaigns under party auspices, only party leaders in New York City adopted this policy. Everywhere else, Socialist Party women and independent left suffragists joined mainstream organizations, and, where feasible, built their own groups to represent working-class interests in the larger suffrage movement. Often working in close collaboration, they spearheaded the recruitment of working-class women, gained the support of organized labor, and introduced a new level of tactical militance. They played particularly forceful and effective roles in suffrage campaigns in the western states, as well as in Wisconsin, and New York.[1]

Despite their vital contributions to the revitalization and expansion of the suffrage movement, socialists often faced marginalization by mainstream suffragists seeking to distance themselves from radical and working-class politics. Attempts to downplay the socialist contribution were most pronounced in the industrial Northeast and Midwest, where the predominantly native-born, elite leadership feared association with the immigrant masses, and after the onset of World War I, when socialism became identified with disloyalty and subversion. In the southern states, social conservatism prompted the suffragists with socialist and trade union sympathies to avoid making public connections between radicalism and the suffrage cause.[2]

California's Fertile Ground for Political Experimentation

California socialist women achieved an apparently unprecedented level of integration, leadership, and influence in the suffrage coalition. The construction of their substantial left-wing presence depended, in part, on the fertile ground of the state's political climate and social context. During the late nineteenth century, the state provided space for the growth of numerous indigenous protest movements, such as Bellamy Nationalism and Populism, that sought to combat the harsh consequences of corporate capitalism. California's speedy economic development, accompanied by glaring economic inequalities, nurtured an openness to radical ideas and political alternatives. This climate of political experimentation gave rise to a sizeable and well-organized socialist women's movement that flourished in California from the 1890s until World War I. Beginning in the 1890s, several generations of radical women active in suffrage and temperance crusades found in socialism the basis for an egalitarian society guaranteeing women's freedom. In the early 1900s, local activists built a network of autonomous socialist women's clubs, under the umbrella of the Woman's Socialist Union of California (WSU), and worked within both the male-dominated socialist movement and the mainstream woman's movement.[3]

The Woman's Socialist Union represented hundreds of the most active socialist-feminists in the state. A number of like-minded radical women remained independent, but developed close ties to their sisters in the WSU. Information gathered on thirty-five state and local leaders of the WSU suggests a social portrait of the leadership cadre of the socialist women's movement. Most were born in the United States in the 1860s and 1870s, attained either stable working-class or middle-class status, and came to the socialist women's movement through participation in the woman and left movements of the 1890s. Many of these activists had been raised in Protestant households, had married and borne one or two children, and were surrounded by socialist family members. Relatively well educated, these women worked in professional or clerical occupations, particularly in teaching and newspaper work, for at least part of their adult lives. They were joined by a number of veteran activists born in the United States between the 1820s and the 1840s who had had formative political

Postcard from the 1911 California campaign. Courtesy of the Bancroft Library

experiences in abolitionism, early women's rights, and spiritualism. A younger generation of women born in the United States in 1880s and 1890s joined the socialist women's movement around 1910.[4]

The same climate of openness to political alternatives that nurtured a vigorous socialist women's movement also enabled socialists to establish a strong presence within California's suffrage movement from its inception. In fact, prominent radical women founded the suffrage movement in Northern California in the 1870s and in Southern California a decade later. A favorable social context undergirded their leadership and eased their early efforts to expand the movement's base of support along the lines of class and culture. In Southern California, socialist women and their working-class allies largely shared the native-born, Protestant backgrounds of mainstream suffragists, which meant that radicalism did not suffer from association with "foreignness." In Northern California, where Northern European immigrants and their children comprised a majority of the urban working class, socialism appeared somewhat more threatening to mainstream suffragists. As the suffrage demand moved from the margins to the center of organized white womanhood's political agenda in the late 1880s and 1890s, socialist women remained at the forefront of the movement, especially in the southern part of the state.[5]

Cross-Class Coalition Building, 1900–1910

The founding of the Woman's Socialist Union in 1902 coincided with, and contributed to, the revival of the state suffrage movement and the creation of a diverse suffrage coalition. After the defeat of a state suffrage amendment in 1896, suffrage activism declined as many demoralized participants left the movement. But during the first decade of the century, California women, like their counterparts across the nation, created new voluntary associations and social movements, through which they exerted an enormous collective influence on public policy and pursued woman suffrage. As the membership of mainstream suffrage clubs associated with the California Equal Suffrage Association (CESA) expanded from 100 to over 50,000, white clubwomen, college-educated reformers, working-class labor activists, African American clubwomen, as well as socialists, established their own organizations dedicated to the suffrage cause.[6] The demand for suffrage unified women in the early twentieth century because it encompassed their sense of commonality as well as their differences. Disfranchisement was a powerful symbol of women's socially constructed unity and an indicator of their common oppression in male-dominated society. Conceptualized as a tool of group interests, as well as a means of individual self-expression, the ballot also came to be understood as a means of achieving the goals considered important to different subgroups of women. The demand for suffrage constituted a "capacious umbrella" under which a large diversity of women, organizations, and beliefs, could temporarily stand. A genuine mass movement for women's enfranchisement emerged for the first time, one that embodied the widest spectrum of ideas and opinion, as well as participants, in its long history.[7]

As the suffrage coalition expanded after 1900, socialist women increased their numbers and their visibility as a distinctive left-wing entity within the movement. By 1907, WSU leader Josephine Cole celebrated the fact that every "Socialist woman [she knew] in this part of the country [was] a suffragist and almost every one of them [was] in a suffrage club." While Cole may have exaggerated, many WSU activists, female party members, and independent socialist-feminists joined mainstream suffrage groups. Although neither local suffrage clubs nor the CESA maintained good records, we know from scattered newspaper accounts that at least thirty-six socialists led local suffrage organizations and that most of them also served as delegates to or officers of the CESA. At least one socialist, and more often two or three, held important posts on the CESA's executive committee from 1903 to 1911. Under WSU guidance, socialist women exerted a strong, collective presence at state and local CESA conventions and in the Pacific Coast's suffrage press.[8]

Although few in-depth analyses of state suffrage movements are now available, in no other state did socialist women appear to gain so much prominence within the mainstream suffrage movement. Socialist women became leaders of the CESA based on their own dedication and commitment and because mainstream suffragists welcomed and acknowledged the participation of the left. This openness developed from the history of radical women's leadership in California suffrage, the context of political experimentation in California politics, and the public support offered by the state Socialist Party after its founding in 1902. Prominent suffragist Sarah M. Severance maintained in 1910 that "Socialists have [long] been our consistent friends" and she thanked them for their "just attitude" and "consistent record on woman's suffrage."[9]

Equally important in helping socialist women become "an acknowledged factor" in the state suffrage movement from 1902 to 1911 was the dual strategy of autonomous collaboration and full integration they devised to expand their influence. Rooted in their experience as participants in multiple and overlapping movements, dual strategy allowed them to collaborate with mainstream suffragists without losing their independent identity and separate base of power. "One woman lifting up her voice is not so well listened to as when she represents a body of women," WSU president Ethel Whitehead reasoned. The leaders of the WSU believed that socialist women's voices would carry greater weight when associated with independent organizations of radical suffragists.[10]

Socialist women self-consciously attempted to expand the boundaries of the suffrage coalition as leaders of the CESA and local mainstream organizations who remained based in, and coordinated their actions with, the WSU and other independent socialist suffrage groups. They believed that their "special mission...in the woman-suffrage field" involved enlarging the movement's constituency and political vision. The WSU leaders made the recruitment and integration of working-class women a major priority, arguing that no group was "better fitted" for the task. Socialist women also dedicated themselves to providing an "entering wedge" for the "Socialist thought" that would undergird a "more progressive, more democratic" movement. They hoped to convince non-socialists that women's emancipation depended upon economic independence, as well as political rights, and that such independence could be achieved only through a major restructuring of class relations and social resources. Likewise they sought to demonstrate that the social problems female reformers frequently attacked—child labor, prostitution, and poverty—could be eliminated only if women used their ballots to undermine capitalism. They envisioned the construction of an inclusive woman's movement dedicated to the emancipation of both women and the working class.[11]

In WSU affiliates, socialist women refined their arguments for enfranchisement. Many of their arguments paralleled those utilized by their non-socialist comrades. Both "sameness" and "difference" arguments appeared often in early twentieth-century suffrage literature. Suffragists argued that to the extent women were the same as men they deserved the ballot as a matter of justice, and to the extent they possessed special qualities, they needed a direct means of affecting public decision making.[12] Members of the WSU asserted that women deserved the ballot based on their inherent equality with men and their right to represent themselves. Most WSU activists also maintained that women's distinctive qualities—their socially constructed moral, maternal, and altruistic sensibilities—were desperately needed in the public sphere where male competitiveness and self-interest had been unable to combat the harsh social consequences of capitalist development. In combining these two strands of suffrage thought, Josephine Cole insisted that "possession of the ballot" would allow woman "the opportunity to alter many existing conditions which bear cruelty upon her, to her own injury and that of the race, but which...receive little attention from male legislators, be they Socialist or otherwise."[13]

Socialists also generated several new and distinctive arguments for suffrage shaped by their understandings of modern transformations in women's labor and the relation of women's work to women's emancipation. As socialist women pioneered these arguments in California, other members of a new generation of suffrage activists, many of them middle-class, college-educated reformers influenced by and sympathetic to radicalism, popularized them in New York and introduced them to the National American Woman Suffrage Association. Proponents of these new arguments drew upon the contributions of Charlotte Perkins Gilman, the most influential feminist theorist of their time, who insisted that gender equality depended upon women's economic independence achieved through wage labor outside the home and the socialization of housework and child rearing. Interestingly, Gilman developed her "sexuo-economic" theory of social relations in the early 1890s when she began her public career as a member of California's emerging socialist-feminist community.[14]

Socialist women proposed that women's economic contributions entitled them to political rights. The heart of their argument rested on the idea that women's labor, inside and outside the home, had always contributed to "social wealth" and that women, as social producers, deserved the ballot. But they highlighted the ways in which women's increasing involvement in the paid labor force provided a new rationale for suffrage. As women's "field of labor" shifted from the home to the factory, they became, in the words of Josephine Cole, permanent "financial factor[s]" who would "necessarily" be regarded as independent human beings and citizens rather than as "helpless dependents." Indeed the WSU's Jennie Arnott believed that because women's paid employment "forced their recognition as social units," it had "done more than any one thing to make the voters of the country see their need of the ballot." Ultimately, this wage-earners' suffragism not only provided a new rationale for women's entitlement to political rights, but helped socialist women draw working-class women into the suffrage coalition.[15]

A strong identification with working-class women undergirded socialist women's distinctive emphasis on wage-earning women's need of the ballot. Suffrage would provide wage-earning women with an important tool for their own advancement and self-protection, as well as for the empowerment of working-class communities. "That army of women who labor with their hands," WSU leader Mary Garbutt reminded her fellow suffragists, are the ones "whose hard experiences in life, long hours, poor pay and unsanitary conditions...really demand...the ballot for their protection against such untoward conditions."[16]

Wage-earning women never assumed the same importance in the arguments and literature of most mainstream suffragists in California. Socialist and trade-union activists generated most of the materials utilized by suffrage forces to attract such women. In this regard, independent socialist-feminist Alice Locke Park, a longtime ally of the WSU, played a key role as a prominent leader of the CESA's literature committee from 1906 to 1911. She issued several CESA leaflets directed towards working-class and wage-earning women, highlighted socialist and trade union endorsements, and helped her colleagues in the WSU and union movement produce their own literature.[17]

Park's work on the literature committee was only part of an intensive effort on the part of socialist women, networked through the WSU, to broaden the arguments and constituency of the suffrage movement. At CESA conventions in 1906 and 1907, substantial and well-organized socialist delegations, in concert with Progressive suffragists sympathetic to working women, advocated the recruitment of wage-earning women, outreach to working-class communities, and efforts to obtain greater support from organized labor. The 1906 convention featured a discussion devoted to securing the "interest and co-operation of the wage-earning women" led by WSU leader Anna Ferry Smith, a veteran feminist labor activist, and several other socialist and trade union women. They advised suffragists to meet with the leaders of women's unions, as the Los Angeles county suffrage organization had recently done. In 1907, a proposal drafted by the socialist-dominated resolutions committee pledged the CESA to widen the "scope of the suffrage movement by enlisting in its service the tremendous force of the women who work for wages and bringing to bear the pressure which organized labor can exert." The resolution invited trade union women to join the suffrage movement, stressing that their "struggle for better economic conditions" was hampered by their lack of political power.[18]

The approval of this resolution solidified the commitment of mainstream suffragists to working-class recruitment. Pragmatism, as well as socialist organizing within the CESA, underlay this strategic shift. Suffrage leaders saw in the rise of Progressivism a political climate conducive to social reform and women's enfranchisement. But they also believed that a suffrage victory depended on a new and enlarged base of suffrage activists, the backing of male-dominated institutions, better organization, and coordinated legislative lobbying. Whether sympathetic to organized labor or not, mainstream suffragists understood by 1906 that unions had become a powerful force in state politics and that the passage of a constitutional amendment depended on working-class votes.[19]

The success of working-class outreach and integration differed by city and region. Social context and socialist leadership proved critical factors in coalition-building efforts. In Southern California, and particularly in Los Angeles, relative ethnic homogeneity among whites and longstanding socialist leadership within organized womanhood facilitated class-bridging. But even as mainstream suffragists relied on their socialist comrades and supported the recruitment of wage-earning women, they felt uneasy in working-class environs. Socialist sympathizer Helen Bary recalled that elite and middle-class suffragists in Los Angeles thought her "very brave" to visit the Labor Temple, located in a downtown working-class district. In general, mainstream suffragists left the work of class-bridging to socialist women and their labor-identified allies.[20]

From 1906 to 1911, the Los Angeles WSU, a member of the local suffrage coalition, began to sponsor class-bridging activities in the form of meetings, conferences, and actions that brought mainstream suffragists and union women together. In 1908, Socialist Party member and WSU supporter Frances Nacke Noel emerged as the most prominent and effective organizer of class-bridging efforts. Under Noel's guidance, the California branch of the Woman's International Union Label League, an organization that promoted the consumption of union-made goods, became an important champion of female unionization, protective labor legislation, and woman suffrage.[21]

Label League activists drawn from the WSU's and the Socialist Party helped the organization become the grassroots, working-class component of the suffrage coalition in Southern California from 1908 to 1911. In Los Angeles, San Diego, and elsewhere, socialist women arranged joint meetings for label leaguers and mainstream suffragists in which they shared their thoughts on suffrage strategies and social reform proposals. In the winter of 1910, Los Angeles' Label League, Votes for Women Club, and WSU also collaborated on a Christmas benefit for the wives and children of local striking workers.[22] These activities culminated in the short-lived Woman's Conference of Los Angeles County,

HOMBRES Y MUJERES

¿Quien Dio Al Hombre El Derecho De Votar Y Cuando?

¡Pueden votar todos los hombres en Los Estados Unidos?

Si, si son mayores de 21 años y son nacidos en el país ó naturalizados. (En algunos Estados deben tambien saber leer).

¡Han pedido todos estos hombres el derecho de votar?

No, Ninguno lo ha pedido. El derecho les ha sido concedido por las leyes del país.

¡Cuando las leyes fueron hechas pidieron todos estos hombres el derecho de votar?

No, los representantes que hicieron las leyes, fueron suficientemente previsores para saber que no podrian formar una república con los pocos ciudadanos, á quienes era permitido votar en los tiempos Coloniales—aquellos hombres que llenaban los requisitos de religion, nacimiento y que tenian propiedades—y en consecuencia todos éstos requisitos fueron suprimidos y á la mayoria de los hombres les fué concedido el derecho de votar.

NOTA, ésto fué hecho por razones politicas y no porque los hombres pidieron el derecho de votar.

LOS DESCENDIENTES de estos hombres han votado desde entonces.

¿ Quien Dara a Las Mujeres el Derecho de Votar ?

¡Pueden todas las mujeres votar en Los Estados Unidos?

No, solamente aquellas que viven in Los Estados de Colorado, Idaho, Utah, Wyoming y Washington.

¡Han pedido todas las mujeres en Los Estados Unidos el derecho de votar?

No, pero el NUMERO DE MUJERES QUE HAN PEDIDO el derecho de votar es mayor que el NUMERO DE HOMBRES QUE HAN PEDIDO ALGUNA cosa en toda la historia de nuestro pais.

Las mujeres son ciudadanas de este pais, "aunque sean ó no sean oficialmente reconocidas."

La mujer debe obtener el derecho de votar por las mismas razones politicas por las que el hombre lo ha obtenido y no PORQUE lo pide.

La mujer forma parte del pueblo y nadie se atreveria á negar ésto. Abraham Lincoln definió una república ideal "como un gobierno, formado del pueblo, elegido por el pueblo y para el pueblo," pero el nuestro esta formado del pueblo por la mitad del pueblo.

El pais necesita la cooperación de todos sus ciudadanos.

Los hombres y las mujeres necesitan la oportunidad, de trabajar juntos para el mismo fin y en igualdad de condiciones.

Votese por Dar la Mujer de California el Derecho de Votar

EN LA ELECCION DEL 10 DE OCTUBRE, 1911

Political Equality League, Choral Hall, Auditorium Building. Los Angeles, California. Precio, cien por 20 centavos

Leaflet in Spanish from the 1911 California campaign. Sophia Smith Collection

which Noel and her socialist comrades envisioned as a permanent cross-class umbrella organization devoted to advancing the welfare of women and children, particularly those from the laboring classes. Called by the Label League and women's unions, the conference attracted over one hundred delegates to its first meeting in January 1911, many of them from mainstream women's organizations. After demanding that the legislature place a constitutional amendment for woman suffrage on the ballot, the conference conducted investigations of housing, industrial working conditions, and protective labor legislation. The conference disbanded in March 1911 as many of its constituent groups found a more pressing collaborative venture in the upcoming suffrage amendment campaign.[23]

Modern Methods and Militant Tactics in the 1911 Campaign

In February 1911, shortly after the California legislature voted to place a suffrage amendment on the October ballot, CESA leaders approved a plan to coordinate suffrage activism during the campaign that lay ahead. Led by Elizabeth Lowe Watson, a longtime socialist ally, the CESA called for collaboration among the thousands of suffragists in the state, including members of the California Federation of Women's Clubs (CFWC), the Woman's Christian Temperance Union (WCTU), women's trade unions, socialist organizations, and independent suffrage groups. The commitment to cooperation among diverse "kinds of suffrag[ists]," and the inclusion of radical and trade union organizations, rested on the preceding decade of socialist leadership and class-bridging efforts in the state association, as well as on the practical notion that a broad and well-organized suffrage coalition had the best chance of success. Although the Cooperative Council faced difficulty in "dove-tailing" precinct work and nurturing "new methods of propaganda and [an] exchange of talent" on the state level, regional coordinating bodies, especially in Southern California, facilitated cooperation among the many groups that comprised the suffrage coalition in 1911.[24]

Across California, and particularly in the southern part of the state, socialist women pioneered some of the most innovative tactics of the first state-level campaign to demonstrate the modern, militant, and often flamboyant methods characteristic of the suffrage movement's final decade. California suffragists perfected door-to-door canvassing and precinct organization, engaged in street speaking and car campaigning, coordinated press work, designed "modern" literature for mass distribution featuring concise arguments and catchy slogans, developed billboard ads and electric signs, staged plays and pageants, and held outdoor meetings and rallies. Socialist women helped to make press work and door-to-door canvassing—two modern tools of organization first introduced in the 1890s—more systematic and widespread. But they contributed most by experimenting with new styles of protest. Suffrage militance involved taking suffrage agitation aggressively into the streets. First employed to gain working-class support, militant methods became an effective means of acquiring widespread publicity because they challenged the bourgeois notions of female respectability that had mitigated against women's vigorous participation in public life. First in New York and then in California, socialists and working-class feminists helped popularize and expand the use of these militant methods nationwide.[25]

As the CESA formulated its plans for the suffrage campaign, WSU leaders prepared to mobilize their troops and the state Socialist Party. They were overjoyed by the party's pledge to work actively for suffrage, a commitment they had attempted to secure for nearly a decade, and formed a State Woman's Committee to coordinate the party's effort. Committee chairs Mary Garbutt and Georgia Kotsch quickly realized, however, that the state party's commitment consisted primarily of generous use of its weekly newspaper, the *California Social-Democrat*. While few party locals developed sustained campaigns, socialist women in all regions stepped up their suffrage activism in mainstream organizations and autonomous groups. Through WSU branches, socialist suffrage clubs, wage-earners' suffrage leagues, and Socialist Party locals, they worked to gain the support of organized labor and working-class voters, often collaborating with mainstream suffrage organizations and regional coordinating committees in which their comrades exercised influence.[26]

In Los Angeles County, socialist women played a highly visible role in the regional campaign that achieved the greatest success in constructing a diverse, cross-class coalition. As the campaign began, socialist women occupied leadership positions in all of the county's major suffrage organizations—the Political Equality League, the Votes for Women Club, and the WCTU. Although socialists and other labor-identified suffragists secured commitments for outreach to immigrant and working-class communities, these organizations remained focused on gaining the support of middle-class women and men.[27] In order to conduct an intensive campaign among the county's working-class population, WSU veterans and their allies founded two new suffrage groups: the Socialist Suffrage Club (SSC) and the Wage Earners' Suffrage League (WESL). Delegates from the SSC, WESL, and several mainstream groups represented the socialist/labor forces on the county's Equal Suffrage Central Committee, which loosely coordinated the overall campaign and facilitated an extraordinary interchange of personnel among its constituent groups.[28]

Under the direction of Mary Garbutt, Ethel Whitehead, and Frances Noel, the SSC and the WESL developed distinctive, but complementary, niches in the campaign. The Socialist Suffrage Club, founded in March 1911 and led by WSU veterans, organized public meetings and conducted house-to-house canvasses in working-class communities throughout the county.[29] The WESL, initiated by Frances Noel in May 1911, attracted labor as well as socialist activists, especially working-class homemakers from the label leagues and members of the garment workers union. Modeled after a similar organization founded by elite labor reformer Maud Younger in San Francisco in 1908, the WESL focused on mobilizing the support of the county's trade unions. The WESL maintained a visible presence at the Labor Temple, distributed literature to union members, and brought street speaking and outdoor meetings to neighborhoods in which union members resided. Both groups sought to empower working-class women, as well as to gain the support of working-class men.[30]

The actions of the SSC and the WESL reveal both the breadth and the limits of socialist women's conceptions of community and coalition, and the boundaries that circumscribed their political vision. Although their efforts focused on the predominantly white and native-born sector of Los Angeles' working-class community and labor movement, socialists campaigned in immigrant communities. In August, Noel promoted the suffrage cause in German at one of the first foreign-language meetings in the county. Similar meetings may have been held at the party's Jewish, Hungarian, Finnish, Latvian, and Mexican branches, and socialists probably distributed more foreign-language materials than any other sector of the county suffrage coalition. But many socialist women excluded Asian immigrants from their conception of the working class, despite a theoretical commitment to international solidarity. Socialists active in the labor movement internalized the hostility towards Asians that had ironically helped to unify California's white workers since the 1860s. Although their own suffrage materials were implicitly inclusive, socialist women widely distributed Maud Younger's "Why Wage-Earning Women Should Vote," first reproduced by Alice Park for the CESA in 1908, which decried the fact that native-born "Mongolians" (men) could vote and (white) women could not. In addition, socialist women apparently failed to challenge the exclusion of African American suffragists from mainstream suffrage groups and the county coordinating committee, even though their party had a small African American branch. Although socialist women clearly included ethnic and immigrant Euro-Americans and Latinos in their "imagined communities," the constructions of racial difference shared by most white reformers in California during the Progressive Era impoverished the vision of female solidarity they possessed and the diversity of the suffrage coalition they worked to build.[31]

Through the SSC and the WESL, socialist suffragists experimented with modern methods of suffrage organization, many of which challenged the Victorian notion that respectable women should not seek public attention. An extensive use of the socialist and labor press reflected the suffrage movement's growing emphasis on the importance of systematic and sustained publicity. Leaders of the SSC and the WESL coordinated the publication of a steady stream of suffrage propaganda in the *Citizen,* the newspaper of the Los Angeles labor movement, and the *California Social-Democrat.* The September 29, 1911 "Votes for Women" issue of the *Citizen* featured seventeen articles on the subject.[32]

In July and September, the SSC organized forty neighborhood suffrage meetings held in socialist halls throughout the city, in order to reach systematically a predominantly white, native-born working-class population that comprised more than fifty percent of the residents of all but one of Los Angeles' wards, and more than seventy percent in East Side wards.[33] The SSC also conducted a house-to-house canvass that sent pairs of socialist suffragists into selected precincts in order to speak personally with female homemakers and registered male voters about the suffrage cause. The club's canvass appears to have dovetailed with that of the Political Equality League (PEL), the largest and most powerful suffrage organization in the county. While the PEL focused on the middle-class and elite West Side, socialists concentrated on the precincts with large populations of working people and socialist voters (primarily in central and eastern Los Angeles). Although canvassing has not been regarded by historians as a particularly militant method of suffrage organizing, WSU leaders Ethel Whitehead and Georgia Kotsch argued that it was an effective strategy in part because of the curiosity and interest that women's presence in the streets engendered about their new public roles. Kotsch reported that many women treated her as an "amusing creature" and welcomed the "break" from the "monotony [of] their lives" that her presence offered. Whitehead, who encountered more hostility, relished the excitement of "assailing the enemy on his own doorstep," as the embodiment of the modern woman fully engaged in public life.[34]

The WESL focused on gaining grassroots labor support through equally modern methods. The WESL sent a circular letter to hundreds of labor organizations in the county and throughout the state. The San Francisco WESL, the key working-class suffrage organization in the Bay Area, published the letter in the newspaper of the San Francisco Labor Council and mailed it to local unions that could not be personally contacted. Maud Younger believed that the letter "brought endorsements that otherwise might not have been forthcoming," increased agitation among new converts, and garnered attention in the press. An innovative tear-off informed the WESL that the targeted organization had endorsed the suffrage amendment.[35]

As part of their effort to mobilize working-class support, socialist women pioneered the use of the most aggressively militant street tactics employed by California suffragists. Street tactics were certainly familiar to socialist women, since most had participated in the street demonstrations common to American labor and socialist protest. Socialist leaders of the CESA, including Alice Park and Jennie Arnott, had also been impressed with the militance of British suffragists since 1908.[36]

The WESL sponsored the first open-air meeting of the Southern California campaign on July 13 in Hollenbeck Park, located in an ethnically mixed, working-class neighborhood on Los Angeles' East Side. This move showed daring, not only because open-air meetings had not been part of conventional suffrage organizing, but also because the WESL had to find a way to circumvent a city ordinance prohibiting political speeches in public parks. Instead of speaking, the hundred suffrage supporters in attendance sang their arguments for the ballot and informally discussed the issue around picnic tables where coffee and doughnuts were served. Excellent press coverage in papers across the state emphasized the innovativeness of the outdoor gathering and the courage displayed in challenging local police. Good coverage, in turn, encouraged many suffrage groups to sponsor outdoor meetings in other areas of the county and state.[37]

The WESL also "broke the way for street speaking, going into the highways and byways to talk to the men who would not come to [them]." During the last three weeks of the campaign, the league conducted daily street speaking in working-class wards of central and eastern Los Angeles. Before street meetings held near the Labor Temple, WESL speakers would drive about the neighborhood "with votes for women banners flying in the breeze" in order to draw a larger crowd.[38] Many mainstream suffragists in Los Angeles and elsewhere found the courage to speak on the streets with the example and encouragement of socialists. Alice Park reported that by September street speaking had become so popular that many suffragists were engaging in it who had "no idea three months ago they would ever do such a thing."[39]

Victory and Its Aftermath

The broad, militant, and well-organized suffrage campaign, waged in the context of popular enthusiasm for "direct democracy" and Progressive reform,

A woman casts her first vote in San Francisco after California passed woman suffrage, November 12, 1912. The New York Public Library

resulted in the enfranchisement of California women on October 10, 1911. But the suffrage amendment remained one of the most contested of all ballot measures in 1911, approved by the state's voters by a narrow margin of 3,587 out of 246,487 votes cast. The amendment won in Southern California and in most of the rural regions of the state, but it lost in San Francisco and Oakland. A complex set of demographic and political factors contributed to these regional differences. In San Francisco, a largely German and Irish Catholic population associated woman suffrage with temperance activists and moral reformers who appeared to threaten their traditional social customs. The union movement remained ambivalent or opposed, Progressive political forces failed to make suffrage a priority, and a well-organized opposition funded by liquor interests campaigned vigorously against the amendment. Although mainstream suffragists went after the working-class and immigrant vote, an undercurrent of nativism and anti-union sentiment informed their campaign and strained relations with working-class suffragists. In the southern cities and rural counties, the population tended to be native-born and Protestant, and hence theoretically more favorable to temperance and suffrage. In Los Angeles, Progressive reformers, organized labor, and a popular Socialist Party endorsed suffrage with more fervor. And the opposition, aligned with the anti-reform and anti-union Merchants and Manufacturers Association, may have actually increased support for the amendment among both working-class and middle-class voters. The suffrage coalition, with socialist women serving as an important class-bridging force, more successfully united women from divergent backgrounds.[40]

It is difficult to assess the precise impact of socialist women on the outcome of the suffrage campaign. In many cities, their contributions cannot be separated from those of their non-socialist sisters, although they no doubt took the lead in agitating in working-class communities and in the streets.[41] In Los Angeles, however, socialist women clearly made a difference, playing a major role in securing a victory for suffrage in working-class neighborhoods and therefore in the city overall. Of Los Angeles' seven assembly districts, five supported the amendment, and four of those contained working-class majorities. Contemporary accounts suggest that working-class precincts provided greater margins of victory than the middle-class and elite precincts that favored the amendment. The voters most likely to reject the amendment lived on the "respectable, stylish West Side" and in the downtown neighborhoods that housed the city's most transient and impoverished residents. The precinct surrounding the Labor Temple, in which many union members lived, carried the amendment by a two-to-one margin.[42]

Mainstream suffragists freely acknowledged the critical importance of working-class and socialist support and praised socialist suffragists for their activism. The *Western Woman Voter,* the organ of the West Coast suffrage movement, credited the victory in Southern California to the fact that "the labor unions and the Socialists there…[had] actively lined up in favor of the amendment." Progressive suffragist Helen Bary considered the campaign to get out the labor and socialist vote conducted by the WESL and the SSC more "productive" than the "whole elaborate campaign" devised by mainstream groups to gain support among the elite and middle classes.[43]

For socialist women, the 1911 campaign seemed to represent the fulfillment of their "dream of solidarity among women," of a sisterhood that crossed the boundaries of class, political ideology, and organizational affiliation. Tensions between mainstream and socialist activists surfaced periodically in the post-suffrage period, however, especially during partisan elections. But overall, enfranchisement contributed to greater collaboration among socialist and mainstream women on a wider variety of political projects, rather than to a fragmentation of the woman's movement. Socialist women, in alliance with a small group of labor-oriented Progressive clubwomen, continued to comprise a left-wing of the woman's movement from 1911 to 1917. During this period, radical women became the leading proponents of labor legislation and unionization, the most outspoken advocates of a redistributive social welfare state, and the earliest supporters of birth control. In fact, socialist women's influence on the legislative proposals advocated by mainstream women's groups helps explain why California was at the forefront of social welfare legislation for women during the Progressive Era. Socialist women's activism appears to offer an important reason why California devised better protection for women workers than most other states and debated more comprehensive and less oppressive mothers' pension programs than were considered elsewhere.[44]

The activism of Josephine Cole and her comrades highlights the ways in which socialist women reinvigorated and expanded the suffrage movement in the early twentieth-century United States. An influential sector of California's suffrage coalition, socialist women broadened its boundaries by recruiting working-class women, emphasizing new arguments, and introducing militant methods. They also demonstrated a fruitful strategy for coalition-building, one that made them a distinctive and independent tendency within the larger movement. Their grassroots activism in working-class communities contributed to a critical suffrage victory that, following on the heels of the successful Washington State campaign in 1910, ignited expectations nationwide. As the California campaign served to emphasize the importance of collaborative and class-bridging efforts, innovative methods, and working-class support, the socialist suffragists of the state helped shape the course of the national suffrage movement.

Notes

This essay is part of a forthcoming book to be published by Routledge, *Dual Commitments: Feminism, Socialism, and Women's Political Activism in California, 1890-1920.*

1. Ellen Carol DuBois, "Woman Suffrage and the Left: An International Socialist-Feminist Perspective," *New Left Review*, no. 186 (March/April 1991), 29-45; Mari Jo Buhle, *Women and American Socialism, 1870-1920* (Urbana, 1981), chpt. 6; Nancy F. Cott, *The Grounding of Modern Feminism* (New Haven, 1987), chpt. 1.; John D. Buenker, "The Politics of Mutual Frustration: Socialists and Suffragists in New York and Wisconsin," in Sally M. Miller, *Flawed Liberation: Socialism and Feminism* (Westport, Conn., 1981), 113-144.

2. Buhle, *Socialism*, 231-238; Buenker, "Politics," 113-144; Marjorie Spruill Wheeler, *New Women of the New South: The Leaders of the Woman Suffrage Movement in the Southern States* (New York, 1993), 74-75, 184.

3. Michael Kazin, "The Great Exception Revisited: Organized Labor and Politics in San Francisco and Los Angeles, 1870-1940," *Pacific Historical Review* 55 (August 1986), 381-388; Sherry Jeanne Katz, "Dual Commitments: Feminism, Socialism, and Women's Political Activism in California, 1890-1920," (Ph.D. diss., University of California, Los Angeles, 1991), chpts. 1-3.

4. Katz, "Dual Commitments," 106-112; and Sherry Katz, "Socialist Women and Progressive Reform," in William Deverell and Tom Sitton, eds., *California Progressivism Revisited* (Berkeley, 1994), 119.

5. Gayle Ann Gullett, "Feminism, Politics, and Voluntary Groups: Organized Womanhood in California, 1886-1896," (Ph.D. diss., University of California, Riverside, 1983), esp. 19-21, 144-150, 176-184, 196-201, 297-313; Susan L. Englander, "The San Francisco Wage Earners' Suffrage League: Class Conflict and Class Coalition in the California Woman Suffrage Movement, 1907-1912," (M.A. thesis, San Francisco State University, 1989), 54-80; Katz, "Dual Commitments," 54-69.

6. Donald Waller Rodes, "The California Woman Suffrage Campaign of 1911," (M.A. thesis, California State University, Hayward, 1974), 10-11, 23-31; Ronald Schaffer, "The Problem of Consciousness in the Woman Suffrage Movement: A California Perspective," *Pacific Historical Review* 45 (Nov. 1976), 469-493; Douglas Flamming, "African-Americans and the Politics of Race in Progressive-Era Los Angeles," in Deverell and Sitton, eds., *California Progressivism*, 206-208; Bess Marjory Munn, "Activ-

ity of the Suffragette," *Citizen* (Los Angeles), Sept. 29, 1911.

7. Nancy F. Cott, "Feminist Theory and Feminist Movements: The Past Before Us," in Juliet Mitchell and Ann Oakley, eds., *What Is Feminism?* (New York, 1986), 52-54.

8. Josephine R. Cole, "In Defense of Woman Suffrage," *Common Sense* (Los Angeles), March 30, 1907; Katz, "Dual Commitments," 259-277.

9. Katz, "Dual Commitments," 263-264; n. 47-48, 317-320; "For Political Equality," *People's Paper* (Los Angeles), September 24, 1910.

10. M[ary] E. G[arbutt], "Notes from the Convention of the Socialist Women's Union of California," *Los Angeles Socialist*, Oct. 4, 1902; Ethel Whitehead, "Woman and the Socialist Movement," *People's Paper*, Oct. 28, 1910; Ethel Whitehead, "The Woman's Movement in California," *Progressive Woman* 2 (May 1909), 7.

11. Josephine R. Cole, "Women's Unions," *Appeal to Reason*, June 13, 1903; report by M[ary] E. G[arbutt], *Los Angeles Socialist*, Jan. 3, 1903; Josephine R. Cole, "A Reply to Mrs. Corbin," *Los Angeles Socialist*, June 20, 1903; Agnes Halpin Downing, "Woman's Needs," *Socialist Woman* 1 (March 1908), 2; Whitehead, "Woman and the Socialist Movement."

12. Cott, "Feminist Theory," 50-54; Cott, *Grounding*, 19-21, 29-30.

13. Sallie E. Bowman, "Why Women Should Have the Ballot," *Citizen*, March 5, 1909; Georgia Kotsch, "The Mission of the Socialist Woman," *Progressive Woman* 5 (Aug. 11), 13-14; J[osephine] R. Cole, "Political Power for Women," *Los Angeles Socialist*, April 4, 1903.

14. Ellen Carol DuBois, "Working Women, Class Relations, and Suffrage Militance: Harriot Stanton Blatch and the New York Woman Suffrage Movement," in this volume; Cott, *Grounding*, 24-25, 41-42; Ann J. Lane, *To "Herland" and Beyond: The Life and Works of Charlotte Perkins Gilman* (New York, 1990), chpts. 6-10.

15. Josephine R. Cole, "The Economic Cause of Woman's Advancement," *Yellow Ribbon* 1 (Feb. 1907), 1-3; Jennie Arnott, "Forces Which Are Working For Suffrage," *Yellow Ribbon* 1 (Jan. 1907), 1.

16. [Mary Garbutt], *Los Angeles Socialist*, Feb. 28, 1903.

17. Alice Park, "The Ballot," *Yellow Ribbon* 1 (Oct. 1906), 3; CESA leaflet, "Woman Suffrage Endorsed by California

Conventions," [1906], box 4, Keith-McHenry-Pond Family Papers, Bancroft Library, University of California, Berkeley; "California Literature," *Woman's Journal*, April 29, 1911; [Alice] Park to [Agnes] Downing, March 8, 1911, box 3, Alice Locke Park Collection, Huntington Library, (hereafter cited as Park Coll., HL.)

18. M[able] C[raft] D[eering], "Annual Convention of California Equal Suffrage Association," *Yellow Ribbon* 1 (Nov. 1906), 1-2; *San Francisco Call*, Oct. 6, 1907; CESA convention program, *Western Woman* 1 (Oct. 1907), 12.

19. Report of the San Francisco Equal Suffrage League, *Yellow Ribbon* 1 (Dec. 1906), 1; Rodes, "Woman Suffrage Campaign," 23-57; Englander, "San Francisco Wage Earners' League," 81-86.

20. Helen Valeska Bary, "Labor Administration and Social Security: A Woman's Life," interview by Jacqueline K. Parker, 1972-1973, Regional Oral History Office, Bancroft Library, 1974, 20-21, (hereafter cited as Bary OH, BL).

21. Georgia Kotsch, "State Conference of the Women's Socialist Union," *World*, May 22, 1909; Mary E. Garbutt to Mrs. [Mary] Wilshire, May 20, 1909, in *Wilshire's Magazine* 13 (Aug. 1909), 18; Katz, "Dual Commitments," 273, n. 70, 329-330, 578-580, n. 28, 614-615.

22. "San Diego Women Study Laws for Women," *Citizen*, March 4, 1910; "The Union Label and Votes For Women," *Citizen*, Dec. 9, 1910; "Christmas for Strikers' Children," *People's Paper*, Dec. 23, 1910.

23. See recruitment letters and Noel's "The Woman's Conference of Los Angeles County: It's Aim and Object," folder 12, box 4, Frances Noel Papers, Department of Special Collections, University Research Library, UCLA, (hereafter cited as Noel Papers, UCLA); "Council of Women Formed," *Citizen*, Jan. 20, 1911; "Woman's Conference of L.A. County," *Citizen*, Feb. 24, 1911.

24. Elizabeth Lowe Watson, "To the Members of the California Equal Suffrage Association and friends who favor Votes for Women, throughout the State of California," March 2, 1911, box 227, John Randolph Haynes Papers, Special Collections, University Research Library, UCLA (hereafter cited as Haynes Papers, UCLA); "Denver Woman Will Conduct Local Battle," *San Francisco Call*, Sept. 19, 1911; list, Equal Suffrage Campaign Committee, n.d., [1911], box 10, Elizabeth Morrison (Boynton) Harbert Collection, Huntington Library (hereafter cited as Harbert Coll., HL).

25. Buhle, *Socialism*, 230; Cott, *Grounding*, 24-29; DuBois, "Woman Suffrage and the Left," 35-41; DuBois, "Suffrage Militance," 52-58.

26. "Official Bulletin of the Socialist Party of California," *California Social-Democrat* (Los Angeles), Sept. 9, 1911; State Woman's Committee, "Suffrage Amendment Must Be Carried at the Polls," *California Social-Democrat*, July 22, 1911; Agnes H. Downing, "Woman Suffrage In California," *Progressive Woman* 5 (Sept. 1911), 1; Katz, "Dual Commitments," 279-296.

27. Katz, "Dual Commitments," 287-288, n. 106, 346-347; Bary, OH, BL, 17-22, 24; Helen V. Bary to Adella M. Parker, Nov. 23, 1911, box 3, Park Coll., HL.

28. Downing, "Woman Suffrage in California"; list, Equal Suffrage Central Committee, [1911], and Lloyd Galpin to "Dear Madam," Aug. 30, 1911, box 10, Harbert Coll., HL; *California Social-Democrat*, Sept. 9, 1911.

29. "Socialists Open Woman Suffrage Campaign," *Citizen*, June 2, 1911; Ethel Whitehead, "The Socialists' Fight," *California Social-Democrat*, Sept. 9, 1911.

30. "Wage-Earners' Suffrage Rally," *Citizen*, June 2, 1911; WESL circular letter, "To All Union Men of California," [1911] and Estelle Lawton Lindsey, "The Wage-Earners Suffrage League Plans Great Educational Campaign," *Los Angeles Record*, n.d., folders 7 and 14, box 1, Noel Papers, UCLA.

31. "Next Municipal Election May Be Open to Women," n.p., n.d., Woman's Suffrage Scrapbook, compiled by Mrs. M.A. Holmes, Pasadena Historical Society, Pasadena, California (hereafter cited as Suffrage Scrapbook, PHS); Leonard Pitt, "Red Flag Over City Hall? The Socialist Labor Ticket in the Los Angeles Mayoral Election of 1911," (Paper delivered at AHA Convention, 1989), n. 12, 29; Bary, OH, 20-22; Bary to Parker, Nov. 23, 1911, box 3, Park Coll., HL; "Report on Publicity of the Political Equality League of Southern California," box 227, Haynes Papers, UCLA; Kazin, "Great Exception," 378-380, 384, 389-392; and Maud Younger, "Why Wage-Earning Women Should Vote," folder 1, box 1, Noel Papers, UCLA; Flamming, "Politics of Race," 207-210.

32. On the increased use of publicity among suffragists, see DuBois, "Suffrage Militance."

33. *People's Paper*, July 1, 1911; *Citizen*, July 14, Sept. 8, 1911; Whitehead, "The Socialists' Fight"; *California Social-Democrat*, July 22, Sept. 9, 1911; Downing, "Woman Suffrage in California"; Pitt, "Red Flag?" 14-18.

34. "Workers are Wanted," *People's Paper*, July 1, 1911; report from Mary Garbutt, *Citizen*, July 21, 1911; *Woman's Journal*, April 15, June 17, 1911; Whitehead, "The Socialists' Fight"; Georgia Kotsch, "Through Battle's Smoke," *Citizen*, Oct. 20, 1911.

35. *Citizen*, July 28, 1911; WESL circular letter; "Wage Earners' Suffrage League," *Labor Clarion* (San Francisco), Sept. 1, 1911; Maud Younger to [Frances] Noel, Oct. 24, 1911, Knox Mellon Collection (a collection of Frances Nacke Noel materials held privately by historian Knox Mellon, hereafter cited as Mellon Coll.)

36. *Woman's Journal*, Oct. 10, 1908; Sofia M. Loebinger to Alice Park, Aug. 4, 1909 and Alice Park, "American Suffragette," n.p., n.d., box 2, Park Coll., HL.

37. "Suffrage Battle Hymn Swells in City Park," *Los Angeles Herald*, July 14, 1911; "Musical Pleas for Votes By Women Thwart Police," *San Francisco Call*, July 15, 1911; 1911 clippings, Suffrage Scrapbook, PHS; *Woman's Journal*, Aug. 26, 1911.

38. "Behold the Advent of the Woman Orator," *Los Angeles Tribune*, Oct. 20, 1911; *Citizen*, Sept. 15, 1911; [Frances Noel] to E[thel Duppy Turner], Oct. 19, 1911, Mellon Coll.; "Suffrage Message Carried to Men in Territory Before Neglected," n.p., n.d., Suffrage Scrapbook, PHS.

39. Letter from Elizabeth Lowe Watson, *Woman's Journal*, Aug. 12, 1911; Alice Park, "The California Campaign," *Western Woman Voter* 1 (Oct.-Nov. 1911).

40. Katz, "Dual Commitments," 277-297, n. 140, 356-358.

41. Ibid., 283-287.

42. Pitt, "Red Flag?" 19-20; *California Social-Democrat*, Oct. 14, 1911; Bary OH, BL, 18-24, esp. 24; "At Los Angeles," *Progressive Woman* 5 (Dec. 1911), 5; Citizen, Oct. 13, 1911.

43. *Western Woman Voter* 1 (Oct.-Nov. 1911), 1; Bary to Parker, Nov. 23, 1911, box 3, Park Coll., HL.

44. Bary to Parker, Nov. 23, 1911, box 3, Park Coll., HL; Katz, "Dual Commitments," 299-301; Katz, "Socialist Women and Progressive Reform," 117-143.

Fourteen

Ida B. Wells-Barnett and the Alpha Suffrage Club of Chicago

Wanda A. Hendricks

Editor's Introduction: Wanda A. Hendricks's article on Ida B. Wells-Barnett and the first African American woman suffrage club in Chicago, like the articles by Ellen DuBois and Sherry Katz that precede it, underscores the diversity of the suffrage movement in the early twentieth century. Though black women encountered much discrimination from white suffragists, they were active participants in the movement nonetheless. One of the most famous of the African American suffragists was the indomitable Ida B. Wells-Barnett, under whose leadership black women in Chicago not only worked for suffrage but played a significant role in the city's politics.

Beginning with her refusal to move from the "ladies car" to the "colored car" on a train in Mississippi in 1884, Ida B. Wells-Barnett did not allow anyone to deny her or her race their rights without a challenge—and the National American Woman Suffrage Association (NAWSA) was no exception. The famous incident Hendricks describes below, in which Wells-Barnett refused to obey the NAWSA's instructions to march with an all-black contingent at the end of the 1913 suffrage parade in Washington, D.C. rather than with the Illinois delegation, would have come as no surprise to those who knew her. She was well known for her opposition to accommodation and gradualism and for her fearless advocacy of justice and equality.

Wells-Barnett was convinced that the vote was crucial for black Americans—including as a weapon in the crusade against lynching to which she devoted much of her life—and thus she fought *against* the disfranchisement of African American men and *for* the enfranchisement of African American women. And through the Alpha Suffrage Club, the first and most important of several black suffrage clubs in Chicago, she helped African American women and Chicago politicians realize that black women could play a decisive role in city elections.

The fact that in 1913 Illinois gave women the right to vote in presidential and municipal elections (the first state east of the Mississippi River to do so), meant that Illinois suffragists had the opportunity to be politically active and influential—even while working for *full* suffrage. As Wanda Hendricks clearly demonstrates, these African American suffragists took full advantage of this opportunity. The women of the Alpha Suffrage Club worked hard and successfully to get more black women and men to register and vote in Chicago elections, thus encouraging African Americans to run for office. Their support was a decisive factor in the election of Oscar DePriest, the first black alderman in Chicago's history, who later (1928) made history as the first northern black to be elected to Congress and the first black congressman since the disfranchisement of southern blacks in the 1890s.

★　★　★　★　★

IDA BELL WELLS-BARNETT played an important role in the municipal politics of Chicago during the second decade of the twentieth century. She sought civic representation for the masses of black women and men who fled the South seeking economic, social, and political opportunity. In defense of the rights of African Americans and women, she had by 1915 formed the largest black women's suffrage club in Illinois, defied the National American Woman Suffrage Association's ban on allowing African American women to march under their state banners alongside their white counterparts at the landmark 1913 suffrage parade in Washington, and played a crucial role in the election of the first African American alderman in Chicago.

Like most African Americans growing up in the Jim Crow South, Wells's early life was wrought with strife and conflict. She was the eldest of eight children, born in Holly Springs, Mississippi, on July 16, 1862 to a former slave from Virginia named Lizzie Warrenton and Jim Wells, the son of his master.[1] Despite the ravages of segregated Mississippi, the Wells educated their children at Shaw University in Holly Springs, later renamed Rust College. A community activist, Jim Wells became a trustee at Shaw while Lizzie Wells accompanied her children to classes so that she could learn to read and write.[2]

In 1878, the yellow fever epidemic that swept through the area drastically changed Ida Wells's life. Her father, mother, and a nine-month-old sibling, died in the epidemic, leaving sixteen-year-old Ida to care for the other children.[3] Financially responsible for the family, she passed the teachers' exam for the county schools and gained employment at a school six miles from her home that paid a monthly salary of $25. A year later, invited by her mother's sister in Memphis, Tennessee, Wells left Holly Springs. She took the two younger girls with her and left a sister and two brothers with relatives. Another brother had died several years earlier of spinal meningitis.[4]

Post-Reconstruction Memphis, like much of the South, began a program built on the usurpation of African American rights. With the aid of the Supreme Court, southern states implemented a pervasive system of Jim Crow rules. The Court, in a series of cases, had by 1883 upheld the right of southern states to enforce laws that violated the civil rights gained by African Americans in the post-Civil War era. Deeply disturbed over the events leading to the restoration of white supremacy, Wells challenged the legality of the system. In May 1884, twenty-two-year-old Wells boarded a train owned by Chesapeake and Ohio Railroad and chose a seat in the "ladies" coach. Though informed by the conductor that as a black woman she could not sit in the car reserved for white females, Wells stood her ground and refused to move to the all-black Jim Crow car. Rather than allow Wells to remain seated, the conductor attempted forcefully to remove her. In retaliation, she bit his hand. Refusing to be outdone, the conductor sought the aid of the baggage man who assisted in dragging Wells from the coach.

Seeking justice, Wells hired a lawyer, and sued the railroad. Though she was initially victorious, the settlement of $500 was bittersweet. The state supreme court reversed the ruling of the lower court. Though disappointed, she understood that hers' "was the first case in which a colored plaintiff in the South had appealed to a state court since the repeal of the Civil Rights Bill by the United States Supreme Court," and if she had won, it "would have set a precedent which others would doubtless have followed."[5] The case and its subsequent reversal served as a springboard for her career to fight racism and discrimination. Over the years Wells pushed the system to its limit by persistently defending her rights as an African American woman. She advocated protest, demanded equality, and sought redress for crimes committed against the race.

One of the media Wells used to publicize her message was the newspaper. Before she reached thirty years of age, she had been co-owner of the *Memphis Free Speech and Headlight* and contributed articles to local and national publications such as the *Memphis Watchman* and the *Living Way,* the *New York Age,* and the *Indianapolis World.*[6] Many of the articles centered on the lynchings of African American men. The deaths of three colleagues, Thomas Moss, Calvin McDowell, and Henry Stewart by a lynch mob on March 9, 1892 in Memphis prompted these writings.

The three successfully managed the People's Grocery in a heavily populated black section just outside Memphis. Accompanied by a police deputy, a competing white grocery store owner whose business was failing, harassed two of the African American owners. In the ensuing altercation, McDowell knocked the white grocer down and confiscated his gun. Stewart and McDowell were charged with assault and battery and arrested. McDowell later posted bond and they were released. The following Saturday night, the white grocer accompanied by a mob of white men entered the back door of People's Grocery. Fear compelled the African American men inside to fire several shots. Three of the white men were wounded. Chaos erupted when several black men were dragged from their homes and questioned or incarcerated. Eventually, Moss, McDowell, and Stewart were indicted and thrown in jail. During the night they were removed from the county jail, shot, mutilated, and hanged.[7]

The African American community responded in several ways. The *Free Speech* ran an editorial that indicted the entire white community for the deaths of the three men and encouraged blacks to leave the city. Pushed by fear, many black

Memphis residents heeded the call of the *Free Speech* and migrated to Oklahoma. So many departed that black ridership on the City Railway Company's trains rapidly deteriorated. Reduced profits for the owners of the railway company and other businesses heavily trafficked by African Americans resulted. Concern over the massive out-migration forced mainstream white newspapers to discourage such moves and declare Oklahoma to be a major disappointment and plagued by hardships.

Wells refused to bow to pressure from white business owners to join them in their efforts to terminate the movement. Lost profits, she believed, were such a small price to pay for the lives of three responsible citizens. She even visited several black churches and urged members "to keep on staying off the [railway] cars." Too, she quietly "rejoiced" when many more blacks sought refuge in Oklahoma.[8]

Wells also decided to do her own investigation of the murders. The fates of Moss, McDowell, and Stewart forced her to question the rationale of white mob action and rethink her own ideas about the reasons for lynchings. Like most Americans, black and white, she had been heavily influenced by white myths that suggested that lynchings happened to accused rapists; that is, black men raping white women. The men brutally murdered in Memphis, however, did not fall into that category. They were outstanding community citizens whose only crime involved competing with a white grocer. The realization compelled Wells to examine previous lynching cases. After extensive research, she concluded that more often than not, the cry of rape masqueraded as a legitimate device for white men to eliminate African American competitors.

Subsequently, she wrote a scathing editorial: "Eight Negroes lynched since last issue of the *Free Speech*. Three were charged with killing white men and five with raping white women. Nobody in this section believes the old thread-bare lie that Negro men assault white women. If southern men are not careful they will overreach themselves and a conclusion will be reached which will be very damaging to the moral reputation of their women."[9] The editorial attacked southern white male honor and suggested that white women could be attracted to black men. And, it infuriated the white community.

Fortunately, when the editorial appeared, Wells was en route to Philadelphia to attend the African Methodist Episcopal General Church Conference. Warnings from an enraged white mob persuaded the co-owner of the paper to flee. The mob destroyed the newspaper office and in their rage threatened Wells's life should she dare return to Memphis. Exiled from her home, she went to New York, joined the staff of the *New York Age* and continued her exposé on lynchings.[10]

Ida B. Wells had met the editor of the *New York Age*, Timothy Thomas Fortune, in the summer of 1888 and maintained her contact with him. When Fortune called for the formation of the National Afro-American League, she supported him. Through the *Age* and the encouragement of Fortune, Americans were alerted to the inherent problems of disfranchisement, lynching, inequitable distribution of educational funding, the convict lease system, and Jim Crow.[11]

Wells's research on lynching culminated in the pamphlet *Southern Horrors: Lynch Law In All Its Phases*. Published in October 1892, Wells prefaced it with "Somebody must show that the Afro-American race is sinned against [rather] than sinning, and it seems to have fallen upon me to do so." She was determined to prove that blacks were not a "bestial race" and to "arouse the conscience of the American people to a demand for justice to every citizen."[12]

Creating the Alpha Suffrage Club

By the time Wells married newspaper publisher and attorney Ferdinand Barnett in 1895, she had visited England twice, caused an uproar at the Columbian Exposition of 1893, held in Chicago, by publishing and handing out the pamphlet *The Reason Why The Colored American is not in the World's Columbian Exposition,* and become an active club woman by establishing the Ida B. Wells Club. Marriage to Barnett brought part ownership in his newspaper, the *Conservator,* two step-children and four of her own. Domestic duties as a wife and mother did not deter Wells from public life. She joined the National Association of Colored Women, organized in 1896, actively pursued the suffrage cause for both disenfranchised African American men and all women, and heeded the call for the development of the National Association for the Advancement of Colored People (NAACP) in the aftermath of the 1908 Springfield, Illinois, race riot. She also continued her exposés on lynching. In 1910 she wrote "How Enfranchisement Stops Lynching," for *Original Rights Magazine.*[13]

The Barnetts resided on the South Side of Chicago in the Second Ward. By the second decade of the twentieth century, the largest majority of African Americans in the city also lived in the area. In 1910 African Americans comprised twenty-five percent of the 42,801 population in the Ward and by 1915 represented nearly forty percent of the 63,342 residents.[14] Voting-age women in the ward developed a keen interest in the electoral process, particularly because of the pending female suffrage bill in the state legislature. They founded several suffrage clubs, developed voter education classes and held mass rallies.[15]

One of the most important and the first African American suffrage club in the city was the Alpha Suffrage Club. Wells-Barnett and a white colleague, Belle Squire, established the organization in January 1913.[16] Ida B. Wells-Barnett used the Suffrage Club as a basis to demonstrate the significance of the ballot to the masses of black women in Chicago. During her early years in Chicago she toured the state for the Women's State Central Committee encouraging women to organize and develop political knowledge. She found on one of these trips that "in only a few instances did I see any of my own people." From this she concluded that "if the white women were backward in political matters, our own women were even more so."[17]

Lacking the skills to understand the political process, Wells-Barnett concluded, hindered African American women from full participation in civic matters. The necessity for the suffrage club took on new urgency when it became clear "that we were likely to have a restricted suffrage, and the white women of the organization [Women's Suffrage Association] were working like beavers to bring it about."[18]

To generate interest in the Suffrage Club and the ballot, she pooled her meager resources, organized meetings and insisted that the club hold membership in national, state, and local organizations such as the National Federation of Colored Women, the State Federation of Colored Women's Club, the Illinois Federation of Colored Women's Clubs and the City Federation of Colored Women's Clubs. The Club's goals included showing black women how to use their "vote for the advantage of ourselves and our race" and acting as a liaison to the city, state, and national organizations. Within less than three years of its founding two hundred women claimed membership. Ida B. Wells-Barnett was elected president.[19]

Racism in the Suffrage Movement

One of Wells-Barnett's first official duties as president was to attend the March 1913 parade sponsored by the National American Woman Suffrage Association in the nation's capital. Carrying banners representing almost every state in the union, the parade marchers highlighted the demand for universal female enfranchisement. But because of racist attitudes, African American women were relegated to the back of the line regardless of state residency. Sixty-five enthusiastic delegates from Illinois prepared for the march along Pennsylvania Avenue. As they lined up, Grace Wilbur Trout, president of the Illinois Equal Suffrage Association and chairperson of the Illinois delegation, informed the Illinois group that the NAWSA advised them "to keep our delegation entirely white" because many women, especially those from the South, resented the presence of a black woman in the Illinois ranks. They would not march, Trout concluded, if Wells-Barnett remained in the Illinois line. They expected her to march with the black women's contingent at the end of the procession.

Fear of antagonizing southern white women, whose support was worth more to the NAWSA's cause than that of African American women, prompted state colleagues to deny Wells-Barnett's opportunity to march with them. Viewing black women as a threat to white supremacy, white southern women rejected the legitimacy of black female state delegates marching with white state delegates. Historian Steven Buechler argues that the NAWSA became the vehicle for southern white women to "maximize white women's votes, minimize black women's votes, and leave restrictions on black male voters intact." The desire of southern white suffragists to assure the public and their state legislatures that African American suffrage and woman suffrage were unconnected pushed them to devise the Jim Crow strategy and to petition for the assistance of the NAWSA.[20] The NAWSA's acquiescence made it blatantly clear that the organization took advantage of the racist agenda, especially when it proved expedient. Ida B. Wells-Barnett's inclusion in the state delegation in the 1913 parade threatened to impede that tactic by stripping away the veil of Jim Crow and opening the door to other African American women.

When Trout pleaded with Wells-Barnett to march with the black delegates at the back of the procession, she refused; she insisted that "the southern women have tried to evade the question time and again by giving some excuse or other every time it has been brought up. If the Illinois women do not take a stand now in this great democratic parade then the colored women are lost."[21] But, Wells-Barnett's plea fell on deaf ears just as an earlier appeal from Virginia Brooks, a white woman from West Hammond, had. If "[w]e have come down here to march for equal rights," then, "[i]t would be autocratic to exclude men or women of any color," Brooks told the contingent. Furthermore, she continued, "I think that we should allow Mrs. Barnett to walk in our delegation. If the women of other states lack moral courage, we should show them that we are not afraid of public opinion. We should stand by our principles. If we do not the parade will be a farce."[22] The state delegates refused to reconsider and acquiesced to the demands of southern white women. Black women could march only if they maintained a very low profile and stayed in their place—at the back of the line.

Angry at the blatant disregard for her right as a woman and an Illinois resident to take part, Wells-Barnett told delegates that "I shall not march at all unless I can march under the Illinois banner" because "[w]hen I was asked to come down here I was asked to march with the other women of our state, and I intend to do so or not take part in the parade at all." One member of the group retorted "If I were a colored woman, I should be willing to march with the other women of my race." Wells-Barnett replied "there is a difference,...which you probably do not see.... I shall not march with the colored women. Either I go with you or not at all. I am not taking this stand because I personally wish for recognition. I am doing it for the future benefit of my whole race."[23]

After this debate Wells-Barnett disappeared from the parade site. Illinois delegates probably assumed that she had relented and decided to march with the black contingent. But, as the delegates began marching down Pennsylvania Avenue, she quietly stepped out from the crowd of spectators and joined the only white Illinois colleagues sympathetic to her cause, Belle Squires and Virginia Brooks. So important was the event that a photograph of her, flanked by Squires and Brooks, appeared in *The Chicago Daily Tribune* giving the event and its participants local and national exposure.[24] As the marchers proceeded, southerners did not defect. This may be in part because they did not learn of Wells-Barnett's inclusion until after the parade ended. At any rate, the press coverage reassured many black women of their own tenuous place in the suffrage movement and probably convinced many whites, despite the NAWSA's insistence, that the "Negro question" and female suffrage were not separate issues.

The staunch refusal by Wells-Barnett to march with the black contingent impeded the white female prerogative of discriminating against African American women on racial grounds while simultaneously embracing them along gen-

Ida B. Wells-Barnett.
University of Chicago

Leaflet from the 1915 New York campaign. Library of Congress

der lines. Racial xenophobia rather than gender inclusion guided their principles. The endorsement of Jim Crow segregation blinded white participants to the fact that unlike the requirement for their African American counterpart, they did not have to separate their whiteness from their femaleness. Indeed, they could embrace the white, middle-class, nativist, racist sentiments prevalent during the Progressive Era under the guise of expediency. Ultimately, white women could express the desire for the enfranchisement of women while ignoring African American women.

But, Wells-Barnett frustrated their plans. She defined the battle for African American women by intertwining her state citizenship, her African Americanness, and her femaleness. She affirmed African American women's place in the fight for the ballot by confronting white women. For women and for the race, she rejected the notion that she did not belong among her state delegates.

Electing a Black Man as Alderman

On May 7 of that same year, the Illinois Senate passed the Presidential and Municipal Suffrage Bill and on June 11 the House approved the measure. Before the month ended, the legislature ratified the bill that granted partial suffrage to female citizens twenty-one years or older. Illinois became the first state east of the Mississippi River to enfranchise its women.[25] More importantly, for the first time in the city's history, African American females could cast their ballots in the race for alderman of the Second Ward. Mobilizing their forces quickly and instituting a large grassroots campaign, black women became powerful political allies to voting age African American men.

The Alpha Suffrage Club increased its activism in communities with large percentages of African Americans, especially since the aldermanic primary was less than a year away. Under Wells-Barnett's leadership, the Club implemented a block system to canvass neighborhoods. In addition, once-a-week meeting sessions were established as learning centers on the rights and duties of citizens. Women worked as clerks in the voter registration process and provided the necessary civic education.[26]

In the 1914 aldermanic primary the club endorsed the Independent candidate, William Randolph Cowan, a prominent black real estate businessman, against the incumbent machine candidate, Hugh Norris.[27] While black politicians championed the new gender-integrated electorate, several other ward men challenged female entry into their domain. As members of the Alpha Suffrage Club marshalled their forces and canvassed the black community, registering women for the February 1914 primary, some men "jeered at them and told them they ought to be at home taking care of the babies." Other male hecklers accused them of "trying to take the place of men and wear the trousers."[28] The jeers made an impact on these Victorian ladies. Discouraged and unsure of their own place in politics, many of the women questioned the legitimacy of their role in the faction-riddled arena. Reassuring members that their efforts were important, Wells-Barnett refused to allow black women to bow to male pressure. She urged each of the workers to return to the neighborhoods and continue registering women. Under her tutelage, most of the women stuck by their convictions, continued the registration efforts, and, in the process realized the importance of their participation in politics.

Some 7,290 female and 16,327 male potential voters registered during this campaign.[29] Though the club was not solely responsible for the number of registrants, it does suggest that the members aroused considerable interest and probably increased the potential number of African American voters. Ida B. Wells-Barnett proudly proclaimed that due to the impressive demonstration of women, "our men politicians were surprised," especially "because not one of them even our ministers, had said one word to influence women to take advantage of the suffrage opportunity Illinois had given to her daughters."[30]

The black weekly, the *Chicago Defender,* captured the sentiments of many women in its sensational headlines for February 21, 1914: "Women To Show Loyalty By Casting First Ballot For Cowan For Alderman"; "Second Ward Women Determine to Use Their Power to Better Themselves and Strengthen the Race"; "Asserted Men Needed Their Assistance"; and "Garbage Question, Children's Playgrounds, Ventilation in Public Places, Supervision of 'Movies' Important Matters to Them." The paper triumphantly predicted that black women would become "the balance of power" in the aldermanic campaign and would "see their first vote make race history in Chicago."[31]

On primary day, almost 3,000 women cast ballots in the Second Ward. Still, William Cowan lost the election. Though disappointed with the outcome, the Suffrage Club women consoled themselves with the knowledge that they had played a significant role in attracting forty-five percent of the women who voted for Cowan to the polls. For the *Defender*, this showed that black women understood better than the men the interconnection between duty and politics because "they were actuated by principal in politics just as they are in everything else." Moreover, the newspaper article stated that "The women's vote was a revelation to everyone, and after analysis shows them still actuated by the sense of duty to do more" and that because of female votes "Traitorous leaders are to be relegated to the background and citizens of strength and character are to take their places." The *Defender* vigorously promoted both Victorian ideals and female access to the electoral process.[32]

The female vote even compelled another weekly, the *Broad Ax*, to acknowledge that "Cowan and his followers woke things up...for he received 2,700 votes more than one thousand of that number being cast by the ladies." The vote "plainly brought to the front one thing and that is that within the next two or four years at the longest a high class popular solid Colored man of affairs can and will be elected to the city council from that ward." For if only three hundred of the black votes to Norris had been transferred to Cowan, the paper concluded, "nothing could have prevented him from breaking into the city council."[33]

The Alpha Suffrage Club's role generated the most attention. Within a few days after Cowan's defeat, two members of the Republican Party visited the Alpha Suffrage Club. A black Republican and contractor, Oscar DePriest, joined the president of the ward organization, Samuel Ettelson, in an appeal for the women to campaign and vote for the machine candidate in the next election.[34] The two men urged the women not to support an Independent candidate for alderman as they had in the Cowan primary, because if they did so, the black vote would split and the Democratic candidate might win. In turn, the Republican Party "having realized that there was now a demand for a colored man, would itself nominate one at the next vacancy." The next vacancy, they were told would probably be in 1915. In November, 1914, George Harding, a Second Ward alderman, was elected state senator. Keeping its promise, the organization pushed DePriest to the forefront by endorsing him as their black candidate for alderman.[35]

Despite the Chicago political machine's endorsement of DePriest, his candidacy was contested. As a matter of fact, his nomination opened the door for other African American candidates seeking the coveted post of alderman. For the first time in Chicago's political history, three black candidates campaigned for alderman in the primary. Joining DePriest were Louis Anderson, a former journalist from Washington, D.C., and Charles Griffin, an insurance and real estate broker.[36]

With battle lines drawn, the candidates began seeking votes. One of the first forums for the three politicians was at the Alpha Suffrage Club's headquarters. They presented their political platform and entertained questions. The Club decided to "endorse" the Republican ticket and "our young giant Oscar DePriest for alderman of the Second Ward." They pledged "to leave no stone unturned" for his election because "we realize that in no other way can we safeguard our own rights than by holding up the hands of those who fight our battles."[37]

On February 27, 1915, DePriest won the Republican primary. After the victory DePriest appealed to those who did not vote for him. "[A]s all good Republicans," he wrote, I hope that they "give me in my coming fight for election their heartiest loyalty and support."[38] But despite his plea dissenters lingered. For example, Edward Wright, disgruntled over DePriest's victory and his own failed bids for alderman, requested that the Political Equality League endorse William Cowan as an independent candidate against DePriest. As a member of the League and on behalf of the Alpha Suffrage Club, Wells-Barnett recoiled from the appeal. She argued that this scheme was conjured up by "this nameless white man" who "had not been prompted by the desire to secure a better man for nomination. It simply was to get two colored men to fight against each other, and the result would be that neither one of them would secure the place." The League agreed and the Wright-Cowan challenge ended.[39]

The contest between DePriest and three white candidates drew thousands of African Americans in the Second Ward to the polls to cast their ballots. When the votes were tabulated, DePriest was the clear winner—and became the first black alderman of Chicago. The final count was: DePriest, 10,599 (Republican); Al Russell, 6,893 (Democrat); Simon P. Gary, 3,697 (Progressive); Samuel Block, 433 (Socialist).[40]

Oscar DePriest's victory inspired public discussion of the significance of the female electorate. The woman vote was a decisive factor and without it, DePriest would not have been the first black alderman. Women's ballots accounted for more than one third of the ballots cast for DePriest. The nearly 4,000 remaining votes went to the other candidates.[41] Again, reflecting that more than one third of the total votes cast came from women.

DePriest acknowledged his debt to Second Ward women. Soon after the election, he asserted in the national black journal, *The Crisis,* "I favor extension of the right of suffrage to women" because the women in Chicago "cast as intelligent a vote as the men." Although there was a certain degree of "timidity" during "the first campaign in which women voted in Chicago," women educated themselves. And in the 1914 and 1915 campaigns, "the work of the women was as earnest and the interest as keen as that of the men and in some instances the partisanship was almost bitter." Moreover, DePriest asserted that during

the campaign of 1915 when colored men were primary candidates for alderman, the women of the race seemed to realize fully what was expected of them, and, with the men, rolled up a very large and significant vote for the colored candidates; and they were consistent at the election, contributing to a plurality of over 3,000 votes for the successful colored candidate in a field of five. Personally, I am more than thankful for their work and as electors believe they have every necessary qualification that the men possess.[42]

The Legacy

A year after the election, the Alpha Club elected new officers and continued its suffrage work. Ida B. Wells-Barnett retained the presidency.[43] In addition to the Second Ward, the Club also canvassed the Sixth, Fourteenth, and Thirtieth Wards in Chicago because each had high concentrations of African Americans. The lure of jobs opened by America's involvement in World War I and the fear of the continued deterioration of race relations in the South prompted a mass exodus from southern states to large urban areas like Chicago. By 1920, the Second Ward African American population was 47,647 or sixty-nine percent of the residents. Voting-age women accounted for 17,144, while men numbered 19,894.[44] This united force challenged political leaders, elected African Americans to the aldermanic post, and commanded some of the spoils from patronage politics.

Little is known about the Alpha Suffrage Club during those late teen years. It is likely that African American women in the Second Ward and other heavily populated black wards continued canvassing and voting in large numbers, in part because of the preceding labor by Suffrage Club members. Despite the passage of the Nineteenth Amendment in 1920 granting suffrage to all women, the political necessity of a united African American constituency remained. For that reason Wells-Barnett continued to press for black women to vote by making speeches and canvassing throughout Chicago and the state. In 1930 she ran for the Illinois Senate as an Independent candidate. Though she lost, her zeal for political involvement continued.[45]

The year after her political bid for the senate Wells-Barnett died of a kidney disease.[46] She left a legacy of activism in social and civic endeavors. Courageously, she exposed the horrors of lynching to a national audience, inspired the growth of the black female club movement in the state, encouraged African Americans to become a part of the political process, and inspired hundreds of women to enter into the public domain of politics.

Notes

1. Alfreda Duster, ed. *Crusade For Justice: The Autobiography of Ida B. Wells* (Chicago, 1970), 7-8; See also Neil R. McMillen, *Dark Journey: Black Mississippians In The Age of Jim Crow* (Urbana, 1989) for discussion of African American life in Mississippi in the post-Civil War era.

2. Duster, *Crusade*, 8-9.

3. Ibid., 9-17; Monroe A. Majors, *Noted Negro Women Their Triumphs And Activities* (Chicago, 1893; reprint ed., Nashville, Tenn., 1971), 187-188.

4. Duster, *Crusade*, 15-18.

5. Ibid., xvii, 18-20; Mildred Thompson, "Ida B. Wells-Barnett: An Exploratory Study of An American Black Woman, 1893-1930," (Ph.D. diss., George Washington University, 1979), 26-28.

6. Duster, *Crusade*, 22-24, 69, 71; Thompson, "Ida B. Wells Barnett: An Exploratory Study of An American Black Woman, 1893-1930," 29-31; Majors, *Noted Negro Women*, 189.

7. Duster, *Crusade*, 47-51; Ida B. Wells, *Southern Horrors: Lynch Law In all Its Phases* in *On Lynchings* (New York, 1892; reprint ed., New York, 1969), 18-19; David M. Tucker, "Miss Ida B. Wells and Memphis Lynching," *Phylon* 32 (1971): 115-116.

8. Duster, *Crusade*, 53-58.

9. Ibid., 65-66.

10. Ibid., 61-67.

11. Ibid., 71, 77; Thompson "Ida B.WellsBarnett: An Exploratory Study of An American Black Woman, 1893-1930," 36-37, 58; Emma Lou Thornbrough, "The National Afro-American League, 1887-1908," *Journal of Southern History* 27 (1961): 504.

12. Wells, *Southern Horrors*, preface.

13. Duster, *Crusade*, xxiii, 239, 321-327; Ida B. Wells, *The Reason Why The Colored American is not in the World's Columbian Exposition* (Chicago, 1893); Elizabeth Lindsay Davis, *The Story of The Illinois Federation of Colored Women's Clubs* (Chicago, 1922), 26-28, 56; Ida B. Wells-Barnett, "How Enfranchisement Stops Lynching," *Original Rights Magazine* (June 1910), 42-53.

14. *Thirteenth Census Of The United States, 1910: Population*, v. 2: The breakdown of the population was Native White, native parentage = 11,642; Native White, foreign or mixed = 11,225; Foreign-Born White = 9,118; Negro = 10,709; Indian, Chinese, Japanese, and all other = 107. Yearly census data for the area was kept by the *Chicago Daily News*. Corrections and updates can be found in James Langland, M.A. Compiler, *The Chicago Daily News Almanac And Year-Book For 1916* (Chicago, 1916), 585, 586. Also see Allan H. Spear, *Black Chicago: The Making Of A Negro Ghetto 1890-1920* (Chicago, 1967) 15 and 122 for population data from 1915.

15. *Chicago Defender*, February 21, 1914; Also see listing in Ford S. Black, *Black's Blue Book Directory Of Chicago's Active Colored People And Guide To Their Activities* (Chicago, Ill., 1916), 55, Illinois State Historical Library, Springfield, Ill.

16. Katherine E. Williams, "The Alpha Suffrage Club," *The Half Century Magazine* (September 1916): 12.

17. Duster, *Crusade*, 244-245.

18. Ibid., 345.

19. Williams, "The Alpha Suffrage Club," 12; *Alpha Suffrage Record*, 18 March 1914 [1915], Ida B. Wells-Barnett Papers, University of Chicago. Other officers included: Mary Jackson, Viola Hill, Vera Wesley Green, Sadie L. Adams, and K.J. Bills. There is not an "official" roster of members.

20. Carrie Chapman Catt and Nettie Rogers Shuler, *Woman Suffrage and Politics: The Inner Story of the Suffrage Movement* (1923; reprint, Seattle, 1969), 241-242; Rosalyn Terborg-Penn, "Discrimination Against Afro-American Women in the Woman's Movement, 1830-1920," in *The Afro-American Woman: Struggles And Images*, eds. Sharon Harley and Rosalyn Terborg-Penn (New York, 1978), 24-25; Aileen S. Kraditor, *The Ideas of the Woman Suffrage Movement, 1890-1920* (1965; reprint New York, 1981), 212-218; Steven Buechler, *The Transformation of The Woman Suffrage Movement: The Case of Illinois, 1850-1920* (New Jersey, 1986), 149-150, 226; Adade Mitchell Wheeler, "Conflict in the Illinois Woman Suffrage Movement of 1913," *Journal of the Illinois State Historical Society* 76 (Summer 1983): 106; Marjorie Spruill Wheeler, *New Women Of The New South: The Leaders of the Woman Suffrage Movement in the Southern States* (New York, 1993); *The Chicago Daily Tribune*, March 3 and 4, 1913.

21. *The Chicago Daily Tribune*, March 4, 1913.

22. Ibid.

23. Ibid.

24. Ibid.

25. John D. Buenker, "Illinois and the Four Progressive-Era Amendments to the United States Constitution," *Illinois Historical Journal* 80 (Winter 1987): 210-227; Wheeler, "Conflict in the Illinois Woman Suffrage Movement of 1913," 65-114; Anne Firor Scott and Andrew MacKay Scott, *One Half the People: The Fight for Woman Suffrage* (1975; reprint, Urbana, Ill., 1982), 116-121.

26. Williams, "The Alpha Suffrage Club," 12.

27. *Broad Ax*, January 17, 1914; Gosnell, *Negro Politicians*, 74.

28. Duster, *Crusade*, 346.

29. *The Chicago Daily News Almanac And Year-Book For 1915* (Chicago, 1914), 632, Chicago Municipal Library, Chicago, Ill.; Also, the *Chicago Defender*, February 21, 1914, mentions the Alpha Political Club and Josephine Crawford as active in the political process as well.

30. Duster, *Crusade*, 346.

31. *Chicago Defender*, February 21, 1914.

32. Spear, *Black Chicago*, 81-82; *Chicago Defender*, March 28, 1914.

33. *The Chicago Daily News Almanac And Year-Book For 1915*, 632. Spear, *Black Chicago*, 123; *Chicago Defender*, February 21, 1914; *Broad Ax*, February 28, 1914.

34. Duster, *Crusade*, 346.

35. Duster, *Crusade*, 346-348; Gosnell, *Negro Politicians*, 170.

36. Gosnell, *Negro Politicians*, 30, 70, 104-105; Pinderhughes, *Race and Ethnicity*, 77-78.

37. *Suffrage Record*, March 18, 1914 [1915].

38. *Chicago Defender*, February 27, 1915; *The Chicago Daily News Almanac And Year-Book For 1916* (Chicago, 1916), 567.

39. Duster, *Crusade*, 348.

40. *The Chicago Daily News Almanac And Year-Book For 1916*, 567, 591; Gosnell, *Negro Politicians*, 171.

41. *The Chicago Daily News Almanac And Year-Book For 1916*, 567, 591; Gosnell, *Negro Politicians*, 171.

42. Oscar DePriest, "Chicago and Woman's Suffrage," *The Crisis* 10 (August 1915): 179.

43. Williams, "The Alpha Suffrage Club," 12. Other officers were: Sadie L. Adams, E.D. Wyatt, J.E. Hughes, W.N. Mills, and Laura Beasley.

44. *Fourteenth Census of the United States*, 274.

45. See Wanda Hendricks, "Ida Bell Wells-Barnett," In Darlene Clark Hine, ed. *Black Women In America: An Historical Encyclopedia*, v. 2, s.v. (New York, 1993), 1245.

46. Ibid., 1246.

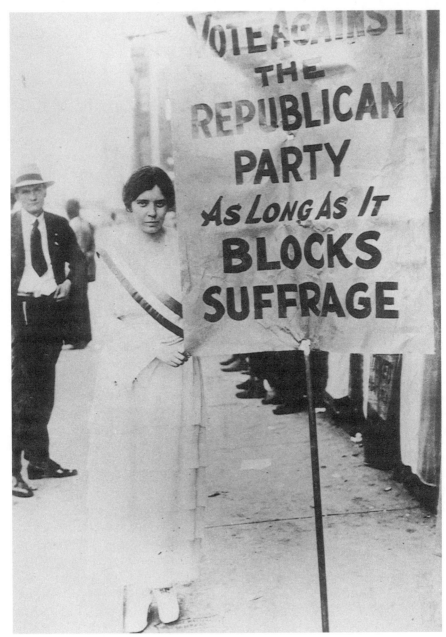

Alice Paul. Smithsonian Institution

Fifteen

Alice Paul and the Triumph of Militancy

Linda G. Ford

Editor's Introduction: As historian Linda G. Ford so clearly illustrates in this article, the spirit of militancy that had been evident in the early
stages of the woman suffrage movement was rekindled near its end. This militant spirit inspired women to bold and dramatic acts that made it impossible for
the public or the politicians to ignore the movement or fail to understand the
determination of suffragists to bring the long battle to a victorious conclusion.

As the movement entered its last decade, a new mood was developing among
American suffragists: there was a growing impatience with the slow progress
and a sense that victory should have come long ago. Indeed, to a generation of
women who had come of age in an era of greater educational and employment
opportunities for women and who witnessed the political activism of women in
the Progressive Era, the denial of the vote to women seemed like an anachro-
nism that must be swiftly rejected—along with the concept of separate spheres
upon which that denial was based. This new generation of suffragists, together
with many veterans of the movement who had buried one revered suffrage
leader after another while politicians still denied them their rights, were responsible for the new wave of suffrage militancy. Militant tactics, as we have seen,
were increasingly evident, including in the states of New York and California.
Suffrage militants were incensed that women were forced to plead and cajole
and to devise arguments as to why woman suffrage was good for society. Equal
suffrage was their right, they declared, and they would *take* it.

Alice Paul soon emerged as the leader of the American militants. Paul had
returned from Great Britain in 1910, but for two years devoted herself to the
completion of her doctoral degree, earning a Ph.D. in sociology from the University of Pennsylvania. During her three years in Great Britain (where she was
a caseworker for a settlement house), Paul had been inspired by Emmeline
Pankhurst and the militant Women's Social and Political Union (WSPU). Radicalized by participation in the bold and defiant British suffrage movement,
Paul was disturbed by the relative docility of the National American Woman
Suffrage Association (NAWSA) under President Anna Howard Shaw, and
appalled that the entire energies of American suffragists were absorbed by
state suffrage campaigns while the federal amendment remained on the back
burner.

Working at first through the NAWSA's Congressional Committee and later the NAWSA-affiliated Congressional Union (CU), Paul tried to refocus the attention of suffragists on the federal amendment and revitalize—and publicize—the national suffrage movement. Paul masterminded the dramatic suffrage parade in 1913 during Woodrow Wilson's inauguration, a grand and dramatic display of the strength of the national movement that became even more sensational when the largely hostile crowd attacked the marchers—provoking massive press coverage and a Congressional investigation, commanding the attention of the nation.

As explained in this essay by Linda Ford and the subsequent essay by Robert Booth Fowler, Alice Paul and the CU soon parted company with the NAWSA (in 1914), largely over the issue of tactics. Influenced by the strategy of the British suffragists, Paul introduced her famous plan of holding the party in power responsible for the failure to enfranchise women. Rather than beg for enfranchisement, Paul sought to direct the full power of the women already enfranchised in western states against President Wilson and the Democrats (who had a majority in Congress), hoping to force the president and his party to abandon their traditional insistence on states' rights and to secure the passage of the federal woman suffrage amendment. Paul's approach violated the NAWSA's traditional nonpartisan strategy, and led to a new schism in suffrage ranks. For the rest of the movement's history, the NAWSA and the militants would be involved in a public dispute over strategy and tactics.

It is interesting to note that one point of disagreement between the two groups was the *name* of the federal amendment. Soon after the CU became an independent organization, its members began referring to the proposed amendment as "The Susan B. Anthony Amendment"—over the objections of the NAWSA and some CU members, including Harriot Stanton Blatch, who believed it was inappropriate to single out any one of the nineteenth-century pioneers for this recognition.

The CU continued to exist as a separate organization and was renamed the National Woman's Party (NWP) when it merged with its western affiliate (the Woman's Party) in 1917. As Ford describes, the NWP gradually but steadily became more militant, engaging in acts of non-violent civil disobedience that provoked a stern—even violent—response from the Wilson administration. But the harsh and unjust treatment the suffragists received only cemented their determination. Women became the first in the United States to picket the White House, a form of protest that lasted nearly three years before the Nineteenth Amendment was ratified. During this time hundreds of suffragists were arrested illegally and jailed, with some organizing hunger strikes while in jail, and facing forced feedings by prison officials. These actions, and more, continued to focus the public's and the politicians' attention on woman suffrage.

Militancy, Ford insists, was a success. Not only did suffrage militancy successfully focus attention on woman suffrage and reawaken the "slumbering issue of a national woman suffrage amendment," it "made the government and politicians acutely aware of women's potential political power." Though reviled by many politicians—and suffragists—the militants "created a situation in which something had to be done." The violent reaction to their uncompromising demand for political equality solidified their determination to win the vote and also to wipe out all vestiges of discrimination against American women; it was this group that drafted and introduced the Equal Rights Amendment in 1923—an amendment they called the "Lucretia Mott Amendment."

☆ ☆ ☆ ☆ ☆

THE STRONG, FEMINIST MILITANCY of the National Woman's Party (NWP) evolved as a logical response to the intransigence of male-centered government in the first decades of this century. Feminist militancy, which I define as the readiness to resist governmental authorities and break the law for the cause of women's rights, developed gradually from men's (non)reaction to women's political claims to equal citizenship. Woman militants for suffrage were not shy about critiquing the male monopoly on power, and, in turn, male authorities responded to the perceived threat, describing the suffragists as "unnatural, iron-jawed" females—even "revolutionaries." Militant suffragists were *feminist* revolutionaries, "striking the blow" themselves to secure drastic political change for women, and with that, change in women's social role, status and image.

Women's New Independence

In the early twentieth century angry women—potential militants—were beginning actively to change their lives. Time and time again, in autobiographies of women of this period, there emerges a strong sense of impatient resentment and desire for independence. A growing number of women wanted independence from the nineteenth-century concept of a stiffly corseted, rigidly role-stereotyped woman. These women wanted freedom from centuries of having to depend on men for identity, sustenance, and decision-making.

In the twentieth century, cultural and economic change would slowly make a difference in the social role a woman could play. Virginia Woolf wrote that if a woman had the means to support herself, all sorts of possibilities arose; she might even be able to do something with her anger. The American feminist theorist Charlotte Perkins Gilman echoed Woolf, arguing that the time had come for women to be completely independent, especially economically, of men. Early twentieth-century women were a rapidly growing presence in the labor force, in offices and factories, and even in "male" professions such as law and medicine. And along with a greater presence, these women's expectations were growing.[1]

In the United States, the women who joined Alice Paul in a new militant suffrage movement were, as Paul put it, not of any particular class, but shared a "feeling of loyalty to our own sex and an enthusiasm to have every degradation that was put upon our sex removed." *The Suffragist,* the militants' weekly jour-

Members of the Congressional Union travel west to rally women voters.
Rose Winslow, Lucy Burns, and Doris Stevens are on the left.
Schlesinger Library, Radcliffe College

nal, was decidedly feminist in tone and subject matter. These new suffrage leaders saw revolutionary social implications in their struggle for political rights, and they were not the only ones to see them. A 1916 *New York Times* editorial called the "threat of sex vs. sex" carried out by the suffragists:

> political blackmail...an ugly portent, whose possibilities of damage are not limited to politics, but may extend to other parts of the social structure. These [women] leaders have justified to the extent of their powers the worst that has ever been said about the danger of giving votes to women.

That same year a Georgia woman wrote western suffrage leader Anne Martin: "A female creature, queer and quaint, Who longs to be just what she ain't/ We cannot efface—we can't forget her—We love her still—the stiller the better."[2] Suffrage militants were not at all within the bounds of proper womanhood.

American and English Suffragists

"Improper" woman suffragists revealed their impatience with passive roles in both England and the United States. There was a very direct relation between the arch-militant Women's Social and Political Union (WSPU) of England and the National Woman's Party of the United States. Women who were very important to the woman suffrage movement had long traveled the Atlantic to inspire and inform each other. Many of them advocated a new sort of independence for women featuring a determination to act—strike their own blows—to take matters into their own hands. The feminism of mid-nineteenth century reformer Elizabeth Cady Stanton was directly inspired by English women like Mary Wollstonecraft, author of the 1792 *A Vindication of the Rights of Woman,* and Frances Wright, who spoke out for women's rights when she came to America in the 1820s. *The Revolution,* published by Stanton and feminist reformer Susan B. Anthony, kept close track of the English scene.[3]

By 1887 the American/English Women's Franchise League included among its members the British Emmeline Pankhurst, along with Stanton and her daughter, Harriot Stanton Blatch (who had married an Englishman). Both the Pankhursts and the Stantons advocated a certain aggressive style of seeking reform. According to both Emmeline and her daughter Christabel Pankhurst, when Susan B. Anthony visited London in 1901, she was a great inspiration for British feminists. Realizing that Anthony would die without gaining the franchise for women, Christabel Pankhurst decided that "deeds, not words" should be the motto of the WSPU's organized fight for woman suffrage.[4]

American graduate student Alice Paul was "extremely thrilled" when she joined the parliamentary deputations of the WSPU while in England. Alice Paul, like her idol Susan B. Anthony before her, had a feminist philosophy that demanded full equality for women and a belief that moral principles should be committed to action. Paul was born in 1885 in the Quaker community of Moorestown, New Jersey, and was brought up with the Quaker maxim that women were equal before God and were entitled, even obliged, to address social problems. Paul had a serious-minded childhood, during which she developed a strong sense of right and wrong, and the belief that any life without a cause was empty. For Paul, although trained as a social worker, that cause would single-mindedly be women's rights.

Although not without hesitation and much trepidation, Paul first became involved in women's rights advocacy in England by interrupting the speeches of Foreign Secretary Edward Grey and Home Secretary Winston Churchill. In addition, she went to Scotland to organize and rabble-rouse—traveling with fellow American Lucy Burns and Emmeline Pankhurst herself. It was while working with the WSPU in England that Paul and Burns first felt a "blazing" feminist anger, both at the rough treatment they received at the hands of male police and jailers—including forced feeding in jail—*and* at the continued indifference of male political authorities.[5]

Their militant experiences in England gave Paul and Burns a credibility and a notoriety of sorts with American suffragists upon their return to the United States in 1910. Their English experiences also left Paul and Burns with a lasting adulation for the Pankhursts and the WSPU, although they never did use the

Pankhurst's "violent" tactics such as destroying property. After deputations to Parliament were repeatedly dispersed with violence, and after suffering harsh jail terms, the women of the WSPU reasoned that the violent actions against them demonstrated that property—not human life—was most important to the English government. The British authorities unleashed a tremendously hostile counterattack and in the process spurred a large portion of public opinion to shift to the WSPU side. Only World War I would put an end to the war between the WSPU and the British government.[6] What Alice Paul learned from the British movement was a resentment of male domination, a desire for full equality, and a determination to organize women to act aggressively on their demands—to *take* their rights.

A Militant Approach in America

The fame they gained in England culminated in an invitation for Alice Paul and Lucy Burns to speak to the National American Woman Suffrage Association (NAWSA) in 1910. Two years later, through the auspices of social reform paragon Jane Addams, Paul and Burns were asked to chair a "congressional committee" for the NAWSA that would work for a federal woman suffrage amendment in Washington. The two young militants brought a new excitement—an aggressive spirit—to what had become a lethargic woman suffrage movement in America.

The flamboyance of the militants' new committee was directed toward overcoming indifference to women's issues in the United States. In time, their concerted militant actions generated hostility and violence—directed at them as "unnatural" women. How would a movement to revive the campaign for the middle-class, Progressive reform of woman suffrage come to be considered a dangerously militant, antigovernment conspiracy? The coming of World War I certainly helped shape events, but Woman's Party policy—a direct reaction to government non-action—went through gradual, increasingly militant stages, leading to the women's arrest and imprisonment.

The Congressional Committee was defiant and aggressive from the beginning. That brand of impatient, militant feminism, coupled with competition over NAWSA-held suffrage territory and money, soon offended the NAWSA's deliberately moderate leaders. The Congressional Committee evolved into the Congressional Union (CU), a more independent, and stronger group. The CU approach of strong feminism and militant-spirited strategies—obviously influenced by the British—became a liability and an embarrassment to a NAWSA leadership determined not to erode the legislative and public support they had painstakingly won for suffrage. NAWSA officers were sure that the aggressive CU was doing damage by pushing too hard, alienating President Woodrow Wilson and antagonizing the public with their incessant, unladylike lobbying. The CU promoted militancy, an aggressive, unapologetically egalitarian, militant style, which the more moderate NAWSA members could not countenance. In

1914, Paul and Burns' group was expelled from the NAWSA for being "too British."[7]

As an independent organization, the CU used increasingly militant methods between 1914 and 1917, trying to force the Wilson administration to secure the passage of woman suffrage. They began with "heckling" Wilson—interrupting speeches and asking pointed questions—and combined that with strenuous speaking and petitioning campaigns for suffrage. A small but dedicated new suffrage organization, the CU was particularly well-known for the British-inspired tactic of organizing women voters in the West to vote against recalcitrant Democrats in 1914 and again in 1916. In the 1916 elections, under a strict "party responsibility" policy, the Democrats were held responsible for nonaction on the newly formed western Woman's Party's one and only plank, "the enfranchisement of the women of America through a Federal Amendment." Through the efforts of traveling organizers and helped by their own increasingly popular journal, *The Suffragist,* the militants did their best to convince women in the western states, many of whom had had the vote for years, to vote "Republican, Socialist, Prohibitionist or Progressive—anything but Democratic." Although studies have shown that the Woman's Party did affect those elections with their appeals to western women to "help their sisters in the East," the Wilson administration was not impressed enough to pass the suffrage amendment. However, a few years later, Wilson *was* persuaded to favor woman suffrage due to a shift in public opinion. Unquestionably this change of heart was influenced by the NWP pressure and propaganda, yet personally Wilson remained "repelled" by women who, by speaking in public, "reversed the social order."[8]

Organizing the National Woman's Party

When the assertive policy of holding the party in power responsible did not secure woman suffrage, the Woman's Party began overt acts of militancy in defiance of authority and the law. This group of militant women decided in March of 1917 that in order to further a united, politically powerful campaign, they needed to merge the western campaign's Woman's Party with the Washington-based CU, and to call themselves the National Woman's Party (NWP). The militants' tactics, including their shrewd use of women's existing political power and their obvious courage and iron-willed determination, continued to reflect their belief that women were worthy of political power. Increasingly resentful of the men who held power over them, NWP suffragists used progressively more militant actions against an unyielding government. At the same time, they sharpened their feminist critique. They slowly shifted from just insisting on a greater democracy that included women, to a condemnation of an oppressive, "autocratic," patriarchal society, including their effort to show that the "women's" militancy—picketing and civil disobedience—was different from and highly superior to, the current manifestation of "men's" militancy—war. Paradoxically, the NWP used the weapon of nonviolence very effectively to illustrate their enormous strength as women. Furious that the war-harried Wilson decided to receive no more NWP suffragist delegations, the militant women, in the first stage of their open militancy, began a perpetual delegation of White House pickets in January 1917, continuing almost daily pickets even after the United States entered the war in April.

The first stage of outright militancy was characterized by beautifully staged and deliberately peaceful, nonviolent demonstrations—consisting of banner-holding suffragists arranged outside the White House—protesting the Wilson government's inaction on suffrage. The NWP's suffrage strategy is a classic example of nonviolent resistance against a government, with the intent to defy and coerce authorities. A typical NWP banner would mock the president by using his own lofty moral rhetoric. One example of this was the use of Wilson's war message: "We shall fight for the things which we have always held nearest our hearts —for democracy, for the right of those who submit to authority to have a voice in their own government."[9] The peaceful and perfectly legal picketing method was adopted from several sources, including labor activists as well as the British militant suffragists. The tactic also in part reflected Alice Paul's adherence to a tradition of Quaker civil disobedience. To some NWP leaders, such demonstrations were particularly appropriate for women, "peace-loving by nature," to show that "woman's" militancy was brave and defiant, but peaceful, whereas "male" militancy, in 1917, was violent and destructive. Paul said it was clear that "women were the peace-loving half of the world and that by giving power to women we would diminish the possibilities of war."[10] Whether they thought women naturally more peaceful or not, all NWP pickets demanded that Wilson act on woman suffrage immediately, and give women a voice in decisions on war.

Suffragists Arrested

The first mob attacks, arrests, and jailings began the second stage of open militancy in June 1917. The government began to regard the women as more than a nuisance when the pickets raised new banners that were sharply critical of the Wilson government, proclaiming that America, fighting a war for freedom in Europe, was not as democratic as "free Russia," which had enfranchised its women. Banners lambasted "Kaiser Wilson" and his "dictatorial and oppressive" policies toward women. The Wilson administration's violent reaction, including jailing many of the protesters and exposing them to harsh treatment and terrible conditions, brought the NWP to the third stage of open militancy— the October demands for political prisoner status in the face of what the women called "administration terrorism" against their members.

The abusive treatment meted out to the NWP demonstrators was suffered by rich and poor, old and young suffragists alike. Co-leaders Alice Paul and Lucy Burns—both from very comfortable backgrounds, highly educated and progressive "New Women" professionals (one an educator, the other a social worker/scholar) initially attracted other impatient feminists of similar backgrounds. The core membership of the NWP in the suffrage period, 1912-1920, tended to be of two types: the state and local officers, either mature (over forty) social reformer/clubwomen, inspired to greater militancy; or speaker/organizers, young college-educated "New Women," with very liberal, modern ideas of women's equality and economic independence. There was, therefore, conflict within the NWP, over race and class issues, over how inclusive their "united sisterhood" should be. But to all NWP suffrage leaders and organizers, the defiant stance against the Wilson administration, as part of the battle against sexism, always came first.

Other groups of antigovernment dissenters directed their protests directly against war itself, or against the capitalist system which made a war of "imperialist aggression" possible. The antigovernment, feminist demonstrators of the NWP also wanted to change the system, but their vision was one in which women should be included, not just in government, but in full equality in all aspects of American society. Some NWP feminists stressed women's "superior" qualities, evolved over centuries of being "other directed," but many others stressed that all women must be given the opportunity to participate fully in their culture, whatever qualities they did or did not possess.[11] National Woman's Party feminists shared a radical vision of completely equal opportunity, and were not willing to wait for their goal. In fact, they were more than willing to act, to fight against their opponent, the Wilson government.

Political Prisoners

The government started jailing militant suffragists in June 1917, but the sentences were not more than a few days in length until mid-August and the

Police arrest suffrage pickets, Washington, DC 1917.
Woman Suffrage Media Collection

"Kaiser" banners, when sixty-day sentences at Occoquan Workhouse in Virginia began to be meted out. By mid-September, sympathetic socialist women began to be more apparent among the arrested, including newspaper writer Peggy Baird Johns, one of the first to suggest demanding political prisoner status. The women at Occoquan, including Lucy Burns, readily assented to the plan, agreeing that they were not "traffic obstructors," as charged, but in reality, political offenders. The women drafted a letter to the district commissioners in Washington demanding political prisoner privileges and protesting their unjust and erratic sentences that ranged from a suspended sentence to sixty days for the same offense.[12] Their letter went unanswered, but the women continued to demand recognition as political prisoners.

Government and prison authorities had little patience for the women's demands and showed their growing irritation in late October by giving Alice Paul a seven-month sentence for picketing. Paul was placed in a psychopathic ward and force-fed after she decided to go on a hunger strike along with socialist Rose Winslow. Alice Paul and Winslow decided to go on hunger strikes in order to get political prisoner status "in accordance with the plan started by the sixty-day group"—the group led by Peggy Baird Johns and arrested back in September. Paul had not wanted other NWP suffragists to hunger strike, but only wanted to take the sacrifice on herself. As she wrote national board member Dora Lewis, "Things took a more serious turn than I had planned, but it's happened rather well because we'll have ammunition against the Administration, and the more harsh and repressive they seem the better."[13] The administration's reaction to her hunger strike was to forcibly feed her in order to "save" her. Lewis protested to District Commissioner Gwynne Gardener, insisting that Paul and the other prisoners be given political offender status as "government enemies."[14]

The Night of Terror and Forced Feedings

On November 14, thirty-three NWP women, arrested for picketing the White House in protest against the treatment of Alice Paul, suffered Superintendent Raymond Whittaker's infamous "night of terror." The terror began immediately when two soldiers attacked the picketing Boston matron Agnes Morey, jabbing her broken, splintered banner pole between her eyes. Philadelphia grandmother Dora Lewis, always in the forefront, was knocked about by three youths. All the arrested suffrage militants regarded themselves as political prisoners of the Wilson administration, and were quite willing to undergo whatever was necessary to have prison and government authorities recognize them as such. After the women were taken to Occoquan Workhouse, their demands for political offender status were not even delivered to prison superintendent Whittaker before his men seized Lewis. The guards seemed in a frenzy of rage. After Louisiana suffragist Alice Cosu was clubbed into her cell, Whittaker told her that "in her work she could stand anything." Cosu later wrote that she "was completely unnerved....I was sick all night long from this treatment." When the other women suspected Cosu had had a heart attack, their cries to Whittaker's guards for help were ignored. NWP vice president Lucy Burns, a vocal leader at Occoquan, was singled out for especially rough treatment. When she resisted being hauled away, she was beaten and then eventually had her wrists handcuffed high on her cell door. A young suffrage organizer, Julia Emory, stood in the same position as Burns in sympathy. Dorothy Day (founder of the Catholic Workers' Movement) said she "naturally...tried to pull away" from the guards, so they responded by pinching her arms, twisting her wrists, then wrestling her down over an iron bench, bruising her back and shoulders. One man had his hand at her throat. By morning, Day was "in an hysterical and sick condition." No one treated Day's or anyone else's injuries; they were not even allowed to use a toilet. This was true although most of the women reported later they were at least bruised and shaken, and felt "terrorized." [15]

Their night of terror ended, but the women did not relinquish their insistence on being considered Wilson's political prisoners. The only practical resistance seemed to be to use the hunger strike, just as the British had, to secure public sympathy and move the government to act on woman suffrage. But the hunger strike had its own horrors. It was met by the counterforce of "forcible feeding," ostensibly done to save lives, but a harsh and cruel procedure. Feeding was done with tubing forced down the mouth or nostrils, and the suffragists faced it stoically but with dread. Rose Winslow, who experienced forcible feeding three times a day during her imprisonment, smuggled out notes saying:

> I had a nervous time of it, gasping a long time afterward, and my stomach rejecting during the process.... The poor soul who fed me got liberally besprinkled during the process. I heard myself making the most hideous sounds.... One feels so forsaken when one lies prone and people shove a pipe down one's stomach.... Yesterday was a bad day for me in feeding. I was vomiting continually during the process. The tube had developed an irritation somewhere that is painful.... The same doctor feeds both Alice Paul and me. Don't let them tell you we take this well.... We think of the coming feeding all day. It is horrible.

Besides using forcible feeding, doctors and matrons tried to "persuade, bully and threaten" the women out of "sticking to their purpose, hunger striking to gain political offender status." But on November 23, Judge Edmund Waddill decided the suffragists had been illegally committed to Occoquan, and should be remanded to the District Jail; all were released on November 27 and 28. [16]

The Wilson Administration Versus the Militants

The violence of the night of November 14, 1917, and the trauma of forcible feedings that NWP suffragists endured, were all done for a cause about which they were deadly serious. The women insisted that the Wilson government was oppressing and discriminating against American women, while hypocritically fighting a war for democracy in Europe. The government considered the suffragists' on-going, defiant presence near the White House to be a threat to national security, and therefore did not stop mob abuse of the pickets and freely arrested demonstrators for "obstructing traffic."

In March of 1918, the Federal Court of Appeals decided that the women arrested in 1917, some serving several months in jail, had been tried and imprisoned under no existing law.[17] The pickets had been caught up in a wave of war hysteria. (They might arguably have been tried under the Sedition Act on expressing "scurrilous" opinions of the administration, but that act was not passed until May of 1918.) The militant suffragists were deprived of their civil liberties in the same way numerous others would soon be, from high school teachers and ministers with antiwar opinions to radical socialists. The suffragists had been arrested for obstructing traffic, a misdemeanor, but their lengthy sentences were far from appropriate punishment for such a crime. The sentences backfired as a deterrent however, since the jail experience thoroughly radicalized the suffragists in terms of their feminism and sense of solidarity with all women, as well as in terms of their disillusionment with the government, leading to still further acts of militancy.

In the highest circles of government, NWP suffragists had made themselves very unpopular since their 1914 presidential heckling. Between 1914 and 1917 President Wilson had become more and more respectful and attentive to the moderate NAWSA, as he became more convinced that NWP women were unreasonable radicals. In October of 1917 he had written NAWSA President Carrie Chapman Catt, saying that he realized her group should not be associated with the militants, who had "laid themselves open to serious criticism." Wilson was convinced "the treatment of the woman picketeers [sic] has been grossly exaggerated" and there had been "an extraordinary amount of lying about the thing." He also wrote his secretary, Joseph Tumulty, on November 16, stating that the United States had no political prisoners, but the militant suffragists "offended against an ordinance of the District and are undergoing the punishment appropriate in the circumstances."[18] Wilson apparently thought that the misdemeanor of disobeying a traffic regulation required a punishment of harsh treatment at the workhouse with some sentenced to six months or more.

The Wilson administration had also tried to thwart the militants in other ways besides imprisonment. The NWP militancy was designed to reach the public through the media; its effectiveness depended on public support, sympathy and outrage. Therefore, the administration thought press control of the suffragists' activities might be an effective curb. In July of 1917, Tumulty suggested to the president a press blackout of NWP stories. Wilson thought that "bare, colorless chronicles" might be better, but many papers, particularly the Washington *Times, Star,* and *Post,* eventually adopted a policy of rarely covering NWP activities, or covering them in an unfavorable light.[19] The NWP organizers testified time and again that the lack of coverage by the press became a problem. Also, after the June "Russian" banner appeared, contrasting Russia's franchise for women with "democratic" America's lack of one, the government's brand-new Secret Service kept tabs on the NWP all across the country. Western NWP leader Anne Martin was especially plagued by agents in October and November of 1917, with several of them usually in attendance at her suffrage rallies; she even found one listening at her hotel door. One reason for such vigilance may have been Martin's proclivity for making statements like "Russia fears the world war is only a capitalistic war" because the United States' "democracy" jails its women. In Los Angeles, a government agent informed her that she would not hold a meeting. In response, she told him America had guarantees of freedom of speech and assembly, and he could come arrest her if she said something "seditious." Martin wrote to NWP activist Pauline Clarke: "The hand of the administration is certainly reaching out after us. The prison story gets the women and they fear it." Martin argued strongly that criticizing Wilson's blocking of woman suffrage was not treason.[20] Obviously, the Wilson government disagreed.

A week after the "night of terror," the *New York Tribune* accused the NWP of having incriminating links with radical socialists and "anarchists." From 1917 to 1919 the militants would be accused of "bolshevism," charges they would usually not even bother to answer. The Wilson administration and the public considered the NWP's feminist views and their militant actions "radical," and many (leftist) political radicals agreed. The socialist *Liberator* reported in early 1918, "Alice Paul and her young army of militants are one of the leading radical forces in American politics in the near future."[21] Beginning in 1917, socialist women joined the NWP in droves to demonstrate against the Wilson government. "Laboring women," particularly Connecticut munitions workers protesting their lack of suffrage as workers and as women, also joined the fray.[22] Obviously, many NWP members did not wholeheartedly embrace the anticapitalist stance of the socialists, but at least for a time they were united with socialists in feeling left out of American society and in their grievances against the Wilson government for suppressing their rights to free speech, and for sustaining a war in which they felt they had had no say.

Fighting Hypocrisy

The violence that NWP suffragists suffered at the hands of the Wilson administration, beyond showing that the government perceived the NWP as a threat to national security along with other dissenters, served to radicalize further and to disillusion the largely middle-class and relatively sheltered woman suffragists. The jail experience made the NWP feel alienated from their own government. However, it strengthened their radical feminism and identification with other women; for some of them this identification extended even to the poor and black women in prison. The suffragists all recoiled in disbelief from the way in which the government had had them punished, simply for fighting for women's rights. In essence, the Woman's Party suffragists were angry at the hypocrisy of the Wilson government in fighting for democracy in

Europe while denying American women the right to vote—or even the right to free speech.

When Alice Paul and Lucy Burns first founded the NWP, they staunchly believed, as good Progressive reformers, in the promise of American democracy. They also expected a superior generosity of American men as compared to the unyielding British political system and brutish "bobbies" who had put down the Pankhurst rebellion. By 1917 the NWP saw the promise of American liberty as empty. Upon being released after the November terrors, Paul asked how "people fail to see our fight as part of the great American struggle for democracy? We are bearing on the American tradition, living up to the American spirit." [23]

It would be difficult for women jailed by their society for exercising their rights of free speech to look upon that society in the same way ever again. Perhaps because they were middle-class reformers, the NWP suffragists reacted to their brutal treatment with incredulity and anger. The Occoquan prisoners felt desolate, alienated, and very bitter. New York suffragist, Kathryn Lincoln, who participated in the hunger strike, said the days in jail were "an eternity." She would throw herself on her bed sobbing, feeling that she was "gradually losing my hold upon life." Buffalo newspaper columnist Ada Davenport Kendall testified that Occoquan was "a place of chicanery, sinister horror, brutality and dread" from which "no one could come out without just resentment against any government which could maintain such an institution." [24] These women reformers had come to a conclusion similar to that of socialists and other radical dissidents—that there was no justice, no real democracy in America in 1917.

The NWP suffragists blamed the government, and Wilson in particular, for their harsh treatment, for the suppression of their rights, and for their continued political powerlessness as women. As Boston NWP leader Agnes Morey wrote: "So far as democracy and liberalism goes it is for men—that politicians speak—women are outside their cosmos." [25] Inasmuch as the government ignored their claims as women, the militants felt their grievance as feminists more pointedly. Perceived common oppression increased the "bonds of sisterhood." Many imprisoned suffragists saw life in prison as a microcosm, in extreme form, of women's situation in American society. They experienced utter powerlessness and violent attacks at the hands of male authorities.

In prison, the women saw more clearly the particular injustice of women's vulnerable position vis-à-vis men, a view amplified by a new knowledge of the condition of their fellow women, especially black women, prisoners. As Estelle Freedman wrote in *Their Sisters' Keepers,* under the control of male jail keepers, woman prisoners represent "an extreme case of sexual powerlessness," symbolizing the constraints placed on all women by authoritarian institutions. Many of the guards at Occoquan seemed to carry out their duties with relish. Linda Gordon, author of *Woman's Body, Woman's Right: A Social History of Birth Control in America,* has argued that guards were "hostile and violent" to women imprisoned for working for birth control, because they seemed to "violate every male fantasy about what women should be like." [26] Militant suffragists were

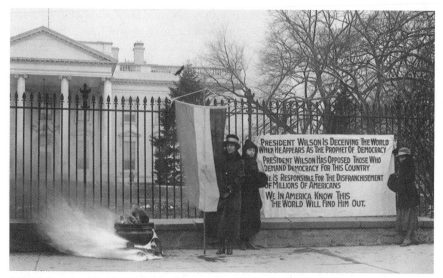

Watchfire outside of the White House was maintained by National Woman's Party pickets, 1919. National Archives

regarded as unnatural members of their sex outside the prison, from the mobs in the streets to the President of the United States. They were also perceived as unwomanly within prison walls and treated accordingly.

For most Woman's Party activists, harsh treatment by prison guards did not dampen their feminist ardor, but only intensified it. As Texas suffragist Lucille Shields explained: "In jail as one empty hour succeeds another, you realize more keenly the years that women have struggled to be free and the tasks that they have been forced to leave undone for lack of power to do them." Or note Massachusetts NWP leader Katharine Fisher's statement: "In prison or out, American women are not free....Disfranchisement is the prison of women's power and spirit." If disillusion and anger at injustice was one effect of jail, inspiration and renewed faith in their fellow women and in their cause, was another. Although, as mentioned above, she had at first despaired in prison, Kathryn Lincoln testified upon her release in late November 1917: "Prison bars mean only freedom.... The cause of women must advance."[27] Many of the released prisoners insisted the government had not daunted their spirit, and their continued militancy made that clear.

In spite of physical injury and illness, and of deeply felt disillusion and anger, most suffrage prisoners came out of jail renewed in purpose. As middle-class Progressive reformers, which most of them were, they had first believed in the process of American democracy, although they went well beyond the bounds of Progressive reformism with their militancy. When the Wilson government cracked down on the pickets, unleashing mob and police attacks and leaving the imprisoned suffragists to the vagaries of Occoquan Superintendent

Whittaker and his guards, the radical suffragists' militancy and determination only increased. As established feminist radicals in 1918 and 1919, they would persist with demonstrations pointedly critical of the Wilson administration and would continue to be jailed.

More Militant Action

The National Woman's Party did not shrink from further acts of militancy when woman suffrage was still not won in 1918. In January, President Wilson finally endorsed woman suffrage by federal action and the House passed the suffrage amendment. According to the NWP all this political progress was made as a direct result of the Woman's Party's actions.[28] But by the fall of 1918, the Senate had not yet passed the amendment, lacking one vote. This necessitated further militancy by the NWP. Picketing and arrests began again. In early 1919, the demonstrations were intent upon forcing the Wilson administration's hand. With World War I over, Wilson was triumphant on the world stage; but to frustrated suffrage militants, the battle was not yet won. The NWP kept "watchfires" burning in front of the White House, fueling the flames with Wilson's hypocritical words as well as with his effigy. In February 1919, a "welcome party" of protesting NWP women met Wilson in Boston, upon his return from the peace talks in Europe. Using nonviolent resistance against the Boston police, a line of silent pickets held banners calling for the president's aid. Women also gathered on Boston Common and burned the parts of Wilson's Boston speech that spoke of democracy and liberty. Additionally a group of Woman's Party luminaries—women who had been (as NWP leader Doris Stevens wrote) "jailed for freedom"—toured on a "Prison Special" train, wearing replicas of their prison uniforms and taking the cause to cities throughout the country.[29] The men of the Senate remained unmoved.

What turned out to be the NWP's last militant protest provoked the harshest response from authorities and bystanders yet. It was held outside the New York Metropolitan Opera House in March of 1919. On March 3, Congress had adjourned without a Senate vote. When President Wilson stopped in New York to speak at the Opera House, Alice Paul planned to burn immediately a copy of anything he said about democracy. Bearing banners protesting Wilson's "autocracy" at home, a picket line of twenty-five women marched toward the Opera House, but were soon met by two hundred policemen in close formation. The police were joined by a crowd made up of mostly soldiers and sailors, rushed the pickets, and the ensuing battle went on for hours. Doris Stevens, a participant, wrote:

> Not a word was spoken by a single officer of the 200 policemen in the attack to indicate the nature of our offense. Clubs were raised and lowered and the women beaten back with such cruelty as none of us had ever witnessed before.... Women were knocked down and trampled under foot, some of them almost unconscious, others bleeding from

the hands and face; arms were bruised and twisted; pocket-books were snatched and wrist-watches stolen.

Called a "bunch of cannibals and Bolsheviks" by the police, the militants were charged with "disorderly conduct" and "assaulting the police," and arrested, but then released.[30]

Until victory was finally achieved, the NWP moved from one action to another, continually keeping the pressure on the authorities. By late spring 1919, victory was finally in sight for the militant suffragists. In May, the House passed the amendment again, and in June, Wilson secured the last Senate vote for passage. After another long and arduous lobbying campaign, including picketing the Republican convention, the Susan B. Anthony Woman Suffrage Amendment was finally ratified by a sufficient number of states in August 1920. The National Woman's Party took full credit for the victory, saying the Wilson administration had "yielded under the gunfire" of the NWP.[31]

The Woman's Party was certainly instrumental in moving the "center" of the woman suffrage movement toward greater activity by its own radical actions. The militants demanded attention for the cause of woman suffrage and got it. They reawakened the slumbering issue of a national woman suffrage amendment, revitalized the entire movement and made the government and politicians acutely aware of women's potential political power. The militants' stubborn protests, however reviled they may have been, created a situation in which something had to be done. Each act of open militancy was followed by government action: feminist militancy worked.

In the process, feminist militancy—which insisted on the vital importance of a woman's right to participate in the political life of her society—transformed the suffragists themselves. Feminist militancy was a tactic, but it was also a state of mind. Doris Stevens wrote that the militants' campaign compelled women to "stop being such good and willing slaves." In June of 1919 Alice Paul declared that, "Freedom has come not as a gift but as a triumph, and it is therefore a spiritual as well as a political freedom which women receive."[32]

And the NWP emphasized that winning suffrage was only the first step in "woman's emancipation." As The Suffragist observed just after the victory: "The ballot is the symbol of a new status in human society, it is the greatest possible single step forward in the progress of women, but it does not in itself complete their freedom." For the members of the NWP, then, the struggle did not end with gaining the vote. They knew there was much more to do to secure women's equality in all facets of American society. In a press release just after the ratification was announced, Alice Paul stated her determination to use the vote as "the tool with which [women] must end completely all discriminations against them." "Our victory," she said, "cannot be a signal for rest."[33] Thus began the fight for the Equal Rights Amendment, spearheaded by the NWP, and first introduced in Congress only three years after ratification of the Nineteenth Amendment.[34]

Notes

This essay is drawn largely from Linda Ford's *Iron-Jawed Angels: The Suffrage Militancy of the National Woman's Party, 1912-1920* (Lanham, Md.: University Press of America, Inc., 1991), and appears here with the permission of the publisher.

1. See George Dangerfield, *The Strange Death of Liberal England* (London, 1936); Marian Ramelson, *Petticoat Rebellion: A Century of Struggle for Women's Rights* (London, 1967); Charlotte Perkins Gilman, *Women and Economics* (Boston, 1900).

2. *New York Times*, July 14, 1916, 10; Nelly Gordon to Anne Martin, Feb. 4, 1916, Reel 23 of the National Woman's Party Papers, Suffrage Years, on microfilm, Microfilming Corporation of America, 1981, hereafter referred to as NWPP.

3. On militance in the American suffrage movement before Alice Paul, see Ellen DuBois, "Taking the Law into Our Own Hands: *Bradwell, Minor,* and Suffrage Militance in the 1870s," and "Working Women, Class Relations, and Suffrage Militance: Harriot Stanton Blatch and the New York Woman Suffrage Movement, 1894-1909," in this volume.

4. Harriot Stanton Blatch and Alma Lutz, *Challenging Years: The Memoirs of Harriot Stanton Blatch* (New York, 1940), 73; Emmeline Pankhurst, *My Own Story,* (New York, 1917), 19-30, 33-40; Andrew Rosen, *Rise Up, Women! The Militant Campaign of the WSPU, 1903-1914* (London, 1974), 80-85; Katharine Anthony, *Susan B. Anthony: Her Personal History and Her Era* (Garden City, N.Y., 1954), 366, 484.

5. Katharine Anthony, *Susan B. Anthony,* Amelia Fry, interview with Alice Paul in 1972-73, "Woman Suffrage and the Equal Rights Amendment," Bancroft Library Suffragists Oral History Project, University of California at Berkeley; Sylvia Pankhurst, *The Suffragettes: The History of the Women's Militant Suffrage Movement, 1905-1910* (New York, 1912), 416-417.

6. Pankhurst, extended accounts in *My Own Story; Rosen, Rise Up!,* 80-85.

7. See NAWSA's Mary Ware Dennett to Paul, Oct. 30, 1913, Reel 5, NWPP; Robert Gallagher's interview with Alice Paul, "I Was Arrested, Of Course," *American Heritage,* Feb. 1974, 17-24; 92-94; *New York Times,* Jan. 5, 1914, 3. On the "too British" accusation, see Shaw to Burns, Nov. 29, 1913, Reel 5, NWPP.

8. Inez Irwin, *Alice Paul and the National Woman's Party,* (1921: Fairfax, Va., 1964), 158-160; Sidney Bland, "'Never Quite as Committed as We'd Like': The Suffrage Militancy of Lucy Burns," *Journal of Long Island History,* (Summer/Fall 1981): 12-13; Meredith Snapp, "Defeat the Democrats: The Congressional Union for Woman Suffrage in Arizona, 1914 and 1916," *Journal of the West,* (1975): 131-138; Edwin A. Weinstein, *Woodrow Wilson; A Medical and Psychological Biography* (Princeton, 1981), 83.

9. Banner is quoted in Irwin, *Paul and the NWP,* 214.

10. Fry interview with Paul, 551.

11. NWP activist Rheta Childe Dorr wrote for *The Suffragist* (April 1920, 36) that if women voted as a group on social and political problems, improvements would occur. However, Mabel Vernon argued that women had a right to vote, no matter their views or qualities. Fry interview with Vernon, "Mabel Vernon: Speaker for Suffrage and Petitioner for Peace," Bancroft Project 1976, 164.

12. See Sherna Gluck, ed., *Parlor to Prison: Five American Suffragists Talk About Their Lives* (New York, 1976), 228,

242-243; Doris Stevens, *Jailed For Freedom* (1920: New York, 1976), 177.

13. Alice Paul to Dora Lewis, Nov. 1917, Reel 53, NWPP.

14. Dora Lewis to Gwynne Gardener, Nov. 7, 1917, Reel 52, NWPP.

15. Papers of Camilla Whitcomb, Schlesinger Library, Radcliffe, n.d., *Worcester Telegram* article; Cosu affidavit, Nov. 28, 1917, Reel 53; Emory affidavit, Nov. 1917, Reel 53; Burns's Nov. 1917 statement, Reel 52; Day affidavit, Nov. 28, 1917, Reel 53; Nolan affidavit, Nov. 23, 1917, Reel 52, NWPP.

16. Rose Winslow quotation from Doris Stevens, *Jailed for Freedom,* (1920: Troutdale, Ore., 1995), 118-119; Day, *The Long Loneliness,* (New York, 1952), 89-90; NWP Press Release, Nov. 27, 1917, Reel 92, NWPP.

17. In 1918 and 1919 the NWP protesters would receive sentences of up to fifteen days, first for holding public meetings without a permit and climbing on a public statue, and then for building fires. Stevens, *Jailed,* 229; Irwin, *Paul and the NWP,* 273, 418.

18. Wilson to Catt, Oct. 13, 1917, Reel 210; Wilson to Tumulty, Nov. 12, 1917; Wilson to "WFJ, Secretary," Nov. 16, 1917, Reel 210, Wilson Papers, Library of Congress.

19. A. Brisbane to Joseph Tumulty, July 20, 1917; Tumulty to Wilson, July 21, 1917; Wilson to Tumulty, July 21, 1917, Reel 210, Wilson Papers.

20. Author's interview with Rebecca Hourwich Reyher, April 23, 1983; Anne Martin to Pauline Clarke, Oct. 31, 1917, Reel 51 and Nov. 19, 1917, Reel 51; Martin to a Eugene, Oregon editor, Nov. 1, 1917, Reel 51, NWPP.

21. *New York Tribune*, Nov. 22, 23, 1917, Reel 95, NWPP; *Suffragist*, March 2, 1918.

22. See NWP Press Releases, Jan. 19 and 23, 1918, Reel 92, NWPP.

23. NWP Press Release, Nov. 27, 1917, Reel 91, NWPP.

24. Lincoln affidavit, Nov. 28, 1917, Reel 53; Kendall affidavit, Nov. 2, 1920, Reel 83, NWPP.

25. Morey to Mabel Vernon, May 3, 1917, Reel 42, NWPP.

26. *Their Sisters' Keepers: Woman's Prison Reform in America, 1830-1930* (Ann Arbor, 1981), 1; Gordon, *Woman's Body, Woman's Right: A Social History of Birth Control in America* (New York, 1974), 233.

27. Shields, NWP Press Release, Jan. 18, 1919, Reel 92, NWPP; Stevens, *Jailed,* 156; Lincoln affidavit, Nov. 28, 1917, Reel 53, NWPP.

28. Irwin, *Paul and the NWP,* 344-345, 349; Stevens, *Jailed,* 248.

29. Stevens, *Jailed.*

30. Stevens, *Jailed.* 331-332; *New York Times,* March 5, 1919, 3, 10; *Suffragist,* March 15, 1919, 4-5.

31. *Suffragist,* June 4, 1919, 10-11; Sept. 1920, 191; NWP Press Release, March 20, 1920, Reel 92, NWPP.

32. Stevens, "Militant Campaign," Stevens Papers, Schlesinger Library, Radcliffe, Cambridge, Mass.; *Suffragist,* March 29, 1919, 8.

33. NWP Press Release, 1920, in Folder 24, Anna Kelton Wiley Papers, Radcliffe.

34. *The Suffragist,* Sept. 1920, 191.

Sixteen

Carrie Chapman Catt, Strategist

Robert Booth Fowler

Editor's Introduction: Political scientist Robert Booth Fowler discusses the strategic decisions made by Carrie Chapman Catt, president of the National American Woman Suffrage Association (NAWSA). Catt's decisions were of vital importance for the woman suffrage movement, and as president of the NAWSA twice—from 1900 to 1904 and from 1915 to 1920—she had a major influence on the strategy pursued by the organization in both periods. In this essay, a chapter from his book *Carrie Catt: Feminist Politician,* Fowler focuses primarily on Catt's second presidency, analyzing her decisions that he claims were crucial to the success of the federal suffrage amendment in 1920.

Fowler emphasizes that, though Catt cared deeply about other reforms and political issues, during the last years of the suffrage battle she focused her energies on woman suffrage alone. Like Susan B. Anthony with whom she had worked closely in the 1890s, Catt was determined not to allow other issues to divide suffragists, dispel their energy, or alienate potential supporters. Continuing the strategy of making woman suffrage appear respectable and in keeping with widely shared American values and goals, she was particularly eager to distance the movement from unpopular causes or radical tactics that could undermine the steady growth in support for woman suffrage between 1910 and 1920. This strategy disappointed many within the movement as well as would-be allies outside the movement. Fowler insists, however, that Catt's pragmatism was strategically sound, even if it seems—then and now—cynical or unethical. As a single-issue campaign, the woman suffrage movement was more efficient, united, and less vulnerable to its critics.

A dramatic example of Catt's implementation of this policy was her decision to put aside her own strong antiwar sentiments and shun an alliance between the woman suffrage and peace movements during World War I. As public opinion shifted rapidly from an insistence upon American neutrality to an overwhelming prowar fervor that tolerated no dissent, Catt aligned the NAWSA and its leaders first with "preparedness" and then the war effort. Though some suffragists, notably peace advocate Jane Addams, were dismayed by this turn of events, Fowler argues that this decision saved Catt and the NAWSA from the extreme hostility and loss of influence that Addams and other peace advocates endured during the war, and aided the suffrage cause significantly with Wilson and the public—creating the impression that women deserved the vote as a reward for war service.

A second example of Catt's pragmatic strategy discussed by Fowler is "The Plan" that Catt devised soon after she returned to the NAWSA presidency late in 1915. "The Plan" was approved by NAWSA members at an "Emergency Convention" in Atlantic City in September 1916. Often called "The Winning Plan," this strategy was designed to centralize authority within the massive but disorganized NAWSA, and coordinate the efforts of suffragists nationwide in a final campaign that would at last secure the adoption of the federal amendment. It is interesting to note that, as Fowler observes, this decision does not seem at all controversial today; indeed, both Catt and Alice Paul are celebrated for their role in finally returning the suffrage movement to an emphasis on the federal approach to winning woman suffrage. Yet in 1916, this decision was far more controversial than Catt's alignment of the suffrage movement with the war effort.

Catt's "Winning Plan," was a significant departure from the policy of her predecessor Anna Howard Shaw, whose highly decentralized administration had given scant attention to the federal amendment. Shaw was influenced to an extent by southern suffragists including Laura Clay and Kate Gordon who served for years as self-appointed "watch-dogs" for the South on the NAWSA Executive Board and who opposed suffrage by federal amendment. Catt, however, had no difficulty finding other southern women to work with such as Madeline McDowell Breckinridge, Pattie Ruffner Jacobs, Anne Dallas Dudley, and Minnie Fisher Cunningham who, frustrated by repeated rejections of state suffrage initiatives in the South, enthusiastically supported the federal amendment. As Fowler explains, Catt believed that the state approach would never enfranchise *all* American women, and that the national approach was more in keeping with "women's dignity," allowing suffragists to bypass at least some of the state-by-state pleading that, even back in the 1870s, Elizabeth Cady Stanton and Susan B. Anthony rejected as demeaning.

Fowler also analyzes Catt's dealings with the militant suffragists, emphasizing that while Catt agreed with Paul on the need to refocus on the federal amendment, she objected strenuously to the tactics employed by Alice Paul and the National Woman's Party and believed that Paul lacked the "pragmatic sense" essential in a leader. Catt was particularly critical of Paul and the NWP for engaging in partisanship and picketing, believing that they were alienating Democrats in Congress whose votes were so desperately needed—not to mention President Wilson himself. Catt was convinced that the NAWSA's lobbying campaign directed by Maud Wood Park and Helen Gardener between 1917 and 1919—dignified, diplomatic, non-partisan, non-threatening and nicknamed by the press the "Front Door Lobby"—was the only way of persuading Congressmen to approve the federal amendment.

Historians *still* debate this issue—the strategic effectiveness of both Paul and Catt's tactics—as we try to explain why the woman suffrage amendment was finally adopted and assess the relative contributions of the NAWSA and the

NWP to that victory. Most would agree with Fowler that both groups played a positive role and that "the Woman's Party's tactical radicalism helped enormously to legitimate the NAWSA."

Catt's "Winning Plan" was clearly a major factor in the final victory. Historian Eleanor Flexner described Catt as bringing "order out of chaos and victory out of apparent stagnation," and a genius at uniting all of the disparate elements within the massive NAWSA into a "potent political force." Instead of allowing suffragists in the various states to adopt whatever policy they wished and launch campaigns as they chose, Catt assigned a role to each state and demanded that state suffrage leaders adhere to an over-arching national strategy. As Maud Wood Park later explained in her 1960 autobiography *Front Door Lobby*, Catt divided the states into four categories and "assigned a particular form of legislative work" to each. First, she directed suffrage organizations in the equal suffrage states and in Illinois (which had presidential and municipal suffrage) to obtain from their legislatures resolutions requesting that Congress approve the federal amendment and send it to the states. Second, Catt identified several states including the key state of New York where she believed there was a good chance of winning a state suffrage amendment, and urged workers from those states to prepare at once for a new campaign. Third, she advised the remaining states to try for presidential suffrage, as this could be granted by legislatures without having to be approved by the voters in referenda. Last, Catt advised suffragists in the southern, one-party states to try for "primary suffrage," which could also be granted by the legislatures. Much to the disappointment of suffragists in states such as Kentucky, in which local women were far more optimistic than Catt about the chances of successful state amendment campaigns, the NAWSA president demanded that they defer to her judgment, and play their assigned part in "The Plan."

Catt's plan, then, did not abandon state campaigns, but coordinated them with unprecedented care to insure that a series of victories would together build momentum for the federal amendment, and that defeats in states she considered "hopeless" would be avoided. The Plan was not announced to the public. Swearing everyone to secrecy, Maud Wood Park recalled Catt explained that these initiatives would be launched at the beginning of legislative sessions the following January (1917), catching the opposition off-guard, and requiring the anti-suffragists to fight on "many fronts at once." Catt presented a "compact" to be signed by suffragists representing at least thirty-six states—the number needed for ratification. As the signing ceremony ended, wrote Park, "I felt like Moses on the mountain top after the Promised Land had been shown to him and he knew the long years of wandering in the Wilderness were soon to end. For the first time I saw our goal as possible of attainment in the near future." Park concluded:

> Often since then, remembering how hard it was at best to win our vote in the Congress and the subsequent ratification by thirty-six states, I

have speculated as to what would have happened if Mrs. Catt's plan had not been presented on that sultry afternoon in 1916. Undoubtedly a woman suffrage amendment would have been adopted at some time, even if Mrs. Catt had never been born; but, if success had not come when it did, the cause might easily have been caught in a period of postwar reaction, and victory postponed for another half-century. That women all over the United States were able to vote in 1920 is due, I believe, to the carrying out of the plan prepared and presented by an incomparable leader.

★   ★   ★   ★   ★

A NYONE WHO KNOWS the story of the struggle for the enfranchisement of women in the 1915-1920 period knows that Carrie Catt's strategic decisions were of fateful importance. Their pragmatic wisdom is clear, though their ethical wisdom is now, as it was then, a good deal more controversial.

Catt's Progressive agenda was wide-ranging, and suffrage for her was in large part a *means* to realize other reform objectives. Nevertheless, during the suffrage fight Catt focused all her energies on that issue. Her conscious strategy was to allow no other cause to enter the NAWSA's agenda: "As a matter of fact we do not care a ginger snap about anything but that Federal Amendment."[1] She did not object when the NAWSA Convention adopted all sorts of resolutions favoring a number of this or that measures to assist women in economic, professional, and legal realms. But she insisted that the NAWSA would be doing nothing about them. She did not think it could and at the same time promote women's enfranchisement: "we cannot...until the Federal Amendment is through, spare any force for the support of any bill...we haven't the power to do anything but merely pass a resolution. It is of no avail."[2]

Catt made sure her wishes were followed as she fashioned her version of that very contemporary phenomenon, the single-issue pressure group. Her rationale was simple, one goal would mobilize women and the NAWSA's resources in a focused direction. It was efficient and—equally valuable—it freed the NAWSA of the conflicts and attacks that involvement with other causes inevitably generated.

This was not a self-evident strategic choice, however, and it drew opponents. On the one hand, some earlier feminist leaders, such as Elizabeth Cady Stanton, objected to this approach as too narrow. On the other, some groups, especially the WCTU, the Anti-Saloon League, and, later, peace groups sought alliance with Catt and the NAWSA and were not happy when they did not get it. But Catt pushed all such complaints aside, arguing that even hints of such links were a formula for disaster.[3]

Woman Suffrage and World War I

A remarkable illustration of Carrie Catt's willingness to pursue this strategy—even at the cost of compromise with other of her values—came in her much disputed strategic moves before and during World War I. All her life, Catt proudly identified with efforts to end war. In the decades after 1920 this became her principal field of public activity. However, when the First World War began in Europe, Catt was caught between her antiwar inclinations and her suspicion that suffragist peace activity could adversely affect the struggle for women's enfranchisement. Catt calculated even before the United States became a direct belligerent in the Great War that the situation was out of control and suffragists' efforts would be a costly venture for nothing. Concerned women, led by Jane Addams, might try, but the unleashed forces of war could not be stopped by their necessarily "puny effort." She doubted that anything could stop "these men in whom the furious beast" had been unchained.[4] Trying to stop them was "like throwing a violet at a stone wall." "There is no power on earth that is going to stop that war until there has been perhaps the most terrible battle that the world has ever seen."[5]

At first Catt tried to have it both ways. While accounts differ as to whom credit belongs for initiating organized opposition to the war among women, in 1914 Catt and Addams worked together in this cause. In general, Catt worked behind the scenes lest she create the kind of backlash toward suffrage that so worried her. She specifically refused to accept a public leadership post. On the other hand, Catt did not avoid public appearances altogether, and her participation with Addams and others undoubtedly lent peace forces prestige without which its modest endeavor might have collapsed even sooner than it did. Catt did, for example, go to the White House on several occasions in 1914 to urge American neutrality to Woodrow Wilson and to Secretary of State William Jennings Bryan. She felt that she took a great risk in such public actions. That risk certainly did not diminish when Catt continued, albeit as quietly as possible, to support Addams when she founded the Woman's Peace Party.[6]

Nonetheless, Catt's heart was not in the Woman's Peace Party or any other part of the active but tiny women's peace movement in the United States from 1914 to 1917. She insisted she had to be concerned about votes for women above all else. She observed with dismay the barrage of attacks on her and woman suffrage by anti-suffragist publications once war broke out in Europe. She feared that if she were more active in the peace cause she might confirm their propaganda that the woman's movement was a harbor for pacifists at best and for disloyal American women at worst. Most of the main organs of the anti-suffragists were early on the bandwagon of United States preparedness and outspoken hostility to Germany and they ridiculed every effort of peace groups and every peace plan. Such ideas, they challenged, were dangerous and had a large part in encouraging the weakness that led to war in the first place. Moreover, as time went on, anti-suffragists lost the distinction between pacifist "disloyalty" and outright support for Germany and the Kaiser. It all became rather ugly and the charges specifically toward Catt were as ugly as the rest.[7]

As war approached for the United States, Catt moved with the tide. She had no intention of allowing enemies of her crusade to get away with their antiwar, pro-German charges and thus damage it. In February 1917, Catt convened the NAWSA, recognizing that war for the United States was imminent. It was necessary for the NAWSA to get its house in order because "The future of our movement depends upon the right action being taken now."[8] What Catt wanted was a willingness on the part of the NAWSA to support national war readiness. She got it, successfully steering past both extremist doves and hawks. In her terms the convention was a great success also because it attracted favorable publicity from the growing prowar segments in American society and brought the NAWSA into contact with such influential government notables as Secretary of War Newton Baker and Secretary of the Navy Josephus Daniels.

When the United States did declare war on Germany and the contest she had long expected (and dreaded) began in earnest, Catt quickly offered her personal endorsement; she made sure that the NAWSA was in line with national war policy in every way; and she repudiated suffragists who disagreed, notably Montana Congresswoman Jeannette Rankin, who voted against the war.[9]

These actions led to Catt's ejection from the Woman's Peace Party and a good many hard feelings between her and its small cohort of pacifists. Her decision could not have come as a surprise to them, but it still led to some bitter denunciations. They did not really bother her because she had absolutely no hesitation about paying this price. For her, opposition to the war, once the United States had entered it, was courting martyrdom and taking the suffrage movement down in the process. And so Carrie Catt began her war work, publicly working to get women involved in the Red Cross, canteen service, food production, and the like. She campaigned in Liberty Loan drives, and she accepted appointment to the Woman's Committee of the Council of National Defense (under Anna Howard Shaw's leadership).[10]

These activities, especially service on the Woman's Committee of the Council of National Defense, were not easy. Catt hated war and now she found herself busy supporting one, albeit one she eventually convinced herself was legitimate. Equally difficult was the treatment Catt, along with the other members of the committee (especially Shaw), received from the male leaders of the Council of National Defense and assorted government agencies. They found themselves, once again, treated as second-class citizens, bossed, patronized, or ignored. The situation was often acutely frustrating, but Catt remained convinced that working for the war was vital to the suffrage cause.[11]

There clearly were a great many enemies waiting to pounce. Once the United States entered the war, they crossed the already thin line between criticism of suffragists and wild, even frenzied accusations. Without any shame, critics called suffragists disloyal and pro-German. "Woman suffrage is proving of more potent assistance to the Kaiser than his wonderful army." In addition, anti-suffragists repeatedly tried to tar them with the brush of socialism, bolshevism, and just about anything that might make suffragists seem anti-American in what became a time of unpleasant xenophobia.[12]

Once again, the anti-suffragists singled out Catt for special charges and smears. How intensely the anti-suffragists, now garbed in the most patriotic of uniforms, hated Catt is difficult to comprehend unless one actually reads the flood of denunciatory articles on her in their press during World War I. In their portrait Catt was a knowing opponent of the war, a virtual traitor who continued to criticize her government in disgusting fashion during wartime. Her work for the war was a sham, hiding her conspiratorial actions for woman suffrage, and often for the Germans. In at least one article deportation was suggested as the way to deal with Catt.[13]

It is only in this context that Catt's own strategy can be understood. And it is only in this context, despite the loud cries of the anti-suffragists, that its success can be understood. For, despite the cries of the anti-suffragists, Catt's strategy regarding World War I worked. All over the country she gained praise as a patriot actively behind the war effort. Though publicly abused, Catt and the NAWSA escaped the almost unbelievable hostility that befell some others, Jane Addams in particular, which undercut their political influence for a time. When charges of disloyalty and other ugly words flew, Catt could and did reply with her war record and that of the NAWSA.

It would be wrong, however, to portray Catt's strategic purposes in World War I, as only defensive. She looked in this direction, but she also realized that there was another, much more positive side to her strategy. Patriotic service could create "opportunity" for the cause of women's enfranchisement. It could greatly increase the respectability of suffragists and their cause, and thus advance the cause, which is exactly what happened both with the public at large and with many Washington decision-makers including Woodrow Wilson. It happened in part because Catt made sure every contribution by the NAWSA and prominent members of the NAWSA received as much publicity as possible. The not very subtle point was that the vote for women was American, was patriotic. Meanwhile, Catt sought to foster the impression that women, while they gave their service freely, nonetheless deserved something in return, and that something of course, was the vote.[14]

Catt did not hesitate to make sure that people got the point that suffragist war service deserved repayment with enfranchisement. In fact, Catt relentlessly kept up the pressure for woman suffrage throughout the war. A frequent argument was that women's enfranchisement was needed "as a war measure."[15] Her argument that, if it was to fight a war for democracy, the United States should advance democracy at home by making women full citizens was effective—just how effective is indicated by the outrage it provoked from anti-suffragists. They stormed at Catt, accusing her of being a monomaniac, pursuing her cause at all

Carrie Chapman Catt leads a Suffrage School class in New York, c. 1915.
Smithsonian Institution

costs, and thus threatening American democracy when such divisive matters ought to be laid aside in the name of wartime unity.[16]

Catt paid no attention. Just as she spurned those who expected her peace concern would lead her to oppose the war, so she rejected those who urged she drop the cause of the vote during the war. For her the central issue never changed.

Overall, Catt was proud of her strategy during the Great War, though she hoped it would never be required again and dreamed that once women got the vote they might well end all wars. But questions were raised then—and have been since. Shouldn't she of all people have known the shortsightedness of her strategy? After all, from her own perspective, war corrupted progressive impulses in history. Some historians agree, regarding World War I.[17] But this analysis does not apply to votes for women. World War I hardly killed the chance for enfranchisement.

The uneasiness over Catt's strategy mostly derives from a sense that it was cynical. Cynical it was, but Catt did not see it this way. She never had any interest in a politics of purity in the impure world. To her the fact was that she could not stop the war, but the NAWSA's opposition to war could seriously delay women's enfranchisement. And her belief was that she was called to help women. Her devotion in subsequent decades of her public life to the cause of world peace was not an act of expiation. It was rather a resumption of the peace mission, which she had never lost sight of. But it was a long-range goal and she had no intention of losing momentum for women's enfranchisement because of it.

The Winning Plan

Much less controversial in retrospect, but much more so at the time, was the adoption of "The Plan," in 1916, to push for congressional passage of the Anthony Amendment to the United States Constitution, giving women the right to vote. Catt had long looked toward the Anthony Amendment as a way of overcoming the slow and cumbersome process of achieving women's enfranchisement state-by-state.[18] But by 1915-1916, she was sure it was absolutely necessary to concentrate NAWSA resources on this strategy, a major shift in NAWSA focus.

"The Plan" was adopted in 1916 at an emergency meeting of the NAWSA which Catt had called at Atlantic City, New Jersey.[19] Catt was by then president of the NAWSA, and she reflected dissatisfaction with the NAWSA's drift during Shaw's long reign towards (unsuccessful) campaigning for the extension of suffrage at the state level, including support for the Shafroth-Palmer constitutional amendment intended to encourage opportunities for state electorates to vote on woman suffrage. The Shafroth-Palmer proposal would have required any state to hold a vote on woman suffrage where eight percent of the voters in the previous presidential election petitioned for such a referendum.

The drift during the Shaw years towards action on the state level was the result of several factors. One was fealty to those in the NAWSA, including Catt, who had been struggling for success state-by-state. Another was the necessity of placating southern members of the NAWSA who were states' rights oriented and strongly against the Anthony Amendment. A third was anger at Alice Paul and her supporters, who were committed exclusively to the federal strategy—a knee-jerk resistance on the NAWSA's part to whatever Paul and her faction favored.[20]

But by 1916 Catt was convinced that reversal of strategy was essential. She based her strategic judgment on what she thought was the practical situation. The old approach now seemed what Catt frankly called "negative—not positive."[21] It simply was not working, certainly not fast enough. No doubt, the memory of the loss of the suffrage referendum in New York State in 1915 was a painful factor in this assessment. As she looked ahead, moreover, Catt increasingly doubted the state approach alone could ever work. Its chances in many states were nearly hopeless. State election laws and constitutional provisions often made state constitutional revision almost impossible. Even worse, Catt doubted whether there was a majority of men in many states who would soon vote for women's enfranchisement if they got the chance. She continued to be haunted by "the others," the "groups of recently naturalized and even unnationalized foreigners, Indians, Negroes, large numbers of illiterates, ne'er-do-wells, and drunken loafers," who she felt resisted women's enfranchisement.[22] Catt also worried that even if she was wrong, and some states did begin to approve enfranchisement, this might represent a victory of distinctly mixed blessings. Concern with national enfranchisement might decline in every state that granted women the vote. Valuable energy and talent might be lost to the NAWSA; and "disintegration" would increase.[23] Thus, from every angle it seemed imperative to Catt to redirect attention to the national effort to obtain congressional passage of the Anthony Amendment.

Catt's expectation was that Congress would prove more cooperative than many of the resistant states. She understood that this was a gamble and intended to keep some pressure on the states while hoping that suffrage states and those with strong pro-suffrage forces would help by pressuring Congress. Pressure from the states was needed, after all, to impress Congress that there was popular support for woman suffrage. Moreover, the states could not be ignored because, when Congress finally capitulated, the Anthony Amendment would need approval by three-fourths of the state legislatures. Yet Catt was convinced emphasis had to shift to the federal level. Victory there would lead to victory everywhere.[24]

Catt also argued that the national approach best fit her long-run ideal for women. It acknowledged women's dignity, she insisted, because it took them seriously. It made the issue of woman suffrage a national matter, as it should be, and it left behind the image of women pleading state-by-state for something that was basic to democracy and human rights.[25]

At the Atlantic City convention Catt pushed her strategy through largely on the force of her personal and political leadership. In a mood for strong leadership and attracted by her effective plea for her strategic gamble, the convention swung behind "The Plan" with an enthusiasm that overcame earlier positions and earlier doubts.[26]

Undoubtedly, Catt was aided in her coup by the decision of Anna Howard Shaw to back her plan fully (except for moving the national headquarters [from New York] to Washington). While Shaw had lost much respect within the NAWSA during her presidency, she was still, second only to Catt, the most formidable force to be reckoned with. Her enthusiasm for "The Plan" was strong. She helped arrange the special Atlantic City meeting, in fact, and thereafter repeatedly backed its decisions, probably in part because she thought it would undermine the appeal of the Woman's Party.[27]

On the other hand, there were costs. There were personal costs: Catt drove herself night and day as she built support within the NAWSA for her shift in strategy. There were organizational costs: there was serious opposition to "The Plan" from significant southern voices in the NAWSA. Kate Gordon, of Louisiana, and Laura Clay, of Kentucky, both prominent during the Shaw presidency, argued that suffrage could (and should) have appeal in the South only if it did not remind southerners of earlier national attempts to change the South at the behest of federal edicts. And they feared that if a national effort were successful in this instance a similar attempt to dictate to the South on the subject of race might follow.

Moreover opponents of several stripes felt that Catt bulldozed her plan through in Atlantic City with precious little concern for them or for a diverse

NAWSA. From their perspective, they were quite right. But Catt wanted action in response to the strategic imperative at hand. They had had their way for a long time; now their day was over. Indeed, Catt believed it should have ended long before, since an honest evaluation would have revealed that the "littleness of the view, which our states' rights' [sic] plan has stimulated for a hundred years, is the greatest enemy of woman suffrage."[28]

Privately, Catt had arranged to resign if "The Plan" was not adopted by the NAWSA. She insisted there just was no point in continuing the struggle in the old, humiliating, and ineffective fashion. This issue went beyond compromise or temporizing. But Catt won in Atlantic City and she used "The Plan" as her vehicle towards victory, defending it as she went.[29]

Dealing with Divisiveness

Catt's strategic analysis is further illuminated by her attitude towards and dealings with "the Militants" in the later suffrage movement. The first major sign of division in the suffrage crusade occurred in 1907 when Harriot Stanton Blatch, daughter of Elizabeth Cady Stanton, turned against the NAWSA. Influenced by the more active and more militant movement in Great Britain, Blatch founded a more radical organization in 1907, which became the Women's Political Union in 1910. While Blatch's tiny splinter movement played a minor role, it was a harbinger of the future.

A far more serious split in the suffrage forces became apparent in 1913 with the emergence of the remarkable Alice Paul. Paul's first serious work for votes for women began in England, where she associated with the British militants and went to prison for her militancy.[30] With this background, the young Alice Paul arrived in Washington in 1913 and went to work for the NAWSA's Congressional Committee. Through the force of her charismatic personality, Paul soon transformed the committee. She changed it from the inactive, sleepy arena it had been under Anna Howard Shaw's regime into a permanent committee that was a busy lobbying center determined to push the Susan B. Anthony Amendment through Congress. In spite of the changes, Paul became dissatisfied with the unwieldy committee, linked as it was to the "conservative" NAWSA and its multileveled strategies. As an alternative, Paul set up the Congressional Union to concentrate exclusively on the Anthony Amendment, ignoring state efforts for suffrage and efforts to get Congress to encourage enfranchisement of women by the states. At first Paul acted within the NAWSA and with the approval of President Shaw, but Paul's focus and her sometimes brash style soon aroused opposition within NAWSA circles. Moreover, as the Congressional Union took on the unmistakable appearance of a separate and independent organization, still others within the NAWSA became uncomfortable. Aware of the criticisms by the end of 1913, Paul defended herself by claiming that the Congressional Union existed only to assist the Congressional Committee.

In reality, however, the Congressional Union was an almost separate organization—empire, critics charged—which used NAWSA stationery to raise money and recruit membership while not accepting direction from the NAWSA board. Indeed, as Anna Howard Shaw eventually argued, it pursued policies never approved by the NAWSA. Not surprisingly, the NAWSA board sought to force Paul to do its bidding. The result was that in 1914 Paul was asked to resign as head of the Congressional Committee. She did so and she soon took the Congressional Union with her, feeling very much that she had been rejected and forced to secede. While in later years Paul conceded that she had erred in not communicating along the way with the NAWSA leadership, she doubted at the time that compromise was possible—and it was not, in fact.[31]

Paul did not act alone. She had support from others who had tired of the NAWSA's largely fruitless pursuit of votes for women via state referenda. They wanted to get the Anthony constitutional amendment passed, and they wanted to move fast. Among them were Blatch, whose Women's Political Union fused with the Congressional Union in 1916, and Alva Belmont, who contributed a great deal of her considerable wealth to the cause. By 1916 the Woman's Party had emerged, with Anne Martin as first chair. Martin was a former NAWSA board member from Nevada who, like a number of others from western states where woman suffrage was a reality, was impatient with the slow progress of the NAWSA towards national enfranchisement of women. Finally, in 1917 the National Woman's Party was founded with Alice Paul as its acknowledged leader.[32]

It was Anna Howard Shaw who took the role of chief and consistent opponent and who rallied those within the NAWSA seeking to control Paul. Shaw detested Paul. "I wish something would happen to Miss Paul," she wrote, and one senses she did not mean something pleasant.[33] But her larger complaint went to Paul's followers, who were "blank fools"[34] and who, Shaw insisted, hurt the suffrage cause by their divisiveness, disloyalty, and tactical militance.

Shaw blamed herself for not attacking Paul's tendency to go her own way from the first, stopping her before she was in a position to make a cause célèbre out of the affair. Shaw suspected that would have ended the entire affair, since in her judgment it was not at bottom a fight over tactics or policy but a matter of willful ambition on the part of Paul and her coworker Lucy Burns.[35]

Shaw's opinion was widely shared among other suffragists. One of the most important, and most hostile, was Alice Stone Blackwell, [editor of *The Woman's Journal* and daughter of Lucy Stone and Henry Blackwell], who was still denouncing the Woman's Party in the late 1920s. She would not forgive them for the divisions she felt they had brought to the suffrage cause, and she thought it incredible that they blithely took credit for the passage of the Anthony Amendment. And yet even Blackwell acknowledged their appeal. They might be "pestiferous," but they had "cleverness and enthusiasm"—which made them continually "dangerous."[36]

In 1913 and 1914, while Catt shared Shaw's doubts about the organizational loyalty of the Paul group, Catt did not join President Shaw in her assault on them.[37] Nor did she share the antagonism that some in the NAWSA felt toward Paul and her allies because they wished to push Congress to adopt the Anthony Amendment. Indeed, Catt favored the same approach. This fact explains why informed critics of the NAWSA did not single out Catt nearly as much as they did Shaw as a major cause of the split.[38]

1915 was a decisive year in Catt's relations with the Alice Paul group, by then gone from the NAWSA. On the one hand, Catt made efforts to heal the wounds between the NAWSA and Paul. She met with Paul, despite Shaw's intense disapproval and fear,[39] though to no good result.[40] And she moved rapidly, upon her election to the presidency of the NAWSA in 1915, towards adoption of a national strategy for women's enfranchisement (which Paul had supported with no success within the NAWSA), a goal she accomplished when "The Plan" was approved in 1916.

By then, however, the split was too deep, too personal, and too institutionalized for the two groups to get back together. Moreover, new conflicts arose that sealed a split between Catt and her NAWSA and Paul and her associates. As a consequence, while all of Catt's contacts with Woman's Party supporters did not dissolve,[41] Catt made her decision. Alice Paul and her group—soon to be the National Woman's Party—were a destructive influence on the cause, and the NAWSA must keep free from them. While never denying that they sometimes were "doing some good work," Catt concluded that there was a fundamental split and all suffragists had to choose: "No one can carry water on both shoulders."[42] At the same time Catt unrealistically hoped to avoid open warfare. A choice had to be made but that did not mean each group should continually waste energy "battling each other when they should be more concerned to help the big cause on."[43]

The source of conflict between Catt and Paul concerned tactics, and whether Paul and her allies had a realistic understanding of practical politics. The question Catt asked of any strategy or tactic was: will it help the cause, will it maximize votes in referenda and in Congress? In Catt's judgment this pragmatic sense was missing among people such as Alice Paul. A "sharp tongue," radical pronouncements, radical actions did not produce votes. They were the products of those who chose self-indulgence over practicality.[44]

In the suffrage fight two tactics of the Paul group drew Catt's opposition, partisanship and picketing. The militants' eagerness to abandon nonpartisanship, enter the world of party and electoral politics, and campaign against political enemies appealed to some women activists more than nonpartisanship did.[45] Catt claimed to appreciate the appeal of activism by recognizing that nonpartisanship "lacks the avenger's satisfaction."[46] She could also agree with those such as Rose Young who thought more in terms of positive action and wondered if using a "big stick" such as electoral politics might not speed progress by striking fear into politicians.[47]

But Catt thought this was a dangerous idea, a judgment undoubtedly encouraged by her natural suspicion of partisan politics in every situation. Catt insisted, first, that alliances for or against a political party invariably proved costly in terms of independence. In this case, she feared that suffrage would be swallowed up by other party concerns and the compromising, self-promoting ethic of all parties. Second, even if one were to enter party politics to the extent of endorsing candidates—which was too much involvement to begin with—the endorsements had to cross party lines or else one would find oneself saddled with a partisan label and the bitter opposition of at least one political party.

Catt's position was faithful to the long-time gospel of the women's movement, especially the ideas of Susan B. Anthony. Had there been a party prepared to endorse "Freedom to Women" on its banner, Anthony and, later, Catt would have rallied to it. In the meantime, Catt was prepared to follow Anthony's classic advice to appeal to both parties and to serve as "a balance of power" when possible, never accepting a marriage to one party or a crusade against another.[48] It was incredible to her that Paul and her allies sought to go after all Democrats in the 1914 and 1916 elections, blaming Democratic President Wilson and all congressional Democrats for the failure of Congress to pass the Anthony Amendment. The policy of nonpartisanship failed to distinguish between Democrats who favored suffrage and those who did not. Moreover, it was bound to alienate desperately needed Democrats in Congress where the Anthony Amendment had to gain a two-thirds majority if it were to start its way to final enactment.

It was also bound to alienate President Wilson, whose support was needed, especially to persuade reluctant southern Democrats in Congress to give their support. Nor was it the way to promote success in state referenda. As she wrote Jane Addams, any crusade against the Democrats was "exceedingly distasteful to most of us because it committed the stupendous stupidity of making an anti-democratic campaign when the suffrage question was pending in eleven states and depending for success upon Democratic votes."[49]

Instead, Catt preferred to work closely with friends in both parties while exerting pressure in all legal (but nonelectoral) ways on senators, members of the House, and the president. She gave full support to Maud Wood Park's direct lobbying work on Capitol Hill and kept in close lobbying touch with Park's "Front Door" effort, the joint strategy sessions, and "machinations," which were (and are) part of the game there. She worked the White House personally, convinced that dignified lobbying was the way to get results.[50]

Yet Catt did not object only because she considered entering partisan, electoral politics a strategic mistake. The Woman's Party's strategy also offended her ideals. It was natural for her to skate away from playing partisan electoral politics. Such a strategy clashed with her nonpartisan ideal for a democracy and activated her substantial ambivalence about politics in general and party politics in particular. The Woman's Party was guilty of a tactical blunder, in her mind, but it also seriously offended Catt's dream for a politics without politics. Catt fought for her perspective with all her energy, challenging Charles A. Beard when he defended the Woman's Party's partisanship in that bosom of

Progressivism, the *New Republic*. And she fought back against other critics. A lot was at stake for her that went beyond strategy, though her replies invariably stressed her claim that only her approach would work—and was working. And Catt had the considerable satisfaction (if that is the word) of watching the radicals' adventures into partisan electoral politics fail in both 1914 and 1916.[51]

Nonpartisanship remained a fixed star in her belief, but by 1918 Catt became open to the idea of bringing women's muscle to bear on congressional opponents of women's enfranchisement through the electoral process. Her impatience with the manifest dilatoriness of Congress from 1915 to 1917 had grown. She began to issue unmistakable warnings that votes for women was an idea that would "not perish," but "the party which opposed it may," and she told the 1917 convention to expect to take action against individual senators who were up for re-election in 1918 if they opposed woman suffrage.[52] When the 1918 campaign came, Catt led the NAWSA into a carefully circumscribed, nonpartisan battle to defeat four recalcitrant senators (three Republicans and one Democrat), and was delighted by the defeat of one of them in November. Of course—though not for the first time—this move reflected the adoption of a part of Paul's strategy, yet it did so only within Catt's nonpartisan strategic constraints, which, she asserted once again, preserved the NAWSA's freedom while advancing its effectiveness.[53]

A far more rigid position was adopted by the head of the NAWSA towards the other major "radical" tactic of the Woman's Party, the aggressive picketing of the president which began in 1917. Women picketers caused a sensation and, in many circles including within the NAWSA, they created a scandal. Nor were the Woman's Party picketers necessarily modest and sedate. As time went on they became more aggressive in pursuit of their mission, refusing to cooperate when police arrested them.[54]

Once again the issue here was not solely a matter of strategic effectiveness. Catt put it this way. So did her opponents. Interminable arguments followed over whether militant picketing and what became civil disobedience were, or ever could be, effective. Catt was convinced that suffrage was past its strictly agitational phase. What it needed now was male support, and especially the support of the male who was president of the United States. Picketing could not accomplish this goal. It was better to work mostly on education, particularly during the war, as that would produce more male acquiescence or support.[55]

Though Catt and everybody else treated the matter in these terms, the enormous national controversy over a few picketers suggested much more was at stake. The fight over the picketers actually involved an intense and significant dispute over the definition of a good woman. Were women pushing for suffrage always to be proper ladies and law-abiding citizens? Or was it appropriate for free women in control of their lives to break convention and law in pursuit of the vote? Most of the leadership and members of the NAWSA were outraged at the tactics of the picketers, in part because they seemed brash and unfeminine—and thus were detrimental to their cause.

Carrie Chapman Catt, however, was not among those who joined the assault on the picketers as unladylike women. Given Catt's resentment over undignified treatment of women, indeed their daily humiliation, it is no surprise that she had more than a sneaking sympathy with the picketers' tactical militance—especially when they were safely located in Great Britain. At home the problem for Catt, as always, concerned their political effectiveness.[56] She knew the public reaction would be negative—as it was. She also observed the picketers' negative effects on Congress.

As a result, Catt publicly appealed in 1917 for the Woman's Party to stop damaging the chances for passage of the Anthony constitutional amendment by its picketing. She privately wrote Alice Paul deploring the "futile annoyance to the members of Congress."[57] She worried too about picketing as "an insult to President Wilson," which could alienate his needed support. (She tried to compensate by quietly notifying the White House of planned embarrassments to Wilson, which her friends in the Woman's Party leaked to her.) Finally, Catt saw only unfortunate effects on the state level also, since she was certain that "the picket party" had hurt the 1917 New York campaign for the enfranchisement of women.[58]

Everywhere she heard opponents denouncing the picketing. They charged it showed the danger of women in politics and the foolishness of granting women the vote. They insisted that to give women the ballot while they were picketing would reward tactics that should have no place in American politics. At another, lower level, anti-suffragists consciously used the uproar over the picketers as an opportunity to denounce the suffragists as exemplars of "fanaticism," and as "freaks" and "spoiled" children undeserving of suffrage. Moreover, intent on destroying all suffragists through public disapproval of the picketers, they worked as hard as they could to collapse any distinction between them and Catt and the NAWSA. Over and over they asserted that Catt and the NAWSA were in league with the militants, equally deserving of popular condemnation.[59]

Throughout much of 1917 and thereafter, Catt tried to repair the continuing damage she believed the picketers caused the movement. Her private assistance to the White House was an illustration of this, but mostly Catt did her work in public. She succeeded in getting the NAWSA to disavow the picketing tactic and she led the NAWSA to publish its objections in some 350 newspapers across the country. She spoke out personally, arguing that all suffragists should not be judged by what she correctly insisted was a tiny minority. She was especially anxious to establish that suffragists were not against Wilson (and thus not unpatriotic) in what was wartime.

Catt's course offended (and still does) those who contended that Catt should have embraced the picketers as fellow participants in the struggle who were determined to get action quickly. Such judgments did not impress Catt. Her constant refrain was that one had to be practical, to make trade-offs, and to ask about the consequences of tactics. Catt thought she, and not the Woman's

Party, recognized how to play politics. And those who did not know its rules had to be neutralized because, though naive, they could hurt the work of those who did. The danger was always that the Woman's Party might become the tail that wagged the suffrage dog, that the work of two million women might be lost in the actions of a group that never was larger than 50,000.[60]

Pragmatism was not the only root of Catt's objections to the picketers, however. She may not have found their "unladylike" activities offensive to her ideal of womanhood, but their actions did clash with her ideal of the kind of politics she wanted suffragists to model for society at large. When Carrie Catt looked at the Woman's Party, she saw individuals who had already proven themselves "untrustworthy and extremely disloyal."[61] They operated by churning up dark forces of emotion and conflict, not at all the kind of politics she wanted anything to do with. After all, Catt was to devote almost as many years of her life to world peace as to woman suffrage. She could not see how promoting "warfare" in any realm for any reason was acceptable. In this Catt's thought was identical to that of Jane Addams and many other Progressives. Conflict was their enemy. It could not and did not facilitate a harmonious democracy or a peaceful world. In effect, Catt's complaint was that the militants were merely reflecting the world in their tactical moves. They did not represent change and were not reformers at all. They had surrendered to the world and were trying to beat men at their own game.

Of course, Catt respected toughness and employed military language often enough that she had no business being too self-righteous in condemning the Woman's Party. Moreover, all along she suspected that emotional appeals could at times be more effective than rational ones. Yet none of these things were quite to the point in Catt's calculations. To her, the Woman's Party gloried in confrontation and seemed to operate under the illusion that conflictual emotionalism was somehow laudatory. It would not work, nor, she thought, should it work if the woman suffrage movement was to herald the new politics of Catt's Progressive dreams.[62]

Another factor that alienated Catt from the radicals was clashing temperaments. It cannot be neatly separated from more straightforward issues. We know Catt loved order and organization; that inclination automatically recoiled from the milieu of Alice Paul and the Woman's Party, which Catt believed housed a good many unconventional souls, organizational arrangements, and, of course, tactics. Even the NAWSA sometimes attracted what Catt saw as strange people, but Catt was pleased that they rarely stayed long. She felt they were welcome in the Woman's Party, where disorder was a way of life.

Catt misunderstood how the Woman's Party actually functioned. It may have been unconventional in many ways, but it was not disorganized. In practice Alice Paul commanded it in a remote but far tighter fashion than Catt ever dreamed of doing with the NAWSA. Moreover, the picketers were extremely disciplined generally. But to Catt the Woman's Party was another part of America out of control in a country already blighted by too many other instances of the same thing.[63]

Eventually Peck and Catt conceded that both the NAWSA and the Woman's Party had contributed to the success of the suffrage crusade. While it was true that "an icy gulf existed" between the two groups, "the two organizations worked side by side" in effect.[64] Each had done so by compensating for the limitations of the other. The limitations of the NAWSA spurred the creation of the Woman's Party as a home for militants who could not work for suffrage elsewhere and provided a base for the development of more radical and experimental tactics and strategies. For instance, the Woman's Party and its predecessors created the idea of the suffrage parade and it argued for the federal amendment strategy, both of which Catt's NAWSA adopted. Above all, the Woman's Party's tactical radicalism helped enormously to legitimate the NAWSA: it turned the NAWSA into a respectable vehicle for reform and increased its effectiveness both in attracting women and the public at large. Catt went a bit far in later years when she pretended that "there was no serious quarrel between the two." She was more convincing in her perception that each organization had nothing to apologize for in its respective endeavors.[65] By her lights neither organization was flawless, neither was totally "right," and neither deserved full credit for the adoption of the suffrage amendment.[66]

Conclusion

In reflecting on Carrie Catt as a strategist, we can see how much strategy mattered to her and how much she was involved in its formation and defense. Thinking strategically was natural to her, integral to Catt's very being. No one can have a sense of her as a politician, or recognize her as one, without understanding that strategy was foremost on her mind. This is what it means to say she had an intensely political mind. She had goals, of course, and they meant a lot to her, but she never visualized them apart from strategy. It was not just that she did not approve of "unrealistic" or "unstrategic" idealists. She was totally different from such people just as, in turn, her Progressive form of idealism prevented her from being merely another politician.

Her single-minded pursuit of woman suffrage led her to be flexible in strategy and tactics, so flexible indeed that she sometimes seemed to compromise far too much, as in her response to World War I or her tolerance of racism. But she insisted that being practical in this fashion was being moral. It was not the whole of morality, but without it moral idealism was more a self-righteous pose than a relevant program to change the world.

Notes

This essay was originally published as "Strategy," Chapter Nine of Robert Booth Fowler's *Carrie Catt: Feminist Politician* (Boston: Northeastern University Press, 1986), and appears here with the permission of the publisher.

1. C.C. Catt to Ethel M. Smith (Aug. 3, 1917), Carrie Chapman Catt Papers, Library of Congress, Washington, D.C., (hereafter designated as Catt Papers), box 8.

2. C.C. Catt in "Proceedings," 1919 NAWSA Convention, 418, National American Woman Suffrage Association Papers, Library of Congress, Washington, D.C. (hereafter designated as NAWSA Papers), box 84.

3. As they often were. See, for example, Abigail Duniway to Alice Stone Blackwell (Dec. 12, 1913), NAWSA Papers, box 10.

4. C.C. Catt to Jane Addams (Dec. 14, 1914), Catt Papers, box 4; Loretta E. Zimmerman, "Alice Paul and the National Woman's Party," Ph.D. diss., Tulane University, 1964, 245.

5. C.C. Catt to Jane Addams (Nov. 12, 1915), Catt Papers, box 4.

6. Robert E. Riegel, *American Women: A Story of Social Change*, (Rutherford, N.J., 1970), 290; Marie Louise Degen, *The History of the Woman's Peace Party* (1939: New York, 1974), 36, 30; Mercedes M. Randall, *Improper Bostonian: Emily Greene Balch* (New York, 1964), 162, 138; Barbara J. Steinson, *American Women's Activism in World War I* (New York, 1982), chpts. 1 and 3; also see Steinson for "Minutes of the Peace Parade Committee" (Aug. 12, 1914), 10; William L. O'Neill, *Everyone Was Brave: The Rise and Fall of Feminism in America* (Chicago, 1969), 174.

7. "The Flag," *Woman's Protest* 9 (Oct. 1916): 3; "The Suffragist Peace Fiasco," *Woman's Protest* 7 (July 1915): 6-7; "Peace of Politics," *Woman's Protest* 6 (March 1915): 4; "For Woman's Service or Woman Suffrage?" *Woman's Protest* 10 (March 1917): 8; Alice Hill Chittendon, "Our Duty to the State," *Woman's Protest* 10 (April 1917): 3; "Questions for Mrs. Catt To Answer," *Woman's Protest* 11 (Sept. 1917): 16; Grace D. Goodwin, *Anti-Suffrage: Ten Good Reasons* (New York, 1912), 142.

8. C.C. Catt to Executive Council, (Feb. 5, 1917), NAWSA Papers, box 82.

9. Ida Husted Harper, *History of Woman Suffrage*, (New York, 1922), vol. 5: 722-730 and 517; C.C. Catt, "Organized Womanhood," *Woman Voter* 8 (April 1917): 9; J. Stanley Lemons, "The New Woman in the New Era: The Woman Movement From the Great War to the Great Depression," Ph.D. diss., University of Missouri, 1967, 27-28.

10. Steinson, *American Women's Activism*, 237-240 and 308-312; "Third Liberty Loan Drive," *Woman Citizen* 2 (March 30, 1918): 355; also see Mary Summer Boyd, "The Menace to War Workers," *Woman Citizen* 1 (June 9, 1917): 31, for a characteristic expression of concern for mobilized women.

11. "Mrs. Catt Urges Big Drive For More Food," *Woman's Journal* 48 (April 14, 1917): 85-86; Lemons, "The New Woman," 26; Mary G. Peck, *Carrie Chapman Catt* (New York, 1944), 270-272; Ida Tarbell, *All In The Days Work* (New York, 1939), 320-327; David Howard Katz, "Carrie Chapman Catt and the Struggle for Peace," Ph.D. diss., Syracuse University, 1973, 41, 44-45; Steinson, *American Women's Activism*, 313-315.

12. Margaret Robinson, "Woman Suffrage and Pacifism," *Woman Patriot* 1 (April 27, 1918): 3; Margaret Robinson, "Germany's Strongest Allies," *Woman Patriot* 1 (July 6, 1918): 4; "Woman's Suffrage To Please Germans Is Now Urged By Suffrage Leaders," *Woman Patriot* 1 (Sept. 14, 1918): 1; "Is Suffrage Pro-German?" *Woman Patriot* 1 (Oct. 26, 1918): 3; "How Pro-Germans and Pacifists Carried Suffrage In New York," *Woman's Protest* 11 (Nov. 1917): 4-5.

13. "Mrs. Catt and the Schwimmer Peace Plan," *Woman's Protest* 11 (Oct. 1917): 10-11; "Suffragists Have No Part in This War," *Woman Patriot* 1 (July 13, 1918): 4; "Mrs. Catt's Defamation of Her Country," *Woman Patriot* 4 (June 19, 1920): 6; "War Record of Mrs. Carrie Chapman Catt," *Woman Patriot* 1 (Nov. 16, 1918): 3, 5; "Unscrupulous Suffrage Leaders Playing Politics Without Stint Limit with Council of Defense," *Woman Patriot* 1 (Oct. 12, 1918): 1; "Mrs. Catt Again Attacks the Government," *Woman Patriot* 3 (Dec. 27, 1919): 3.

14. C.C. Catt to Maud Wood Park (April 13, 1918), Catt Papers, box P80-5453; HWS 5: 736; Steinson, *American Women's Activism*, 319-320.

15. C.C. Catt, speech, "Woman Suffrage As A War Measure," *Woman Citizen* 3 (June 1918), and other speeches on the same theme, see NAWSA Papers, box 83.

16. "Suffrage As A War Measure," *Remonstrance* (Oct. 1917): 7; "Is Suffrage A War Measure?" *Woman Patriot* 1 (Sept. 28, 1918): 4; "Suffrage vs. Patriotism," *Woman's Protest* 11 (May 1917): 5.

17. Richard Hofstadter, *The Age of Reform: From Bryan to F.D.R.* (1955; New York, 1960), 275.

18. For example, C.C. Catt, statement, Committee on Judiciary, House of Representatives (1904), 19, Catt Collection, Box 1, folder 13, Sophia Smith Library, Smith College.

19. "The Plan" was in Catt's "Report: Campaign and Survey Committee" (1916), NAWSA Papers, box 82.

20. David Morgan, *Suffragists and Democrats: The Politics of Woman Suffrage in America* (East Lansing, Mich., 1972), chpts. 6 and 7.

21. C.C. Catt, "Report: Campaign and Survey Committee" (1916), 32, NAWSA Papers, box 82.

22. Ibid., 1-2 and passim; C.C. Catt, editor, *Woman Suffrage by Federal Constitutional Amendment* (New York, 1917), 6-7, 35, and passim; C.C. Catt, speech, "The Crisis" (Sept. 7, 1916), "Suffrage: U.S." Catt Collection, Box 6, folder 117.

23. C.C. Catt, "Report: Campaign and Survey Committee" (1916), 34-35, NAWSA Papers, box 82.

24. Morgan, *Suffragists and Democrats*, 112; C.C. Catt to Ida H. Harper (Oct. 14, 1921), Catt Papers, box 5; Inez Haynes Irwin, *Angels and Amazons: A Hundred Years of American Women*, (1933; New York, 1974), 372; Mari Jo Buhle and Paul Buhle, eds. *The Concise History of Woman Suffrage* (Urbana, Ill., 1978), 38; also see Alice Blackwell's report on Catt's calculations in the Blackwell Papers, Library of Congress, box 36.

25. C.C. Catt, *An Address to the Legislature of the United States* (New York, 1919), 19-22; C.C. Catt, An Address to the Congress of the United States (New York, 1917), 8, 17, 19.

26. See "Handbook" and "Proceedings," 1916 Convention.

27. See, for example, Anna Howard Shaw to C.C. Catt, (July 1916 [two letters], Sept. 1916, and Jan. 4, 1916, NAWSA Papers, box 27.

28. C.C. Catt to Sue White (May 16, 1918), Sue White Collection, Box 2, folder 21, Schlesinger Library, Radcliffe College; Aileen S. Kraditor, *Ideas of the Woman Suffrage Movement: 1890-1920*, (New York, 1965), 173; Paul E. Fuller, *Laura Clay and the Woman's Rights Movement*, (Lexington, 1975), chpt. 9, and the 1919 NAWSA Convention "Proceedings," 13-27, NAWSA Papers, box 84; also see Dewey W. Grantham, *Southern Progressivism: The Reconciliation of Progress and Tradition*, (Knoxville, 1983), 200-217.

29. C.C. Catt, *An Address to the Legislature*, 1-23.

30. Amelia R. Fry, interviewer, *Conversations with Alice Paul: Woman Suffrage and the Equal Rights Amendment*, (Berkeley, 1976), section I, Schlesinger Library, Radcliffe College.

31. Ibid., 96 and 106-107.

32. Robert McHenry, *Liberty's Women*, (Springfield, Mass., 1980), 28, 37-38, 272, 319-320; Zimmerman, "Alice Paul and the National Woman's Party," 40; Caroline Katzenstein, *Lifting the Curtain*, (Philadelphia, 1955), 165-200; Inez Haynes Irwin, *The Story of the Woman's Party*, (1921; New York, 1971), 12 and Part 1, chpt. 5; HWS 5: 380-381; Penelope P.B. Huse, "Appeals to Congress," in NAWSA, *Victory: How Women Won It*, (New York, 1940), 103; Anna H. Shaw, "Tells of the Stand of the Union," *Woman's Journal* 45 (Feb. 14, 1914): 54; also see *Woman's Journal* throughout 1913 and 1914 (vols. 44-45) on the Congressional Union; Andrew Sinclair, *The Better Half: The Emancipation of the American Woman*, (New York, 1965), 300-304; Irwin, *Angels and Amazons*, 357;

Carrie Chapman Catt and Nettie Rogers Shuler, *Woman Suffrage and Politics: The Inner Story of the Suffrage Movement*, (1923; Seattle, 1970), 255; Inez H. Irwin to Maud Wood Park (March 14, 1921), NAWSA Papers, box 17.

33. Anna Howard Shaw to Harriet Laidlaw (Aug. 16, 1917), Laidlaw Collection, Box 8, folder 137, Schlesinger Library, Radcliffe College.

34. Ibid.

35. See, for example, Anna H. Shaw to Rosamond Danielson (March 11, 1914) and Anna H. Shaw to C.C. Catt (Oct. 14, 1916, and March 12, 1916), all in NAWSA Papers, box 27.

36. Alice Stone Blackwell to C.C. Catt (Sept. 4, 1929), Blackwell Papers, box 12; by the 1930s, however, Blackwell and Alice Paul were corresponding fairly regularly; see NAWSA Papers, box 23.

37. Fry, *Conversations with Alice Paul*, 96-98.

38. Zimmerman, "Alice Paul and the National Woman's Party," chpt. 3 and, 65; Sinclair, Better Half, 303-304; C.C. Catt to Harriet Laidlaw (May 23, 1912), Laidlaw Collection, Box 7, folder 101; Fry, *Conversations with Alice Paul*, 324.

39. Anna Howard Shaw to Harriet Laidlaw (June 5, 1915), Laidlaw Collection, Box 7, folder 101.

40. Paul claimed that Catt announced no compromise was possible; Fry, *Conversations with Alice Paul*, 202-203.

41. For example, Sue White to C.C. Catt (April 27, 1918; May 9, 1918; and May 16, 1918), Sue White Collection, Box 2, folder 21.

42. C.C. Catt to Mrs. Leslie Warner (April 24, 1918), Sue White Collection, Box 2, folder 21; C.C. Catt to Maud Wood Park (Dec. 11, 1918), Carrie Chapman Catt Collection, Box 4, folder 33, Schlesinger Library, Radcliffe College.

43. C.C. Catt to Sue White (July 20, 1918), Sue White Collection, Box 2, folder 21.

44. C.C. Catt to Clara Hyde (May 29, 1911), Catt Papers, box 6; Eleanor Flexner, *Century of Struggle: The Woman's Rights Movement in the United States*, (1959; New York, 1973), 287; C.C. Catt, "Their First Convention" (1920), Catt Papers, box P80-5456; Sinclair, *Better Half*, 330.

45. C.C. Catt to Sue White (May 6, 1918), Sue White Collection, Box 2, folder 21.

46. Catt, "Report: Campaign and Survey Committee" (1916), 30.

47. Rose Young to C.C. Catt (Aug. 8, 1916), Blackwell Papers, box 36.

48. Susan B. Anthony to Alice Stone Blackwell (June 14, 1872), Blackwell Papers, box 9, in which she enunciates the classic position that Catt followed.

49. C.C. Catt to Jane Addams (Jan. 4, 1915), Catt Papers, box 4.

50. C.C. Catt to Joseph Tumulty (Jan. 19, 1917), Catt Papers, box 9; Catt and Shuler, *Woman Suffrage and Politics*, chpt. 11; *HWS* 5: 714; C.C. Catt to Joseph Tumulty (May 3, 1918), Catt Papers, box 9; C.C. Catt, statement (May 21, 1915), Catt Papers, box P80-5459; Morgan, *Suffragists and Democrats*, chpts. 9 and 10; Grace Sample McClure to Alda Wilson (March 20, 1947), Catt Papers, box 9; Maud Wood Park, *Front Door Lobby* (Boston, 1960), is the fullest account.

51. C.C. Catt, "The Suffrage Platform," *Woman's Journal* 46 (June 12, 1915): 184; C.C. Catt, "If We Win in New York," *Woman's Journal* 46 (Oct. 30, 1915): 345; C.C. Catt, "Opening of the Convention," *Woman Citizen* 2 (Dec. 15, 1917): 54.

52. C.C. Catt, "Opening of the Convention," 54.

53. C.C. Catt, "What Every Senator Knows," *Woman Citizen* 2 (March 2, 1918): 263; C.C. Catt to Maud Wood Park (April 18, 1933), Catt Papers, box 7; Catt and Shuler, *Woman Suffrage and Politics*, 327-328.

54. Fry, *Conversations with Alice Paul*, 209-241.

55. C.C. Catt, "Why We Did Not Picket the White House," *Good Housekeeping* 66 (March 1918): 32.

56. C.C. Catt to Mary G. Peck (April 20, 1913), quoted in Peck, *Carrie Chapman Catt*, 210.

57. C.C. Catt to Alice Paul, quoted in Zimmerman, "Alice Paul and the National Woman's Party," 238-239.

58. C.C. Catt, "Excuses Only," *Woman Citizen* 1 (Aug. 11, 1917): 179.

59. "Militant Methods In Action," *Woman's Protest* 10 (Nov. 1916): 5-6; "Organized Obtrusion for a Campaign of Clamor," *Woman's Protest* 9 (July 1916): 3; "Pickets Determine to Persecute President," *Woman Patriot* 1 (Aug. 3, 1918): 1; "Recent Militant Freaks," *Remonstrance* (Oct. 1913): 1; "More Proof that `Pickets and Conservative' Suffragists Have a `Mutual Working Agreement,'" *Woman Patriot* 2 (Jan. 4, 1918): 8; "Do American Suffragists Favor Militancy?" *Woman Patriot* 4 (Dec. 1913): 12; "Picketing and `Pestering,'" *Woman Patriot* 1 (Aug. 24, 1918): 8.

60. See, for example, C.C. Catt, "Pickets Are Behind the Times," *Woman Citizen* 1 (Nov. 1917): 470; Zimmerman, "Alice Paul and the National Woman's Party," 243; 50,000 is undoubtedly too high a figure for the Woman's Party; so is two million for the NAWSA. But the proportions are roughly correct.

61. C.C. Catt to Sue White (May 6, 1918), Sue White Collection, Box 2, folder 21.

62. C.C. Catt to Millicent G. Fawcett (Oct. 19, 1909), Catt Papers, box 5; C.C. Catt to E. Garrison (Aug. 1, 1914), quoted in Riegel, *American Feminists*, 178; "Mrs. Catt's International Address," *Woman's Journal* 39 (June 27, 1908): 101-103; C.C. Catt, "Their First Convention" (1920), Catt Papers, box P80-5456; Harriot Stanton Blatch and Alma Lutz, *Challenging Years: The Memoirs of Harriot Stanton Blatch*, (New York, 1940), 129, 203.

63. Susan D. Becker, *The Origins of the Equal Rights Amendment: American Feminism Between the Wars*, (Westport, Conn., 1981), 89; C.C. Catt to Millicent G. Fawcett (Oct., 19, 1909), Catt Papers, box 5; Shaw, "Tells of the Stand of the Union," *Woman's Journal* 45 (Feb. 14, 1914): 54; Zimmerman, "Alice Paul and the National Woman's Party," 97.

64. Mary G. Peck, "Changing the Mind of a Nation: The Story of Carrie Chapman Catt," *World Tomorrow* 13 (Sept. 1930): 358-361.

65. C.C. Catt to Eileen Morrissey (March 4, 1933), Catt Papers, box P80-5458; on NAWSA borrowings, see, for example, Rheta Childe Dorr, *A Woman of Fifty*, (New York, 1924), 222.

66. Others agree: Morgan, *Suffragists and Democrats*, 186; Blatch and Lutz, *Challenging Years*, 131, 199; Buhle, *Concise History*, 38; Irwin, *Angels and Amazons*, 392-393; Sinclair, *Better Half*, 304.

Seventeen

Minnie Fisher Cunningham's Back Door Lobby in Texas:

Political Maneuvering in a One-Party State

Judith N. McArthur

Editor's Introduction: In this essay, Judith McArthur tells the fascinating story of the Texas suffragists who, shrewdly exploiting a rift within the state's Democratic Party, achieved something that had long seemed impossible: they made it politically expedient to support woman suffrage in a southern state. In keeping with Carrie Chapman Catt's "Winning Plan," Texas suffragists in 1918 sought primary suffrage, the right to vote in the state-wide elections through which the political parties selected their candidates—an important gain in a one-party state. More significantly, this victory was a major breakthrough in the virtually "Solid South," setting the stage for ratification in Texas, which became one of the few southern states to approve the Nineteenth Amendment. If the South had remained solidly opposed to ratification, the amendment would have failed.

This victory did not come easily. Texas suffragists were opposed by anti-suffrage forces that were powerful and entrenched, and amply funded by the liquor industry. Their implacable enemy, Governor James E. Ferguson, a well-known "wet" (opponent of prohibition), had led the anti-suffrage forces at the 1916 National Democratic Convention. Driven from office in 1917 in a scandal, he was down but not out—and he was determined to return to office.

Texas suffrage leader Minnie Fisher Cunningham and her supporters, however, outfoxed even the wily Ferguson, beating him at his own game of political maneuvering. By 1918, suffragists had long since learned that, if they were to win, they would have to convince politicians that it was in their interest to support woman suffrage. But this was particularly difficult to accomplish in the South where there was such hostility to woman suffrage and (in most southern states) no two-party competition to exploit. Yet Cunningham and her associates found a way to convince politicians it was expedient to assist them by skillfully playing one faction within the Democratic Party against another, and making it clear that women voters would support a politician who welcomed them into the political fold. Cunningham and the Texas suffragists also demonstrated their ability—and willingness—to exploit ethnic tensions and war-time anxieties and cater to racial prejudice, as did the male politicians. But in the process, they prevented the re-election of James Ferguson, who, if victorious, would have been in office at the time of the ratification campaign and, in all likelihood, prevented Texas from ratifying the Nineteenth Amendment.

This essay is a vivid reminder of the fact that suffragists did not win the battle in 1920 by appealing to politicians' sense of justice alone. As McArthur clearly illustrates, "front door lobbying" was aided and abetted by "back door lobbying." To win, suffragists found it necessary to master the intricacies of partisan politics and, at times, embrace demagogic tactics—as unsavory as it might seem. Some suffragists found political maneuvering distasteful; others found it exciting. Some, including Minnie Fisher Cunningham, found that they were quite good at it.

Impressed with her success in Texas, Carrie Chapman Catt called Cunningham to Washington to be the Secretary for the NAWSA's Congressional Committee headed by Maud Wood Park. Thus Cunningham became part of the core group of suffragist-politicians that successfully lobbied Congress for the passage of the Nineteenth Amendment.

★　　★　　★　　★　　★

IN THE SPRING OF 1893, thirty-nine women and nine men met in Dallas to form the Texas Equal Rights Association, the state's first suffrage organization. One of the most outspoken feminists in the small group, Dr. Grace Danforth, warned that hard work and justice alone would probably not bring success. "Every concession of right or suffrage that has ever been made to the people has proceeded from the need of the powers that be for the votes of the people," she pointed out. Danforth then made a perceptive prediction: "The Republican party needed the votes of the negroes and the negroes were enfranchised. It will not be long until some party will need the votes of the women, and then we will be granted the right of suffrage."[1]

Grace Danforth's observation was optimistic as well as cynical, for in the 1890s it appeared that southern Democrats might be receptive to votes for women—white women—as the "solution" to Negro suffrage that the Republican Party had imposed after the Civil War. As southern legislatures pondered ways to restore white supremacy, the National American Woman Suffrage Association (NAWSA) created a special Southern Committee to launch an organizing effort in the former Confederacy. Money from the Southern Committee helped bring the Texas Equal Rights Association and other southern suffrage societies into being, but their aspirations were thwarted as state legislatures and local vigilantes invented ways to reestablish white supremacy without sacrificing patriarchy. Legal restrictions—especially the poll tax (which Texas approved in

1902) and the literacy test—now supplanted violence, fraud, and intimidation in disfranchising the majority of blacks. Many lower-class whites who had been attracted to the Populist Party's challenge to conservative Democratic rule in the 1890s were also winnowed out of the electorate in the process.[2]

The result was one-party government that, in combination with deeply rooted cultural obstacles, made the South barren ground for suffragists. Anti-feminism, negrophobia, and the gospel of states' rights created formidable obstacles to the suffrage movement. The lack of viable Republican opposition in most of the southern states made it impossible for suffragists to exploit party competition, a strategy that helped advance the cause in the North. Consequently, most suffrage campaigns below the Mason-Dixon line met repeated failure. None of the southern states gave women full suffrage, and the opposition of their Senators and Congressmen killed, year after year, the federal bill that eventually became the Nineteenth Amendment. When it finally passed in 1919, seventy percent of southern congressional representatives voted in opposition.[3]

By that time, however, southern suffragists had won three partial victories that were to have important consequences nationally: the right to vote in primary elections in Arkansas (1917) and Texas (1918); and in presidential elections in Tennessee (1919). The NAWSA still needed to persuade thirty-six state legislatures to ratify the amendment, and some of those votes would have to be found in the South. Southern Democratic opponents of ratification, led by Governor Ruffin Pleasant of Louisiana, called upon the thirteen southern state legislatures to unite to defeat the amendment, and several of them passed rejection resolutions.[4] The three partial-suffrage states, however, helped clinch the victory in just fourteen months by providing the only ratifying votes from the former Confederacy.

What accounts for these isolated successes in the most anti-suffrage region in the country? In the case of Texas, the victory was the result of skillful political maneuvering by state suffrage leaders, who found a way to exploit political rivalry even in the absence of a two-party system. The women and their male allies left a paper trail that clearly contradicts the legislators' public professions that primary suffrage was a reward for women's patriotic work on the homefront during World War I. Although Grace Danforth did not live to see it, the supposedly impossible came to pass in a one-party southern state: women were enfranchised because politicians needed their votes.

In 1918 the Texas Democratic Party was temporarily rent by issues that divided it into bitterly feuding factions. The president of the Texas Equal Suffrage Association shrewdly exploited the rift by back door lobbying; she invited collusion with a group of legislators who had self-interested motives for helping the cause. Facing a hotly contested primary election that it appeared likely to lose, the Progressive-prohibitionist wing of the party made a quiet bargain with suffrage leaders. It pushed a bill permitting women to vote in primary elections through the legislature in return for a promise that they would turn out en masse to vote for its gubernatorial candidate.

Early Failures

Until 1918 the Texas suffrage movement shared the same history of discouragement and defeat as its counterparts in the rest of the South. Like the other southern societies that the NAWSA helped establish in the 1890s, the Texas Equal Rights Association had a short, unproductive life. Still tainted in southern eyes by its abolitionist origins, woman suffrage evoked little positive response among women whose conservative culture idealized retiring, refined ladyhood "protected" by chivalrous manhood. One by one, the southern suffrage associations disbanded, lapsed into dormancy, or ceased to be more than sporadically active. Unsuccessful in recruiting members and raising money, the Texas Equal Rights Association had stopped holding meetings by 1896. Another organizing attempt in 1903 produced the Texas Woman Suffrage Association that expired in all but name two years later when its president moved to New York.

In the 1910s, as increasing numbers of women were drawn into the Progressive movement and discovered the ballot's potential usefulness as a weapon for social reform, the southern suffrage movement was reborn and revitalized. New associations were founded and dormant ones like the Texas Woman Suffrage Association revived; it was reactivated in 1913 and within three years had eighty local affiliates.[5] Yet the second generation of southern suffrage leaders, enthusiastic, hard-working, and backed by state associations that now counted membership in the thousands, faced the familiar pattern of defeat as they lobbied state legislatures for constitutional amendments to enfranchise women. The experience of the Texas organization, which changed its name to Texas Equal Suffrage Association (TESA) in 1916, was typical: constitutional amendments were voted down decisively in the biennial legislative sessions of 1915 and 1917. The margin of defeat was even larger in 1917 than in 1915, and alternative bills for primary and presidential suffrage failed to come to a vote.[6]

Discouraging results like these in every part of the nation helped convince NAWSA president Carrie Chapman Catt to devise a new strategy, the famous "Winning Plan" adopted in 1916. Thereafter the NAWSA gave priority to securing a federal amendment and continued state work selectively, mounting campaigns only where there was a strong likelihood of success. State presidents in the unpromising South were instructed to focus on partial enfranchisement—primary or presidential suffrage.[7] Legislators could grant these partial measures as amendments to existing election laws without the public referenda required for constitutional amendments, which had often been expensive failures. And since "white primary" laws restricted black participation, primary suffrage would circumvent the conservative argument that woman suffrage would bring huge numbers of black women to the polls. (This reality unfortunately proved no obstacle to anti-suffragists determined to manipulate debate on the "negro problem.") When Texas suffragists failed again in 1917, it appeared that the state would remain part of the "Solid South" against woman suffrage.

Suffragists Versus Governor Ferguson

In the months that followed, the governor of Texas, James E. Ferguson, and the president of the TESA, Minnie Fisher Cunningham of Galveston, emerged as protagonists in a political drama that unexpectedly made Texas women voters. Both were strong personalities and they first clashed publicly at the Democratic National Convention in 1916 in St. Louis, where suffragists were demonstrating for a plank supporting suffrage by federal amendment. The convention's compromise endorsement of suffrage on a state-by-state basis merely stiffened the conservatives' determination to keep it out of their own states. Governor Ferguson, leading the Texas delegation, infuriated the women by presenting the dissenting minority report in a theatrical speech studded with injunctions about "woman's place." A member of the Resolutions Committee who defended the suffrage plank was howled down by the Texas delegation. Minnie Fisher Cunningham, who had a flair for political theater herself, retorted by leading the state suffrage delegation in a counter demonstration: the Texas suffragists carried a Lone Star Flag draped with mourning that Cunningham improvised by cutting up a black crepe dress.[8]

Both Cunningham and Ferguson shared a common allegiance to the Democratic party, but their political supporters came from different ends of the socioeconomic spectrum. Suffragists were disproportionately urban women from the middle and upper classes, the wives and daughters of professional men. Minnie Fisher Cunningham, who in 1901 had become one of the first women to earn a pharmacy degree from the University of Texas, was married to an attorney and belonged to the selective Woman's Wednesday Club of Galveston and the Woman's Health Protective Association, a citywide coalition of activists and reformers. Although Cunningham's interest in suffrage far exceeded her rather nominal involvement in voluntary associations, many TESA women were active in club-inspired civic work and often at odds with entrenched political interests over social reform issues.[9]

Governor Ferguson had started out as a struggling farm youth, but after several years of drifting and manual labor he had studied law, married well, and opened a bank. He had promoted himself for governor as a successful self-made businessman and a populist who sympathized with farmers' problems, especially the high rate of tenancy (in excess of fifty percent) and the poor quality of rural schools. Ferguson's studied platform image of folksy but shrewd "Farmer Jim" won him a large following among native-born rural whites. He made education a focal point of his populism, denouncing the University of Texas as an elitist institution where rich men's sons were educated with the tax dollars of struggling farmers and workers. When he tried to purge the university of half a dozen professors whose politics he disliked and vetoed its appropriation in 1917, organized women were prominent in the coalition that rallied to its defense. An Austin suffragist, fuming in her diary, expressed the common opinion of elite women: the governor was "an ignorant, common personage."

Stronger adjectives tempted her, "—but not having the vocabulary of a sea captain…I can't express what I think of Jim Ferguson." [10]

Elite women particularly disliked Ferguson because he enjoyed strong support among opponents of prohibition, including the state's substantial populations of German, Czech, and Mexican immigrants. Prohibition had been the dominant political issue in Texas for a decade, splitting the Democratic party into "wet" and "dry" camps. More than a moral question or a social problem, prohibition took center stage as an issue of political corruption and the power of special interests. Since most organized women sympathized with the drys, anti-prohibitionism went hand in hand with anti-suffragism. The politically strong brewing interests helped fund the "Texas Business Men's Association," a powerful and underhanded lobbying organization that distributed anti-suffrage and anti-prohibition boilerplate to hundreds of county newspapers. Brewery money, raised by a sixty-cents-per-barrel-sold assessment, and the organized ethnic vote helped put Ferguson in office and regularly elected anti-prohibition, anti-suffrage majorities in the Texas Legislature. [11]

Consequently, Cunningham and the TESA rejoiced when the governor's enemies began scrutinizing his questionable administrative expenditures and flexible ethics in the summer of 1917. Suffrage activity was put on hold while they quietly assisted the legislative investigation against Ferguson and publicized his misdeeds. [12] When he was impeached in August 1917 on multiple counts of misusing public funds and barred from again seeking public office, the Democratic Party was left bitterly divided in Texas and the political future unpredictable.

A New Governor Hesitates

Governor Ferguson's departure elevated the young lieutenant governor, William P. Hobby, to the governorship. A thirty-nine-year-old newspaper publisher nurtured in the party's conservative inner circle, Hobby, like Ferguson, had been elected as an anti-prohibitionist; the influential conservatives who backed him also opposed woman suffrage. Hobby himself took no public stand on the issue, but Cunningham knew from his response to a legislative questionnaire sent out by her predecessor that he was privately receptive. This and the post-impeachment political climate encouraged her to seek the NAWSA's approval for another attempt to secure primary suffrage. The revelations of the legislative investigation had lent credence to the demand for the woman's ballot to "clean house" in political affairs. "It has been a full six weeks since I have found any man with the temerity to look us in the eye and say he opposed women's voting in the face of the outrageous condition that has been proven to prevail in our state government," Cunningham reported to Carrie Chapman Catt that fall. [13]

Cunningham pinned her hopes on the near certainty that Hobby would have to call the Thirty-fifth Legislature back into special session to deal with problems caused by the Ferguson impeachment and mobilization for the First World

War. But she had no illusions that women could succeed solely on the claim of morality and political housecleaning unless they could make these issues seem more compelling than in the past. The fact that the state constitution disfranchised men in uniform while permitting resident aliens, many of whom were German-born, to vote after applying for their preliminary citizenship papers seemed to Cunningham to open a window of opportunity for a suffrage bill. Women's votes could be presented as a way of compensating for those of husbands and brothers in the army, offsetting the ballots of unnaturalized aliens, who were known to be "wet" and pro-Ferguson and suspected of being disloyal. The TESA hoped to arouse public sentiment against the fact that "enemy aliens" could vote, while loyal American women were disfranchised. If the legislators held a fourth special session, Cunningham told Catt, "Perhaps we can prove to them that they need us even if they do not want us!"[14]

Cunningham could not make the case to the legislators, however, unless Hobby summoned them back to Austin, and he deliberately delayed. War mobilization was inflaming the divisive prohibition question, and a special session would make it a front-page issue. Hobby would have to run for the gubernatorial nomination in his own right in the July 1918 primary and feared that any position he took on the liquor question would cost votes. It would be safer not to convene another session until after the election, by which time Congress would probably have passed a prohibition amendment and resolved the issue. Governor Hobby took the same approach to suffrage, putting off the TESA representatives as they repeatedly tried to extract a promise that primary suffrage would be part of the agenda of any special session.[15]

Pressure from the Progressive spokesmen in the party, and increasing public and War Department concern over reports of free-flowing liquor and open prostitution near Texas's numerous army training camps and military airfields, eventually persuaded Hobby to capitulate and call the special session. Popular sentiment was increasing for prohibition as a war measure, and Hobby himself was beginning to think it might be justifiable.[16] But he remained immovable on woman suffrage; there was no reason to think that it would pass the same legislature that had already rejected three different bills, and endorsement would cost him votes among the anti-prohibitionists. His message to the legislature did not mention suffrage or even amending the election laws, which would have opened the door for a primary suffrage bill. Since a special session could not consider any measures except those submitted by the governor, the TESA's options once again appeared to have been foreclosed.

The Back Door Lobby

A potential friend had failed the Texas suffragists, but a confirmed enemy would inadvertently be their salvation. The impeached James Ferguson had declared himself a candidate for governor in 1918, contending that the legal ban against him was invalid because he had resigned from office before the sen-

Minnie Fisher Cunningham.
Austin Public Library

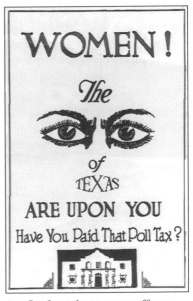

Leaflet from the woman suffrage campaign in Texas.
Austin Public Library

ate voted for conviction. A peerless stump speaker, Ferguson had the backing of the powerful brewing interests, and he stood a good chance of winning a plurality in the primary. His political resurrection worried the Progressive-prohibitionist wing of the Democratic Party, who knew he would get the wet vote, especially the manipulated Hispanic portion of it along the Mexican border, where political bosses ruled. James Ferguson's candidacy also worried the old-line conservatives, who shared Ferguson's aversion to prohibition and woman suffrage but feared his strong appeal to tenant farmers and the working class. When the suffragists called on Governor Hobby late in January 1918, Cunningham reported, "We found him somewhat exercised over Mr. Ferguson's activity, and we left him more so. We had nothing cheerful to tell him along that line." [17]

However, Cunningham was an astute politician, and as Ferguson's star rose she quietly began to negotiate a back door approach to suffrage. She knew that Representative Charles Metcalfe of San Angelo, a friend of the TESA, was actively supporting Hobby's campaign and that he had a son in the army. Before the date for the special session had even been announced, Cunningham asked Metcalfe by letter to help persuade Hobby to submit a primary suffrage bill. She offered two reasons: the necessity to support the troops overseas by electing a loyal American government and not one chosen by "a solid pro-German vote"; and the very real possibility that a divided vote among the prohibitionists would allow Ferguson to win the governor's race by a plurality. She hinted broadly that it would be in Hobby's own best interest to submit the suffrage bill:

"A large number of new and grateful voters would be his salvation, I should think!"[18]

Representative Metcalfe ignored the reference to the "German menace" and took the hint, as Cunningham had hoped, about the real danger to his candidate. The prohibitionists had lost the gubernatorial election in 1910 by fielding multiple candidates who split the dry vote. They had lost again in 1914 (to Ferguson) by offering a weak candidate with doubtful prohibition credentials (like Hobby) who had failed to rally the drys. Several prohibitionists had already announced their interest in running for governor, and as Ferguson's campaign gathered momentum, it appeared that the Progressives were once again poised to snatch defeat from the jaws of victory. Metcalfe asked Cunningham if she could truly guarantee to deliver the woman vote for Hobby. He cautioned her to keep their discussion confidential:

> Please write me at once saying how the women of the state to your knowledge would vote in the Governors [sic] race if they have the ballot: not officially—but so I can use your letter if I wish to do so, not for publication, but as I see fit otherwise. It seems to me very probable if you know they will vote right, that...a bill may be passed....

He added bluntly that success would also depend on the suffragists' maintaining a low profile, that he did not want to be pestered by "the old maids and *masterful* women, or *militants*. They get in the way & tire me and the others."[19]

Immediately, Cunningham furnished the "unofficial" letter for Metcalfe to circulate. In it she explained that at the last TESA board meeting the suffrage leaders had passed a resolution to support Hobby's candidacy if he submitted their primary suffrage bill with a recommendation for passage. Some of the other candidates were strong friends of suffrage, but their chances of winning were slim. It was better strategy to back the incumbent and persuade him to adopt suffrage convictions. Knowing full well what cards the other political players were holding, Cunningham laid her aces on the table:

> ...vote in hand we will quite naturally concentrate on the man who enfranchised us. And with the Pro's divided, with the purchasable, corrupt, ignorant, pro-German vote going to Ferguson, whomsoever the women of Texas concentrate on in the July primaries, that man is just as good as elected. But without us, it is Ferguson with a plurality,...[20]

Representative Metcalfe had worked with the suffragists long enough to know that they had amassed complete political profiles of every representative and senator. He asked Cunningham for a breakdown of legislators according to their views on suffrage—supportive, opposed, or undecided—for his "confidential use" so that he could begin "all the lining up possible" before the lawmakers assembled in Austin at the end of February.[21] Although Metcalfe felt certain that women's ballots could offset the wet vote that Hobby would lose by supporting suffrage, the young acting governor was not inclined to take the risk.

His promise to support dry zones around the military cantonment towns, which he could justify to wets by pleading pressure from the War Department, prompted the dry candidates to withdraw and throw him their support. Expecting to draw votes from both sides with his "win the war" platform, Hobby avoided the controversial suffrage issue like a virus. When the suffragists urged him to reconsider, he replied that he would ask to have the election laws brought up *only* if presented with a petition signed by a majority of both houses of the legislature.

It was a clever response: whether they succeeded or failed, he would be absolved of responsibility. If Hobby anticipated failure he underestimated the determination of women like Nonie B. Mahoney, of the TESA's Dallas chapter, who helped staff the special suffrage headquarters set up during the called session. An anti-suffrage Dallas representative told Mahoney that he would not believe women really wanted the vote unless five thousand of his townswomen petitioned for it; four days later Mahoney lugged a suitcase to the speaker's rostrum and presented the petition—with *ten* thousand signatures. When the suffragists had succeeded "after many hours of labor" in collecting signatures from two-thirds of the legislators, prompting the necessary action from Hobby's office at last, Metcalfe and several co-sponsors immediately introduced a primary suffrage amendment.[22]

Since the deadline for paying the poll tax had passed, Metcalfe and company were careful to specify that women would be exempted for the current year. Fear of Ferguson pushed wet anti-suffrage conservatives into a reluctant alliance with the Progressive-prohibitionist faction, and the bill moved through the legislature quickly. Within four days after it was introduced on March 12 the bill had been passed to its third reading and cleared the House with seventy-one percent of the vote. Less than a week later, the Senate gave it an even larger majority.[23] Governor Hobby signed the bill on March 26, four months before the primary election.

Sidestepping the "Negro Problem"

As Cunningham had foreseen, woman suffrage passed in Texas in 1918 because it was a subtle and effective way of outflanking Ferguson.[24] Restricting women to primary suffrage secured the benefit of their votes without subjecting legislators to accusations of betraying the white race. A provision requiring each woman to fill out her registration blank in her own hand was added as a de facto literacy test to keep out the "illiterate negro women and the Mexican women along the border" who would be likely to vote for Ferguson. Minnie Fisher Cunningham was personally opposed to this restriction but conceded that it was necessary to appease influential conservatives like the senate's Rienzi M. Johnston. Editor and part owner of the *Houston Post,* Johnston was Hobby's political and journalistic mentor and a spokesman for the party's conservative wing. The edition of the *Post* that announced the bill's passage carried Johnston's dire warning that allowing black women to vote would bring black men into the primaries and put an end to the state's political sovereignty. The paper refrained from mentioning that Johnston, like other conservatives torn between personal conviction and political necessity, had quietly cast an affirmative vote.[25]

Like other southern suffragists of this era, Cunningham countered that the "negro problem" was a smoke screen; the majority of blacks had long been disfranchised. In Texas some 100,000 black men had voted in the 1890s; by the early twentieth century the poll tax and the white primary had reduced the number to about 5,000. Anti-suffragists nevertheless thundered about the danger of "placing the ballot in the hands of 300,000 negro women and prostitutes." Rienzi Johnston claimed that 10,000 northern women were prodding the federal government to enforce the Fifteenth Amendment in the South.[26]

The TESA's decision not to admit African American members needs to be judged within this context. Perpetually on the defensive and unable to puncture this emotional negrophobic rhetoric with logic and facts, Cunningham and her followers had no realistic hope of succeeding unless they distanced themselves from black women. Consequently, the suffrage leadership was taken aback when, in the midst of the post-victory registration campaign to enroll the new women voters, a black women's club applied for TESA membership. In the letters they exchanged pondering the dilemma none of the white suffragists expressed any personal objection to admitting the black women; the issue was their enemies' potential reaction. What the legislature had given it could take away, and conservatives would have raised an angry cry that they had been right all along: black women were flocking to the polls.

Ultimately, the TESA officers made the politically expedient decision. Minnie Fisher Cunningham followed Carrie Chapman Catt's advice to tell the black women "that you will be able to get the vote for women more easily if they do not embarrass you by asking for membership." On her own, she added resourcefully that since the application was without precedent it would require a convention vote and the next convention would not meet until 1919, by which time she hoped that the federal amendment enfranchising all women would have passed.[27]

Suffragists Keep Their Promise

The more immediate concern for Cunningham was fulfilling her part of the political bargain that had brought the suffragists' victory. Representative Metcalfe urged a massive registration campaign, reminding her of the danger that many women would not want to vote, and some country women would even vote for Ferguson. "I hope tho [sic] to be vindicated in my statements that they *will vote* and for the *right men*," Metcalfe reminded Cunningham. The NAWSA was equally concerned. If Ferguson regained control of the statehouse, Texas would vote against ratifying the federal suffrage amendment that was almost certain to pass within the next year. Carrie Chapman Catt quietly diverted a thousand dollars to the Texas suffragists, with instructions to use it to get out the anti-Ferguson vote.[28]

Characteristically, Cunningham had an inspiration of her own: a woman candidate on the ticket to help draw women to the polls. At its convention in May, the TESA unanimously adopted a resolution urging Annie Webb Blanton, a professor of English at North Texas State Normal College to run for state superintendent of public instruction. Since public education was conceded to be woman's domain and several other states had already elected female superintendents, a woman candidate was unlikely to arouse significant male criticism. In Blanton the suffragists also had a proven candidate: she had just completed a term as the first woman president of the Texas State Teachers' Association. As a professional, she could also be expected to appeal strongly to educated urban women, the ones most likely to vote for Hobby.[29]

Once Blanton had been persuaded to make the race, Cunningham channeled all of the TESA's energy and resources into signing up as many women as possible during the seventeen-day registration period that had been substituted for the poll tax. Local equal franchise societies transformed themselves into precinct committees and "suffrage schools" that taught women how to mark ballots. "Women's Hobby Clubs" chauffeured women without transportation to the courthouse and volunteered as hostesses at the registration booths; in the larger cities suffragists persuaded officials to authorize registration substations in popular department stores, permitting women the easy option of registering while they did their errands. "Hobby Club" women stood on downtown street corners to hand out campaign literature and urge registration; they distributed yellow badges, signifying intention to vote, for women to pin on their street clothes.[30]

The suffragists astutely linked registration and voting to war patriotism, stressing women's "duty" to take the place of their absent husbands and brothers at the polls, and urged every woman to turn out in defense of her home and not be a "slacker." Since some 100,000 men were away in the army, it was possible that a large female turnout might decide the election, which added news interest to the registration drive. The large metropolitan newspapers published running tallies of local registrations and speculated that between seventy-five to ninety percent of these women would vote for Hobby. Some 386,000 women ultimately signed up, and Cunningham exulted that "the registration figures are enough to make Ferguson sick."[31]

Faced with an apparent groundswell of female support for Hobby, "Farmer Jim" worked to divide women along rural-urban lines, appealing to country women to vote against "an aristocracy that doesn't care anything more about you than a hog does for a side-pocket." He urged farm wives not to be influenced by the "pink tea and poodle dog nursing women" of the cities.[32] Ferguson was justly feared for the effectiveness of such rhetoric, and suffragists met it with action. Although residents of towns under 10,000 in population were not legally required to register, suffragists organized Hobby Clubs and registration drives in country precincts to draw out rural women. While Ferguson mounted a populist assault, suffrage leaders countered with a cross-class appeal for gender solidarity by presenting Hobby as the "woman's" candidate.

First, they emphasized how much Hobby's tenure in office had benefitted the female sex. Speakers stressed that a Ferguson victory would mean the repeal of primary suffrage: "If your first vote is not cast for the man who made it possible for you to have a vote, you may never cast a second vote." To engage women who had not actively sought suffrage, they promoted the connection between the candidate and the unprecedented reform legislation or "Hobby laws" passed during the special session: liquor and prostitution outlawed within ten miles of military training camps; the age of consent for girls raised from fifteen to eighteen years of age; and statutory prohibition for the entire state. All were reforms for which women's voluntary associations had lobbied. Campaign flyers addressed "To the Women of Texas" stressed women's indebtedness to Hobby for the realization of their legislative goals. One signed by five women's organizations, including the Woman's Christian Temperance Union, the Federation of Women's Clubs, and the Congress of Mothers, exhorted women to elect "by an OVERWHELMING MAJORITY OUR SPLENDID YOUNG GOVERNOR who speaks through deeds rather than words." [33]

Second, the suffragists made political capital from the old tradition of separate spheres and cultural assumptions about female moral superiority, appealing to women across divisions of class and geography to help save the state. Governor Hobby and his advisors were accusing Ferguson of ties to the German-American Alliance, which had admitted during a United States Senate investigation to having taken an "interest" in his 1914 gubernatorial race. There was also the matter of $156,000 that Ferguson had once borrowed to cover a business debt from friends whose names he refused to reveal; speculation ranged from the brewing interests to the Kaiser himself. The suffragists helped the Hobby forces invert Ferguson's populism and define the contest as a struggle against brewery-manipulated, special-interest politics by urging women to stand together for good government and morality. The cards they distributed for Hobby proclaimed him to be "The Man Whom Good Women Want." [34]

Ferguson on the Defensive

So successful were Cunningham and the suffrage leadership in mobilizing vocal female support for Hobby and helping shape public debate that they made the unimaginable happen in a southern state: it actually became politically expedient to be *for* suffrage rather than against it. The once reluctant Hobby began to cultivate his new female constituency and to embrace the pro-woman image that the suffragists had manufactured for him. He urged women to help make Texas safe for democracy by going to the polls and even promised to recommend a constitutional amendment for full suffrage to the next legislature. [35]

Noting the direction of the prevailing political wind, Ferguson abruptly switched tactics and made his own pitch for the female vote. He claimed he had never opposed the *principle* of suffrage for women, only the idea of forcing them to become voters without their consent. His weekly paper, the *Ferguson Forum*, played up the occasional endorsement from a prominent woman, the formation of women's Ferguson clubs, and supportive letters from female readers. By June the *Ferguson Forum* was regularly running long pieces supposedly by "Sally Jane Spottswood," represented as a school teacher in mythical Pine Hollow, Texas, who addressed women directly. Lauding Ferguson as "the proven friend of every mother in the state," she urged country women to register. "Follow your intuition and you can't go wrong," Sally Jane exhorted. "Intuitively you will vote for Ferguson!" [36]

The Ferguson camp repeatedly tried to make an issue of the fact that Hobby's recently acquired enthusiasm for woman suffrage and prohibition was an eleventh-hour conversion for political advantage. The claim that Hobby had given women the vote was "sheer political buncombe," Ferguson jeered. He offered a new hat to any woman who could show that the governor had ever done anything to assist suffrage except sign the bill. A two-part article in the *Ferguson Forum* by "One Who Was There" described how the primary suffrage bill had passed without any assistance from "our young Christian governor and reformed anti-prohibitionist for political reasons." "After this year they are going to charge you good women $1.75 [in poll taxes] to vote," Ferguson pointed out, "but this year you can vote for Hobby for free. Instead of wanting to do something for the women, he wants you to do something for him." [37]

The charge was perfectly true, but it failed to stick. The superheated passions of wartime provided the suffragists with the same kind of political cover that their enemies had so long exploited with the "negro problem." Now the "German menace" made women's enfranchisement appear not only necessary but patriotic. The Progressives who had persuaded Hobby to change his position on the liquor issue had astutely predicted that it could be pulled off with "a show of patriotism" that would smother charges of "flopping to the pros overnight." The same strategy worked for suffrage, as southern-bred Woodrow Wilson had already demonstrated by taking up the NAWSA's claim that women deserved the vote as a reward for their war work. Using the TESA's variation of this rationale, Hobby, who turned out to be better than anticipated on the hustings, claimed that women had been admitted to the primaries "to offset the votes of those whose carcasses are in this country but whose souls are in Germany." Former governor Tom Campbell hit the campaign trail declaring that "every slacker and every pro-German will vote for James E. Ferguson for Governor and it is up to the good women of this State to kill those votes." [38]

Women Clench Hobby's Victory

When the ballots were counted, both Hobby and Annie Webb Blanton won enormous victories. "'Hurrah for the women!'" R.M. Dudley, who had won nomination to the state senate, wrote jubilantly to Cunningham. "We probably would have elected Hobby anyway, but we know the women clenched it and nailed it down." Governor Hobby's total was more than twice as large as Ferguson's; Blanton won nearly 70,000 more votes than the incumbent superintendent of public instruction and a minor third candidate combined and carried every county except one. About the voters themselves, only anecdotal evidence exists. A Hobby chairman in East Texas, a Ferguson stronghold, reported during registration that many women were saying that they planned to vote for Hobby even though their husbands supported Ferguson. They may well have done so. Ferguson had predicted that he would win only twenty percent of the urban women but that eighty percent of the country women would support him; afterward he admitted that women had apparently voted ten to one for Hobby. Analysis of the election returns for San Antonio, where the newspaper published the candidates' total votes by precinct as well as a numerical breakdown of men and women registered in each precinct, indicates that at least eighty percent of women voters cast their ballots for Hobby for governor and eighty-six percent voted for Blanton as superintendent of public instruction.[39]

This impressive show of "voting right" notwithstanding, Cunningham soon discovered that her allies of convenience had not altered their underlying convictions. Rienzi Johnston's *Houston Post,* for years the anti-suffrage foil of the progressive *Houston Chronicle,* had done a sharp editorial about-face after the suffrage bill passed. During the registration campaign it monitored the rising totals in a regular front page feature, urging the city toward a goal of 15,000 enrolled women. Rienzi Johnston abruptly ceased agitating the race issue and became so indifferent to the black women who signed up that the *Post* did not even bother to tally them beyond round numbers. In the end, black women made up less than eight percent of the female registrants in Houston, home to the state's largest black community, and surrounding Harris County. The *Post* celebrated Hobby's victory by declaring that "the hand that rocks the cradle is the hand that rules the ballot box."[40] But when Cunningham asked Hobby for a resolution endorsing the federal suffrage amendment on the eve of the state Democratic convention six weeks later, he declined because his mentor, Johnston (who would be acting governor later that month while Hobby was out of the state), was adamantly opposed.

Minnie Fisher Cunningham "still feeling a little pert," as she later said, from the election victory, promptly declared that she would organize a women's floor fight for the resolution and was reproached for threatening to embarrass a young governor with "a fine political future." "If he doesn't support this amendment, he doesn't *have* any future," Cunningham retorted. Weeks before, Cunningham had been named to chair the convention as a reward for the women's campaign, but on the opening day she coolly rose and declined the honor. Her only purpose as a delegate was to secure endorsement for the federal suffrage amendment, she announced, and she reserved the right to speak on the subject if the committee report was unsatisfactory. "We really did organize a fine floor fight; it's a pity we didn't have to have it," she recollected forty years later. "We would have shown them something in termagants they had never seen." The opposition backed down and the convention endorsed the federal amendment, virtually guaranteeing the NAWSA a vote for ratification when the Nineteenth Amendment passed the following summer.[41]

Only two years earlier, in 1916, Cunningham and two other TESA suffragists had appeared before the state Democratic convention to ask for suffrage and been rebuffed; James Ferguson, fresh from his performance in St. Louis, had been in control. Nothing then seemed less likely than that the suffragists' implacable enemy would soon be their means to victory. As historian Aileen Kraditor noted long ago, political considerations often override personal convictions when legislators vote, and a reform movement has the best chance of succeeding if its leadership is "politically sophisticated" and has "something to offer the potential ally,... something to trade." The lack of such opportunities in the one-party South, she pointed out, doomed suffragists there to failure.[42] In 1918 Texas suffragists unexpectedly found themselves possessed of precisely those essentials for success: [intra-] party competition, something to trade, and a leader politically shrewd enough to recognize it.

Prudently, Cunningham and her inner circle kept the details of their legislative bargain to themselves. Political trading did not fit the self-image suffragists projected as earnest pleaders for simple justice, a "front door lobby" that shunned back room deals and politicking. It appeared that hardworking women had persevered until fair-minded men had seen the light of reason, when in fact temporary political expediency camouflaged in patriotic rhetoric had secured the suffrage victory. Years later, in a letter to one of her closest associates, Cunningham neatly summed up in words what they had earlier demonstrated in deed: "At the moment, we were the smartest group of politicians in the state."[43]

Notes

1. Grace Danforth, "Struggling for Freedom," *Dallas Morning News*, May 11, 1893. On the founding of the Texas Equal Rights Association, see Ruthe Winegarten and Judith N. McArthur, eds., *Citizens at Last: The Woman Suffrage Movement in Texas* (Austin, Tex., 1987), 87-93.

2. Marjorie Spruill Wheeler, *New Women of the New South: The Leaders of the Woman Suffrage Movement in the Southern States* (New York, 1993), 13-14, 113-116; *Proceedings of the Twenty-sixth Annual Convention of the National American Woman Suffrage Association, February 15-20, 1894*, edited by Harriet Taylor Upton (Warren, Ohio, [1894]), 47-49.

3. On the "Solid South" see Carrie Chapman Catt and Nettie Rogers Shuler, *Woman Suffrage and Politics: The Inner Story of the Suffrage Movement* (1926; reprint, Seattle, 1969), 323-26; Eleanor Flexner, *Century of Struggle: The Woman's Rights Movement in the United States* (1959; reprint, New York, 1974), 302-305; and David Morgan, *Suffragists and Democrats: The Politics of Woman Suffrage in America* (East Lansing, 1972), 122-23, 155-56, 165-77. Anne Firor Scott, *The Southern Lady: From Pedestal to Politics, 1830-1930* (Chicago, 1970), chpt. 7, and Wheeler, *New Women of the New South*, chpt. 1, analyze the difficulties of southern suffragists.

4. Wheeler, *New Women of the New South*, 37.

5. For the history of the Texas suffrage movement, see A. Elizabeth Taylor, "The Woman Suffrage Movement in Texas" *Journal of Southern History*, 27 (May 1951): 194-215.

6. 63 percent of the Texas House of Representatives voted for the amendment in 1915; 59 percent did in 1917. In both sessions the amendment failed to come to a vote in the Senate. Calculated from tallies in Taylor, "The Woman Suffrage Movement in Texas," 208-212.

7. Wheeler, *New Women of the New South*, 160-62.

8. Catt and Shuler, *Woman Suffrage and Politics*, 255-56; Jane Y. McCallum, "Activities of Women in Texas Politics," in *Texas Democracy: A Centennial History of Politics and Personalities of the Democratic Party, 1836-1936*, 2 vols., Frank Carter Adams, ed. (Austin, 1937), 1: 470-74; *Dallas Times-Herald*, June 16, 1916; Maud Wood Park, *Front Door Lobby*, Edna Lamprey Stantial, ed., (Boston, 1960), 14-15.

9. Elizabeth Hayes Turner, "'White-Gloved Ladies' and 'New Women' in the Texas Woman Suffrage Movement," in *Southern Women: Histories and Identities*, Virginia Bernhard et al, eds. (Columbia, Mo., 1992), 129-156.

10. Lewis L. Gould, *Progressives and Prohibitionists: Texas Democrats in the Wilson Era* (Austin, 1973), 130-32, 185-221, and Gould, "The University Becomes Politicized: The War with Jim Ferguson," *Southwestern Historical Quarterly*, 86 (Oct. 1982): 255-76; Janet Humphrey, ed., *A Texas Suffragist: Diaries and Writings of Jane Y. McCallum* (Austin, 1988), quotations 64, 80-81.

11. "Brewing Propaganda," *New Republic*, Aug. 21, 1915, 62-64; Anti-Saloon League, *The Brewers and Texas Politics*, 2 vols. (San Antonio, 1916), 1: 109-112. Catt and Shuler, *Woman Suffrage and Politics*, list Texas as one of the eight states where the "organized German-liquor vote was hurled into woman suffrage referenda campaigns with the unerring accuracy claimed for it," 148.

12. See Judith N. McArthur, "Motherhood and Reform in the New South: Texas Women's Political Culture in the Progressive Era," (Ph.D. diss., University of Texas at Austin, 1992), 479-490.

13. Minnie Fisher Cunningham to Carrie Chapman Catt, Sept. 26, 1917, box 1, folder 8, Minnie Fisher Cunningham Papers, Houston Metropolitan Research Center, Houston Public Library.

14. Cunningham to Catt, July 31 (quotation), Aug. 27, 1917, ibid.

15. Hobby to Thomas B. Love, Oct. 22, Nov. 16, Dec. 31, 1917; Feb. 9, 1918, Thomas B. Love Papers, Dallas Historical Society. Cunningham to Hortense Ward, Sept. 27, 1917; Ward to Cunningham, Dec. 7, 22, 1917, box 13, folder 193, Cunningham Papers; Cunningham to Carrie Chapman Catt, Jan. 25, 1918, box 1, folder 9, ibid.

16. Gould, *Progressives and Prohibitionists*, 227-33; Hobby to Thomas B. Love, Dec. 31, 1917; Feb. 9, 1918, Love Papers.

17. Cunningham to Tom Finty, Jan. 28, 1918, box 4, folder 3, Jane McCallum Family Papers (Part I), Austin History Center, Austin Public Library.

18. Cunningham to C.B. Metcalfe, Jan. 28, 1918, box 14, folder 213, Cunningham Papers.

19. Metcalfe to Cunningham, Feb. 10, 1918, ibid.

20. Cunningham to Metcalfe, Feb. 13, 1918, ibid.

21. Metcalfe to Cunningham, Feb. 18, 13, 1918, ibid.

22. McCallum, "Activities of Women in Texas Politics," 481.

23. Texas Legislature, *House Journal*, 35th Leg., 4th Called Sess., (Austin, 1918), 264, 328-36. Final vote appears in *Senate Journal*, 355. Only the previous summer sentiment against suffrage had been so strong that Cunningham had not dared to attempt a second try at bringing a primary suffrage bill to a vote before the third special session ended. See Cunningham to Hortense Ward, Sept. 5, 1917, box 13, folder 193, Cunningham Papers.

24. The primary suffrage bill was only one of several election law changes passed during the special session in an attempt to keep Ferguson ·from winning. See Robert Maxwell, "Texas in the Progressive Era," in *Texas: A Sesquicentennial Celebration* (Austin, 1984), 191-92; Gould, *Progressives and Prohibitionists*, 234; and *Austin American*, March 19, 24, 1918.

25. *Austin American*, March 21, 1918 (quotation); Cunningham to Catt, March 25, 1918, box 1, folder 9, Cunningham Papers; *Houston Post*, March 21, 1918; *Farm and Ranch*, April 6, 1918.

26. Alwyn Barr, *Black Texans: A History of Negroes in Texas, 1528-1971* (Austin, 1981), 79-80; *Houston Post*, April 11, 1915, March 21, 1918.

27. Mrs. E. Sampson to Mrs. [Maud Wood] Park, June 1918; Belle C. Critchett to Edith Hinkle League, July 1, 1918; League to Ruth White, July 8, 1918, and White to League, July 12, 1918; Catt to League July 17, 1918; Cunningham to Sampson, Aug. 31, 1918. All in box 3, folder 4, McCallum Papers, (Part I).

28. Metcalfe to Cunningham, April 12, 1918, box 14, folder 213, Cunningham Papers; "Minutes of Special Meeting of Executive Board of the Leslie Woman Suffrage Commission, Inc., Held June 20, 1918," Mrs. Percy V. Pennybacker Papers, Center for American History, University of Texas at Austin; Carrie Chapman Catt to Minnie Fisher Cunningham, June 20, 1918, box 18, folder 5, McCallum Papers (Part II).

29. Debbie Mauldin Cottrell, *Pioneer Woman Educator: The Progressive Spirit of Annie Webb Blanton* (College Station, Tex., 1993), 53-55.

30. *Austin American, Dallas Morning News, Fort Worth Star-Telegram, Houston Post*, and *San Antonio Express*, June 26 through July 12, 1918,.

31. McCallum, "Activities of Women in Texas Politics," 482; Cunningham to T.N. Jones, July 13, 1918, box 3, folder 4, McCallum Papers (Part I).

32. *Dallas Morning News*, July 27, 1918, July 19, 1918.

33. Humphrey, ed., *A Texas Suffragist*, 18, "To the Women of Texas," campaign flyer, box 19, folder 279, Cunningham Papers.

34. *Home and State*, June 1, 1918; "Vote for HOBBY for Governor," box 15, folder 234, Cunningham Papers.

35. *Austin American*, May 30, 1918.

36. "Extract from speech by James E. Ferguson, at City Auditorium, Houston, Texas, May 22, 1918—stenographic report by J.A. Lord," typescript, box 15, folder 227, Cunningham Papers; *Ferguson Forum*, March 28, April 25, 1918; July 11, 1918, June 20, 1918.

37. *Dallas Morning News*, June 27, 1918, July 19, 1918; *Ferguson Forum*, April 18, 1918, May 21, 1918.

38. M.M. Crane to Hobby, Feb. 2, 1918, box 3N98, folder 4, Martin McNulty Crane Papers, Center for American History, University of Texas at Austin; Thomas B. Love to Hobby, Jan. 26, 1918, Love Papers; *Dallas Morning News*, July 3, 1918, June 30, 1918.

39. R.M. Dudley to Cunningham, July 31, 1918, box 14, folder 206, Cunningham Papers; Seth Shepard McKay, *Texas Politics, 1906-1944* (Lubbock, Tex., 1952), 82; Cottrell, *Pioneer Woman Educator*, 61; Blanton to Anna Pennybacker, Aug. 9, 1918, Pennybacker Papers; M.M. Crane to Walter Crawford, July 12, 1918, box 3N98, Crane Papers; *Ferguson Forum*, July 18, Aug. 1, 1918; McArthur, "Motherhood and Reform in the New South," 554-556; Hobby received 461,479 votes to Ferguson's 217,012. Ferguson carried only 22 counties of 245, including 6 of the 9 "German" counties in the central part of the state.

40. *Houston Post*, July 4, 9, 12, 13, 29 (quotation), 1918. In Harris County black women were allowed to register at a separate table in the courthouse after the NAACP filed a protest. *The Houston Post*, on July 13, 1918, reported a final total of 14,400 white and 1,200 Negro women who registered. The 1920 census recorded 25,528 Negroes age 21 and over in the county; 1,200 is less than ten percent of the female half. Newspaper reports indicate in Texas black women were permitted to register in some counties, turned away in others, and in still others permitted to register but told that they would not be allowed to vote.

41. "Spanning the Old to the New South," *Texas Observer*, Nov. 21, 1958 (Cunningham quotations).

42. McCallum, "Activities of Women in Texas Politics," 206; Gould, *Progressives and Prohibitionists*, 170-73; Aileen S. Kraditor, "Tactical Problems of the Woman Suffrage Movement in the South," *Louisiana Studies*, 4 (Winter 1966): 295, 300 (quotations).

43. Cunningham to Jane Y. McCallum, April 5 [ca. 1939], box 7, folder 3, McCallum Papers (Part I).

Members of the Southern Women's League for the Rejection of the Susan B. Anthony Amendment, August 1920. Tennessee State Library

Eighteen

Armageddon in Tennessee:

The Final Battle Over the Nineteenth Amendment

Anastatia Sims

Editor's Introduction: In 1917, with the adoption of a suffrage amendment by the influential state of New York, the suffrage bandwagon seemed to be gaining momentum. As the list of "suffrage states" grew and the numbers of Congressmen accountable to women voters rose, the prospects for passage of the federal suffrage amendment brightened. In 1918 President Wilson finally endorsed the measure and urged Democrats on Capitol Hill to give it their support. To the great delight of the suffragists, the House of Representatives approved the amendment in January 1918. But, despite a personal plea from Wilson, the Senate failed to give it the two-thirds vote required for adoption. Before Congress met again, the National American Woman Suffrage Association and the National Woman's Party—joined by national political leaders well aware of the electoral votes now controlled by suffrage states—sought desperately to gain the two votes yet needed for Senate approval. In May of 1919, the House of Representatives again overwhelmingly approved the amendment, and this time the Senate concurred. On June 4, 1919, the Congress of the United States finally approved the woman suffrage amendment.

Even as they celebrated, however, suffragists were all too aware of the challenge that remained: getting three-fourths of the states (thirty-six) to ratify the amendment. The task did indeed prove to be difficult, and seemed to grow more difficult as it neared completion. As historian Anastatia Sims tells us in this dramatic and colorful essay, the battle for the thirty-sixth state was a virtual "Armageddon," in which suffragists fought opponents whose determination and willingness to resort to any means necessary to defeat the amendment astounded even seasoned veterans of the suffrage movement including Carrie Chapman Catt.

By mid-June 1920, a year after Congress had sent the amendment to the states for approval, thirty-five states had ratified. Needing only one more state, suffragists were extremely frustrated when Delaware unexpectedly defeated the amendment—the only state north of the Mason-Dixon line to do so—and no other state was slated to hold a legislative session before the November 1920 presidential election. Polls of the Republican-dominated legislatures in Connecticut and Vermont indicated that they would ratify if called into special session, but the anti-suffrage, anti-Prohibition governors of the two states refused to do so—despite frantic efforts by local and national suffragists to persuade them. Woodrow Wilson was able to convince Democratic governors in North Carolina and Tennessee to call special sessions, but North Carolina legislators defeated the amendment—and urged Tennessee to follow their example. Wilson exhorted these predominantly Democratic legislatures to ratify for the sake of the national Democratic Party, but North Carolina anti-suffrage legislators declared that "they were not going to sacrifice their honor upon the fickle altar of supposed political expediency" and urged their counterparts in Tennessee to "fight to the last ditch, and then some." The Tennessee anti-suffragists did exactly that.

As both sides mobilized for the fight, writes Sims, suffragists had reason to be encouraged. In keeping with Catt's "Winning Plan," Tennessee suffragists had persuaded these legislators to enact presidential and municipal suffrage for women in 1919, and many powerful political leaders, businessmen, and newspaper editors were pro-suffrage. However, as Catt warned, the anti-suffragists would spare no tactic or expense to dissuade legislators from supporting the amendment.

Anti-suffragists made use of anti-feminist arguments now nauseatingly familiar to the suffragists, including the idea that woman suffrage would ruin women and destroy the home. And familiar corporate opponents—particularly the liquor industry—were clearly operating in Tennessee. Sims describes the liquor industry, allied with the railroads and the cotton textile industry, as playing a leading role in the struggle.

That this final battle took place in the South clearly added to the difficulties of the suffragists, as anti-suffragists used race and states' rights arguments lavishly to arouse public sentiment against the amendment. Since the 1890s, southern suffragists had struggled against anti-suffragists who denounced the suffrage movement as anathema to southern values including white supremacy, state sovereignty, and reverence for traditional womanhood, and the antis now presented the fight over ratification as a battle to save "Southern Civilization." Earlier in the year, when Mississippi rejected the amendment, the Jackson *Clarion-Ledger* proclaimed (inaccurately) that "the vile old thing is as dead as its author [Susan B. Anthony], the old advocate of social equality and intermarriage of the races, and Mississippi will never be annoyed with it again." The leader of the Tennessee Division of the Southern Women's League for the Rejection of the Susan B. Anthony Amendment, Josephine Pearson, declared to her followers that Tennessee "could not fail in this most crucial test of Southern rights and honor, when Tennessee became the pivotal battle-ground of the Nation!" Ironically, two southern suffragists and former NAWSA officers, Laura Clay and Kate Gordon, agreeing that the federal amendment was a threat to states' rights, actually came to Nashville and lobbied against ratification—though Clay hated being associated with the antis.

Leaders from both sides of the suffrage battle flocked to the state to assist their allies in Tennessee. Anti-suffrage leaders including Anne Pleasant, the wife of the Louisiana governor who had attempted to unite the South against the amendment, was there, for example, as was Charlotte Rowe of the National Association Opposed to Woman Suffrage. From the NAWSA, Marjorie Shuler, and finally President Carrie Chapman Catt herself, came to Nashville to assist Tennessee suffrage leaders, including Nashville socialite and former NAWSA Vice President Anne Dallas Dudley who had played a leading role in the NAWSA's lobbying of Congress. Alice Paul of the NWP did not come, but lobbied actively from a distance and dispatched capable assistants to the state. This was a wise decision: leading Tennessee Democrats greatly resented the NWP's campaign against their party and the picketing of President Wilson, and NWP orators on a 1917 speaking tour in the state had difficulty even obtaining a lecture hall. However, Paul was well represented by Sue Shelton White, formerly editor of the NWP's national organ *The Suffragist* and chair of the NWP in Tennessee, who worked well with all suffrage factions.

As the long, hot, summer progressed, suffragists struggled to retain their supporters and win new ones, but the anti-suffragists nearly succeeded in their dogged and unscrupulous fight to block ratification. It is amazing but true, as Sims explains, that after the seventy-two-year-long struggle for woman suffrage, the outcome was determined by an elderly mother in the Tennessee mountains who instructed her son (from an anti-suffrage district) to vote for woman suffrage if it became necessary. May her name live in the annals of the movement: Febb King Ensminger Burn, mother of twenty-four-year-old Harry Burn who did indeed cast the deciding vote.

The anti-suffragists believed that, had they been able to prevent ratification of the suffrage amendment until after the November 1920 national elections, this "fad" that Wilson had promoted as a war measure would lose momentum and they might be able to block it permanently. They may have been right. As Catt and Shuler reported in *Woman Suffrage and Politics,* there was only one other ratification between that of Tennessee and the November election: in September, the Connecticut legislature was called into session to make provisions for registering women and took the occasion to ratify the Nineteenth Amendment—against the instructions of their anti-suffrage governor. This put the Nineteenth Amendment on firmer ground—since, as Sims describes below, anti-suffragists were *still* contesting the validity of Tennessee's ratification. However, the Connecticut legislature would not have had the *opportunity* to ratify had it not been for Tennessee's action. Without Tennessee's ratification, it is possible that in the conservative climate of the 1920s, the amendment would have failed—a scenario that seems more plausible after the failure of the Equal Rights Amendment in more recent times.

Suffragists, however, celebrated August 26, 1920, the day Tennessee's ratification reached Washington and was signed by the Secretary of State, as the day of their great victory. As the news spread, bells rang and whistles blew, and politicians of many stamps offered congratulations and attempted to take credit for enfranchising women. Carrie Chapman Catt returned to Washington to a giant victory celebration, and went on to New York for another. Alice Paul sewed the last star—the thirty-sixth—on a suffrage banner and hung it from the balcony of the NWP headquarters in Washington. In Seneca Falls a flag was draped over the tablet that marked the site where it had all begun.

★　★　★　★　★

I N JUNE 1919 Congress passed the Nineteenth Amendment and sent it on to the states.... By the summer of 1920 thirty-five states had ratified it. If suffragists could win the approval of just one more state, they would, at long last, achieve their goal. When the Delaware legislature unexpectedly defeated the amendment in early June, women pinned their hopes on Tennessee. During a steamy southern summer, Nashville, the "Athens of the South," became the site of one of the most fiercely fought contests in American political history. For the amendment's friends and foes alike it was Armageddon—the final battle in the long, bitter struggle that had, in the words of one observer, pitted "powers that pray" against "powers that prey."[1]

Suffragists were by no means certain of victory. Tennessee, like the rest of the South, had a history of hostility toward women's rights. In 1908, for example, Governor Malcolm R. Patterson offered this comment on woman suffrage: "Let the women pray and the men vote."[2] Twelve years later many Tennesseans—male and female alike—still agreed with the governor. Woman's place was at home, in church, in the schoolroom or even in the factory—but not at the polls.

At the same time, there appeared to be reasons for cautious optimism. In 1919, just two months before Congress submitted the Nineteenth Amendment to the states, the Tennessee General Assembly had passed a law giving women the right to vote in presidential and municipal elections, and the same men would consider the amendment. The state Democratic party had endorsed woman suffrage, and so had most of the state's major newspapers.

As suffragists knew from past experience, however, appearances could be deceiving, and close examination revealed a grim picture in Tennessee. The first obstacle was a section of the state constitution that prohibited ratification by a legislature elected before Congress submitted an amendment to the states. (Members of the current legislature had been elected in 1918.) When the United States Supreme Court handed down a decision that nullified that provision, suffragists immediately began clamoring for a special session. Sue Shelton White, chair of the National Woman's Party (NWP) in Tennessee, requested the session in a letter to Governor Albert H. Roberts on June 19. Two days later, Catherine Talty Kenny and Kate Burch Warner of the Tennessee Equal Suffrage Association (an affiliate of the National American Woman Suffrage Association) led a delegation of women who urged the governor to call the session in time for women to vote in the state primaries August 5. At the request of the Tennessee League of Women Voters and the NAWSA, pro-suffrage politicians from Tennessee and elsewhere wrote the governor. The United States attorney general, the state attorney general and other prominent jurists assured Roberts that such a session would be legal. Even President Woodrow Wilson bowed to the suffragists' pleas, and telegraphed his support.[3]

But the governor stalled. During his campaign two years earlier Roberts had spoken out against woman suffrage. According to Catherine Kenny, he had signed the presidential and municipal suffrage bill only because he believed it was unconstitutional. Subsequently, he had blocked women's attempts to expand their political power further when he refused to call a special session to give women the right to vote in party primaries.[4]

Roberts had good reason to want to keep women out of politics. There were persistent rumors that his highly paid private secretary, who had been working for him on the state payroll since 1915, was a woman of questionable reputation. He was firmly allied with the "wet" [anti-prohibition] wing of the Democratic Party, and his advisers were hostile to votes for women. As a candidate, he was unlikely to appeal to women voters.[5]

And it was his appeal as a candidate that was foremost in A.H. Roberts's mind in the summer of 1920. He was embroiled in a bitter fight for renomination. He confronted challengers within his own party, as well as strong Republican opposition. His tax reform program had alienated farmers, while his support for management during the strikes of 1919 turned industrial workers against him. Opponents accused him of raising taxes and increasing the state's debt.[6]

With his political career hanging in the balance, Governor Roberts faced a seemingly impossible choice. If he endorsed woman suffrage, perhaps women would forgive his other transgressions, and maybe their support would offset disillusioned farmers and workers. On the other hand, if women voted (as suffragists predicted they would) on moral issues alone, he might be ensuring his own defeat. Whatever women did, Roberts was under increasing pressure from his own party. Democratic leaders at the national level, including President Wilson himself, were staking the party's honor (and chances for victory in the November elections) on their ability to ratify the Nineteenth Amendment and enfranchise women who, they presumed, would then express their gratitude by voting the Democratic ticket. Uncertain of his own chances for reelection, Roberts could not afford to repudiate the national platform. Within Tennessee, however, he drew his support from men likely to oppose votes for women. If he followed Wilson's lead, he risked offending some of his staunchest friends. Finally, however, the governor capitulated. On June 25 he announced that he would convene the legislature later in the summer—*after* the Democratic primary August 5.

The Battle Begins

The governor's announcement set off one of the most heated political fights ever witnessed in Tennessee, a state hardly known for political tranquility. Professor Edwin Mims observed that "The Battle of Nashville in 1864 was a five o'clock tea in comparison with this one." Writing fifty years after the fact, journalist Joe Hatcher described the special session as "the bitterest, bare-fisted, name-calling, back-biting session in the state's history." The stakes were high, and both sides were hard at work long before the session opened.[7]

Suffragists initiated their campaign by recruiting a Men's Ratification Committee composed of some of the most prominent men in the state. With former governor Tom Rye as chair, the committee included newspaper publishers (George Fort Milton of the *Chattanooga News,* Edward B. Stahlman of the *Nashville Banner* and Luke Lea of the *Nashville Tennessean*), politicians (speaker of the Tennessee house Seth Walker, Memphis political boss Edward H. Crump, United States Senator Kenneth D. McKellar, former Republican Governor Ben Hooper, and Republican gubernatorial candidate Alfred A. Taylor) and businessmen (Guilford Dudley, among others). It was an eclectic coalition, representing diverse political factions and economic interests. Such strange bedfellows were unlikely to rest easily together. Before the end of the summer, some of the men who had allowed themselves to be named to the Ratification Committee had joined the opposition, and the committee itself played only a limited role in the campaign.[8]

Suffragists expected that in Tennessee, as elsewhere, they would lead the fight to win votes for women. Accordingly Abby Crawford Milton, president of the Tennessee League of Women Voters, appointed a Women's Ratification Committee, with Catherine Kenny as chair. To their dismay, Governor Roberts decided to form his own Women's Ratification Committee. He named as its head Kate Warner, "a lady of culture and refinement," and a lady who, unlike Milton and Kenny, was firmly aligned with the Roberts camp.[9] Abby Milton's husband edited the *Chattanooga News,* which had endorsed Roberts's rival for the Democratic gubernatorial nomination. Catherine Kenny was a friend of Luke Lea, publisher of the anti-Roberts, pro-suffrage *Nashville Tennessean,* and arch-rival of Major Edward B. Stahlman, one of Roberts's strongest supporters. Factionalism was the keynote of Tennessee politics; factionalism had earlier torn apart the suffrage movement in Tennessee. "You know we Tennesseans and Kentuckians are rather strong on 'feuds,'" Catherine Kenny wrote the NAWSA president Carrie Chapman Catt. "Sorter [sic] drunk it in with our mother's milk." Now factionalism jeopardized the ratification of the Nineteenth Amendment. "I don't believe there's a ghost of a chance of ratification in either Tennessee or North Carolina," Catt told Nashville suffragist Anne Dallas Dudley on July 12. "Tennessee has always been torn by factions in all men's and women's work, and it was these factions which defeated us in Delaware."[10]

The existence of two "official" women's ratification committees implied that there was disagreement among the suffragists themselves (and, in fact, the two groups were not always in harmony). Suffrage leaders recognized that the appearance of disunity could seriously damage their cause. The NAWSA's representative in Nashville, Marjorie Shuler, negotiated a compromise, persuading

Governor Roberts, the League of Women Voters, and the NAWSA to recognize both committees. Through letters, telegrams, and telephone calls Shuler kept in close touch with Carrie Chapman Catt in New York. In mid-July, Catt decided the situation required her personal attention. She arrived in Nashville on July 17, expecting to stay only a few days. Instead, she remained more than a month.[11]

Upon her arrival Catt told reporters, "I have no definite plan of action for my stay in Nashville." At least one reporter knew better. After describing her "pleasing personality," "kindly but animated face," and "soft, musical voice," he added, "yet there is about her expression something that strongly suggests that she can be firm when the occasion requires, and, if need be, aggressive."[12] Catt had worked for suffrage for thirty years. She was an intelligent woman, and a shrewd politician. She came to Tennessee determined to win the final victory.

Catt had been coordinating the campaign from New York long before she set foot in Nashville. In June she instructed Tennessee suffragists to begin polling the legislators to determine how they would vote on the amendment. They should not rely on hearsay, she warned; they should accept only the word of "bona fide" suffrage workers. She urged volunteers to get firm commitments, but cautioned them that these might not be binding. At the same time the women undertook to poll the legislators, they conducted another survey to find out which lawmakers might be susceptible to bribes. Catt was a seasoned politician, with few illusions about the political process. "[N]o matter how well the women may work or how effective their results may be," she wrote Catherine Kenny, "ratification in Tennessee will go through the work and actions of men, and the great motive that will finally put it through will be political and nothing else. We have long since recovered from our previous faith in the action of men based upon a love of justice. That is an animal that doesn't exist."[13]

The Anti-suffragists

While suffragists organized, their opponents also went into action. On the same day that Carrie Chapman Catt arrived in Nashville, Josephine Anderson Pearson, an educator from east Tennessee who had been tapped to lead the fight against suffrage in 1917, was entertaining guests in her mountain home when she received a telegram summoning her to Nashville to fight the *"invasion by foreign forces."* She caught the train to the capital city that afternoon. That night she checked into the cheapest room available at the Hermitage Hotel, and reserved assembly rooms on the mezzanine and the first floor for the Tennessee branch of the Southern Women's Rejection League (full name: Southern Women's League for the Rejection of the Susan B. Anthony Amendment). For the next six weeks the Hermitage Hotel would be her home, and anti-suffrage headquarters.[14]

Although the anti-suffragists (or antis) criticized suffragists for bringing in "foreign forces" they did not hesitate to call in their own reinforcements. Mrs.

*NWP lobbyists with U.S.
Senator Jones.
Mrs. William (Elizabeth)
Kent (left), Mrs. Richard
(Clara) Wainwright,
Maud Younger, and Mrs.
Abby Scott Baker.*
National Woman's
Party Corporation

James Pinckard of Alabama, Mrs. Ruffin Pleasant of Louisiana, and Miss Charlotte Rowe of New York were among the women who came to Nashville to fight the Nineteenth Amendment. These women were not really outsiders, Josephine Pearson declared, because "Tennessee considers no influence as 'outside' that is southern, or invited to this state by united southern sentiment for the preservation of our state constitution and white civilization."[15] Like the suffragists, female anti-suffragists recognized that this confrontation was crucial, and, like the suffragists, they believed they acted for the good of women and of society.

"A few women representatives of the National Association Opposed to Woman Suffrage are in Nashville," Marjorie Shuler reported in early August, "but far more deadly is the corps of men who have quietly stolen into the state and whose work is evident in the wavering of certain legislators and in the organization of a Tennessee Constitutional League." The League, a subsidiary of the American Constitutional League and the anti-suffrage counterpart to the Men's Ratification Committee, was dedicated to the defeat of the Susan B. Anthony Amendment. It included "prominent lawyers and business men," men who would use their wealth and influence in their attempt to block ratification in Tennessee.[16]

Suffragists faced formidable adversaries. They believed that "sinister forces" were working against them, and they set out to discredit their opponents. In late July, Carrie Chapman Catt and Abby Crawford Milton embarked on a statewide speaking tour, to convince the public that the "whiskey lobby, manufacturers' lobby, and the railroad lobby" were united against "the women of Tennessee."[17] After the fight was over, Catt declared: "Never in the history of politics has there been such a nefarious lobby as labored to block ratification in Nashville." Other participants and observers agreed with Catt's assessment. George Fort Milton described the antis as "insidious," and "a well-organized

Anti-suffragists strategize against passage of the Nineteenth Amendment in the final days, Hermitage Hotel, Nashville, Tennessee, 1920.
Tennessee State Library

and unscrupulous opposition." The *Christian Science Monitor* compared the anti lobbyists to "a horde of locusts," and characterized the battle over ratification as "justice against vested influence." Writing four months after the suffragists had won, Abby Crawford Milton insisted that the devil himself had been at work in Tennessee in the summer of 1920, collaborating with the antis to keep the ballot from women.[18]

"Nefarious." "Insidious." "Unscrupulous." These are strong words, even when hurled in the wake of a feverish political contest. Were the suffragists prone to hyperbole, or were their accusations on target? Certainly by 1920 the suffragists were skilled publicists for their own cause, and they recognized the advantages of portraying themselves as defenseless women fighting ruthless political machines and heartless corporate giants. The portrait was an effective piece of public relations. It was also rooted in fact. Across the nation distillers, brewers, and manufacturers (particularly those who employed large numbers of women and children) subsidized campaigns against state suffrage referenda and against the federal woman suffrage amendment, although they worked, for the most part, in secrecy. A Senate investigation of the United States Brewers' Association in 1918 revealed that that organization had actively tried to defeat woman suffrage in several states.[19] In some states textile manufacturers joined with liquor interests. Walter Clark, Chief Justice of the North Carolina Supreme Court, believed that "the Whiskey Interests and the Cotton Mill owners of the South" underwrote anti-suffrage campaigns. Clark was one of the South's leading Progressive reformers, but his son, David, edited the *Southern Textile Bulletin,* mouthpiece of the region's cotton industry.[20]

These forces had been evident on the political scene in Tennessee for years, and it is likely that they were in Nashville in the summer of 1920. Prohibition had been the central issue of Tennessee politics during the first fifteen years of the twentieth century, and distillers and brewers had mobilized to protect their businesses. The Manufacturers' Association was also active politically, opposing bills to regulate child labor, set minimum wages, and establish employers' responsibility for workers' safety on the job. Finally, the Louisville and Nashville Railroad (L&N) had been involved in Tennessee politics since the 1880s. The L&N's generosity in distributing free passes to legislators in 1913 (while the General Assembly was considering a railroad bill) led to an Interstate Commerce Committee investigation in 1916. Woman suffrage—with its promise to deliver women's votes for the enforcement of Prohibition, regulation of child labor, and reforms to end political corruption—threatened vital interests of all three of these powerful lobbies.[21]

Suffragists charged that these groups "paid the bills" for the antis in 1920. There is no concrete evidence to confirm or refute their accusations. We do know that some of the men who led the fight against the Nineteenth Amendment in Tennessee were affiliated with the businesses that had opposed woman suffrage elsewhere. For example, John Vertrees, one of the best-known opponents of suffrage, was also associated with the liquor industry. Although he denied being part of the "whiskey ring," he represented at least one executive of George A. Dickel and Company in both personal and business matters, and was closely identified with liquor interests.[22] Garnett Andrews, one of the founding members of the Tennessee Constitutional League, was involved with several knitting and hosiery mills, and, according to John Trotwood Moore, was "one of the most prominent representatives of the knitting industry in the South."[23] Mr. and Mrs. George A. Washington both participated in the fight against woman suffrage; Mr. Washington was a director of the L&N.[24]

Finally there was Edward Bushrod Stahlman, "the Major," publisher of the *Nashville Banner* and one of the most colorful (and powerful) figures in Tennessee politics. Stahlman had come to the United States from Germany before the Civil War. He got a job with the L&N in 1863, and worked his way up to a vice presidency. In 1884 he led a successful attempt to abolish the state railroad commission, established only two years earlier. During that debate Stahlman not only presented the L&N's case to the General Assembly, he also attempted to curry favor with Nashville newspapers. His attempts failed. By the time the fight was over, all the papers in the capital city were hostile to the railroad, a situation that could weaken the L&N in future legislative contests. In 1885, Stahlman bought the Banner. He left the L&N in 1890 to become commissioner of the Southern Railway and Steamship Association, a post he held until 1895. After that he devoted his attention to his family, the *Banner,* and Tennessee politics.[25] Although he officially severed his ties with the railroad industry, his critics (notably Luke Lea) suspected that he continued to represent the L&N's interests in Nashville. In 1914 Lea's *Nashville Tennessean* ran an editorial cartoon with the following caption: "Tennessee is governed by [Republican Governor Ben] Hooper; Hooper is manipulated by Stahlman; Stahlman is dominated by L&N; find the real ruler of Tennessee."[26] Stahlman dismissed Lea's accusation as "a malicious lie"; nevertheless, some Tennesseans continued to regard the *Banner* publisher as an agent of the L&N. In the summer of 1920, Stahlman waffled on woman suffrage. After being named to the Men's Ratification Committee, he changed his mind, and, through the pages of the *Banner* as well as in public addresses, became an outspoken opponent of votes for women.[27]

...[T]he...influential men who fought the Nineteenth Amendment may have acted from conviction instead of (or in addition to) self-interest. Many antis sincerely believed that women had no business in politics, and that enfranchising them would only create problems. But connections between prominent antis and liquor, textile, and railroad companies convinced the suffragists that these men represented larger interests. Events like Stahlman's change of heart and what Marjorie Shuler described as "the wavering of certain legislators" persuaded the women that their enemies were employing underhanded tactics. As the special session drew near, more and more lawmakers who had pledged themselves to suffrage switched sides. Two days before the legislature was to meet, suffragists lost one of their most valuable allies, Seth Walker, Speaker of the House of Representatives. Just a week earlier, a newspaper had announced that Walker was firmly committed to ratification. He had even promised to introduce the resolution. His defection, according to *The Suffragist*, official journal of the NWP, was a "sure indication of the strength of the opposition forces at work."[28] Support for the amendment eroded steadily. By the time the session opened, suffragists who earlier in the summer had been confident of victory were worried. "All that we can say at this writing," reported the NAWSA's *Woman Citizen*, "is that the signs are favorable, but that the opposition is massed as it was never massed before." Before the final vote on the amendment, every single legislator who the suffragists had identified as bribable moved from the pro column to the anti list.[29]

The Battle Intensifies

At the same time that both sides worked behind the scenes to influence lawmakers, they also waged massive publicity campaigns to sway public opinion. Anti-suffragists took the offensive with assertions that representatives and senators who voted for the amendment would violate their oath of office. Attempting to circumvent the Supreme Court decision, they maintained that legislators pledged to uphold the state constitution as it was written, not as it was interpreted by the United States Supreme Court. Suffragists countered with numerous opinions from legal authorities within Tennessee and throughout the United States.[30]

Anti-suffragists also relied on arguments that had been used ever since the idea of woman suffrage was introduced in 1848. They predicted that female enfranchisement would result in nothing less than the end of civilization. It would destroy the home and the family. Wives would divorce their husbands when they disagreed about politics. Mothers, preoccupied with their new status as voters, would neglect their children. Women would become "masculinized" and men "feminized." One anti-suffrage leaflet warned men: "A Vote for Federal Suffrage is a Vote for Organized Female Nagging Forever."[31]

Suffragists quickly responded to the anti attack. They affirmed their loyalty to domesticity and motherhood. A widely circulated photograph showed Anne Dallas Dudley, a Tennessee suffrage activist with an impeccable pedigree, reading to her children. Suffragists argued that circumstances of modern life required housewives to get involved in politics, because politics affected family life. The vote would not make women forsake their home duties, suffragists insisted. Instead, it would enable them to fulfill their domestic obligations more effectively.[32]

At the beginning of the campaign, Carrie Chapman Catt warned Tennessee suffragists that "The anti suffragists will flood Tennessee with the most outrageous literature it has ever been your lot to read.... It will be extremely harmful, and the 'nigger question' will be put forth in ways to arouse the greatest possible prejudice."[33] Catt was right. For many southern opponents of suffrage, the central issue in 1920 was race. Josephine Pearson identified "three deadly principles" in the Nineteenth Amendment: "1st, surrender of state sovereignty. 2nd, Negro woman suffrage. 3rd, Race equality."[34] A leaflet addressed to the "Men of the South" reminded voters of the similarity between the Fifteenth and Nineteenth Amendments, and predicted that ratification would lead to "another period of Reconstruction horrors," when African American men and "female carpetbaggers" would rule. Anti leaders informed white southerners that Congress had three "force bills" ready for consideration, bills similar to those used during Reconstruction.[35] A broadside entitled "Woman Suffrage, A Menace to the South" warned that the Nineteenth Amendment would destroy state sovereignty and increase the number of African American voters in the South because it would enable black women to vote.[36] Anti-suffrage propaganda quoted feminists and African American leaders who favored social equality between blacks and whites, and concluded that woman suffrage would lead to interracial marriage. Again and again southern antis declared that woman suffrage would result in the downfall of white supremacy, which, they implied, would leave white southern women vulnerable to assaults by black men. According to Mrs. Ruffin Pleasant of Louisiana, "the passage of the Nineteenth Amendment would embolden both the negro [sic] woman and the negro man to give us even greater trouble than they are doing now."[37]

To counter the anti assault, suffragists pledged to uphold white supremacy, and argued that the same measures that disfranchised African American men would also disqualify African American women. Privately, some suffragists defended the contributions black women could make to politics. Because of the presidential and municipal suffrage bill enacted in 1919, African American women had already begun to vote in Tennessee. In January, 1920, Catherine Kenny told Carrie Chapman Catt that the record of black women voters in Nashville was "one of which every southern suffragist may not only feel proud but hopeful for the future." In July she repeated her endorsement: "[I]n every instance...they voted with the best white women thereby eliminating any political prejudice." After the ratification fight was over, Kenny wrote in the Tennessee chapter of the *History of Woman Suffrage* that African American woman suffrage "was anything but the 'bugaboo' politicians had tried to show it would be and in some instances it was a contributing factor to good government." In Tennessee, as in other southern states, black women had joined in the campaign for woman suffrage, working in segregated organizations.[38]

The special session was scheduled to open on Monday, August 9. Lawmakers began arriving in Nashville on Saturday, and they, along with suffragists and antis, converged on the Hermitage Hotel. There were others at the Hermitage, too, "mysterious men," whom the suffragists did not recognize, but who clearly had a stake in the outcome of the vote. Suffragists observed these unidentified men escorting legislators to a room on the eighth floor, a room where liquor flowed freely. By late in the evening, Carrie Chapman Catt recalled, "legislators, both suffrage and anti-suffrage men, were reeling through the hall in a state of advanced intoxication." Horrified suffragists asked officials to enforce the Prohibition laws. They were told that this was the "Tennessee way," and that "in Tennessee, whiskey and legislation go hand in hand."[39]

Armageddon: The Final Showdown

The legislature convened at noon on Monday, August 9. The Senate was solidly pro-suffrage. The ratification resolution was introduced on August 10, and referred to the committee on constitutional amendments the following day. On Friday, August 13, the committee recommended its adoption. "National woman's suffrage is at hand," the majority report stated; "it may be delayed but it cannot be defeated, and we covet for Tennessee the signal honor of being the thirty-sixth and last State necessary to consummate this great reform." That same day, the Senate passed the resolution by a vote of 25 to 4.[40]

With the question settled in the Senate, suffragists and their opponents focused their attention on the House. The antis immediately invoked a number of delaying tactics, and continued their efforts to win over lawmakers. Each side accused the other of foul play. Carrie Chapman Catt claimed that anti-suffrage men tapped phones, listened at transoms, and intercepted telegrams in order to anticipate the suffragists' plans. According to Catt, they used liquor, loans, bribes, promises of high office and "every other device which old hands at illicit politics could conceive or remember"[41] to get legislators to vote their way. On August 12 a newspaper reported that "Nashville looks like a real oasis in the dry desert. Moonshine corn whiskey is flowing freely."[42]

The suffragists, meanwhile, allegedly employed tactics that were more subtle but no less persuasive. "Automobile rides, hugs, kisses, even the absurdity of powdering the members' noses and rouging their cheeks in the assembly hall were frequently witnessed," *The Lookout* of Chattanooga told its readers. The suffragists were testing the boundaries of ladylike behavior with their aggressive tactics, the journal implied, and *The Lookout* clearly disapproved. According to *The Lookout's* vigilant observer, one suffragist—"a very pretty lady"—eager to convert a dubious legislator "grabbed his tie...and held him in a grip that one would suppose invincible." As the woman kept talking, the man pulled a knife out of his pocket, cut himself loose, and walked away, leaving the startled suffragist holding the remnants of his tie. "Just keep it," he remarked as he strolled away.[43]

In the House, as in the Senate, a ratification resolution had been introduced on August 10. But day after day passed; the House took no action. On August 17, the committee on constitutional convention and amendments issued a favorable report. Dismissing the arguments that ratification would be unconstitutional or a violation of the oath of office, the committee agreed with its Senate counterpart that it would be "an honor" for Tennessee to be the final state to ratify the amendment, "giving to our mothers, wives, daughters, sisters and sweethearts a precious right which they have so long been unjustly denied."[44]

The debate began. In an impassioned speech, Seth Walker urged his colleagues to vote against the ratification resolution on states' rights grounds. He also defended his reputation. He resented the charge that he had changed his mind on the issue because of pressure from "a certain railroad," he declared. But, as Marjorie Shuler noted, he "made no specific denial." Speaking for the suffragists, Joe Hanover of Memphis condemned the interference of antis from other states, and denounced the tactics of Tennessee's own anti-suffragists. "What is a greater crime," he demanded, "than for certain newspapers connected with the opposition to threaten you as they have been doing for the last ten days?" The debate continued for several hours, but the House adjourned without voting.[45]

That night was a long one for suffragists. They patrolled the corridors of the Hermitage Hotel and stationed sentries at the train station to prevent the untimely departure of any of the men still pledged to support them. They met in Carrie Chapman Catt's room for yet another strategy session. But this time even Catt had exhausted her political resources. "There is one more thing we can do—only one," she said. "We can pray."[46] After all the careful organization, the years of winning over public opinion, the arduous task of wooing legislators, the women were still left to pray while the men voted.

The galleries were packed when House Speaker Seth Walker called the session to order on August 18. The atmosphere was tense; both sides knew the vote was too close to call. An anti motion to table the ratification resolution ended in a tie.[47] It was a victory for suffragists, but the real test lay ahead.

"The hour has come!" Seth Walker shouted. The roll call began. There were two votes for, followed by four against. The seventh name on the list was Harry Burn. At twenty-four, he was the youngest man in the legislature, a Republican from McMinn County in east Tennessee. Suffrage polls listed him as undecided. He had voted with the antis on the motion to table. Although Burn had promised suffrage leaders he would vote with them if they needed his vote to ratify, suffragists feared he would continue to side with the antis. They knew that political leaders in his home district opposed the Nineteenth Amendment. But they did not know that in his pocket was a letter from his mother telling him to "be a good boy" and vote for ratification. When his name was called, Harry Burn voted yes.[48]

It took a few moments for the suffragists to absorb what had happened, but before the roll call was over they realized that Harry Burn had given them the last vote they needed. The antis realized it, too. As soon as the clerk announced the vote—49 to 47—Seth Walker changed his vote from no to aye, and introduced a motion to reconsider. (Under House rules, only a representative voting with the winning side could move to reconsider). That parliamentary maneuver did not diminish the suffragists' joy. "Emancipated at last!" some exclaimed. That night, Carrie Chapman Catt sent a telegram to North Carolina suffragist Gertrude Weil: "The thirty-sixth state is won."[49]

The story should have ended there, but it continued. For two days Walker refused to bring up the motion to reconsider, while he and the antis tried to round up enough votes to defeat the measure on the second vote. They sent telegrams to pro-suffrage representatives, reproaching them for their votes. Two legislators, T.O. Simpson and S.F. Stovall, complained that they "were called up every half hour day and night so that they had no sleep." Assemblyman Simpson received threats that he would lose his teaching job if he did not change sides. But the pro-suffrage majority held firm. Late on the night of August 20, thirty-eight anti-suffrage representatives fled to Decatur, Alabama, on an L&N train ("very suitably indeed in their choice of conveyance" was Marjorie Shuler's caustic comment). Members of the "Red Rose Brigade" (named after the anti-suffrage emblem, the red rose; suffragists adopted the yellow rose) hoped that their absence would break the quorum, and prevent further action on the amendment.[50]

Meanwhile, antis appealed to public opinion. On August 19, they held a mass meeting at Ryman Auditorium "to save the South." E.B. Stahlman was the featured speaker. Antis organized similar rallies throughout the state later in the month. Observers disagreed on the response to the meetings. "Indignation Spreads Over Whole State" declared a headline in the anti-suffrage *Chattanooga Daily Times,* while the pro-suffrage *Nashville Tennessean* reported "Little Interest Manifested in Mass Meetings."[51] Antis all over the nation condemned the Tennessee legislators who voted with the suffragists. Martin Lee Calhoun of Selma, Alabama, compared them to "assassins of the night who have stabbed the heart of the South and its traditions to the core."[52]

Antis directed much of their outrage at Harry Burn. Josephine Pearson labelled him a "traitor to manhood's honor," while anti newspapers reported that Joe Hanover paid him $10,000 to change his vote.[53] In response to the antis' attacks on his integrity, Burn inserted a personal statement in the House journal, explaining that he cast his vote for morality, justice, his mother, and the glory of the Republican party. Charges of bribery did not stick to Harry

Burn, but they persisted against the antis. In September, a grand jury investigated the activities of lobbyists during the campaign. It returned no indictments against either side.[54]

House custom gave the representative who introduced a motion to reconsider three days to bring the motion before the floor; after that, any member could call the question. Pro-suffrage legislators were determined to resolve the issue once and for all on August 21; if Walker did not call for a vote on his motion, they would. The legislature convened, with all the suffrage men in their places, and women occupying the desks of the absent members, sitting in silent protest against the retreat of the Red Rose Brigade. Fifty-eight members of the legislature were present that morning—forty-nine suffrage men and nine antis. T.K. Riddick, one of the amendment's strongest supporters, moved to reconsider the ratification resolution. Speaker Walker ruled him out of order. There was no quorum, he said. Besides, he announced, just that morning antis had won an injunction to prohibit the governor from certifying Tennessee's ratification. Riddick appealed the Speaker's decision to the members of the House. They voted 49 to 8 to overturn Walker's ruling (Walker abstained) then went on to table the motion to reconsider. Walker's procedural ploy had failed.[55]

On August 23, the Tennessee Supreme Court overturned the injunction against the governor. Governor Roberts signed the certificate of ratification on August 24 and sent it on to Washington. On the morning of August 26, Secretary of State Bainbridge Colby issued a proclamation declaring the Nineteenth Amendment ratified and part of the United States Constitution.[56]

Still the antis refused to surrender. When members of the Red Rose Brigade returned to the House August 31, they moved to expunge the activities of August 21 from the record. The motion carried, largely because pro-suffrage members refused to vote. "I consider that the Nineteenth Amendment has been legally adopted," one stated, "and that any other action by this House would be a farce." Having erased August 21 from history, anti legislators went on to reconsider the Nineteenth Amendment, and vote it down. Most pro-suffrage representatives were recorded as present and not voting.[57]

Anne Dallas Dudley found it highly amusing. "Tennessee enacted a little farce to add to the gayety [sic] of the nation today," she wired Carrie Chapman Catt. A day later she was not laughing. "Find out from Washington if action yesterday seriously injures our case," her next telegram read. "Lawyers here differ. Must know at once."[58] She had no reason to worry. Ratification was secure, despite Tennessee's attempt to rescind its approval, and despite Seth Walker's ongoing efforts to prevent the amendment from taking effect. In September, he and other antis went first to Washington, to persuade Secretary of State Colby that Tennessee's ratification was unconstitutional (the Secretary was not convinced) then on to Connecticut, where the legislature was considering ratification. There, as well, too few men heeded their pleas. Connecticut ratified in mid-September, and American women's right to vote was at last assured.[59]

Aftermath

The antis were no more gracious in defeat than they had been during the battle. Unable to stop woman suffrage, in the fall of 1920 they encouraged women voters to vote against the men who had enfranchised them. In Tennessee, they set their sights on Harry Burn and A.H. Roberts. Roberts was particularly vulnerable. Already unpopular because of his tax program and hostility to organized labor, he had alienated his political allies with his stand on suffrage. The special session of the General Assembly, after acceding to his request to ratify the Nineteenth Amendment by the narrowest of margins, proceeded to turn down every other proposal he submitted. E.B. Stahlman's *Nashville Banner,* which had supported him in the Democratic primary, now turned against him. The *Chattanooga Daily Times* even demanded that he be removed from the ticket.[60]

Suffragists rallied to the aid of their champions. Abby Crawford Milton traveled around the state, defending Burn and organizing women for Roberts. In Nashville, Catherine Kenny appealed to working women to support the governor. Still, suffragists recognized that Roberts's campaign was in serious trouble. In early October, a member of the women's committee of the state Democratic Party turned to Carrie Chapman Catt for help. "This is private and confidential and TNT," she began. "The Antis have concentrated their campaign against Governor Roberts and intend to defeat him at any cost." She pleaded with Catt to use her influence to raise money for the governor's campaign, and concluded: "If I knew anyway to make this appeal stronger I would do it. I shall feel forever disgraced if Roberts is repudiated. This is a woman's fight and we can't afford to lose."[61]

But they did lose. "Election Returns Prove Strength of Anti-Suffragists" proclaimed the *Woman Patriot,* official newspaper of the National Association Opposed to Woman Suffrage. Harry Burn won reelection, but A.H. Roberts went down to defeat, and Republican presidential candidate Warren G. Harding carried Tennessee. Female anti-suffragists—women who had not wanted the vote in the first place—now claimed that they had used the franchise to drive their enemies from office.[62] Democratic politicians blamed women for the defeat as well—black women, who, they said, had turned out in large numbers and voted Republican. The day after the election, Edward H. Crump of Memphis wrote: "I was never so certain in all my life as I was that with woman suffrage and no poll tax provision it would be harmful to the Democratic party in Tennessee."[63]

The outcome of the election troubled suffragists, and they, too, cast about for scapegoats. Catherine Kenny attributed Roberts's loss to labor, farmers, and the Democrats themselves. The state party made only feeble attempts to turn out white women's votes, she reported, while Republicans actively recruited black female voters. She conceded, too, that the governor was an unattractive candidate. "He was pathetic," she told Carrie Chapman Catt, and unable to overcome the scandals that had tainted his reputation.[64]

Woman suffrage undoubtedly played a crucial role in Roberts's loss. The large turnout of both men and women in Republican east Tennessee meant a strong anti-Democratic vote.[65] The governor's half-hearted support of suffrage, along with the rumors surrounding him and his secretary, alienated potential women voters. Most important, when he called the special session and endorsed ratification of the Nineteenth Amendment, he turned many of his own allies against him. Roberts was an unpopular incumbent facing a beloved Republican opponent. When powerful friends like E.B. Stahlman deserted him because of his stand on woman suffrage, Roberts's candidacy was doomed.

Suffragists had staked their honor on a Roberts victory, and his loss hurt them. In January 1921, Catherine Kenny forecast a cold political season for women voters. "I believe the effect of our successful fight here in Tennessee will be to nullify any real power or influence of the women in either party," she told Carrie Chapman Catt. The newly elected legislators—"about 70% [sic] new men, inexperienced, and not even up to the usual poor standard"—seemed uniformly hostile to any measures of interest to women. Antis continued their efforts to dilute women's political strength. They introduced a bill to abolish primaries. Since women had little influence within party organizations, if the proposal succeeded it would, in the words of Abby Crawford Milton, "about disfranchise the women of Tennessee." Although the General Assembly voted to retain the primary, women's political prospects remained bleak. "Just now in Sunny Tennessee, we are certainly 'dead ones,'" Kenny concluded.[66]

Woman suffrage had, for the moment, failed to live up to its promise. But Kenny, Milton, and other suffragists never abandoned their faith in their cause and, in spite of their disappointments, they continued to believe that the prize was worth the price. "I shall never be as thrilled by the turn of any event as I was at that moment when the roll call that settled the citizenship of American women was heard," Abby Crawford Milton declared. "It seemed too dramatic to happen in real life, with the real thrill of history making, not the excitement of the stage or movies. Personally, I had rather have had a share in the battle for woman suffrage than any other world event."[67] It was, indeed, an historic occasion. The women and men who secured the ratification of the Nineteenth Amendment acknowledged the truth of the message suffragists had been spreading since 1848: that women and men *were* equal, with the same rights, privileges, and responsibilities. In that hot Nashville August, suffragists faced their Armageddon and emerged victorious; "powers that pray" vanquished "powers that prey." They demonstrated once and for all that, when it came to politics, women were capable of far more than prayer, and they moved the nation one step closer to realizing its ideal of equality.

Notes

This essay is drawn from, "'Powers That Pray and Powers That Prey': Tennessee and the Fight for Woman Suffrage," *Tennessee Historical Quarterly* 50(4), 1991, and is reprinted with permission of the journal.

1. "Why?," newspaper clipping, *Nashville Tennessean*, Aug. 22, 1920, Harry T. Burn Scrapbook, Manuscripts Department, Special Collections, University of Tennessee Library, Knoxville; [For further information on the ratification struggle in Tennessee, including reprints of many of the pro- and anti-suffrage documents mentioned in this article, see Marjorie Spruill Wheeler, ed. *Votes for Women! The Woman Suffrage Movement in Tennessee, the South, and the Nation,* (Knoxville, 1995)].

2. Quoted in Wilma Dykeman, *Tennessee Women, Past and Present,* Narrative by Wilma Dykeman with selected additional material edited by Carol Lynn Yellin (Memphis, Nashville, 1977), 25.

3. Carrie Chapman Catt and Nettie Rogers Shuler, *Woman Suffrage and Politics: The Inner Story of the Suffrage Movement* (New York, 1923), 424-28; Sue Shelton White to Gov. Albert H. Roberts, June 19, 1920, box 26, folder 4, Albert H. Roberts Papers, Tennessee State Library and Archives, Nashville (hereafter cited as TSLA); "Special Session in Tennessee!" *The Suffragist* 8 (July 1920): 121-22; Catherine Talty Kenny to Rose Young, June 21, 1920, box 1, folder 13; Charles Evans Hughes to Mary Garrett Hay, June 25, 1920, box 1, folder 10; Catherine Kenny to Carrie Chapman Catt, July 11, 1920, box 1, folder 14, all in Carrie Chapman Catt Papers, TSLA; "What's The Matter With Tennessee?" *Woman Citizen* 5 (July 3, 1920): 125.

4. Catherine T. Kenny to Ida Husted Harper, Dec. 16, 1919, box 1, folder 13; Catherine T. Kenny to Carrie Chapman Catt, Jan. 5, 1920, box 1, folder 13; Catherine T. Kenny to Mrs. Shuler, June 28, 1920, box 1, folder 14; Catt Papers; Albert H. Roberts, March 11, 1920, box 36, folder 1, Roberts Papers.

5. Catherine T. Kenny to Mrs. Shuler, June 28, 1920; Sue Shelton White, "The Tennessee Campaign at Close Range," *The Suffragist* 8 (Aug. 1920): 164; Gary W. Reichard, "The Defeat of Governor Roberts," *Tennessee Historical Quarterly* 30 (1971): 94-110.

6. Reichard, "Defeat of Governor Roberts"; "How Leading Democratic Newspapers Size Up Gov. Roberts and His Administration," (Nashville, [1920]), pamphlet, TSLA. See also Kenneth S. Braden, "The Wizard of Overton: Governor A.H. Roberts," *Tennessee Historical Quarterly* 43 (1984): 273-94.

7. Edwin Mims, *The Advancing South: Stories of Progress and Reaction* (1926; reprint, Port Washington, N.Y., 1969), 238; Joe Hatcher, "1920: Amendment and a Perfect 36," *Nashville Tennessean,* March 26, 1972, Vertical File—Woman Suffrage, TSLA.

8. Taylor, *Woman Suffrage Movement in Tennessee,* 108 and 140 n.

9. Albert H. Roberts to Carrie Chapman Catt, July 10, 1920, box 1, folder 18, Catt Papers.

10. Catherine T. Kenny to Carrie Chapman Catt, July 11, 1920; Carrie Chapman Catt to Mrs. Guilford Dudley, July 12, 1920, box 1, folder 6, Catt Papers.

11. Catt and Shuler, *Woman Suffrage and Politics,* 432-33; Taylor, *Woman Suffrage Movement in Tennessee,* 109.

12. "Mrs. Carrie C. Catt Arrives in City," clipping, n.p., n.d., Vertical File—Woman Suffrage, TSLA.

13. Carrie Chapman Catt to Mrs. John M. [Catherine Talty] Kenny, June 29, 1920, box 1, folder 6, Catt Papers; Catt and Shuler, *Woman Suffrage and Politics,* 435-37; "Tennessee—The 36th," *The Suffragist* 9 (Sept. 1920): 199.

14. Josephine Anderson Pearson, "My Story!", 1, 19, box 1, folder 17, Josephine Anderson Pearson Papers, TSLA.

15. "Antis Gather New Strength," clipping, *Chattanooga Daily Times,* Aug. 9, 1920, box 2, folder 6, Catt Papers.

16. Marjorie Shuler, "Outside Influences Fight Suffrage in Tennessee," clipping, *Public Ledger,* Philadelphia, Pa., Aug. 8, 1920, box 2, folder 4; "Anti-suffrage Faction Busy," clipping, *Chattanooga Daily Times,* July 30, 1920, box 2, folder 5, both in Catt Papers.

17. Ida Husted Harper, ed., *History of Woman Suffrage,* (New York, 1922), vol. 6: 620; NAWSA, *VICTORY: How Women Won It: A Centennial Symposium, 1840-1940* (New York, 1940), 149.

18. *HWS* 6: 621 n.; G.F. Milton, "Editorial Correspondence," clipping, *Chattanooga News,* Aug. 19, 1920, Burn Scrapbook; "Winning the Vote in Tennessee," clipping, *Christian Science Monitor,* Sept. 4, 1920, Burn Scrapbook; Abby Crawford Milton to Carrie Chapman Catt, Jan. 13, 1921.

19. Catt and Shuler, *Woman Suffrage and Politics,* 135-38.

20. Walter Clark to Henry Watterson, April 12, 1919, in Aubrey Lee Brooks and Hugh Talmage Lefler, eds., *The Papers of Walter Clark* (Chapel Hill, 1950) 2: 396. See also David Morgan, *Suffragists and Democrats: The Politics of Woman Suffrage in America* (East Lansing, Mich., 1972), 157-77, and Jane Jerome Camhi, "Women Against Women: American Antisuffragism, 1880-1920," (Ph.D. diss., Tufts University, 1974), 183-94.

21. See Joe Michael Shahan, "Reform and Politics in Tennessee, 1906-1914," (Ph.D. diss., Vanderbilt University, 1981); Paul E. Isaac, *Prohibition and Politics: Turbulent Decades in Tennessee 1885-1920* (Knoxville, 1965); and Maury Klein, *History of the Louisville and Nashville Railroad* (New York, 1972), 368-94.

22. Paul E. Isaac, historian of the prohibition movement in Tennessee, identified Vertrees as "an attorney for liquor concerns"; see Isaac, *Prohibition and Politics,* 46.

23. John Trotwood Moore, *Tennessee: The Volunteer State 1769-1923* (Chicago, Nashville, 1923), 4: 650-51.

24. "Speaker Walker Lauded From Many States," *Woman Patriot* 4 (Aug. 28, 1920): 1.

25. Will T. Hale and Dixon C. Merritt, *A History of Tennessee and Tennesseans: The Leaders and Representative Men in Commerce, Industry and Modern Activities* (Chicago, New York, 1913) 5: 1401-02; Dumas Malone, ed., *Dictionary of American Biography* (New York, 1936) 9: 493-94; *National Cyclopedia of American Biography* (New York, 1898) 8: 224; Klein, *History of the Louisville and Nashville Railroad,* 376-78.

26. "The Power Behind the Throne," clipping, *Nashville Tennessean,* July 11, 1914, box 1, folder 3, Edwin A. Price Scrapbook, TSLA.

27. Clipping, *Nashville Banner,* July 11, 1914, box 1, folder 3, Price Scrapbook; Catt and Shuler, *Woman Suffrage and Politics,* 443.

28. Marjorie Shuler, "From the Tennessee Firing Line," *Woman Citizen* 5 (Aug. 28, 1920): 331; "Tennessee—The 36th," 200.

29. Quotation, "The Crisis," *Woman Citizen* 5 (Aug. 14, 1920): 277; Catt and Shuler, *Woman Suffrage and Politics,* 441, 446.

30. "Supreme Law of Tennessee Prohibits Ratification," broadside, box 1, folder 4; "Foster V. Brown, Champion of Suffrage, Declares That Ratification is Violation," broadside, box 1, folder 4; "The Federal Suffrage Amendment WILL NEVER BE RATIFIED If The People of Tennessee Guard Their Rights," broadside, box 1, folder 4; "Can The Present Legislature Act?" pamphlet, box 1, folder 5; Josephine A. Pearson to "Dear Sir or Madam," box 1, folder 7, all in Pearson Papers; "Vertrees Says There is No Excuse for Ratification," *Woman Patriot* 4 (Aug. 7,

1920): 1-2; Shuler, "Outside Influences Fight Suffrage in Tennessee"; "History of the Bitter Struggle to Ratify Suffrage," clipping, *Nashville Tennessean*, Aug. 29, 1920, Burn Scrapbook; Catherine T. Kenny to Carrie Chapman Catt, July 11, 1920; Catt and Shuler, *Woman Suffrage and Politics*, 434-36, 440; NAWSA, *VICTORY: How Women Won It*, 149.

31. "America When Feminized," broadside, box 1, folder 4, Pearson Papers. For other examples see broadsides in box 1, folder 4, and pamphlets in box 1, folder 3, Pearson Papers.

32. The photograph of Mrs. Dudley and her children is reprinted in John Egerton, *Nashville: The Faces of Two Centuries*, (Nashville, 1979), 184.

33. Carrie Chapman Catt to Mrs. John M. [Catherine T.] Kenny, June 29, 1920, box 1, folder 6, Catt Papers.

34. Josephine Pearson to "Dear [blank]," form letter, Aug. 9, 1920, box 1, folder 18, Pearson Papers.

35. "Beware!" broadside, box 1, folder 4. See also "That Deadly Parallel," "Can Anybody Terrorize Tennessee Manhood," and other leaflets and broadsides, folders 3, 4, and 5; "Three Federal Suffrage Force Bills in Congress," press release, May 15, 1920, *Woman Patriot*, all in Pearson Papers.

36. "Woman Suffrage, A Menace to the South. A Protest Against Its Imposition Through Federal Authority," pamphlet, box 1, folder 3, Pearson Papers.

37. Quotation from "Statement of Mrs. R.C. Pleasant, Leader of Anti-Federal Suffrage Ratification Forces of Louisiana," Burn Scrapbook.

38. Catherine T. Kenny to Carrie Chapman Catt, Jan. 5, 1920; Kenny to Catt, July 11, 1920; *HWS* 6: 606.

39. Catt and Shuler, *Woman Suffrage and Politics*, 442.

40. *House and Senate Journals of the Extraordinary Session of the Sixty-First General Assembly of the State of Tennessee*, (Nashville, 1920), 254, 263, 292-96; quotation, 293.

41. *HWS* 6: 621 n.; Catt and Shuler, *Woman Suffrage and Politics*, 445-46.

42. "Tennessee Likely To Vote Suffrage in Next Few Days," clipping, Aug. 12, 1920, n.p., box 2, folder 7, Catt Papers.

43. "The People Against the Politicians," *The Lookout: A Journal of Southern Society* 25 (Aug. 24, 1920): 1, box 1, folder 8, Pearson Papers. Carol Lynn Yellin identified the suffragist and the solon as Anne Dallas Dudley and Senator Lon McFarland; see Carol Lynn Yellin, "Countdown in Tennessee, 1920" *American Heritage* 30 (1978): 29-30.

44. *House Journal*, 33, 86-88; quotation, 87.

45. Quotations, Marjorie Shuler, "From the Tennessee Firing Line," 331. See also "Winning the Vote In Tennessee"; *House Journal*; 89; *HWS* 6: 623; Catt and Shuler, *Woman Suffrage and Politics*, 447.

46. Catt and Shuler, *Woman Suffrage and Politics*, 447.

47. *House Journal*, 91; Catt and Shuler, *Woman Suffrage and Politics*, 448-49.

48. Shuler, "From the Tennessee Firing Line," 331; Catt and Shuler, *Woman Suffrage and Politics*, 449; *HWS* 6: 623; "Suffrage Amendment Adopted By House," clipping, *Nashville Tennessean*, Aug. 19, 1920; G.F. Milton, "Burn Vote Was Influenced By His Mother's Views," clipping, *Chattanooga News*, Aug. 19, 1920; "Burn Changed Vote On Advice of His Mother," clipping, *Nashville Tennessean*, Aug. 20, 1920; Zoe Beckley, "Mother Proud of Boy Who Cinched Suffrage Victory," clipping, *Memphis Press*, Aug. 31, 1920; all in Burn Scrapbook.

49. Quotations from "Shouts of Joy and Groans of Dismay Greet News of Action of Legislature on Suffrage," clipping, *Knoxville Journal and Tribune*, Aug. 19, 1920,

Burn Scrapbook, and telegram, Carrie Chapman Catt to Gertrude Weil, box 3, folder 4, Catt Papers; *House Journal*, 92-94; Catt and Shuler, *Woman Suffrage and Politics*, 449; "History of Bitter Struggle to Ratify Suffrage."

50. Quotations, Shuler, "On The Tennessee Firing Line," 332, 334. See also "Suffragists Inspired With House Victory," clipping, *Chattanooga News*, Aug. 20, 1920, Burn Scrapbook; Pearson, "My Story!" n.p.; *HWS* 6: 624; Catt and Shuler, *Woman Suffrage and Politics*, 450-54.

51. "MASS MEETING *TONIGHT* TO SAVE THE SOUTH," broadside, box 1, folder 2, Catt Papers; "Indignation Spreads Over Whole State," *Chattanooga Daily Times*, Aug. 26, 1920; "Little Interest Manifested in Mass Meetings," clipping, *Nashville Tennessean*, Aug. 29, 1920, box 1, folder 2, Price Scrapbook.

52. Martin Lee Calhoun, "God of Our Fathers Spare Us Yet!" *Woman Patriot* 4 (Sept. 11, 1920): 3.

53. Pearson, "My Story!" 13; "Burn Strongly Denies Charges" and "Nashville Papers Publish Affidavits Alleging Burn Was Approached on Subject," clippings, *Knoxville Sentinel*, Aug. 19, 1920, Burn Scrapbook; "The Truth About The Tennessee Campaign," *Woman Patriot* 4 (Sept. 11, 1920):6.

54. *House Journal*, 94-95; telegram, Carrie Chapman Catt to Frank J. Shuler, Aug. 20, 1920, box 3, folder 4, Catt Papers; "Reconsideration of Ratification Comes Up Today," clipping, *Nashville Tennessean*, Aug. 20, 1920, Burn Scrapbook; *HWS* 6, 621.

55. Catt and Shuler, *Woman Suffrage and Politics*, 450, 453-54; *House Journal*, 117-21; *HWS* 6: 624.

56. *HWS* 6: 624-25; Catt and Shuler, *Woman Suffrage and Politics*, 454-55.

57. *House Journal*, 130-35; quotation, 136-37.

58. Telegram, Anne Dallas Dudley to Carrie Chapman Catt, Aug. 31, 1920; telegram, Anne Dallas Dudley to Carrie Chapman Catt, Sept. 1, 1920, box 3, folder 5, Catt Papers.

59. Catt and Shuler, *Woman Suffrage and Politics*, 459-60.

60. "Anti-Suffrage Party Declares Bitter War," clipping, n.p., July 21 [1920], box 2, folder 4, Catt Papers; A.H. Roberts to Carrie Chapman Catt, Sept. 13, 1920, box 1, folder 18, Catt Papers; "Tennessee Antis Wage Campaign Against Roberts," *Woman Patriot* 4 (Oct. 16, 1920): 1-2; "The Truth About the Tennessee Campaign," 6; Braden, "The Wizard of Overton," 287-91; Reichard, "Defeat of Governor Roberts," 106-08.

61. Ellis Meredith to Carrie Chapman Catt, Oct. 5, 1920, box 1, folder 15, Catt Papers. See also Catherine T. Kenny to Carrie Chapman Catt, Sept. 10, 1920; Abby Crawford Milton to Carrie Chapman Catt, Sept. 1, 1920, box 1, folder 16, Catt Papers.

62. "Election Returns Prove Strength of Anti-Suffragists," *Woman Patriot* 4 (Nov. 6, 1920): 1; "Governors Who Forced Ratification Defeated," *Woman Patriot* 4 (Nov. 13, 1920): 6.

63. Edward H. Crump to Hill McAlister, Nov. 5, 1920, box 9, folder 5, Hill McAlister Papers, TSLA.

64. Catherine Talty Kenny to Carrie Chapman Catt, Nov. 16, 1920, box 1, folder 14, Catt Papers; "Where the Suffrage Issue Counted," *Woman Citizen* 5 (Nov. 20, 1920): 682.

65. Reichard, "Defeat of Governor Roberts," 108-09.

66. Catherine T. Kenny to Carrie Chapman Catt, Jan. 21, 1921, box 1, folder 14; Abby Crawford Milton to Carrie Chapman Catt, Feb. 5, 1921, box 1, folder 17, both in Catt Papers.

67. Abby Crawford Milton to Carrie Chapman Catt, Feb. 5, 1921, box 1, folder 17, Catt Papers.

Nineteen

Across the Great Divide:

Women in Politics Before and After 1920

Nancy F. Cott

Editor's Introduction: It is appropriate to conclude this anthology in which we "rediscover" the woman suffrage movement with this thought-provoking essay by eminent historian Nancy Cott in which she challenges widespread assumptions concerning women and politics "across the Great Divide." The passage of the Nineteenth Amendment in 1920 was unquestionably one of the great turning points in American history. However, as Cott argues, "too great a focus on the achievement of the Nineteenth Amendment obscures the similarities in women's political behavior before and after it and the relation of that behavior to broader political and social context."

In fact, from the immediate aftermath of the suffrage victory to the present, political analysts and historians have posited theories concerning the impact of the Nineteenth Amendment on American politics and women's political behavior that definitely warrant re-examination. The often-told story goes something like this: despite suffragists' claims that women would transform politics, many failed to vote, and those who voted did not vote as a "bloc." As a result, politicians quickly lost their new-found respect for women voters, and women were relegated to a minor role in party politics. Furthermore, the massive and cohesive women's movement, having lost—by winning—the issue that held it together, disintegrated, with many former suffragists becoming politically apathetic and the few that remained active locked in bitter combat with one another over the Equal Rights Amendment introduced in 1923. Such theories imply that woman suffrage was a failure, or, at best, a great victory that led (ironically) to a decline in women's political activism.

As Cott acknowledges, these widespread perceptions are correct in part. No significant "gender gap" emerged in the immediate aftermath of the Nineteenth Amendment. The massive NAWSA converted itself into the League of Women Voters, but the League retained only a small percentage of the giant suffrage organization's membership. The NWP, which continued under the same name, introduced the Equal Rights Amendment, hoping to wipe out all remaining legal discrimination against women. But this proposal alarmed the LWV and many women (that historians call "social feminists") who insisted that working women desperately needed the laws that "discriminated" in their *favor*—the "protective legislation" for women that had been a primary goal during the Progressive Era and that was under attack in the conservative climate of the 1920s.

However, as Cott explains (and readers of *One Woman, One Vote* are by now well aware), the woman suffrage movement was never a "unity"; there was diversity and factiousness in the women's movement *before* and *after* 1920. From the debate in the 1860s over whether or not to support the Fifteenth Amendment, to the dispute over the picketing of the White House as the movement neared an end, suffragists disagreed fervently over tactics—even as they agreed upon a goal. Furthermore, the suffrage coalition included women of diverse racial, ethnic, religious, regional, and class backgrounds, as well as party identifications, who could not reasonably be expected to fall into a solid "bloc" after enfranchisement. Indeed, as Cott suggests, those who lament—or merely point out—the fact that enfranchised womanhood failed to "bloc vote" are quite unrealistic. Given the natural divisions among women (as among men), Cott considers the idea of a "woman's bloc" as an imaginary construct, "an interpretive fiction rather than a realistic expectation." Furthermore, re-examining the pronouncements of the suffragists on this subject, Cott makes it clear that "even when maintaining that women would exercise civic duties differently from men, suffragists rarely if ever portrayed a future voting 'bloc' of women." They spoke of issues about which they expected women voters to be concerned, such as children's health, political corruption, and the liquor traffic, but they "rarely specified by what means, exactly, the injection of women's votes into the polity was to bring about change."

Cott also objects strongly to the suggestion that 1920 ushered in a great decline in women's political and social activism. On the issue of voter turnout, she points out that women's political participation can only be understood when studied in the context of overall voter turnout—which *declined* in the 1920s. She also explains that both before and after 1920, women were involved in a range of political activities besides voting or even party politics. Cott is particularly disdainful, however, of the idea that women's participation in voluntary organizations declined sharply after 1920, and suggests that to measure women's political activity, as many have done, by comparing the size of the NAWSA and the dissimilar League of Women Voters is absurd. For a more accurate picture, Cott insists, one must examine (as she does in this essay) the broad range of women's voluntary associations from the PTA to the DAR to the American Birth Control League. Indeed, writes Cott, the years between the two world wars were marked by an extremely high level of political activity on the part of women, though they often were engaged in organizations with conflicting—or directly competing—agendas. The disagreement among feminists over the ERA in the 1920s was only one of many areas in which female activists of all persuasions exercised their right to pursue their diverse political goals. Indeed, it might be argued that, with its success, the Nineteenth Amendment freed women to disagree among themselves, as well as to work for a wide variety of causes other than suffrage, whether individually, in women's groups, or in mixed-gender organizations.

Cott's reminder about the diversity among politically active women before and after 1920 not only sets the record straight, but, combined with her point about the impossibility of a woman's bloc, it clearly demonstrates (in her words) "the unique power of disenfranchisement to bring diverse women into coalition." Millions of American women who became suffragists agreed on one point if nothing else: they were weary of a social and political system based on the idea of separate spheres and wanted full recognition of their individuality, equality, and right to participate fully and directly in making the laws under which they lived.

★ ★ ★ ★ ★

THE NINETEENTH AMENDMENT is the most obvious benchmark in the history of women in politics in the United States. To neglect the political watershed of 1920 when assessing the history of women's politics would be obtuse, since the sex barrier to the ballot was eliminated then and also the decades-long campaign for the vote, which had mobilized millions of women, ended. Yet too great a focus on the achievement of the Nineteenth Amendment obscures the similarities in women's political behavior before and after it and the relation of that behavior to broader political and social context.

There were striking continuities in women's political choices and actions on both sides of 1920. After women gained the ballot, they continued to engage in a range of politics broader than simply electoral activity. While it may be impossible to compare the influence women as a group had in politics before and after the Nineteenth Amendment, it is possible to consider more carefully suffragists' promises and their results. Women's voting must be put in the context of men's voting—that is, in the context of popular political participation in the period. Perhaps most important, the organizational and political roles of women's voluntary associations—which, far from declining, multiplied in membership—must be considered within rather than outside of politics.

The Suffrage Coalition—A Woman's Bloc?

Although historians usually present the campaign for suffrage as a unity, in contrast to the disunity among women's groups of the 1920s, there is reason to see disunity among politically active women as typical of both the 1910s and 1920s. For instance, suffragists were opposed by female anti-suffragists; white suffragists raised racial bars to blacks. In other matters great and small, from the conflicts between clubwomen and entertainers over the status and standards of dance halls to standoffs between pacifists and preparedness advocates during World War I, there were strategic, ideological, class-based and race-based differences among groups of women that were acted out in the public arena before as well as after 1920. From 1869 on, within the suffrage movement itself there were successive deep divisions over strategy and method. Intense internal conflicts over leadership, finances, and tactics so racked the National American Woman Suffrage Association (NAWSA) in 1911 that longtime suffragist, the Reverend Olympia Brown, called her colleagues' "shallow false talk of love excellence harmony &c &c ...so false that it makes me vomit."[1] The bitter split between the National American Woman Suffrage Association and the Congressional Union (CU) leaderships beginning in 1913 was the latest but not the only such cleavage.

The way that suffragists built coalitions during the 1910s acknowledged that women had variant and perhaps clashing loyalties. Suffrage leaders purposely addressed defined groups (mothers, wage-earners, black women, white women, professionals) with specifically designed instrumental appeals, tacitly acknowledging that not all women shared the same definition of self-interest. Even nonvoting women took on partisan affiliations, which mattered: In the final years of the suffrage campaign Maud Wood Park, head of Congressional lobbying for the NAWSA, was so aware of Republican and Democratic partisan loyalties clashing within her own Congressional Committee that she preferred to meet with its members individually. The women were so "inclined to be suspicious" of one another that full meetings of the committee were unproductive. Though distressed by the division, Park took it for granted that "party women could not be expected to free themselves from the prevailing currents of thought."[2]

Even when maintaining that women would exercise civic duties differently from men, suffragists rarely if ever portrayed a future voting "bloc" of women. It is striking that the one time that a small minority of suffragists *did* attempt to marshal women's votes into a voting bloc, they were condemned by the majority of their colleagues. That was in 1914 and 1916, when the Congressional Union (predecessor of the National Woman's Party) campaigned among enfranchised women of the western states to defeat all Democrats. They intended to "punish the party in power" in Washington for failure to adopt a constitutional amendment for woman suffrage. Their effort to make women's power at the polls count on a single issue inspired horrified rejection from mainstream suffragist leaders and little agreement from women voters. Alice Paul, architect of the CU plan, had a definite conception of a single-issue feminist bloc—not a generalized "woman bloc"—operating in a two-party system to swing the balance: "To count in an election you do not have to be the biggest Party; you have to be simply an independent Party that will stand for one object and that cannot be diverted from that object."[3]

Very likely the CU strategy failed to evoke support from the bulk of suffragists not only because of its approach but because of its object—to unseat all Democrats, whether they as individuals supported woman suffrage or not. There was the thorn on the rose of any such proposal: a woman's bloc, to cohere and have an impact, had to make a single issue its clear priority, while candidates' positions on so-called women's issues would not stand alone but would combine with their positions on other questions that concerned women. The NAWSA's judgment that the CU was misguided gave more evidence that women had differing priorities and tactics; perceiving that division, suffragists were unlikely to imagine women voting as one. When the National Woman's Party moved on to militant demonstrations, which the NAWSA also deplored, Maud Wood Park found nothing more exasperating than having to answer Congressmen's questions: "'Why don't you women get together? You can't expect us to vote for you if you can't agree among yourselves.'" She pointed out as "mildly" as possible "that men, even within the same party, were not without their differences. But sauce for the gander was rarely accepted as sauce for the goose." Lest we assume that suffragists were too naive to recognize the coalition nature of their association, they remind us, as Harriot Stanton Blatch reminded a colleague in 1918, "altho [sic] all sorts and conditions of women were united for suffrage...they are not at one in their attitude towards other questions in life."[4]

Suffragists spoke of issues—safeguarding children's health, eliminating political corruption, ending the liquor traffic, improving the economic leverage of women wage-earners—but rarely addressed exactly how or for whom women's votes would be collected, whether electing women to office was a high priority, or whether women's votes were adjuncts or substitutes for the established practice of lobbying and educational work by women's voluntary associations. As much as suffragists talked about women's inclinations, duties, and contributions, they rarely specified by what means, exactly, the injection of women's votes into the polity was to bring about change. Suffragists usually made very general or else modest claims, and (interestingly) rarely touched on the subject of women in political office. True, there were some overarching retorts such as Anna Howard Shaw's to an anti-suffragist who objected that voting women would have little time for charity, "Thank God, there will not be so much need of charity and philanthropy!" There was rhetoric—equally vague—regarding women's inclination against war, such as the Congressional Union's claim that "A government responsible to all women, as well as all men, will be less likely to go to war, without real necessity." There were particular anticipations of women's efficacy, such as Florence Kelley's that "the enfranchisement of women is indispensable to the solution of the child labor problem." Typically, however, suffragists' proposals and predictions in the 1910s were locally relevant: it was claimed at the New York Woman Suffrage Party's 1910 convention, for instance, that women's votes would help to alleviate the evils of inadequate inspection of milk, high prices, overcrowded classrooms, crime, prostitution, and child labor; the ballot would enable women to preside as associate justices in children's court and women's night court. During the 1915 New York campaign, Carrie Chapman Catt even warned suffragist speakers against promising "what women will do with the vote."[5]

The idea that women's votes would line up in one direction certainly existed in an implicit imprecise form, in the views of both suffragists and their opponents. As prospective voters, women were often expected to punish candidates who did not show deference to women's organizations' aims and to embrace those who supported Prohibition and social legislation. There was some evidence in the 1910s (mainly from Scandinavia) that women were "conservative" voters and some claims (from New York City) that women swelled the "radical" vote. When Washington, Oregon, and Arizona each adopted Prohibition shortly after adopting woman suffrage, women's votes were presumed to have turned the tide. Since the western states that enfranchised women early did not have extensive industries employing women and children, they gave little evidence whether women's ballots would decisively protect such vulnerable wage-earners. Shortly after New York women got the right to vote, however, four state legislators who had opposed minimum-wage legislation for women, child-labor laws, and other social legislation were unseated. Two of the four were replaced with assembly*women*. In Columbus, Ohio, in 1919, after women received municipal suffrage, their organizing and voter-registration work through voluntary associations succeeded in dumping the city boss who had been mayor for sixteen years, despite his organization's labeling them a "shrieking sisterhood." However, most big-city machine politicians had dropped objections to woman suffrage by the late 1910s after observing and reasoning that enfranchised women had *not* shown a habit of voting together to oppose existing political organizations. Claims about the impact of women's votes were so speculative and contradictory by 1919, in fact, that social scientists William Ogburn and Inez Goltra, after studying "how women vote," could conclude only that there might be some significant sex differences *or* that "the enfranchisement of women will have no other effect than approximately to double the number of votes previously cast." With more evidence, a 1923 study drew the similarly ambivalent conclusion that women neither "merely vote the same as men" nor vote "with marked independence."[6]

Voter Turnout

The unspoken notion that adding women to the electorate should transform politics did prompt some suffragists to be disappointed at the lack of outcome in the 1920s, but they were not the only ones looking dourly at the scene. Both popular journalists and political scientists expressed a mood of skepticism, if not downright cynicism, about mass political participation. Social scientists stressed the irrational motivations driving individual political behavior, the inability of the mass public to make objective judgments in popular government, and the likelihood that politicians would manipulate these failings.[7] Observers' discouragement about democratic participation found corroboration in the deepening decline in voter participation, a trend continuous from 1896 and intensifying from the 1910s to the 1920s. Mean national turnout in the presidential election years 1920, 1924, and 1928 was just over half of the eligible electorate, as compared to an average of almost eighty percent in the late nineteenth century. In the off-year elections between 1922 and 1930, little more than a third of the electorate voted, whereas nearly two-thirds, on the average, had voted in the off-years between 1876 and 1896.[8]

The meaning of the decline in voter turnout is not absolutely clear, in great part because of the debatable meaning of early twentieth-century Progressive reform—that is, whether its intents and/or effects were democratic or elitist. In light of such reforms as direct election of senators, direct primaries, the initiative, referendum and recall, it seems ironic, even tragic, that the Progressive Era should have ushered in the decade of the lowest voter participation ever. But if Progressive reforms intended to keep the reins of the state in the hands of the expert or the economically powerful few—as some reforms more than others indicate—then the decline in voter turnout fulfilled rather than undid that aim. Voting "reforms" included the continuing disfranchisement of blacks and Populist or Republican whites in the South by means of poll taxes, literacy tests, and other bars to registration and balloting; more complicated and rigorous residency and registration requirements in northern states which limited immigrant voting; and, at the municipal level, replacement of district voting with at-large elections, which predestined minority interest-group candidates to fail.

While Progressive reformers embraced the salutary aim to eliminate corrupt influence-peddling and substitute neutral and informed standards, their emphasis on expert presence and management in the state also diverted control away from the populace, to an elite of professional and business-managerial experts. The results could be seen institutionalized in the 1920s in various forms, from city-manager rule in municipalities, to federal and state commissions, to such quasi-governmental institutions as the National Bureau of Economic Research. "It is a misfortune for the woman's movement," mordantly commented Suzanne La Follette, a feminist and pacifist of anti-statist leanings, in 1926, "that it has succeeded in securing political rights for women at the very period when political rights are worth less than they have been at any time since the eighteenth century." The most persuasive explanations of downsliding voter turnout from 1896 to the 1920s also have to do with the entrenchment of the Democratic Party's hold on the South and the Republican Party's domination of the North and West (and thus of the national government) to the extent that the interest of voters in partisan contest, and voter sense of efficacy, collapsed. The portrait of increasingly dispirited voters does not account for the vigor of third parties during the period, but it does account for the overall trend.[9]

Analyses in the 1920s pinned much of the blame for the contemporary drop in voter turnout on newly eligible women. Just before the presidential election in 1924, journalists and political scientists turned the spotlight on the "failure" of women to flock to the polls, although dependable data on voting behavior were very scarce.[10] Votes were not counted by sex except in the state of Illinois. In the 1920 national elections, slightly less than half of the eligible women in

Illinois cast a ballot, while three-quarters of the eligible men did. Early discussions based on that evidence generalized only downward, on the reasoning that Illinois women were more likely than most to vote since they had had the ballot since 1913.

Women's voting participation actually varied greatly from place to place, group to group, and issue to issue. Fewer women than men voted, but the difference in their voting behavior was not as stark as initial extrapolations from the Illinois data established. Analysis via regression techniques have now made it clear that the 1920s low in turnout was not due to women's behavior alone, but also to male voters' sinking interest. Hull House leader Jane Addams was on the mark when to a magazine's 1924 question, "Is Woman Suffrage Failing?" she responded that the question ought to be "is suffrage failing?"[11]

Voting Women and Their Organizations

As Addams noted, the context in which to look at women's voting behavior in the 1920s is that of declining voter participation overall. A few vigorous female voices, such as that of former National Woman's Party leader Anne Martin of Nevada, urged women to enter the electoral arena in force and move directly to claim "woman's share, woman's *half* in man-controlled government."[12] The much more general trend—and one deplored by Martin as merely "indirect influence"—was women's reliance on voluntary associations rather than the electoral arena for political efficacy. Since the early nineteenth century, women had influenced what took place in electoral and legislative halls from outside, not only by seeking suffrage but by inquiring about a range of health, safety, moral, and welfare issues. They had built a tradition of exercising political influence (one admittedly hard to measure), which continued vigorously once the vote was gained. Women's organizations' lobbying route should be seen as pioneering in the modern mode of exerting political force—that is, interest-group politics. This voluntarist mode, with its use of lobbying to effect political influence, and the kinds of interests pursued (i.e., health, safety, moral, and welfare issues), prevailed in women's political participation both before and after 1920.[13]

From recent histories one might gain the impression that women's voluntary organizations waned after 1920, but nothing is further from the truth. In her 1933 history of women, author and former NWP suffragist Inez Haynes Irwin observed that women were, if anything, *over*organized in voluntary associations during the 1920s and 1930s. She closed her book with a staggering list, from professional to civic to patriotic to social welfare to charitable to ethnic and religious women's organizations.[14] Although historians often cite as evidence of decimation in activism the contrast between the two million women in the NAWSA in the 1910s and the tiny fraction of that membership—probably five percent—who joined in the NAWSA's successor group, the National League of Women Voters (LWV), the two figures are not really comparable. The

Jeannette Rankin at Suffrage House, 1917, before becoming the first woman in Congress. Library of Congress

two organizations differed widely in form and intent: the first was a federation that pursued one specific goal, made few demands on its local members, imposed no homogeneity upon affiliates, and used all volunteer labor; the subsequent organization stated many aims (including civic reform, citizenship education, international peace, and women's rights), made strenuous demands on its local members, attempted standardized national procedure, and employed professional staff.

Quickly evolving into a "good government" rather than a feminist organization, its premise being to ready women for political life, the LWV found itself, ironically, competing with women's partisan activity as much as preparing women for it. When all women became fair game for party organizations, Republican and Democratic women's divisions vied with the nonpartisan League for the time and loyalty of women interested in politics. Some leading NAWSA suffragists went directly into party organizations instead of into the League. Lillian Feickert, for example, a prominent New Jersey suffragist who was named vice-chairman of the Republican state committee in 1920, built the New Jersey Women's Republican Club on the grassroots model of the New Jersey Woman Suffrage Association. Feickert claimed that three-quarters of the suffragists joined; by the spring of 1922 the club claimed 60,000 members. Women's divisions in state and national party committees should be seen, as logically as the League, as successor organizations to the NAWSA.[15]

More generally, where one large or vital pre-1920 women's organization declined or ended, more than one other arose to take its space, if not its exact task. While the General Federation of Women's Clubs seemed to decline in vigor (although not clearly in membership), the National Congress of Parents and Teachers Associations (PTA) rose into a mass membership whose local units took up efforts similar to those of many unnamed women's clubs of the earlier generation, working to establish playgrounds, libraries, and health clinics, as well as lobbying at the national level, on issues from film standards to international peace. More than quintupling during the 1920s, the membership of the PTA reached over a million and a half by 1931. Its color bar led (in effect) to the founding in 1926 of a National Colored Parent-Teachers Association, which had at least the cooperation of the older group.[16]

The two national organizations that had labored most avidly on behalf of wage-earning women in the pre-World War I era did show drastic reductions in membership and resources in the 1920s. These were the National Consumers' League (NCL)—not strictly but for the most part a women's group—and the National Women's Trade Union League (WTUL). Although both had set out auspicious programs in 1919, neither gained members nor momentum, their experience more like that of labor unions than of women's associations. Both the WTUL's and the NCL's efforts had informed public consciousness to the extent that unions themselves and agencies of government took up the concerns raised by those voluntary associations. As pressure from women's voluntary organizations was instrumental in making local public health and school departments assume some responsibilities for sanitation and for children's safety, and in inducing states to institute social welfare and protective labor legislation and the federal government to establish pure food and drug laws, likewise it was pressure from the WTUL and NCL (and other women's groups) that led to establishing the Women's Bureau in the United States Department of Labor. The Women's Bureau's mandate was to investigate the conditions and protect the interests of wage-earning women; it also took on the WTUL's aim to educate the public, and, in alliance with the WTUL, staunchly defended sexbased protective legislation.[17]

The WTUL's intention to raise the trade-union consciousness of industrially employed women as well as sweeten their lives through association was seized by Industrial Clubs formed by the YWCA. In 1926, the YWCA stopped requiring that members be Protestant Christians, and membership grew; by 1930 the organization boasted over 600,000 members, 55,000 volunteer advisors, and a dispersed professional staff of almost 3,500. The YWCA Industrial Clubs educated and helped to organize both black and white women workers in southern textile mills, and brought them to testify before legislatures about industrial conditions. These clubs also served as recruitment grounds for summer schools for women workers. The summer schools themselves, founded during the 1920s by labor reformers and academics, formed a sequel to the WTUL cross-class efforts earlier in the century.[18]

The YWCA was also instrumental in bringing together white-collar women workers. The founding in 1919 of the National Federation of Business and Professional Women's Clubs resulted from a conference of businesswomen called by the YWCA during World War I. Lena Madesin Phillips, a Kentucky-born lawyer who was drafted from her wartime YWCA position to become the first executive secretary of the National Federation, warmed to the subject of encouraging business and professional women's teamwork, courage, risk-taking, and self-reliance. The slogan the federation used to develop hundreds of local educational fundraising efforts during the 1920s, "at least a high school education for every business girl," indicated its orientation toward ordinary white-collar workers. Lawyers, teachers, and independent entrepreneurs also formed an important part of its membership. The clubs affiliated with the federation (required to have three-quarters of their members actively employed) numbered 1,100 by 1931, including about 56,000 individuals. Scores of new associations of women professionals were also founded between 1915 and 1930, as were two more federations of such clubs, called Zonta International and Quota International.[19]

The alliance with professionals—social workers, social researchers, college and university professors—so noticeably important in efforts on behalf of women workers and in the YWCA in the 1920s was also apparent in the birth control movement. In 1919 Margaret Sanger, leader in the American Birth Control League, left behind her former socialist politics, along with her purposeful lawbreaking and agitation in working-class communities and her emphasis on women's control of their own bodies. Sanger thenceforward emphasized eugenic reasoning about better babies. The American Birth Control League organized and educated the public and lobbied for the legalization of birth control on the premise of allowing "doctors only" to provide information and methods. Women who saw the virtues of that approach and volunteered their time for birth control in the 1920s were mainly middle-class matrons, more socially and politically conservative than the birth control advocates of the 1910s, and also more numerous. The American Birth Control League claimed over 37,000 members in 1926, almost ninety percent female. Fewer women followed the approach of civil libertarian Mary Ware Dennett, founder of the Voluntary Parenthood League, which stood on First Amendment rights and aimed to decriminalize birth control by removing it from federal obscenity statutes.[20]

While major women's organizations founded earlier, such as the Woman's Christian Temperance Union, persisted, a host of organizations that women could and did join in the 1920s were new ones, founded during or after World War I. The American Association of University Women (AAUW), whose members had to be graduates of accredited collegiate institutions, evolved from the Association of Collegiate Alumnae into a truly national operation in 1921 under the new name and a decade later had 36,818 members in 551 branches. Black collegiate alumnae, excluded by the spirit if not the letter of the AAUW, founded their own national association in 1924, not only to promote mutual benefit, educational standards, and scholarship among their own race, but also to work toward "better conditions of contact" between white and black college women. In 1932 it had eight branches and almost 300 members.[21]

Group consciousness among minority-group women was a major source of new organizations. Both Jewish women and Catholic women founded numerous voluntary associations during the 1920s and 1930s.[22] Black women continued the National Association of Colored Women (NACW), the organizational hub that had been central to black suffragist efforts and had linked black clubwomen in communities across the nation. Its umbrella covered between 150,000 and 200,000 members in forty-one states in the mid-1920s. Many of its leaders also pursued their aims of racial uplift through male-dominated black organizations, especially the NAACP, the Urban League, and the Commission on Interracial Cooperation. All through the decade, black women campaigned vigorously against lynching and for the federal antilynching bill languishing in the southern-dominated United States Senate—their numbers far beyond Ida B. Wells-Barnett's lone crusade in an earlier generation. Despite (or, perhaps, because of) the way that the NACW had brought women into political activism, its numbers declined by the end of the decade to about 50,000. Civil rights and welfare organizations of men and women were conducting the kinds of activities the NACW had begun, and they had more benefit of white financial support. Lacking resources, in 1930 the NACW cut its departments from thirty-eight to two: the home, and women in industry. But five years later Mary McLeod Bethune, a former president of the NACW and longtime laborer in the black struggle for freedom, led the way in establishing a new national clearinghouse, the National Council of Negro Women. She was emphatic that neither organizations dominated by black men nor by white women had given black women sufficient voice.[23]

Other new organizations women joined in the 1920s were patriotic, security-minded societies formed in the wake of World War I, including the American War Mothers and the American Legion Auxiliary, which grew from an initial 131,000 to over 400,000 members after ten years. The American Legion Auxiliary often worked in concert with the longer-established Daughters of the American Revolution (DAR), which more than doubled in size between 1910 and 1932, reaching 2,463 chapters and almost 170,000 members by the latter date. During the 1920s and 1930s these women's organizations—loudly anti-communist and enthusiastic in red-baiting—advocated military preparedness.[24] They positioned themselves against women's peace organizations, for international peace was *the* major item of concern among organized women in the 1920s.

In an unprecedented tide of public concern, a range of peace groups from the conservative and nationalistic American Peace Society, through Protestant church agencies, to the left-wing pacifist War Resisters League formed during and after the war. In the 1920s they proposed competing alternatives, including the League of Nations, the World Court, international arbitration conferences, disarmament, and noncooperation with the military. Women could follow a number of avenues instigated and dominated by men; they appeared in all the peace societies, but clustered in their own organizations. Two groups were founded in 1919: the Women's International League for Peace and Freedom, whose American section included such luminaries of social reform as Jane Addams, Lillian Wald, and Alice Hamilton, and the much smaller, more extremely nonresistant Women's Peace Society. The foundings of the Women's Peace Union of the Western Hemisphere, and the Women's Committee for World Disarmament, followed in 1921. In addition, the major women's organizations—the LWV, the AAUW, the WCTU, the NFBPW, and the PTA—all put international peace prominently on their agendas. In 1925 Carrie Chapman Catt, the former general of NAWSA, assembled from the memberships of the major women's organizations with peace departments the National Committee on the Cause and Cure of War (NCCCW). That collectivity met annually for many years and formed a basis for peace lobbying; it claimed cumulative membership over five million at the start and eight million—or one out of five adult women in the United States—by the 1930s.[25]

The Politics of Women's Voluntary Associations

The level of organization among American women after 1920 thus appears to compare very favorably to that before, even considering that voluntary memberships would have to increase by slightly more than a fifth to keep up with the growth in the adult female population. The number of women in organizations is compelling although memberships in the various organizations could and often did overlap, as had been no less true of the pre-war generation. Repeated foundings and aggregate memberships make it clear that women were still joining women's organizations, as they had for generations. By their very constitution of specialized memberships (professional women, religious women, mothers, women of a particular political bent) and purposes (birth control, education, antilynching, peace, and so on), such organizations were as likely to sustain or even to rigidify the differentiations and diversities among women according to racial, ethnic, class, and political grounds, however, as to make women feel a common cause. The more purposive and specialized a women's organization was, the more likely it was to be instrumentally allied with professional expertise and involved with the bureaucratic machinery of institutions, commissions, and conferences that developed rapidly in and outside government during the 1920s. It was also more likely to be working in concert with male-dominated organizations pursuing similar purposes. These women's organizations were not purporting to emanate from or to operate in a separate sphere, as had many of their forebears in the nineteenth century. Consequently, there was an omnipresent potential for the groups working on issues not peculiar to women—peace, for example—to self-destruct by routing their members toward male-dominated organizations that had more funds and thus seemed more effective (as it happened with the NACW).

Carrying on the voluntarist legacy of pre-war (unenfranchised) women's groups, women's organizations in the 1920s and 1930s had the benefit of the ballot and the ethos that women were full citizens. Such organizations benefitted from the much increased rate of high school and college education among women and the lower birth rate, which together meant that there were many more women knowledgeable about social issues and not entirely occupied with child care. At the same time, three-quarters of all adult women were not gainfully employed. These factors created the pool of enfranchised women who peopled voluntary associations in the era between the two world wars, very probably the highest proportion of women so engaged in the whole history of American women.

Not all women's organizations entered politics, but most of the national organizations did. They adopted the mode of pressure politics rather than fielding their own candidates: that is, they aimed to educate the public and lobbied for specific bills as they had during the suffrage campaign. As the first president of the LWV, Maud Wood Park took the lead in 1920 in forming among ten women's organizations a Capitol Hill lobbying clearinghouse, the Women's Joint Congressional Committee (WJCC). The National League of Women Voters, the General Federation of Women's Clubs, the Woman's Christian Temperance Union, the National Congress of Parents and Teachers, the National Federation of Business and Professional Women's Clubs, were all charter members. The WJCC promised to establish a lobbying committee on behalf of any item that at least five of its constituent members wished to forward, and it immediately started working on two different attempts, one for federal funds for maternity and infancy health protection (realized in 1921 in the Sheppard-Towner Act), the other for removal of citizenship discrimination against American women who married aliens (partially realized in the Cable Act of 1922).

Describing the WJCC in 1924, by which time it included twenty-one organizations, Mary Anderson, Director of the United States Women's Bureau, asserted with pride that "American women are organized, highly organized, and by the millions. They are organized to carry out programs of social and political action." She called the WJCC the "cooperative mouthpiece" of American women, conveying its members' opinions to Washington and bringing back to them news of legislators' doings. Women's organizations operated from motives and resources different from those of men's chambers of commerce, fraternal organizations, manufacturers' associations and so on, in Anderson's view. Where men's pressure groups relied on economic power in politics and looked for commercial or financial advantage or professional gain, women's organizations were working without self-interest, for the public good, for social welfare, on largely volunteer talent, relying on their influence on public opinion and "upon their voting strength for their success."[26] Anderson's commentary highlighted how far women leaders such as she persisted in assumptions formed before suffrage about women citizens' salutary disinterestedness. It also, unintentionally, explained why women's organizations (lobby as they might, and did) commanded only a weak position. Women could marshal only votes (in an era of widespread voter resignation) and public opinion. Men had the economic clout.

Voluntary Conflicts

The considerable unity of method among women's organizations contrasted with the diversity—often acrimony—among their specific goals.[27] Although women formed groups of probably greater number and variety in the 1920s than ever before, that did not necessarily mean they could work together nor could any particular group claim—without being countered—to speak politically for women. Differences among women's groups were at least as characteristic as their techniques of pressure politics. The controversy over the Equal Rights Amendment in the 1920s is well known: when the National Woman's Party had introduced into Congress in December 1923 an amendment to the Constitution reading "Men and women shall have equal rights throughout the United States and every place subject to its jurisdiction," it was immediately—and for decades after—opposed by the LWV and most other major women's organizations, which supported sex-based protective labor legislation, presumed to be put at risk by an ERA.[28] What is not so well recognized are the other equally important divisions among politically active women, and the fact that these divisions might cross-cut. Partisan loyalty has been wrongly slighted in historians' assessments of women's political behavior in the 1920s: women loyal to one party not only conflicted with women loyal to another, but also, importantly, partisan women conflicted with women who wanted to organize nonpartisan alliances.[29]

On the peace issue—where at first glance women seemed most wholeheartedly united—women's groups urging disarmament were opposed by patriotic women's organizations who boosted military preparedness. To counter the antimilitarist impact that WILPF was making, the DAR and allied groups in 1924 formed a National Patriotic Council. When WILPF speakers testified in Congress in 1928 against the naval building program, for instance, members of the DAR and the Dames of the Loyal Legion were also present, and Mrs. Noble Newport Potts, president of the National Patriotic Council, outspokenly warned the House Naval Affairs Committee Chairman about Dorothy Detzer, executive secretary of the WILPF, "That's a dangerous woman you've been talking to!" In that particular instance WILPF and other antimilitarists had the desired effect, and the House Committee, deluged by adverse mail, cut their authorization from seventy-one to sixteen naval vessels. Still, confidence that antimilitarism was "women's" stance was shattered.[30]

The impact that women activists made on one side or another of the pacifism/militarism question proved, ironically, the absence rather than the substance of gender solidarity. Right-wing women's confrontation and red-baiting of women pacifists and antimilitarists also led Carrie Chapman Catt, who intended to be moderate and mainstream, to leave out the WILPF and the Women's Peace Union when she organized the National Committee on the Cause and Cure of War. Regardless, ultra-patriotic women's organizations tarred Catt with the same brush that they used on the pacifists.[31]

On Prohibition—generally presumed in the 1910s to command women's support—the late 1920s revealed another crevasse. Pauline Morton Sabin recalled being motivated to found the Women's Organization for National Prohibition Reform when she heard Ella Boole, president of the WCTU, announce to the Congress, "I represent the women of America!" Sabin felt, "Well, lady, here's one woman you don't represent." A New Yorker born to wealth and elite social position, Sabin was president of the Women's National Republican Club, an active Republican fund-raiser and director of eastern women's activities for the Coolidge and Hoover presidential campaigns. Sabin first brought together women of her own class and acquaintance, but after she launched her organization formally in Chicago in 1929 with a national advisory council of 125 women from twenty-six states, it gathered much broader middle-class membership. Its numbers grew to 300,000 by mid-1931 and doubled that a year later, vastly exceeding the membership of the longer-established men's Association Against the Prohibition Amendment and surpassing the membership claimed by the WCTU. The WONPR actively challenged the stereotype that

Anne Martin of Nevada, in the front passenger seat, on the campaign trail, 1920.
Nevada Historical Society

women supported Prohibition. For instance, it disputed the WCTU's public assurance that the three million women under the aegis of the General Federation of Women's Clubs endorsed the Eighteenth Amendment. After WONPR leaders dared the GFWC to poll its membership on Prohibition—emphasizing that WONPR members also belonged to GFWC clubs—the WCTU no longer made that assertion.[32]

The Fiction of a Woman's Bloc

"The woman 'bloc' does not tend to become more and more solidified but tends to become more and more disintegrated," journalist William Hard observed in 1923.[33] The quantity of evidence that women arrayed themselves on opposing political sides (even if they used gender-dependent justifications to do so) calls into question the very possibility of a woman bloc. Given the divisions among women and given the nature of the political system, a women's voting bloc—or, even the possibility of a lobbying bloc representing *all* women—must be considered an interpretive fiction rather than a realistic expectation, useful perhaps to some minds, but requiring a willing suspension of disbelief.

In the 1920s most politically active women (and the LWV as an organization) eschewed the notion of a women's voting bloc in favor of women's diverse individuality. In her early leadership of the LWV, Carrie Chapman Catt made clear that it was not a woman's party intending to mobilize women's votes but a group dedicated to guiding women into the male-dominated political process and parties where change could be effected from the inside. Only a very few spokeswomen pointedly disagreed: Anne Martin, for instance, excoriated the decision to "train women for citizenship," saying that it handed women over to the Republican and Democratic parties "exactly where men political leaders wanted them, bound, gagged, divided, and delivered." The head of the Republican Women's Division believed, however, that voting women "do not want to differ from men on lines of sex distinction" and predicted that women would never vote for female candidates because of their sex alone but would choose the most qualified individuals. Grace Abbott, head of the Children's Bureau, said that women's voting record by 1925 showed that they were "trying hard to vote as citizens rather than as women, measuring a party or candidate in terms of their judgment on general community needs." Cornelia Bryce Pinchot, a leading Pennsylvania Republican, believed that women should enter politics to improve the position of their sex; nonetheless, as a candidate for Congress she found it counterproductive to isolate women as such in politics. She wanted to be listened to as an individual with views on many issues. Freda Kirchwey, influential left-leaning writer for *The Nation,* emphasized that "women are going to vote according to the dictates of class interest and personal interest as well as sex interest." To urge women otherwise, she contended, was to make them "forget they are human beings."[34]

Such remarks suggest that feminist impulses might scuttle the notion of a woman's bloc as reasonably as champion it. The fiction that women were unified in the political arena laid a foundation for feminist action, but also involved risks—most pointedly, the risks of denying women's diversity and individuality or prescribing a "woman's sphere" in politics. As much as suffragist rhetoric had stressed women's need to represent themselves and women's duty to become voters because their interests and expertise differed from men's, it had also stressed that women and men were equally citizens and individuals in relation to the state. A *New York Times* editorialist heard the suffragists' clarion to be that "women are people—human beings sharing certain fundamental human interests, aspirations, and duties with men." That very important strand of suffragist rationale was renewed in the 1910s along with rationales stressing women's differences from men; it justified and anticipated women's integration into men's political associations rather than the formation of a woman bloc.[35]

There were also strategically defensive reasons why most women active in politics did not pursue nor speak of their goals in terms of mobilizing a woman bloc. The notion of a woman bloc was portrayed as the deployment of destructive sex antagonism and was condemned in the harshest terms by mainstream male politicians as well as by right-wing ideologues. Once when the fledgling LWV did try to marshal a women's voting bloc—in New York in 1920, trying to unseat Republican Senator James Wadsworth, an intransigent opponent of woman suffrage whose wife headed the National Association Opposed to Woman Suffrage—the organization was violently condemned by New York's Republican governor as *"a menace to our free institutions and to representative government."* In the two-party system, Governor Nathan Miller said, "there is no proper place for a *league of women voters,* precisely as I should say there was no proper place for a *league of men voters."* His attack differed only in degree rather than in kind from the blast of *The Woman Patriot,* a right-wing hyper-patriotic "news"-sheet published during the 1920s by former anti-suffragists, which trumpeted that women's organizations on Capitol Hill formed an "interlocking lobby dictatorship" bent on "organizing women for class and sex war." *The New York Times,* too, censured the forming of a political organization by women, claiming that such formation presupposed that women were "a class, a group, something apart,...a class which apparently hates and distrusts men." In *The New York Times'* editorialist's view, such thinking not only signaled a "revival of sex-antagonism" but even amounted to a "socialist" theory, of "a world divided into hostile classes."[36]

Although rarely proposed or envisioned by women leaders as desirable or likely, the notion of a woman bloc was denigrated, repressed and ridiculed by defenders of "politics as usual" as fiercely as if it threatened them. Although the woman bloc could only have been an interpretive fiction, it was, curiously, a large enough looming specter for male politicians to slay it again and again. Those who have imagined that women entering politics in the 1920s should have or could have constituted a bloc of women voters similar to the coalition formed on behalf of woman suffrage have underestimated how profoundly at cross purposes to the existing party system such a proposition really was. Yet how else could women lobbyists, without economic resources to speak of (as Mary Anderson admitted) swing any weight? Women leaders in the political arena faced a classic double bind: damned outright for attempting to form a woman bloc, damned (in effect) by male politicians' indifference or scorn for failing to form one. There was the dilemma for women who intended to make it clear that politics was no longer a man's world.

Conclusion

An improved view across the great divide of 1920 clarifies the accomplishments of women in American politics and the limits to those accomplishments. A more continuous view highlights not only the immense organizational implications of women's lack of the ballot until the early twentieth century but also the unique power of disenfranchisement to bring diverse women into coalition. By taking fuller account of women's political efforts (including voluntary associations and lobbying as well as candidacies and voting), and by acknowledging that political efforts by various subsets of women may be mutually counterpoised, we might move the focus of inquiry after 1920 from the "woman bloc" to the possibility of a feminist bloc—the latter admittedly a grouping by politics and ideology rather than by sex.

Notes

This is a revised version of Cott's article by the same title that appeared in *Women, Politics, and of Change*, Louise A. Tilly and Patricia Gurin, eds., published by the Russell Sage Foundation, 1990 and is printed here with permission of the Russell Sage Foundation.

1. Olympia Brown to Catharine Waugh McCulloch, June 25, 1911, folder 236, Dillon Collection, Schlesinger Library, Radcliffe College; Rosalyn Terborg-Penn, "African American Women and the Woman Suffrage Movement," in this volume, *One Woman, One Vote;* Gayle Gullett, "City Mothers, City Daughters, and the Limits of Female Political Power in San Francisco, 1913," in Barbara J. Harris and JoAnn McNamara, eds., *Women and the Structure of Society* (Durham, N.C., 1984), 149-159; Barbara Steinson, *American Women's Activism in World War I* (New York, 1982).

2. Maud Wood Park, *Front Door Lobby*, Edna Stantial, ed. (Boston, 1960), 179-80.

3. Paul's statement, from 1916, is quoted in Inez Haynes Irwin, *The Story of the Woman's Party* (New York, 1921), 151. On the CU, see Eleanor Flexner, *Century of Stuggle* (New York, 1968), 261-70, 275-77, 282-89; Nancy F. Cott, *The Grounding of Modern Feminism* (New Haven, 1987), 53-59; Christine A. Lunardini, *From Equal Suffrage to Equal Rights: Alice Paul and the National Woman's Party, 1913-1928* (New York, 1986).

4. Park, *Front Door Lobby*, 23; Harriot Stanton Blatch to Anne Martin, May 14, [1918], Anne Martin Collection, Bancroft Library, University of California, Berkeley; On the mixed nature of the suffrage coalition, see Cott, *Grounding*, 24-33.

5. Quotations from Shaw, CU, and Kelley cited by Aileen S. Kraditor, *The Ideas of the Woman Suffrage Movement, 1890-1920* (New York, 1971), 50; Ronald Schaffer, "The New York City Woman Suffrage Party, 1910-1919," *New York History*, 43 (1962): 273; Catt quotation, Doris Daniels, "Building a Winning Coalition: The Suffrage Fight in New York State," *New York History*, 60 (1979): 71.

6. J. Stanley Lemons, *The Woman Citizen: Social Feminism in the 1920s* (Urbana, Ill., 1973), 92-93; John D. Buenker, "The Urban Political Machine and Woman Suffrage," *The Historian*, 33 (1970-71): 264-79; William Ogburn and Inez Goltra, "How Women Vote: A Study of An Election in Portland, Oregon," *Political Science Quarterly*, 34 (1919): 413-33; Stuart A. Rice and Malcolm M. Willey, "American Women's Ineffective Use of the Vote," *Current History*, 20 (1924): 641-47.

7. See Edward A. Purcell, Jr. *The Crisis of Democratic Theory* (Lexington, Ky., 1973), 95-114, on political scientists.

8. Walter Dean Burnham, "The Changing Shape of the American Political Universe," *American Political Science Review*, 59 (1965): 10; see also E.E. Schnattsneider, *The Semisovereign People* (Hinsdale, Ill., 1960).

9. See Schattsneider, *SemiSovereign;* Burnham, "Changing Shape"; Samuel P. Hays "The Politics of Reform in Municipal Government in the Progressive Era," *Pacific Northwest Quarterly*, 55 (1964): 157-69; James Weinstein, *The Corporate Ideal in the Liberal State, 1900-1918*

(Boston, 1968), esp. 92-116; J. Morgan Kousser, *The Shaping of Southern Politics* (New Haven, 1974); David W. Eakins, "The Origins of Corporate Liberal Policy Research, 1916-1922: The Political Economic Expert and the Decline of Public Debate," in Jerry Israel, ed., *Building the Organizational Society: Essays on Associational Activities in Modern America* (New York, 1972), 163-179, 288-291. Quotation from Suzanne LaFollette, *Concerning Women* (New York, 1926), 268.

10. Susan C. Bourque and Jean Grossholz, "Politics an Unnatural Practice: Political Science Looks at Female Participation," *Politics and Society*, (1974): 225-266, very effectively shows that early 1920s analyses of female non-voting—especially Charles Meriam and Harold Gosnell, *NonVoting: Causes and Methods of Control* (Chicago, 1923) were still being repeated in political science texts of the 1960s.

11. Addams quoted in "Is Woman Suffrage Failing?" *Woman Citizen*, n.s. 8 (April 19, 1924): 14-16. Early analyses are Stuart A. Rice and Malcolm M. Willey, "American Women's Ineffective Use of the Vote," *Current History*, 20 (1924): 641-47, and Hugh L. Keenleyside, "The American Political Revolution of 1924," *Current History*, 21 (1925): 833-40; see also Meriam and Gosnell, Non-Voting. Recent treatments are Paul Kleppner, "Were Women to Blame? Female Suffrage and Voter Turnout," *Journal of Interdisciplinary History*, 12 (1982): 621-643, and Sara Alpern and Dale Baum, "Female Ballots: The Impact of the Nineteenth Amendment," *Journal of Interdisciplinary History*, 16 (1985): 43-67.

12. Anne Martin, "Woman's Vote and Woman's Chains," *Sunset Magazine*, April 1922, 14; see also Anne Martin, "Feminists and Future Political Action," *Nation*, 115 (Feb. 18, 1925): 165-166; Frances Kellor, "Women in British and American Politics," *Current History*, 17 (Feb. 1923): 831-35.

13. Viz. Edward B. Logan, "Lobbying," *Annals AAPSS*, 144 supplement, (1929), 32; Dorothy Johnson, "Organized Women as Lobbyists in the 1920s," *Capitol Studies*, 1 (1972): 41-58; Paula Baker, "The Domestication of Politics: Women and American Political Society, 1780-1920," *American Historical Review*, 89 (1984): 620-48, Anne Firor Scott, *Making the Invisible Woman Visible* (Urbana, Ill., 1984), 259-294, have stressed the voluntarist political tradition among women in the nineteenth century, but its continuity after 1920 has received little attention, except very recently in the N.J. study by Felice D. Gordon, *After Winning: The Legacy of the New Jersey Suffragists, 1920-1947*, (New Brunswick, N.J., 1986).

14. Inez Haynes Irwin, *Angels and Amazons* (Garden City, N.Y., 1934), 408-11 and Appendix.

15. The League had branches in 45 states in 1931, with total membership probably under 100,000; see Sophonisba Breckinridge, *Women in the Twentieth Century: A Study of their Political, Social and Economic Activities* (New York, 1933), 66-68. On the LWV program, Lemons, *Woman Citizen*, 49-55; on Feickert, Gordon, *After Winning*, 79.

16. On GFWC, see Margaret Gibbons Wilson, *American Woman in Transition: The Urban Influence 1870-1920* (Westport, Conn., 1979), 98, 100-101, 107 n. 26; William P. O'Neill, *Everyone Was Brave: A History of Feminism in America* (Chicago, 1969), 256-62; Breckinridge, *Women*, 39; on Parent-Teacher Associations, 53-54, 79-80.

17. Allis Wolfe, "Women, Consumerism, and the National Consumers League in the Progressive Era, 1900-23," *Labor History*, 16 (1975): 378-92; Nancy Schrom Dye, *As Equals and As Sisters: Feminism, Unionism, and the Women's Trade Union League of N.Y.* (Columbia, Mo., 1980); Lemons, *Woman Citizen*, 25-30, 122-23; O'Neill, *Everyone*, 231-49.

18. Breckinridge, *Women*, 56-57; Alice Kessler-Harris, *Out to Work: A History of Wage-Earning Women in the U.S.* (New York, 1982), 243-45; Theresa Wolfson, "Trade Union Activities of Women," *Annals AAPSS*, 143 (1929):

130-131; Mary Frederickson, "The Southern Summer School for Women Workers," *Southern Exposure*, 4 (1977): 70-75; Mary Frederickson, "'I know which side I'm on': Southern Women in the Labor Movement in the Twentieth Century," in Ruth Milkman, ed., *Women, Work and Protest* (Boston, 1985), 169-171; Dolores Janiewski, *Sisterhood Denied: Race, Gender and Class in a New South Community* (Philadelphia, 1985), 83, 151; Rita Heller, "The Bryn Mawr Workers' Summer School, 1921-1933: A Surprising Alliance," *History of Higher Education Annual*, (1981), 110-31.

19. Lemons, *Woman Citizen*, 58-59 n.8; Breckinridge, *Women*, 63-64.

20. See Linda Gordon, *Woman's Body, Woman's Right* (New York, 1976), 295-98; Joan Jensen, "The Evolution of Margaret Sanger's Family *Limitation Pamphlet*, 1914-21," *Signs* 6 (1981): 548-67; Ellen Chesler, *Woman of Valor* (New York, 1992).

21. Breckinridge, *Women*, 54-55, 79.

22. Breckinridge, *Women*, 49-51, 58-59; June Sochen, *Consecrate Each Day: The Public Lives of Jewish American Women 1880-1980* (Albany, 1981); Norma Fain Pratt, "Transitions in Judaism: The Jewish American Woman Through the 1930s," in Janet James, ed., *Women in American Religion* (Philadelphia, 1978), 222.

23. Breckinridge, *Women*, 77-79; Rosalyn Terborg-Penn, "Discontented Black Feminists: Prelude and Postscript to the Passage of the Nineteenth Amendment," in Lois Scharf and Joan Jensen, eds., *Decades of Discontent* (Westport, Conn., 1983), 269-70, 272-73; Paula Giddings, *When and Where I Enter: The Impact of Black Women on Race and Sex in America* (New York, 1984), 177, 183-185, 203-204. On southern white women's antilynching efforts, see Jacqueline Dowd Hall, *Revolt Against Chivalry: Jessie Daniel Ames and the Women's Campaign against Lynching* (New York, 1979).

24. Breckinridge, *Women*, 43-49, 58.

25. Charles De Benedetti, *Origins of the Modern American Peace Movement, 1915-1929* (Millwood, N.Y., 1978), esp. 90-97; Charles Chatfield, *For Peace and Justice: Pacifism in America, 1914-1941* (Knoxville, Tenn., 1971); Florence Brewer Boeckel, "Women in International Affairs," *Annals AAPSS*, 143 (1929): 231-32; Joan Jensen, "All Pink Sisters: the War Department and the Feminist Movement in the 1920s," in Scharf and Jensen, eds., *Decades of Discontent*; Breckinridge, *Women*, 85-87.

26. [Mary Anderson,] "Organized Women and their Program," typescript, c. 1924, folder 84, Mary Anderson Collection, Schlesinger Library.

27. See Kay Lehman Schlozman, "Representing Women in Washington: Sisterhood and Pressure Politics," in Tilly and Gurin, eds., *Women, Politics, and Change*, 339-382.

28. In 1943 the NWP changed the wording of the ERA to its current reading. On the controversy between women's organizations over the ERA see O'Neill, *Everyone*, 274-94; William Chafe, *The American Woman: Her Changing Political, Social and Economic Roles, 1920-1970* (New York, 1972), 112-43; Lemons, *Woman Citizen*, 184-99; Sheila Rothman, *Woman's Proper Place* (New York, 1978), 153-65; Kessler-Harris, *Out to Work*, 205-12; Susan Becker, *The Origins of the Equal Rights Amendment: American Feminism between the Wars* (Westport, Conn., 1981), 121-51; Lunardini, *From Equal Suffrage*; Cott, *Grounding*, 115-42.

29. Partisan/nonpartisan controversies bulked large in the first year or two of the LWV; see Lemons, *Woman Citizen*, 49-53, and Gordon, *After Winning*, 34-39.

30. Carrie Foster-Hayes, "The Women and the Warriors: Dorothy Detzer and the WILPF," Ph.D. diss., University of Denver, 1984, 318-21.

31. See Jensen, "All Pink Sisters," and Cott, *Grounding*, 244-61.

32. David Kyvig, "Women Against Prohibition," *American Quarterly*, 28 (1976): 465-82, and *Repealing National Prohibition* (Chicago, 1979), 118-127.

33. William Hard, quoted in "What the American Man Thinks," *Woman Citizen*, Sept. 8, 1923, cited by O'Neill, *Everyone*, 264.

34. On Catt, see Lemons, *Woman Citizen*, 90-91; Anne Martin, "Feminists," 185; on Pinchot, John Furlow, "Cornelia Bryce Pinchot: Feminism in the Post-Suffrage Era," *Pennsylvania History*, 95 (1976): 329-346; all other quotations are cited from Alpern and Baum, "Female Ballots," 60-62.

35. *New York Times*, Nov. 30, 1918, 16. See Cott, *Grounding*, 29-30, 37-38.

36. Lemons, *Woman Citizen*, 98-100; "Are Women a Menace?" *Nation*, 112 (Feb. 9, 1921): 198; "The Interlocking Lobby Dictatorship," *The Woman Patriot*, 6 (Dec. 1, 1922); "Organizing Women for Class and Sex War," *The Woman Patriot*, 7 (April 15, 1923); *New York Times*, Nov. 30, 1918, 16.

October 28, 1920

Life

Vol. 76.   Copyright, 1920, Life Publishing Company   No. 1982

Price 15 Cents

"Congratulations"

The Electoral Thermometer

Woman Suffrage Won by State
Constitutional Amendments and
Legislative Acts Before the Proclamation
of the Nineteenth Amendment

Electoral Vote

Year		Electoral Vote
1890	Wyoming was admitted to statehood with woman suffrage, having had it as a territory since 1869.	3
1893	Colorado adopted a constitutional amendment after defeat in 1877.	6
1896	Idaho adopted a constitutional amendment on its first submission.	4
1896	Utah, having had woman suffrage as a territory since 1870, was deprived of it by Congress in 1887. It was reinstated by constitutional referendum when admitted to statehood.	4
1910	Washington adopted a constitutional amendment after defeats in 1889 and 1898. The territorial legislature twice enacted woman suffrage, but lost it by court decisions.	7
1911	California adopted a constitutional amendment after defeat in 1896.	13
1912	Oregon adopted a constitutional amendment after defeats in 1884, 1900, 1906, 1908, 1910.	5
1912	Kansas adopted a constitutional amendment after defeats in 1867 and 1893.	10
1912	Arizona adopted a constitutional amendment submitted as a result of referendum petitions.	3
1913	Illinois was the first state to get presidential suffrage by legislative enactment.	29
1914	Montana adopted a constitutional amendment on its first submission.	4

1914   Nevada adopted a constitutional amendment on its first submission.   3

1917   North Dakota secured presidential suffrage by legislative enactment, after defeat of a constitutional amendment in 1914.   5

1917   Nebraska secured presidential suffrage by legislative enactment after defeats of a constitutional amendment in 1882 and 1914.   8

1917   Rhode Island secured presidential suffrage by legislative enactment after defeat of a constitutional amendment in 1887.   5

1917   New York adopted a constitutional amendment after defeat in 1915.   45

1917   Arkansas secured primary suffrage by legislative enactment.   9

1918   Michigan adopted a constitutional amendment after defeats in 1874, 1912, and 1913. Secured presidential suffrage by legislative enactment in 1917.   15

1918   Texas secured primary suffrage by legislative enactment.   20

1918   South Dakota adopted a constitutional amendment after six prior campaigns for suffrage had been defeated, each time by a mobilization of the alien vote by American-born political manipulators. In that state, as in nine others in 1918, the foreign-born could vote on their "first papers" and citizenship was not a qualification for the vote. The last defeat, in 1916, had been so definitely proved to have been caused by the vote of German-Russians in nine counties that public sentiment, in addition to the war spirit, aroused a desire to make a change in the law that resulted in victory.   5

1918   Oklahoma adopted a constitutional amendment after defeat in 1910.   10

1919   Indiana secured presidential suffrage by legislative enactment in 1917. Rendered doubtful by a court decision, the law was re-enacted with but six dissenting votes.   15

1919   Maine secured presidential suffrage by legislative enactment after defeat of a constitutional amendment in 1917.   6

1919   Missouri secured presidential suffrage by legislative enactment after defeat of a constitutional amendment in 1914.   18

1919   Iowa secured presidential suffrage by legislative enactment after defeat of a constitutional amendment in 1916.   13

1919	Minnesota secured presidential suffrage by legislative enactment.	12
1919	Ohio secured presidential suffrage by legislative enactment after defeat of referendum on the law in 1917 and of a constitutional amendment in 1912 and 1914.	24
1919	Wisconsin secured presidential suffrage by legislative enactment after defeat of a constitutional amendment in 1912.	13
1919	Tennessee secured presidential suffrage by legislative enactment.	12
1920	Kentucky secured presidential suffrage by legislative enactment.	13

Total of presidential electors for whom women were entitled to vote before the Nineteenth Amendment was adopted, 339. (Full number 531).

In 1913 the territory of Alaska had adopted woman suffrage. It was the first bill approved by the governor.

———————

From: The National American Woman Suffrage Association, *VICTORY: How Women Won It* (New York: H.W. Wilson Company, 1940), Appendix 4, 161-164.

Chronology of Congressional Action

1868   Passage of the Fourteenth Amendment, which introduced the word male into the Constitution.

1869   First woman suffrage bill introduced into the House.

1869   Hearing on woman suffrage.

1878   Introduction by Senator Sargent of the Woman Suffrage Amendment in its final form.

1887   January 25, first vote in the Senate, yeas 16, nays 34, 50 voting.

1914   March 19, second vote in the Senate, yeas 35, nays 34, 69 voting.

1915   January 12, first vote in the House, yeas 174, nays 204, 378 voting.

1917   September 24, creation of Woman Suffrage Committee in the House.

1918   January 10, second vote in the House, yeas 274, nays 136, 410 voting.

1918   October 1, third vote in the Senate, yeas, including pairs, 62,

1919   February 10, fourth vote in the Senate, yeas, including pairs, 63, nays 33.

1919   May 21, third vote in the House, yeas 304, nays 89.

1919   June 4, fifth vote in the Senate, yeas, including pairs, 66, nays 30.

1920   August 26, proclamation by the Secretary of State of the Nineteenth Amendment.

From: The National American Woman Suffrage Association. *VICTORY: How Women Won It* (New York: H.W. Wilson Company, 1940), Appendix 8, 172.

The Contributors

Beverly Beeton is the author of *Women Vote in the West: The Woman Suffrage Movement, 1869-1896,* (Garland Publishing, Inc., 1986). She has also published numerous articles on the western suffrage movement, including "Susan B. Anthony's Woman Suffrage Crusade in the American West," (with co-author G. Thomas Edwards) in *Journal of the West* (1982). Beeton is the former Provost and Vice Chancellor for Academic Affairs at the University of Alaska, Anchorage. She received her Ph.D. at the University of Utah in Salt Lake City.

Victoria Bissell Brown is an associate professor of United States History at Grinnell College in Iowa, where she specializes in gender and social history. She received her Ph.D. from the University of California, San Diego. Brown has published articles on female socialization and female education at the turn of the century. She is currently writing *The Education of Jane Addams,* a two-volume study of Addams's development as a social reformer.

Nancy F. Cott, Stanley Woodward Professor of History and American Studies at Yale University, is the author of *The Grounding of Modern Feminism,* (1987) and *The Bonds of Womanhood: "Woman's Sphere" in New England, 1780-1835,* (1977), both published by Yale University Press. She is the editor of *A Woman Making History: Mary Ritter Beard Through Her Letters,* (Yale University Press, 1991); *Root of Bitterness: Documents of the Social History of America,* (Northeastern University Press, 1986); and *A Heritage of Her Own: Families, Work, and Feminism,* (Simon and Schuster, 1980). Her Ph.D. is from Brandeis University.

Ellen Carol DuBois, professor of history at the University of California, Los Angeles, is the author of numerous works on the woman suffrage movement, including *Feminism and Suffrage: The Emergence of an Independent Woman Suffrage Movement, 1848-1869,* (Cornell University Press, 1978), and *The Elizabeth Cady Stanton-Susan B. Anthony Reader: Correspondence, Writings, Speeches,* (Northeastern University Press, revised edition, 1992). Her biography of second-generation suffragist Harriot Stanton Blatch is forthcoming from Yale University Press. Her publications also include *Unequal Sisters: A Multi-Cultural Reader in U.S. Women's History,* (Routledge, 1994), co-edited by Vicki L. Ruiz. She received her Ph.D. from Northwestern University.

Linda G. Ford is an assistant professor of history at Keene State College in New Hampshire. She received her Ph.D. in 1984 from Syracuse University. Her book, *Iron-Jawed Angels: The Suffrage Militancy of the National Women's Party, 1912-1919,* (University Press of America, Inc., 1991) received the Gustavus Myers Award for Human Rights. Ford has also published articles on farm women and agrarian activism in the 1930s, coeducation at Syracuse, and William Penn's views on women.

Robert Booth Fowler is Hawkins Professor of Political Science at the University of Wisconsin-Madison specializing in American political thought and the intersection between ideas and actual politics in American history. He received his Ph.D. from Harvard. Fowler is the author of *Carrie Catt: Feminist Politician,* (Northeastern University Press, 1986). His other publications include *The Dance with Community: The Contemporary Debate in American Political Thought,* (University of Kansas Press, 1991), and *The Greening of Protestant Thought: 1970-1990,* (University of North Carolina Press, 1995).

Carolyn De Swarte Gifford is the editor of *"Writing Out My Heart": Selections from the Journal of Frances E. Willard, 1855-1896,* (University of Illinois Press, 1995). She is an associate editor of the *Historical Encyclopedia of Chicago Women* to be published by Indiana University Press. Gifford is a visiting associate in the Women's Studies Program, Northwestern University. Her publications also include several articles about Willard and the Woman's Christian Temperance Union. She earned her doctorate at Northwestern University.

Sara Hunter Graham is an associate professor of history at Louisiana State University. She received her Ph.D. from the University of Texas, Austin. In addition to articles on the woman suffrage movement, Graham is the author of *Woman Suffrage and the New Democracy,* forthcoming from Yale University Press. She is currently at work on a study of poverty and charity among New Orleans women and children, 1800-1920.

Wanda A. Hendricks, an assistant professor of history at Arizona State University, received her Ph.D. from Purdue University. She published the article "'Vote for the Advantage of Ourselves and Our Race': The Election of the First Black Alderman in Chicago," in the *Illinois Historical Journal* (Autumn, 1994). Hendricks also contributed to *Black Women in America: An Historical Dictionary* (1993), and *Encyclopedia of African-American Civil Rights: From Emancipation to the Present* (1992). She is currently revising her dissertation, "The Politics of Race: African American Women in Illinois, 1890-1920," for publication.

Sherry J. Katz received her Ph.D. from the University of California, Los Angeles. She is currently an affiliated scholar of the Beatrice M. Bain Research Group at the University of California, Berkeley, and teaches history at UCLA and the University of California, San Diego. Her forthcoming book on socialist women, social reform, and the welfare state in Progressive Era California will be published by Routledge.

Linda K. Kerber is the author of *Women of the Republic: Intellect and Ideology in Revolutionary America,* (University of North Carolina Press, 1980), and co-editor (with Jane DeHart), of *Women's America: Refocusing the Past,* (Fourth Edition, Oxford University Press, 1995). With Alice Kessler-Harris and Kathryn Kish Sklar, she is co-editor of *U.S. History As Women's History: New Feminist Essays* (University of North Carolina Press, 1995). Kerber, who received her Ph.D. from Columbia University, is May Brodbeck Professor in the Liberal Arts and Professor of History at the University of Iowa. She has served as President of the American Studies Association and in 1996-97 will be President of the Organization of American Historians.

Andrea Moore Kerr is a women's historian and independent scholar in Washington, D.C. She is the author of *Lucy Stone: Speaking Out for Equality,* (Rutgers University Press,1992). She is now at work on an historical novel based upon Shays's Rebellion.

Judith N. McArthur received her Ph.D. from the University of Texas, Austin, and is a lecturer in history at the University of Houston-Victoria. She is the co-editor (with Ruthe Winegarten) of *Citizens at Last: The Woman Suffrage Movement in Texas* (Ellen C. Temple, 1987). She is also the co-editor (with Orville Vernon Burton) of *A Gentleman and An Officer: The Military and Social History of James B. Griffin's Civil War,* forthcoming from Oxford University Press. McArthur is currently working on a study of Texas women and Progressive reform.

Alice S. Rossi, retired in 1991 as Professor Emerita of the University of Massachusetts, Amherst, is currently a member of the MacArthur Foundation research network on midlife development. Her extensive publications include the classic anthology, *The Feminist Papers: From Adams to de Beauvoir,* (1973: second edition, Northeastern University Press, 1988). She is also the author of seven books, including her most recent work, *Sexuality Across the Life Course,* (University of Chicago Press, 1994), and editor of four books in addition to *The Feminist Papers.* Rossi received her Ph.D. from Columbia University. A former president of the American Sociological Association, she was a founder and member of the original governing board of the National Organization for Women.

Anastatia Sims, an associate professor at Georgia Southern University, received her Ph.D. from the University of North Carolina at Chapel Hill. She has published numerous articles on the Woman's Christian Temperance Union, women's missionary societies, and other women's organizations, and two articles on suffrage and anti-suffrage in Tennessee. Sims is the author of *The Power of Femininity in the New South: Women and Politics in North Carolina, 1883-1920,* forthcoming from the University of South Carolina Press.

Rosalyn Terborg-Penn is a professor of history at Morgan State University in Baltimore, and the Director of the doctoral program in history at the university. She received her Ph.D. from Howard University. Terborg-Penn has published extensively on topics in African American women's history, and edited (with Sharon Harley) *The Afro-American Woman: Struggles and Images,* (Kennikat Press, 1978). She was one of the editors of *Black Women in America: An Historical Encyclopedia.* Most recently she has been completing "African American Women Struggle for the Vote, 1850-1920," which is forthcoming as a book.

Manuela Thurner is a doctoral student in the American Studies Program at Yale University. She received M.A. and M.Phil. degrees from Yale, and a B.A. from Ludwig Maximilians University in Munich, Germany. She is currently at work on her dissertation, "Visions of Europe, Visions of Empire: American High Culture and Western Imperialism." Her article, "'Better Citizens Without the Ballot': American Anti-suffrage Women and Their Rationale During the Progressive Era," appeared in the *Journal of Women's History,* (Spring, 1993).

Marjorie Spruill Wheeler, an associate professor at the University of Southern Mississippi, received her doctorate at the University of Virginia. She is the author of *New Women of the New South: The Leaders of the Woman Suffrage Movement in the Southern States,* (Oxford University Press, 1993). In addition to *One Woman, One Vote: Rediscovering the Woman Suffrage Movement,* she has edited two books: *Votes For Women! The Woman Suffrage Movement in Tennessee, the South, and the Nation,* (University of Tennessee Press, 1995); and a new edition of Mary Johnston's 1913 pro-suffrage novel, *Hagar,* (University Press of Virginia, 1994).

Suggested Readings

Armitage, Susan and Elizabeth Jameson, eds. *The Women's West.* University of Oklahoma Press, 1987.

Banner, Lois W. *Elizabeth Cady Stanton: A Radical for Woman's Rights.* Little, Brown and Co., 1980.

Barry, Kathleen. *Susan B. Anthony: A Biography of a Singular Feminist.* New York University Press, 1988.

Beeton, Beverly. *Women Vote in the West: The Woman Suffrage Movement, 1869-1896.* Garland Publishing, Inc., 1986.

Bordin, Ruth. *Frances Willard: A Biography.* University of North Carolina Press, 1986.

Buechler, Steven. *The Transformation of the Woman Suffrage Movement: The Case of Illinois, 1850-1920.* Rutgers University Press, 1986.

Buhle, Mari Jo, and Paul Buhle, eds. *The Concise History of Woman Suffrage.* University of Illinois Press, 1978.

Buhle, Mari Jo. *Women and American Socialism, 1870-1920.* University of Illinois Press, 1983.

Catt, Carrie Chapman and Nettie Rogers Shuler. *Woman Suffrage and Politics: the Inner story of the Suffrage Movement,* 1923; Reprint, University of Washington Press, 1970.

Cott, Nancy F. *The Grounding of Modern Feminism.* Yale University Press, 1987.

DuBois, Ellen Carol, ed. *The Elizabeth Cady Stanton-Susan B. Anthony Reader.* Northeastern University Press, 1992.

DuBois, Ellen Carol. *Feminism and Suffrage: The Emergence of an Independent Women's Movement in America, 1848-1869.* Cornell University Press, 1978.

DuBois, Ellen Carol, with Vicki L. Ruiz. *Unequal Sisters: A Multi-Cultural Reader in U.S. Women's History.* Routledge, 1994.

Flexner, Eleanor. *Century of Struggle: The Woman's Rights Movement in the United States.* 1959: Belknap Press, 1976.

Foner, Philip S. *Frederick Douglass on Women's Rights.* 1976: Da Capo Press, 1992.

Ford, Linda G. *Iron-Jawed Angels: The Suffrage Militancy of the National Woman's Party, 1912-1920.* University Press of America, Inc., 1991.

Fowler, Robert Booth. *Carrie Catt: Feminist Politician.* Northeastern University Press, 1988.

Frankel, Noralee and Nancy S. Dye, eds. *Gender, Class, Race & Reform in the Progressive Era.* University Press of Kentucky, 1991.

Fuller, Paul E. *Laura Clay and the Woman's Rights Movement.* 1975: University of Kentucky Press, 1994.

Giddings, Paula. *When and Where I Enter: The Impact of Black Women on Race and Sex in America.* William Morrow, 1984.

Gifford, Carolyn De Swarte. *"Writing Out My Heart": Selections from the Journal of Frances E. Willard.* University of Illinois Press, 1995.

Graham, Sara Hunter. *Woman Suffrage and the New Democracy.* Yale University Press, forthcoming.

Griffith, Elisabeth. *In Her Own Right, The Life of Elizabeth Cady Stanton*. Oxford University Press, 1985.

Gurko, Miriam. *The Ladies of Seneca Falls: The Birth of the Woman's Rights Movement*. 1974; Reprint, Easton Press, 1990.

Johnston, Mary. *Hagar*. 1913; new edition with introduction by Marjorie Spruill Wheeler, University Press of Virginia, 1993.

Kerr, Andrea Moore. *Lucy Stone: Speaking Out for Equality*. Rutgers University Press, 1992.

Kimmel, Michael S. and Thomas E. Mosmiller, eds. *Against the Tide: Pro-Feminist Men in the United States 1776-1990*. Beacon Press, 1992.

Kraditor, Aileen S. *The Ideas of the Woman Suffrage Movement, 1890-1920*. 1965; Reprint, W.W. Norton, 1981.

Lunardini, Christine A. *From Equal Suffrage to Equal Rights: Alice Paul and the National Woman's Party, 1910-1928*. New York University Press, 1986.

Mathews, Glenna. *The Rise of Public Woman: Woman's Power and Woman's Place in the United States, 1630-1970*. Oxford University Press, 1992.

McArthur, Judith N., and Ruthe Winegarten. *Citizens at Last: The Woman Suffrage Movement in Texas*. Ellen C. Temple, 1987.

Rossi, Alice S. *The Feminist Papers from Adams to de Beauvoir*. 1973; Second edition, Northeastern University Press, 1988.

Ryan, Mary. *Women in Public: Between Banners and Ballots, 1825-1880*. Johns Hopkins University Press, 1990.

Scott, Anne F. and Andrew M. Scott. *One Half the People: The Fight for Woman Suffrage*. J.B. Lippincott and Co., 1975.

Scott, Anne Firor. *Natural Allies: Women's Associations in American History*. University of Illinois Press, 1991.

Sheppard, Alice. *Cartooning for Suffrage*. University of New Mexico Press, 1993.

Sherr, Lynn. *Failure Is Impossible: Susan B. Anthony in Her Own Words*. Random House, 1995.

Soloman, Martha M., ed. *A Voice of Their Own: The Woman Suffrage Press, 1840-1910*. University of Alabama Press, 1991.

Sterling, Dorothy. *Ahead of Her Time: Abby Kelley and the Politics of Antislavery*. W.W. Norton and Company, 1991.

Stevens, Doris. *Jailed For Freedom*. 1920; Reprint, Carol O'Hare, ed., NewSage Press, 1995.

Tilly, Louise A., and Patricia Gurin., eds. *Women, Politics, and Change*. Russell Sage Foundation, 1990.

Terborg-Penn, Rosalyn. *The Afro-American Woman: Struggles and Images*. Kennikat Press, 1978.

Wheeler, Marjorie Spruill. *New Women of the New South: The Leaders of the Woman Suffrage Movement in the Southern States*. Oxford University Press, 1993.

Wheeler, Marjorie Spruill, ed. *Votes for Women! The Woman Suffrage Movement in Tennessee, the South, and the Nation*. University of Tennessee Press, 1995.

Yellin, Jean Fagan. *Women and Sisters: The Antislavery Feminists in American Culture*. Yale University Press, 1989.

Index

One Woman, One Vote: Rediscovering the Woman Suffrage Movement is the companion book to the documentary "One Woman, One Vote," for the PBS "American Experience" series. NewSage Press has also published *Jailed for Freedom: American Women Win the Vote*, by Doris Stevens, edited by Carol O'Hare (1995).

For more information on the documentary or other books by NewSage Press, call or write: PO Box 607, Troutdale, OR 97060.

(503) 695-2211 or fax (503) 695-5406